Denmark

a Lonely Planet travel survival kit

Glenda Bendure
Ned Friary

Denmark

1st edition

Published by
    Lonely Planet Publications
    Head Office: PO Box 617, Hawthorn, Vic 3122, Australia
    Branches: 155 Filbert St, Suite 251, Oakland, CA 94607, USA
                     10 Barley Mow Passage, Chiswick, London W4 4PH, UK
                     71 bis rue du Cardinal Lemoine, 75005 Paris, France

Printed by
    Colorcraft Ltd, Hong Kong

Photographs by
    Ned Friary
    Glenda Bendure

    Front cover: Frescoes, Fanefjord Kirke, Møn (Ned Friary)

Published
    July 1996

Although the authors and publisher have tried to make the information as accurate as possible, they accept no responsibility for any loss, injury or inconvenience sustained by any person using this book.

National Library of Australia Cataloguing in Publication Data

Bendure, Glenda.
    Denmark

    1st ed.
    Includes index.
    ISBN 0 86442 330 6.

    1. Denmark – Guidebooks.
    I. Friary, Ned. II. Title.
    (Series: Lonely Planet travel survival kit).

914.890459

Glenda Bendure & Ned Friary

Glenda grew up in California's Mojave Desert and first travelled overseas as a high school AFS exchange student to India.

Ned grew up near Boston, studied Social Thought & Political Economy at the University of Massachusetts in Amherst and upon graduating headed west.

They met in Santa Cruz, California, where Glenda was completing her university studies. In 1978, with Lonely Planet's first book, *Across Asia on the Cheap*, in hand, they took the overland trail from Europe to Nepal. The next six years were spent exploring Asia and the Pacific, with a home base in Japan where Ned taught English and Glenda edited a monthly magazine. They now live on Cape Cod in Massachusetts – at least when they're not on the road.

Ned and Glenda have visited Denmark four times in the past four years, exploring the country extensively, twice using public transport and twice self-touring by car.

They are also the authors of Lonely Planet's guides to *Micronesia, Hawaii, Honolulu* and the *Eastern Caribbean* and they write the Norway and Denmark chapters of LP's *Scandinavian & Baltic Europe on a shoestring*.

From the Authors

Thanks to the staff of the Danish Tourist Board who provided information and answered queries, especially Lillian Hess and Rikke Olsen in New York and Kurt Nielsen in Copenhagen.

A special thanks to Thomas Hadrup, the Information Officer of the Danish Embassy in Washington, DC, who dug deep into his files for us, and to the helpful folks at Use It, in particular Jeanett Geoffrey and Gunnar Dahlgaard. Many thanks also to Svend Ravnkilde of the Dansk Musik Informations Center, Nina Skriver Dahl of the Danish Literature Information Center, Mette Dahl-Jensen of Wonderful Copenhagen, Charlotte Christiansen of the Traffic Information Centre at the Ministry of Transport and Jette Sandahl, curator of the Kvindemuseet in Århus.

A particularly hearty thanks to the various travellers and friends we met along the way and to those who took time to write us after we returned home: Stig Albeck, James Bohannon, Trine & Birthe Bøtkjær, Jan Buschardt, Peter Byberg, Caroline Dye, Thomas Dyvik, Anton Jansen, Susan

Kenning, Anne Morris, Mick Rasmussen, Gudrun Rishede and Ole Skram.

From the Publisher

This first edition of *Denmark* was edited in Lonely Planet's Melbourne office by Rowan McKinnon, Kirsten John, Miriam Cannell and Bethune Carmichael. They were assisted by the eagle eyes of proofreaders Katie Codie, Jane Fitzpatrick and Brigitte Barta. The mapping was coordinated by Tamsin Wilson and Glenn Beanland, and Dorothy Natsikas, Lyndell Taylor and Tony Fankhauser helped with the map drawing. Tamsin Wilson laid out the book and drew the illustrations, and Andrew Tudor helped with the colour pages. The cover was designed by David Kemp and the climate charts were designed by Marcel Gaston.

Thanks to Dan Levin for help with some curly Icelandic fonts and to Lou Callan for her work on the Danish language section. Special thanks to Tamsin 'the unflappable' and to Jane Fitzpatrick for their help and guidance. Special thanks also to our authors, Glenda & Ned, who did what they do so very well.

Warning & Request

Things change – prices go up, schedules change, good places go bad and bad places go bankrupt – nothing stays the same. So if you find things better or worse, recently opened or now closed, please write and tell us so we can make the next edition better.

Your letters will be used to help update future editions and, where possible, important changes will also be included as an update section in reprints.

We greatly appreciate all information that is sent to us by travellers. Back at Lonely Planet we employ a hard-working readers' letters team to sort through the many letters we receive. The best ones will be rewarded with a free copy of the next edition or another Lonely Planet guidebook if you prefer. We give away lots of books, but, unfortunately, not every letter or postcard receives one.

Contents

Map Legend

BOUNDARIES

...............International Boundary
...................Regional Boundary

ROUTES

....................................Freeway
....................................Highway
................................Major Road
........Unsealed Road or Track
...............................City Road
................................City Street
.....................................Railway
...........Underground Railway
....Tram
............................Walking Track
.............................Walking Tour
......................................Ferry Route
.............Cable Car or Chairlift

AREA FEATURES

...................................Parks
.............................Built-Up Area
..........................Pedestrian Mall
..................................Market
...................................Cemetery
....................................Reef
.................Beach or Desert
....................................Rocks

HYDROGRAPHIC FEATURES

.................................Coastline
...............................River, Creek
.............Intermittent River or Creek
....................Rapids, Waterfalls
...........Lake, Intermittent Lake
.....................................Canal
.....................................Swamp

SYMBOLS

✪ CAPITAL	.......................National Capital	
◉ Capital	........................Regional Capital	
🌀 CITY	.................................Major City	
● City	....City	
● Town	....Town	
● Village	.....................................Village	
■ ▼	.........Place to Stay, Place to Eat	
☕ 🍺	......................Cafe, Pub or Bar	
✉ ☎	...............Post Office, Telephone	
❶ ❾	............Tourist Information, Bank	
◕ 🅿	...................Transport, Parking	
🏛 ⛺	...............Museum, Youth Hostel	
🏕 ⛺	Caravan Park, Camping Ground	
✝ ✚	...............Church, Cathedral	
☪ ✡	..................Mosque, Synagogue	
卍 卐	Buddhist Temple, Hindu Temple	
✚ ★	..............Hospital, Police Station	

◔ ℗	.............Embassy, Petrol Station	
✈ ✝	..........................Airport, Airfield	
▭ ❁	..........Swimming Pool, Gardens	
❖ 🐘	..............Shopping Centre, Zoo	
⚲ ▣	...Winery or Vineyard, Picnic Site	
← A25	One Way Street, Route Number	
🏛 ▲	...........Stately Home, Monument	
🏰 ▣	...........................Castle, Tomb	
⌂ ⌂	.........Cave, Hut or Chalet	
▲ ✳	...........Mountain or Hill, Lookout	
🗼 ⚓	.............Lighthouse, Shipwreck	
)(◎	...........................Pass, Spring	
🐫 ⚑	...................Beach, Surf Beach	
∴	......Archaeological Site or Ruins	
	..................Ancient or City Wall	
	.......Cliff or Escarpment, Tunnel	
	.......................Railway Station	

Note: not all symbols displayed above appear in this book

Introduction

The world first took notice of Denmark a millennium ago when Danish Vikings took to the seas and ravaged vast tracts of Europe. Much has changed since then. These days Denmark is the epitome of civilised society, noted for its progressive policies, widespread tolerance and liberal social-welfare system.

The smallest and most southern of the Scandinavian countries, Denmark offers visitors an interesting mix of lively cities and rural countryside. The country abounds with medieval churches, Renaissance castles and tidy 18th century fishing villages.

Copenhagen, Scandinavia's largest and most cosmopolitan capital, has renowned museums, a wealth of cultural activities and a spirited music scene.

Denmark's historic treasures include the preserved bodies of 2000-year-old 'bog people', a scattering of Neolithic dolmens and some impressive Viking ruins. Denmark also boasts quaint towns lined with period half-timbered houses, white-sand beaches and scores of unspoiled islands.

Denmark is a maritime nation, bordered on the west by the North Sea and on the east by the Baltic Sea. Most Danes live within a couple of kilometres of the coast, and no place in Denmark is more than an hour's drive from the sea. The only part of Denmark that is connected by land to Continental Europe is the Jutland peninsula, with the remainder of the country comprised of some 400 islands.

While much of the coast of Denmark is

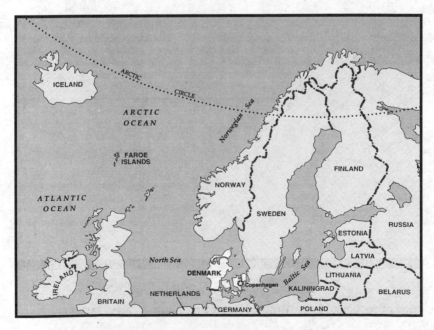

dominated by dunes and heathland, most of the interior is given over to farmland. Despite gentle hills here and there, Denmark is largely flat which, combined with an extensive network of cycle routes, makes it a great place to explore by bicycle.

Facts about the Country

HISTORY
The Stone Age
There are indications that Denmark may have had intermittent periods of human habitation during the interglacial period, but the first permanent settlements were probably around 12,000 BC. By that time the glacial ice, which had covered all of Denmark, had receded, exposing a low shelf tundra. The tundra's vegetation of lichen and mosses attracted drifting herds of reindeer, which were in turn followed by nomadic hunters. A Stone Age culture that relied primarily on hunting developed, but as the climate gradually warmed and the tundra gave way to forest, the reindeer migrated farther north. Eventually the hunters were compelled to resettle near the sea and subsisted by fishing and catching seabirds and seals.

As time went on Stone Age people began to grow more of their own food crops and by 4000 BC agriculture and the keeping of stock animals had become common practice. Woods were cleared by slash-and-burn methods and grain was sown in the ash. Villages developed around the fields and the villagers began to bury their dead in dolmens, graves comprised of upright stones topped by a large capstone; a number of these ancient dolmens can still be found in the meadows today. There are no indications that social organisation extended beyond that of village life during the Stone Age.

The Bronze Age (1800 BC to 500 BC)
Bronze made its way to Denmark around 1800 BC and gave rise to a skilled society of artisans who used this pliable metal to make weapons, tools, jewellery and finely crafted works of art. Trade routes to the south were opened to maintain a supply of bronze; influences from as far away as Crete and Mycenae are found in Danish bronze works of the period.

In pre-historic Denmark, objects of great value were often buried in bogs as sacrificial offerings. One superb artefact of this era is the *Sun Chariot*, which was crafted in bronze 3500 years ago by followers of a sun cult and was found by a farmer in a Zealand field in 1902. It's now on display at the National-museet in Copenhagen, along with bronze-age *lurs*, curved metal horns which were blown to call villagers to meetings and which now are amongst the world's oldest surviving musical instruments.

The Iron Age (500 BC to 800 AD)
Iron began to replace bronze around 500 BC. Since iron ore was readily available domestically, long-distance trade trickled off during this period. The iron proved useful for creating plough to till fields and consequently large agricultural communities developed.

Present-day Denmark can trace its linguistic and cultural roots back to the late Iron Age with the arrival of the Danes, a tribe that is thought to have migrated south from Sweden around 500 AD.

The Threat of the Franks
At the dawn of the 9th century Denmark was still on the outer perimeter of Europe when an expansion-oriented Charlemagne (771-814) extended the power of the Franks northward to present-day northern Germany. Hoping to ward off a Frankish invasion of Denmark, the Jutland king Godfred reinforced an impressive earthen rampart that ran along the entire length of his southern border, all the way from the North Sea to the town of Hedeby (present-day Schleswig, now part of Germany). However, the rampart, known as the Danevirke, was breached by the advancing Franks who combined their military adventures in Denmark with attempts to establish Christian missions. Both measures encountered widespread resistance.

To some degree the Viking expeditions – at least those that spread southward – were a

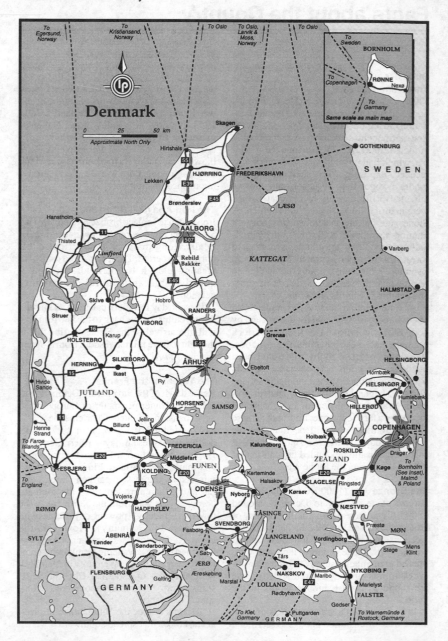

reaction to the challenges posed by the powerful Frankish Empire which had changed the political and economic landscape of Western Europe.

Early Viking Era

Although unrecorded raids had probably been occurring for decades, the start of the Viking Age is generally dated from 793 AD, when Nordic Vikings brutally raided Lindisfarne Monastery in Northumbria, off the coast of north-eastern England. Survivors of the Lindisfarne attack described the Vikings' sleek square-rigged vessels as 'dragons flying in the air' and the raiders as 'terrifying heathens'.

The early Viking raiders often targeted churches and monasteries, not for their religious significance but because they held rich repositories of gold and jewels. As the churches also served as centres of learning, many invaluable documents, books and other cultural artefacts went up in flames during the raids. So fearsome were the Vikings that a special prayer was instituted into British church services: 'From the fury of the Northmen, good Lord, deliver us'.

The Vikings were by and large adventurous opportunists who took advantage of the turmoil and unstable political conditions that prevailed elsewhere in Europe. In time their campaigns evolved from the mere forays of pirates to organised expeditions that established far-flung overseas colonies.

The Vikings came from Denmark, Norway and Sweden and each group had its own dominant sphere of influence. The Swedes colonised the Baltic states, which became bases for adventures deep into Russia, with Swedish Viking ships sailing as far east as the Caspian Sea. The Norwegian sphere included Scotland, Ireland and the Shetland, Orkney and Hebrides islands. It was a Norwegian explorer, Erik the Red, who colonised Iceland and Greenland; his son, Leif Eriksson, went on to explore the coast of North America.

The main Danish sphere of influence was along the coast of Western Europe and in north-eastern England, with the first documented raid by Danish Vikings occurring in the year 835. In 845 a Danish fleet devastated Hamburg and in the same year other Viking raiders attacked Paris and successfully forced its citizens to pay a hefty ransom in silver. With the concept of ransom established, Viking fleets began to terrorise other parts of the Frankish Empire.

In the 860s, the French monk Ermentarius wrote:

The number of ships is growing. Endless flocks of Vikings keep pouring in. Everywhere the Christians are massacred, burned and pillaged. The Vikings take everything that comes their way. Nobody is able to resist them. They have captured Bordeaux, Périgeux, Limoges, Angoulême and Toulouse. Angers, Tours and Orléans have been annihilated. A countless fleet moves up the Seine and all over the country viciousness is growing. Rouen has been devastated, plundered and sacked. Paris, Beauvais and Meaux are captured, the strong fortress of Melun has been razed to the ground, Chartres is occupied, Evreux and Bayeaux plundered and all towns besieged.

Still the Danes' main focus was on England, in part because it was comprised of a number of warring kingdoms, which made it a suitable target for conquest. By 850 Danish Vikings had established a settlement in Kent and in the years that followed sizeable groups of Danish colonists arrived. The Danes soon came to control all of north-west England, although the Anglo-Saxon king Alfred the Great (871-901) successfully repelled their advances to the south and forced the Danes to accept a boundary which recognised his reign over the kingdom of Wessex.

Unification of Denmark

Denmark's lands, like the rest of Scandinavia, have a long history of being ruled by rival regional kings, although by the early 800s Jutland (and parts of southern Norway) appears to have been more or less united under a single king. In the late 9th century a final move towards Danish unification occurred when warriors, led by the Norwegian chieftain Hardegon, conquered the Jutland peninsula and then began extending

ᛁᚾᚱ·ᛏᛁᚾ·ᚠ᛬ᚷᚾᛈᛘ᛬ᛚᛈᚠᛈᚾᛁᚾ·ᚠᛈᛈᛁᚾᚱ·ᛏᛁᚾ·ᚠ᛬ᚷᚾᛈᛘ᛬ᛚᛈᚠᛈᚾᛁᚾ·ᚠᛈᛈᛁᚾᚱ·ᛏᛁᚾ·ᚠ᛬ᚷᚾᛈᛘ᛬ᛚᛈᚠᛈᚾᛁᚾ·ᚠᛈᛈᛁᚾᚱ·ᛏᛁᚾ·ᚠ᛬ᚷᚾᛈᛘ᛬ᛚᛈᚠᛈᚾᛁᚾ·ᚠᛈᛈᛁᚾᚱ

Danish King & Queens

The Danish monarchy began in the 900s with Gorm the Old and has continued to the present day. The official name for the country is Kongeriget Danmark (Kingdom of Denmark). The monarchs, and the dates of their reign, are as follows:

Gorm (The Old)	–950	Christian III	1534–59
Harald I (Bluetooth)	950–85	Frederik II	1559–88
Sweyn I (Forkbeard)	985–1014	Christian IV	1588–1648
Harald II	1014–18	Frederik III	1648–70
Canute I (The Great)	1018–35	Christian V	1670–99
Hardecanute	1035–42	Frederik IV	1699–1730
Magnus (The Good)	1042–47	Christian VI	1730–46
Sweyn II (Estridsen)	1047–74	Frederik V	1746–66
Harald II	1074–80	Christian VII	1766–1808
Canute II (The Holy)	1080–86	Frederik VI	1808–39
Oluf I	1086–95	Christian VIII	1839–48
Erik I (The Kind)	1095–1103	Frederik VII	1848–63
Niels	1104–34	Christian IX	1863–1906
Erik II	1134–37	Frederik VIII	1906–12
Erik III (The Lame)	1137–46	Christian X	1912–47
Sweyn III & Canute III (both		Frederik IX	1947–72
claimed the throne)	1146–57	Margrethe II	1972–
Valdemar I (The Great)	1157–82		
Canute IV (Son of Valdemar)	1182–1202		
Valdemar II (The Victorious)	1202–41		
Erik IV (Ploughpenny)	1241–50		
Abel	1250–52		
Cristopher I	1252–59		
Erik V	1259–86		
Erik VI	1286–1319		
Christopher II	1320–26		
Valdemar III	1326–30		
Valdemar IV (Atterdag)	1340–75		
Oluf III (Håkonsson)	1376–87		
Margrethe I	1387–96		
Erik VII (of Pomerania)	1396–1439		
Christopher III (of Bavaria)	1440–48		
Christian I	1448–81		
John (Hans)	1481–1513		
Christian II	1513–23		
Frederik I	1523–33		

Christian IX, whose six children married into many European royal families.

ᛁᚾᚱ·ᛏᛁᚾ·ᚠ᛬ᚷᚾᛈᛘ᛬ᛚᛈᚠᛈᚾᛁᚾ·ᚠᛈᛈᛁᚾᚱ·ᛏᛁᚾ·ᚠ᛬ᚷᚾᛈᛘ᛬ᛚᛈᚠᛈᚾᛁᚾ·ᚠᛈᛈᛁᚾᚱ·ᛏᛁᚾ·ᚠ᛬ᚷᚾᛈᛘ᛬ᛚᛈᚠᛈᚾᛁᚾ·ᚠᛈᛈᛁᚾᚱ·ᛏᛁᚾ·ᚠ᛬ᚷᚾᛈᛘ᛬ᛚᛈᚠᛈᚾᛁᚾ·ᚠᛈᛈᛁᚾᚱ

Hardegon's power base to the rest of Denmark.

The Danish monarchy, the oldest kingdom in Europe, dates back to Hardegon's son, Gorm the Old, who established his reign in the early 10th century, ruling from Jelling in central Jutland.

Gorm's son, Harald Bluetooth, took the throne in 950 AD and, during his 35-year rule, he completed the conquest of Denmark.

He also spearheaded the conversion of Danes to Christianity, apparently in part to appease his powerful Frankish neighbours to the south, who a century earlier had sent the Christian missionary Ansgar to build churches in the Danish towns of Ribe and Hedeby.

End of the Viking Era

Under the reigns of Harald Bluetooth's son

ᛁᚱᚠ᛬ᛏᛁᚱ᛬ᚠᛉᛏᛈᛘ᛬ᛏᛈᚠᛈᛘᛑ᛬ᚠᛈᛈᛁᚱᚠ᛬ᛏᛁᚱ᛬ᚠᛉᛏᛈᛘ᛬ᛏᛈᚠᛈᛘᛑ᛬ᚠᛈᛈᛁᚱᚠ᛬ᛏᛁᚱ᛬ᚠᛉᛏᛈᛘ᛬ᛏᛈᚠᛈᛘᛑ᛬ᚠᛈᛈᛁᚱᚠ᛬ᛏᛁᚱ᛬ᚠᛉᛏᛈᛘ᛬ᛏᛈᚠᛈᛘᛑ᛬ᚠᛈᛈᛁᚱᚠ

Viking Fortresses

The remains of four Viking ring fortresses have been discovered in the Danish countryside. Two sites, the Trelleborg fortress in Zealand and the Fyrkat fortress near Hobro in Jutland, have been extensively excavated. Both have been developed as sites of historic significance, with educational displays and reconstructed Viking-style buildings.

The other two fortress sites have been identified by archaeologists but are not readily discernible to the untrained eye. They are the Nonnebakken fortress, in Odense on Funen, and the Aggersborg fortress, on the north shore of the Limfjord in Jutland.

These Viking fortresses were constructed in a ring shape with thick earthen walls and gates at the four points of the compass. They were built using the Roman foot (29.33 cm) as the unit of measurement and were mathematically precise and strikingly symmetrical. The long wooden stave buildings that once stood inside the walls were all of an equal measure and were clearly used as barracks for soldiers – there were no houses for nobility, as would have been found inside castle walls.

Although the purpose of these Viking camps is not entirely understood, it's now known that all were erected in the early 900s. Researchers, including Poul Nørlund, who excavated Trelleborg in the 1930s, once believed these impressive camps served as staging grounds for the invasion of England by King Sweyn Forkbeard. Current research, however, including the more precise dating (to 981) of the timbers used in the Trelleborg fortress, place the construction time far in advance of Sweyn Forkbeard's raids on England in 993. Furthermore, most of the four base sites were not well located for naval purposes. In the case of Trelleborg, archaeologists now believe the marsh streams that connect the camp with the sea probably weren't navigable in Viking times.

A popular current theory suggests that these fortified military camps may have been used by the monarchy to strengthen its domestic position, rather than being involved in Viking forays overseas. The massive earthen walls and moats of the fortresses certainly lend support to that theory, as they suggest a more defensive function than an offensive one.

Whatever their exact function, the two excavated fortresses, at Trelleborg and Hobro, are intriguing places to visit. Their perfectly symmetrical walls are still intact after more than a thousand years. ■

ᛁᚱᚠ᛬ᛏᛁᚱ᛬ᚠᛉᛏᛈᛘ᛬ᛏᛈᚠᛈᛘᛑ᛬ᚠᛈᛈᛁᚱᚠ᛬ᛏᛁᚱ᛬ᚠᛉᛏᛈᛘ᛬ᛏᛈᚠᛈᛘᛑ᛬ᚠᛈᛈᛁᚱᚠ᛬ᛏᛁᚱ᛬ᚠᛉᛏᛈᛘ᛬ᛏᛈᚠᛈᛘᛑ᛬ᚠᛈᛈᛁᚱᚠ᛬ᛏᛁᚱ᛬ᚠᛉᛏᛈᛘ᛬ᛏᛈᚠᛈᛘᛑ᛬ᚠᛈᛈᛁᚱᚠ

Sweyn Forkbeard (985-1014) and Blue-tooth's grandsons Harald II (1014-18) and Canute the Great (1018-35), England was conquered and a short-lived Anglo-Danish kingdom was formed.

Canute the Great was the first true Danish king on the throne of England, reigning in much the same manner as an English king except that he employed Scandinavian soldiers to maintain his command. Danish rule in England ended when Canute's son Hardecanute died in 1042, after which power shifted to the English heirs of Alfred the Great. Many of the Danes who had settled in England stayed on to live under English rule.

There were a couple of later unsuccessful attempts by the Danes to take back England, but the Viking era was clearly on the wane. The defeat of Norwegian Vikings by Harold of England at the Battle of Stamford Bridge in 1066 marked the final end of the Viking period.

The Middle Ages

During the medieval period Denmark was marked by internal strife, plots, counter plots and assassinations. Rival nobles, wealthy landowners and corrupt church leaders all vied for power and influence.

In 1060, King Sweyn II, wary of the influence of the bishop of Hamburg who ruled the Danish church, divided Denmark into eight domestic dioceses and appointed his own bishops, all trusted members of the aristocracy. Two decades later Sweyn's son, King Canute II, introduced the first personal tax and sent heavy-handed bailiffs into the countryside to collect it. The resistance to the new tax was so widespread that in 1086 Canute II was chased from Jutland by a band of rebellious farmers and was eventually cornered in an Odense church where he was stabbed to death.

Following a brief period of stability the monarchy was again thrown into turmoil in 1131 when Knud Lavard, a nephew of the ageing King Neils, was coaxed into the forest and slain in cold blood by his cousin Magnus the Strong. Although Magnus, King Niels' oldest son, was the rightful heir to the throne, he feared Knud Lavard's popularity as a war hero might put his cousin in a position to declare himself king.

The murder of Knud Lavard incited a civil war that resulted in the death of Magnus the Strong, King Neils and five of his bishops. Knud's brother Erik Emune, who led the campaign against Magnus the Strong, ascended to the throne in 1134 but his tyrannical rule ended abruptly with his assassination at a council meeting just three years later. The civil strife continued unabated through a series of short-lived reigns until Knud Lavard's son Valdemar finally took the throne in 1157.

King Valdemar I united the country, which was weary from civil war, and enacted Denmark's first written laws, known as the Jyske Lov (Jutland Code). With the cooperation of Bishop Absalon, the militaristic church leader from Roskilde, a series of successful crusades into eastern Germany were launched against the Wends, who had long raided the Danish coast with impunity.

Successor kings of the Valdemar reign enacted other laws that in some respects were quite progressive for their times. In 1282 King Erik V signed a coronation charter outlawing imprisonment without just cause and agreed to hold an annual assembly of the *hof*, a national council. In 1360 King Valdemar IV, under pressure from the *hof*, established the first supreme court and instituted a new and more powerful national council, known as the Rigsråd, which was comprised of nobles and bishops.

The Kalmar Union

Dynastic ties during the 14th century formed the basis for a union between Denmark, Norway and Sweden. In 1363 Norway's King Haakon married Margrethe, the daughter of the Danish king Valdemar IV. When Valdemar IV died in 1375 without a direct male heir, Oluf, the five-year-old son of Margrethe, was selected to become king of Denmark. In 1380, after King Haakon died, Oluf became the king of Norway as well.

It was actually Margrethe, not Oluf, who became leader of the two countries. Margrethe had assumed de facto control of the Danish crown upon Valdemar IV's death and became the official head of state in 1387 after Oluf died before reaching majority.

In 1388, Swedish nobles rebelled against their unpopular German-born king, Albert of Mecklenburg, and then turned to Margrethe for assistance. Sweden and Norway had long had royal ties and, indeed, prior to the selection of Albert, King Haakon had sat on the throne of Sweden as well as Norway.

The Swedes hailed Margrethe as their regent and in turn she sent Danish troops to Sweden who captured Albert and secured victory over his forces.

In 1397, Queen Margrethe established a union between Denmark, Norway and Sweden, known as the Kalmar Union. A primary objective of the union was to counter the influence of the powerful Hanseatic League which had come to dominate the region's trade. Three decades earlier the Hanseatic League, from its base in northern Germany, had initiated a campaign of ransacking Danish coastal cities, stopping only after the Danish crown agreed to pay an annual ransom and give the league a voice in Danish affairs.

In 1410, King Erik of Pomerania, Margrethe's grandson, staged an unsuccessful attack on the Hanseatic League and then went on to exhaust the resources of the tri-national government in a petty war on Denmark's southern Jutland border. Erik's penchant for appointing Danes to public offices in Sweden and Norway further soured native aristocrats in those countries and in 1438 the Swedish council withdrew from the union, whereupon the Danish nobility deposed Erik.

Erik's successor, Danish king Christopher III, promised to keep the administration of the countries separate and was accepted as king by both Norway and Sweden. The union continued to be rocky one, however, marred by Swedish rebellions and a few fully fledged wars between Denmark and Sweden. In 1523 the Swedes elected their own king, Gustav Vasa, and the Kalmar Union was permanently dissolved. Norway, however, would remain under Danish rule for another three centuries.

The Lutheran Reformation

A pivotal power struggle involving the monarchy and the Catholic church was played out during the Danish Reformation.

King Frederik I ascended to the throne in 1523 promising to fight heresy against Catholicism, but in an attempt to weaken the influence of Danish bishops he switched course and instead invited Lutheran preachers to Denmark. Their fiery messages against the corrupt power of the Catholic church, which over the centuries had accumulated an ungodly amount of property and wealth, caught a ready ear amongst the disenchanted.

After Frederik I died in 1533, the Catholic majority in the Rigsråd postponed the election of a new king, afraid that heir-apparent Prince Christian, Frederik's eldest son and a declared Lutheran, would favour the further spread of Lutheranism. Instead they attempted to position Christian's younger brother Hans as a candidate for the throne.

The country, already strained by social unrest, erupted in civil war in 1534. Mercenaries from the Hanseatic city of Lübeck, which hoped to gain control of Baltic trade by allying with Danish merchants against the Danish nobility, invaded southern Jutland and Zealand. By and large the Lübeckers were welcomed as liberators by the peasants and middle class.

Alarmed by the revolt against the nobility, the Rigsråd now threw its support behind Prince Christian and his father's skilful general, Johan Rantzau. Even the Catholic bishops, who realised the coronation of Christian would signal the end of the Catho-

lic church in Denmark, felt compelled to sign on rather than face the consequences of a peasant uprising. In 1534 the prince was crowned King Christian III.

The rebellion raged strongest in Jutland where manor houses were set ablaze and the peasants made advances against the armies of the aristocracy. General Johan Rantzau took control and quickly secured Jutland's southern boundary by cutting Lübeck off from the sea. He then made a sweeping march northward through Jutland, smashing the peasant bands in brutal fighting. Copenhagen, whose merchants supported the uprising and the idea of becoming a Hanseatic stronghold, was taken siege by General Rantzau's troops for more than a year. Protected by its ramparts, but totally cut off from the outside world, Copenhageners suffered widespread starvation and epidemics before finally surrendering in the summer of 1536, marking the end of the civil war.

With the war's end, Christian III took advantage of the opportunity to consolidate his power. He took a surprisingly lenient approach to the merchants and Copenhagen burghers who had revolted, and in turn they now offered their allegiance to the crown, seeing opportunities for themselves in a more stabilised Denmark. On the other hand, the Catholic bishops were arrested and their churches, monasteries and other ecclesiastical estates became property of the crown.

The Danish Lutheran church was established as the only state-sanctioned church and was placed under the direct control of the king. For all practical purposes the church officials, appointed at the whim of the king, were now civil servants. They were reliant upon the government for approval and financial support.

With only the nobility to share power with, the monarchy emerged from the civil war more powerful than ever, buoyed by a treasury that was greatly enriched by the confiscated church properties.

Wars with Sweden

No Danish monarch has had such a lasting impact on the Danish landscape as King

Christian IV (1588-1648), who succeeded his father, King Frederik II, at the age of 10 and ruled for more than half a century.

When Christian IV took power, Denmark held a firm control over Baltic trade, providing strong export markets for Danish agricultural products and reaping handsome profits for landowners and merchants. With a robust economy and a seemingly boundless treasury at hand, the ambitious king established trading companies, a stock exchange and went on to build new Renaissance cities, castles and fortresses throughout his kingdom.

A wealthy upper class prospered during Christian IV's reign and many of Denmark's most lavish mansions, palaces and public buildings were erected during that period. There was also an awakening of the arts and sciences.

Unfortunately, the king's foreign policies weren't nearly as brilliant as his domestic undertakings. When the Swedes began to vie for greater influence in the Baltic, Christian IV, hoping to neutralise Swedish expansion, dragged Denmark into a protracted struggle known as the Thirty Year War.

The war drained Danish resources and resulted in substantial territory losses for Denmark. The king himself lost an eye to shrapnel when his flagship was attacked in battle. A treaty of 1645, after a Swedish invasion of Jutland, signed the Baltic island of Gotland and two Norwegian provinces over to the Swedes, while a second treaty in 1648 relinquished the western half of Pomerania and the bishoprics of Bremen and Verden.

In 1655 the Swedish king invaded Poland and, although the victory was swift, the Swedes found themselves bogged down trying to secure that vast country. Word of the Swedish troubles ignited nationalistic fervour throughout a Denmark that was seething for revenge. In 1657, Christian IV's successor, King Frederik III, hoping to take advantage of the Polish situation, declared war once again on the Swedes. For the Danish government, itself ill-prepared for battle, it was a tremendous miscalculation.

Sweden's King Gustave, looking for an honourable way out of war-ravished Poland, which had already been pillaged to the limit, gladly withdrew from Poland and readied his forces for an invasion of Denmark. He lead his troops through Germany and into Jutland, plundering his way north.

In the winter of 1658 – the severest winter in Danish history – King Gustave marched his soldiers across the frozen seas of the Lille Bælt, between Fredericia and the island of Funen. His uncanny success unnerved the Danes and he proceeded without serious resistance across the frozen Store Bælt to Lolland and then on to Falster.

The Swedish king had barely made it across the frozen waters of the Storstrømmen to Zealand when the thawing ice broke behind him, separating Gustave and his advance detachment from the main body of his forces. But the Danes, who had amassed most of their troops in Zealand to protect Copenhagen, were in such a state of panic that they failed to recognise their sudden military advantage, and instead of capturing the Swedish king they sued for peace and capitulated to yet another treaty.

On 26 February 1658, the Treaty of Roskilde, the most lamented treaty in Denmark's history, was signed. The territorial losses were staggering, with Denmark's borders shrinking by a third. The Danes relinquished the island of Bornholm and lost the old Danish province of Skåne and all of its other territories on the Swedish mainland. Only Bornholm, which eventually staged a bloody revolt against the Swedes, would ever again fly the Danish flag.

Absolute Monarchy

Denmark emerged from the Swedish wars heavily in debt. In 1660 Frederik III convened an assembly of nobles, clergymen and burghers. The royal tax base had been compromised during the war years when the king had granted nobles and burghers (and the citizens of Copenhagen) exemptions from taxation, in return for their war efforts. During the assembly, only the nobility steadfastly refused to relinquish its tax exemption, setting off a division between themselves and the other participants.

The clergy and burghers, egged on by Frederik III, resolved to clip the wings of the nobility, which over the years had secured for itself a disproportionate voice in government affairs. The Copenhagen gates were closed and the capital put under a state of siege until the nobles finally agreed to declare the charter by which they had assumed their powers of council to be now null and void.

With the nobility no longer entitled to a central role in government, Frederik III introduced the Act of Absolutist Succession, which conferred the king and his heirs the unrestricted right of absolute rule. In 1665, the king enshrined the new system in an absolutist constitution called Kongeloven (The Royal Act), which was to stand as the Danish constitution for almost two centuries. In the spirit of the day, the exact content of the constitution was not made public at the

time of its enactment and for nearly 50 years no copies were allowed to be printed. In its essence the document was simple enough: it declared the king to be the highest head on earth, above all human laws and inferior to God alone. Supreme legislative, judicial and military authority was placed solely in the hands of the king.

So concentrated were the royal powers under the new constitution that when King Christian V ascended to the throne in 1670 as the first king to be anointed under absolute rule, it was decided that he alone had the authority to coronate a king, requiring Christian to place the crown upon his own head during the church services.

Frederik III, after effectively using his new powers to break the self-serving influence of the nobility, established a predecessor to the civil service. The new bureaucracy was divided into departments that ran the foreign service, military affairs and commercial activities. Membership was

Palace Follies

One of the pivotal players behind the early reforms of the 18th century was not a Danish king but a German doctor named Johan Struensee. In 1768 Struensee was appointed court physician for King Christian VII, who suffered from bouts of insanity. The doctor managed to win favour both with the ailing king, who granted Struensee broad powers of state, and with the 18-year-old queen, Caroline Matilda, who became Struensee's lover.

Emboldened by his new powers, the 34-year-old physician dismissed the prime minister and over the next 16 months succeeded in proclaiming some 2000 decrees in the name of the monarch. Contemptuous of the aristocracy, he applied the same laws for all citizens across class lines. The exploitation of peasants for the benefit of landlords was restricted and ill treatment in prisons, orphanages and poorhouses was outlawed. Trade barriers were lifted and money from the king's treasury was transferred to public sources for the support of new social endeavours.

Unfortunately for Struensee, he was ahead of his time – the French Revolution which would stir similar passions was still some 20 years away. Instead of broad support, Struensee elicited widespread resentment that was inflamed by unfounded rumours of his ill treatment of the ailing king. However, in actuality it seems that the mad king had taken some comfort in being relieved of both his stately and marital duties.

In January 1772 a coup d'état was instigated at a palace ball and the conspirators, led by the queen mother, forced the king to sign a statement against Struensee, who was being arrested elsewhere in the palace. Unable to prove that Struensee had forcibly taken control of the government, or even that he had been corrupt, the courts instead condemned him to death for his illicit relations with the young queen, which it deemed lese-majesty.

The queen, incidentally, had her marriage dissolved by a special court and was subsequently taken by a British frigate to England to live on the Hanover estate of her brother, King George III. Forbidden to take her young daughter (who was deemed Christian VII's heir although fathered by Struensee) with her to England, Caroline Matilda died a broken woman at the age of 24. ■

open to the sons of privileged landholders, but it was based upon wealth rather than noble lineage.

Crown holdings, consisting largely of manor estates and other church properties that had been confiscated in the wake of the Reformation, were sold off en masse to satisfy the war debt.

The monarchy managed to rebuild the military and put up a reasonable fight in three more wars with Sweden (1675-79, 1699-1700 and 1709-20), but none of these campaigns were able to regain the lost territories in southern Sweden. In the end the resistance of other countries, such as Holland, which were concerned that a more expansive Denmark could block their own access to the Baltic, ensured defeat for the Danes.

Throughout the rest of the 18th century the Danes and Swedes managed to relate without serious hostilities, and there was even some reconciliation with a Danish princess marrying the Swedish king Gustav III.

Age of Reforms

The peace of the 18th century gave Denmark a badly needed economic boost and set the stage for political and social change.

In 1784, Crown Prince Frederik VI, then 16 years old, assumed control of the government. More benevolent and intelligent than his predecessors, Frederik VI brought progressive landowners into government and introduced a sweeping series of reforms. With the French Revolution brewing elsewhere on the continent, the government now took an interest in improving the lot of the Danish peasantry, who in centuries past had drawn scant attention from the powers that be.

Under the leadership of Frederik VI, long-held feudal obligations were abolished, including those that had required peasants to reside within prescribed geographic boundaries and to provide compulsory labour in the domain of landlords. Large tracts of land were broken up and redistributed to the landless. The reforms extended to other areas and included the liberalisation of trade and the

introduction of compulsory, universal education for all children under the age of 14. When his father died in 1808 Frederik acceded to the throne.

Despite these domestic reforms, Denmark found itself once again swallowed up in a mire of international power struggles with the outbreak of the Napoleonic Wars (1796-1815).

Napoleonic Wars

At the turn of the 19th century, Britain, which dominated the seas, was not altogether keen on the growth of Denmark's foreign trade. In 1800, trying to counter potential threats posed by the British, Denmark signed a pact of armed neutrality with Sweden, Prussia and Russia. Britain regarded the act as hostile and in 1801 sent a naval expedition to attack Copenhagen, inflicting heavy damage on the Danish fleet and forcing Denmark to withdraw from the pact.

Denmark managed to avoid further conflicts and actually profited from war trade until 1807, when a new treaty between France and Russia once again drew the Danes closer to the conflict. The British, weary of Napoleon's growing influence in the Baltic, feared that the Danes might soon be convinced to place their fleet at the disposal of the French. This fear was unfounded.

Without resorting to diplomacy, in September 1807 a British fleet unleashed a brutal bombardment upon neutral Copenhagen, setting much of the city ablaze and destroying its naval yard. The British then proceeded to confiscate the entire Danish fleet, sailing away with nearly 170 gunboats, frigates, transports and sloops. Ironically, the only ship left standing in Copenhagen harbour was a private yacht which the king of England had bestowed upon his nephew, Denmark's crown prince Frederik, two decades earlier.

Although the unprovoked attack was unpopular enough back home to have been roundly criticised by the British parliament, England nonetheless kept the Danish fleet. The British then offered the Danes an alliance – something that might have been accepted by Denmark a few months earlier, but which in the wake of the recent British assault was now unthinkable. In October 1807 the Danes joined with the continental alliance against England. In turn, England blockaded Danish and Norwegian waters, resulting in poverty in Denmark and outright famine in Norway. When Napoleon fell in 1814, the Swedes, by then allied with England, successfully demanded that Denmark cede Norway to them.

The Golden Age

Although the 19th century started out dismal and lean, by the 1830s Denmark had awakened to a cultural revolution in the arts, philosophy and literature. The times gave rise to such prominent figures as philosopher Søren Kierkegaard, theologian Nikolaj Frederik Severin Grundtvig and writer Hans Christian Andersen. It was a golden age for the arts, with sculptor Bertel Thorvaldsen bestowing his grand neoclassical statues on Copenhagen and Christoffer Wilhelm Eckersberg introducing the Danish School of Art, which paid homage to everyday life.

Spurred on by new ideas and the rising expectations of a growing middle class, the crown was challenged by an unprecedented interest in democratic principles. Provincial assemblies were formed and, although their jurisdiction was nominal, they provided a vehicle for debate and gave rise to the formation of political parties. While the crown vacillated on how far it wanted to take the democratisation of power, two growing factions – farmers and liberals – joined forces to form a united liberal party in 1846.

The powers of the absolute monarch were already on the wane when revolution swept across the continent from Paris to Germany in the spring of 1848. The new Danish king Frederik VII, under pressure from the liberal party, convened a national assembly to abolish the absolute rule of the monarchy and to draw up a democratic constitution.

The constitution, enacted on 5 June 1849, established a parliament with two chambers,

the Folketing and the Landsting, whose members were elected by popular vote. Although the king retained a limited voice, legislative powers were now shifted to parliament. An independent judiciary was established and citizens were guaranteed the rights of free speech, religion and assembly. Denmark changed overnight from a virtual dictatorship to one of the most democratic countries in Europe.

Schleswig & Holstein

The duchies of Schleswig and Holstein in southern Jutland, which had long been under Danish rule, became restless during the nationalist fervour of the 1840s. Holstein, which was linguistically and culturally German, had already affiliated itself with the German Federation. Schleswig, on the other hand, was inhabited by people of both Danish and German heritage. When Denmark's new constitution threatened to incorporate Schleswig outright as an integral part of Denmark, the German population in Schleswig allied with Holstein and sparked a war against the Danes. The three-year revolt didn't end until 1851, when Denmark agreed to accept the status quo rather than further tighten its bonds with Schleswig.

In 1864 the Prussian prime minister Otto von Bismarck declared war on a militarily weak Denmark and within a matter of months had captured Schleswig. Denmark's new border in southern Jutland was now drawn at the Kongeå river, on the southern outskirts of Kolding. This further erosion of Denmark's domain opened the question of the very survival of Denmark as a nation.

In the aftermath of the 1864 defeat, a conservative government took hold in Denmark and retained power until the end of the century. Although reforms had come to a standstill, the conservatives oversaw a number of economic advancements: the railroad was extended throughout the country; Danish farmers found a ready grain market in Britain; and Denmark's major industries – shipbuilding, brewing and sugar refining – came into maturity.

Early 20th Century

In 1901 the conservative landowners, who had long held a stronghold on government, were ousted by the Venstrereformparti (Left Reform Party). The Venstrereformparti carried through a number of broad-minded reforms, including the application of the progressive principles of Grundtvig to the education system and revising the constitution to extend the right to vote to women.

Denmark remained neutral during WW I. The northern part of Schleswig was returned to Denmark following a plebiscite that took place in 1920 under the accords of the Treaty of Versailles. In the period between the two world wars a social-democratic government emerged, passing landmark legislation that not only softened the effects of the Great Depression but also laid the foundations for a welfare state.

WW II

Denmark again declared its neutrality at the outbreak of WW II, but with the growing Allied presence in Norway, Germany became intent on acquiring advance coastal bases in northern Jutland.

In the early hours of 9 April 1940, the Germans crossed the frontier in southern Jutland and simultaneously landed troops at half a dozen strategic points throughout Denmark. A military airfield in Copenhagen was attacked and commando troops landed in the city, promptly taking the citadel. The Germans proceeded to Amalienborg Palace, where they met resistance from the royal guards. In the meantime the German envoy delivered an ultimatum, warning that if Danish resistance was not halted Copenhagen would be bombed.

With German warplanes flying overhead, King Christian X and parliamentary heads hastily met at Amalienborg and decided to yield, under protest, to the Germans. The Danish government did manage to get assurances from the Nazis that Denmark would be allowed to retain a degree of internal autonomy.

The Danes, with only nominal military forces, had no capacity to ward off a German attack and little alternative but to submit. In all, the lightning blow lasted only a matter of hours, and before nightfall Denmark was an occupied country.

For three years the Danes managed to walk a thin line, basically running their own domestic affairs but doing so under Nazi supervision, until in August 1943 the Germans took outright control. The Danish Resistance movement mushroomed and 7000 Jewish Danes were quickly smuggled into neutral Sweden. In 1944 Iceland, under Danish rule since 1380, declared itself an independent republic.

Although the island of Bornholm was heavily bombarded by Soviet forces, the rest of Denmark emerged from WW II relatively unscathed.

Postwar Developments

Denmark joined NATO in 1949 and the European Community (now the European Union) in 1973.

The Danes have been hesitant to support expansion of the European Union (EU). Indeed when the Maastricht Treaty, which established the terms of a European economic and political union, came up for ratification in Denmark in June 1992, Danish voters rejected it by a margin of 51% to 49%. After being granted exemptions from the Maastricht Treaty's common defence and single currency provisions, the Danes, by a narrow majority, voted to accept the treaty in a second referendum held in May 1993. Danish support for the EU continues to be tepid as many Danes fear the loss of local control to a European bureaucracy dominated by stronger nations.

Under the leadership of the Social Democrats a comprehensive social-welfare state was established in postwar Denmark. Although a tax revolt in the 1980s led to some revisions, those revisions in large part also assured the viability of the system, and Denmark still provides its citizens with extensive cradle-to-grave securities.

GEOGRAPHY

Denmark is a small country with a land area

Greenland & the Faroe Islands

When Norway broke its political ties with Denmark in the early 19th century, the former Norwegian colonies of Iceland, Greenland and the Faroe Islands stayed under Danish administration. Iceland became an independent state within the Danish realm in 1918 and became completely independent in 1944.

The Kingdom of Denmark still includes Greenland and the Faroe Islands. The political situation of the two are not identical, but both are essentially self-governing. The Faroe Islands has had home rule since 1948, Greenland since 1979.

In part because Denmark retains responsibility for their banking, defence and foreign relations, Greenland and the Faroe Islands each have two parliamentary representatives in the Danish Folketing. Unlike Denmark, however, neither Greenland nor the Faroe Islands is part of the EU.

Greenland is the world's largest island (if Australia is regarded as a continent), with a total area of 2,175,600 sq km (of which 341,700 sq km is not under permafrost) and a population of 55,000. The Faroe Islands have a land area of 1399 sq km and a population of about 48,000.

For more information see Lonely Planet's *Iceland, Greenland & the Faroe Islands.* ■

of 42,930 sq km, just slightly larger than Switzerland.

The Jutland (Jylland) peninsula, whose 69-km border with Germany is Denmark's only land connection to the European mainland, encompasses more than half of the land area, stretching 360 km from north to south. In addition, Denmark has 406 islands, about 90 of which are inhabited. The capital city, Copenhagen, is on Zealand (Sjælland), the largest island. The next largest islands are Funen (Fyn), the twin islands of Falster and Lolland, and Bornholm.

Denmark is bordered on the west by the North Sea and on the east by the Baltic Sea. To the north, separating Denmark from Norway and Sweden, are the Skagerrak and Kattegat straits. Sweden is just five km away at its closest point, across a narrow strait called the Øresund.

Most of Denmark is a lowland of fertile farms, rolling hills, beech woods and heather-covered moors. The country hasn't a single mountain; the highest elevation, at Yding Skovhøj in Jutland's Lake District, is a mere 173 metres.

There are numerous small rivers, lakes and streams. The largest lake is Arresø on the island of Zealand and the longest river is the 158-km Gudenå on Jutland.

The coastline, which includes many inlets and bays, measures 7314 km in length. No place in Denmark is more than 52 km from the sea.

CLIMATE

Denmark is at a northern latitude of 54° 34' to 57° 45', approximately the same as Moscow, central Scotland and southern Alaska. Considering its northerly location the climate is relatively mild, moderated by the effects of the warm Gulf Stream, which sweeps northward along the west coast.

In the coldest winter months of January and February, the average daily temperature hovers around the freezing point – and while that may be cold, it's nearly 10°C above average for this latitude. Winter, however, also has the highest relative humidity (90%) and the cloudiest weather (with greater than 80% cloud cover an average of 17 days a month), both of which can make it feel much colder than the actual mercury reading.

From May through September, there are about nine cloudy days a month and the humidity drops to a comfortable level of around 70% at noon.

Expect to see rain and grey skies in Denmark. Measurable rain falls on average from 11 days in June (the month with the fewest rainy days) to 18 days in November, with the greatest amount of precipitation from July to December – although all said and done, rain is fairly evenly spread over

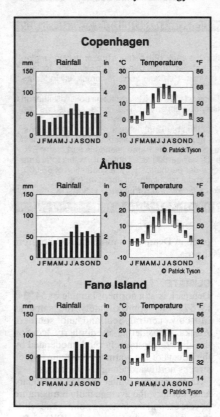

Copenhagen

Rainfall / Temperature graphs

© Patrick Tyson

Århus

Rainfall / Temperature graphs

© Patrick Tyson

Fanø Island

Rainfall / Temperature graphs

© Patrick Tyson

Daylight Hours

Throughout the summer, visitors to Denmark can enjoy long lingering hours of daylight. The longest days are in late June, when the sun rises around 4.30 am and sets around 10 pm, providing nearly 17½ daylight hours.

month	sunrise	sunset
1 January	8.40 am	3.48 pm
1 February	8.08 am	4.39 pm
1 March	7.06 am	5.40 pm
1 April	6.36 am	7.51 pm
1 May	5.29 am	8.46 pm
1 June	4.36 am	9.40 pm
1 July	4.33 am	9.54 pm
1 August	5.17 am	9.23 pm
1 September	6.16 am	8.02 pm
1 October	6.14 am	5.43 pm
1 November	7.15 am	4.31 pm
1 December	8.23 am	3.37 pm

the year. During the most popular months to visit of May, June, July and August, there's an average of 48 mm, 55 mm, 66 mm and 67 mm of rain, respectively.

The normal mean temperature for Denmark is 2.1°C in March, 10.8°C in May, 15.6°C in July and August, 9.1°C in October and 1.6°C in December.

With its low-lying terrain and proximity to the sea, variations in climate throughout Denmark are minimal. There's a prevalent westerly wind, averaging 13 knots.

For the local weather forecast call ☎ 153; for a weather forecast of all Denmark call ☎ 154; and for a five-day forecast call ☎ 156.

ECOLOGY & ENVIRONMENT

The Danish environment is one that has been heavily exploited. In the early 1800s, after centuries of deforestation and overgrazing, less than 4% of Denmark remained forested and encroaching heathlands and meadows covered nearly 50% of the total land area. In the late 19th century, much of that marginal heathland was turned into agricultural land, heavily reliant upon fertilisers and the alteration of waterways.

In all, about 20% of farmland is at or near sea level, much of it on environmentally sensitive wetlands that have been made arable by draining the water with pumps. The landscape has been so intensely altered that only about 2% of Denmark's naturally winding streams remain intact, the rest having been artificially straightened.

Recent international trade agreements and EU quotas have brought an end to many agricultural subsidies for Danish farmers and the most marginal farmland is no longer economically viable. These conditions, along with a growing environmental awareness, have created a backdrop for the implementation of widespread restoration projects. Under a nature management act implemented in 1990, the government has instituted an ambitious programme to restore wetlands, reestablish salt marshes and realign streams to their original courses. That same act calls for the doubling of forests over the next 100 years.

On other fronts, Denmark has vowed not to build nuclear power plants. Instead, it's developed an extensive network of alternative energy sources, most notably wind power. Recycling is extensive, with the majority of paper production created from used paper and roughly 50% of all wastes recycled. Over recent decades many air-pollution levels, including those of sulphur dioxide, have dropped by nearly 50%, and since 1993 Danish businesses have been required to pay a tax based on their carbon dioxide emissions.

In 1971, Denmark created a cabinet-level ministry to deal specifically with environmental matters. It was the first industrialised country to do so. The EU has placed its European Environment Agency in Copenhagen and the Danes have taken an active role in promoting international efforts to reduce pollution.

FLORA & FAUNA
Flora
About 12% of Denmark has tree cover but primary forest is rare. Instead, most woods are planted, the bulk of them having been reforested either for conservation and recreation purposes or for timber production. Most of the commercial forests are now planted with fast-growing conifers such as spruce and fir.

Denmark's natural woodlands are largely deciduous with a prevalence of beech and oak trees. Other common trees found in mixed woodlands are elm, hazel, maple, pine, birch, aspen, lime (linden) and chestnut.

Heath, bogs and dunes cover about 7% of land area, and are particularly common in western Jutland. In an effort to stem coastal erosion, large tracts of the dunes have been planted with lyme and marram grasses,

whose deep root systems help hold the sand in place. Wild pink-and-white beach roses, of the variety *Rosa rugosa*, are common to sand dunes as well.

In the spring, cultivated fields of brilliant yellow rapeseed flowers, a member of the mustard family, are a particularly lovely addition to the farm-belt areas.

In the summer, gardens throughout Denmark are planted with the usual colourful mix of temperate-climate flowers. The national flower is the marguerite, a white daisy with a yellow centre.

Fauna
The loss of natural wilderness habitat to cultivated farmland has spelt the end for numerous animal species in Denmark. Approximately 30% of all mammal species and breeding birds in Denmark are listed as either threatened, vulnerable or rare.

Among the mammals that have disappeared are elk, bears, wolves, wild boars and beavers. The freshwater otter, which was plentiful as late as the 1950s, is today the most endangered mammal in the country, with perhaps as few as 100 remaining.

The largest wild species still found is the red deer, which can weigh over 200 kilos. Denmark also has roe deer, fallow deer, wild hare, foxes, squirrels, hedgehogs and badgers.

Nearly 400 bird species have been observed and of these about 160 are breeders. Some of the more commonly seen birds are magpies, urban pigeons, coots, geese and ducks.

The west coast of Jutland attracts migrating waterbirds and breeding waders, such as avocet, dunlin, ruff, redshank, lapwing and black-winged godwit. The gull-billed tern, which is a threatened species in Europe, breeds on the uninhabited fjord island of Fjandø, as do some of the country's largest colonies of sandwich terns, arctic terns and black-headed gulls.

The easternmost island of Bornholm has relatively large numbers of rooks and nightingales and is a resting spot for migratory ducks and waders. The nearby Ertholmene islands are a bird refuge that attract breeding eider ducks, razorbills, guillemots and other seabirds.

Birds threatened by extinction, mostly due to the destruction of habitat, include the wood sandpiper, golden plover and black grouse, all once common birds of the heathland. The national bird is the swan, which is common to urban parks and suburban ponds throughout the country.

There are 68 indigenous butterfly species, though many are rare and since 1950 nine species have vanished altogether. The national butterfly is the small tortoiseshell, a pretty brownish-orange butterfly with a blue fringe; it's common in all areas of the country from early July and is unusual in that it hibernates as a fully grown insect.

There are 11 species of frogs and toads, including the common toad, green tree frog and fire-bellied toad. However because of the loss of wetlands, amphibians have disappeared from approximately 50% of their breeding sites in the past half-century. Efforts are being made to turn the situation around, most notably in Bornholm where 400 waterholes have recently been restored to create habitat for the green tree frog, whose breeding area on the island had diminished by 90%.

National Parks

Because Denmark does not have large expanses of wilderness, it's not surprising that it does not have a system of national parks. Its largest contiguous area of woodlands is Rold Skov, a 77-sq-km public forest that contains Denmark's only national park, Rebild Bakker.

Although sizeable tracts of wilderness don't exist, there are numerous state-administered nature conservation areas spread around the country, which collectively encompass about 4% of the nation's land area. These areas include beaches, coastal forests, heathlands and inland woods and lakes. Many are quite scenic and have been selected for some particular natural quality or historic significance. Most are crossed with hiking and biking trails and although the majority can be walked in an hour or two, some areas are long and narrow and thus suitable for longer outings.

GOVERNMENT & POLITICS

Denmark is a constitutional monarchy with a single-chamber parliamentary system. The parliament, called Folketing, is responsible for enacting legislation. The prime minister leads the government with the assistance of cabinet ministers who head the various government departments. Queen Margrethe II, who has been on the throne since 1972, has a largely ceremonial role but her signature is required on the enactment of new legislation.

The voting age is 18 and parliamentary elections are held at least once every four years. The Social Democrats, Liberals (a right-of-centre party), Conservatives and Socialists are the four main political parties, though in recent times there have been close to a dozen parties represented in the 179-seat parliament. All parties are quite moderate and, with the exception of the anti-tax Progressive Party, all essentially support the continuation of the welfare state.

The largest of the parties, the Social Democrats, is a moderate socialist party. It's founded on the belief in the right of guaranteed security to all in the form of extensive social-welfare programmes that are funded by high taxes. The Social Democrats first came to power in 1924 and have been in power, either alone or as part of a coalition government, most of the time since. They were, however, ousted in the 1980s by a Conservative-Liberal minority coalition that ruled for a decade until a political scandal over discriminatory immigration policies lead to the downfall of that government in January 1993.

In the wake of the conservative collapse, a four-party central-left majority coalition was formed, headed by Poul Nyrup Rasmussen, the leader of the Social Democrats. As prime minister, Rasmussen has attempted to minimise the boundaries between politicians and the general population. He drew widespread attention in August 1995 by joining a

ᛁᚱᚠ·ᛏᛁᚱ·ᚠᛉᚾᛈᛁ·ᚨᛈᚠᛈᛁᚾ·ᚠᛈᛈᛁᚱᚠ·ᛏᛁᚱ·ᚠᛉᚾᛈᛁ·ᚨᛈᚠᛈᛁᚾ·ᚠᛈᛈᛁᚱᚠ·ᛏᛁᚱ·ᚠᛉᚾᛈᛁ·ᚨᛈᚠᛈᛁᚾ·ᚠᛈᛈᛁᚱᚠ·ᛏᛁᚱ·ᚠᛉᚾᛈᛁ·ᚨᛈᚠᛈᛁᚾ·ᚠᛈᛈᛁᚱᚠ

Denmark's Royal Family

Denmark's current monarch, Queen Margrethe II, was born on 16 April 1940, the eldest daughter of King Frederik IX (1899-1972), who had no sons. As a result of a 1953 referendum that amended the sex-bias of the Danish constitution to allow women to succeed to the throne, Margrethe was proclaimed queen on 15 January 1972, the first female monarch of Denmark since 1412.

Queen Margrethe II is a popular queen who has been credited with giving a fresh perspective to the Danish monarchy and minimising the privilege that has traditionally separated royalty from commoners.

In addition to performing her ceremonial roles as head of state, the queen is an accomplished artist. She has illustrated a number of books, including Tolkien's *Lord of the Rings*, and has also designed Christmas seals for UNICEF and stamps for the Danish postal service. The queen has been active in the theatre as well, designing costumes for a production of HC Andersen's *The Shepherdess and the Chimney Sweep* and creating both the settings and costumes for the Royal Theatre's ballet *Et Folkesage* (The Legend). Together with her French-born husband, Prince Henrik, the queen translated Simone de Beauvoir's novel *Tous les hommes sont mortels* (All Men Are Mortal) from its original French to Danish.

Queen Margrethe and Prince Henrik have two sons. Crown Prince Frederik was born in 1968 and, like his mother, is a graduate of Århus University, where he studied politics and law. Prince Joachim was born in 1969 and attended a smaller Danish college. Both princes did stints in the armed services following their graduation and also have performed work internships overseas, Joachim on a farm in Australia and Frederik at a Californian winery. ∎

Queen Margrethe II

ᛁᚱᚠ·ᛏᛁᚱ·ᚠᛉᚾᛈᛁ·ᚨᛈᚠᛈᛁᚾ·ᚠᛈᛈᛁᚱᚠ·ᛏᛁᚱ·ᚠᛉᚾᛈᛁ·ᚨᛈᚠᛈᛁᚾ·ᚠᛈᛈᛁᚱᚠ·ᛏᛁᚱ·ᚠᛉᚾᛈᛁ·ᚨᛈᚠᛈᛁᚾ·ᚠᛈᛈᛁᚱᚠ·ᛏᛁᚱ·ᚠᛉᚾᛈᛁ·ᚨᛈᚠᛈᛁᚾ·ᚠᛈᛈᛁᚱᚠ

bicycle protest to Paris in protest of the resumption of French nuclear testing in the South Pacific.

The main domestic issues revolve around reforming taxes in the hope of lowering the nation's 50%-plus income-tax rate, the highest in the EU. As major cuts in social services aren't on the table, however, any significant income tax reform is likely to be accomplished by raising other fees and consumption taxes such as those levied on petrol and motor vehicles.

In addition to the national government, Denmark is divided administratively into 14 counties and 273 municipalities. Many government services, such as metropolitan transportation, health services and primary education, are administered on a local level.

ECONOMY

Denmark has the world's 12th highest per-capita GNP and its citizens enjoy a high standard of living. It has a work force of 2,900,000 almost evenly divided between men and women. Relative to other European countries the Danish economy remains strong, despite the fact that the government impounds almost half of the gross domestic product for social services and transfer payments to the disadvantaged.

Unlike its Scandinavian neighbours to the north, Denmark has maintained low inflation and fiscal stability over the past decade – good for the economy overall, but tough on unemployment, which hovers around 11%. However, generous income-transfer payments, including early retirement pay, pensions and unemployment benefits, have buffered the impact on those without work.

Almost all government funding is derived from taxes; one-third comes from the value-added tax (VAT) and taxes on petrol, alcohol and other dutiable items; 53% comes from income taxes; and a mere 3.7% is derived from corporate taxes. The government, while having a socialist bent on social welfare issues, is not involved in the ownership of capital. To the contrary a number of state-funded services, including such basics as ambulance service and firefighting, are provided by privately owned companies.

Nearly two-thirds of Denmark's land area is under cultivation. Of the country's 77,000 farms, the vast majority are still owned and operated by families. The average farm size is 36 hectares. Although family-operated, farms are highly mechanised and efficient, and 75% of their output is exported abroad. Important crops include wheat, barley, sugar beets and rapeseed, which is used to make canola oil.

Livestock raising is also important. Denmark is the world's leading exporter of canned ham and Danish dairy farms supply the milk used to make the country's famous cheeses and butter cookies.

Fishing remains economically important. Denmark boasts the EU's largest fish catches, with a fleet of about 2700 trawlers. The main consumer fishes caught are cod, herring, sprat, mackerel and plaice, but about 20% of the catch is industrial fish that's used to produce fish oil and fish meal. Fish waste from the fish processing plants is utilised as feed for mink farms.

Danish industry provides for roughly 20% of the nation's employment. Important industrial exports include beer, home electronics, furniture, silverware and porcelain. Food processing and the manufacturing of machinery are significant industries as well.

POPULATION & PEOPLE

Denmark's population is about 5.2 million, with 70% living in urban areas. The four largest cities are Copenhagen (1.4 million),

Århus (265,000), Odense (173,000) and Aalborg (155,000).

Denmark is almost entirely inhabited by ethnic Danes; people of the same Teutonic ancestry common to all Scandinavia. Foreign nationals account for just 3% of Denmark's population, and 8% of Copenhagen's population. About 40% of those come from Western European countries, particularly from Germany and the Nordic countries. A relaxation of immigration policies during the economic expansion of the 1960s attracted 'guest workers', many of whom established a permanent niche, and there are now sizeable Turkish, Pakistani and Yugoslav communities. More recent humanitarian policies, in response to famine and drought crises in Africa, have resulted in small Somalian and Ethiopian immigrant communities as well.

The average life expectancy is 72 years for men and 77.7 years for women. There's been a sharp decline in the birth rate in recent decades and the population is expected to fall below five million by the year 2020. Currently only 21% of Danes are age 17 or younger. The disparity between the age groups could bode poorly for the future of

What's in a Name?

Of the five-million-plus Danes on the planet today, two-thirds have a surname ending in 'sen'. The three most common – Jensen, Nielsen and Hansen – account for 23% of all Danish surnames. Next in order are Pedersen, Andersen, Christensen, Larsen and Sørensen.

You may notice a trend here. The most common Danish surnames are derived from the most common given names with 'sen' suffixed on. This is because up until the mid-19th century most peasants and other rural folk did not have a permanent family name but simply added 'sen', meaning 'son', onto their father's first name. Thus if your father was Peder Hansen and your name was Eric, you would be known as Eric Pedersen. ■

the social-welfare system, as there will be increasingly fewer people of working age supporting a proportionately larger number of pensioners.

EDUCATION

Education is free and nine years of education from the age of seven is compulsory. Preschool and kindergarten are optional, and about two-thirds of children aged five and six attend them.

About half of all Danish students who graduate from secondary school continue on to higher education. Slightly more than half of the graduates enrol in vocational programmes for business, nursing, maritime studies and other career-specific fields. Most others attend one of the five state-supported universities, of which the most élite is Copenhagen University (founded in 1479). The others are Århus University, Aalborg University, Odense University and Roskilde University. Men and women are evenly represented in higher education, though female students tend to enrol in shorter courses and male students in longer ones.

ARTS

Fine Arts

Prior to the 19th century, Danish art tended to centre around formal portraits of the bourgeoisie, the aristocracy and the royal family. One of the most highly regarded portrait painters was Jens Juel (1745-1802).

Denmark's 'Golden Age' of the arts (1800-50) produced such artists as CW Eckersberg (1783-1853), who depicted more universal scenes of everyday Danish life, and Eckersberg's student Christen Købke (1810-48), who was little known in his time but is now regarded as one of the most important painters of the era. The leading Danish sculptor of the day was Bertel Thorvaldsen (1770-1844), who recreated classical sculptures during a long sojourn in Rome and returned to Copenhagen to establish his own museum.

Another artistic movement was the Skagen school, which was active in the late 18th and early 19th centuries and specialised in romantic beachside subjects with an emphasis on the effects of natural light. Leading Skagen painters were PS Krøyer, Michael Ancher and Anna Ancher.

The COBRA (COpenhagen-BRussels-Amsterdam) movement, which was formed in 1948 with the aim of exploiting free artistic expression of the unconscious, had an impact on 20th century Danish art. One of its founders, Danish artist Asger Jorn (1914-73), achieved an international following for his abstract paintings, many of which evoke imagery from Nordic mythology.

Architcoture & Design

Of Denmark's contemporary architects, the most internationally notable are Jørn Utzon and Johan von Spreckelsen. Utzon designed the Sydney Opera House in Australia, which was constructed in the 1960s, and von Spreckelsen designed a European landmark, La Grande Arche in Paris, in 1984.

Several Danish architects have crossed over to furniture design, where they've had an even broader impact. Modern Danish furniture focuses on the functional refinement of style, and the principle that design should be tailored for the comfort of the user. In 1948 Hans Wegner designed the 'round chair', whose smooth curving lines made it an instant classic and a model for many furniture designers to follow. So popular was the chair at the time that it appeared on the cover of a number of international interior-design magazines. A decade later architect Arne Jacobsen produced The Ant, a form chair designed to be mass produced, which became the model for the stacking chairs found in schools and cafeterias worldwide.

The cool clean lines of industrial design are applied to Danish silver and porcelain, both of which merge aesthetics and function. Danish silverworks are highly regarded both in Denmark and abroad, with the company named after the late silversmith Georg Jensen the most renowned.

One of the world's most famous sets of porcelain is the Royal Porcelain Manufactory's Flora Danica dinner service. No two pieces of this 1800-piece set are

ᛁᚾᚠ:ᛏᛁᚾ:ᚠᛉᚾᛈᛘ:ᚥᛈᚠᛈᚾ:ᚠᛈᛈᛁᚾᚠ:ᛏᛁᚾ:ᚠᛉᚾᛈᛘ:ᚥᛈᚠᛈᚾ:ᚠᛈᛈᛁᚾᚠ:ᛏᛁᚾ:ᚠᛉᚾᛈᛘ:ᚥᛈᚠᛈᚾ:ᚠᛈᛈᛁᚾᚠ:ᛏᛁᚾ:ᚠᛉᚾᛈᛘ:ᚥᛈᚠᛈᚾ:ᚠᛈᛈᛁᚾᚠ

Hans Christian Andersen

Hans Christian Andersen, born 2 April 1805 in Odense, was the son of a poor cobbler. At the age of 14 he ran away to Copenhagen 'to become famous' and the following year entered the Royal Danish Theatre as a student of dance and music. In 1822, upon the recommendation of the theatre board, he was sent to a preparatory school in Helsingør, and in 1828 he passed his university entrance exams.

The following year Andersen self-published his first book, *A Walk From Holmen's Canal to the Eastern Tip of Amager*. In 1831, after being jilted in a love affair with Riborg Voight of Faaborg, Andersen travelled to Germany and wrote the first of a number of stories about his travels abroad.

In 1835 he finally made a name for himself with the successful novel *The Improvisators*. He followed that with his first volume of fairy tales, *Tales, Told for Children*, which included such classics as 'The Tinderbox' and 'The Princess and the Pea'. Over the next few decades, he continued writing accounts of his travels, as well as novels, but it was his fairy tales that brought him worldwide fame.

Andersen had a superb talent for humanising animals, plants and innate objects without compromising their original character. In his stories the villains are not evil characters like witches or trolls, but rather, they have human weaknesses such as indifference and vanity, and his tales are imbued with moral realism rather than wishful fantasy. Some of his most famous fairy tales are 'The Emperor's New Clothes', 'The Ugly Duckling', 'The Snow Queen', 'The Constant Tin Soldier', 'The Little Fir Tree' and 'The Nightingale'.

Besides his fairy tales and poems, Andersen wrote six novels, numerous travel books and many dramatic works. All in all, he had 156 stories and works published.

Andersen had a penchant for travel and over his lifetime made 29 journeys abroad, several of them lasting many months. On 4 August 1875, at the age of 70, he died of liver cancer at a villa outside Copenhagen. His grave is in the capital's Assistens cemetery. ∎

ᛁᚾᚠ:ᛏᛁᚾ:ᚠᛉᚾᛈᛘ:ᚥᛈᚠᛈᚾ:ᚠᛈᛈᛁᚾᚠ:ᛏᛁᚾ:ᚠᛉᚾᛈᛘ:ᚥᛈᚠᛈᚾ:ᚠᛈᛈᛁᚾᚠ:ᛏᛁᚾ:ᚠᛉᚾᛈᛘ:ᚥᛈᚠᛈᚾ:ᚠᛈᛈᛁᚾᚠ:ᛏᛁᚾ:ᚠᛉᚾᛈᛘ:ᚥᛈᚠᛈᚾ:ᚠᛈᛈᛁᚾᚠ

alike, each hand-painted with a different native Danish wildflower or other plant, and then rimmed with gold. Some of the pieces have trompe l'oeil features, such as cup handles that appear as flower stems. Commissioned in 1790, the original set took 13 years to complete, and is still part of the Danish royal collections today. Pieces of the set are on display at Copenhagen's Rosenborg castle.

Literature

The first half of the 19th century has been characterised as the 'Golden Age' of Danish literature. Forefront writers of that period include Adam Oehlensschläger (1779-1850), a romantic lyric poet who also wrote short stories and plays; Steen Steensen Blicher (1782-1848), a writer of tragic short stories; Hans Christian Andersen (1805-75), whose fairy tales have been translated into more languages than any other book except the Bible; and philosopher Søren Kierkegaard (1813-55), who is considered the father of existentialism.

In around 1870 a trend emerged towards realism, focusing on contemporary problems of the day. A writer of this genre, novelist Henrik Pontoppidan, won the Nobel Prize in 1917 shortly after publishing the epic *The Realm of the Dead*, which attacked materialism. Another Dane who won the Nobel Prize for Literature was Johannes Vilhelm Jensen (1873-1950), who wrote the six-volume novel *The Long Journey*, and *The Fall of the King*, a story about Danes in Renaissance times. Better known outside of Denmark is Martin Andersen Nexø (1869-1954), whose novels about the proletariat, the four-volume *Pelle the Conqueror* and *Ditte, Child of Man*, helped bring attention to the conditions of the poor and spurred widespread reform in Denmark.

The most famous Danish writer of the 20th century, Karen Blixen (1885-1962), started her career with *Seven Gothic Tales*, which was published in New York under the pen name Isak Dinesen. She is best known for *Out of Africa*, the memoirs of her farm life in Kenya, which she wrote in 1937.

Denmark's foremost contemporary novelist is Peter Høeg, who wrote the international best seller *Miss Smilla's Feeling For Snow* (1992; published in the USA as *Smilla's Sense of Snow*), a suspense mystery set in Copenhagen and Greenland.

Theatre & Dance

The Royal Theatre (Det Kongelige Teater) in Copenhagen first opened in 1748 as a court theatre, performing the plays of Denmark's most famous playwright, Ludvig Holberg

Søren Kierkegaard

Søren Kierkegaard, Denmark's most famous philosopher, was born into a prosperous Copenhagen family on 5 May 1813. When he was in early 20s, his father died and left Søren with an inheritance that freed him from the need to work. He studied theology and philosophy at the University of Copenhagen and devoted his entire life to studying and writing.

Kierkegaard was vehemently opposed to the philosophy of Georg Wilhelm Friedrich (GWF) Hegel, which was prevalent in 19th century Europe and embraced by the Danish Lutheran church. In contrast, Kierkegaard's writings confronted the individual to make choices entirely of his or her own among the alternatives that life offered. In his first great work, *Either/Or*, published in 1843, the alternative was between aesthetic pleasures or an ethical life. This work, like many that followed, was in part inspired by Kierkegaard's lifelong pains over breaking off an engagement to a young woman named Regine Olsen. He continued to wrestle with the implications of his broken engagement in subsequent writings, including *Fear and Trembling* (1843), which relates Abraham's biblical sacrifice of Isaac to Kierkegaard's own sacrifice.

Kierkegaard's greatest attack on Hegelianism, and his most philosophically important work, was *Concluding Unscientific Postscript to the Philosophical Fragments* (1846), which passionately put forward the tenets of existentialism.

Kierkegaard was considered by many in the establishment to be a fanatic, and his friends were few, even in the literary world. His works would remain virtually unknown outside Denmark until the 20th century.

The last years of Kierkegaard's life were dominated by a bitter, acrimonious battle with the established church. The toll was so great that it slowly drained his health and he died of exhaustion in a Copenhagen hospital in 1855 at the age of 42. At the time of his death, Kierkegaard felt his works had largely fallen upon deaf ears, but posthumously his writings have become a vanguard for existentialist philosophers worldwide. ■

(1684-1754). Today its repertoire encompasses international works, including Shakespearian plays, as well as classical and contemporary Danish plays.

In the mid-18th century, the Royal Danish Ballet (Den Kongelige Ballet), which also performs at the Royal Theatre, took its present form under the leadership of the French choreographer and ballet master August Bournonville (1805-79). Today the Royal Danish Ballet, which has a troupe of nearly 100 dancers, still performs a number of Bournonville's romantic ballets, such as *La Sylphide* and *Napoli*, along with more contemporary works. Considered the finest ballet company in northern Europe, it is currently directed by Peter Schaufuss, who started his career here as a dancer and pre-

viously directed the English National Ballet and the Berlin Ballet.

Also in the Royal Theatre is the Royal Danish Opera (Den Kongelige Opera), which has an ensemble of 32 singers and a renowned 60-member opera chorus. It performs about 18 operas each season.

The Royal Danish Orchestra (Det Kongelige Kapel), which was founded in 1448, giving it claim to be the oldest orchestra in the world, accompanies the ballet and opera performances at the Royal Theatre.

Film

The best-known Danish director of the early 20th century was Carl Theodor Dreyer (1889-1968), who directed numerous films, including the 1928 French masterpiece *La*

Nobel Prize Winners

Twelve Danes have received Nobel Prizes since 1901, the year the prizes were first awarded. They are as follows:

1903 – Physiology/Medicine: Niels R Finsen, who introduced light-radiation treatment for diseases such as lupus

1908 – Peace: Fredrik Bajer, a peace activist and writer

1917 – Literature: Karl A Gjellerup, for poetry inspired by lofty ideals, and Henrik Pontoppidan, for his insightful descriptions of everyday life in Denmark

1920 – Physiology/Medicine: Auguste Krogh, for discovering the capillary motor-regulating mechanism

1922 – Physics: Niels Bohr, one of the fathers of atomic power, for his investigation into radiation and the structure of atoms

1926 – Physiology/Medicine: cancer researcher Johannes AG Fibiger, for his discovery of the Spiroptera carcinoma

1943 – Physiology/Medicine: Henrik CP Dam (with Edward Doisy of the USA), for the discovery of Vitamin K

1944 – Literature: Johannes V Jensen, for the strength of his poetic imagination

1975 – Physics: Aage Bohr and Ben Mottelson (with James Rainwater of the USA), for the discovery of the link between collective motion and particle motion in atomic nuclei and the development of the theory of the structure of the atomic nucleus

1984 – Physiology/Medicine: Niels K Jerne (with Georges JF Koehler of Germany and Cesar Milstien of the UK), for theories on the development and control of the immune system and the discovery of the principle of monoclonal antibody production ∎

Niels Ryberg Finsen's work led to the development of radiation therapy

Passion de Jeanne d'Arc, which was acclaimed for its rich visual textures and innovative use of close-ups. In the midst of WW II, Dreyer boldly filmed *Vredens Dag* (Day of Wrath), which made so many allusions to the tyranny of Nazi occupation that he was forced to flee to Sweden.

Still it wasn't until the 1980s that Danish directors attracted a more widespread international audience. In 1988 *Babette's Feast*, directed by Gabriel Axel, won the Academy Award for Best Foreign Film. *Babette's Feast* was an adaptation of a story written by Karen Blixen, whose novel *Out of Africa* had been turned into an Oscar-winning Hollywood movie just three years earlier.

In 1989, Danish director Bille August won the Academy Award for Best Foreign Film as well the Cannes Film Festival's Palme d'Or award for *Pelle the Conqueror*, adapted from the book by Danish author Martin Andersen Nexø. August is currently filming his adaptation of *Miss Smilla's Feeling For Snow*, the best seller by Peter Høeg, which will star Julia Ormond and is expected to be released by late 1996.

CULTURE

Danes pride themselves on being thoroughly modern, and the wearing of folk costumes, the celebration of traditional festivals and the clinging to old-fashioned customs is less prevalent in Denmark than in most other European countries. There are, of course, traditional aspects of the Danish lifestyle that aren't apparent at first glance.

Perhaps nothing captures the Danish perspective more than the concept of *hygge* which, roughly translated, means cosy and snug. It implies shutting out the turmoil and troubles of the outside world and striving instead for a warm intimate mood. Hygge affects how Danes approach many aspects of their personal lives, from designing their homes to their fondness for small cafés and pubs. There's no greater compliment that a Dane can give their host than to thank them for a cosy evening.

Visitors will find Danes to be relaxed, casual and not given to extremes. They are tolerant of different lifestyles. Indeed, in 1989 Denmark became the first European country to legalise same-sex marriages and offer gay partnerships the same rights as heterosexual couples.

The national sport is football (soccer), while cycling, rowing, sailing and windsurfing are also popular. Despite the country's small size, over the years Denmark has won Olympic gold medals in sailing, kayaking, cycling, swimming and platform diving.

RELIGION

More than 90% of all Danes officially belong to the state supported national church of Denmark, an Evangelical Lutheran denomination, though fewer than 5% are regular church-goers.

Although the Lutheran church is connected to the state, Danes enjoy freedom of religion. In larger cities, there are places of worship for Catholics, Anglicans and Jews.

LANGUAGE

The Danish language belongs, together with Swedish, Norwegian, Icelandic and Faroese, to the northern branch of the Germanic language group. Consequently, written Danish bears a strong resemblance to these languages. Spoken Danish on the other hand has evolved in a different direction, introducing sounds and pronunciation not found elsewhere.

Grammatically, Danish has the same general rules and syntax as the other Germanic languages of Scandinavia. The nouns have two genders – masculine, *en*, and neuter, *et*. Articles are suffixed to the noun: *-en* for masculine singular nouns and *-et* for feminine singular nouns. Plural nouns take the suffixes *-ne* (indefinite) and *-ene* (definite), regardless of gender.

Danish has a polite form of address, using the personal pronouns *De* and *Dem*. The translations in this chapter are mostly in the familiar form using *du* and *deg*, except where it is appropriate and/or wise to use the formal form. In general, use the formal form when speaking to senior citizens and officials, and the familiar form the rest of the time.

Most Danes speak English, and many also speak German. However, an effort to at least learn the basics, such as memorising the Danish words for 'Thank you', 'Goodbye', 'Hello' and 'I'm sorry', will be appreciated. With an increased command of the language, you will be rewarded by gaining a greater insight into Denmark and the Danes.

Note that Danish has all of the letters of the English alphabet plus three others, æ, ø and å. These fall at the end of the alphabet and we have used this order thoughout the book.

Pronunciation

You may find Danish pronunciation difficult. Consonants are drawled, swallowed and even omitted completely, creating, in conjunction with vowels, the peculiarity of the glottal stop or stød. Its sound is rather as a Cockney would say 'bottle'. Stress is usually placed on the first syllable or on the first letter of the word. In general though, the best advice is to listen and learn. Good luck.

Vowels

a	as in 'father'
a, æ	as in 'act'
u(n), å, o	as in 'walk'
e (g)	as in 'eye'
e, i	short, flat 'e' as in the French et
i	as in 'see'
æ	as in 'bet'
ø	as the 'er' in 'fern', but shorter
o, u	as in 'zoo'
o	as in 'pot'
o(v)	like 'out' or 'vow', but shorter
o(r)	as in 'more' but with less emphasis on the 'r'
u	as in 'pull'
y	a long, sharp 'u' as in the German über

Semiconsonants

w	similar to the 'v' in 'Volkswagon'
j	as in 'yet'

Consonants

Consonants are pronounced as in English with the exception of the following:

sj	as in 'ship'
ch	as in 'cheque', but sharper
c	as in 'cell'
(o)d	like the 'th' in 'these'
ng	as in 'sing'
g	as in 'get', if before a vowel
h	as in 'horse'
k	as in 'cat'
b	as in 'box'
r	a rolling 'r' abruptly cut short

Greetings & Civilities

Hello (formal/ informal).	Goddag/Heg.
Goodbye.	Farvel.
Yes.	Ja.
No.	Nej.
Please.	Må jeg bede/Værsgo.
Thank you.	Tak.
That's fine. You're welcome.	Det er i orden. Selv tak.
Excuse me (Sorry).	Undskyld.
May I/Do you mind?	Må jeg/Tillader De?

Language Difficulties

Do you speak English?
  Taler De engelsk?
Does anyone speak English?
  Er der nogen som taler engelsk?
I (don't) understand.
  Jeg forstår (ikke).

Small Talk

What is your name?
  Hvad hedder du?
My name is ...
  Mit navn er ...
Where are you from?
  Hvorfra kommer du?
I am from ...
  Jeg er fra ...
How old are you?
  Hvor gammel er du?
I am ... years old.
  Jeg er ... år gammel.

Getting Around

What time does the ... leave/arrive?	Hvornår går/ ankommer ...?
boat	båden
bus (city)	bussen
bus (intercity)	rutebilen
train	toget

I would like a ...	Jeg vil gerne have en ...
one-way ticket	enkeltbillet
return ticket	tur-retur billet

1st class	første klasse
2nd class	anden klasse

Directions

Where is ...?
  Hvor er ...?
I want to go to ...
  Jeg vil gerne til ...
Can you show me (on the map)?
  Kunne de vise mig (på kortet)?

far/near	fjern/nær
Go straight ahead.	Gå ligefrem.
Turn left ...	Drej til venstre ...
Turn right ...	Drej til højre ...

Around Town

I'm looking for ...	Jeg søger efter ...
a bank	en bank
the city centre	centrum
the ... embassy	den ... ambassade
my hotel	mit hotel
the market	markedet
the museum	museet
the police	politiet
the post office	postkontoret
a public toilet	et offentligt toilet
the telephone centre	telefoncentralen
the tourist information office	turist- informationen

beach	strand
castle	slot
cathedral	katedral/domkirke
church	kirke

Useful Signs

CAMPINGPLADS	CAMPING GROUND
INDGANG	ENTRANCE
UDGANG	EXIT
GÆSTGIVERI	GUESTHOUSE
VANDRERHJEM	HOSTEL
KRO	INN
INGEN ADGANG	NO ENTRY
IKKE-RYGERE	NO SMOKING
ÅBEN	OPEN
LUKKET	CLOSED
POLITI	POLICE
POLITISTATION	POLICE STATION
FORBUDT	PROHIBITED
JERNBANESTATION/ BANEGÅRD	RAILWAY STATION
TOILETTER	TOILETS
HERRER/DAMER	MEN/WOMEN

main square	hovedtorv/torvet
monastery	kloster
old city	den gamle by
palace	palads
ruins	ruiner
synagogue	synagoge

Accommodation

Where is a cheap hotel?
  Hvor er et billig hotel?
What is the address?
  Hvad er adressen?
Could you write the address, please?
  Kunne De være så venlig at skrive adressen ned?
Do you have any rooms available?
  Har I ledige værelser?

I would like ...	Jeg vil gerne have ...
a single room	et enkeltværelse
a double room	et dobbeltværelse
a room with a bathroom	et værelse med bad
to share a dorm	plads i en sovesal
a bed	en seng

How much is it per night/per person?
Hvor meget koster det per nat/per person?
Can I see it?
Må jeg se værelset?
Where is the bathroom?
Hvor er toiletet?

Food

breakfast	*morgenmad*
lunch	*frokost*
dinner	*middag*

I would like today's special meal, please.
Jeg tager dagens ret, tak.
I am a vegetarian.
Jeg er vegetar.

Shopping

How much is it ...?
Hvor meget koster det ...?

bookshop	*boghandel*
camera shop	*fotohandel*
clothing store	*klædemagasin*
delicatessen	*delikatesse*
laundry	*vaskeri*
market	*marked*
newsagency	*aviskiosk*
souvenir shop	*souvenirbutik*

Health

My friend is/I am sick.
Min ven er/Jeg er syg.

I'm ...	*Jeg er ...*
diabetic	*diabetiker*
epileptic	*epileptisk*
asthmatic	*astmatisk*

I'm allergic to antibiotics/penicillin.
Jeg er allergisk overfor antibiotikum/penicillin.
I need medication for ...
Jeg behøver et medikament imod ...
I have a prescription.
Jeg har en recept.
I have a toothache.
Jeg har tandpine.

My gums hurt.
Mit tandkød gør ondt.
I don't want it extracted.
Jeg vil ikke have den trukket.

chemist	*apoteker*
dentist	*tandlægen*
doctor	*lægen*
hospital	*hospitalet*

antiseptic	*antiseptisk*
aspirin	*aspirin*
condoms	*kondomer*
contraceptive	*præventiv*
medicine	*medicin*
nausea	*kvalme*
sunblock cream	*solcreme*
tampons	*tamponer*

Time & Dates

What time is it?
Hvad er klokken?

today	*i dag*
tonight	*i nat*
tomorrow	*i morgen*
in the morning	*om morgenen*
in the evening	*om aftenen*

Monday	*mandag*
Tuesday	*tirsdag*
Wednesday	*onsdag*
Thursday	*torsdag*
Friday	*fredag*
Saturday	*lørdag*
Sunday	*søndag*

January	*januar*
February	*februar*
March	*marts*
April	*april*
May	*maj*
June	*juni*
July	*juli*
August	*august*
September	*september*
October	*oktober*
November	*november*
December	*december*

Numbers

0	*nul*	30	*tredive*
1	*en*	40	*fyrre*
2	*to*	50	*halvtreds*
3	*tre*	60	*tres*
4	*fire*	70	*halvfjerds*
5	*fem*	80	*firs*
6	*seks*	90	*halvfems*
7	*syv*	100	*hundrede*
8	*otte*	1000	*tusind*
9	*ni*	one million	*en million*
10	*ti*		
11	*elleve*		
12	*tolv*		
13	*tretten*		
20	*tyve*		
21	*enogtyve*		

Emergencies

Help!	*Hjælp!*
I'm lost.	*Jeg har gået vild.*
Call a doctor!	*Ring efter en læge!*
Call the police!	*Ring efter politiet!*
Go away!	*Forsvind!*

Facts for the Visitor

PASSPORT

Your most important travel document is a passport, which should remain valid until well after your trip. If it's about to expire, renew it before you go. This may not be easy to do overseas, and some countries insist your passport remain valid for a specified period (usually three months) after your visit.

Applying for or renewing a passport can take anything from a few days to several months, so don't leave it until the last minute. Bureaucracy usually grinds faster if you do everything in person rather than relying on the mail or agents. First check what is required: passport photos, birth certificate, exact payment in cash, whatever.

Australian citizens can apply at a post office, or the passport office in their state capital; Britons can apply at major post offices; Canadians can apply at regional passport offices; New Zealanders can apply at any district office of the Department of Internal Affairs; and US citizens must apply in person (but may usually renew by mail) at a US Passport Agency office or some courthouses and post offices.

Citizens of many European countries don't always need a valid passport for travel within Europe; a national identity card may be sufficient. An EU citizen travelling to another EU country will generally face the least problems. Check with your travel agent or the Danish embassy in your home country before you go.

Once you start travelling, carry your passport (or national identity card) at all times and guard it carefully. It's a good idea to also carry a photocopy of it in a separate place.

VISAS & PERMITS

A visa is a stamp in your passport permitting you to enter the country in question and stay for a specified period of time. There's a wide variety including tourist, transit and business visas. In most cases, however, travellers are allowed to stay up to three months in Denmark without a visa.

Therefore, most readers of this book will have little to do with visas unless they're also going on to other countries that require a visa, such as the Baltic States or other parts of the former USSR.

Visa requirements can change and you should always check with embassies or a reputable travel agent before travelling.

It's generally easier to get your visas as you go along, rather than arranging them all beforehand. If you're travelling widely before or after Denmark, carry plenty of spare passport photos (you'll need between one and four every time you apply for a visa).

Danish Visas

Visa regulations are always subject to change, so it's essential that you check the situation with your local Danish embassy or consulate before leaving home.

Citizens of the USA, Canada, Australia and New Zealand need a valid passport to enter Denmark, but they don't need a visa for stays of less than three months. In addition, no entry visa is needed by citizens of any of the following countries: Andorra, Argentina, Austria, Bahamas, Barbados, Belgium, Belize, Benin, Bolivia, Bosnia-Hercegovina, Botswana, Brazil, Brunei, Chile, Colombia, Costa Rica, Cote d'Ivoire, Croatia, Cuba, Cyprus, Czech Republic, Dominica, Dominican Republic, Ecuador, El Salvador, Fiji, Finland, France, Gambia, Germany, Great Britain, Greece, Grenada, Guatemala, Guyana, Haiti, Honduras, Hungary, Iceland, Ireland, Israel, Italy, Jamaica, Japan, Kenya, Kiribati, Republic of Korea, Lesotho, Liechtenstein, Lithuania, Luxembourg, Malawi, Malaysia, Malta, Mauritius, Mexico, Monaco, Namibia, Netherlands, Nicaragua, Niger, Norway, Panama, Paraguay, Peru, Poland, Portugal, St Lucia, St Vincent & the Grenadines, San Marino, Seychelles, Sierra Leone, Singapore, Slovakia, Slovenia, Solomon Islands, Spain, Suriname, Swaziland, Sweden, Switzerland, Tanzania, Thailand, Togo, Trinidad & Tobago, Tuvalu, Uganda, Uruguay, Vatican City, Venezuela, Zambia and Zimbabwe.

Nationals of other countries must apply for a visa from a Danish embassy or consulate before arrival in Denmark.

Work Permits
Citizens of Scandinavian countries have the right to reside and work in Denmark without restrictions.

Citizens of other EU countries are entitled to look for work in Denmark and it's fairly straightforward to get a residency permit if you find work. The main prerequisite is that your job provide an income that's high enough to cover your living expenses. No work permits are required of citizens from EU countries.

Citizens of other countries are required to get a work permit before entering Denmark. This requires first securing a job offer and then applying for a work-and-residency permit at a Danish embassy or consulate while you're still in your home country (or the country where you've had legal residency for the last six months). You can enter Denmark only after the permit has been granted. Currently these permits are extraordinarily rare for anyone without a specialised skill.

Educational Permits
Although the situation is considerably relaxed for Nordic and EU citizens, people from other countries must obtain a residency permit in order to enter Denmark for the purposes of study. This can be applied for after the applicant has been accepted for enrolment at a Danish university or college. If you enter the college for more than a short exchange, such as with the intention of graduating, there will be further conditions, the main one being that the course should be one that is not available in your home country. If your purpose is simply to learn Danish, that's generally not enough to qualify for a resi-

dency permit. In order to obtain the permit, students must be able to show that they are capable of paying all costs attendant to their stay. Normally, work permits are not issued to students who hold a residency permit for the purpose of attending a college or university in Denmark.

EMBASSIES
Danish Embassies
Danish embassies abroad include:

Australia
Royal Danish Embassy, 15 Hunter St, Yarralumla, ACT 2600 (☎ 06-273 2195, 06-273 3864). There's also a consulate in Sydney.
Austria
Königlich Dänische Botschaft, Führichgasse 6 (Postfach 298) 1015 Vienna (☎ 222-512 79 04, fax 222-513 81 20)
Belgium
Ambassade Royale de Danemark, Avenue Louise 221, Bte 7, 1050 Brussels (☎ 2-648 25 25, fax 2-647 07 09)
Canada
Royal Danish Embassy, 85 Range Road, Apt 702, Ottawa, Ontario K1N 8J6 (☎ 613-234-0704, fax 613-234-7368). There's also a consulate in Toronto.
Czech Republic
Royal Danish Embassy, U Páté Baterie 7 (Box 70), Prague (☎ 2-35 31 09, fax 2-35 06 59)
Estonia
Royal Danish Embassy, Rävala Avenue 9, 6th Floor, 0100 Tallinn (☎ 22-445 260, fax 30 33 73 53)
Finland
Kgl Dansk Ambassade, Centralgatan 1 (PB 1042), 00100 Helsinki (☎ 0-17 15 11, fax 0-17 17 41)
France
Ambassade Royale de Danemark, 77 Avenue Marceau, 75116 Paris (☎ 1-44 31 21 21, fax 1-44 31 21 88). There's also a consulate in Marseilles.
Germany
Königlich Dänische Botschaft, Pfälzer Strasse 14 (Postfach 180220), 53032 Bonn (☎ 228-72 99 10, fax 228-729 9131). There are also consulates in Berlin, Dresden, Düsseldorf, Flensburg, Frankfurt, Hamburg and Munich.
Greece
Royal Danish Embassy, 11 Vassillissis Sofias, 106 71 Athens (☎ 1-360 8315, fax 1-363 6163)
Iceland
Kgl Dansk Ambassade, Hverfisgata 29 (Postboks 1540), 101 Reykjavík (☎ 1-62 12 30, fax 1-62 33 16)

Ireland
> Royal Danish Embassy, 121 St Stephen's Green, Dublin 2 (☎ 1-475 6404, fax 1-478 4536)

Israel
> Royal Danish Embassy, 23 Bnei Moshe St, PO Box 21080, Tel Aviv 61210 (☎ 3-544 2144, fax 3-546 5502)

Italy
> Ambasciata di Danimarca, Via dei Monti Parioli 50, 00197 Rome (☎ 6-3200 441, fax 6-3610 290). There's also a consulate in Milan.

Japan
> Royal Danish Embassy, 29-6 Sarugaku-cho, Shibuya-ku, Tokyo 150 (☎ 3-34 96 30 01, fax 3-34 96 34 40)

Latvia
> Royal Danish Embassy, Liela Pils iela 11, 1863 Riga (☎ 2-226 210, fax 2-229 218)

Lithuania
> Royal Danish Embassy, T Kosciuskos 36, Vilnius (☎ 2-628 028, fax 8-290 110)

Netherlands
> Royal Danish Embassy, Koninginnegracht 30 (Postbus 85654), 2508 GJ Den Haag (☎ 70-365 5830, fax 70-360 2150)

New Zealand
> Contact the embassy in Australia

Norway
> Kgl Dansk Ambassade, Olav Kyrres Gate 7, 0244 Oslo (☎ 22 44 18 46, fax 22 55 46 34)

Poland
> Ambasada Dúnska, Ul Rakowiecka 19, 02-517 Warsaw (☎ 22-490 056, fax 22-487 580)

Russia
> Royal Danish Embassy, 9 Pereulok Ostrovskovo, Moscow (☎ 095-201 7860, fax 095-201 5357). There's also a consulate in St Petersburg.

Singapore
> Royal Danish Embassy, 101 Thomson Road 13-01/02, United Square, Singapore 1130 (☎ 250-3383, fax 253-3764)

South Africa
> Royal Danish Embassy, 8th Floor, Sanlam Centre, Pretorius & Andries Sts, PO Box 2942, 0001 Pretoria (☎ 12-322 0595, fax 12-322 0596)

Spain
> Embajada Real de Dinamarca, Claudio Coella 91, 28006 Madrid (☎ 1-431 8445, fax 1-431 9168).

Sweden
> Kgl Dansk Ambassade, Jakobs Torg 1 (Box 1638), 11186 Stockholm (☎ 8-231860, fax 8-791 7220)

Switzerland
> Ambassade Royale de Danemark, Thunstrasse 95, 3006 Bern (☎ 31-352 5011, fax 31-351 2395)

UK
> Royal Danish Embassy, 55 Sloane St, London SW1X 9SR (☎ 0171-333 0200, fax 0171-333 0270)

USA
> Royal Danish Embassy, 3200 Whitehaven St NW, Washington DC 20008 (☎ 202-234-4300, fax 202-328-1470). There are also consulates in Los Angeles, Chicago and New York.

Foreign Embassies & Consulates

The following foreign diplomatic representatives to Denmark are in Copenhagen:

Australia
> Kristianiagade 21 (☎ 35 26 22 44)

Austria
> Sølundsvej 1 (☎ 39 29 41 41)

Belgium
> Øster Allé 7 (☎ 35 26 03 88)

Canada
> Kristen Bernikowsgade 1 (☎ 33 12 22 99)

Czech Republic
> Ryvangs Allé 14 (☎ 31 29 18 88)

Finland
> Sankt Annæ Plads 24 (☎ 33 13 42 14)

France
> Kongens Nytorv 4 (☎ 33 15 51 22)

Germany
> Stockholmsgade 57 (☎ 35 26 16 22)

Greece
> Borgergade 16 (☎ 33 11 45 33)

Hungary
> Strandvejen 170, Charlottenlund (☎ 31 63 16 88)

Iceland
> Dantes Plads 3 (☎ 33 15 96 04)

India
> Vangehusvej 15 (☎ 31 18 28 88)

Ireland
> Østbanegade 21 (☎ 31 42 32 33)

Israel
> Lundevangsvej 4, Hellerup (☎ 31 62 62 88)

Italy
> Gammel Vartov Vej 7, Hellerup (☎ 31 62 68 77)

Latvia
> Rosbæksvej 17 (☎ 39 27 60 00)

Lithuania
> Bernstorffsvej 214, Charlottenlund (☎ 31 63 62 07)

Japan
> Pilestræde 61 (☎ 33 11 33 44)

Luxembourg
> Fridtjof Nansens Plads 5 (☎ 35 26 82 00)

Netherlands
> Toldbodgade 33 (☎ 33 15 62 93)

New Zealand
> Contact the British embassy

Norway
> Trondhjems Plads 4 (☎ 31 38 89 85)

Portugal
   Hovedvagtsgade 6 (☎ 33 13 13 01)
Russia
   Kristianiagade 5 (☎ 31 42 55 85)
South Africa
   Gammel Vartov Vej 8, Hellerup (☎ 31 18 01 55)
Spain
   Upsalagade 26 (☎ 31 42 22 66)
Sweden
   Sankt Annæ Plads 15A (☎ 33 14 22 42)
Switzerland
   Amaliegade 14 (☎ 33 14 17 96)
Turkey
   Rosbæksvej 15 (☎ 31 20 27 88)
UK
   Kastelsvej 40 (☎ 35 26 46 00)
USA
   Dag Hammarskjølds Allé 24 (☎ 31 42 31 44)

DOCUMENTS
Apart from your passport there are a number of other documents that may be worth taking with you.

International Health Certificate
You'll need this yellow booklet only if you're coming into the region from areas, such as Africa and South America, where diseases like yellow fever are prevalent.

International Driving Permit (IDP)
Bring your home driving licence, as Denmark accepts many foreign driving licences without restriction, including those issued in the USA, Canada, the UK and other EU countries. If you don't hold a European driving licence and plan to drive elsewhere in the region, it's a good idea to obtain an IDP from your local automobile association before you leave – you'll need a passport photo and a valid licence. IDPs are usually inexpensive and valid for one year only. An IDP helps Europeans make sense of your unfamiliar local licence (make sure you take that with you, too) and can make life much simpler, especially when hiring cars and motorbikes.

While you're at it, if you're a member of the local automobile association, ask for a Card of Introduction – or at least take your association card. This may entitle you to services offered by affiliated organisations in Europe, usually free of charge (touring maps and information, help with breakdowns, technical and legal advice, for example).

Camping Carnet
In many countries, local automobile associations issue a Camping Carnet, which is basically a camping ground ID. Carnets are also issued by local camping federations and sometimes on the spot at camping grounds. Once in Denmark, they can also be purchased at a number of tourist offices. They incorporate third-party insurance for any damage you may cause. In Denmark your camping card will be accepted if it's an international one and has the current year's stamp.

Hostelling Card
If you have an international hostel card be sure to bring it. Some European hostels don't require that you be a hostelling member, but often charge less if you have a card. In Denmark, if you don't have an international card you must either buy a one-night Hostelling International guest card for 25 kr or an annual card for 100 kr; both are available on the spot at hostels.

Another advantage of hostel cards is that they'll get you discounts at some museums and sightseeing spots. A complete list of the discounts available are found in the free Danish hostelling booklet. See Hostelling International in the later Accommodation section.

Student & Youth Cards
The most useful of these is the International Student Identity Card (ISIC), a plastic ID-style card with your photograph, which can provide discounts on many forms of transport and cheap or free admission to some museums and sights.

There is a worldwide industry in fake student cards, and many places now stipulate a maximum age for student discounts or, more simply, they've substituted a 'youth discount' for a 'student discount'. If you're aged under 26 but not a student, you can apply for a Federation of International Youth

Travel Organisations (FIYTO) card or a Euro26 card, which gives much the same discounts as an ISIC.

Both types of card are issued by student unions, hostelling organisations or student travel agencies. They don't automatically entitle you to discounts, but you won't find out until you flash the card.

CUSTOMS

The following items can be brought into Denmark duty free: one litre of hard liquor or two litres of fortified or sparkling wine, as well as two litres of table wine; 200 cigarettes, 50 cigars or 250 grams of tobacco; and general items of a personal nature. The age requirement for tax-free importation of alcohol is 17.

If obtained from an EU country, the duty-free allowances on many goods, including spirits and cigarettes, are 50% higher.

When you arrive in Denmark, there will be two channels. You must use the red channel if you're bringing in more than the usual allowance of duty-free goods or any restricted items (guns, drugs etc). Use the green channel – which is generally a quick exit – if you have nothing to declare.

MONEY

The general rule holds doubly true in expensive Denmark: bring as much money as you can!

It's convenient to have Danish currency on hand when you arrive. Fortunately the Copenhagen airport bank is open to meet most incoming flights. If you're on an international ferry to Denmark, they'll not only exchange US dollars and local currencies to Danish kroner on board, but if you buy a meal or use the duty-free shops, irregardless of the currency you pay in, most will give you change in Danish kroner upon request.

Because of its widespread acceptance, the US dollar is generally the handiest foreign currency to carry, particularly if you're travelling farther afield than Denmark. Danish banks will convert a wide range of currencies, however, including the US dollar, Canadian dollar, British pound, Irish pound,

German mark, French franc, Japanese yen, Dutch guilder, Belgian franc, Swiss franc, Austrian schilling, Italian lira, Spanish peseta, Portuguese escudo, Greek drachma, Finnish markka and kroner from Norway, Sweden and Iceland. Keep in mind that foreign coins are seldom accepted by banks, so try to unload those before arriving in Denmark.

Cash

Nothing beats cash for convenience…or risk. If you lose it, it's gone forever.

Travellers' Cheques

The main idea of carrying travellers' cheques is to offer some protection from theft. American Express and Thomas Cook cheques are widely accepted and have efficient replacement policies.

Keeping a record of the cheque numbers and those you have used is vital when it comes to replacing lost cheques. You should keep this separate from the cheques themselves. Cheques are available in various currencies; choose the currency you're likely to need most, particularly if you'll be travelling through more than one country.

When you change cheques, don't look at just the exchange rate; ask about fees and commissions as well. Danish banks add hefty fees when cashing travellers' cheques. Because the charges are a flat per-cheque fee, it's best to bring travellers' cheques in high denominations.

International Transfers

Transferring money from your home bank will be easier if you've authorised someone back home to access your account. Specify the city, the bank and the branch to which you want your money directed, or ask your home bank to tell you where there's a suitable one, and make sure you get the details right. If you have the choice, find a large bank and ask for the international division.

Money sent by telegraphic transfer (which typically costs US$30 or more) should reach you within a week; by mail, allow at least two weeks.

You can also transfer money by American Express and pick it up at their office in Copenhagen. There are also Western Union agents in Denmark; call ☎ 80 01 07 11 (a toll-free number) for locations.

Plastic Cards & ATMs

If you're not familiar with the options, ask your bank to explain the workings and relative merits of credit, debit, charge and cash cards.

Plastic cards are an ideal travelling companion – not only can you make purchases without carrying a wad of money but you can use them to withdraw cash from selected banks and automatic teller machines (ATMs). As ATMs are linked up internationally, you can often use them in Denmark the same way as back home. However, credit cards usually aren't hooked up to ATM networks unless you specifically ask your bank to do this and request a PIN number, so be sure to do that before you travel.

Keep in mind that ATMs aren't 100% fail-safe; if an ATM in Europe swallows a card that was issued outside Europe, it can be a major headache, so you may be better off trying to make your transaction with a human teller.

Cash cards, which you use at home to withdraw money directly from your bank account or savings account, are slowly becoming more widely linked internationally – ask your bank at home for advice. Currently, the Cirrus network is fairly widespread in Europe, and is used by ATM machines at Den Danske Bank (Denmark's largest banking network) as well as a few other banks. Cirrus cards, as well as Visa and MasterCard, can also be used at all Danish cash dispensers marked 'Kontanten'.

Credit cards like Visa and MasterCard (also known as Access or Eurocard) are widely accepted in Denmark. However, these cards can be difficult to replace if lost abroad. On the other hand, charge cards like American Express and Diners Club have offices in the major centres of most countries which will replace a lost card within 24 hours. However, charge cards are not quite as universally accepted as credit cards.

The best advice is to not put all your eggs in one basket. If you want to rely heavily on bits of plastic, bring at least two different cards. Better still is a combination of plastic cards and travellers' cheques so you have something to fall back on if an ATM swallows your card or the banks in the area don't accept it.

Eurocheques

Guaranteed personal cheques are another way of carrying money or obtaining cash. The most popular of these is the Eurocheque. To get Eurocheques, you need a European bank account; it takes at least two weeks to apply for the cheques, which may be too long for most visitors.

Throughout Europe, when paying for something in a shop or withdrawing cash from a bank or post office, you write out a Eurocheque (up to its maximum limit, otherwise simply write out two or more cheques) and show the accompanying guarantee card with your signature and registration number. You may also have to show your passport. Once the shopkeeper or bank clerk has checked the cheque's signature with that on the card and copied your registration number onto the cheque, it's guaranteed by the issuing bank, which will deduct the amount from your account when the paperwork comes through.

The card can double as an ATM card, and should obviously be kept separate from the cheques for safety.

Currency

The Danish *krone* is most often written DKK in international money markets, Dkr in northern Europe and kr within Denmark.

The krone is divided into 100 øre (pronounced ore-a). There are 25 øre, 50 øre, one krone, two kroner, five kroner, 10 kroner and 20-kroner coins. Notes come in 50, 100, 500 and 1000-kroner denominations.

Exchange Rates

The following currencies convert at these approximate rates:

Australia A$1	=	4.29 Dkr
Canada C$1	=	4.11 Dkr
France FF1	=	1.12 Dkr
Germany DM1	=	3.87 Dkr
Japan ¥ 100	=	5.38 Dkr
New Zealand NZ$1	=	3.38 Dkr
Norway 1 Nkr	=	0.88 Dkr
Sweden 1 Skr	=	0.81 Dkr
UK £1	=	8.73 Dkr
USA US$1	=	5.68 Dkr

Changing Money

All common travellers' cheques are accepted at major banks in Denmark. It's best to bring travellers' cheques in higher denominations as bank fees for changing money are a hefty 20 kr per cheque with a 40 kr minimum. Cash transactions are charged a 20-kr fee (25 kr at a few banks) for any size transaction; that doesn't necessarily make cash more favourable however, as travellers' cheques command about a 1% better exchange rate.

Post offices have recently begun to exchange foreign currency (cash only) with the same 20-kr fees that banks charge – the main benefit for travellers being Saturday morning opening hours.

Most major banks have ATMs, many of them accessible outside normal banking hours, which give cash advances on Visa, MasterCard and Cirrus cards. A few banks, especially in Copenhagen, have also installed 24-hour cash-exchange machines that change major foreign currencies, such as the US dollar and the British pound, into Danish kroner.

Costs

By anything other than Scandinavian standards, Denmark is certainly an expensive country. Part of the credit lies with the 25% value-added tax (VAT), called *moms* in Danish, which is included in every price from hotel rooms and restaurant meals to car rentals and shop purchases. See Consumer Tax Refunds in this section.

Still, your costs will depend on how you travel and it's possible to see Denmark without spending a fortune. If you're travelling on a budget, one way to cut down on expenses is to take advantage of Denmark's extensive network of camping grounds and hostels. The latter are widely used by all age groups and are usually set up more like small hotels than cavernous drop-in centres.

In terms of basic expenses, if you camp and stay in hostels and prepare your own meals you might get by on 175 kr a day. If you stay in modest hotels and eat at inexpensive restaurants, you can expect to spend about 400 kr a day if you're doubling up, 500 kr if you're travelling alone. Interestingly, 1st-class hotels, which commonly have good weekend and holiday rates, are often only about 30% more than low-end hotels.

On top of the amounts given above you'll need to budget for local transport (about 10 kr a ride), admission fees to museums and other sights, entertainment and incidentals. Long-distance public transport is reasonably priced and it helps that Denmark is small – the most expensive train ticket between any two points costs just 231 kr.

If you're travelling by car, it's going to be more expensive. Petrol is around 5.5 kr a litre, car ferries are reasonable but the charges can add up, and if you opt to rent a car in Denmark the costs range from high to exorbitant. Expect to pay 650 kr for daily car rental, although the daily rate on week-long rentals can average about half that – in either case this is for the cheapest economy car! One cost advantage of travelling by car is that you can often find economical accommodation options outside the city centre – so you should save a bit on hotel bills.

Of course there are always ways to circumvent some of the high costs. For instance if you're willing to enter Denmark via Germany you can pick up a rental car there for about one-third of the Danish car-rental fees and then drive north into Denmark.

Tipping & Bargaining

Restaurant bills and taxi fares include service charges in the quoted prices. Further tipping is unnecessary, although rounding up the bill is not uncommon when the service has been particularly good. Bargaining is not a common practice in Denmark.

Consumer Tax Refunds

Foreign visitors from countries outside the EU or Norway who buy goods in Denmark can get a refund of the 25% value-added tax (VAT), less a handling fee, if they spend at least 300 kr at any retail outlet that participates in the Tax-Free plan. This includes most shops catering to tourists. The 300 kr can be a single item or several items, as long as they're purchased from the same shop.

Be sure to obtain the tax-refund 'cheque' from the store when you make the purchase; it should include the date, both the buyer's and seller's name and address, the number and type of goods, the selling price and the VAT amount.

Contact the VAT refund bureau at your point of departure from Denmark to get the refund. At Copenhagen Airport, you'll find a booth in the departure hall; if you're leaving by international train, inform the conductor when you board; if you depart by ship, enquire at the port. If you have questions about VAT refunds call ☎ 32 52 55 66, or pick up a brochure on the programme from participating shops.

WHEN TO GO

Considering its northern latitude, Denmark has a fairly mild climate all year round. Still, the winter months – cold and with short daylight hours – are certainly the least hospitable. Correspondingly, many tourist destinations come alive in late April, when the weather begins to warm up and the daylight hours start to increase, and by October they again become sleepers.

May and June can be delightful months to visit: the earth is a rich green accented with fields of yellow rapeseed flowers, the weather is generally warm and comfortable, and you'll beat the rush of tourists. While autumn can also be pleasant, it's not nearly as scenic because the rural landscape has largely turned to brown and the air quality

suffers as many Danish farmers burn crop waste in the fields.

The high tourist season occurs between July and August and this is the time for open-air concerts, lots of street activity and basking on the beach. Other bonuses for travellers during midsummer are longer hours at museums and other sightseeing attractions, and potential savings on accommodation as some hotels drop their rates. Of course you won't be the only tourist during summer, as many Danes and other Europeans travel during their summer holidays and celebrate midsummer with gusto. The Danish school year is back into full swing by mid-August, so the last half of August can be a particularly attractive time to travel, as it still has summer weather but far fewer crowds.

Before planning a trip, see also the Climate section in the earlier Facts about the Country chapter.

WHAT TO BRING

Travelling light is always the best policy. It's very easy to find almost anything you need along the way. However, keep in mind that because of the value-added tax and the overall high price of goods, most people won't want to be stocking up excessively in Denmark.

Travelpacks, a combination of backpack and shoulder bag, are very popular for carrying gear. The backpack straps zip away inside the pack when not needed so you almost have the best of both worlds – a smart-looking soft bag for checking in at hotels, and a suitable backpack for walking. Some packs have sophisticated shoulder-strap adjustment systems so you can use them comfortably even on long hikes. Travelpacks can be reasonably thief-proofed with small padlocks.

As for clothing, the season you travel in will have a major bearing on what you should bring along. Keep in mind that even during the warmest months, it's good to carry at least a light jacket, as cool weather can sweep across Denmark at any time.

A minimum packing list could include:

- underwear, socks and swimming gear
- a pair of jeans and trousers
- a pair of shorts or a skirt
- a few T-shirts and shirts
- a warm sweater
- a comfortable pair of shoes
- sandals or thongs for shared showers
- a coat or jacket
- a raincoat, umbrella, or waterproof jacket
- a medical kit and sewing kit
- a combination padlock
- a Swiss Army knife
- soap and towel
- toothpaste, toothbrush and toiletries
- a small daypack

Bringing a tent and a sleeping bag is vital if you're camping. A sleeping sheet with pillow cover is necessary if you plan to stay in hostels – you'll have to hire or purchase one if you don't bring your own. You can make one of these sleeping sheets yourself out of old sheets or buy one from your hostel association. A bath towel is also necessary if you're staying in hostels.

A Swiss Army knife is useful for all sorts of things (any pocket knife is fine, so long as it includes a bottle opener and a strong corkscrew). Note than in Denmark an anti-gang law makes it illegal in most cases to carry a knife with a blade more than seven cm long.

A small daypack will prove convenient for city sightseeing. Other items might include a compass (to help orient yourself in large cities), a torch (flashlight), an alarm clock or a watch with an alarm function, an adaptor plug for electrical appliances, a cup water heater to save on buying tea and coffee, sunglasses and an elastic clothesline.

The secret of successful packing is using plastic carry bags inside your travelpack: they keep things organised, and also keep things dry if the bag gets soaked.

Airlines do lose luggage from time to time, but you've got a better chance of it being retrieved if it's tagged with your name and address *inside* as well as outside. Outside tags can always fall off or be removed.

SUGGESTED ITINERARIES
Depending on the length of your stay and your interests, you might like to see and do the following:

Two days
    Copenhagen – get a Copenhagen Card and explore the city
One week
    Copenhagen, North Zealand's castles and beaches, Roskilde, Trelleborg and a bit of southern Zealand
Two weeks
    Sights listed above plus Odense, Ærø, Århus, Skagen, Ribe and other Jutland sights of interest (or Bornholm)
One month
    As above plus Bornholm, south Funen (including Faaborg and the islands of Tåsinge and Langeland), Møn and Falster islands
Two months
    As above but at a slower pace, possibly much of it by bicycle

TOURIST OFFICES
The 111 tourist offices found throughout Denmark can be amazingly helpful, providing you with information on virtually anything from what's happening at the concert theatre to the location of the nearest coin laundry or bicycle-rental shop. Of course they can also help with booking accommodation, finding a certain type of restaurant or providing specific advice on local sightseeing.

Most have multilingual staff who can handle inquiries in English, German and Danish.

Local Tourist Offices
Virtually every good-sized town in Denmark has a tourist office, most often found in the town hall (*rådhus*) or elsewhere on the central square (*torvet*).

Phone and fax numbers and addresses of tourist offices are given under individual towns. You can pick up general literature at these local tourist offices once you arrive, or upon request most will send out a package of tourist materials specific to their area.

If you want to stock up on materials before heading off to the countryside, brochures and booklets about all parts of Denmark are available to walk-in visitors at the main tourist office: Danish Tourist Board, Bernstorffsgade 1, 1577 Copenhagen V. Although the Copenhagen office is the best stocked tourist office in Denmark, other major city offices, such as those in Odense, Århus and Aalborg, can also pile visitors high with a good range of brochures pertaining to all parts of Denmark.

Overseas Representatives
You can receive general information on travel in Denmark, including a road map and an annually updated hotel guide, from Danish tourist offices abroad.

Overseas representatives of the Danish Tourist Board include:

Belgium
Deens Verkeersburo/Office du Tourisme de Danemark, Avenue Louise 221, bte 7, 1050 Brussels (☎ 2-648 37 89, fax 2-647 07 09)
Canada
Danish Tourist Board, PO/CP 636, Mississauga, Ontario LCM 2C2 (☎ 905-820-8984, fax 519-576-7715)
Finland
Danska Turistbyrån, Bensowgränd 6, 02701 Grankulla (☎ 0-505 0036, fax 0-505 0004)
France
Le Conseil du Tourisme du Danemark, 4 rue Henry Monnier, 75009 Paris Cedex 18 (☎ 1-45 96 02 72, fax 1-49 95 03 63)
Germany
Dänisches Fremdenverkehrsamt, Glockengiesserwall 2, Postfach 101329, 20008 Hamburg (☎ 40-327 803, fax 40-337 083)
Dänisches Fremdenverkehrsamt, Friedrichstrasse 180, 10117 Berlin (☎ & fax 30-229 3056)
Dänisches Fremdenverkehrsamt, Postfach 320326, 40418 Düsseldorf (☎ & fax 211-464 438)
Dänisches Fremdenverkehrsamt, Postfach 2021, 23508 Lübeck (☎ & fax 45-081 019)
Italy
Ente Danese per il Turismo, Via Cappuccio 11, 20 123 Milano (☎ 2-87 48 03, fax 2-86 07 12)
Japan
Scandinavian Tourist Board, Sanno Grand Building, Room 912, 2-14-2 Nagata-cho, Chiyoda-ku, 100 Tokyo (☎ 3-35 80 50 30, fax 3-35 03 44 57)
Luxembourg
Office du Tourisme de Danemark/Dänisches Fremdenverkehrsamt, 4 Boulevard Royal, 2449 Luxembourg (☎ 22 21 22, fax 22 21 24)

Netherlands
Deens Verkeersburo, Shipholweg 96a, Postbus 266, 2300 AG Leiden (☎ 71 233 283, fax 71 211 794)
Norway
Danmarks Turistkontor, Tollbugaten 27, Postboks 406 Sentrum, 0103 Oslo (☎ 22 41 17 76, fax 22 41 38 02)
Sweden
Danska Turistbyrån, Biblioteksgatan 25, Box 5524, 114 85 Stockholm (☎ 86 11 72 22, fax 86 11 72 35)
UK
Danish Tourist Board, 55 Sloane St, London SW1X 9SY (☎ 0171-259 5959, fax 0171-259-5955)
USA
Danish Tourist Board, 655 Third Avenue, Suite 1810, New York, NY 10017 (☎ 212-949-2333, fax 212-286-0896)
Danish Tourist Board, PO Box 2722-18, Huntington Beach, CA 92649 (☎ 714-893-7248, fax 714-893-7327)

USEFUL ORGANISATIONS
Organisations in Denmark
The following organisations in Denmark may prove useful:

Danmarks Vandrerhjem (the national Hostelling International (HI) organisation) is at Vesterbrogade 39, 1620 Copenhagen V (☎ 31 31 36 12).
Kilroy Travels (specialising in youth travel) has offices at Skindergade 28 (☎ 33 11 00 44) in Copenhagen, Fredensgade 40 (☎ 86 20 11 44) in Århus, and Pantheonsgade 7 (☎ 66 17 77 80) in Odense.
FDM, or Forenede Danske Motorejere (Denmark's main motoring organisation) has its central office at Firskovvej 32, 2800 Lyngby (☎ 45 93 08 00, fax 45 93 36 80). There are branches in major towns and cities.
Dansk Handicap Forbund (which can help disabled travellers with specific questions) is at Kollektivhuset, Hans Knudsens Plads 1A, 2100 Copenhagen (☎ 31 29 35 55). However, start first with the comprehensive book *Access in Denmark – a Travel Guide for the Disabled* available from Danish tourist offices.
Kvindehuset (Women's House; for information on women's issues) is at Gothersgade 37, 1123 Copenhagen K (☎ 33 14 28 04).
LBL, or Landsforeningen for Bøsser og Lesbiske (the national association for gays and lesbians) is at Knabrostræde 3, 1210 Copenhagen K (☎ 33 13 19 48).

DK-Camp (the largest of several camping associations in Denmark) is at Vestergade 37C, 7100 Vejle (☎ 75 82 49 55, fax 75 82 45 77). It publishes a free bilingual catalogue listing 300 member camping grounds.

Danes Worldwide Archives (helps people of Danish descent trace their roots) is at Postboks 1731, Ved Vor Frue Kirke, 9100 Aalborg (☎ 98 12 57 93).

Dansk Cyklist Forbund (Denmark's main cycling organisation) is at Rømersgade 7, 1362 Copenhagen (☎ 33 32 31 21, fax 33 32 76 83).

Overseas Organisations

The Danish Cultural Institute distributes information on various aspects of Danish culture through its branches in the following countries:

Austria
  Dänisches Kulturinstitut, Ferstelgasse 3/4, 1090 Vienna (☎ 222-48 67 90, fax 222-408 70 86)
Belgium
  Deens Cultureel Instituut/Institut Culturel Danois, Av Expo Universelle 9-Bte 15, 1080 Brussels (☎ 2-428 87 46, fax 2-426 37 16)
Estonia
  Taani Kultuuriinstituut, Mürivahe 11, 0001 Tallinn (☎ 22-446 836, fax 22-601 247)
Germany
  Dänisches Kulturinstitut, Steinstrasse 48, Postfach 100945, 44009 Dortmund (☎ 231-81 16 82)
Hungary
  Dán Kulturális Intezét, Zimay u 4, 6000 Kecskemét (☎ 76-32 39 23, fax 76-32 30 23)
Latvia
  Danijas Kulturas Instituts, Kr Barona iela 12, 1426 PDP Riga (☎ & fax 2-289 994)
Lithuania
  Dank Kulturos Institutas, Vilniaus 39/6, 2600 Vilnius (☎ 2-222 412, fax 2-222 832)
Poland
  Dunski Instytut Kultury, ul Piwna 36/39, 80 831 Gdansk (☎ 58-311 764, fax 58-310 161)
UK
  The Danish Cultural Institute, Carlsberg House, 3 Doune Terrace, Edinburgh EH3 6DY (☎ 0131-225 7189, fax 0131-220 6162)

In the USA, the American-Scandinavian Foundation (☎ 212-879-9779, fax 212-249-3444), 725 Park Avenue, New York, New York 10021, fills much the same function as does the aforementioned Danish Cultural Institute.

BUSINESS HOURS

Office hours are generally from 9 am to 4 pm Monday to Friday. Most banks are open from 9.30 am to 4 pm Monday to Friday (and to 6 pm on Thursday), though banks at international ports and at Copenhagen's Central Station are open longer hours and on weekends.

Most stores are open from 9.30 am to 5.30 pm on weekdays and to 2 pm on Saturday, although the trend in larger cities, such as Copenhagen, is towards longer hours.

HOLIDAYS

Summer holidays for schoolchildren begin around 20 June and end around 10 August. Schools also take a break for a week in mid-October and during the Christmas and New Year period. Many Danes take their main work holiday during the first three weeks of July.

Banks and most businesses are closed on public holidays, and transport schedules are commonly reduced as well. Public holidays observed in Denmark are:

New Year's Day, 1 January
Maundy Thursday, the Thursday before Easter
Good Friday, the Friday before Easter
Easter Day
Easter Monday, the day after Easter
Common Prayer Day, the fourth Friday after Easter
Ascension Day, the fifth Thursday after Easter
Whitsunday, the seventh Sunday after Easter
Whitmonday, the eighth Monday after Easter
Constitution Day, 5 June
Christmas Eve, 24 December (from noon)
Christmas Day, 25 December
Boxing Day, 26 December

EVENTS & FESTIVALS

There are lots of small local festivals, agricultural shows, regattas and fairs all around Denmark that can be fun to attend if chanced upon. In addition, most towns of any size have a weekly market in the town square on either Wednesday or Saturday.

The following is a list of some of Denmark's larger annual events. As the dates and venues can change a bit from year to year, it's suggested that you check with tourist offices for current schedule information.

Handy to pick up is the English-language *Coming Events* booklet, which is published twice a year by the Danish Tourist Board and contains updated schedules and details for all events nationwide.

January

New Year concerts of classical music are performed in major cities in early January by the Zealand, Århus, Odense, Aalborg and West Jutland symphony orchestras.

February & March

Major festivals hibernate during the cold, dark Danish winter but there are concerts by local musicians, changing museum exhibitions and full programmes by the royal ballet and opera companies.

Gardens at Forum, a horticultural exhibition, is held in mid-March at the Forum in Copenhagen.

Bakken, an amusement park outside Copenhagen, opens for the season at the end of March.

April

The *Queen's birthday* on 16 April is celebrated at Amalienborg in Copenhagen with the royal guards in full ceremonial dress and the queen waving from the palace balcony.

Denmark's two major amusement parks, *Tivoli* in Copenhagen and *Legoland* in Billund, open for the season in April.

May

The *Viking Market* held in Ribe the first weekend in May re-enacts a Viking marketplace with costumed vendors, craft demonstrations, riding and archery. During the week that follows, Ribe holds its annual *Tulip Festival* with sporting events, music and entertainment.

The *Wonderful Copenhagen Marathon*, a 42-km race through the streets of Copenhagen, is held on a Sunday in mid or late May and is open to both amateur and professional runners.

The *Fyrkatspillet* Viking play is presented for two weeks from late May to early June at the Viking-era Fyrkat ring fortress outside Hobro.

The *Copenhagen Carnival*, a three-day event in the heart of the capital, takes place on Whitsunday weekend (usually late May). Highlights include an offbeat parade, samba dancing in the streets and a boat carnival. On Whitmonday children have their own parade to Kongens Have, where there are puppet shows and other activities for kids.

June

The *Hjallerup Horse Fair*, on a weekend in early June in Hjallerup (near Aalborg), is Denmark's largest horse fair and also features tilting at the ring (a type of jousting) and entertainment.

The *Riverboat Jazz Festival*, held in mid-June in Silkeborg, attracts about 25,000 jazz enthusiasts with numerous performances. Many concerts are free; there's a fee for events that take place on boats.

Midsummer Eve, on 23 June, is a time for evening bonfires at beaches all around Denmark.

5-Øren, a Midsummer Eve music festival at Femøren beach on Amager, is held on 23 June. This is also the venue for free outdoor concerts – rock, funk, hip hop, jazz and pop – held each weekend throughout the summer.

The *Danish Derby*, Denmark's most important horse race, is held in late June at Klampenborg near Copenhagen.

The *Skagen Festival*, held in late June at various indoor venues in Skagen, features folk and world music by Danish and international performers.

The *Round Zealand Boat Race*, one of Europe's largest yacht races, is held over an 84-hour period in late June, starting and ending in Helsingør.

The *Roskilde Festival*, northern Europe's largest rock music festival, is held in Roskilde over four days in late June or early July. More than 100 singers and bands, including big-name international performers, attract nearly 100,000 concert-goers.

Actors in traditional Viking costume perform in the *Fyrkatspillet*, near Hobro, in late May

The *Viking Festival* in Frederikssund is spread over a two-week period in late June and early July. Costumed 'Vikings' present an open-air drama, followed by a banquet with Viking food and entertainment.

The *Viking Fair* at Lindholm Høje, north of Aalborg, re-enacts the Viking era with a marketplace and other activities for three days in late June or early July.

At the *Jels Viking Play*, held outdoors by lake Jels Sø near Rødding in southern Jutland, a local troupe re-enacts the Viking Age in an open-air play. It takes place over two weeks in late June or early July.

July

The *Tilting Festival*, held in Aabenraa for four days in early July, is one of the largest of its kind in Europe. About 500 uniformed tilters (jousters) parade on horseback and there's a big fair and fireworks.

The *Midtfyns Festival* in Ringe, held for five days in early July, features international rock, pop, world, folk and jazz musicians on four stages for 120 concerts. Past musicians have included Bon Jovi, Bryan Adams, Miles Davis and Joe Cocker.

Fourth of July celebrations to commemorate US Independence Day are held each 4 July in Rebild Bakker, with thousands of Danes and Danish-Americans in attendance.

Fannikerdage, held in Nordby on Fanø during a weekend in early July, features islanders wearing traditional costumes and performing folk dances.

The *Copenhagen Jazz Festival*, held for 10 days in early July, is one of the world's major jazz festivals, with indoor and outdoor concerts all around the city.

The *Århus Jazz Festival*, held the week following the Copenhagen Jazz Festival, features modern and traditional jazz in venues all around Århus.

Djurs Bluesland, a blues festival with both international and Danish groups, is held near Randers during the second weekend in July.

The *Maribo Jazz Festival*, held in Maribo for three days in mid-July, features traditional New Orleans jazz and big bands.

At the *Hans Christian Andersen Festival*, from mid-July to mid-August, children perform an HC Andersen fairy tale on an open-air stage in Odense.

The *Copenhagen Summer Festival* features chamber and classical music concerts in Copenhagen during the last week of July and the first two weeks of August.

The *Viking Moot*, held for two days in late July at the Moesgård Prehistoric Museum in Århus, has a Viking-style market with crafts, food, equestrian events and a Viking ship cruise.

August

The *Odense Film Festival*, an international film festival, is held in Odense for six days in early August.

The *Copenhagen Water Festival*, in mid-August, features concerts, ballet and other events on floating stages in Copenhagen harbour and along the waterfront from Nyhavn to the Little Mermaid. It's held over 10 days and most events are free.

At the *Ullerup Junk and Horse Fair*, 500 vendors sell antiques, clothing and second-hand goods at the fairgrounds in Dragør for three days in mid-August. One of Denmark's largest such events, it draws 300,000 people.

Randers Week, held in Randers for 10 days in mid-August, features music, dance, theatre, sports and fireworks. A bicycle race (30, 70 and 100 km) attracts 2500 cyclists. On the last Saturday there's a regatta on the Randers Fjord with sailing ships and a tugboat carrying jazz musicians.

The *SCC Country Music Festival* features country bands and soloists in Silkeborg for three days in mid-August.

Danmarks Smukkeste Festival features Danish and international rock, pop and blues bands in Skanderborg over three days in mid-August.

The *Tønder Festival*, one of northern Europe's largest folk festivals, is held for four days at the end of August with numerous indoor and outdoor performances in Tønder. It attracts the likes of Ramblin' Jack Elliot, Arlo Guthrie and The Chieftains.

Ny Music in Suså, held over a weekend in mid-August, features Danish contemporary music (saxophone quartets, wind quintets etc) at the Suså school in Skelby, between Sorø and Næstved.

The *Danish Trotting Derby*, Denmark's major trotting event, is held in late August at the Charlottenlund Travbane near Copenhagen.

September

The nine-day *Århus Festuge* (Århus Festival), beginning on the first Saturday in September, turns that city into a stage for nonstop revelry with jazz, rock, classical music, drama and dance. As one of Scandinavia's largest cultural festivals, it encompasses hundreds of events, from street theatre to concert-hall performances, as well as the popular Marselis Run, a six or 12-km run through the Marselisborg forest.

A three-day *kite flying festival* is held in early September on Lakolk beach on Rømø.

The *Tour de Gudenaa*, one of the world's longest kayak and canoe races, takes place in early September on the river Gudenå, from Skanderborg to Randers via Ry and Silkeborg. Open to both amateurs and professionals.

The *Copenhagen Film Festival*, held for a week in

mid-September at various cinemas in Copenhagen, is a showcase for about 70 feature films.

The *Amager Musikfestival*, held from mid-September to early October, features music performances by Danish and international soloists and ensembles at 14 churches in Amager, all with free admission.

October

The *Copenhagen Choir Festival*, held for one week in late October, features a cappella chorale performances in churches and concert halls around Copenhagen.

November

The *Copenhagen Irish Festival* features traditional Irish and Scottish music in Copenhagen for three days in early November.

The *Musikhøst* (Music Harvest), held in Odense for five days in November, features contemporary music from Denmark and abroad. Soloists, ensembles and orchestras perform at Odense Koncerthus and other city venues.

December

Tivoli in Copenhagen reopens its gates from mid-November to Christmas with a holiday market and fair. Some Tivoli restaurants offer menus with hot mulled wine and traditional holiday meals. Unlike in the summer, at this time of year admission to Tivoli is free.

Christmas fairs, with food booths, arts and crafts stalls, and sometimes parades, take place all around Denmark throughout December. Particularly atmospheric is the Christmas fair held for two days in early December at Den Gamle By in Århus.

POST & TELECOMMUNICATIONS
Post

Most post offices are open either from 9 am to 5.30 pm or from 10 am to 5 pm on weekdays and to noon on Saturday. You can receive mail poste restante at any post office in Denmark, but many places, including the Copenhagen post office, will hold it for only two weeks.

It costs 3.75 kr to airmail a postcard or letter weighing up to 20 grams to Scandinavia or Western Europe, 5 kr to other countries. Heavier letters weighing up to 50 grams cost 5 kr within Denmark, 5.50 kr to other Scandinavian countries, 9.50 kr to Western Europe and 12 kr to other countries. International mail sent from Copenhagen is generally out of the country within 24 hours.

Music Festivals

More than 175 music festivals are held each year in Denmark. Concerts run the gamut from hard rock to classical, Nordic ballads to hip hop, gospel to jazz, and everything in between. The festivals are spread from May to November, with the vast majority held in July and August.

The two largest rock festivals are the Roskilde Festival held in Roskilde and the Midtfyns Festival in Ringe. Both are large Woodstock-like events that take place in early summer. The festivals last four to five days, bring in big-name international musicians and attract crowds from throughout Europe.

For jazz fans, the major attraction is the 10-day Copenhagen Jazz Festival, which is held in early July. It's followed the next week by the smaller but still significant Århus Jazz Festival. The largest folk festival is held in Tønder in late August and features both Danish and top international folk musicians.

Some festivals hold all their concerts indoors in music halls and clubs, while others mix it up, with both indoor and outdoor venues. Fees vary with the festival. For some events you pay for the individual performances you attend, while on others there's a single price for the entire festival. The outdoor Roskilde Festival, for instance, costs 600 kr and includes all concerts as well as space to pitch a tent.

In Denmark, most concerts can be booked in advance through BilletNet (☎ 38 88 70 22), the national on-line ticket system.

To get a free pamphlet with an updated listing of all music festivals, including dates, featured performers and admission fees, contact the Dansk Musik Informations Center (☎ 33 11 20 66, fax 33 32 20 16), Gråbrødretorv 16, 1154 Copenhagen K. ■

Telephone

Denmark has an efficient phone system.

If you're going to be making many calls, consider buying a debit phonecard (*telekort*), which is sold in denominations of 20, 50 and 100 kr. These cards, which can be used for making both local and international calls, are used in special card phones and are more convenient than pumping in coins. The cards can be bought at post offices, Telecom shops and many kiosks, especially those at railway stations.

Card phones are found in busier public places side by side with coin phones. Card phones work out slightly cheaper than coin phones, as you pay for the exact amount of time you speak; an LCD-readout keeps you posted on how much time is left on the card. It's possible to replace an expiring card with a new card without breaking the call. Card phones are posted with information in English detailing their use as well as the location of the nearest place that sells phonecards.

Domestic Calls All telephone numbers in Denmark have eight numbers. There are no area codes; all eight numbers must be dialled, even when making calls within the same city.

It generally costs 2 kr minimum to make a local call at coin phones. Local calls are timed and you get twice as much calling time for your money on domestic calls made between 7.30 pm and 8 am daily and all day on Sunday. For directory assistance, dial 118.

International Calls to Denmark The country code for Denmark is 45. To call Denmark from another country, dial the international-access code for the country you're in, followed by 45 and the local eight-digit number.

International Calls from Denmark The international-access code for Denmark is 00. To make direct international calls from Denmark dial 00, followed by the country code for the country you're calling, the area code and local number.

You can dial 113 for international directory assistance, but there's a hefty fee of about 20 to 40 kr, depending on the length of the call.

For other assistance, including information on rates for international calls, dial 141. While the 141 call is toll free, if you do decide to place your international call, you're better off hanging up and then dialling direct, rather than having the operator connect you through, as there's a 35 kr service charge for operator-assisted calls.

As an example of costs, the per-minute charge for calls made from Denmark's public Telecom system are: 6 kr to other Scandinavian countries; 7 kr to Germany or Poland; 8 kr to the UK, France, Switzerland or the Netherlands; 20 kr to the USA or Canada; 26 kr to Australia or Israel; and 32 kr to Hong Kong, Japan or Singapore.

In addition to placing direct calls via the Danish telephone system, you can also call home using the 'country direct system' that will charge the call to your home phone bill or calling card. To reach an operator in your home country using the country direct system, simply dial the following toll-free numbers from any phone:

Australia
  ☎ 80 01 00 61
Canada ·
  ☎ 80 01 00 11
France
  ☎ 80 01 00 33
Germany
  ☎ 80 01 00 49
Italy
  ☎ 80 01 00 39
Netherlands
  ☎ 80 01 03 31
New Zealand
  ☎ 80 01 00 64
Norway
  ☎ 80 01 00 47
Sweden
  ☎ 80 01 00 46
UK
    BT ☎ 80 01 04 44
    MCL ☎ 80 01 00 14

USA
    AT&T ☎ 80 01 00 10
    MCI ☎ 80 01 00 22
    Sprint ☎ 80 01 08 77

Fax, Telex & Telegram
Faxes, telexes and telegrams can be sent from public telephone offices (marked by a blue TELE logo), which commonly are found side-by-side with larger post offices. Many hotels can provide fax services, but enquire first about any surcharge fees. Telegrams can also be sent by phone by dialing 122.

TIME
Time in Denmark is normally one hour ahead of GMT/UTC, the same as in neighbouring European countries. When it's noon in Denmark, it's 11 am in London, 6 am in New York and Toronto, 3 am in San Francisco, 9 pm in Sydney and 11 pm in Auckland.

Clocks are moved forward one hour for daylight-saving time from the last Sunday in March to the last Sunday in September. Denmark uses the 24-hour clock system and all timetables and business hours are posted accordingly.

Dates are written with the day followed by the month, thus 3/6 means 3 June and 6/3 means 6 March.

ELECTRICITY
Voltage & Cycle
Most of Europe, including Denmark, runs on 220 V (volts), 50 Hz (cycles) AC. By the end of the 1990s, the EU countries should become standardised at 230 V, but like everything else in the EU, this may take longer than anticipated.

Check the voltage and cycle (usually 50 Hz) used in your home country. Most appliances that are set up for 240 V (such as those used in the UK) will handle 220 V without modifications (and vice versa). It's always preferable to adjust your appliance to the exact voltage if you can – a few items, such as some electric razors and radios, will do this automatically. If your appliance doesn't have a built-in transformer, don't plug in a 110/125 V appliance (the kind used in the USA and Canada) into a Danish outlet without using a separate transformer.

Several countries outside Europe (such as the USA and Canada) have 60 Hz AC, which will affect the speed of electric motors even after the voltage has been adjusted to European values, so CD and tape players (where motor speed is all-important) will be useless. But things like electric razors, hair dryers, irons and radios will be fine.

Plugs & Sockets
Most of Europe, including Denmark, uses the 'europlug' with two round pins. Many europlugs and some sockets don't have provision for earth since most local home appliances are double-insulated; when provided, earth usually consists of two contact points along the edge.

If your plugs are of a different design, you'll need an adaptor. These are usually available in stores specialising in travel needs; get one before you leave, since the adaptors available in Denmark usually go the other way.

LAUNDRY
Coin laundries (møntvaskeri) are relatively easy to find in cities and towns, but hostels and camping grounds often have coin-operated machines as well. The cost to wash and dry a load of clothes is generally around 40 kr.

WEIGHTS & MEASURES
Denmark uses the metric system. Petrol and beverages are sold by the litre, meats and vegetables are weighed in kg, distance is measured by the km or metre, and speed limits are posted in km per hour (km/h).

Fruit is often sold by the piece (stykke), abbreviated 'stk'. Decimals are indicated by commas and thousands by points.

For those unaccustomed to the metric system, there's a conversion table at the back of this book.

BOOKS & MAPS
History
There are numerous books about Viking-era

culture and history. *The Viking World*, by James Graham-Campbell, is a paperback book with handsome photos that outlines the history of the Vikings by detailing excavated Viking sites and artefacts. *The Viking*, by Bertil Almgren, is an authoritative hardcover book that traces Viking history in both the Old and New World.

Denmark: A Modern History, by W Glyn Jones in hardback, is one of the more comprehensive and insightful accounts of contemporary Danish society.

The pocketsize *Facts About Denmark*, published by the Ministry of Foreign Affairs, provides a readable history of Denmark, with statistics and cultural background information.

General

Danmark, by John Roth Andersen, is an attractive hardback, four-colour, coffee-table-style pictorial of the country with multilingual commentary.

Discover Denmark – on Denmark and the Danes; Past, Present and Future, by the Danish Cultural Institute, provides a comprehensive overview of Danish society, covering topics such as history, politics, arts, culture and social issues.

Philosopher Søren Kierkegaard produced volumes of works, including *The Concept of Dread* (1844), which is considered by many to be the first work of depth psychology ever written, and *Concluding Unscientific Post-script to the Philosophical Fragments* (1846), which passionately put forward the tenets of what would become existentialism. *A Kierkegaard Anthology*, by Robert Bretall, has a broad cross-selection of major works by Kierkegaard.

Travel Guides

If your travels will include other parts of Scandinavia or Baltic Europe, you'll find these destinations covered in *Scandinavian & Baltic Europe* from Lonely Planet's 'on a shoestring' series.

The hardback *Drive Around Denmark*, by Robert Spark, has ideas on auto routes, itineraries and what to see along the way.

Camping Danmark, published annually by Campingrådet (Danish Camping Board), includes detailed information on all approved camping grounds in Denmark.

Literature

The much acclaimed *Pelle the Conqueror*, by Martin Andersen Nexø, is an intriguing novel about the harsh reality of life as an immigrant in 19th century Denmark.

Works by Karen Blixen (written under the pen name Isak Dinesen), Denmark's best-known 20th century writer, are widely available in English. Her best-selling novel *Out of Africa*, the memoirs of her life in Kenya, was penned in 1937 and turned into a Hollywood movie in the 1980s. Other works include *Winter's Tales* in 1942, *The Angelic Avengers* in 1944, *Last Tales* in 1957, *Anecdotes of Destiny* in 1958 and *Shadows on the Grass* in 1960. Three of Blixen's books were published after her death: *Daguerreotypes and Other Essays*, *Carnival: Entertainments and Posthumous Tales* and *Letters from Africa 1914-1931*.

There's an avalanche of books by and about Hans Christian Andersen. His first volume of fairy tales, *Tales, told for Children* (1835), included such classic stories as 'The Tinderbox' and 'The Princess and the Pea.' Today these and other children's stories, including the timeless *The Little Mermaid* and the satirical *The Emperor's New Clothes*, are found in bookshops throughout the world. Besides works by Andersen himself, there are numerous biographies of the author, including the definitive *Hans Christian Andersen* by Elias Bredsdorff. Andersen published two autobiographies, of which the most highly regarded is *The Fairy Tale of My Life*.

Denmark's pre-eminent contemporary novelist is Peter Høeg, who became *Time* magazine's Author of the Year with the best seller *Miss Smilla's Feeling For Snow* (1992; published in the USA as *Smilla's Sense of Snow*), a thriller set in Copenhagen and Greenland that touches upon Danish colonialism and the struggle for Greenlandic cultural identity. In 1995 Høeg's first novel,

The History of Danish Dreams, a narrative that sweeps through many generations of a Danish family, was published in English, as was his third novel, *Borderliners*, which deals with social issues surrounding private schooling in Denmark.

Maps

Denmark's larger cities, such as Copenhagen, Århus, Aalborg and Odense, have excellent city maps that can be picked up for free from tourist offices. Tourist offices in smaller cities and towns can generally provide simpler maps that are suitable for local sightseeing.

The *Denmark Map & General Travel*, a quality fold-out, four-colour road map, can be obtained free in advance from Denmark's overseas tourist offices.

If you're renting a car, you can usually get a good fold-out Denmark road map free from the rental agency when you pick up your car.

While the aforementioned maps will suit most travellers' needs, if you enjoy exploring backroads, nooks and crannies you may also want to pick up the detailed road map of Denmark which is published by Kort-og Matrikelstyrelsen in a handy atlas format (1:200,000). It's sold in Danish bookshops for 95 kr.

MEDIA
Newspapers & Magazines

Denmark has 48 daily newspapers, of which *Politiken* has the largest circulation. None are in English, but foreign English-language newspapers and magazines are readily available at railway-station kiosks in larger towns. Among the more common English-language newspapers sold in Denmark are the *International Herald Tribune, USA Today, Wall Street Journal, The European* and the *Guardian*. In the news-magazine category, *Time*, *Newsweek* and *The Economist* are widely available.

Radio & TV

You can hear a five-minute news brief in English at 8.30 am Monday to Friday on Danmarks Radio channel 3 (93.8 FM in Copenhagen, 91.7 FM in Århus). The BBC World Service is broadcast in Denmark at 9410 kHz and at 106.9 MHz.

British and US network programmes are common on Danish TV and are often presented in English with Danish subtitles. Many hotels have live CNN news, Sky TV and other English-language cable and satellite TV programming.

FILM & PHOTOGRAPHY

Print and slide films are readily available in major cities and towns. A 24-exposure roll of Kodacolor Gold 100 will cost about 50 kr without processing. A 36-exposure roll of Kodachrome 64 slide film with processing costs about 110 kr.

In many larger cities you can find photo centres that offer a range of photo-processing options. The cost to develop and print a roll of 24-exposure film averages around 125 kr for one-hour photo processing, 100 kr for same-day service and 75 kr for three-day service.

HEALTH

Denmark is a healthy place and travellers don't need to take any unusual health precautions.

Visitors whose countries have reciprocal agreements with Denmark are covered by the national health-insurance programme.

All visitors, however, receive free hospital treatment in the event of an accident or sudden illness, including the aggravation of a chronic disease, provided the patient has not come to Denmark for the purpose of obtaining the treatment and is not strong enough to return home.

In Denmark, controlled medicine is only available from a pharmacy with a prescription that is issued by a Danish or other Scandinavian doctor. While most pharmacies have the same opening hours as other shops, in major population centres there's usually at least one pharmacy (*apotek*) open 24 hours; there'll be an additional charge for using the pharmacy outside normal opening hours. When a pharmacy is closed, it's required to display the address of a nearby shop that's open.

For medical emergencies dial ☎ 112; the call can be made without coins from public phones.

Predeparture Preparations

Health Insurance A travel-insurance policy to cover theft, loss and medical problems is a good idea. There is a wide variety of policies and your travel agent will have recommendations. If you're a student, the international travel policies handled by STA Travel or other student-travel organisations are usually good value. Some policies offer lower and higher medical expenses options. Check the small print:

Some policies specifically exclude 'dangerous activities' such as scuba diving, motorcycling, skiing, mountaineering or even trekking.

A policy that pays doctors or hospitals directly may be preferable to one where you pay on the spot and claim later. If you have to claim later, make sure you keep all documentation. Some policies ask you to call back (reverse charges) to a centre in your home country where an immediate assessment of your problem is made.

Check if the policy covers ambulances or helicopter rescue, and an emergency flight home. If you have to stretch out you will need two seats and somebody has to pay for them!

Citizens of EU countries are covered for emergency medical treatment in the EU on presentation of an E111 form. Enquire about these at your national health service or travel agent well in advance; in some countries post offices have them. Similar reciprocal arrangements exist between the Nordic countries. You may still have to pay on the spot but you'll be able to reclaim these expenses at home (keep all documentation). However, travel insurance is still advisable because of the flexibility it offers in where and how you're treated, as well as covering expenses for ambulance and repatriation.

Medical Kit A small, straightforward medical kit is a good thing to carry. It should include:

- Aspirin or Panadol – for pain or fever
- Antihistamine (such as Benadryl) – useful as a decongestant for colds, allergies, to ease the itch from insect bites or stings, or to help prevent motion sickness
- Kaolin preparation (Pepto-Bismol), Imodium or Lomotil – for possible stomach upsets
- Antiseptic, such as Betadine, and antibiotic powder or a similar 'dry' spray – for cuts and grazes
- Calamine lotion – to ease irritation from bites or stings
- Bandages and Band-aids – for minor injuries
- Scissors, tweezers and a thermometer (note that mercury thermometers are prohibited by airlines)
- Insect repellent, sun block and chapstick

If you're travelling to Denmark in the summer, when sunlight hours are long, you'll find an eye mask helpful to fall asleep while it's still light and to avoid being awoken by an early dawn.

Health Preparations If you wear glasses, take a spare pair and a copy of your prescription. Losing your glasses can be a problem, but you can usually get new spectacles made up quickly.

If you need a particular medication, take an adequate supply. Also take the prescription, or better still, part of the packaging showing the generic rather than the brand name (which may not be available), as it will make getting replacements easier.

It's a good idea to have a legible prescription to show that you legally use the medication. Keep the medication in its original container. If you're carrying a syringe for some reason, have a note from your doctor to explain why you're doing so.

A Medic Alert tag is a good idea if your medical condition is not always easily recognisable (heart trouble, diabetes, asthma, allergic reactions to antibiotics, for example).

Immunisations Jabs are generally not necessary for Denmark or elsewhere in Europe. However, they may be an entry requirement if you're coming from an infected area – a yellow fever vaccination is the most likely requirement. If you're going to Europe with stopovers in Asia, Africa or Latin America, check with your travel agent or with the embassies of the countries you plan to visit.

There are, however, a few routine vaccinations that are recommended whether you're travelling or not, and this Health section assumes that you've had them: polio (usually administered during childhood), tetanus and diphtheria (usually administered together during childhood, with a booster shot every 10 years), and sometimes measles. See your physician or nearest health agency about these.

All vaccinations should be recorded on an International Health Certificate, which is available from your physician or government health department. Don't leave this till the last minute, as the vaccinations may have to be spread out a bit.

Basic Rules

Water Tap water is safe to drink throughout Denmark.

Always be wary of drinking natural water. The burbling stream may look crystal clear and very inviting, but it can be polluted by animals upstream.

The simplest way of purifying water is to boil it thoroughly. Technically this means boiling for 10 minutes, something which happens very rarely!

Simple filtering will not remove all dangerous organisms, so if you cannot boil water it should be treated chemically. Chlorine tablets (Puritabs, Steritabs or other brand names) will kill many but not all pathogens. Iodine is very effective for purifying water and is available in tablet form (such as Potable Aqua), but follow the directions carefully and remember that too much iodine can be harmful.

Food Stomach upsets are a possibility anywhere you travel, but in Denmark these are likely to be relatively minor.

As a general rule, at home and abroad, take care with fish and shellfish (for instance, cooked mussels that have not properly opened can be dangerous), and avoid undercooked meat.

If a place looks clean and well run and if the vendor also looks clean and healthy, then the food is probably safe. In general, places that are packed with travellers or locals will be fine. Be careful with food that has been cooked and left to go cold.

Mushroom-picking is a favourite pastime in Europe as autumn approaches, but make sure you don't eat any mushrooms that haven't been positively identified as safe.

Nutrition If you don't vary your diet, and are travelling hard and fast and therefore missing meals, or you simply lose your appetite, you can soon start to lose weight and place your health at risk.

If you rely on fast foods, you'll get plenty of fats and carbohydrates but little else. Remember that overcooked food loses much of its nutritional value. If your diet isn't well balanced, it's a good idea to take vitamin and iron pills. Fruit and vegetables are good sources of vitamins, but can be expensive in Denmark.

In hot weather make sure you drink enough – don't rely on feeling thirsty to indicate when you should drink. Not needing to urinate or very dark-yellow urine is a danger sign. Carry a water bottle on long

---

Everyday Health

Normal body temperature is 98.6°F or 37°C; more than 2°C higher is a 'high' fever. A normal adult pulse rate is 60 to 80 per minute (children 80 to 100, babies 100 to 140). You should know how to take a temperature and a pulse rate. As a general rule the pulse increases about 20 beats per minute for each °C rise in fever.

Respiration (breathing) rate is also an indicator of illness. Count the number of breaths per minute: between 12 and 20 is normal for adults and older children (up to 30 for younger children, 40 for babies). People with a high fever or serious respiratory illness (like pneumonia) breathe more quickly than normal. More than 40 shallow breaths a minute usually means pneumonia. ∎

trips. Excessive sweating can lead to loss of salt and therefore muscle cramping. Salt tablets are not a good idea as a preventative, but in situations where salt is not used much, adding salt to food can help.

Medical Problems & Treatment

Local pharmacies or neighbourhood medical centres are good places to visit if you have a small medical problem and can explain what it is. Hospital casualty wards will help if it's more serious, and will tell you if it's not. Major hospitals and emergency numbers are indicated on the maps in this book or mentioned in the text. Tourist offices, pharmacies and hotels can put you on to a doctor or dentist.

Sunburn Anywhere on water, sand or snow, you can get sunburnt surprisingly quickly, even through cloud. Use a sunblock and take extra care to cover areas that don't normally see sun – eg your feet. A hat provides added protection, and it may be a good idea to use zinc cream or some other barrier cream for your nose and lips. Calamine lotion is good for mild sunburn.

Remember that too much sunlight, whether it's direct or reflected (glare), can damage your eyes. If your plans include being near water, sand or snow, then good sunglasses are doubly important. Good quality sunglasses are treated filter out ultraviolet radiation. However poor quality lenses will actually do more harm than good: tinted lenses cause your pupils to dilate and they will thereby absorb more ultraviolet light than they would if you wore no sunglasses at all. Excessive ultraviolet light can damage your retinas.

Cold Too much cold is just as dangerous as too much heat, particularly if it leads to hypothermia. Cold combined with wind and moisture (ie soaking rain) is particularly risky. If you are cycling or hiking in a cool, wet environment, be prepared.

Hypothermia occurs when the body loses heat faster than it can produce it and the core temperature of the body falls. It is surpris-

ingly easy to progress from very cold to dangerously cold due to a combination of wind, wet clothing, fatigue and hunger, even if the air temperature is above freezing. It is best to dress in layers – silk, wool and some of the new artificial fibres are all good insulating materials. A hat is important, as a lot of heat is lost through the head. A strong, waterproof outer layer is essential, as keeping dry is vital. Carry basic supplies, including food that contains simple sugars to generate heat quickly, and lots of fluid to drink.

Symptoms of hypothermia are exhaustion, numb skin (particularly toes and fingers), shivering, slurred speech, irrational or violent behaviour, lethargy, stumbling, dizzy spells, muscle cramps and violent bursts of energy. Irrationality may take the form of sufferers claiming they are warm and trying to take off their clothes.

To treat hypothermia, first get the person out of the wind and/or rain, remove their clothing if it's wet and replace it with dry, warm clothing. Give them hot liquids – not alcohol – and some high-kilojoule, easily digestible food. Do not rub victims; place them near a fire or, if possible, in a warm (not hot) bath.

Motion Sickness Eating lightly before and during a trip will reduce the chances of motion sickness. If you are prone to motion sickness, try to find a place that minimises disturbance – near the wing on aircraft, close to midships on boats, near the centre on buses. Fresh air and a steady reference point like the horizon usually help, whereas reading or cigarette smoke don't. Commercial antimotion-sickness preparations, which can cause drowsiness, have to be taken before the trip commences – when you're feeling sick, it's too late. Ginger is a natural preventative and is available in capsule form.

Jet Lag Jet lag is experienced when a person travels by air across more than three time zones (each time zone usually represents a one-hour time difference). It occurs because many of the functions of the human body (such as temperature, pulse rate and emptying of the bladder and bowels) are regulated by internal 24-hour cycles called circadian rhythms. When we travel long distances rapidly, our bodies take time to adjust to the 'new time' of our destination, and we may experience fatigue, disorientation, insomnia, anxiety, impaired concentration and loss of appetite. These effects will usually be gone within three days of arrival, but there are ways of minimising the impact of jet lag:

• Rest for a couple of days prior to departure; try to avoid late nights and last-minute dashes for travellers' cheques, passport and the like.
• Try to select flight schedules that minimise sleep deprivation; arriving late in the day means you can go to sleep soon after you arrive. For very long flights, try to organise a stopover.
• Avoid excessive eating (which bloats the stomach) and alcohol (which causes dehydration) during the flight. Instead, drink plenty of non-carbonated, non-alcoholic drinks such as fruit juice or water.
• Avoid smoking, as this reduces the amount of oxygen in the airplane cabin even further and causes greater fatigue.
• Make yourself comfortable by wearing loose-fitting clothes and perhaps bringing an eye mask and ear plugs to help you sleep.

Diarrhoea A change of water, food or climate can all cause the runs; diarrhoea caused by contaminated food or water is more serious. Despite all your precautions, you may still have a bout of mild travellers' diarrhoea if you travel beyond the relatively safe confines of Europe, but a few rushed toilet trips with no other symptoms is not indicative of a serious problem.

Moderate diarrhoea, involving half-a-dozen loose bowel movements in a day, is more of a nuisance. Dehydration is the main danger with any diarrhoea, particularly for children, so fluid replenishment is the number one treatment. Weak black tea with a little sugar, soda water, or soft drinks allowed to go flat and diluted by 50% with water are all good.

With any diarrhoea more severe than this, go straight to the casualty ward of the nearest hospital and have yourself checked out. You may need a rehydrating solution to replace minerals and salts. Stick to a bland diet as you recover.

Viral Gastroenteritis This is caused not by bacteria but, as the name suggests, by a virus. It is characterised by stomach cramps, diarrhoea, and sometimes by vomiting and a slight fever. All you can do is rest and drink lots of fluids.

Hepatitis B This disease, also called serum hepatitis, is spread through contact with infected blood, blood products or bodily fluids, for example through sexual contact, unsterilised needles and blood transfusions. Other risk situations include tattooing and ear-piercing. The symptoms are fever, chills, headache and fatigue followed by vomiting, abdominal pain, dark urine and jaundiced skin. Hepatitis B can lead to irreparable liver damage, even liver cancer. There is no treatment (except rest, drinking lots of fluids and eating lightly) but an effective prophylactic vaccine is readily available in most countries.

Rabies Though rare in Europe, rabies is caused by a bite or scratch from an infected animal. Dogs are a noted carrier, but cats, foxes and bats can also be affected. Any bite, scratch or even lick from a warm-blooded, furry animal should be cleaned immediately and thoroughly. Scrub with soap and running water, and then clean with an alcohol solution. If there is any possibility that the animal is infected, particularly if it froths at the mouth and behaves strangely, medical help should be sought immediately. Even if it is not rabid, all bites should be treated seriously as they can become infected or can result in tetanus.

Sexually Transmitted Diseases (STDs) Sexual contact with an infected partner spreads these diseases. Abstinence is the only 100% preventative, but using condoms is also effective. Gonorrhoea and syphilis are the most common of these diseases: sores, blisters or rashes around the genitals, discharges, or pain when urinating are common symptoms. Symptoms may be less marked or not observed at all in women. Syphilis symptoms eventually disappear completely but the disease continues and can cause severe problems in later years. The treatment of gonorrhoea and syphilis is by antibiotics. STD clinics are widespread in Europe. Don't be shy about visiting them if you think you may have contracted something.

HIV/AIDS HIV, the Human Immunodeficiency Virus, may develop into AIDS, Acquired Immune Deficiency Syndrome. HIV is a major problem in many countries, including Denmark. Any exposure to blood, blood products or bodily fluids may put the individual at risk. Apart from sexual abstinence, the most effective preventative is always to practise safe sex using condoms. It is impossible to detect the HIV-positive status of an otherwise healthy-looking person without a blood test.

HIV/AIDS can also be spread through infected blood transfusions or by dirty needles – vaccinations, acupuncture, tattooing and body-piercing can potentially be as dangerous as intravenous drug use if the equipment is not clean. If you have any questions regarding AIDS while in Denmark, there's an AIDS Hotline (☎ 33 91 11 19) centred in Copenhagen that's open from 9 am to 11 pm daily.

Cuts, Bites & Stings Treat any cut with an antiseptic solution such as Betadine. Where possible avoid bandages and Band-aids, which can keep wounds wet.

Bee and wasp stings are usually painful rather than dangerous. Calamine lotion will give relief or ice packs will reduce the pain and swelling. There are some spiders with dangerous bites (rare in Europe) but antivenenes are usually available. In warm weather, mosquitoes may be a nuisance, but mosquito-borne diseases such as malaria are unknown in Denmark.

Snakes tend to keep a very low profile, but to minimise your chances of being bitten always wear boots, socks and long trousers when walking through undergrowth or rocky areas where snakes may be present. Tramp heavily and they'll usually slither away before you come near. Don't put your hands into holes and crevices, and be careful when collecting firewood.

Snake bites do not cause instantaneous death and antivenenes are usually available. Keep the victim calm and still, wrap the bitten limb tightly, as you would for a sprained ankle, and then attach a splint to immobilise it. Then seek medical help, if possible with the dead snake for identification. Do not attempt to catch the snake if there is even a remote possibility of being bitten again. Tourniquets and the process of sucking out the poison are now comprehensively discredited.

All lice cause itching and discomfort. They make themselves at home in your hair (head lice), your clothing (body lice) or in your pubic hair (crabs). You catch lice through direct contact with infected people or by sharing combs, clothing and the like. Powder or shampoo treatment will kill the lice, and infected clothing should then be washed in very hot water.

Women's Health

Some women experience irregular periods when travelling, due to the upset in routine. Don't forget to take time zones into account if you're on the pill; if you run into intestinal problems, the pill may not be absorbed. Ask your physician about these matters.

Poor diet, lowered resistance due to the use of antibiotics for stomach upsets, and even contraceptive pills, can lead to vaginal infections when travelling in hot climates. Maintaining good personal hygiene, and wearing skirts or loose-fitting trousers and cotton underwear will help to prevent infections.

Yeast infections (thrush), characterised by a rash, itch and discharge, can be treated with a vinegar or even lemon-juice douche or with yoghurt. Nystatin suppositories are the usual medical prescription. Trichomonas is a more serious infection; symptoms are a discharge and a burning sensation when urinating, and if a vinegar-water douche is not effective, medical attention should be sought. Metronidazole (Flagyl) is the prescribed drug. In both cases, male sexual partners must also be treated.

WOMEN TRAVELLERS
While women travellers are less likely to encounter problems in Denmark than in most other countries, the usual common-sense precautions apply when it comes to potentially dangerous situations like hitchhiking and walking alone in cities at night.

Good places to contact for women's issues are Kvindehuset (☎ 33 14 28 04), Gothersgade 37, 1123 Copenhagen K, and Kvindemuseet (☎ 86 13 61 44), Domkirkeplads 5, 8000 Århus C.

TRAVEL WITH CHILDREN
Successful travel with young children requires planning and effort. Try not to overdo things; even for adults, packing too much into the time available can cause problems. And make sure the activities include the kids as well – balance that day at the Nationalmuseet in Copenhagen with a day at Legoland. Include children in the trip planning; if they've helped to work out where you will be going, they will be much more interested when they get there. See Lonely Planet's *Travel with Children* by Maureen Wheeler for more information.

DISABLED TRAVELLERS
If you have a physical disability, get in touch with your national support organisation (preferably the 'travel officer' if there is one) and ask about the countries you plan to visit. They often have libraries devoted to travel, and can put you in touch with travel agents who specialise in tours for the disabled.

For instance, the British-based Royal Association for Disability & Rehabilitation (RADAR) publishes a useful guide entitled *Holidays and Travel Abroad: A Guide for Disabled People*, which gives a good overview of the facilities available in Europe. Contact RADAR (☎ 0171-250 3222) at 12 City Forum, 250 City Rd, London EC1V 8AF.

Most Danish tourist literature, such as the Danish Tourist Board's hotel guide, the camping association listings and the hostel booklet, indicate which places have rooms and facilities accessible to wheelchair users.

In addition, the Danish Tourist Board, in association with the Committee for Housing, Transportation and Technical Aids, puts out a free 100-page, English-language publication entitled *Access in Denmark – a Travel Guide for the Disabled*. The book has practical information for disabled travellers, including a list of accommodation with suitable access, information on using public transportation and the wheelchair accessibility of museums and sights. It's obtainable from larger tourist offices, but unfortunately the current edition is overdue for an update.

GAY & LESBIAN TRAVELLERS
Denmark is a popular destination for gay and lesbian travellers. Copenhagen in particular has an active gay community and lots of nightlife options, but you'll find gay and lesbian venues in other cities and large towns as well.

The *Spartacus International Gay Guide*, published by Bruno Gmünder (Berlin), is a good international directory of gay men's entertainment venues in Europe. It's best used in conjunction with listings in local papers. For lesbians, *Places for Women* (Ferrari Publications) is the best international guide. Another good book to pick up is *Are You Two...Together? A Gay and Lesbian Travel Guide to Europe*, by Lindsy Van Gelder & Pamela Robin Brandt (Random House), which has a particularly enjoyable chapter on Copenhagen.

SENIOR TRAVELLERS
Senior citizens are entitled to many discounts on things like public transport and museum admission fees, with proof of age, although in some cases a special pass is required. The minimum qualifying age is generally 60 to 65. One example is on the DSB national railway, which offers discounts of 25% to 50% to seniors age 65 and older for travel on most days (see the Getting

Around chapter for more information). Private companies also offer discounts. SAS hotels, for example, has an interesting senior programme that offers those over 65 a discount on rates equivalent to their age – thus if you're age 75, the room rate is discounted 75%.

In your home country, a lower age may already entitle you to all sorts of interesting travel packages and discounts (on car rentals, for instance) through organisations and travel agents that cater for senior travellers.

TRAVELLERS WITH SPECIAL DIETS

If you have dietary restrictions – you're a vegetarian or you require kosher food, for example – tourist organisations may be able to advise you or provide lists of suitable restaurants. You'll find a number of places serving vegetarian food listed in this book.

Many eating places in Denmark feature food for diabetics. Such restaurants post a sign at the main entrance with a circular logo showing a smiling chef and the words *Diabetes mad – sund mad for alle* – 'food for diabetics – healthy food for everyone'.

DANGERS & ANNOYANCES

Denmark is by and large a very safe country and travelling presents no unusual dangers. Travellers should nevertheless be careful with their belongings, particularly in busy places such as Copenhagen's Central Station.

In cities, you'll need to quickly become accustomed to the busy cycle lanes that run beside roads between the vehicles and the pedestrian pavement, as these lanes (and fast-moving cyclists) are easy to veer into accidentally.

Throughout Denmark, dial 112 for police, fire or ambulance emergencies.

Theft

As a traveller, you're often fairly vulnerable and when you do lose things it can be a real hassle. The most important things to guard are your passport, papers, tickets and money. It's best always to carry these next to your skin or in a sturdy leather pouch on your belt.

Carry your own padlock for hostel lockers. Be careful even in hotels; don't leave valuables lying around in your room.

Never leave valuables unattended in parked cars. If you must leave your luggage in a vehicle, be sure your car has a covered area that keeps it out of sight and carry the most important items with you in a day pack. Remove all luggage overnight, even if the car is in a parking garage.

Precautions

The hassles created by losing your passport can be considerably reduced if you have a record of its number and issue date, or even better, photocopies of the relevant data pages. A photocopy of your birth certificate can also be useful.

In addition, keep a record of the serial numbers of your travellers' cheques (cross them off as you cash them in) and photocopies of your credit cards, airline tickets and other travel documents. Keep all this emergency material separate from your passport, cheques and cash, and leave extra copies with someone you can rely on back home. Add some emergency money, say US$50, to this separate stash as well. If you do lose your passport, notify the police immediately to get a statement, and then contact your nearest consulate.

Drugs

Always treat drugs with a great deal of caution. There is a fair bit of marijuana available in the region, sometimes quite openly, but that doesn't mean it's legal. Even a little seemingly harmless hashish can cause a great deal of trouble.

No traveller should consider bringing drugs home with them either. With 'suspect' stamps in a passport (including Amsterdam Airport!) energetic customs officials could well decide to take a closer look.

WORK

Denmark has a double-digit percentage of unemployment and the job situation is bleak for those who are not Danes, doubly so for those who don't speak Danish.

In terms of qualifying to work in Denmark, foreigners are divided into three categories: Scandinavian citizens, citizens of EU countries and other foreigners. Essentially, Scandinavian citizens have the easiest go of it. EU citizens are also legally allowed to work in Denmark but there can be snarls and employers aren't always eager. Other foreigners can expect to find it very difficult unless they have a unique skill that's in demand and in any case they'll need to obtain a work permit before they arrive in Denmark. For more information see Work Permits in the Visas section near the beginning of this chapter.

If you do decide to look for work in Denmark, the AF Arbejdsmarkedsservice (☎ 33 93 43 53), a labour-exchange office at Kultorvet 17, 1019 Copenhagen K, helps link up the unemployed with employers looking for workers. The newspapers with the best jobs-wanted columns are the Sunday issues of *Politiken* and *Berlingske Tidende*. If you don't mind being a waiter, kitchen helper or cleaning person, restaurants and hotels are two types of businesses that are more likely to offer jobs to foreigners, so you might try inquiring directly.

ACTIVITIES
Cycling
Denmark prides itself on being a bicycle-friendly country. With a gentle terrain that tops out at a mere 173 metres, cycling routes are well suited for recreational cyclers, including families with children. The country is crossed with thousands of km of established cycling routes, some parallelling lightly trafficked roads and others through nature preserves and woods.

There are 10 long-distance national cycling routes. The shortest is a 100-km route around the perimeter of Bornholm, while the longest runs along the west coast of Jutland some 500 km from the German border to Skagen.

The Danish cycling federation, Dansk Cyklist Forbund (☎ 33 32 31 21), Rømersgade 7, 1362 Copenhagen K, publishes *Cykelferiekort*, a 1:510,000 cycling map of the entire country, with commentary in English. It also publishes *Overnatning i det fri*, which lists over 200 farmers who provide cyclists with a place to pitch a tent for only 10 kr a night.

In addition, Danish counties also publish their own detailed topographical cycling maps with legends and other information in both Danish and English.

The cycling maps make it easy to self-plan your own tour as they not only show places of interest, such as castles and museums, but also the locations of hostels and camping grounds. Cycling maps can be purchased throughout Denmark at bookshops and larger tourist offices.

Walking
While Denmark does not have substantial forests, there are numerous small tracts of woodlands crisscrossed by a few km of walking trails. The Skov og Naturstyrelsen (Forest & Nature bureau) produces brochures with sketch maps that show trails in nearly 200 such areas. The brochures can be picked up for free at public libraries and tourist offices.

There's public access to the coast in Denmark whether it's publicly or privately owned and in many areas there are walking tracks along the shoreline. Access is also granted to virtually all forests; in publicly owned areas you can walk about freely, while in privately owned woodlands you must stick to the established trails.

Swimming
Denmark is well endowed with beaches. There are attractive sandy strands all around the country, from the southern shores of Bornholm to the northernmost tip of Jutland.

While topless sunbathing is common on all beaches, nude sunbathing is more restricted and is generally practiced only on the more private and remote sections of beaches. Unless the beach is specifically set aside for nude bathing, follow local custom.

Don't expect tropical conditions. Even in July, water temperatures in the seas around Denmark average just 16°C (61°F) in the

Tracing Your Danish Roots

Many visitors of Danish descent take advantage of their trip to Denmark to trace their roots and seek out the birthplace of their ancestors. If your family hasn't kept ties with relatives still living in Denmark, establishing your genealogy will generally require some careful investigation.

The best place to begin your research is at home before you go. People generally hold on to their naturalisation papers, and these and other official forms can indicate such vital information as an immigrant's birth date and place of birth. Any old letters from Denmark that have been stowed away may also reveal important clues, including the return addresses of relatives. Another possible source for immigration records is the national archives in your home country.

Once you've determined the birthplace or last Danish address of your ancestors, the Danes Worldwide Archives, which maintains the history of Danish emigrants and their offspring, can help you establish your genealogy and make contact with distant relatives. Their address is: Danes Worldwide Archives, Udvandrerarkiv Det Danske, Postboks 1731, Ved Vor Frue Kirke, 9000 Aalborg.

Among the resources maintained by the Danes Worldwide Archives are copies of the old emigration lists compiled by the police and numerous manuscripts and periodicals relating to emigration. If you contact them in advance of your trip, they can help you place ads in local newspapers in an effort to make contact with distant relatives. Once in Denmark, you can use their library and research facilities to learn more about your family history.

In addition, the Danish national archives in Copenhagen keeps various records. The most important for genealogical research are census forms and military draft registers, which date back as far as 1787. Note, however, that only people of the peasantry had to register for the draft prior to 1849. The address is: Rigsarkivet, 9 Rigsdagsgården, 1218 Copenhagen K.

There are also four provincial archives that keep birth, death and marriage certificates and other similar records. They are: Landsarkivet for Sjælland (Zealand), 10 Jagtvej, 2200 Copenhagen N; Landsarkivet for Fyn (Funen county), 36 Jernbanegade, 5000 Odense; Landsarkivet for Nørrejylland (northern Jutland), 5 Lille Sankt Hansgade, 8800 Viborg; and Landsarkivet for de Sønderjyske Landsdele (southern Jutland), 45 Haderslevvej, 6200 Aabenraa. ■

---

north and 17.3°C (63°F) in the south, so most beach-goers are Germans and Scandinavians, rather than visitors from warmer climes.

If you find the waters chilly, most larger towns and cities have heated public swimming pools that are open to all for a modest fee. Additionally, there are numerous 'water world' parks with pools and water slides that are geared for children.

Windsurfing

Denmark has excellent conditions for windsurfing (called 'surfing' in Danish), varying from open seas favoured by pros to inland fjords and sheltered coastal areas with calm waters that are ideal for beginners. If you want to rent equipment or take lessons, there are a few dozen windsurfing shops/schools around Denmark. Most are in Jutland, the west coast of which has some of the country's top wind and wave conditions, but you'll also find a few along the Zealand coast within easy reach of the capital.

Rental equipment typically costs 50 to 80 kr an hour, and 250 to 350 kr a day, with the lower prices for beginners' gear. You can get a three-hour introductory lesson for about 350 kr, a more substantial lesson for double that price, which includes the use of the equipment.

The largest windsurfing organisation, Surf & Ski, publishes the Danish-language magazine *Surf News*, which lists the locations of windsurfing shops, gives dates and details of windsurfing tournaments and advertises windsurfing equipment. It can be picked up at windsurfing shops around the country, or by contacting Surf & Ski (☎ 75 22 02 11, fax 75 22 51 37), Håndværkervej 10a, 6800 Varde.

Doorways of Denmark

NED FRIARY

NED FRIARY

NED FRIARY

NED FRIARY

GLENDA BENDURE

NED FRIARY

NED FRIARY

People of Denmark

Yacht Chartering

With over 7300 km of coastline and hundreds of islands, Denmark offers some excellent yachting possibilities. There are lots of calm-water fjords and protected seas, such as Smålandshavet (the area nestled between Zealand and Lolland) and the island-dotted waters south of Funen.

While most sailors in Danish waters are Scandinavians and Germans with their own boats, it's also possible to charter boats in Denmark. Charter Group Denmark consists of five different yacht chartering companies with locations from the Limfjord in Jutland to the island of Møn. Collectively they offer a wide range of boats that can be rented on a weekly basis. The boats come equipped with everything from cutlery and crockery to navigational equipment. Prices vary with the season and the size of the boat, but generally begin at around 6000 kr per week. You can get a booklet on Charter Group Denmark, with information in English, from Det Nordatlantiske Compagni (☎ 98 79 06 99, fax 98 18 71 66), Gøteborgvej 12, 9200 Aalborg.

Fishing

Denmark abounds with streams and lakes, many of which are stocked with pike, perch and trout. In addition, with so much shoreline, the saltwater fishing possibilities are nearly endless; the most common saltwater fish are cod, mackerel, plaice and sea trout.

Anglers between the ages of 18 and 67 must buy a fishing licence, which costs 25 kr a day or 75 kr a week and can be purchased at tourist offices and post offices. There are also a number of privately run 'put and take' fishing holes that allow you to fish for an established fee (no licence required).

Golf

In Denmark you are seldom far from a golf course – there are about 100 courses scattered around the Danish countryside. By Danish standards, green fees are reasonable, about 125 kr on weekdays, double that on weekends. Some of the courses are private clubs, so if you have a membership card from

a golf club at home bring it along as it'll sometimes grant you temporary membership at Danish golf clubs. You can get a complete list of golf courses from Danish tourist offices.

COURSES
Folk High Schools

Scandinavia's unique *folkehøjskole*, literally 'folk high school' (the 'high' meaning institute of higher learning), provides a liberal education within a communal living environment. Folk high schools got their start in Denmark, inspired by philosopher NFS Grundtvig's concept of 'enlightenment for life'. The curriculum varies between schools but includes such things as drama, Danish culture, peace studies and organic farming. People aged 19 and older can enrol and there are no entrance exams and no degrees. For more information, including a catalogue of the nearly 100 schools, contact Højskolernes Sekretariat (☎ 33 13 98 22), Nytorv 7, 1450 Copenhagen K.

While most schools teach in Danish only, at the International People's College (☎ 49 21 33 61), Montebello Allé 1, 3000 Helsingør, students and teachers come from around the world and instruction is in English. The fees are quite reasonable considering the high cost of living in Denmark. Eight-week courses cost 12,500 kr including meals, accommodation, tuition and outings.

HIGHLIGHTS
Castles

Denmark is full of castles, some with turrets and towers, some with dungeons and others just misnamed manor houses. The most strikingly set is Egeskov Castle, surrounded by a moat and formal gardens in the Funen countryside. For the most elaborately decorated Renaissance interior, Frederiksborg Castle in Hillerød is unequalled. In Copenhagen, the king of castles is Rosenborg, where the dazzling crown jewels are on display.

Historic Towns

Half-timbered houses, cobblestone streets and ancient churches are thick on the ground in Denmark, but a few places are unique. Ribe, the oldest town in Denmark, has an exquisite historic centre encircling a 12th century cathedral.

The tiny fortress island of Christiansø, off Bornholm, retains its ramparts and 17th century buildings, with almost no trace of the 20th century. And Ærøskøbing on Ærø has a town centre of 18th century houses that's arguably the most picturesque in Denmark.

Museums

Denmark has several open-air folk museums with period buildings. The most impressive is Den Gamle By in Århus, which is set up as a provincial town, while the folk museum in Odense has the most engaging natural setting.

The best preserved bog people – intact Iron Age bodies found preserved in peat bogs – are at the Silkeborg Museum in Silkeborg and the Moesgård Prehistoric Museum in Århus. In Zealand, the top art museums are Ny Carlsberg Glyptotek in Copenhagen and Louisiana in Humlebæk. The National-museet in Copenhagen has a superb collection of Danish historical artefacts, including Viking weaponry and rune stones.

Viking Sites

The Danish countryside holds a number of Viking sites, including Viking fortresses dating back to around 980 AD. Their circular earthen walls remain intact and surround the faint remains of house sites where timbered stave-style structures once stood. The two best preserved are the Trelleborg fortress in Zealand, six km outside Slagelse, and the Fyrkat fortress in Jutland, three km outside Hobro; both have reconstructed Viking houses.

There are Viking ships on display at the Viking Ship Museum in Roskilde, the Bangsbo Museum in Frederikshavn and the Ladbyskibet museum outside Kerteminde. The impressive Lindholm Høje outside Aalborg contains the largest plot of Viking and Iron Age graves in Scandinavia.

In the summer, several Danish towns hold Viking festivals and open-air Viking plays.

One of the most atmospherically set plays is held at the Fyrkat fortress outside Hobro, but there are also plays in Frederikssund in North Zealand and in Jels and Jelling in Jutland. Some of the more interesting Viking festivals are held at Lindholm Høje, the Moesgård Prehistoric Museum in Århus and the new Viking centre in Ribe.

ACCOMMODATION

Denmark has a wide range of accommoda-tion options, and your budget will be greatly affected by which types you select. While truly cheap hotels are virtually unknown in Denmark, there are some good alternatives. If you're on a tight budget, you'll save money by camping, staying in hostels or booking rooms in private homes.

If you do opt to stay in hotels there are some schemes, especially in the summer and on weekends, that can bring hotel rates down to a more reasonable level. You may find it works out best to combine different types of accommodation to suit your travelling needs. For example, on a moderate budget, you could stay in hostels (most have private rooms for couples or families) on weekdays and in comfortable chain hotels which offer discounted rates on weekends. Self-catering flats and cottages may be worth considering if you're with a group and are planning to stay in one place for a while.

Local tourist offices are generally very helpful and can provide lists of in-town and nearby accommodation options. Sometimes they can also call round and do the actual booking for you, for which there may be a nominal fee.

During high-season periods, accommoda-tion can be hard to find and it's advisable to book ahead. Even camping grounds can fill up, especially popular big-city ones. Because most people travel in Denmark with advance reservations, in this book you'll find the phone number, fax number and mailing address listed under each hostel, camping ground and hotel.

Accommodation rates quoted in Denmark, including those listed in this book, already include all taxes and service charges.

Camping

Camping is very popular in Denmark and there were, at last count, 525 camping grounds spread around the country. No matter where you're travelling you'll seldom be far from one. In resort areas there are commonly camping grounds right in the thick of it all, while in cities and large towns they tend to be on the outskirts of the municipality. For this reason camping is most popular for people with their own vehicles. If you're on foot the money you save by camping can quickly be outweighed by the money you spend commuting to and from a town centre. Of course you'll also need a tent, sleeping bag, cooking equipment and other bits and pieces – easier to cart around if you have a vehicle.

Although most camping grounds are seasonal, about 100 places stay open all year round. The rest vary quite a bit in their opening season; some, particularly those in seaside resort areas, are open only in the summer months, while others operate from spring through autumn. Many of those that have a longer season offer discounted rates outside of midsummer.

Although other factors come into play, the cost for camping is largely dependent upon the camping ground's rating (see the following Ratings section), with the fee rising roughly 10% with each additional star. The per-night charge to pitch a tent or park a caravan ranges from 32 to 45 kr for each adult, and 18 to 24 kr for each child. In the summer, some places also tack on a per-site surcharge of 15 to 25 kr.

A camping pass is required by all camping grounds. If you don't have a valid International Camping Carnet, then you can purchase a Danish carnet at the first camping ground you visit or from tourist offices. The cost for an annual pass is 24 kr for an individual or 48 kr for a family. See Camping Carnet in the Documents section of this chapter.

Camping is regulated in Denmark and is only allowed in established camping grounds, or on private land with the owner's permission. While it may seem tempting, camping in a car or caravan at the beach, in a parking lot or along the street is prohibited and can result in an immediate fine.

If you're camping with a car or caravan, particularly in the high season it's wise to make reservations. If you're backpacking or travelling by bicycle, note that even if a camping ground is signposted as fully booked to motorists, it's worth stopping to talk to the warden, as he or she will usually be able to find a site for a camper who is travelling light.

Most road maps show camping grounds and the Danish Tourist Board publishes a free brochure listing the locations of camping grounds throughout Denmark. If you're camping your way around Denmark, a very useful book is the annually updated *Camping Denmark*, published by the Campingrådet (Danish Camping Board), which lists all approved camping grounds in Denmark and gives details on their exact facilities, ratings and opening dates. It can be bought in most any bookshop for 70 kr.

Cabins & Caravans Many camping grounds also rent cabins (and/or on-site caravans) that sleep four to six people and cost from roughly 200 to 450 kr a day in midsummer, a bit cheaper in the low season. Although cabins often have cooking facilities, bed linen and blankets are rarely provided so it's best to bring your own sleeping bag. Toilet and shower facilities are not in the cabins but are shared with other campers.

Most camping grounds in Denmark gear their facilities to people touring by caravan – in fact, many Danish camping grounds look more like car parks than nature preserves. All sites classified two-star or higher are equipped to service caravans with facilities for emptying toilets, cleaning tanks and replenishing drinking water.

Ratings Camping grounds in Denmark are rated by the Danish Camping Board using a star system, with the number of stars relating to the facilities. That rating is displayed at the camping ground, as well as in literature that lists camping areas.

One-star camping grounds fulfil minimum standards, such as providing running water, toilets, at least one shower and at least one electric outlet for shavers.

Two-star places have a minimum of one shower for every 25 sites, a kitchen with hot tap water and a minimum of one hot plate per 50 sites, as well as a playground for children. To qualify for a two-star rating, the site must also be within two km of a grocery store.

Camping grounds with three stars, the most common rating, have more elaborate facilities, including hot water in the wash basins, a communal lounge, a larger play area for children, nursing rooms for babies, and sinks or washing machines for laundry. Also, they must be within one km of a grocery store.

In 1995 the system was expanded to make way for four-star and five-star ratings. The higher standards required to earn the additional stars are mostly along the lines of greater creature comforts, but these higher ratings also require that there be a separate pitch area for tents and an equipped cycle repair area. Currently only a few camping grounds have received the new top ratings, but it has provided an incentive for many three-star places to upgrade their facilities, so camping – already of a high standard in Denmark – should become an increasingly comfortable option in the next few years.

When selecting a camping ground keep in mind that while the stars give a good indication of what to expect, they don't tell the whole story. For example, if a place meets all of the qualifications for a three-star rating but is more than a km from one grocery store, it still can't be rated higher than two stars

---

Danish Camping Terms
Here are common Danish words that campers are apt to come across on camping signs and price lists:

voksne	adult
børn	child
hund	dog
campingvogn	caravan, house trailer
campingbil	motorised caravan
hytte	cabin, hut
udlejning	rental
strøm	electricity charge
handicap-rum	an area accessible by wheelchair
dag/uge	day/week

Danish Camping logo

Hostelling International

Denmark's 100 hostels (*vandrerhjem*) are members of the Hostelling International (HI) organisation, which in recent years has changed its name from International Youth Hostel Federation (IYHF) in order to attract a wider clientele and move away from the emphasis on youth. Not all countries have made the switch to HI yet, so if your home hostel card says IYHF, HI or YHA, it's all the same thing.

Most of Denmark's hostels have private rooms in addition to dormitory rooms, which makes them a good-value alternative to hotels. Danish hostels appeal to a wide range of guests in all age categories and are oriented as much towards families and groups as they are to backpackers, students and other budget travellers.

Facilities in hostels vary, but most newer hostels have two-bed and four-bed rooms and thus are well suited for use by couples and small groups. Most hostels list rates for singles and doubles, although during the busier periods some are loathe to rent private rooms to individuals or couples unless you're willing to pay for all the beds in that room.

Hostelling International logo

Hostels are categorised from A+ to C; generally those highest rated have private baths in the rooms and dorms with fewer beds squeezed in. It's not uncommon for a hostel to have rooms in more than one category, giving guests a bit of choice in price and comfort. Depending on the hostel category, dorm beds cost from 53 to 85 kr, while private rooms range from 125 to 225 kr for singles and 150 to 250 kr for doubles, plus 40 to 50 kr for each additional person.

With few exceptions, Danish hostels have single bunk-style beds with comfortable foam mattresses. Blankets and pillows are provided at all hostels but if you don't bring your own sheets you'll have to hire them for around 35 kr per stay. Sleeping bags are not allowed. A handy, lightweight pouch-style sleeping sheet with an attached pillow cover can be purchased at many hostels worldwide and will save you a bundle on sheet rental charges.

Travellers who don't have an international hostel card can buy one once they arrive in Denmark for 125 kr (annual fee) or pay 25 kr extra for each night's stay. If you're not sure whether you'll be staying at hostels often enough to make it worth buying an annual card, ask for a sticker each time you pay the 25 kr per-night fee; if you accumulate six stickers you'll have yourself an annual hostel card.

In the summer and other holiday periods, many hostels book out in advance, so it's always a good idea to call ahead to make reservations. This can be done by telephone, fax or letter. Outside Copenhagen, check-in is generally between 4 and 9 pm, and the reception office is usually closed (and the phone not answered) between noon and 4 pm.

In the spring and autumn, hostels can get crowded with children on school outings; many hostels require reservations from individual travellers from 1 September to 15 May. Most Danish hostels close in the winter for any time from a few weeks to several months.

You can pick up the handy, 170-page *Danmarks Vandrerhjem* guide free from hostels or tourist offices; it gives information on individual hostels, including each hostel's facilities and a simple sketch map showing its location.

All Danish hostels provide an all-you-can-eat breakfast for 38 kr or less and some provide lunch (50 kr maximum) and dinner (60 kr maximum). Most hostels also have guest kitchens with pots and pans where you can cook your own food.

To join the HI before you leave, ask at your nearest hostel or contact your national hostelling association. Some national offices are:

Australia
 Each state has its own Youth Hostel Association. The National Administration Office is the Australian Youth Hostels Association, Level 3, 10 Mallett St, Camperdown NSW 2050 (☎ 02-9565 1699).
Canada
 Hostelling International – Canada, 1600 James Naismith Drive, Suite 608, Gloucester, Ontario K1B 5N4 (☎ 613-748-5638)
England & Wales
 Youth Hostels Association, Trevelyan House, 8 St Stephen's Hill, St Alban's, Herts AL1 2DY (☎ 01727-855215)
Ireland
 An Oige, Irish Youth Hostel Association, 61 Mountjoy St, Dublin 7 (☎ 01-304555)
New Zealand
 Youth Hostels Association of New Zealand, PO Box 436, 173 Gloucester St, Christchurch 1 (☎ 03-379 9970)
Northern Ireland
 Youth Hostels Association of Northern Ireland, 56 Bradbury Place, Belfast BT7 1RU (☎ 0232-324733)
Scotland
 Scottish Youth Hostels Association, 7 Glebe Crescent, Stirling FK8 2JA (☎ 0786-451181)

USA
    Hostelling International – American Youth Hostels, 733 15th St NW, Suite 840, Washington, DC 20005 (☎ 202-783-6161)

Home Stays

Many tourist offices can book rooms in private homes in their region for a small fee, or can provide a free list of the rooms so travellers can phone on their own. Rates vary widely, but average about 150/250 kr for singles/doubles. In most cases, breakfast is available for an additional 30 to 40 kr per person. This is not only a cheaper accommodation option than the hotels, but can also be a good opportunity to meet local families.

In addition, Dansk Bed & Breakfast (☎ 31 61 04 05), Postbox 53, 2900 Hellerup, publishes a useful booklet of nearly 100 Danish homes offering private rooms. The homes are listed by town and include virtually all of Denmark, from Bornholm to Skagen.

Farm Stays

If you'd like to be in the country, Horsens Turistbureau (☎ 75 62 38 22), Søndergade 26, 8700 Horsens, books stays on farms throughout Denmark. There's an interesting variety of farmhouses, ranging from modern homes to traditional straw-roofed timber-framed places. The cost, including breakfast, is 175 kr a person a day (half-price for children under 12 years), with a three-night minimum. They also book self-contained flats and small houses that can accommodate up to six people for 2100 kr a week. Upon request, Horsens Turistbureau will mail you a booklet containing a colour photo and brief description of each place as well as details on booking.

Landsforeningen for Landboturisme (☎ 86 52 41 50, fax 86 52 13 50), Låsbyvej 20, 8660 Skanderborg, produces a similar picture booklet listing farmhouses around Denmark that welcome holiday visitors. The main difference is that the booklet has mailing addresses for each farm and you book them directly yourself; correspondingly, the rates are slightly cheaper.

Although it's wise to make plans in advance, if you're cycling or driving around Denmark on your own, you're also likely to come across farmhouses with 'room' (*værelse*) signs posted.

Manor Houses

Danske Slots og Herregårdshoteller (☎ 39 40 02 77, fax 39 40 11 77), Annasvej 9, 2900 Hellerup, books rooms in a dozen manor houses and small castles around Denmark. The cost is from 850/1400 kr for singles/doubles, including breakfast and a three-course dinner. A glossy brochure with photos and descriptions of each site can be obtained by mail in advance or picked up at some of the larger tourist offices once you arrive in Denmark.

Hotels

Hotels can be found in the centre of all major Danish cities and towns. Prices at the lower end average around 325/450 kr for singles/doubles. Though the cheapest places tend to be spartan, Danish hotels are rarely seedy or unsafe. Interestingly, while 'low-end' hotels tend to be pricey for what you get, the difference in rates between categories is relatively small. Standard 1st-class hotels are generally only about a third higher than low-end hotels, particularly if you use weekend rates or other hotel schemes.

Kro, a name that implies a country inn but is more commonly the Danish version of a motel, is a type of accommodation typically found along major motorways near the outskirts of town and are generally cheaper than hotels. However, they're usually not a practical option unless you have your own transport.

Both hotels and kros usually include an all-you-can-eat breakfast, which can vary from a simple meal of bread, cheese and coffee to a generous full-table buffet.

Hotel Schemes

There are a number of hotel schemes that can pare down room costs in Danish hotels and inns. The main programmes, outlined below, cover many of Denmark's middle and top-end hotels, so if you plan to use hotels as your main accommodation, these schemes are worth considering.

Dansk Kroferie Dansk Kroferie (☎ 75 64 87 00, fax 75 64 87 20), Vejlevej 16, 8700 Horsens, operates an 'Inn Cheques' programme valid at the 86 inns that belong to its association. The cheques can be purchased at Danish tourist offices and travel agencies for 390/575 kr for singles/doubles. Each cheque covers breakfast and a room with a private bath; there is an additional charge for children over the age of four. Although most of the association's hotels and inns accept the cheques at face value, some add on a 125 kr surcharge. The association publishes a 50-page booklet that provides a brief description of member hotels and notes which ones add the surcharge.

Dansk Familie Hoteller Dansk Familie Hoteller (☎ 98 10 38 11, fax 98 13 31 66), Boulevard 41, Postboks 1360, 9100 Aalborg, is an association of about 30 hotels that participate in the 'Familie Check' programme. These cheques, which are sold at tourist offices, cost 445 kr for a single room and 525 kr for a double room. Rooms have private bath and breakfast is included. About a quarter of the hotels, including many of the most convenient city hotels, add a surcharge of 100 to 200 kr per room. Still this scheme offers a sizeable discount off the walk-in rate

at a number of places and, like the Dansk Kroferie Inn Cheque programme, doesn't require a lot of advance planning. A brochure listing participating hotels is available at tourist offices or from the association.

Scandic Hotels The Scandic Holiday Card, which costs 100 kr and is valid for one year, can be used at Scandic hotels to obtain one night's accommodation for 595 kr per room, breakfast included. Rooms have private bath, TV and minibar. The price covers two adults and up to two children aged 13 or under. The card can be used at Scandic hotels on Friday to Sunday year round and on any day during Danish school holidays, including summer. The cards can be purchased on the spot at any Scandic hotel and come with a voucher good for a 100 kr discount at the hotel restaurant.

Best Western Hotels This chain also has a cheque plan. Best Western Hotel Cheques Scandinavia are valid at 33 Best Western hotels in Denmark between 15 May and 15 September. The cheques, which cost 680 kr and can be purchased from travel agents or directly from Best Western, can be exchanged for a double room with private bath, breakfast included. Some hotels add on a surcharge.

If your travel dates coincide with their effective dates, the Best Western 'Holiday

Danish Hotel Terms
Here are some words you'll come across on hotel brochures:

værelse	room
enkeltværelse	single room
dobbeltværelse	double room
eget bad og toilet	with shower and toilet
bad og toilet på gangen	shower and toilet in the hallway
morgenmad inkl i prisen	breakfast included in the price
senge; køjsenge	beds; bunk beds
med opredning	with extra bed
lejlighed	flat, apartment
adgang til køkken	access to kitchen
vaskemaskine og tørretumbler	washing machine and tumbler drier

Package' rates are a better deal than the cheques and don't require vouchers or advance payment. Rates under this plan cover up to two adults and two children (aged 15 or under) in the same room for 650 kr a night, breakfast included. These rates are in effect on Friday, Saturday and Sunday all year round and during school holiday periods, including from mid-June to early August. It's best to book as far in advance as possible as the offer is valid on a limited number of rooms.

Seaside Cottages and Flats
In many seaside resort areas, cottages and flats account for a significant slice of the places to stay. These are suited mostly to visitors who are planning to holiday at one specific location, as they are generally booked by the week and require reservations. Rates vary greatly, depending upon the type of accommodation and the season, but generally work out cheaper than hotels.

The following two agencies handle cottage bookings on a nationwide basis and publish free catalogues listing rentals with a colour photo of each place:

DanCenter (☎ 33 33 01 02, fax 33 33 75 92), Søtorvet 5, 1371 Copenhagen K

Go Denmark (☎ 75 25 56 00, fax 75 25 51 20), Strandvejen 436, 6854 Henne Strand

FOOD & DRINK
Food
Nothing epitomises Danish food more than smørrebrød (literally 'buttered bread'), an open-face sandwich that ranges from very basic fare to elaborate sculpture-like creations. Typically it's a slice of rye bread topped with either roast beef, tiny shrimps, roast pork or fish fillet and finished off with a variety of garnishes. Although smørrebrød is served in most restaurants at lunch time, it's cheapest at bakeries or at specialised smørrebrød takeaway shops found near railway stations and office buildings.

Also distinctively Danish is the koldt bord (literally 'cold table'), a buffet-style spread of cold foods, including herrings, salads, cold cuts, smoked fish, cheeses, vegetables, condiments, breads and crackers, and usually a few hot dishes such as frikadeller (meatballs) and fried fish.

Apart from Danish food, there are also plenty of other international cuisines available, including expensive French fare; moderately priced Indian, Turkish and Chinese food; and generic American fast food such as McDonald's and Burger King. Some of the most common and cheapest places to eat are Italian restaurants, all of which serve the standard pizza-and-pasta menu. Simple Greek eateries serving inexpensive shawarma, a filling pitta-bread sandwich of shaved meat, are also common in larger towns and cities. You can find a cheap, if not particularly healthy, munch at one of the ubiquitous pølsemandens, the wheeled carts which sell a variety of hot dogs and sausages.

The rich pastry known in most places as 'Danish' is called wienerbrød in Denmark, and nearly every second street corner has a bakery with mouthwatering varieties.

Dagens ret, which means daily special, is usually the best deal on the menu, while the børnemenu is for children. Larger cities usually have restaurants featuring vegetarian dishes, cafés commonly serve a variety of salads, and vegetarians can often find something suitable at the smørrebrød counter.

Drinks
Denmark's Carlsberg and Tuborg breweries both produce excellent beers. Beer (øl) can be ordered as draught beer (fadøl), lager (pilsner), light beer (lyst øl), dark lager (lagerøl) or stout (porter).

The most popular spirit in Denmark is the Aalborg-produced aquavit (akvavit). There are several dozen types, the most common of which is spiced with caraway seeds. In Denmark aquavit is not sipped but is swallowed straight down as a shot and most commonly followed by a chaser of beer. A popular Danish liqueur, made of cherries, is Peter Heering, which is good sipped straight or served over vanilla ice cream.

Common wine terms are hvidvin (white

wine), *rødvin* (red wine), *mousserende vin* (sparkling wine) and *husets vin* (house wine). *Gløgg* is a mulled wine that's a favourite speciality during the Christmas season.

Beer, wine and spirits are served in most restaurants and cafés. They can be purchased at grocery stores during normal shopping hours and prices are quite reasonable compared to those in other Scandinavian countries. The minimum legal age for purchasing all alcoholic beverages is 18 years.

Danish Cuisine

Danish cuisine relies heavily on fish, meat and potatoes. The following are some typical Danish dishes:

Flæskesteg – roast pork, usually with crackling and served with potatoes and cabbage

Frikadeller – fried ground-pork meatballs, commonly served with boiled potatoes and red cabbage

Fyldt hvidkålshoved – ground beef wrapped in cabbage leaves

Gravad laks – cured or salted salmon marinated in dill and served with a sweet mustard sauce

Hakkebøf – a ground-beef burger that's usually covered with fried onions and served with boiled potatoes, brown sauce and beets

Hvid labskovs – Danish stew made of square cuts of beef boiled with potatoes, bay leaves and pepper

Kogt torsk – poached cod, usually in a mustard sauce and served with boiled potatoes

Mørbradbøf – small pork fillets, commonly in a mushroom sauce

Stegt flæsk – crisp-fried pork slices, generally served with potatoes and a parsley sauce

Stegt rødspætte – fried, breaded plaice, usually served with parsley potatoes

Food & Drink Terms

Here is a glossary of food and drink terms you're likely to come across on menus in Denmark:

Danish Beer

Danes are great producers and drinkers of beer. Denmark's United Breweries, an amalgamation of Carlsberg and Tuborg breweries, is the largest exporter of beer in Europe. Not all of the brew makes its way out of Denmark however. Danes down some seven million hectolitres (roughly two billion bottles) of brew a year, ranking them sixth among beer drinkers worldwide.

The best-selling beers in Denmark are pilsners, lagers with an alcohol content of 4.6%, but there are scores of other beers to choose from as well. These range from light beers with an alcohol content of 1.7% to hearty stouts that kick in at 8%. You'll find the percentage of alcohol listed on the bottle label and all Danish beers are classified with ascending numbers according to the amount of alcohol they contain, with *klasse 1* referring to the common pilsners and *klasse 4* to the strongest stouts. ■

abrikos – apricot
agurk – cucumber
agurkesalat – sliced cucumber with vinegar dressing
alkoholfri – nonalcoholic
ananas – pineapple
and, andesteg – duck, roast duck
ansjoser – anchovies
appelsin – orange
artiskok – artichoke
asparges – asparagus

bagt – baked
bagt kartoffel – baked potato
bambusskud – bamboo shoots
banan – banana
benfri – boneless
blomkål – cauliflower
blomme – plum
blæksprutte – octopus
blødkogt æg – soft-boiled egg
blåbær – blueberry
bolle – soft bread roll; also a meatball or fishball
brombær – blackberry
brød – bread
bønner – beans
bønnespirer – bean sprouts

champignon – mushroom
chokolade – chocolate, also hot chocolate
citron – lemon
citronvand – lemonade
creme fraiche – sour cream

dampet – steamed
dild – dill
dyresteg – roast venison

eddik – vinegar
engelsk bøf – steak, commonly served with onions

fadøl – draught (draft) beer
fersken – peach
fisk – fish
fiskefilet – fish fillet
fiskefrikadelle – fried fishball
fiskeretter – fish dishes
fiskesuppe – fish soup, usually creamy

flute – type of French bread
flynder – flounder
flæskesteg – roast pork, often served with crackling
flæskeæggekage – scrambled eggs with bacon
fløde – cream
flødeøst – cream cheese
flødeskum – whipped cream
forårsrulle – spring roll, egg roll
forel – trout
frisk – fresh
friturestegt – deep fried
fromage – a pudding
frugt – fruit
fyld – stuffing
fyldt – stuffed
fårekød – mutton

gennemstegt – well-done
glasur – glaze, frosting
grapefrugt – grapefruit
grilleret, grillstegt – grilled
gryderet – casserole or stew
grøn bønne – green bean
grøn salat – green salad
grøntsager – vegetables
gulerødder – carrots
gås – goose

hakkebøf – ground-beef burger
hakket – chopped, minced
haresteg – roast hare
hasselnød – hazelnut
helleflynde – halibut
hindbær – raspberry
hjemmebagt, hjemmelavet – home baked, home made
honning – honey
honningmelon – honeydew melon
hummer – lobster
hvide – white (as in white potatoes, rice etc)
hvidløg – garlic
hytteost – cottage cheese
høns, hønsekød – hen, chicken meat
hønsebryst – chicken breast
hønsekødsuppe – chicken soup
hårdkogt æg – hard-boiled egg

ingefær – ginger

ingefærbrød – gingerbread
is – ice cream, ice
iskold – ice cold

jordbær – strawberry
jordnød – peanut
jordnødsmør – peanut butter

kaffe – coffee
kage – cake
kalkun – turkey
kalvekød – veal
karry – curry
kartoffel – potato
kartoffelmos – mashed potatoes
kartoffelsalat – potato salad
kirsebær – cherry
klar suppe – clear soup
klipfisk – dried salt cod
koffeinfri – caffeine-free
kogt – boiled
kold – cold
kotelet – cutlet
krabbe – crab
kringle – type of Danish pastry
kryddere – crispy bread rolls
krydderi – spice
kryddersild – herring pickled in various
    marinades
kuller – haddock
kylling – chicken
kærnemælk – buttermilk
kød – meat
kødbolle – meatball
kål – cabbage

lagkage – layer cake
laks – salmon
lamme, lammekød – lamb
lammesteg – roast lamb
letmælk – low-fat milk
lever – liver
leverpostej – liver paté
løg – onion

majs – corn
makrel – mackerel
mandel, mandler – almonds
marineret – marinated
marineretsild – marinated herring

mellemstegt – medium cooked
mineralvand – mineral water
musling – mussel
mælk – milk

nudler – noodles
nødder – nuts

oksehaleragout – oxtail stew
oksekød – beef
oksemørbrad, oksefilet – fillet of beef,
    tenderloin
oksesteg – roast beef
olie – oil
oliven – olive
ost – cheese
ovnstegt – roasted

pandekage – pancake or crepe
parisertoast – toasted ham and cheese
    sandwich
peber – pepper
pebermynte – peppermint
peberrod – horseradish
persille – parsley
pocheret – poached
pommes frites – French fries, chips
porre – leek
purløg – chives
pære – pear
pølse – sausage, hot dog

rejer – shrimp
remoulade – mayonnaise-based tartar sauce
ris – rice
ris à l'amande – rice pudding with almonds
ristet – toasted
rugbrød – rye bread
rundstykke – crispy poppy-seed roll
rødbeder – beets, commonly served pickled
rødkål – red cabbage
rødspætte – plaice
røget – smoked
røget laks – smoked salmon
røget sild – smoked herring
røræg – scrambled eggs
rå – raw

salat – salad, lettuce
saltet – salted, cured

selleri – celery
sennep – mustard
sild – herring
skaldyr – shellfish
skinke – ham
skive – slice
skummetmælk – skim (nonfat) milk
sky – gravy
smør – butter
smørrebrød – open sandwich
snittebønner – string beans
sodavand – soft drink, carbonated water
sovs – sauce
spejlæg – fried egg, sunny side up
spinat – spinach
stegeretter – meat dishes
stegt – fried
sukker – sugar
suppe – soup
sursød – sweet-and-sour
surt – pickled cucumbers
svinekød – pork
syltetøj – jam
sød – sweet
sødmælk – whole milk
søtunge – sole

te – tea
tilberedt – cooked
torsk – cod
torskerogn – cod roe
tun, tunfisk – tuna
tunge – tongue
tykmælk – a pourable yoghurt
tærte – tart

vaffel – waffle
valnød – walnut
vand – water
vandmelon – watermelon
vanilleis – vanilla ice cream
varm – warm, hot
vegetar, vegetarianer – vegetarian
vildt – game

wienerbrød – Danish pastry

æble – apple
æg – egg
æggeblomme – egg yolk

ægekage – scrambled eggs with onions, potatoes and bacon
ærter – peas
ærter gule – split pea soup served with pork

øl – beer
ørred – trout
østers – oyster

ål – eel

Useful menu terms include:

børnemenu – children's menu
dagens middag – set menu
dagens ret – daily special
diabetes mad – dishes for diabetics
forretter – starters, appetisers
frokost – lunch
hovedretter – main dishes
middag – dinner
morgenmad – breakfast
retter – dishes, courses
spisekort – menu
udvalg af – assorted

ENTERTAINMENT

Denmark's cities have some of the most active nightlife in Europe, with live music wafting through numerous side-street cafés, especially in the university cities of Copenhagen, Århus and Odense. You'll find a wide range of music, including current alternative trends, rock, folk, jazz and blues. Little begins before 10 pm or ends before 3 am.

Copenhagen's Royal Danish Ballet is one of the most highly regarded in Europe. The larger Danish cities have concert halls with their own symphony orchestras; these halls also double as a venue for big-name Danish and international musicians of all genres, including classical music, pop and jazz.

Most towns have cinemas showing first-run English-language films (from 35 to 50 kr). Foreign films are not dubbed – movies are shown in their original language with Danish subtitles.

Denmark has introduced casino gambling and now has six casinos, all in hotels: SAS

Scandinavia Hotel in Copenhagen, Hotel Marienlyst in Helsingør, SAS HC Andersen Hotel in Odense, Hotel Royal in Århus, Hotel Munkebjerg in Vejle and Limfjordshotellet in Aalborg.

THINGS TO BUY

Because prices tend to be high, few people come to Denmark to go on shopping sprees. However, there are some distinctively Danish products that can make fine items to bring home. Danish amber, which washes up on Jutland's west coast beaches, makes lovely jewellery and prices are relatively reasonable.

Other popular purchases are silverwork, ceramics and hand-blown glass – all in the sleek style that typifies Danish design – of which Georg Jensen silverworks, Royal Copenhagen Porcelain and Holmegaard Glass & Crystal are the biggest names in their fields. You can find their shops as well as scores of others along Strøget, Copenhagen's famed shopping street. In addition to speciality shops, Denmark has large department stores (Magasin du Nord, Illum, Salling) which carry virtually anything you can think of, from souvenir picture books to goose-down quilts (down comforters) and Scandinavian-design furniture.

Getting There & Away

The information in this chapter details the various ways of getting directly to Denmark – by air, land and sea.

As Copenhagen is one of northern Europe's main gateway cities, there is a multitude of international flights to Denmark. However, depending on the particular airline deals available at the time of travel, overseas visitors might sometimes find that it's cheaper to fly to another city in Europe first and then travel onward to Denmark by boat, train, bus or car. This is particularly true of travellers who are including Denmark as just one destination in a larger European trip. But even other travellers might want to compare prices of airfares to Copenhagen with the cost of flying to, say, Frankfurt and using a rail pass or renting a car from there.

TRAVEL INSURANCE

Whichever way you're travelling, you should take out travel insurance, which usually covers medical expenses, luggage theft or loss, and cancellation and delays in your travel arrangements (such as falling seriously ill right before departure). Ticket loss is also covered by travel insurance, but make sure you have a separate record of all the details – or better still, a photocopy of the ticket. The exact coverage depends on the insurance policy you buy, so get your insurer or travel agent to explain the details.

It's a good idea to purchase travel insurance as early as possible. If you buy it the week before you fly, you might find, for instance, that you're not covered for delays to your flight caused by strikes or other industrial action that may have been in force before you took out the insurance.

Paying for your ticket with a credit card often provides limited travel accident insurance and you may also be able to reclaim the payment if the operator doesn't deliver – in the UK, for instance, credit card providers are required by law to reimburse consumers if a company goes into liquidation and the amount in contention is over £100. Ask your credit card company what it will cover.

WARNING

The information in this chapter is particularly vulnerable to change: prices for international travel are volatile, routes are introduced and cancelled, schedules change, special deals come and go, and rules and visa requirements get amended.

Airlines and governments seem to take a perverse pleasure in making price structures and regulations as complicated as possible. You should check directly with the airline or a travel agent to make sure you understand how a fare (and a ticket you may buy) works.

The upshot of this is that you should get opinions, quotes and advice from as many airlines and travel agents as possible before you part with your hard-earned cash. The details given in this chapter should be regarded as pointers and are not a substitute for your own careful, up-to-date research.

AIR

The vast majority of overseas flights to Denmark arrive at Copenhagen International Airport, which is conveniently located on the outskirts of Copenhagen, a 15-minute drive from the city centre.

A few international flights, mostly coming from other Scandinavian countries or the UK, land at small regional airports in Århus, Aalborg, Esbjerg and Billund.

Scandinavian Airlines (SAS) is the largest carrier servicing Denmark. Other scheduled international carriers flying into Copenhagen include: Aer Lingus, Aeroflot, Air France, Alitalia, Austrian Airlines, British Airways, British Midland, Delta Air Lines, Egypt Air, El Al, Finnair, Iberia, Icelandair, Kenya Airlines, KLM, LOT, Lufthansa, Mærsk Air, Olympic Airways, PIA Pakistan, Sabena, Singapore Airlines, Swissair, TAP Air Portugal, Thai Airways, Turkish Airlines and Varig Airlines.

Numerous charter carriers fly into Copenhagen as well, including Air Liberté, Air Ukraine, Canada 3000, Premiair, Sterling European and Transwede.

Visitors who fly SAS to Scandinavia from Europe, North America or Asia can purchase tickets on a Visit Scandinavia Air Pass which allows one-way travel on direct flights between any two Scandinavian cities serviced by SAS for US$80 to US$140. Tickets must be purchased in advance before arriving in Scandinavia and in conjunction with a return SAS international ticket. You can buy from one to six tickets. A similar deal applies with the SAS Visit Europe and Visit Baltic Air Passes. You can buy from three to eight Visit Europe Air Passes, valid for a one-way flight on any of a number of routes within Europe, for US$120 each. The Visit Baltic Air Pass, valid for a one-way flight between Scandinavian and Baltic countries, costs US$110 and is sold in units of two to four tickets.

Buying a Plane Ticket

For overseas travellers, the plane ticket will probably be the single most expensive item in your travel budget and it's worth putting aside some time to research the market. Start early because some of the cheapest tickets have to be bought months in advance, and some popular flights sell out early, particularly in the high season. Look at the ads in newspapers and magazines, watch for special offers, and call the airlines and ask if they're running any special promotions.

Cheap tickets are available in two distinct categories: official and unofficial. Official ones have a variety of names including advance-purchase fares, budget fares, Apex and super-Apex. Unofficial tickets are discounted tickets that the airlines release through selected travel agents, travel clubs and discount-ticket brokers.

Airlines or good travel agents can supply information on routes and timetables, as well as provide specific fares for the time you want to travel. Low-season, student and senior-citizen fares can be very competitive.

Normal full-fare airline tickets can also be worth examining as they sometimes include one or more side trips in Europe free of charge and generally have fewer restrictions.

Return (round-trip) tickets usually work out *much* cheaper than two one-way fares and can often work out cheaper than a single one-way fare!

If you're coming from a distant corner of the Earth, Round-the-World (RTW) tickets can sometimes work out to be no more expensive, or even cheaper, than an ordinary return ticket. RTW prices start at about A$2800 or US$2000 depending on the season. The official airline RTW tickets are usually put together by a combination of two airlines, and permit you to fly anywhere you want on their route systems so long as you don't backtrack. As a rule, you must book your itinerary in advance; after being issued a ticket the dates can usually be changed without a penalty, but if you want to add or drop destinations there's typically a charge of US$50. There may be restrictions on how many stops you are permitted and usually the tickets are valid from 90 days up to a year. An alternative type of RTW ticket is one put together by a travel agent using a combination of discounted tickets.

Discounted tickets are usually available at prices as low as, or lower than, the official Apex or budget tickets. Phone around the travel agencies for bargains and ask about fares, routes, ticket duration, if stopovers and open jaws are allowed, and any restrictions and cancellation penalties.

You may be told that those impossibly cheap flights are 'fully booked, but we have another one that costs a bit more…'. Or that the flight is on an airline notorious for its poor safety standards which will leave you in the world's least favourite airport mid-journey for 14 hours. Don't panic – keep ringing around.

If you are travelling from the USA or South-East Asia, or trying to get out of Europe, you may find that the cheapest flights are being advertised by obscure agencies whose names haven't even reached the telephone directory. Many such firms are

Air Travel Glossary

Apex Apex ('advance-purchase excursion') is a discounted ticket which must be paid for in advance. There are penalties if you wish to change it.

Baggage Allowance This will be written on your ticket: usually one 20-kg item to go in the hold, plus one item of hand luggage.

Bucket Shop An unbonded travel agency specialising in discounted airline tickets.

Bumped Just because you have a confirmed seat doesn't mean you're going to get on the plane (see Overbooking).

Cancellation Penalties If you have to cancel or change an Apex ticket there are often heavy penalties involved – insurance can sometimes be taken out against these penalties. Some airlines impose penalties on regular tickets as well, particularly against 'no show' passengers (see No Shows).

Check In Airlines ask you to check in a certain time ahead of the flight departure (usually two hours on international flights). If you fail to check in on time and the flight is overbooked the airline can cancel your booking and give your seat to somebody else.

Confirmation Having a ticket written out with the flight and date you want doesn't mean you have a seat until the agent has checked with the airline that your status is 'OK' or confirmed. Meanwhile you could just be 'on request'. It's also wise to reconfirm onward or return bookings directly with the airline 72 hours before departure (see Reconfirmation).

Discounted Tickets There are two types of discounted fares: officially discounted (see Promotional Fares) and unofficially discounted. The lowest prices often impose drawbacks like flying with unpopular airlines, inconvenient schedules or unpleasant routes and connections. A discounted ticket can save you other things than money – you may be able to pay Apex prices without the associated Apex advance booking and other requirements. Discounted tickets only exist where there is fierce competition.

Full Fares Airlines traditionally offer first-class (coded F), business-class (coded J) and economy-class (coded Y) tickets. These days there are so many promotional and discounted fares available from the regular economy class that few passengers pay full economy fare.

Lost Tickets If you lose your airline ticket an airline will sometimes treat it like a bank would treat a travellers' cheque and issue you with another one, although there may be a lengthy waiting period and a reissue fee. Legally, however, an airline is entitled to treat a ticket like cash and if you lose it then it's gone forever. Take good care of your tickets.

No Shows No shows are passengers who fail to show up for their flight, sometimes due to unexpected delays or disasters, sometimes due to simply forgetting, sometimes because they made more than one booking and didn't bother to cancel the one they didn't want. Full-fare passengers who fail to turn up are sometimes entitled to travel on a later flight. The rest of us are penalised (see Cancellation Penalties).

On Request An unconfirmed booking for a flight (see Confirmation).

Open Jaws A return ticket where you fly out to one place but return from another. If available, this can save you backtracking to your arrival point.

honest and solvent, but there are a few rogues who will take your money and disappear. If you feel suspicious about a firm, don't give them all the money at once – leave a deposit of 20% or so and pay the balance when you pick up the ticket. If you use a credit card you may have certain protections through your credit card company if the deal falls through. If they insist on cash in advance, you should go somewhere else or be prepared to take a very big risk. And once you have the ticket, ring the airline to confirm that you are actually booked on the specified flight.

You may decide to pay more than the rock-bottom fare by opting for the safety of a better known travel agent. Firms such as STA Travel, which has offices worldwide, Council Travel in the USA, Travel CUTS in Canada and Trailfinders in London offer good prices to most destinations and are all competitive and reliable.

Use the fares that are quoted in here as a guide only, as it is quite possible that they

ᛁᚠᚨ·ᛏᛁᚠ·ᚠᚷᚾᛗ·ᚨᛈᚠᛗᚾ·ᚠᛈᛈᛁᚠᚨ·ᛏᛁᚠ·ᚠᚷᚾᛗ·ᚨᛈᚠᛗᚾ·ᚠᛈᛈᛁᚠᚨ·ᛏᛁᚠ·ᚠᚷᚾᛗ·ᚨᛈᚠᛗᚾ·ᚠᛈᛈᛁᚠᚨ·ᛏᛁᚠ·ᚠᚷᚾᛗ·ᚨᛈᚠᛗᚾ·ᚠᛈᛈᛁᚠ

Overbooking Airlines hate to fly empty seats, and since every flight has some passengers who fail to show up (see No Shows), airlines often book more passengers than they have seats for. Usually the excess passengers balance those who fail to show up but occasionally somebody gets bumped. If this happens guess who it is most likely to be? The passengers who check in late.

Promotional Fares Officially discounted fares like Apex fares which are available from travel agents or direct from the airline.

Reconfirmation At least 72 hours prior to departure time of an onward or return flight you must contact the airline and 'reconfirm' that you intend to be on the flight. If you don't do this the airline can delete your name from the passenger list and you could lose your seat. You don't have to reconfirm the first flight on your itinerary or if your stopover is less than 72 hours. It doesn't hurt to reconfirm more than once.

Restrictions Discounted tickets often have various restrictions on them – advance purchase is the most usual one (see Apex). Others are restrictions on the minimum and maximum period you must be away, such as a minimum of 14 days or a maximum of one year (see Cancellation Penalties).

Standby A discounted ticket where you only fly if there is a seat free at the last moment. Standby fares are usually only available on domestic routes.

Tickets Out An entry requirement for many countries is that you have an onward or return ticket – in other words, a ticket out of the country. If you're not sure what you intend to do next, the easiest solution is to buy the cheapest onward ticket to a neighbouring country or a ticket from a reliable airline which can later be refunded if you do not use it.

Transferred Tickets Airline tickets cannot be transferred from one person to another. Travellers sometimes try to sell the return half of their ticket, but officials can ask you to prove that you are the person named on the ticket. This is unlikely to happen on domestic flights, but on international flights, tickets may be compared with passports.

Travel Agencies Travel agencies vary widely and you should use one that suits your needs. Some simply handle tours while full-service agencies handle everything from tours and tickets to car rental and hotel bookings. A good one will do all these things and can save you money, but if all you want is a ticket at the lowest possible price, then you're probably better off with an agency specialising in discounted tickets. A discounted ticket agency, however, may not be useful for other things, like hotel bookings.

Travel Periods Some officially discounted fares, Apex fares in particular, vary with the time of year. There is often a low (off-peak) season and a high (peak) season. Sometimes there's an intermediate or shoulder season as well. At peak times, when everyone wants to fly, not only will the officially discounted fares be higher but so will unofficially discounted fares, or there may simply be no discounted tickets available. Usually the fare depends on your outward flight – if you depart in the high season and return in the low season, you pay the high-season fare. ■

ᛁᚠᚨ·ᛏᛁᚠ·ᚠᚷᚾᛗ·ᚨᛈᚠᛗᚾ·ᚠᛈᛈᛁᚠᚨ·ᛏᛁᚠ·ᚠᚷᚾᛗ·ᚨᛈᚠᛗᚾ·ᚠᛈᛈᛁᚠᚨ·ᛏᛁᚠ·ᚠᚷᚾᛗ·ᚨᛈᚠᛗᚾ·ᚠᛈᛈᛁᚠᚨ·ᛏᛁᚠ·ᚠᚷᚾᛗ·ᚨᛈᚠᛗᚾ·ᚠᛈᛈᛁᚠ

will have changed by the time this book is published.

Travellers with Special Needs

If you have special needs of any sort – you require a special diet, you're travelling in a wheelchair or with a baby, or you have a medical condition that warrants special consideration – let the airline know as soon as possible so that they can make arrangements. Remind them when you reconfirm your booking (at least 72 hours before departure)

and again when you check in at the airport. It may also be worth ringing around the airlines before you make your booking to find out how each of them can handle your particular needs.

Most international airports will provide an escorted cart or wheelchair from check-in desk to plane where needed, and there should be ramps, lifts, accessible toilets and reachable phones. Aircraft toilets, on the other hand, are likely to present a problem for some disabled passengers; travellers should discuss this with the airline at an early stage and, if necessary, with their doctor.

Children under two travel for 10% of the standard fare (or free on some airlines) as long as they don't occupy a seat. They don't get a baggage allowance either. 'Skycots', baby food and diapers should be provided by the airline if requested in advance. Children between two and 12 can usually occupy a seat for half to two-thirds of the full fare, and do get a baggage allowance.

To/From the USA

The North Atlantic is the world's busiest long-haul air corridor and the flight options are bewildering. Larger newspapers such as the *New York Times*, the *Chicago Tribune*, the *San Francisco Chronicle* and the *Los Angeles Times* all produce weekly travel sections in which you'll find any number of travel agents' ads for airfares to Europe.

You should be able to fly return from New York to Copenhagen or any other major Scandinavian city for around US$600 in the low season and around US$700 in the high season. These fares include connecting flights from other major East Coast cities such as Boston or Washington DC. Add about US$100 more for flights from the Midwest and about US$200 more from the West Coast. You might be able to beat these rates if the airlines are battling for passengers with promotional fares, or you could end up with a higher fare if all the cheapest fares are booked out on the day you want to leave. Most low-end fares between the USA and Denmark are valid for either a 30-day or 60-day stay.

With most tickets you can travel 'open jaws' even with its cheapest fares, allowing you to land in one city (Copenhagen for example) and return from another (either a Danish city such as Rønne or Aalborg, or another Scandinavian city such as Oslo or Stockholm) at no extra cost.

An interesting alternative to a direct flight is offered by Icelandair (☎ 800-223-5500), which allows a three-day stopover in Iceland's capital, Reykjavík, on flights from Boston, Washington or New York to Copen-

hagen. Their prices are competitive with direct East Coast-Copenhagen fares offered by other airlines. In addition, Icelandair has a New York-Luxembourg flight via Reykjavík that can be a real bargain (as low as US$350 in the low season) for those willing to fly to Luxembourg and travel overland to Copenhagen from there.

There are other options for getting to Europe, including purchasing tickets through an agency that specialises in discount fares. Make sure you thoroughly understand all of the conditions before paying any money, and realise these tickets are seldom refundable. In addition you'll often need more flexibility, and may have to fly into a nearby country rather than directly to your intended destination. For example, Airhitch (☎ 212-864-2000), a New York company specialising in stand-by tickets, can get travellers to Europe one way from US$169/269 from the East Coast/West Coast. Airhitch also has offices in Santa Monica (☎ 310-394-0550), Paris (☎ 1-47 00 16 30) and Amsterdam (☎ 020-627 24 32), but you have to be a US or Canadian resident to fly one way to North America.

Another option is a courier flight, where you accompany a parcel or freight to be picked up at the other end. The drawbacks are that your stay in Europe may be limited to one or two weeks, that your luggage is usually restricted to carry-on luggage (the freight you carry comes out of your luggage allowance), and that you may have to be a resident and apply for an interview before they'll take you on. It's best to make your initial contact with the courier services a few months before you plan to travel.

Find out more about courier flights from Discount Travel International in New York (☎ 212-362-3636), Now Voyager in New York (☎ 212-431-1616) and Way to Go in Los Angeles (☎ 213-466-1126). They all work slightly differently. Now Voyager, for example, charges a $50 annual registration fee, after which most flights to Europe (including some to Copenhagen) cost US$199 return and allow a stay of seven days. When they're in a bind they do occasionally have great last-minute specials as low as US$99 return.

The *Travel Unlimited* newsletter, PO Box 1058, Allston, MA 02134 publishes details of the cheapest airfares and courier possibilities for destinations all over the world from the USA and other countries including the UK. It's a treasure-trove of information. A single monthly issue costs US$5 and a year's subscription costs US$25 (US$35 abroad).

To/From Canada

Travel CUTS offers good prices to most destinations and has offices in all major cities. Scan the budget travel agents' ads in the *Toronto Globe & Mail*, the *Toronto Star* and the *Vancouver Province*.

See the previous To/From the USA section earlier in this chapter for general information on courier flights. For courier flights originating in Canada, contact FB On Board Courier Services (☎ 514-633-0740 in Montreal or Toronto, or ☎ 604-338-1366 in Vancouver). A courier return flight to Europe will set you back about C$350 from Toronto or Montreal, or C$425 from Vancouver.

For scheduled commercial flights directly to Copenhagen, you'll generally have to fly first to New York or Chicago and pick up a connecting flight from there.

However, Icelandair (☎ 800-223-5500) has recently introduced a new direct service from Halifax to Reykjavík, Iceland, with connections on to Copenhagen.

To/From Australia

STA Travel and Flight Centres International are major dealers in cheap airfares. Check the travel agents' ads in the Yellow Pages and ring around.

The Saturday travel sections of the *Sydney Morning Herald* and Melbourne's *Age* newspapers have many ads offering cheap fares to Europe, but don't be surprised if they happen to be sold out when you contact the agents: they're usually low-season fares on obscure airlines with conditions attached.

Discounted return fares on mainstream airlines through a reputable agent like STA Travel cost between A$1600 (low season)

and A$2500 (high season). Flights to/from Perth are a couple of hundred dollars cheaper.

To/From New Zealand

As in Australia, STA Travel and Flight Centres International are popular travel agencies. Not surprisingly, the cheapest fares to Europe are routed through the USA, and a RTW ticket can be cheaper than an advance-purchase return ticket.

To/From Africa

Nairobi, Kenya, is probably the best place in Africa to buy tickets to Europe, thanks to the strong competition between its many bucket shops. A typical one-way/return fare is about US$550/800.

From South Africa, Air Namibia has particularly cheap return youth fares to London from as low as R2819. The big carriers' return fares range from R2900 to R3815. The South African Students' Travel Service (SASTS; ☎ 011-716 3045) in Johannesburg and the Africa Travel Centre (☎ 021-235 555) in Cape Town are worth trying for cheap tickets.

To/From Asia

Hong Kong is the discount plane-ticket capital of Asia, and its bucket shops are at least as unreliable as those of other cities. Ask the advice of other travellers before buying a ticket. Many of the cheapest fares from South-East Asia to Europe are offered by Eastern European carriers. STA Travel has branches in Hong Kong, Tokyo, Singapore, Bangkok and Kuala Lumpur.

From India, the cheapest flights tend to be with Eastern European carriers like LOT and Aeroflot, or with Middle Eastern airlines such as Syrian Arab Airlines and Iran Air. Bombay is the air-transport hub, with many transit options to/from South-East Asia, but tickets are slightly cheaper in Delhi. Try Delhi Student Travel Services (☎ 332-4788) in the Imperial Hotel, Janpath.

To/From the UK

London is the major centre for discounted

fares in the UK. The Trailfinders (☎ 0171-937 5400) head office, at 194 Kensington High St W8, is an amazing place complete with travel library, bookshop, visa service and immunisation centre. The nearby Campus Travel (☎ 0171-938 2188), at 174 Kensington High St W8, also has many interesting deals. STA Travel, the world's largest student travel agency, has its London branch (☎ 0171-937 9962) at 74 Old Brompton Rd SW7.

The listings magazine *Time Out*, the Sunday papers, the *Evening Standard* and *Exchange & Mart* carry ads for cheap fares. Also look out for the free magazines and newspapers widely available in London, especially *TNT* (recommended) and *Southern Cross* – you can often pick them up outside the main train and tube stations.

It's advisable to use an agent who is a member of some sort of traveller-protection scheme, such as that offered by the ABTA (Association of British Travel Agents). If you have paid for your flight to an ABTA-registered agent who then goes out of business, ABTA will guarantee a refund or an alternative. Unregistered bucket shops are riskier, but they're also cheaper – for example, you can often find a return ticket from London to Copenhagen or a nearby city, such as Frankfurt, for around £100.

There are many scheduled commercial flights between Denmark and the UK, including five daily flights with SAS (☎ 0171-734 4020) between London and Copenhagen; the unrestricted one-way fare is £226, while a non-refundable 30-day return fare costs £160. SAS also operates a daily flight from London to Århus with the same fares.

Although the London-Copenhagen route is the busiest, numerous other flight options exist. For example, Business Air flies 31-passenger SAAB 340 turboprops to Esbjerg from Aberdeen, Edinburgh and Manchester. However, these fares are generally higher than those charged on the more competitive London-Copenhagen route. For information on Business Air call ☎ 0382-566345 in Scotland, ☎ 75 16 07 77 in Esbjerg.

To/From Continental Europe

While the cheapest way to travel between Denmark and the rest of Continental Europe is usually by land, cheap discount charter flights are often available to full-time students aged under 30 and to other young travellers aged under 26 through student travel agencies.

Many travel agents in Europe have ties with STA Travel, where cheap tickets can be purchased. Outlets in important transport hubs include: Voyages et Découvertes (☎ 1-42 61 00 01), 21 Rue Cambon, Paris; SRID Reisen (☎ 069-43 01 91), Berger Strasse 118, Frankfurt; and Student and Youth Travel Service (☎ 01-323 3767), Nikis 11, Athens.

Other agencies specialising in discount fares include Alternativ Tours (☎ 030-8 81 20 89) in Berlin, and Maliu Travel (☎ 623 68 14) and NBBS (☎ 638 17 36) in Amsterdam.

LAND
Bus

If you're coming from elsewhere in Europe, it's often cheaper to get to Denmark by bus than it is by train or plane, although this may not hold true if you're using a rail pass. Long bus rides can be tedious, so bring along a good book. On the plus side, some of the coaches are quite luxurious with toilet, air-con, stewards and snack bar.

Small bus companies come along from time to time with cut rates, although most of them don't remain in business for more than a year or two. Ask around at student and discount travel agencies for the latest information.

Eurolines, one of the biggest and longest established express-bus services, connects many cities in Denmark with the rest of Europe. Most of the buses operate daily (or near-daily) in summer, and between two and five days a week in winter.

Sample one-way fares from Copenhagen are 470 kr to Brussels, 420 kr to Amsterdam, 595 kr to Paris, 610 kr to London, 565 kr to Helsinki and 885 kr to St Petersburg. Between Copenhagen and Germany, fares are 200 kr to Hamburg, 340 kr to Berlin and

425 kr to Frankfurt. Between Copenhagen and Sweden, fares are 90 kr to Helsingborg, 195 kr to Gothenburg and 395 kr to Stockholm.

There's a discount of 10% to 15% for youth (aged 12 to 25) and seniors (over 60 years) and a discount of about 50% for children aged 4 to 11. Children aged 3 and under can travel free. The return fare is about 20% less than two one-way fares.

Eurolines' representatives in Denmark are:

Eurolines Scandinavia, Reventlowsgade 8, 1651 Copenhagen V (☎ 33 25 10 44)
Eurolines Scandinavia, Rådhuspladsen 3, 8000 Århus C (☎ 86 12 36 11)
Eurolines Scandinavia, JF Kennedys Plads 1, 9000 Aalborg (☎ 99 34 44 44)
Eurolines Scandinavia, Kongensgade 53, 5000 Odense C (☎ 66 14 21 00)

Eurolines' representatives elsewhere in Europe include:

Eurolines, 52 Grosvenor Gardens, London SW1 (☎ 0582-40 45 11)
Budget Bus, Rokin 10, Amsterdam (☎ 020-627 51 51)
Eurolines, 55 Rue Saint Jacques, Paris (☎ 1-43 54 11 99)
Eurolines, ZOB Adenauer Allee 78, Hamburg (☎ 40 24 71 06)
Deutsche Touring GmbH, Am Römerhof 17, Frankfurt (☎ 069-790 3240)
Deutsche Touring, Arnulfstrasse 3, Munich (☎ 089-59 18 24)
Lazzi Express, Via Tagliamento 27R, Rome (☎ 06-884 0840)
Eurolines/Nor-Way Bussekspress, Karl Johans gate 2, 0154 Oslo (☎ 22 17 52 90)
Eurolines Sweden, Kyrkogatan 40, 411 15 Gothenburg (☎ 31 10 02 40)
Matkakeskus Resecenter, Georgsgatan 23A, Helsinki (☎ 0-68 09 01)

These offices may also have information on other bus companies and deals. Advance reservations may be necessary on international buses; either call the bus companies directly or enquire at a travel agency.

In addition Denmark's national railway, DSB, has arrangements with some international bus companies. For example, DSB couples up with CSAD in the Czech Republic and Swebus in Sweden. A one-way bus ticket from Copenhagen to Prague costs 400 kr, while a ticket to Halmsted, Sweden, costs 100 kr. Tickets are sold at the DSB travel agency in Copenhagen's Central Station; call ☎ 33 14 17 01 for schedule information.

Train

Trains are a popular way of getting around; they are good meeting places and in Scandinavia they are frequent, comfortable at all levels of services and generally on time.

If you plan to travel extensively around Europe by train, it might be worth getting hold of the *Thomas Cook European Timetable*, which gives a complete listing of train schedules and indicates where supplements apply or where reservations are necessary. It is updated monthly and available from Thomas Cook outlets worldwide. If you will be travelling in Denmark only, then the *DSB Køreplan* is a better option; it is published biannually and can be purchased at larger railway stations.

In the discussion of rail passes that follows, keep in mind that Denmark is a small country so domestic fares are quite moderate. Squeezing your money's worth out of a rail pass that is used solely in Denmark can be a real challenge. (For more details on Denmark's domestic fares, see the Train section in the Getting Around chapter that follows.) On the other hand, if you will also be making excursions to neighbouring countries then that will certainly boost the value of your rail pass.

For comparison purposes, standard 2nd-class rail fares from Copenhagen are 871 kr to Frankfurt, 534 kr to Oslo, 252 kr to Gothenburg and 429 kr to Stockholm. For passengers aged under 26 years, discounts lower these fares to 675 kr to Frankfurt, 350 kr to Oslo, 225 kr to Gothenburg and 325 kr to Stockholm.

Rail Passes There is a multitude of rail passes available for travel in Europe and it's important to find a travel agent that's familiar with the various options. Two places in the

USA that specialise in selling rail passes are Budget Europe Travel Service (☎ 800-441-2387 ext 80), 2557 Meade Court, Ann Arbor, MI 48105, and Europe Through the Back Door (☎ 206-771-8303), 120 Fourth Avenue N, PO Box 2009, Edmonds, WA 98020. Among the places selling rail passes in the UK are Wasteels Travel (☎ 0171-834 7066), 121 Wilton Road, London SW1 and Campus Travel (☎ 0171-730 3402), 52 Grosvenor Gardens, London SW1. In Continental Europe, rail passes can be purchased at larger railway stations and travel agencies.

If you buy a rail pass, read the small print. There are certain rules for validation and the pass cannot be transferred. Lost or stolen Eurail passes can only be reissued in certain circumstances and with the correct supporting documents. For ScanRail passes, refunds can only be made if the card is returned unused before the first day of validity, and there are no refunds for theft, loss or partial usage.

Keep in mind that rail passes do not cover seat-reservation costs and fees for supplements, such as sleepers. Pass holders must always carry proper identification, such as a passport or national-identity card. If you take any overnight sleepers they will generally be counted as next-day travel as long as the train departs after 7 pm.

Eurail In Scandinavia, the ScanRail pass is generally a better deal than the Eurail pass, so this information will be of most interest to the traveller who is going to visit other parts of Europe too.

Eurail passes are valid for unlimited travel on national railways and some private lines in Austria, Belgium, Denmark, Finland, France (including Monaco), Germany, Greece, Hungary, Ireland, Italy, Luxembourg, the Netherlands, Norway, Portugal, Spain, Sweden and Switzerland (including Liechtenstein). The UK is not covered nor are Estonia, Latvia and Lithuania.

Eurail is also valid for ferries between Ireland and France (not between the UK and France), between Italy and Greece, and from Sweden to Finland, Denmark or Germany.

Eurail passes offer reasonable value to people aged under 26. A Eurail Youthpass is valid for unlimited 2nd-class travel for 15 days (US$418), one month (US$598) or two months (US$798). The Youth Flexipass, also for 2nd-class travel, is valid for freely chosen days within a two-month period: 10 days for US$438 or 15 days for US$588.

The corresponding passes for those aged over 26 are available in 1st class only. The Eurail Flexipass costs US$616 or US$812 for 10 or 15 freely chosen days in two months.

The standard Eurail pass has five versions, all for 1st-class travel, costing from US$522 for 15 days' unlimited travel up to US$1468 for three months. Two or more people travelling together (minimum three people between 1 April and 30 September) qualify for a Eurail Saverpass, which works like the standard Eurail pass – for example, a 15-day pass under this scheme costs only US$452 per person. Eurail passes for children are available at half price.

Eurail passes can only be bought by residents of non-European countries, and are supposed to be purchased before arriving in Europe. However, Eurail passes can be purchased within Europe, so long as your passport proves you've been there for less than six months, but the outlets where you can do this are limited and the passes will be more expensive than getting them outside Europe. For example, Copenhagen is the only city in Denmark and Oslo is the only city in Norway where you can buy the Eurail passes (at the Eurail Aid counters at the main railway stations). French National Railways (☎ 0171-493 9731), 179 Piccadilly, London, is another such outlet.

If you've lived in Europe for more than six months, you are eligible for an Inter-Rail pass which is a better buy.

Inter-Rail Inter-Rail passes are available to residents of European countries. To purchase this pass, you will be expected to show proof of European residency for a minimum of six months. Terms and conditions vary slightly from country to country. Inter-Rail cards should be treated like cash, as you can make no claims in the event of loss or theft.

Travellers aged over 26 can get the Inter-Rail 26+, valid for unlimited rail travel in Austria, Bulgaria, Croatia, Czech Republic, Denmark, Finland, Germany, Greece, Hungary, Ireland, Luxembourg, Netherlands, Norway, Poland, Romania, Slovakia, Slovenia, Sweden and Turkey. The pass also gives free travel (barring port tax) on shipping routes from Brindisi (Italy) to Patras (Greece), as well as 30% to 50% discounts on various other ferry routes (many more than covered by Eurail) and certain river and lake services. A 15-day pass costs UK£209 and one month costs UK£269.

The Inter-Rail pass for those under 26 has been split into zones. Zone A is Ireland; B is Sweden, Norway and Finland; C is Denmark, Germany, Switzerland and Austria; D' is the Czech Republic, Slovakia, Poland, Hungary, Bulgaria and Romania; E is France, Belgium, Netherlands and Luxembourg; F is Spain, Portugal and Morocco; and G is Italy, Greece, Turkey and Slovenia. The price for any one zone is UK£179 for 15 days. Multi-zone passes are better value and are valid for one month: two-zone passes cost UK£209, three zones costs UK£229, and all zones costs UK£249.

ScanRail This is a flexible rail pass covering travel in Denmark, Norway, Sweden and Finland.

There are three versions of the pass. For travel on any five days within a 15-day period, the pass costs US$222/176 for 1st/2nd class (US$167/132 for travellers under age 26). For travel on any 10 days within a one-month period, the pass costs US$346/278 for 1st/2nd class (US$260/209 for under age 26). For a pass that allows unlimited travel during 30 consecutive days, the cost is US$504/404 for 1st/2nd class (US$378/303 for under age 26).

If you are age 55 or over, then you're eligible for the ScanRail 55+ Pass, which will allow 1st/2nd-class travel over five days in a 15-day period for US$193/153, 10 days in a one-month period for US$301/242 and one month for US$438/351.

Children under the age of four ride for free, while those under 12 pay half price.

To get the ScanRail passes at these prices, they must be purchased before you arrive in Scandinavia. ScanRail passes can also be purchased in Denmark, but they'll cost roughly 35% more. For example, a 2nd-class pass allowing travel five out of 15 days costs 1264 kr when purchased in Denmark; at the current exchange rate, that comes to US$230.

ScanRail passes are valid on trains run by state railways in Denmark (DSB), Finland (VR), Norway (NSB) and Sweden (SJ). The pass also includes free travel on the following boat services:

DSB domestic ferry lines (Denmark)
Helsingør-Helsingborg (ScandLines)
Rødbyhavn-Puttgarden (DSB)
Gedser-Warnemünde (DSB)
Trelleborg-Sassnitz (SJ/DB)

There's a 50% discount if you're travelling on the following services:

Copenhagen-Malmö (DSØ Flyvebådene hydrofoils)
Copenhagen-Rønne (Bornholmstrafikken)
Rønne-Ystad (Bornholmstrafikken)
Copenhagen-Oslo (DFDS)
Hjørring-Hirtshals (train)
Frederikshavn-Oslo (Stena Line)
Frederikshavn-Gothenburg (Stena Line)
Frederikshavn-Moss (Stena Line)
Hirtshals-Kristiansand (Color Line)
Stockholm-Helsinki (Viking Line)

There are about a dozen other boat lines operating between Scandinavian ports outside of Denmark that also allow a 50% discount. Discounts on ferry routes apply only to the basic fares; no discounts are given on cabin supplements, for example.

Other Passes & Cheap Tickets There are also a number of other innovative passes for European rail travel, including some that incorporate rail/drive packages, and others that are geared for travel within one country for a short period of time, such as the EuroDomino pass. To get all of the latest information, contact a good travel agent who is familiar with rail passes.

When weighing up rail-pass options, consider also the cost of other cheap-ticket deals. Travellers aged under 26 can pick up BIJ (Billet International de Jeunesse) tickets which sometimes cut fares by up to 50%. Unfortunately, you can't always bank on a substantial reduction.

Various agents issue BIJ tickets in Europe; Campus Travel (☎ 0171-730 3402), 52 Grosvenor Gardens, London SW1 for example, which also sells Eurotrain tickets. Eurotrain options include circular Explorer tickets, allowing a different route for the return trip. British Rail International (☎ 0171-834 2345) and Wasteels (☎ 0171-834 7066) also sell BIJ tickets.

Car & Motorbike

Denmark's only land border is with Germany. The E45, part of the inter-European motorway network, is the main route between Germany and the Jutland peninsula, though there are several smaller border crossings as well.

Currently it's necessary to take a car ferry to get to Copenhagen from anywhere outside Denmark. However, in the not-too-distant future Copenhagen will be connected to both the Jutland peninsula (via the Store Bælt bridge, scheduled for completion in the late 1990s) and to Sweden (via a new bridge across the Øresund, optimistically projected to be in place for the year 2000).

For information on car ferries to Denmark, see the Sea heading later in this chapter. For information on travelling around Denmark by private vehicle, see the Car & Motorbike section in the Getting Around chapter.

If you plan to do extensive car travelling around Europe, a useful general reference is Eric Bredesen's *Moto Europa* (Seren Publishing). It's updated annually and contains information on renting, buying, necessary documents, tax, road rules and motoring phrases. It can be ordered from US and Canadian bookshops (US$24.95), or direct from Seren Publishing (☎ 800-EUROPA-8) at PO Box 1212, Dubuque, IA 52004, USA (add US$3 for shipping).

Paperwork & Preparations Proof of vehicle ownership should always be carried when driving in Europe (a Vehicle Registration Document for British-registered cars). Also carry your national licence, as well as an International Driving Permit (IDP) from your motoring organisation when appropriate (see Documents in the earlier Facts for the Visitor chapter).

Third-party motor insurance is a minimum requirement in most of Europe. Most UK motor insurance policies automatically provide third-party cover for EU countries and some others. Get your insurer to issue a Green Card (it may cost extra) which is internationally recognised as proof of insurance, and check that it lists all the countries you intend to visit. You'll need this in the event of an accident outside the country where the vehicle is insured. Also ask your insurer for a European Accident Statement form, which can simplify things. Never sign statements you can't read or understand – insist on a translation and sign that only if it's acceptable.

Taking out a European breakdown-assistance policy is a good investment, such as the AA Five Star Service or the RAC Eurocover Motoring Assistance. Ask your motoring organisation for a letter of introduction, which entitles you to free services offered by affiliated organisations around Europe.

Every vehicle travelling across an international border should display a nationality plate of its country of registration. A warning triangle, to be used in the event of breakdown, is compulsory almost everywhere. Recommended accessories are a first-aid kit, a spare bulb kit and a fire extinguisher.

Road Rules You'll drive on the right in all the northern European countries. Vehicles brought over from the UK or Ireland should have their headlights adjusted to avoid blinding oncoming traffic at night (a simple solution on older headlight lenses is to cover up the triangular section of the lens with tape). Priority is usually given to traffic approaching from the right in countries that drive on the right-hand side. The British RAC publishes an annual *European Motoring Guide*, which gives an excellent summary of regulations in each country, including parking rules. Motoring organisations in other countries have similar publications.

Take care with speed limits as they vary significantly from country to country. You may be surprised at the apparent disregard of traffic regulations in some places but as a visitor it is always best to err on the side of caution. In Denmark and a number of other European countries, many driving infringements are subject to on-the-spot fines. Always ask for a receipt if you're fined.

Scandinavian countries are particularly strict with drink-driving regulations. In some places, including the Baltic states of Estonia, Latvia and Lithuania, only a zero blood-alcohol level is tolerated, so don't drive after drinking at all.

For road rules specific to Denmark, see the Car & Motorbike section in the Getting Around chapter that follows.

Bicycle

A bicycle can make a great travelling companion in cycle-friendly Denmark. If you're flying to Denmark, you should be able to take your bicycle along with you on the plane relatively easily. You can take the bicycle to pieces and put it in a bike bag or box, but it's much easier simply to wheel your bike to the check-in desk, where it should be treated as a piece of baggage. You may have to remove the pedals and turn the handlebars sideways so that it takes up less space in the aircraft's hold, but check all this with the airline well in advance, preferably before you pay for your ticket.

It's also possible to send bicycles between Denmark and most other European countries (but not Italy) via train as international luggage. The bicycle must be easy to handle; therefore it cannot be locked and anything bulky, such as baskets and saddlebags, must be removed. The transport time can take as much as three days to other stations in Scandinavia and five days to elsewhere in Europe. If you're sending the bicycle from Denmark to a foreign station, the cost is 205 kr, except for those sent directly from Copenhagen's Central Station or Padborg Station (on the German border) in which case the charge is usually only 75 kr.

If you're travelling between Denmark and Germany, bicycles can be taken with you on certain direct trains, including a number of those from Puttgarden, Hamburg and Berlin. In many cases, you can travel on the same carriage as your bicycle. Reservations should be made and you'll need a special bicycle ticket (58 kr) which can be purchased at stations that sell tickets to foreign destinations. If you're travelling in the high season, book as far in advance as possible, as each train has only a limited amount of space for bicycles.

International ferries allow you to bring your bicycle along with you and the fees are quite reasonable; for example, the ferries plying between Esbjerg and the UK charge only 45 kr.

Once you're in Denmark, you'll find many trains and buses specially equipped to carry bicycles at a nominal fee. Information on travelling around Denmark by bicycle is in the Bicycle section of the Getting Around chapter, and also under Cycling in the Activities section of the Facts for the Visitor chapter.

Ride Services

With the exception of hitchhiking, the cheapest way to get to Denmark from elsewhere in Europe is as a paying passenger in a private car. There are several European organisations that can help you find a ride. In addition, you may want to check notice boards at universities, some of which post 'riders wanted' notices.

If you're leaving from Germany, or travelling within that country, such rides are arranged by Mitfahrzentrale agencies in many German cities. You pay a reservation fee to the agency and your share of petrol to the driver. The local tourist information office will be able to direct you to such agencies, or you can check the entry 'Mitfahrzentrale' in the Yellow Pages phone book.

Here are some other organisations that offer ride services:

Austria
 Daungasse 1a, Vienna (☎ 0222-408 2210)
Belgium
 Marché aux Herbes 27, Brussels (☎ 02-512 10 15)
Denmark
 Interstop, 14 Kjeld Langesgade, Copenhagen (☎ 33 33 08 25)
The Netherlands
 Nieuwezijds Voorburgwal 256, Amsterdam (☎ 020-622 43 42)
Switzerland
 Leonhardstrasse 15, Zürich (☎ 01-261 68 93)

SEA

Ferry travel can be an economical way to get to Denmark as it often includes overnight accommodation, and it's also a pleasant way to travel as the boats are generally of a high standard. The long-distance boats usually have duty-free shops, lounges, nightclubs and both cafeterias and formal restaurants. Many of the boats between Denmark and other Scandinavian countries have floating casinos and small grocery stores on board as well.

Unless otherwise noted, the fares that follow are for one-way travel. There are often discounts on return tickets, particularly for people travelling by car, and occasionally there are some handsome excursion deals – always ask about special promotions. If you're carrying a rail pass or a student card, be sure to flash it when you purchase a ticket, as it may entitle you to a substantial discount. Children's fares are usually half of the adult fares.

Keep in mind that the same ferry company can have a whole host of different prices for the same route, depending upon the time of day or year. Note that cabin fares are quoted on a per-person (not a per-cabin) basis. Car fares given in this section are for a standard car (generally up to six metres in length and two metres in height); most fares inch up as

the vehicle increases in size, and fares for camper vans are higher still.

Particularly if you're bringing along a vehicle, you should always make reservations well in advance – this holds doubly true in summer and on weekends. During busy periods, you'll also get the best cabin selection by booking far in advance.

Boat Companies

Following are the reservation numbers for the largest ferry companies operating international routes to and from Denmark:

Scandinavian Seaways Known also as DFDS, Scandinavian Seaways runs ferries from Copenhagen to Oslo via Helsingborg (Sweden) and also from Esbjerg to Harwich, England.

Booking agents include:

Denmark
 Scandinavian Seaways, Sankt Annæ Plads 30, 1295 Copenhagen (☎ 33 42 30 00, fax 33 15 49 93 in Copenhagen; ☎ 75 12 48 00, fax 75 18 11 01 in Esbjerg)
France
 c/o Navifrance, Paris (☎ 1-42 666 540)
Germany
 Scandinavian Seaways, DFDS Gmbh, Van-der-Smissen-Strasse 4, 22 767 Hamburg 50 (☎ 040-38903-71, fax 403 890 3120)
Ireland
 Irish Ferries, 2-4 Merrion Row, Dublin 2 (☎ 6610511)
Norway
 Scandinavian Seaways, Utstikker II Vippetangen, Oslo (☎ 22 42 93 50, fax 22 41 38 38)
UK
 Scandinavian Seaways, 15 Hanover St, London W1R 9HG (☎ 0171-409 6060, fax 0171-409 6035)
 Scandinavian Seaways, Scandinavia House, Parkeston Quay, Harwich, Essex C012 4QG (☎ 01255-240 240, fax 01255-244382)
 Scandinavian Seaways, Tyne Commission Quay, North Shields, Newcastle (☎ 0191 293 6262, fax 0191 293 6222)
USA
 DFDS Seaways, Cypress Creek Business Park, 6555 NW 9th Avenue, Suite 207, Fort Lauderdale, FL 33309 (☎ 800-533-3755, fax 305-491-7958)

Stena Line Stena operates ferries from Frederikshavn to Gothenburg (Sweden) and Oslo and Moss (Norway) and from Grenaa to Varberg and Halmstad (Sweden).

Booking agents include:

Denmark
  Stena Line, Stenaterminalen, 9900 Frederikshavn (☎ 96 20 02 00, fax 96 20 02 81)
Germany
  Stena Line, Schwedenkai, 2300 Kiel 1 (☎ 431-90 90, fax 431-90 92 00)
Norway
  Stena Line, Jernbanetorget 2, 0154 Oslo (☎ 22 33 50 00, fax 22 41 44 40 in Oslo; ☎ 69 25 75 00, fax 69 25 41 17 in Moss)
Sweden
  Stena Line, 405 16 Gothenburg (☎ 031-77 50 000, fax 031-12 36 13)
UK
  Stena Sealink Line, Charter House, Park Street, Ashford, Kent TN24 8EX (☎ 1233 647022, fax 1233 646021)
USA
  Scantours, 1535 6th St, Suite 205, Santa Monica, CA 90401 (☎ 310-451-0911, fax 310-395-2013)

Color Line The Color Line operates ferries between Hirtshals and the Norwegian cities of Kristiansand and Oslo.

Booking agents include:

Denmark
  Color Line, Færgeterminalen, Postboks 30, 9850 Hirtshals (☎ 99 56 19 66, fax 98 94 50 92)
France
  Color Line, c/o Scanditours, 36 rue Tronchet, 75009 Paris (☎ 47 42 80 00, fax 42 66 45 95)
Germany
  Color Line GmbH, Postfach 2646, 24025 Kiel (☎ 431 9 74 11-0, fax 431 9 74 11 22)
Norway
  Color Line, Postboks 1422 Vika, 0115 Oslo (☎ 22 94 44 00, fax 22 83 07 76 in Oslo; ☎ 38 07 88 00, fax 38 07 88 13 in Kristiansand)
UK
  Color Line, Tyne Commission Quay, North Shields NE29 6EA (☎ 0191-296 1313, fax 0191-296 1540)
USA & Canada
  Bergen Line, 505 Fifth Avenue, New York, NY 10017, USA (☎ 212-986 2711)

Larvik Line The Larvik Line operates ferries between Frederikshavn and Larvik, Norway,
and has a summertime catamaran between Skagen and Larvik.

Booking agents include:

Denmark
  Postboks 30, 9900 Frederikshavn (☎ 99 20 40 60, fax 98 20 40 50)
France
  Bennett Voyages, 28 Boulevard Haussmann, 75009 Paris (☎ 01-48 01 87 77, fax 01-48 01 87 89)
Germany
  Reisebüro Norden GmbH, Ost-West Str 70, 20457 Hamburg (☎ 040-36 00 15 78, fax 040-36 64 83)
Norway
  Hoffsveien 15, Box 265, Skøyen, 0212 Oslo (☎ 22 52 55 00, fax 22 52 15 40 in Oslo; ☎ 33 18 70 00, fax 33 18 72 70 in Larvik)
UK
  Scandinavian Seaways, Scandinavia House, Parkeston Quay, Harwich, Essex CO12 4QG (☎ 0255-24 12 34, fax 0255-24 43 82)

To/From Germany

Rødbyhavn to Puttgarden The busy train, car and passenger ferry from Puttgarden to Rødbyhavn (the quickest way to Copenhagen) goes nearly every half-hour 24 hours a day and takes one hour. Ferries leave Rødbyhavn on the hour and half-hour, and depart from Puttgarden at five and 35 minutes past the hour. A few runs are skipped in the low season and on slow days, but there's always at least one ferry an hour. If you're travelling by train, the cost of the ferry will be included in your ticket. Otherwise the cost is 160 kr for a motorcycle with up to two people and 300 kr for a car with up to five people, plus 100 kr extra for travel on weekends from 1 June to mid-September. For reservations call ☎ 33 15 15 15 in Copenhagen, ☎ 04371 86 51 11 in Puttgarden.

Gedser to Rostock & Warnemünde Two ferry companies operate from Gedser to Rostock, a trip of about two hours. Europa-Linien (☎ 53 87 00 05 in Gedser, ☎ 49 381 67 00 667 in Rostock) makes several runs a day (at least seven in summer) and charges 30 kr for passengers and 160 kr for a motorcycle with two people. A car with up to five people costs 385 kr on summer weekends and 275 kr on other days. The DSB (☎ 33 15 15 15) Gedser-Rostock ferry has three runs a day and charges comparable fares. DSB also operates a car ferry between Gedser and Warnemünde four to five times a day for the same fares.

Korsør to Kiel A car ferry, operated by DSB, runs daily between Korsør (Halsskov harbour) and Kiel. The ferry leaves Halsskov at 9 am, arriving in Kiel at 2.15 pm, and then returns from Kiel at 3.45 pm. Passenger fares are 40 kr, while a motorcycle with two passengers costs 115 kr. The summer fare for a car with up to five passengers is 265 kr from Sunday to Wednesday and 345 kr on other days. Car fares are about 25% lower in winter. Reservations are made through DSB (☎ 53 57 15 77 in Korsør, ☎ 0431 98 11 36 in Kiel).

Bagenkop to Kiel The Langeland-Kiel Linien (☎ 62 56 14 00 in Bagenkop, ☎ 0431 97 41 50 in Kiel) operates a car ferry between Bagenkop and Kiel two or three times a day. The fare is 27 kr (35 kr in July) for a passenger, 90 kr for a motorcycle and 125 kr for a car. The trip takes 2½ hours.

Marstal to Kiel The passenger ferry *Fair Lady* (☎ 04351 5531 in Kiel, ☎ 62 53 10 74 in Marstal) runs between Kiel and Marstal (on the island of Ærø) from early April to late October. The boat leaves Kiel at 8.30 am, arrives in Marstal at 11 am and departs from Marstal at 5 pm. The fare is 60 kr.

Faaborg to Gelting The Faaborg-Gelting line (☎ 62 61 15 00 in Faaborg, ☎ 04643-793 in Gelting) operates between Faaborg and Gelting from mid-February to the end of December, with two to three sailings a day. The passenger fare is 15 kr, the motorcycle fare 20 kr and the car fare 60 kr, except for July when all fares double. The trip takes two hours.

Rømø to Sylt The Rømø-Sylt Linie (☎ 74 75 53 03 in Rømø, ☎ 4652 475 in Sylt) operates car ferries between Havneby on the island of Rømø to List on Germany's island of Sylt at least six times a day. The trip takes one hour and costs 32 kr for adults, 24 kr for children, 100 kr for a motorcycle and driver and 220 kr for a car.

Bornholm Ferries For information on ferries between Rønne and the German ports of Sassnitz and Neu Mukran (Rügen) see the Getting There & Away section of the Bornholm chapter.

To/From Poland
Polferries operates a year-round ferry service between Swinoujscie (☎ 936-3006) and Copenhagen (☎ 33 11 46 45). The trip takes 10 hours. Ferries depart from Copenhagen at 9.30 pm on Monday, Wednesday, Thursday and Friday and at 11 am on Sunday. From Swinoujscie, ferries depart at 10.30 am on Thursday and Friday and at 10.30 pm on Tuesday, Saturday and Sunday. The fare is 290 kr for adults, 180 kr for children, 90 kr for a motorcycle, 430 kr for a car with driver or 795 kr for a car with up to five passengers. There are good discounts on return fares.

For information on the summertime ferry between Swinoujscie and Rønne, see the Getting There & Away section of the Bornholm chapter.

To/From Sweden
Helsingør-Helsingborg The cheapest ferry between Denmark and Sweden is the shuttle between Helsingør and Helsingborg (25 minutes, 18 kr); if you're travelling by train it's included in your rail ticket. Ferries leave opposite the Helsingør railway station about every 15 minutes during the day and once an hour through the night. Ferry passage for a motorcycle and up to two riders costs 105 kr, while a car with up to five people costs 305/395 kr on weekdays/weekends. All return tickets cost 50% more. For car reservations call ScandLines (☎ 49 26 26 83 in Helsingør, ☎ 42 18 61 00 in Helsingborg).

There's also a frequent passenger hydrofoil service offered by Sundbusserne that takes 20 minutes and costs 35 kr.

Dragør to Limhamn The Limhamn-Dragør line (☎ 32 53 15 85 in Dragør, ☎ 040 36 20 41 in Limhamn) operates between Dragør and Limhamn about a dozen times a day. The trip takes 55 minutes and costs 32 kr for passengers, 115 kr for a motorcycle with up to two people and 395 kr for a car with up to five people.

Copenhagen to Malmö There are a couple of companies running hydrofoils from Copenhagen to Malmö. Pilen (☎ 33 32 12 60 in Copenhagen, ☎ 040 23 44 11 in Malmö) has the most frequent service, operating hourly, except on Sunday when it leaves every other hour. The standard fare is 85 kr, however because of price wars it's not uncommon to find a fare for half of that. The crossing takes only 45 minutes.

Frederikshavn to Gothenburg The Stena Line operates six car ferries a day between Frederikshavn and Gothenburg, charging 90 kr for passengers, 140 kr for a motorcycle with driver and 295 kr for a car including the driver and all passengers. The trip takes 3¼ hours.

You can cut your travel time in half by using SeaCat (☎ 98 42 83 00 in Frederikshavn), a sleek catamaran that charges 95 kr for passengers, from 290 to 390 kr for a motorcycle and from 590 to 1190 kr for cars, both vehicle fares including the driver and passengers. The vehicle fares depend on the day of the week and the season of travel. The boat operates three to five times a day.

If you're a cyclist, note that the SeaCat charges from 40 to 60 kr for a bicycle, whereas the Stena Line carries bicycles for free.

Grenaa to Varberg & Halmstad The Lion Ferry operates daily year round between Grenaa and the Swedish ports of Varberg and Halmstad. The crossing takes 4¼ hours. The fare is 90 kr for passengers, 290 kr for a motorcycle with driver and from 350 kr for a car. Reservation numbers are ☎ 86 32 03 00 in Grenaa, ☎ 35 13 51 70 in Halmsted and ☎ 34 01 90 10 in Varberg.

Bornholm Ferries For information on ferries from Ystad in Sweden to Rønne, see the Getting There & Away section in the Bornholm chapter.

To/From Norway

Copenhagen to Oslo Scandinavian Seaways (DFDS) runs daily overnight ferries between Oslo and Copenhagen, with the cheapest cabin fare (passenger fare included) costing from 400 kr from Sunday to Wednesday in the low season up to 745 kr on summer weekends. Car fares are an additional 220 kr, motorcycles 150 kr. This is a great way to travel between these two Scandinavian capitals – the cabins in all categories are quite pleasant and you can linger over a splendid buffet dinner for 149 kr. The departure in either direction is at 5 pm, with arrival at 9 am.

Frederikshavn/Skagen to Larvik The Larvik Line has a daily year-round ferry between Frederikshavn and Larvik. In spring and autumn, the boat leaves Frederikshavn at 1.30 pm and arrives in Larvik at 7.45 pm, then departs from Larvik at 8.30 pm, arriving back in Frederikshavn at 8 am the next morning. In summer and winter, the schedule varies with the day of the week, and it can be a day or overnight ferry in either direction. The boat holds 2200 passengers and has five restaurants, a casino and a cinema.

The passenger fare is 220/260 kr on weekdays/weekends, except from late June to mid-August when it's 320/360 kr. With a car the fare, including the driver, is 500/590 kr on weekdays/weekends except in summer when it's 710/850 kr. Motorcycles cost from 150 to 270 kr. There are 50% discounts for senior citizens, disabled passengers and children aged between four and 15.

Sleeperettes (reclining chairs) are free of charge. Cabin prices begin at an additional 85 kr (105 kr in summer) in a four-berth cabin and 130 kr (200 kr in summer) in a two-berth cabin. The Larvik Line is also planning to begin a daily summertime service between Skagen and Larvik, using an ultramodern 600-passenger catamaran. If the service – which has already been delayed for one season – does begin, the sailing time will be 2¾ hours, while the fares for both passengers and cars will be the same as on the Frederikshavn-Larvik route.

Frederikshavn to Oslo & Moss The Stena Line operates ferries between Oslo and Frederikshavn daily in summer, slightly less frequently the rest of the year. From June to mid-August the ferries leave Oslo at 7.30 pm, arriving in Frederikshavn at 7.45 am, while they operate in the opposite direction as a day ferry leaving Frederikshavn at 9.45 am. In the low season, departure times vary a bit from Frederikshavn but from Oslo it remains an overnight ferry on all runs. Standard passenger fares range from 190 to 410 kr, with discounts for return fares, children and those aged over 67. Cabins are available at an additional fee, varying with the day of the week and season. Motorcycles cost from 124 to 210 kr, cars from 290 to 500 kr.

The Stena Line also operates a daily ferry between Frederikshavn and Moss that leaves Frederikshavn at 5 pm, arrives in Moss at midnight, and then departs from Moss at 12.45 am. Fares range from 140 to 350 kr for a passenger, from 70 to 176 kr for a motorcycle and from 290 to 400 kr for a car. Two-person cabins are available from 130 kr.

Hirtshals to Kristiansand & Oslo The Color Line runs three or four ferries daily between Hirtshals and Kristiansand, the busiest ferry connection between Norway and Denmark. The trip takes 4¼ hours. Passenger fares vary from 130 kr in the low season to 340 kr on summer weekends. A car costs an additional 170 to 460 kr, a motorcycle 120 to 230 kr.

The Color Line also operates a ferry between Hirtshals and Oslo daily except in the low season when there's no Sunday sailing from Oslo and no Monday sailing from Hirtshals. The boat from Oslo operates as an overnight ferry, departing at 7.30 pm, while the boat from Hirtshals leaves at 10 am and arrives in Oslo at 6.30 pm (except for low-season Sundays when it departs from

Hirtshals at 7 pm). The passenger fare ranges from 150 to 200 kr, while the cheapest two-berth cabins cost from 218 to 530 kr. Motorcycles cost from 120 to 230 kr, cars cost from 280 to 470 kr.

Hanstholm to Egersund & Bergen The Fjord Line operates a year-round ferry to Egersund and Bergen from Hanstholm on Tuesday, Thursday, Saturday and Sunday. The boats depart from Hanstholm mid-afternoon, arriving in Egersund seven hours later and in Bergen the next morning (except for the Saturday boat which terminates in Egersund). Fares depend on the day of the week and the season, ranging from 171 to 329 kr to Egersund, from 225 to 576 kr to Bergen. Add another 50 to 144 kr for a couchette and 212 to 306 kr for a two-berth cabin. A car costs from 167 to 419 kr to Egersund, a motorcycle from 95 to 189 kr. A car with five passengers costs from 594 to 1116 kr to Egersund; ask about the special *bilpakket* return fare which is only a few kroner more. Except in midsummer, there's a 50% discount for students, senior citizens and disabled passengers.

Reservation numbers are ☎ 97 96 14 01 in Hanstholm, ☎ 55 32 37 70 in Bergen and ☎ 51 49 33 88 in Egersund.

To/From the UK

Scandinavian Seaways (DFDS) operates car ferries between Esbjerg and Harwich, England. These are pleasant boats, but when the North Sea is choppy the crossing can get a bit rough.

The ferry between Newcastle and Esbjerg operates from April through October, sailing on every fourth day, departing from Newcastle at 5.30 pm and from Esbjerg at 4.30 pm. The trip takes about 20 hours.

The fares range from UK£65 in the low season to UK£115 in the high season for a reclining chair, while economy two-berth cabins begin at UK£80/130 in the low/high season. There's a 25% discount on return tickets and a 35% discount on fares for travellers aged over 60, students and children.

The cost to bring along a car ranges from

UK£40 to UK£62, depending on the season, while a motorcycle costs from UK£23 to UK£35. If you're travelling with four people and a car, there are discount packages.

To/From Iceland & the Faroe Islands

The Smyril Line runs weekly ferries from Esbjerg to Tórshavn (Faroe Islands) and Seyñisfjörñur (Iceland) from early June to the end of August. The boat leaves Esbjerg on Saturday at 10 pm, arriving in Tórshavn on Monday at 10 am. Visitors then have a two-day stopover in the Faroe Islands (while the boat makes a run to Bergen, Norway), departing from Tórshavn at 3 pm Wednesday and arriving in Seyñisfjörñur at 7 am Thursday. The return boat departs from Seyñisfjörñur at 11 am Thursday, arriving in Tórshavn at 6 am Friday and in Esbjerg at 7 pm Saturday.

The cheapest fares are for a couchette, which costs 880 kr to Tórshavn and 1390 kr to Seyñisfjörñur for the first two and last three sailings of the season and 1350/1980 kr to Tórshavn/Seyñisfjörñur in mid-season. Four-person cabins are 90 kr more, while two-person cabins cost 1470/2190 kr in the low/high season to Tórshavn, 2380/3400 kr to Seyñisfjörñur. There's a 25% discount for students aged under 26 and travellers aged over 60. You can bring a bicycle along for 80

kr more, a motorcycle for about 500 kr and a car for about 80% of the passenger fare.

Reservations can be made through the Smyril Line (☎ 97 96 22 44), Auktionsgade 13, 7730 Hanstholm, Denmark.

TOURS

If your time is limited, there are various package tours that include transport to Denmark, hotel accommodation and, in most cases, sightseeing. Standard tours can be arranged through your travel agent or SAS airlines.

An array of package tours can also be arranged through the large ferry companies, such as the Stena Line and Scandinavian Seaways (DFDS), the addresses of which are listed under Boat Companies earlier in this section.

The Danish Cultural Institute and the American-Scandinavian Foundation arrange study tours to Denmark. Contact addresses are listed under Useful Organisations in the Facts for the Visitor chapter.

LEAVING DENMARK

There are no departure taxes when leaving Denmark.

See the Money section in the Facts for the Visitor chapter for details on how to reclaim value-added tax (VAT) when you depart.

Getting Around

AIR

Most of Denmark's domestic air routes are operated by Mærsk Air (☎ 32 31 45 45), which connects Copenhagen with Billund, Esbjerg, Karup, Odense, Rønne and Vojens. The regular one-way fare from Copenhagen is 595 kr to Odense and Rønne, from 680 to 705 kr to the other destinations. The regular return fare is double these.

There are however, a number of discounts. If you travel on specified flights from Monday to Friday, and stay at least two nights, the return fare is the same price as the normal one-way fare. Not only is this a good deal, but many of the discounted flights are simply flights in the middle of the day that are inconvenient for businesspeople but work out fine for travellers.

If you travel on weekends the return fare is about 70% of the regular return fare, with additional discounts for accompanying family members. For example, using the weekend fare, a return flight from Copenhagen to Rønne (Bornholm) costs 840 kr for the first adult, 515 kr for an accompanying spouse or child aged between 12 to 19, and 410 kr for a child aged two to 11. Children under the age of two travel for free.

Travellers aged under 26 years or over 60 are eligible for one-way stand-by fares of 360 kr on all flights.

SAS (☎ 32 32 68 28) flies from Copenhagen to Århus and Aalborg, both about a dozen times a day. The one-way fare is 595 kr every day, while the return fare is 595 kr in midweek and 840 kr from Friday to Sunday.

In addition, Cimber Air (☎ 74 42 22 23) flies from Copenhagen to Sønderborg for 680 kr one way, from 680 to 1360 kr return.

If your travel plans include an international flight to and from Copenhagen you can often work in a free domestic flight by getting an open-jaw ticket. This would allow you, at either the start of your trip or on the return flight, to add a connecting flight between Copenhagen and another Danish city at no extra charge. On two trips to Denmark, we've had tickets written with an open jaw into Copenhagen and out of Aalborg – a convenient combination that allowed us to rent a car in Copenhagen, self-tour one way, and drop the car at Aalborg airport on the last day of our stay.

BUS

All large cities and towns have a local bus system and most places are also served by county-wide regional buses. More often than not, the central bus stand is beside the railway station and in many cases regional buses conveniently time their routes to connect with train schedules.

Stiff competition from trains has left long-distance buses as a very secondary mode of transport in Denmark. Still there are a handful of cross-country bus routes that can save you money under certain circumstances. Overall, travelling by bus on long-distance routes is about 25% cheaper than standard train fares, though comparable to the lower midweek train fares.

Daily express buses include a run between Copenhagen and Århus that takes 4½ hours and costs 140 kr, and another from Copenhagen to Aalborg that takes six hours and costs 160 kr. There's also an express-bus service running a couple of times a day between the Jutland port cities of Frederikshavn and Esbjerg (180 kr, five hours).

TRAIN

Denmark has a good, reliable train system with reasonable fares and frequent service. Most long-distance trains, such as the busy Copenhagen-Aalborg route, operate at least hourly throughout the day. With the exception of a few short private lines, the Danish State Railways (DSB) runs all train services in Denmark. Rail passes such as ScanRail

Copenhagen
Top: Rainbow over Amalienborg Palace
Middle: Building ornamentation, Royal Theatre
Bottom: Canal boat touring Nyhavn

NED FRIARY

NED FRIARY

NED FRIARY

Copenhagen
Left: Detail of the Børsen (Stock Exchange)
Top: Bicycle and mural at Thorvaldsens Museum
Bottom: View of Copenhagen from tower of Frelsers Kirke

Denmark Railways

+-+-+ *Private Railway Lines*

and Eurail are valid on DSB trains, but cannot be used on the private lines.

DSB has two types of long-distance trains and ticket prices are the same on both. The new, sleek intercity (IC) trains have ultra-modern comforts and both 1st-class and 2nd-class cars. Albeit much roomier, the carriage layout otherwise resembles that of an aeroplane interior, complete with cushioned seats, overhead reading lights, individual music headphones and an electronically lit map board that shows the train's progress. IC trains also have play areas for children and large restrooms with nappy-changing facili-

ties. Reservations are required on IC trains, unless you board after 8 pm or are travelling on the sector from Aalborg to Frederikshavn.

Inter-regional (IR) trains are older, a bit slower, solely 2nd class, and don't require reservations except for a few weekend IR trains that go on the ferry between Zealand and Funen. While more ordinary than the IC trains, the IR trains are by all measures quite comfortable. Seat reservations are optional on IR trains and in most cases you can find a seat without one, but if you're travelling a long distance or during rush hour you might prefer to pay the fee and be guaranteed a seat.

Regardless of distance, reservation fees are 30 kr (60 kr for 1st class) for IC trains and 20 kr for IR trains. Rail passes don't cover reservation fees.

Sleepers are available on overnight trains between Copenhagen and Frederikshavn or Esbjerg. The cost per person is 60 kr in a six-person compartment, 160 kr in a two-person cabin, or 300 kr in a private cabin, all in addition to the usual train fare.

Standard 2nd-class fares work out to about 1 kr per km. Travel of more than 100 km on Tuesday, Wednesday, Thursday and Saturday gets an automatic 20% discount. People aged 65 and older are entitled to a 50% discount on those days (and on Monday) and to a 25% discount on Friday and Sunday. Children aged from four to 11 years pay half the adult fare. Three or more adults travelling together are entitled to either a 20% discount or to travel 1st class for standard 2nd-class fares any day of the week – ask for the mini-group rate. In general, travelling in 2nd class is quite comfortable and there's no need to pay the 50% surcharge for 1st-class travel.

Dan Rail (☎ 86 98 02 65) is a special pass available to those aged under 26 years and valid for unlimited travel on DSB trains and ferries during the first two weeks of Danish school holidays (around 19 June to 3 July); the cost is 435 kr. During that period, travellers under 26 are also eligible for free overnight accommodation at 'bed-ins' in 44 schools around Denmark.

For information on ScanRail, Eurail and other rail passes, see the Train section of the Getting There & Away chapter.

TAXI

Taxis are readily available throughout Denmark in city centres, at railway stations and around major shopping centres. If you see a taxi with a lit 'fri' sign, you can wave it down, but you can always phone for a taxi as well. If you do call for a taxi, the meter isn't started until you're picked up.

The fare is typically 18 to 20 kr at flagfall and from 8 to 10 kr per km, with the higher rates prevailing after 6 pm and on weekends.

There's no need for tipping, as a service charge is built into the fare.

CAR & MOTORBIKE

Denmark is a pleasant country for touring by car. Roads are in good condition and almost invariably well signposted, and traffic is quite manageable, even in major cities including Copenhagen, rush hours excepted.

Access to and from motorways is made easy in Denmark as roads leading out of city and town centres are sensibly named for the main city to which they're routed. For instance, the road leading out of Odense to Faaborg is called Faaborgvej, the road leading to Nyborg is called Nyborgvej, and so on.

Denmark's extensive network of domestic ferries carries motor vehicles at reasonable rates. Although fares vary, as a rule of thumb, fares for cars average three times the passenger rate. The motoring organisation FDM distributes a handy timetable listing updated fares and schedules for all car ferries serving Denmark; you can pick it up for free at FDM offices throughout Denmark. It's always a good idea – and sometimes essential – for drivers to call ahead and make reservations, even if you can only do so a couple of hours in advance. More information on car ferries, including reservation numbers, is given under the appropriate destinations throughout this book.

One litre of unleaded petrol costs about 5.5 kr, a litre of super petrol costs about 5.8 kr and a litre of diesel fuel costs about 4.5 kr. You'll generally find the most competitive prices at petrol stations along motorways. If you don't mind using self-service pumps, the unstaffed OK Benzin stations, which are adjacent to Brugsen grocery stores, charge about 25 øre less per litre than the name-brand stations; OK Benzin pumps are open 24 hours and accept 100 kr notes but not credit cards.

Road Rules

In Denmark you drive on the right-hand side of the road. Cars and motorbikes must have

The Marguerite Route

A special network of scenic routes recommended for people touring by car and motorcycle has been designated and signposted throughout Denmark. Known as the Marguerite Route, it is not a single route that can be taken from end to end but rather is a series of routes, combining 3500 km of roadways in all. Sometimes the road is noted for its rural appeal, while at other times it's been selected because it passes tourist attractions.

Most of the Marguerite Route is along secondary highways and minor country roads and consequently, it usually makes an enjoyable alternative to a mundane zip along the main motorway.

The Marguerite Route is marked by a road sign consisting of a white daisy set against a brown backdrop. Virtually all Danish highway maps show the route, either with heavy green dots or solid green outlines. While it's fun to include sections of the Marguerite Route in any self-drive itinerary, at times you'll find alternative country roads parallelling the Marguerite Route to be at least as scenic.

The Marguerite Route is not intended for cars pulling trailers, as some of the roads are narrow and cross small bridges. For more details on the Marguerite Route and sights along the way, pick up the small self-touring book *The Marguerite Route*, which is published in English, Danish and German by the Danish Tourist Board. The book can be purchased in larger tourist offices and at many Statoil petrol stations. ■

Symbol marking the
Marguerite Route

---

dipped headlights on at all times and drivers are required to carry a warning triangle.

Seat belt use is mandatory in the front seats; it's also required for passengers in the back seats as long as the car is equipped with rear seat belts. Children aged under seven must use a child seat or other approved child restraint appropriate to the child's size.

Speed limits are generally 50 km/h in towns and built-up areas, 80 km/h on major roads and 110 km/h on motorways. However, if you're towing a trailer the maximum speed you can travel on major roads and motorways is 70 km/h.

Speeding fines, which can be collected on the spot, vary with the violation. As an example, driving just 10 km over the speed limit in a 50 km/h zone warrants a 400 kr fine, while going 20 km/h over that limit jumps the fine to 1100 kr. On motorways the fine is 600 kr for driving 10 km over the speed limit, 2900 kr for going 175 km/h and 6800 kr for going twice as fast as the speed limit. While the latter condition may be a rare case of madness, Danish drivers do com-

monly exceed speed limits by a good 10 to 20 km an hour, so don't rely upon the flow of traffic as an indication of whether you are moving within legal speed limits.

The authorities are very strict about driving under the influence of alcohol. It's illegal to drive with a blood alcohol concentration of 0.08% or greater; driving under the influence will subject drivers to stiff penalties and a possible prison sentence.

Emergencies

Motorways have emergency telephones at two-km intervals; an arrow on marker posts along the shoulder indicates the direction of the nearest phone. From ordinary pay phones, dial ☎ 112 for emergencies.

For updated information on roadwork and traffic conditions, you can call the Danish Road Directorate (☎ 33 15 64 44), which is open from 5 am to 10 pm from April to October and 24 hours a day in winter.

Parking

To park streetside in city centres, you usually

have to buy a ticket from a kerbside machine, labelled *billetautomat*. The billetautomat has an LCD read-out showing the current time and as you insert coins the time advances. Put in enough money to advance the read-out to the time you desire and then push the button to eject the ticket from the machine. Place the ticket, which shows the exact time you've paid for, face up inside the car's windscreen. The cost is generally from 4 to 16 kr an hour. Unless otherwise posted, street parking is usually free from 6 pm to 8 am, after 2 pm on Saturday and all day on Sunday.

The billetautomat only charges for hours when a ticket is required. So, if you were to park overnight starting at 5 pm, in a space where tickets are required from 8 am to 6 pm, and put in sufficient coins for two hours, the ticket would be valid until 9 am the next morning.

In smaller towns, which are delightfully free of coin-hungry billetautomats, street parking is free within the time limits posted. These parking spaces will be marked by a blue sign with the letter 'P' and beneath it will be the time limit for free parking (*1 time* is one hour, *2 timer* is two hours, etc). You will, however, need to use a windscreen parking disk. This is a flat plastic card with a clock face and a movable hour hand which must be set to show the time you parked the car. Parking disks can be picked up free from tourist offices, banks and petrol stations.

Parkering forbudt means 'no parking' and is generally accompanied by a round sign with a red diagonal slash. You can, however, stop for up to three minutes to unload bags and passengers. A round sign with a red 'X', or a sign saying *Stopforbud*, means that no stopping at all is allowed.

Rental Cars

Rental cars are expensive in Denmark – you could easily pay as much to rent a car for just one day in Denmark as it would cost to rent one for a week across the border in Germany.

This is one area where it certainly can save you a bundle to do a little research in advance. You'll generally get the best deal on a car rental by booking through an international rental agency before you arrive in Denmark. Be sure to ask about promotional rates, pre-pay schemes and the like, and then compare the options. Otherwise if you just show up at the counter at Copenhagen Airport you're likely to find the rates for the cheapest cars (including VAT, insurance and unlimited km) beginning at about 620 kr a day, or 470 kr a day on rentals of two days or more.

One of the better car-rental deals that doesn't require booking before you arrive in Denmark is the weekend rate offered by some companies. This allows you to keep the car from Friday afternoon to Monday morning and includes VAT, insurance and unlimited km for around 1000 kr.

Europcar/Interrent (known as National in the USA), Avis and Hertz are among the largest operations in Denmark, with offices in major cities, airports and other ports of entry.

BICYCLE

Cycling is not only a practical way to get around Denmark, but it's also an immensely popular one. There are extensive bike paths linking towns throughout the country, as well as bike lanes along the streets of most city centres.

Three out of four Danes own bicycles, and half use them on a regular basis. Postal workers are more likely to deliver mail by bicycle than motor vehicle, and it's not uncommon to see executives beating the rush hour by cycling through city traffic.

It's easy to travel with a bike, even when you're not riding it, as bicycles can readily be taken on ferries and most trains. On shorter ferry routes it'll generally cost about 20 kr to bring along your bike, while the longest routes, such as the one between Copenhagen and Bornholm, charge around 50 kr. On DSB trains, carrying a bicycle costs about 40 kr and reservations should be made at least three hours prior to departure as bikes are generally stored in a place that is away from the passengers.

In Denmark, most long-distance buses

and domestic flights will also carry bicycles for a modest fee, but you'll need to make advance arrangements because the capacity is often limited to a few bikes.

If you're travelling with a bike, pick up the DSB pamphlets *Bikes and Trains in Denmark* (in English) and *Cykler i tog* (Danish only), available at larger railway stations.

If you prefer to leave your bike at home, it's easy to rent bikes throughout Denmark. Prices average around 45/200 kr a day/week, although if you want a fancy multi-speed bike it'll cost more. You might want to bring your own bike helmet, as helmets are not included with most rental bicycles.

Always be careful locking up your bike, especially if you're travelling with an expensive model, as bike theft is common in Denmark, particularly in larger cities such as Copenhagen and Århus.

For more information on cycling, including cycle routes and maps, see Cycling under Activities in the Facts for the Visitor chapter.

HITCHING

Hitching is never entirely safe in any country in the world, and we don't recommend it. Travellers who decide to hitch should understand that they are taking a small but potentially serious risk. People who do choose to hitch will be safer if they travel in pairs and let someone know where they are planning to go.

At any rate hitching in Denmark is rare, usually not rewarding, and outright illegal on motorways. Most Danes who hitch usually only do so when they are travelling outside of their own country, in which case the general rule of thumb is to take a train to Germany and hitch from there.

WALKING

Denmark doesn't have any long-distance national walking trails of the kind found elsewhere in Europe, but it does have some attractive shorter trails. See Walking under Activities in the Facts for the Visitor chapter, as well as individual destinations.

BOAT

An extensive network of ferries links all of Denmark's populated islands. For ferry information see the Getting There & Away section under relevant destinations.

LOCAL TRANSPORT

All cities and towns of any size in Denmark are served by local buses. As a general rule, the main local-bus terminal is adjacent to the railway station or ferry depot. Taxis commonly wait at these transport centres as well.

For more details, see the relevant destination sections.

TOURS

Denmark is so small and public transport systems so extensive that organised tours are not all that common.

However, the national railroad, DSB (☎ 33 14 17 01), does put together a handful of self-guided tour packages that include same-day return train fare and entry fees. From Copenhagen these include a tour to the Louisiana art museum (85 kr), Legoland amusement park (344 kr for adults, 195 kr for children) and southern Sweden (125 kr). The tours can be taken from other cities as well; for example, the Legoland tour from Odense would cost 231/137 kr for adults/ children.

For information on sightseeing tours within a specific city or region, see the relevant destination sections.

Copenhagen

Copenhagen (Danish: København) is Scandinavia's largest and liveliest city, home to a quarter of all Danes.

Despite a population of nearly 1.5 million, Copenhagen is an appealing and largely low-rise city comprised of block after block of period six-storey buildings. Church steeples add a nice punctuation to the skyline and only a couple of modern hotels burst up to mar the scene.

The capital of Denmark since the early 15th century, Copenhagen grew by gradually radiating out from its centre and consequently most of the city's foremost historical and cultural sites remain concentrated in a relatively small area. Parks, gardens, water fountains, squares and green areas lace the city. Along the waterfront you'll find the scenic row houses that comprise Nyhavn, the famed statue of the *Little Mermaid* and the canal-cut district of Christianshavn.

For a big city, Copenhagen is surprisingly easy to get around. It's a particularly pleasant city for walking, as many of the sightseeing areas and shopping districts in the city centre are reserved for pedestrians. For those who prefer to move at a faster pace, there are bicycle lanes on Copenhagen's main roads as well as an excellent metropolitan bus-and-train system.

A cosmopolitan city, Copenhagen abounds with sightseeing and entertainment possibilities. For music lovers and other revellers there's an active nightlife scene which rolls into the early hours of the morning, and for sightseers there's a treasure-trove of museums, castles and old churches to explore.

HISTORY

The city of Copenhagen was founded in 1167 when Bishop Absalon constructed a fortress on Slotsholmen Island, fortifying a small and previously unprotected harbour-side village. The bishop had been granted the land by King Valdemar I, who wanted to put

HIGHLIGHTS

- Tivoli, a classic amusement venue in the city centre
- World-class museums, including most notably the Nationalmuseet and Ny Carlsberg Glyptotek
- Shopping and street entertainment on Strøget, the world's longest pedestrian mall
- Canal tours of the historic waterfront
- Rooftop views of the city from the Rundetårn and Vor Freslers Kirke
- Pavement cafés along scenic Nyhavn canal
- Free weekend summer concerts at Amager, and a spirited nightlife scene throughout Copenhagen
- Walking and cycling paths in Dyrehaven (Klampenborg)

an end to the free movement of marauding Wends who staged frequent raids along the East Zealand coast.

After the fortification was constructed, the harbour-side village grew in importance and took on the name Kømandshavn (Merchant's Port), which over time was condensed to København. Absalon's Fortress stood until

1369, when it was destroyed in an attack on the town by the powerful Hanseatic states.

In 1376 construction on a new Slotsholmen fortification, Copenhagen Castle, and in 1416 King Erik of Pomerania took up residence there, marking the beginning of Copenhagen's role as the capital of Denmark.

Still, it wasn't until the reign of Christian IV, in the first half of the 17th century, that the city took on much of its splendour. A lofty Renaissance designer, Christian IV began an ambitious construction scheme, building two new castles and many other grand edifices, including the Rundetårn observatory and Børsen, Europe's first stock exchange.

By the turn of the 18th century, Copenhagen's population was 60,000, but in 1711 the bubonic plague reduced it by a third. Later two fires, one in 1728 and the other in 1795, wiped out large tracts of the city, including most of its timber buildings.

However, the worst scourge in the city's history is generally regarded as the unprovoked British bombardment of Copenhagen in 1807, which occurred during the Napoleonic Wars. The attack targeted the heart of the city, inflicting numerous civilian casualties and setting hundreds of homes, churches and public buildings on fire. In the melee that followed, British admiral Horatio Nelson captured the Danish fleet and took it as war booty, ostensibly to prevent it from falling into the hands of Napoleon, who had been pressuring a neutral Denmark to close its ports to the English.

Copenhagen flourished in the 19th and 20th centuries, expanding beyond its old city walls and establishing a reputation as a centre for culture and the arts.

ORIENTATION

The main railway station, Central Station (Danish: Hovedbanegården or København H), is flanked on the west by the main hotel zone and on the east by Tivoli amusement park. Opposite the northern corner of Tivoli is Rådhuspladsen, the central city square and the main city bus transit point. Buses connect the airport, nine km south of the centre, with Central Station and Rådhuspladsen.

Strøget, the [...] mall, runs throu[...] Rådhuspladsen a[...] square at the head [...] Strøget, which abo[...] dining and entertaini[...] made up of five co[...] Frederiksberggade, Nyga[...] Amagertorv and Østerg[...] walkways run north from S[...] gular pattern into the Latin Q[...]

INFORMATION
Tourist Offices

The Danish Tourist Board (☎ 33 1[...] fax 33 93 49 69), Bernstorffsgade [...] Copenhagen V, is just north of C[...] Station. Its information desk distributes [...] useful *Copenhagen This Week* booklet, [...] well as free maps and brochures for destina[...] tions throughout Denmark; there's a room [...] and hotel booking service here as well. The tourist office is open from 9 am to 6 pm daily from mid-April to 31 May, from 9 am to 8 pm daily from June to mid-September, and from 9 am to 5 pm on weekdays and 9 am to 2 pm on Saturday the rest of the year.

Use It (☎ 33 15 65 18), Rådhusstræde 13, 1466 Copenhagen K, is a terrific alternative information centre catering to young budget travellers but open to all. They book rooms, store luggage, hold mail, provide information on everything from hitching to nightlife, and have excellent city maps and a useful general guide *Playtime* – all provided free of charge. Opening hours are from 9 am to 7 pm daily from mid-June to mid-September, from 10 am to 4 pm weekdays only for the rest of the year.

Money

American Express (☎ 33 12 23 01), on Strøget at Amagertorv 18, cashes all major travellers' cheques free of any fees. It's open from 9 am to 5 pm on weekdays and from 9 [...] am to noon on Saturday.

Banks, all of which charge transactio[...] fees, are plentiful along Strøget and they c[...] be also found on nearly every second cor[...]

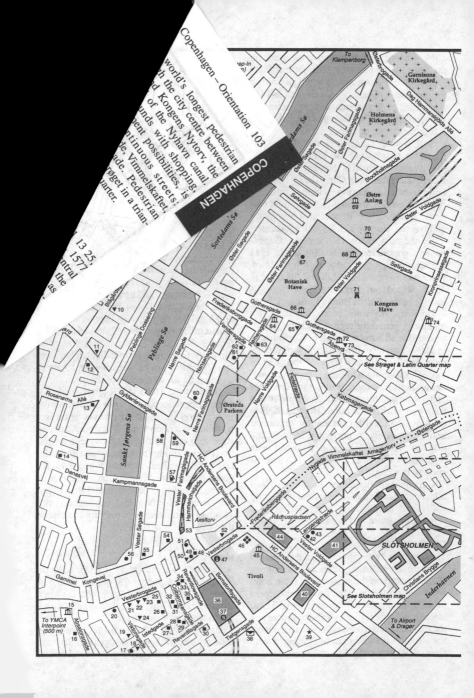

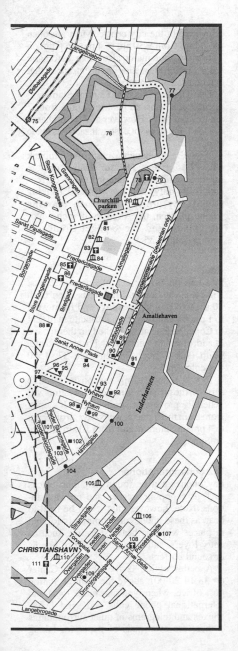

PLACES TO STAY

12 Hotel Sankt Jørgen
13 Cab-Inn Scandinavia
14 Cab-Inn Copenhagen
16 City Public Hostel
25 Hotel Hebron
26 Selandia Hotel
27 Hotel Centrum
28 Absalon Hotel
29 Saga Hotel
30 Turisthotellet
31 Hotel du Nord
32 Hotel Triton
34 Grand Hotel
35 Missionshotellet Nebo
48 SAS Royal Hotel
54 Hotel Imperial
55 Sheraton Copenhagen Hotel
62 Hotel Jørgensen
63 Hotel Windsor
81 Hotel Esplanaden
88 Phoenix
89 Copenhagen Admiral Hotel
90 Sophie Amalie Hotel
92 71 Nyhavn Hotel
94 Neptun Hotel
98 Sømandshjemmet Bethel
101 Hotel Opera
102 Hotel Maritime
103 Hotel City

PLACES TO EAT

3 Quattro Fontane
4 Neelam
5 New Delhi
7 Indian Corner
8 Naturbutik
10 Solsikken
11 Mexicali
18 Indus Restaurant
19 Restaurant Shezan
21 Alanya
22 Restaurant Koh-i-Noor
23 Frugtkælderen
24 Merhaba
50 Centrum Smørrebrød
52 Scala (Food Hall)
65 Mei Chiang
73 Peppe's Pizza (Kongens Have)
93 Pizzabageren
95 Leonore Christine
96 Nyhavns Færgekro

OTHER

1 Rigshospitalet
2 Café Rust
6 Barcelona
9 Bananrepublikken
15 Københavns Bymuseum
17 Coin Laundry

Continued on next page

elsewhere in the city centre. Most are open weekdays from 9.30 am to 4 pm (to 6 pm on Thursday), but many also have automatic teller machines outside their entrances that can be used after hours.

Den Danske Bank, at Central Station, is open beyond normal banking hours from 7 am to 9 pm daily. However a 25% surcharge is added onto fees for cash transactions made after 4 pm.

If you're exchanging cash, the Unibank chain has a few 24-hour cash-exchange machines that accept major foreign currencies (bills only) and use standard banking rates. They are at the branch opposite Rådhuspladsen, the Axeltorv branch opposite Tivoli and the Strøget branch at Vimmelskaftet 35.

Post

The main post office, at Tietgensgade 37, just south-east of Central Station, is open from 10 am to 6 pm on weekdays and from 9 am to 1 pm on Saturday. Poste restante mail sent to Copenhagen can be picked up there; have it addressed to addressee, Poste Restante, Main Post Office, Tietgensgade 37, 1500 Copenhagen V.

If you're not using the poste restante service, the post office in Central Station will generally prove more convenient. It's open from 8 am to 10 pm on weekdays, from 9 am to 4 pm on Saturday and from 10 am to 5 pm on Sunday.

Telecommunications

Pay phones can be found in public places such as shopping arcades and railway stations. Note, however, that it can be hard to hear, as these phones are commonly located in places with the heaviest traffic, such as entry foyers, and lack the benefit of booths or sound buffers.

A better option is the Telecom Center (☎ 33 14 20 00), above the Central Station post office, where you can make local and international phone calls and send faxes, telexes and telegrams in quiet surroundings – there are even pads of paper for taking

Copenhagen Card

The Copenhagen Card allows unlimited travel on buses and trains in Copenhagen Zealand, as well as free admission to most of the region's museums and attractions.

Some of the places within Copenhagen that are covered by the card include Tivoli, Rosen Slot, the Nationalmuseet, Statens Museum for Kunst, Ny Carlsberg Glyptotek, all the Slotsholmen sights, Zoologisk Have (Copenhagen Zoo), Den Hirschsprungske Samling, the Rundtårn (Round Tower) and the Orlogsmuseet (Royal Danish Naval Museum).

The card also gives free admission to the Viking Ship Museum and cathedral in Roskilde; Frederiksborg Castle and ferry in Hillerød; Karen Blixen Museum in Rungsted; Louisiana museum in Humlebæk; and the aquarium in Charlottenlund.

In addition, the card offers some discounts, including half-price theatre tickets, 20% off car rentals and canal tours, and up to 50% off ferry crossings to Sweden.

An adult's card costs 140/230/295 kr for one/two/three days; the cost is half-price for children aged five to 11 years. Cards can be purchased at Central Station, at tourist offices and in some hotels.

If you want to run through a lot of sightseeing in a few days – and plan to hit all the major attractions – the Copenhagen Card can be a real bargain. However, for a more leisurely exploration of select places it may work out better to pay individual admissions and use one of the transport passes (see the Getting Around section later in this chapter). ■

notes. In addition the Telecom Center works out cheaper, as it doesn't round everything off to a krone, but charges in smaller increments. It's also more convenient, as you pay for calls at the desk when you're done, so there's no need for a pocketful of coins. The Telecom Center is open from 8 am to 10 pm on weekdays and from 9 am to 9 pm on weekends and public holidays.

Foreign Embassies

Addresses and phone numbers for foreign diplomatic representatives are under Embassies in the Facts for the Visitor chapter.

Travel Agencies

Kilroy Travels (☎ 33 11 00 44) at Skindergade 28 specialises in discounted travel, primarily for students and people under the age of 26.

There's a general travel agency at the American Express office (☎ 33 12 23 01) on Strøget at Amagertorv 18.

Inter-Travel (☎ 33 15 00 77), Frederiksholms Kanal 2, is a gay-friendly travel agency that sells low-priced tickets to destinations worldwide.

Bookshops

GAD, on Strøget at Vimmelskaftet 32, and Boghallen, at Rådhuspladsen 37, both have good selections of English-language books, including travel guides and maps. Some other shops with notable English-language sections include the British Bookshop, at Badstuestræde 8, and Dickens, at Sankt Pedersstræde 30.

If you're looking specifically for international travel guidebooks, Kupeen, at Kilroy Travels, Skindergade 28, has a comprehensive selection. Nordisk Korthandel, Studiestræde 26-30, stocks an extensive range of guidebooks as well as cycling and trail maps of Denmark.

Two good places for books in French are the aforementioned GAD and the Libraire Française at Badstuestræde 6, which is just south of Strøget.

Interkiosk, a newsstand at Central Station, sells international newspapers and magazines, including *The Guardian, The European, Le Monde, Wall Street Journal, USA Today* and *Time.* You can also buy foreign newspapers at most international hotels and at some of the larger newspaper kiosks, such as those on Rådhuspladsen.

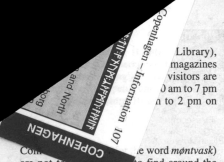

Library),
magazines
visitors are
0 am to 7 pm
n to 2 pm on

Com____ _____ .e word *møntvask*)
are not te__ ____ __ to find around the
city. There's one a____ gade 29 in the main
hotel district and another near Nyhavn at
Herluf Trolles Gade 19. Both are open from
at least 7 am to 9 pm daily.

Emergency

Dial ☎ 112 for police, ambulance or fire
emergencies; the call can be made without
coins from public phone booths.

Several city hospitals have 24-hour emergency wards. The most central are Rigshospitalet (☎ 35 45 35 45), Blegdamsvej 9,
which is in the Østerbro area, north of the
city centre, and Frederiksberg Hospital
(☎ 38 34 77 11), west of the city centre at
Norde Fasanvej 57.

Private doctor visits (☎ 33 93 63 00 for
referrals) usually cost from 250 to 350 kr.

There are numerous pharmacies around
the city; look for the sign *apotek*. Steno
Apotek, at Vesterbrogade 6 opposite Central
Station, is open 24 hours. Like all Danish
pharmacies, it sells both non-prescription
and prescription medications; you'll need a
local doctor's order for the latter.

For any sort of personal crisis, the city's
24-hour social service (☎ 33 66 33 33) can
provide counselling, information and referrals.

THINGS TO SEE

No trip to Copenhagen is complete without
a visit to Tivoli and a stroll down Strøget.
Another area you shouldn't miss is scenic
Nyhavn, from where you can catch a canal
tour for a glimpse of the city's waterfront
sights and a unique perspective into the
history of Copenhagen.

The most outstanding of Copenhagen's
numerous museums are the Ny Carlsberg
Glyptotek and the Nationalmuseet. Of
special interest among churches are Vor Frue
Kirke, the city cathedral with its famed
statues by Bertel Thorvaldsen, and
Christianshavn's Vor Freslers Kirke, which
has an elaborate baroque altar and a spiral
tower with a magnificent city view.

Central Walking Tour

Taking a half-day's walk from Rådhus (City
Hall) to the *Little Mermaid* is a good way to
get oriented to Copenhagen and take in many
of the city's central sights. As you stroll the
narrow streets, be sure to look up now and
then to appreciate the gargoyles and other
ornamentations that decorate many of the
older buildings.

Sights marked with an * are given more
detail in separate headings at the end of this
Walking Tour section.

Before heading off, you might want to
take a closer look at the red-brick **Rådhus**.
The building was completed in 1905 and
encompasses architectural elements of 19th
century national romanticism, medieval
Danish design and northern Italian influences, the latter most notable in the central
courtyard. For no charge you can take a look
at its theatre-like interior, where there are
occasional art exhibits, or for 10 kr you can
go to the top of its 105-metre tower.

Rådhuspladsen, the large central square
fronting Rådhus, is the main transit point for
city buses. At the south-west side of the
plaza, you'll find a statue of Hans Christian
Andersen and a water fountain with spouting
dragons, while on the east side, facing the
Palace Hotel, there's a noteworthy column
capped with a pair of bronze Viking lur-
blowers.

Rådhuspladsen also offers a good view of
the Unibank building, on the north-west
corner of Vesterbrogade and HC Andersens
Blvd. The building is topped with a unique
barometer that displays a girl on her bicycle
when the weather is fair, or with an umbrella
when rain is predicted. This bronze sculpture
was created in 1936 by the Danish artist E
Utzon-Frank.

From Rådhus walk down **Strøget**, which after a couple of blocks cuts between two spirited pedestrian squares, **Gammel Torv** and **Nytorv**. A popular summertime gathering spot in Gammel Torv is the Caritas Fountain, which was erected in 1608 by King Christian IV and marks what was once the old city's central market. As in days past, pedlars still sell jewellery, flowers and fruit on the square. At the south-western corner of Nytorv is the **Domhuset**, an imposing neoclassical building that once served as the city hall and now houses the city's law courts.

Continuing down Strøget, you'll pass **Helligåndskirken** (Church of the Holy Ghost), a wing of which dates from medieval times. The church interior, most of which was rebuilt after a fire in 1732, can be viewed from noon to 4 pm on weekdays. Also along the Amagertorv section of Strøget are some of the city's finest speciality shops including **Royal Copenhagen Porcelain** and **Georg Jensen**; the latter has a small free museum of early 20th century silver work. The WØ Larsen pipe shop, diagonally opposite at Amagertorv 9, boasts another little free speciality exhibit, the **Tobaksmuseet** (Tobacco Museum), which displays hand-carved pipes.

The adjacent square of **Højbro Plads**, marked by a water fountain with bronze storks, is a popular venue for street musicians. At the southern end of this elongated square is a **statue** of city founder Bishop Absalon on horseback, appropriately backdropped by Slotsholmen, where the bishop erected Copenhagen's first fortress. If you look due east from Højbro Plads you'll see the steeple of **Nikolaj Kirke**. The tower of this church dates from the 16th century although most of the church was rebuilt in 1915. No longer consecrated, the church is now owned by the municipality and used for contemporary art exhibits.

At the end of Strøget you'll reach **Kongens Nytorv**, a square boasting a statue of its designer, King Christian V, and circled by gracious old buildings. Notable from Christian V's era are ***Charlottenborg**, a 17th century Dutch baroque palace that

houses the Royal Academy of Arts, and the 1685 Thott's Mansion, which now houses the French Embassy. There are also grand, century-old Victorian buildings including the department store **Magasin du Nord**, with its ornate cupola, and **Det Kongelige Teater** (the Royal Theatre), which is fronted by statues of playwrights Adam Oehlenschläger and Ludvig Holberg. The theatre, home to the Royal Danish Ballet and Royal Danish Opera, has two stages, one on either side of **Tordenskjoldsgade**. An archway with a mosaic of Danish poets and artist spans the road connecting the two stages.

On the east side of Kongens Nytorv is picturesque **Nyhavn** canal, dug 300 years ago to allow traders to bring their wares into the heart of the city. Long a haunt for sailors and writers, including Hans Christian Andersen, who lived at house No 67 for nearly two decades, Nyhavn today is half-salty and half-gentrified, with a line of trendy pavement cafés and restored gabled townhouses. Nyhavn makes an invitingly atmospheric place to break for lunch or an afternoon beer. At the head of the canal you'll find a huge frigate anchor that commemorates Danish seamen who died in WW II serving with the Allied merchant marine.

From the north side of Nyhavn, head north on Toldbodgade, turn right on Sankt Annæ Plads and then left on Havnepromenade and continue walking north along the waterfront. You'll pass a couple of **18th century warehouses** that have been converted for modern use, including the Copenhagen Admiral Hotel, whose interesting lobby is worth a peek.

When you reach the fountain that graces the Amaliehaven (Amalie Gardens), turn inland to get to ***Amalienborg Palace**, home of the royal family since 1794. The palace's four nearly identical rococo mansions, designed by architect Nicolai Eigtved, surround a central cobblestone square and an immense statue of King Frederik V on horseback sculpted by JFJ Saly. From the square you'll get a head-on view of the imposing ***Marmorkirken** (Marble Church), which was designed in conjunction with the

Statue of Hans Christian Andersen's Little Mermaid, designed by Edvard Eriksen in 1913

Amalienborg complex as part of an ambitious plan by Frederik V (1746-66) to extend the city northward by creating a new district geared for the affluent.

From here you could make a detour along *Bredgade, where there are a couple of churches and small museums. Otherwise, continue north on Amaliegade to Churchillparken, where you'll pass *Frihedsmuseet, a museum dedicated to the WW II Danish resistance movement, followed by the attractive gothic-style St Alban's Church, which serves the city's English-speaking Anglican community. The church's location, in the midst of a public park, may seem a bit curious – the site was provided by King Christian IX, following the marriage of his daughter to the Prince of Wales, who later ascended to the British throne as King Edward VII.

Beside the church is the immense Gefionspringvandet (Gefion Fountain), a monument to yet another overseas relationship. According to Scandinavian mythology, when the Swedish king offered the goddess Gefion as much land as she could plough in one night, Gefion turned her four sons into powerful oxen and ploughed the entire area that now comprises the island of Zealand. The bronze statue in the fountain depicts the goddess and her oxen at work.

A 10-minute walk through the park past the fountain and along the waterfront will lead you to the statue of the famed Little Mermaid (Den Lille Havfrue), which was designed by Edvard Eriksen in 1913. This much-photographed bronze figure, perched on a rock at the water's edge, has a certain grace, but don't expect a monument – the mermaid is indeed little, and sports a rather drab industrial harbour backdrop.

From the Little Mermaid continue on the road inland. After just a few minutes you'll reach steps leading down to a wooden bridge that crosses a moat into the Kastellet, a citadel built by King Frederik III in the 1660s. The fortress is still surrounded by some of the city's original ramparts. Although the Kastellet buildings remain in use by the Danish military, the park-like grounds are open to the public from 6 am to sunset daily. Walk south through the Kastellet and you'll pass its main row of historic buildings before reaching a second bridge that spans the moat and leads back into Churchillparken.

Back at the park entrance, you can turn right onto Esplanaden to Store Kongens-

---

Jens Olsen's Clock

This elaborate clock, designed by Danish astro-mechanic Jens Olsen (1872-1945) and built at a cost of 1 million kr, is of special note to chronometer buffs. The clock displays not only the local time, but also solar time, sidereal time, sunrises and sunsets, firmament and celestial pole migration, planet revolutions, the Gregorian calendar and even changing holidays, such as Easter. Of its numerous wheels, the fastest turns once every 10 seconds, while the slowest will finish its first revolution after 25,753 years.

The clock was first put into motion in 1955 and its weights are wound weekly. It can be viewed in a side room off the foyer of Rådhus (City Hall) from 10 am to 4 pm weekdays and from 10 am to 1 pm on Saturday. Admission is 10 kr for adults and 5 kr for children. ■

gade, and from there catch bus Nos 1 or 6 back to Rådhuspladsen.

Charlottenborg Fronting Kongens Nytorv, at the south-west side of Nyhavn, is Charlottenborg, which was built in 1683 as a palace for the royal family. Since 1754 Charlottenborg has housed the Royal Academy of Fine Arts. The academy's exhibition hall, Kunstudstilling, at the east side of the central courtyard, features changing exhibits of modern art, design and architecture by Danish and international artists. It's open from 10 am to 5 pm daily. Admission varies with the exhibit, but is often 20 kr.

Amalienborg Museum The royal family recently opened a wing of Amalienborg Palace as the Amalienborg Museum. The museum features exhibits on the royal apartments through three generations of the monarchy from 1863 to 1947.

The rooms, faithfully reconstructed to the period, are decorated with heavy oak furnishings, gilt-leather tapestries, family photographs and Victorian knick-knacks. They include the study and drawing room of King Christian IX (1818-1906) and Queen Louise, whose six children wedded into nearly as many royal families – one eventually ascending to the throne in Greece and another marrying Russian tsar Alexander III. Also displayed is the study of King Frederik VIII (1843-1912), who decorated it in a lavish neo-renaissance style, and the study of King Christian X (1870-1947), the grandfather of Queen Margrethe II.

The Amalienborg Museum is open from 11 am to 4 pm daily, except in winter when it's closed on Monday. Admission is 35 kr for adults and 5 kr for children.

Marmorkirken Marmorkirken (Marble Church), also known as Frederikskirken, is a stately neo-baroque church at Frederiksgade 4, a block west of Amalienborg Palace.

Changing of the Guard

When the royal family is in residence at Amalienborg Palace, a colourful changing of the guard takes place in the palace square at noon. The ceremony begins with a procession from Rosenborg Slot by the Royal Guard, bedecked in full regalia and marching to the tune of fifes and drums. The guard contingent leaves the Rosenborg Slot gardens at 11.30 am and marches to Amalienborg Palace on a curving route that takes them to Kultorvet in the Latin Quarter, south on Købmagergade and then east along Østergade to Kongens Nytorv. From there they continue to Amalienborg Palace along Bredgade, Sankt Annæ Plads and Amaliegade.

Upon reaching the square, the old guard are ceremoniously relieved of their duties by their fresh replacements, who take up sentry posts in front of the palace. The relieved guards then join the marching band and return to their barracks at Rosenborg Slot, via a route that takes them along Frederiksgade, Store Kongensgade and Gothersgade.

In spring and early summer, when the queen takes up residence at her summer palace in Fredensborg, a version of the changing of the guard occurs there. ■

The church's massive dome, which was inspired by St Peter's in Rome and measures more than 30 metres in diameter, is one of Copenhagen's most dominant skyline features.

The original plans for the church were ordered by King Frederik V and drawn up by Nicolai Eigtved, as part of a grand design that included the Amalienborg mansions. Although church construction began in 1749, it ran into cost overruns, due in part to the prohibitively high price of Norwegian marble, and the project was soon shelved.

It wasn't until Denmark's wealthiest 19th century financier, CF Tietgen, bankrolled the project's revival that it was finally taken to completion. It was consecrated as a church in 1894.

The church's smog-blackened exterior is ringed by statues of Danish theologians and saints. The interior, with its immense circular nave, can be viewed weekdays from 11 am to 2 pm, Saturday from 11 am to 4 pm and Sunday from 1 to 4 pm.

Bredgade Sights There are a cluster of sights on Bredgade between Marmorkirken and Churchillparken.

Heading north, first up, at Bredgade 53, is **Alexander Newsky Kirke**, which was built in Russian Byzantine style in 1883 by Russian tsar Alexander III. The church is usually open only for services.

Medicinsk-Historisk Museum is next, at Bredgade 62, which is housed in a former surgical academy, circa 1786, and displays the history of medicine, pharmacy and dentistry over the past three centuries. It's open only for guided tours, which are offered at 11 am and 1 pm on Wednesday, Thursday, Friday and Sunday. In July and August, the 1 pm tours are given in English. Admission is free.

At 64 Bredgade is **Sankt Ansgars Kirke**, Copenhagen's Roman Catholic cathedral, which has a colourfully painted apse and a small museum on the history of Danish Catholicism. Admission is free and it's open from noon to 4 pm Tuesday to Sunday.

Kunstindustrimuseet, the Museum of Industrial Art, is at Bredgade 68. Housed in the former Frederiks Hospital (circa 1752), it contains a collection of Danish, Oriental and European decorative art and design ranging from the medieval period to the present day. It's open from 1 to 4 pm Tuesday to Sunday. Admission is 30 kr for adults, free for children.

Frihedsmuseet The Frihedsmuseet (Resistance Museum), in Churchillparken, features exhibits on the Danish resistance movement from the time of German occupation in 1940 to liberation in 1945. There are displays on the underground press, the clandestine radio operations that maintained links with England and the smuggling operations that saved Danish Jews from capture by the Nazis.

Admission to the museum is free. From May to mid-September it's open from 10 am to 4 pm Tuesday to Saturday and from 10 am to 5 pm on Sunday. The rest of the year it's open from 11 am to 3 pm Tuesday to Saturday and from 11 am to 4 pm on Sunday.

Latin Quarter

With its cafés and second-hand bookshops, the area north of Strøget that surrounds the old campus of Københavns Universitet (Copenhagen University) is a good place for ambling around. The university, which was founded in 1479, has largely outgrown its original quarters and moved to a new campus on Amager, but parts of the old campus, including the law department, remain here.

At the north side of the Latin Quarter is **Kultorvet**, a lively pedestrian plaza and summertime gathering place with beer gardens, flower stalls and produce stands. On sunny days you'll almost surely find impromptu entertainment, which can range from Andean flute players to local street theatre and dancing.

Ascend the stairs of the **university library** (enter from Fiolstræde) to see one quirky remnant of the 1807 British bombardment of Copenhagen: a glass case containing a cannonball in five fragments and the target it hit, a book entitled *Defensor Pacis* (Defender of

Peace). The library is open from 9 am to 6 pm on weekdays only.

Opposite the university is **Vor Frue Kirke**, Copenhagen's cathedral, which was founded in 1191 and rebuilt on three occasions after devastating fires. The current structure dates from 1829 and was designed in neoclassical style by CF Hansen. With its high vaulted ceilings and columns, Vor Frue Kirke seems as much museum as church – quite appropriate as it's also the showcase for sculptor Bertel Thorvaldsen's statues of Christ and the 12 apostles, his most acclaimed works. Thorvaldsen's depiction of Christ, with comforting open arms, became the most popular worldwide model for statues of Christ and remains so today. Admission to the cathedral is free. It's open from 9 am to 5 pm Monday to Saturday and from noon to 4 pm on Sunday.

Two other handsome places of worship in the Latin Quarter are **Sankt Petri Kirke**, on the corner of Nørregade and Sankt Pedersstræde, a church which dates from the 15th century, and the Jewish synagogue, the **Synagogen**, two blocks to the east at Krystalgade 12, which was built in 1831 in a neoclassical style. Both places can be viewed from the exterior but are not generally open to the public.

Rundetårn

The Rundetårn (Round Tower), at Købmagergade 52, is the best vantage point for viewing the old city's red-tiled rooftops and abundant church spires. This vaulted brick tower, 35 metres high, was built by King Christian IV in 1642 and used as an astronomical observatory in conjunction with the nearby university. Although the university erected a newer structure in 1861, amateur astronomers have continued to use the Rundetårn each winter, which gives it claim to being the oldest functioning observatory in Europe.

A 209-metre spiral walkway winds up the tower around a hollow core; about halfway up is a small hall with changing art exhibitions that's worth a visit.

The Rundetårn is open during the summer from 10 am to 8 pm daily, except on Sunday when it's open from noon to 8 pm. From September to May, it's open from 10 am to 5 pm daily, except on Sunday when it's open from noon to 4 pm. Admission is 15 kr for adults and 5 kr for children, or free to Copenhagen Card holders.

Winter visitors who'd like to view the night sky from the three-metre-long telescope that's mounted within the rooftop dome should make inquiries at the ticket booth. The observatory is generally open on Tuesday and Wednesday night.

Rosenborg Slot

This early 17th century castle, with its moat and garden setting, was built in Dutch renaissance style by King Christian IV to serve as his summer home. A century later King Frederik IV, who felt cramped at Rosenborg, built the Fredensborg Palace in North Zealand. In the years that followed, Rosenborg was used mainly for official functions and as a place to safeguard the monarchy's heirlooms.

In the 1830s the royal family decided to open the castle to visitors as a museum, while still using it as a treasury for royal regalia and jewels. It continues to serve both functions today.

The 24 rooms in the castle's upper levels are chronologically arranged with the furnishings and portraits of each monarch from Christian IV to Frederik VII. But it's the lower level, where the treasury remains, that's the main attraction, with its dazzling collection of crown jewels. These include Christian IV's ornately designed crown, the jewel-studded sword of Christian III and Queen Margrethe II's emeralds and pearls; the latter are displayed here when the queen is not wearing them to official functions.

Rosenborg Slot is open from 10 am to 4 pm daily from 1 June to 31 August; from 11 am to 3 pm daily in spring and autumn; and from 11 am to 2 pm on Tuesday, Friday and Sunday in winter. Admission is 40 kr for adults and 5 kr for children, or free to Copenhagen Card holders. A guidebook that details

COPENHAGEN

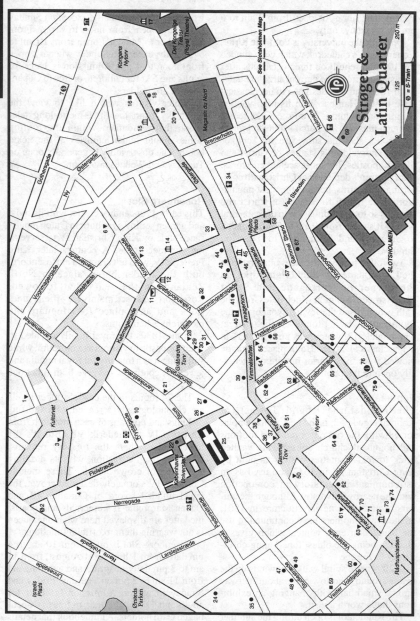

Strøget & Latin Quarter

PLACES TO STAY		63	Shawarma Grill House	35	Dickens Bookshop
		65	RizRaz	39	GAD Bookshop
16	Hotel d'Angleterre	70	Reinh van Hauen	40	Helligåndskirken
59	Hotel Kong Frederik	71	McDonald's	41	American Express
73	Palace Hotel	74	Peppe's Pizza	42	Illums Bolighus
			(Rådhuspladsen)	43	Royal Copenhagen
PLACES TO EAT					Porcelain Shop
		OTHER		44	Georg Jensen
1	St Gertruds Kloster			45	Tobacco Museum
3	Klaptræet	2	Nørreport Station	47	Cosy Bar
4	Hellas	5	Rundetårn	48	Nordisk Korthandel
6	Wessels Kro	7	Jyske Bank	49	After Dark & Metro
13	Café Sommersko	8	Thott's Mansion &		Place de Clichy
20	Restaurant Bali		French Embassy	51	Unibank
21	Det Lille Apotek	9	Synagogen	52	British Book-
26	Ristorante Italiano	10	Central library		shop/Libraire
28	Restaurant Graabrødre	11	Post office & Post-og		Francaise
29	Peder Oxe		Telegrafmuseet	56	Sebastian
30	Jensen's Bøfhus	12	Logotøjemuseet	58	Statue of Bishop
31	Pasta Basta	14	Museum Erotica		Absalon
33	McDonald's	15	Guinness World of	60	Boghallen Bookshop
36	McGrails		Records Museum	62	Sweater Market
37	Chinese Restaurant	17	Charlottenborg	64	Domhuset
	Shanghai	18	Bang & Olufsen	66	La Fontaine
38	La Glace	19	Holmegaard Glass &	67	Canal Tours
46	Haagen-Dazs shop		Crystal		Copenhagen
50	Huset med det Grønne	22	University Library	68	Holmens Kirke
	Træ	23	Sankt Petri Kirke	69	Netto Bådene boats
53	Café Sorgenfri	24	Kul-Kaféen	72	Ripley's Believe It or
54	Café de Paris, Firenze	25	Vor Frue Kirke		Not! Museum
	& Hana Kyoto	27	Kilroy Travels	75	Inter-Travel
55	Bakery	32	Copenhagen Jazz	76	Use It (also Huset &
57	Restaurant Nouvelle		House		Musikcafén)
61	Brasilko	34	Nikolaj Kirke		

each item on display can be purchased for an additional 20 kr.

The entrance to the castle is off Øster Voldgade. There is no entry from Kongens Have, the adjacent gardens. For public transport information see the Gardens section that follows.

Gardens

The green stretch of gardens along Øster Voldgade offers a quiet refuge from city traffic. The following gardens are conveniently located opposite each other, so they can be combined for a lengthier stroll. There are no admission charges.

Kongens Have (King's Gardens), the expansive green space behind Rosenborg Slot, is the city's oldest public park. It has manicured box hedges, lovely rose beds and plenty of shaded areas. Kongens Have is a popular picnic spot and the site of a free marionette theatre on summer afternoons. If your timing coincides, you can include a visit to **Davids Samling**, which is just east of Kongens Have at Kronprinsessegade 30 and houses Scandinavia's largest collection of Islamic art. It's open free from 1 to 4 pm daily except on Monday.

The 25-acre **Botanisk Have** (Botanical Garden), on the west side of Rosenborg Slot, has fragrant paths amidst arbours, terraces, rock gardens and ponds. It's open from 8.30 am to 6 pm daily from April to September, from 8.30 am to 4 pm daily the rest of the year. Within the botanical garden is the **Palmehus** (Palm House), a large walk-through glasshouse with a lush collection of tropical plants, open daily from 10 am to 3 pm all year round. There's also a cacti house and an orchid greenhouse, open only from 1 to 3 pm on Saturday and Sunday. The modest **Botanisk Museum** (Botany Museum), at the southern corner of the garden, features plants from Denmark and Greenland, but is open only on summer afternoons. One entrance to the botanical garden is at the intersection of Gothersgade and Voldgade, while the other is off Øster Farimagsgade.

The **Geologisk Museum**, at Øster Voldgade 5 on the eastern corner of the botanical garden, is Denmark's foremost geological museum. You'll find the usual exhibits of fossils, minerals, crystals and rocks, including one from the moon. In addition it has some interesting Danish displays, such as a 4.5-kg chunk of amber, and some quite notable Greenlandic finds, including the world's sixth-largest iron meteorite, which weighs in at 20 tonnes! The museum has free admission and is open from 1 to 4 pm daily, except on Monday, all year round.

You can get to the gardens and Rosenborg Slot by taking the S-train to Nørreport station and walking north-west for two blocks, or via numerous buses including Nos 14, 16, 31, 42 and 43.

Statens Museum for Kunst

Denmark's national gallery, Statens Museum for Kunst (Royal Museum of Fine Arts), at Sølvgade 48, was founded in 1824 to house art collections belonging to the royal family. Originally at Christiansborg Palace, the museum opened in its current location in 1896.

As might be expected, the museum contains a good fine-arts collection by Danish artists, including Jens Juel, CW Eckersberg, Christen Købke and PS Krøyer. There's also an interesting collection of Old Masters paintings by Dutch and Flemish artists, including Rubens and Frans Hals, as well as more contemporary European paintings by Matisse, Picasso and Munch.

Closed on Monday, the museum is open year round on other days from 10 am to 4.30 pm (to 9 pm on Wednesday). Admission is 20 kr for adults, free for children and Copenhagen Card holders. You can get there via bus Nos 10, 14, 40, 42 and 43.

Den Hirschsprungske Samling

This museum, at Stockholmensgade 20 and a 10-minute walk from the Statens Museum for Kunst, is dedicated to Danish art of the 19th and early 20th century. Originally the private holdings of tobacco magnate Heinrich Hirschsprung, the museum contains works by Golden Age painters such as Christen Købke and CW Eckersberg; a notable collection by Skagen painters PS Krøyer and Anna and Michael Ancher; and works by the Danish symbolists and the Funen painters. The museum is open from 10 am to 5 pm daily, except on Tuesday when it's closed and on Wednesday when it's open from 10 am to 10 pm. Admission is 20 kr for adults (35 kr during special exhibitions) and free for children and Copenhagen Card holders. The museum can be reached via bus Nos 10, 14, 40, 42 and 43.

Nørrebro

The Nørrebro quarter of the city developed in the mid-19th century as a working-class neighbourhood. In more recent times, it's drawn a large immigrant community and has become a haunt for students, musicians and artists. It consequently has lots of interesting Middle Eastern and Asian restaurants and some of Copenhagen's hottest night spots. There are a number of second-hand clothing shops in the streets radiating out from Sankt Hans Torv, antique shops along Ravnsborggade and a Saturday morning flea market a few blocks to the west on Nørrebrogade along the wall of the Assistens Kirkegård.

Assistens Kirkegård This cemetery, in the heart of Nørrebro, is the burial place for some of Denmark's most celebrated citizens, including philosopher Søren Kierkegaard, physicist Niels Bohr, authors Hans Christian Andersen and Martin Andersen Nexø, and artists Jens Juel, Christen Købke and CW Eckersberg. It's an interesting place to wander – as much a park and garden as it is a graveyard.

If you'd like to learn more, the Assistens Kirkegårds Formidlingscenter, a cultural group based at Kapelvej 2, leads summertime guided tours of the cemetery in English (motto: Meet the Danes – both the living and the dead!). The tours, which cost 20 kr, are held a couple of afternoons a week; call ☎ 35 37 19 17 for information.

The cemetery is open from 8 am to 8 pm from May to August, with shorter winter hours. Bus Nos 16, 5 and 7 stop nearby.

Zoologisk Museum This modern zoological museum, a km north of Assistens Kirkegård on the corner of Jaglvej and Universitetsparken, displays all sorts of stuffed animals, from North Zealand deer to Greenlandic polar bears. There are also interesting dioramas, recorded animal sounds, a whale skeleton and insect displays. It's open from 11 am to 5 pm Tuesday to Sunday. Admission is 20 kr for adults and 10 kr for children. You can get there by bus Nos 18, 42, 43 and 184.

Nationalmuseet

If you want to learn more about Danish history and culture, don't miss the Nationalmuseet (National Museum) at Ny Vestergade 10, opposite the west entrance to Slotsholmen. Following an ambitious reconstruction and expansion, the museum has received a number of accolades, including the 1994 European Museum of the Year award.

It holds the country's most extensive collection of Danish historical artefacts, ranging from the Upper Palaeolithic period to the 1840s and including Stone Age tools, Viking weaponry and impressive Bronze Age, Iron Age and rune-stone collections. There are other sections on the Inuit and Norsemen of Greenland, collections of 18th century Danish furniture, a 'Please Touch' exhibition for sight-impaired visitors and a special children's wing.

The museum also boasts a noteworthy coin collection containing Greek, Roman and medieval coins and a Classical Antiquities section covering the Roman Empire, Egypt and Greece. There's a café and gift shop inside the museum and ramps and lifts for the disabled. It's open from 10 am to 5 pm Tuesday to Sunday all year round.

Admission is 30 kr for adults, free for children and Copenhagen Card holders.

Slotsholmen

Slotsholmen is the seat of Denmark's national government and a repository of historical sites. Located on a small island that's separated from the city centre by a moat-like canal, Slotsholmen's centrepiece is **Christiansborg Slot**, a rambling palace that now houses government offices.

Several short bridges link Slotsholmen to the rest of Copenhagen. If you walk into Slotsholmen from Ny Vestergade, you'll cross the west side of the canal and enter Christiansborg's large main courtyard, which was once used as a royal riding grounds. The courtyard still maintains a distinctively equestrian character, overseen by a statue of Christian IX (1863-1906) on horseback and flanked on the north by stables and on the south by carriage buildings.

The stables and buildings surrounding the main courtyard date back to the original Christiansborg Palace, which was built in the 1730s by Christian IV to replace the more modest Copenhagen Castle that previously stood there. The grander west wing of Christian IV's palace went up in flames in 1794, was rebuilt in the early 19th century and was once again destroyed by fire in 1884. In 1907 the cornerstone for the third, and current, Christiansborg Palace was laid by King Frederik VIII and, upon completion, the national Parliament and Supreme Court moved into new chambers there.

Folketinget The Folketinget, or Parliamentary chamber, can be toured on Sunday year round, as well as on weekdays in summer, on the hour from 10 am to 4 pm (except at noon). The tours, which are free and conducted in Danish, visit the chamber where the 179 members of Parliament meet to debate national legislation. The tour also takes in Wanderer's Hall, which contains the original copy of the Constitution of the Kingdom of Denmark.

Slotsholmen

1 Thorvaldsens Museum
2 Slotskirke
3 De Kongelige Repræsentationslokaler
   (Royal Reception Chambers)
4 Ruins under Christiansborg
5 Statue of Frederik VII
6 Holmens Kirke
7 Statue of Christian IX
8 Folketinget (Parliament)
9 Teatermuseet (Theatre Museum)
10 Kongelige Stalde & Kareter
   (Museum of Royal Coaches)
11 Tøjhusmuseet (Royal Arsenal Museum)

Royal Reception Chambers The grandest part of Christiansborg is De Kongelige Repræsentationslokaler (Royal Reception Chambers), an ornate Renaissance hall where the queen holds royal banquets and entertains heads of state. The chambers are closed to the public all of January and also on Monday year round. Tours with commentary in English are given at 11 am and 3 pm Tuesday to Sunday from May to September (also at 1 pm from June to August) and at 11 am and 3 pm on Tuesday, Thursday and Sunday the rest of the year. Admission is 28 kr for adults, 10 kr for children and free to Copenhagen Card holders.

Museum of Royal Coaches Here at Kongelige Stalde & Kareter (Museum of Royal Coaches), visitors can view a collection of antique coaches, uniforms and riding paraphernalia, some of which are still used for royal receptions. However, the museum is only open on weekends between 2 and 4 pm. Admission is 10 kr for adults, 5 kr for children and free to Copenhagen Card holders.

‖‖Ⴙ·ᎢᏐⴼ·ᏞᎧ‖⋈·ᎻᏞᏞᎧ‖·ᎻᏐᏐᏞ‖Ⴙ·ᎢᏐⴼ·ᏞᎧ‖⋈·ᎻᏞᏞᎧ‖·ᎻᏐᏐᏞ‖Ⴙ·ᎢᏐⴼ·ᏞᎧ‖⋈·ᎻᏞᏞᎧ‖·ᎻᏐᏐᏞ‖Ⴙ·ᎢᏐⴼ·ᏞᎧ‖⋈·ᎻᏞᏞᎧ‖·ᎻᏐᏐᏞ

The Workings of Parliament

The Danish Parliament still maintains a seating system rooted in its original national assembly, formed during the era of the French Revolution. Parliament members are grouped by party behind semi-circular tables that face the speaker, who presides over the sessions. Although the growth of splinter parties has eroded the system somewhat, in large measure right-wing parties, such as the Conservative Party, are seated to the right of the speaker, while left-wing parties, such as the Social Democrats, are seated to the left.

One might think that squaring off as opposition parties would foster an environment ripe for heated debate, but instead the parliamentary meetings are markedly subdued and dry. The even Danish temperament prevails – overstatement and passionate discourse are disdained, while self-controlled and carefully scripted speeches are the order of the day. ∎

‖‖Ⴙ·ᎢᏐⴼ·ᏞᎧ‖⋈·ᎻᏞᏞᎧ‖·ᎻᏐᏐᏞ‖Ⴙ·ᎢᏐⴼ·ᏞᎧ‖⋈·ᎻᏞᏞᎧ‖·ᎻᏐᏐᏞ‖Ⴙ·ᎢᏐⴼ·ᏞᎧ‖⋈·ᎻᏞᏞᎧ‖·ᎻᏐᏐᏞ‖Ⴙ·ᎢᏐⴼ·ᏞᎧ‖⋈·ᎻᏞᏞᎧ‖·ᎻᏐᏐᏞ

Ruins under Christiansborg In the basement of the current palace, beneath the tower, you can find the remains of two earlier castles. The most notable are the ruins of Absalon's Fortress, Slotsholmen's original castle built by Bishop Absalon in 1167. The excavated foundations of the early structure consist largely of some low limestone sections of wall, which date back to the city's founding.

Absalon's Fortress was demolished in 1369. Its foundations, as well as those of the Copenhagen Castle that replaced it and stood for over three centuries, were excavated when the current tower was built in the early 1900s.

The ruins can be explored from 9.30 am to 3.30 pm daily in summer and every day except Saturday and Monday from October to April. Admission costs 15 kr for adults, 5 kr for children and is free to Copenhagen Card holders.

Teatermuseet The Teatermuseet (Theatre Museum) occupies the Old Court Theatre, which dates from 1767. Performances over the years have ranged from Italian opera and pantomime to those by local ballet troupes, one of which included fledgling ballet student Hans Christian Andersen. The theatre, which took its current appearance in 1842, drew its final curtain in 1881, but was reopened as a museum in 1922. The stage, boxes and dressing rooms can be examined, along with displays of set models, drawings,

costumes and period posters tracing the history of Danish theatre. It's open year round from 2 to 4 pm on Wednesday and noon to 4 pm on Sunday. Admission is 20 kr for adults, 5 kr for children and free to Copenhagen Card holders.

Thorvaldsens Museum This museum features the works of the famed Danish sculptor Bertel Thorvaldsen (1770-1844), who was heavily influenced by Greek and Roman mythology. After four decades in Rome, Thorvaldsen returned to his native Copenhagen and donated his private collection to the Danish public. In return, the royal family provided this site for the construction of a museum to house Thorvaldsen's drawings, plaster moulds and statues. Thorvaldsens Museum also contains some contemporary paintings and antique art from the Mediterranean region. The museum is free and is open from 10 am to 5 pm Tuesday to Sunday all year round. It's entered from Vindebrogade.

Tøjhusmuseet The Tøjhusmuseet (Royal Arsenal Museum), opposite the entrance to Parliament, contains an impressive collection of historic cannons, hand weapons and armour. The 163-metre-long building housing the arsenal, which was constructed by Christian IV in 1600, boasts Europe's longest vaulted Renaissance hall. Hours are from 10 am to 4 pm Tuesday to Sunday year round. Admission costs 20 kr for adults, 5 kr for children and is free to Copenhagen Card holders.

Royal Library The Kongelige Bibliotek (Royal Library), which dates from the 17th century, is the largest library in Scandinavia. Its main body is housed in a suitably classic building with arched doorways, columned halls, chandeliers and high-ceilinged reading rooms. The library not only serves as a research centre for scholars and university students, but doubles as a repository for rare books, manuscripts, prints and maps. As Denmark's national library it contains a complete collection of Danish printed works, dating from 1482. To handle the increasing demand for storage space, a major extension to the library is underway.

The library, which is fronted by lovely flower gardens containing a fish pond and a statue of Søren Kierkegaard, is entered from Rigsdagsgården, just west of Tøjhusmuseet. It's open to the public from 9 am to 7 pm on weekdays and from 10 am to 7 pm on Saturday.

Børsen Another striking Renaissance building is Børsen, the stock exchange, on Børsgade at the south-east corner of Slotsholmen. Constructed in the 1620s, it's particularly notable for its ornate spire, which is formed by the entwined tails of four dragons, and for its richly embellished gables. This still-functioning stock exchange, which first opened during the bustling reign of Christian IV, is the oldest in Europe.

Holmens Kirke

Just across the canal from Slotsholmen, next to the National Bank, is Holmens Kirke (Church of the Royal Navy). This historic brick structure, whose nave was originally built in 1562 to be used as an anchor forge, was converted into a church for the Royal Navy in 1619. Most of the present structure, which is predominantly of Dutch Renaissance style, dates from 1641. The church's burial chapel contains the remains of important naval figures, including Admiral Niels Juel, who beat back the Swedes in the 1677 Battle of Køge Bay.

It was at Holmens Kirke that Queen Margrethe II took her marriage vows in 1967. The interior of the church, which has an intricately carved 17th century oak altarpiece and pulpit, can be viewed daily, except on Sunday, from 9 am to 2 pm from mid-May to mid-September and from 9 am to noon the rest of the year. There is no admission charge.

Christianshavn

Christianshavn, on the eastern flank of the city, was established by King Christian IV in the early 1600s as a commercial centre and military buffer for the expanding city of Copenhagen. It's cut with a network of canals, modelled after those in Holland, which leads Christianshavn to occasionally be dubbed 'Little Amsterdam'.

Still surrounded by its old ramparts, Christianshavn today is a hotchpotch of newer apartment complexes and renovated period warehouses that have found a second life as upmarket housing and restored government offices. The neighbourhood attracts an interesting mix of artists, yuppies and dropouts. Christianshavn is also home to a sizeable Greenlandic community and was the setting of the public housing complex in the popular novel *Miss Smilla's Feeling For*

An Author's Burden

In 1834, Hans Christian Andersen applied for work at the Royal Library in Copenhagen 'to be freed from the heavy burden of having to write in order to live'. Apparently the library administrators weren't too impressed with his résumé, as he was turned down. Ironically, Andersen's unsuccessful application is now preserved as part of the library's valued archives, along with many of his original manuscripts. They can be viewed by appointment on weekdays with 24 hours advance notice. ■

Snow (1992; published in the USA as *Smilla's Sense of Snow*).

To get to Christianshavn, you can walk over the Knippelsbro bridge from the northeast side of Slotsholmen, take the canal Water Bus or catch bus Nos 8 or 2 from Rådhuspladsen. If you're going to Christiania first, bus No 8 is the best, as it stops near the gate.

Christiania In 1971 an abandoned 41-hectare military camp on the east side of Christianshavn was taken over by squatters who proclaimed it the 'free state' of Christiania, subject to their own laws. The police tried to clear the area but it was the height of the 'hippie revolution' and an increasing number of alternative folks from throughout Denmark continued to pour in, attracted by the concept of communal living and the prospect of reclaiming military land for peaceful purposes.

The momentum became too much for the government to hold back and, bowing to public pressure, the community was allowed to continue as a 'social experiment'. About 1000 people settled into Christiania, turning the old barracks into schools and housing, and starting their own collective businesses, workshops and recycling programmes.

Along with progressive happenings, Christiania also became a magnet for runaways and junkies. Although the Christiania residents felt that the conventional press beat up the image of decadence and criminality – as opposed to portraying Christiania as a self-governing, ecology-oriented and tolerant community – the Christianianites did, in time, find it necessary to modify their free-law approach. A new policy was established that outlawed hard drugs in Christiania and the heroin and cocaine pushers were expelled.

Still, Christiania remains controversial. Some Danes resent the community's rent-free, tax-free situation and more than a few Christianshavn neighbours would like to see sections of Christiania turned into public parks and schoolgrounds.

Although the police don't patrol Christia-

nia they have staged numerous organised raids on the community and it's not uncommon for police training to include a tactical sweep along Pusherstreet.

Visitors are welcome to stroll or cycle through car-free Christiania, though large dogs may intimidate some free spirits. Photography is frowned upon, and outright forbidden on Pusherstreet where hashish is openly (though not legally) smoked and sold.

Christiania has a small market where pipes and jewellery are sold, a few craft shops, a bakery and a couple of simple café-like places to get coffee and light eats. There's also a sit-down dinner restaurant, Spiseloppen, which serves both vegetarian and meat dishes at moderate prices, and also a few entertainment spots.

The main entrance into Christiania is on Prinsessegade, just beyond its intersection with Bådsmandsstræde. Pusherstreet and most of the shops are within a few minutes walk from the entrance.

At 3 pm daily in summer, Christiania residents offer two-hour guided tours (☎ 31 57 96 70) for 20 kr per person that include a commentary on Christiania's background. Anyone can come along, but the tours are mainly targeted for small groups and there's an eight-person (or 100 kr) minimum.

Vor Frelsers Kirke A few minutes walk from Christiania is the 17th century Vor Frelsers Kirke (Our Saviour's Church), at Sankt Annæ Gade 29. The church, which once benefited from close ties with the Danish monarchy, has a grand interior that includes an elaborately carved pipe organ dating from 1698 and an ornate baroque altar with marble cherubs and angels.

For a panoramic city view, make the dizzying 400-step ascent up the church's 95-metre spiral tower – the last 160 steps run along the outside rim of the tower, narrowing to the point where they literally disappear at the top. This colourful spire was added to the church in 1752 by Lauritz de Thurah who took his inspiration from Boromini's tower of St Ivo in Rome.

Entrance to the church is free. It costs 10 kr to climb the tower, which is in the final stages of a lengthy renovation and is expected to be open again in the summer of 1996. Hours are from 9 am to 4.30 pm in summer, from 9 am to 3.30 pm in spring and autumn and from 10 am to 1.30 pm in winter.

Orlogsmuseet The Orlogsmuseet (Royal Danish Naval Museum) occupies a former naval hospital at Overgaden oven Vandet 58 on Christianshavn Kanal. This naval history museum houses more than 300 model ships, many dating from the 16th to the 19th century. Some were built by naval engineers to serve as design prototypes for the construction of new ships. Consequently the models take many forms, from cross-sectional ones detailing frame proportions to full-dressed models with working sails.

The museum also displays a collection of figureheads, ship lanterns, navigational instruments, a Fresnel lens from a lighthouse and the propeller from the German U-boat that sank the *Lusitania*. Opening hours are from noon to 4 pm Tuesday to Sunday all year round. Admission is 25 kr for adults, 15 kr for children and free to Copenhagen Card holders.

Other Christianshavn Sights At Strandgade 1 is **Christians Kirke**, which was designed by Danish architect Nicolai Eigtved and completed in 1759. This church, which once served the local German congregation, has an expansive, theatre-like rococo interior. It's open daily year round from 8 am to 6 pm (to 5 pm in winter), except during church services. Admission is free.

Nearby at Strandgade 4 is the **B & W Museum**, which displays the history of Burmeister & Wein, the shipbuilding company, which in 1912 pioneered the use of diesel engines in ocean-going ships. In January 1943, Burmeister & Wein became the target of the first Allied air raid on Copenhagen, when British bombers levelled the company's Christianshavn factory to put an end to its production of German U-boat engines. The museum is open from 10 am to 1 pm Monday to Friday (and on the first Sunday of the month) year round. Admission is free.

The architectural museum **Gammel Dok**, Strandgade 27B, has changing exhibitions on Danish and international architecture, design and industrial art. It's open from 10 am to 5 pm daily. Admission is 20 kr for adults, free for children.

Tivoli

Situated right in the heart of the city, Tivoli is a tantalising combination of flower gardens, food pavilions, amusement rides, carnival games and open-air stage shows. This genteel entertainment park, which dates from 1843, is delightfully varied. Visitors can ride the roller coaster, take aim at the shooting gallery, enjoy the pantomime of Commedia dell'Arte or simply sit and watch the crowds stroll by.

During the day children flock to Tivoli's ferris wheel, carousel, bumper cars and other rides. In the evening Tivoli takes on a more romantic aura as the lights come on and the cultural activities unfold, with one stage performing traditional folk dancing as another prepares for a theatrical performance.

Each of Tivoli's numerous entertainment venues has a different character. Perhaps best known is the open-air Peacock Theatre, which features mime and ballet and was built in 1874 by Vilhelm Dahlerup, the renowned Copenhagen architect who also designed the city's Kongelige Teater. Tivoli also has an indoor cabaret theatre and a large concert hall with performances by international symphony orchestras and renowned ballet troupes.

Between all the neon and action, Tivoli makes for a fun place to stroll, and if you feel like a splurge there are some good restaurants that enjoy stage views and make for a memorable dining experience (see Places To Eat – Tivoli).

Wednesday, Friday and Saturday are the best nights to visit as they end in a fireworks display shortly before the clock strikes midnight.

Tivoli is open from 11 am to midnight

daily from late April to mid-September. Admission is 38 kr for adults and 19 kr for children, or free with a Copenhagen Card. Amusement ride tickets cost 9 kr (many rides require two tickets), or for 98 kr you can buy a book of 14 tickets. The numerous open-air performances are free, while the indoor performances usually charge admission. For more information, see the Entertainment section.

In recent years Tivoli has begun opening in the winter, a few weeks prior to Christmas, for holiday festivities, a Christmas market and ice skating on the lake. Although access to the usual attractions is limited, admission is free for the pre-Christmas events. If you happen to be there during that season, check with the tourist office for current information.

Ny Carlsberg Glyptotek

This exceptional museum, on HC Andersens Blvd near Tivoli, has an excellent collection of Greek, Egyptian, Etruscan and Roman sculpture and art. The museum was built a century ago by beer baron Carl Jacobsen, who was an ardent collector of classical art. The museum's main building, which was designed by architect Vilhelm Dahlerup, centres around a glass-domed conservatory replete with palm trees and Mediterranean greenery, creating an atmospheric complement to the collection.

Although Ny Carlsberg Glyptotek was originally – and primarily remains – dedicated to classical art, a gift of more than 20 paintings by Paul Gauguin led to the formation of a 19th century French and Danish art collection. The Gauguin works, now numbering 35, are displayed alongside those of Cézanne, Van Gogh, Pissarro, Monet, Renoir and Degas in a new wing of the museum that opened in 1996.

The museum is open daily, except on Monday, from 10 am to 4 pm from 1 May to 31 August. The rest of the year it's open from noon to 3 pm Tuesday to Saturday and from 10 am to 4 pm on Sunday. Admission is 15 kr for adults and free for children and Copenhagen Card holders but it's free for everyone

on Wednesday and Sunday. Guided tours in English are given at 2 pm on Wednesday during the summer. Call the museum (☎ 33 41 81 41) for information on chamber concerts that are presented on some evenings in late summer.

Vesterbro

The Vesterbro district has a varied character that's readily observed by walking along its best-known street, Istedgade, which runs west from Central Station. The first few blocks are lined with rows of respectable hotels that soon give way to the city's main red-light district. When Denmark became the first country to legalise pornography in the 1970s, Vesterbro's porn shops and seedy nightclubs became a magnet for tourists and voyeurs. While it's not necessarily any tamer these days, liberalisation elsewhere has made the area less of a novelty.

About halfway down Istedgade the red-light district recedes and the neighbourhood becomes increasingly ethnic with a mix of Pakistani and Turkish businesses. Vesterbro, and the adjacent district of Nørrebro, are home to much of the city's immigrant community and abound with good ethnic restaurants and interesting shops.

Københavns Bymuseum The Copenhagen City Museum, at Vesterbrogade 59 in the Vesterbro district, features – not surprisingly – displays about the history and development of Copenhagen, largely through paintings and scale models of the old city. Of interest is the small exhibit dedicated to religious philosopher Søren Kierkegaard, who was born in Copenhagen in 1813 and died in the city in 1855.

Also take a stroll along Absalonsgade, which runs along the east side of the museum and retains the character of a bygone era, with its cobblestone road, gas lamps and antique phone box and benches. The museum is open daily, except Monday, from 10 am to 4 pm from May to September and from 1 to 4 pm from October to April. Admission is free.

Tycho Brahe Planetarium

This planetarium (☎ 33 12 12 24), which opened in 1989, is the largest in Scandinavia. Its domed space theatre offers planetarium shows of the night sky using state-of-the-art equipment capable of projecting more than 7500 stars, planets and galaxies. The planetarium also screens Omnimax films on its huge 23-metre screen. Life-like shows range from the experiences of astronauts aboard the space shuttle to divers exploring tropical reefs.

The planetarium was named after the famous Danish astronomer Tycho Brahe (1546-1601), whose creation of precision astronomical instruments allowed him to make more exact observations of planets and stars and paved the way for the discoveries made by other astronomers.

The planetarium is at Gammel Kongevej 10, about one km north-west of Central Station. It's open daily from 10.30 am to 9 pm, except Tuesday, Wednesday, Thursday and school holidays, when it opens at 9.30 am. It costs 65 kr to see either the planetarium show or an Omnimax film, and 100 kr for a combination ticket to both.

Copenhagen Zoo

The Copenhagen Zoo (Zoologisk Have), at Roskildevej 32 in the Frederiksberg area, has the standard collection of caged creatures, including elephants, lions, zebras, hippopotamuses, gorillas and polar bears. Special sections include the Tropical Zoo, Children's Zoo, and the Ape Jungle as well as the African Savanna and South American Pampas displays. It's open daily, from 9 am to 6 pm from June to August, from 9 am to 5 pm in spring and autumn, and from 9 am to 4 pm in winter. Admission is 55 kr for adults, 27 kr for children and free to Copenhagen Card holders. Bus Nos 27 and 28 stop outside the gate.

Other Museums

Musikhistorisk Museum This music history museum, housed in an 18th century building at Åbenrå 30 just north of Kultorvet in the Latin quarter, contains a quality collection of musical instruments dating from 1000 to 1900 AD. The exhibits are grouped according to theme and accompanied by musical recordings. There's special emphasis on the history of music as a social phenomenon, especially its effect on Danish culture. It's open from 1 to 4 pm Friday to Wednesday from May to September and on Monday, Wednesday, Saturday and Sunday the rest of the year. Admission is 15 kr for adults and 3 kr for children. There are occasional concerts and special presentations.

Arbejdermuseet The Arbejdermuseet (Workers' Museum), Rømersgade 22, pays homage to the working class with exhibits portraying the lives of Danish labourers in the 1880s, 1930s and 1950s. From July to October, it's open from 10 am to 5 pm daily; the rest of the year it's open from 10 am to 3 pm from Tuesday to Friday, and from 11 am to 4 pm on weekends. Admission is 30 kr for adults and 15 kr for children. You can get there by taking the S-train to Nørreport and walking west of Frederiksborggade or by catching bus Nos 5, 14 or 16, amongst others.

Nyboders Mindestuer This museum, at Sankt Paulsgade 20, south-west of the Kastellet, stands in the midst of the old residential quarter laid out in 1630 by King Christian IV to provide housing for his naval staff. While the museum is in one of the original buildings, most of the neighbourhood housing – block after block of long ochre-coloured row houses with red-tiled roofs – was built in later years. The museum contains period furnishings and is open from noon to 2 pm on Wednesday and from 1 to 4 pm on Sunday. Admission is 5 kr.

Post-og Telegrafmuseet The post office at Valkendorfsgade 9 houses this small museum, which records the history of the Danish postal and telecommunications system with displays of historic postal vehicles, uniforms, letter boxes, radio equipment etc. It also boasts a fine stamp collection. From May to October the museum is open from 10 am to 4 pm daily except Monday; in winter it's open from 1 to 4 pm on Tuesday, Thursday, Saturday and Sunday. Admission is free.

Legetøjsmuseet A block north of Strøget at Valkendorfsgade 13, the Legetøjsmuseet (Toy Museum) features antique toys dating from 1805 to 1950. Grouped by themes, the displays include a Christmas sitting room, a toy shop and wooden toys carved in prison. It's open daily, except on Friday, from 10 am to 4 pm. Admission costs 25 kr for adults and 12 kr for children.

Guinness World of Records Museum This touristy attraction, on Strøget at Østergade 16, uses displays, photos and film to depict all the world's superlatives – the tallest, fastest, oddest etc. It's open from 10 am to 10 pm (to 8 pm on Sunday) from May to mid-September and from 10 am to 8 pm daily the rest of the year. Admission costs 48 kr for adults and 20 kr for children.

Eksperimentarium This is a hands-on technology and natural science centre that's housed in a former bottling hall of Tuborg Breweries, at Tuborg Havnevej 7 in Hellerup. The centre has some 300 exhibits, many of them environmental, to challenge the senses. Find out how healthy your favourite dishes are from a computerised food menu, test your suntan lotion against the ozone or compare pollution emissions in different cities.

On the lighter side, kids can try composing water music, use parabolas to send whispers across the room and peer through a submarine periscope. It's open from 9 am to 6 pm on Monday, Wednesday and Friday, from 9 am to 9 pm on Tuesday and Thursday and from 11 am to 6 pm on weekends. Admission costs 69 kr for adults and 49 kr for children. To get there catch bus No 6 from central Copenhagen.

Ripley's Believe It or Not! Museum This clichéd museum, at Rådhuspladsen 57, displays the expected collection of unexpected oddities from around the world (such as a

six-legged calf) replicated as wax figures and tableaus. It's open daily from 10 am to 11 pm from May to September and from 10 am to 9 pm from October to April. Admission is 48 kr for adults, 20 kr for children aged between five and 11, and 30 kr for children aged 12 to 15.

Louis Tussaud's Wax Museum At this wax museum, located on the northern edge of Tivoli at HC Andersens Blvd 22, the usual celebrities like Elvis and Frankenstein are in the company of Danish notables, including Søren Kierkegaard, Hans Christian Andersen and the royal family. The exhibits are spruced up with a few lively holograms but admission is a hefty 48 kr for adults and 20 kr for children, making it easier to recommend if you have a Copenhagen Card allowing you to get in for free. It's open daily from 10 am to 11 pm in summer and from 10 am to 9 pm in winter.

Museum Erotica A cross between a museum and a peep show, Museum Erotica, two blocks north of Strøget at Købmagergade 24, is full of erotic paintings, posters, photographs, statues and sex toys. These range from hand-coloured daguerreotype photographs from the 1850s to a nine-screen video room playing modern-day pornographic movies. It's open daily from 10 am to 11 pm from May to September and from 11 am to 6 pm from October to April. Admission is 45 kr.

ACTIVITIES
Swimming
Beaches If brisk water doesn't deter you, the greater Copenhagen area has a number of bathing beaches. The water is tested regularly, and if sewage spills or other serious pollution occurs the beaches affected are closed and signposted.

A popular beach south of Copenhagen is Amager Strandpark (reached by bus Nos 9, 12 or 13). Shallow waters and playground facilities make it ideal for children. Deeper waters can be reached by walking out along the jetties. There's another beach in Amager along the south side of Dragør; to get there catch bus Nos 33, 53 or 73E.

Easily accessible to the north of Copenhagen are beaches at Charlottenlund and Klampenborg; for details see Around Copenhagen at the end of this chapter.

Pools & Saunas Copenhagen has a handful of public saunas and swimming pools that visitors can use for 20 to 25 kr. Following are two of the more central ones.

Øbro Hallen (☎ 31 42 30 65), at Gunnar Nu Hansens Plads 3, near the national stadium in Østerbro, is open from 7 am to 7 pm on weekdays (from 10 am on Monday), from 8 am to 3 pm on Saturday and from 9 am to 2 pm on Sunday.

The Vesterbro Svømmehal (☎ 31 22 05 00), Angelgade 4, is open from 7.15 am to 7 pm on weekdays (from 10 am on Monday, and to 4 pm on Friday), from 9 am to 2 pm on Saturday and from 9 am to 1 pm on Sunday.

Boating

Row boats and pedal boats for paddling around Peblinge Sø and Sortedams Sø, can be hired at Søernes Bådudlejning (☎ 35 37 60 37) on Peblinge Dossering at the city centre's west side. The cost is 35 kr for 30 minutes or 50 kr for an hour. It's open daily from noon to 6 pm (to 10 pm in midsummer) from April to September.

You can hire row boats at similar rates in the Christianshavn area from Christianshavn Bådudlejning (☎ 32 96 53 53) on the canal at Overgaden neden Vandet. It's open from 11 am to sunset from April to September.

For details on boating in the Lyngby area, which has larger lakes and a more natural setting, see Lyngby in the Around Copenhagen section at the end of this chapter.

Cycling

Cycle lanes are found along many city streets and virtually all of Copenhagen can be toured by bicycle, except for pedestrian-only streets such as Strøget. Bicycles (and buses) are allowed to cross Strøget at Gammel Torv and Kongens Nytorv squares.

When touring the city, cyclists should be cautious of bus passengers who commonly step off the bus into the cycle lanes, and of pedestrians (particularly tourists) who sometimes absentmindedly step off the kerb and into the path of oncoming cyclists. This is particularly a problem on roads like Nørregade, where cyclists are allowed to ride against the one-way traffic.

Use It has a free, useful *Copenhagen By Bike* brochure which maps out some suggested cycling routes. For information on bicycle rentals, see Bicycle in the Getting Around section later in this chapter.

Cycle Tour The most popular self-guided cycling tour in the Copenhagen area is the 12-km ride north to Dyrehaven. There's a bike path the entire way, much of it skirting the Øresund coast.

To begin, take Østerbrogade north from the city. After passing the S-train station Svanemølleri, the road continues as Strandvejen, passing through the busy suburb of Hellerup, where the intersections have blue-marked crossings to indicate cyclist right-of-ways, and then up through the quiet coastal village of Charlottenlund. Here the cycle lane widens and there's a beach, an old fort and an aquarium that make for interesting diversions.

Once you reach Klampenborg station, a bike path leads into Dyrehaven, a woodland which is crossed by a network of trails, and a perfect place to break out a picnic lunch; for more details see Klampenborg in the Around Copenhagen section at the end of this chapter. Alternatively, if you want to continue farther north, an off-road cycling path parallels the coastal road to Rungsted.

Either way, you have the choice of returning on the same route, taking an alternative route such as the inland road Bernstorffsvej, or putting your bike on the S-train and making it a one-way cycling tour.

ORGANISED TOURS
Carlsberg Brewery

Carlsberg gives tours of its brewery at 11 am and 2 pm Monday to Friday. The guides speak both English and Danish. There's no fee, but it's a good idea to call (☎ 33 27 13 13) to make sure there's space available before jumping on a bus. After learning a bit about Carlsberg's 150-year history and seeing how barley turns to brew, you get to sample the final product. The brewery is on the west side of the city at the intersection of Valby Langgade and Ny Carlsbergvej. Although the operation is ultramodern, much of the architecture is attractively traditional. Take special note of the Elephant Gate, two elephant pillars at the entrance designed by the renowned architect Vilhelm Dahlerup. To get to the brewery, take bus No 6 westbound from the city centre.

Royal Copenhagen

One-hour multilingual guided tours of the Royal Copenhagen porcelain factory, at Smallegade 45 in the Frederiksberg area, are given weekdays at 9, 10 and 11 am year round and also at 1 and 2 pm from May to mid-September. The factory has been on this site since 1884, although Royal Copenhagen has been making porcelain in Denmark since 1775. The adjacent shop is open from 9 am to 5 pm on weekdays and from 10 am to 1 pm on Saturday. Take bus Nos 1 or 14 from Rådhuspladsen.

Sightseeing Bus

From mid-June to September the city's HT public bus system operates a special sightseeing bus which leaves Rådhuspladsen every 20 minutes between 10 am and 5 pm. It takes a circular route, stopping at Tivoli, Vor Frue Kirke, the Rundetårn, det Kongelige Teater, Amalienborg Palace, Frihedsmuseet, the Little Mermaid, Rosenborg Slot, Botanisk Have, Højbro Plads, Slotsholmen, Nationalmuseet and Gammel Torv. There's no commentary or guide, but you can get on and off as often as you want within 24 hours for a mere 20 kr.

Other Bus Tours

For those who don't want to strike out on their own, conventional bus tours are available from Copenhagen Excursions (☎ 31 54

06 06). They offer 1½-hour city tours, (110 kr) daily in summer at 10 am, noon and 4 pm, which drive by Copenhagen's main sights, including Slotsholmen, Børsen, Kongens Nytorv and Amalienborg Palace, and make a stop at the Little Mermaid. There's also a 2½-hour greater Copenhagen 'grand tour' for 155 kr as well as more expensive day tours from Copenhagen to North Zealand castles (320 kr), Roskilde (395 kr) and Odense (480 kr).

Canal Tours

For a different angle on the city, hop onto one of the boat tours that wind through Copenhagen's canals from late April to mid-September. Though most of the passengers are usually Danes, multilingual guides give a lively commentary in English as well. All the tours make a similar loop route, passing by Slotsholmen, Christianshavn and the Little Mermaid. All rates are half price for children.

The biggest company, Canal Tours Copenhagen (☎ 33 13 31 05), leaves twice an hour from two locations – one at the head of Nyhavn and the other at Gammel Strand, north of Slotsholmen. Tours last 50 minutes and run from 10 am to 6 pm in midsummer and to about 5 pm in the shoulder season. The cost is 38 kr.

A better deal is with Netto-Bådene (☎ 31 54 41 02), which charges just 20 kr. Their cruise, which lasts an hour, includes a swing into the harbour of Trekroner, a U-shaped islet with an old naval base that's used for military training. Netto-Bådene's boats leave from Holmens Kirke, opposite Børsen, on the hour between 10 am and 5 pm. In midsummer they add on extra boats that leave intermittently, averaging three to four boats an hour.

Canal boats also make a fine traffic-free alternative for getting to some of Copenhagen's waterfront sites. Canal Tours Copenhagen charges 30 kr for a one-day pass on its green-route Vandbussen (Water Bus), which runs a route similar to its guided tours but without commentary. These boats leave Nyhavn every 30 minutes from 10.15 am to

4.45 pm daily from mid-April to mid-September and make eight stops – including Christiansborg Slot, Christianshavn, Amalienborg Palace and the Little Mermaid – allowing you to get on and off as often you like. You can also ride just one way from one stop to another for 20 kr.

PLACES TO STAY

Copenhagen is a popular convention city and if you happen to arrive when one is taking place, finding a room could be a challenge. But at most other times a visit to the tourist office reservation service or a stroll through the main hotel district (adjacent to Central Station) can land you a room without advance reservations. Still, if you have a particular place in mind it's a good idea to book in advance – rooms in many of the most popular mid-range hotels fill quickly, particularly during the high season.

Booking Services

The *værelseanvisning* counter (☎ 33 12 28 80) at the tourist office, Bernstorffsgade 1, books rooms in private homes for 150/250 kr for singles/doubles. It also books unfilled hotel rooms, sometimes at discounted rates, although these discounts are the exception during busy periods. The counter is open from 9 am to midnight daily from mid-April to mid-September, from 9 am to 9 pm daily in late September, and from 9 am to 5 pm on weekdays and 9 am to 2 pm on Saturday the rest of the year. The booking fee is 13 kr per person.

Use It, Rådhusstræde 13, books rooms in private homes for about 150/200 kr for singles/doubles (no booking fee), keeps tabs on which hostel beds are available, and is a good source of information for subletting student housing and other long-term accommodation. For more information see Use It in the Information section earlier in this chapter.

Camping

Bellahøj-Camping (☎ 31 10 11 50), Hvidkildevej, 2400 Copenhagen NV, right in the midst of the city near the Bellahøj hostel, is a simple one-star camping ground open from 1 June to 31 August. It costs 44 kr per person. Showers and cooking facilities are available. From Rådhuspladsen take bus No 2 to the Bellahøj stop.

The two-star *Absalon Camping* (☎ 31 41 06 00, fax 31 41 02 93), Korsdalsvej 132, 2610 Rødovre, is nine km west of the city centre in the Rødovre suburb, near Brøndbyøster station on the S-train's line B. There's a coin laundry, kiosk, group kitchen and playground. In addition to camping sites, which cost 45 kr per person, caravans and five-person cabins can be rented from about 200 kr a day, plus the per-person camping fee. It's open all year round.

A delightful alternative is *Charlottenlund Strandpark* (☎ 31 62 36 88), Strandvejen 144B, 2920 Charlottenlund, eight km north of central Copenhagen. This camping ground, on the edge of Charlottenlund beach, is appealingly set amidst the tree-planted grounds of an old moat-encircled coastal fortification. The cost is 60 kr per person. There are showers and a coin laundry and a baker comes every morning to sell bread and milk. The frequent bus No 6 connects the camping ground with Copenhagen's centre.

Hostels

HI Hostels There are two Copenhagen hostels under the auspices of Hostelling International, each about five km from the city centre. The Bellahøj hostel is open all year round except from 16 January to 28 February, while the Amager hostel is closed from 1 December to 15 January. Both hostels have laundry facilities and are accessible by wheelchair, but only the Amager hostel has a guest kitchen. Breakfast (38 kr) and dinner (55 kr) are available at both. These hostels often fill early in summer so it's best to call ahead for reservations.

The more conveniently located *København Bellahøj Vandrerhjem* (☎ 31 28 97 15, fax 38 89 02 10), Herbergvejen 8, 2700 Brønshøj, has 299 dorm beds for 70 kr plus a number of four-bed family rooms. Reception is open 24 hours and lockers are available for 5 kr. From Rådhuspladsen take bus No 2-Brønshøj or the night bus No 902.

The newer, Orwellian *Copenhagen Amager Hostel* (☎ 32 52 29 08, fax 32 52 27 08), Vejlands Allé 200, 2300 Copenhagen S, in Amager just off the E20, is Europe's largest hostel with 528 beds in cell-like two-bed and five-bed rooms. The cost is 70 kr per person and it's usually easy to get a double room for 140 kr. Check-in time is from 1 pm. From Central Station bus No 46 runs directly to the hostel until 6 pm weekdays, otherwise take bus No 16-Vigerslev, change at Mozarts Plads to bus No 37-Holmens Bro and get off at Vejlands Allé.

A third alternative, farther from the city, is the *Lyngby Vandrerhjem* (☎ 42 80 30 74, fax 42 80 30 32), Rådvad 1, 2800 Lyngby, which is in a small hamlet nestled in the woods on the north side of Dyrehaven. The hostel occupies a manor-like house that can accommodate 94 people, mostly in rooms with four to six beds. It costs 70 kr for a dorm bed, 164 kr for a double; meals are available. It's open year round except from mid-December to early January. The area is quite pretty, with swan-filled ponds, and it's within walking distance of the house where silversmith Georg Jensen was born in 1866, but it's not a terribly practical place to make a base if your main focus is exploring central Copenhagen. Bus No 187 goes from Lyngby station to the hostel but only runs on weekdays, six times a day, with the last bus leaving Lyngby at 5.35 pm. Otherwise, it's a two-km walk between the hostel and the nearest regularly serviced bus stop, in Hjortekær.

Other Hostels Even when the HI hostels are full you can usually find a bed at one of the two city-sponsored hostels. Though they tend to be more of a crash-pad scene than the HI hostels, they're also more central and don't require hostel membership.

City Public Hostel (☎ 31 31 20 70, fax 31 23 51 75) or Vesterbro Ungdomsgård, Absalonsgade 8, Vesterbro, 1658 Copenhagen V, has 200 bunk beds in rooms for six to 24 people. It's open from early May to mid-August, has 24-hour reception and costs 100 kr per person. You can use your own sleeping bag or for 30 kr rent bed sheets to use during the length of your stay. Breakfast is available for 15 kr, there's a guest kitchen and you can find some good restaurants within a few blocks of the hostel. To get to City Public Hostel from Central Station, walk 10 minutes west along Vesterbrogade.

The city-run *Sleep-In* (☎ 35 26 50 59, fax 35 43 50 58), 132 Blegdamsvej, 2100 Copenhagen Ø, a few km north of the city centre in the Østerbro district, is open from 1 July to 31 August. The 300 beds are in a badminton hall that has been partitioned into 60 compartments, each containing two, four or six beds; there are no doors, but the compartments have curtains to offer a little privacy. The cost is 70 kr per person. Add another 30 kr if you want breakfast. There are free lockers, free hot showers and a guest kitchen. You can use your own sleeping bag, or rent a set of sheets and a blanket for 30 kr. Reception is open 24 hours. From Rådhuspladsen take bus No 1-Ordrup, 6-Klampenborg or 14, get off at Trianglen and then walk south-west on Blegdamsvej for a couple of minutes; look for the sign on the south side of the road. You can also take night bus Nos 906, 914 or 953 or take the S-train to Østerport station, from where the hostel is about a 15-minute walk to the north-west. There's a bakery, cafeteria, grocery store and a few other eating and drinking places within easy walking distance.

The *YMCA Interpoint* (☎ 31 31 15 74) at Valdemarsgade 15 is open from early July to mid-August and has separate rooms for men and women. There are 28 dorm beds in all; one room has six beds, another 10 and the rest have four. The cost is 65 kr for the bed, another 20 kr to rent sheets. The staff are friendly, breakfast is available for 25 kr and there are good restaurants within walking distance. Reception hours are from 8 am to noon, from 2.30 to 6 pm and from 7 pm to 12.30 am. Interpoint fills up early but reservations can be made by phoning in advance. It's about a 15-minute walk from Central Station (take Vesterbrogade west to

Valdemarsgade, where you turn left), or you can take bus Nos 6 or 16.

B&Bs

There are a couple of informal B&B-style networks in Copenhagen. These are not conventional B&Bs with business names or signs out the front, but rather, private homes or flats with a couple of extra bedrooms that may be booked as guest rooms. While many come and go, the following are two reliable places that not only have recommendable rooms but can also book you with another family when they're full. It's not appropriate to just show up at the door – you should always call to make arrangements before you arrive, even if it's just from the railway station, and it's best to book well in advance, especially in summer.

Annette Hollender (☎ 32 95 96 22, fax 31 57 24 86), Wildersgade 19, 1408 Copenhagen K, has three guest rooms in her cosy half-timbered Christianshavn home, within walking distance to all Christianshavn sights and about 15 minutes by foot from Slotsholmen. Although this four-storey house dates from 1698, it's been restored and has modern conveniences, as well as a little garden area where breakfast is served. One room is a single, the other two are doubles. Annette also books 10 other homes, most in the Christianshavn area. The cost for any room is 210/270 kr for singles/doubles, plus 40 kr per person if you opt for breakfast.

Lise-Lotte Falck (☎ 33 15 50 16, fax 33 13 68 61), Amaliegade 28 3th, 1256 Copenhagen K, has two guest rooms in her restored century-old home near the Amalienborg Palace. It's an attractive place and although the guest rooms are not large they have TVs and small writing desks; a bathroom is shared. This genteel neighbourhood is solidly historic and convenient to a number of sightseeing spots. The cost is 250/320 kr for singles/doubles plus an additional 40 kr if you want breakfast. Mrs Flack is part of a network of a half-dozen homes with guest rooms, all in the same neighbourhood.

For other private rooms, see the earlier Booking Services heading.

Hotels – bottom end & middle

Copenhagen's main hotel quarter (and red-light district) is along the west side of Central Station, where rows of six-storey turn-of-the-century buildings house one hotel after the other. Despite the porn shops and streetwalkers, the area is neither unpleasant nor notably dangerous, at least not by the standards of large cities elsewhere in Europe. In addition, its central location makes it a convenient spot to be based.

While this Central Station area is jammed with mid-range hotels, Copenhagen has very few hotels that are priced affordably enough to really warrant the term 'bottom end'. If you're on a tight budget, the best hotel deals are those with shared bath and toilets in the hall. Even some of the more pleasant mid-range hotels, such as the Hebron and Selandia, have some good-value rooms with shared bath.

By and large, the months from May to September comprise the summer season, October to April the winter season. Many hotels lower their rates by about 10% to 20% in winter. The hotel rates given in this section include service charge and the 25% VAT tax and, except where noted, also include a complimentary buffet-style breakfast.

Around Central Station The area's cheapest hotel, the *Turisthotellet* (☎ 31 22 98 39), Reverdilsgade 5, 1701 Copenhagen V, has a handful of small, worn rooms that are quite basic but are suitable for the price of 200/300 kr with shared bath. Rooms with a private bath cost 100 kr more.

The *Missionshotellet Nebo* (☎ 31 21 12 17, fax 31 23 47 74), Istedgade 6, 1650 Copenhagen V, has a very convenient location, a mere stone's throw from Central Station. The 96 rooms are small and the décor rather drab but each has a sink, TV and phone and the common space includes a front parlour, large, clean showers and toilets, and a bright, cheery breakfast room. The breakfast is simple but adequate with breads, orange juice, yoghurt and cereal. Singles/doubles cost 330/490 kr for rooms with shared bath, 570/720 kr for rooms with private bath.

The *Saga Hotel* (☎ 31 24 49 44, fax 31 24 60 33), Colbjørnsensgade 18-20, 1652 Copenhagen V, has 76 rooms, most of which have recently been renovated. There's no real lobby, no lift and no services to note other than a small breakfast room. The standard rooms are straightforward; some have a TV, but no phone. Singles/doubles cost 350/500 kr with a shared bathroom, 450/600 kr with a private bathroom.

A good low-end option to check is the 81-room *Hotel Centrum* (☎ 31 31 31 11, fax 31 23 32 51), Helgolandsgade 14, 1653 Copenhagen V, which has clean, straightforward rooms with sinks, phones and shared baths costing 350/570 kr for singles/doubles. There are also larger rooms with TVs and private baths for 550/700 kr. Prices are about 25% cheaper in winter. When the hotel's not busy, the management is willing to negotiate a bit on rates, so it can be a good place to start if you're looking for a last-minute bargain.

The 110-room *Hotel Hebron* (☎ 31 31 69 06, fax 31 31 90 67), Helgolandsgade 4, 1653 Copenhagen V, is a quiet hotel with nicely renovated rooms, most with a sofa bed as well as two single beds, a desk, TV and phone. There are 14 rooms with shared baths that cost 390/500 kr for singles/doubles in summer, 330/380 kr in winter. Rooms with private bath cost 680/890 kr in summer, 585/680 kr in winter.

The popular *Selandia Hotel* (☎ & fax 31 31 46 10), Helgolandsgade 12, 1653 Copenhagen V, has a good breakfast buffet and cheery, well-appointed guest rooms. All 84 rooms have a desk, sink and cable TV. The manager once ran the famed Hotel d'Angleterre and there are thoughtful touches throughout, from bedside reading lights and soundproof windows to a secure left-luggage room. A good value option is one of the 27 rooms with shared baths that cost 390/540 kr for singles/doubles year round. Rooms with private baths cost from 650/850 kr in summer, slightly less in winter.

The 75-room *Hotel du Nord* (☎ 31 31 77 50, fax 31 31 33 99), Colbjørnsensgade 14,

1652 Copenhagen V, is a small, tidy hotel with comfortable rooms, most with a desk, TV and phone. Request one of the courtyard rooms, which are larger and quieter than streetside ones. Breakfast is a very simple affair of bread, cheese and coffee. Singles/ doubles cost 395/580 kr in summer. Rates may be negotiable in winter, depending on business.

At the 253-room *Absalon Hotel* (☎ 31 24 22 11, fax 31 24 34 11), Helgolandsgade 15, 1653 Copenhagen V, the cheaper rooms (400/500 kr for singles/doubles) are worn and have shared bathrooms; use the facilities on the upper floors which are better maintained. While not special, these low-end rooms are commonly available at discounted rates from the tourist office's *værelse-anvisning* counter – at which time they can be a good low-end deal. More standard rooms with private baths cost 600/700 kr. The hotel has one of the best breakfast buffets, with Danish pastries, yoghurt, cereals, meats and cheeses.

Hotel Triton (☎ 31 31 32 66, fax 31 31 69 70), Helgolandsgade 7, 1653 Copenhagen V, is popular with business travellers. All 123 rooms are modern and cheery with Scandinavian-design furnishings, TVs, desks, refrigerators, phones and private baths. Standard rooms, which are on par with those at more expensive 1st-class chain hotels, cost 750/880 kr for singles/doubles. Superior rooms, which have additions like trouser presses and hair dryers, cost 50 kr more. There's also a corporate rate that's about 15% cheaper. The management is helpful; telex and fax services are available for guests and there are luggage lockers in the lobby. Non-smoking rooms are available.

Nyhavn & Around A recommendable low-end choice near Nyhavn is *Hotel Maritime* (☎ 33 13 48 82, fax 33 15 03 45), Peder Skramsgade 19, 1054 Copenhagen K, which has 69 renovated rooms that are small but inviting. The rooms vary but most have a sink and desk, and some also have TV. Rates begin at a reasonable 275/430 kr for singles/doubles with shared bath, 395/520 kr with private bath. The staff are friendly and the location, just a few minutes walk from the hydrofoil docks, is convenient for those travelling by boat.

Sømandshjemmet Bethel (☎ 33 13 03 70, fax 33 15 85 70), Nyhavn 22, 1051 Copenhagen K, calls itself a seaman's hotel but it's open to all. This cosy little hotel has a nice location right on Nyhavn canal, a lift to all floors, and two dozen good-sized rooms with private baths and an eclectic variety of furnishings. Many also have unbeatable views of Nyhavn – for the best, ask for a corner room. Singles/doubles cost 395/575 kr. A slightly lower 'seaman's rate' is sometimes available to the general public when things are slow.

The *Hotel Opera* (☎ 33 12 15 19, fax 33 32 12 82), Tordenskjoldsgade 15, 1055 Copenhagen K, is just south of the Royal Theatre. There's a nice Old World character to the place, and while it's not as fancy as top-end period hotels, the rates are more affordable. All 87 rooms have private bath, phone and TV. The hotel has an upmarket restaurant with French and Danish cuisine and a dark-wood pub popular with theatre-goers. Singles/doubles begin at 625/750 kr year round and there's a discounted weekend rate (two-night minimum) of 565/610 kr. Breakfast is available for an additional 65 kr.

Elsewhere in Copenhagen The *Hotel Jørgensen* (☎ 33 13 81 86, fax 33 15 51 05), Rømersgade 11, 1362 Copenhagen K, near Nørreport station, is popular with gay travellers but accepts straight guests as well. The rooms are simple but have some pleasant touches. Singles/doubles cost 380/480 kr for rooms with shared bath, 100 kr more for rooms with private bath. In summer the hotel also has dorm beds for 95 kr, a good breakfast included. There are lockers for dorm guests; laundry service and bicycle rentals can be arranged.

A block away is the *Hotel Windsor* (☎ 33 11 08 30, fax 33 11 63 87), Frederiksborggade 30, 1360 Copenhagen K, an exclusively gay and lesbian hotel in an older building opposite Israels Plads. The 25 rooms are straightforward but all have TV and most have refrigerators. Singles/doubles cost 300/450 kr.

Hotel Sankt Jørgen (☎ 35 37 15 11, fax 35 37 11 97), Julius Thomsens Gade 22, 1632 Copenhagen V, is family-run and pleasantly old-fashioned. There are 19 comfortable and spacious double rooms for 450 kr and two rather cramped single rooms for 350 kr. If space is available, single travellers are usually given a double room for the price of a single room. Bathrooms are shared; there are two toilets and two showers on each floor. It's about a 20-minute walk from the centre.

The modern *Cab-Inn Scandinavia* (☎ 35 36 11 11, fax 35 36 11 14), Vodroffsvej 55, 1900 Frederiksberg C, has 201 sleekly compact rooms that resemble cabins in a cruise ship, complete with upper and lower bunks. Although small, the rooms are quite comfortable, with full amenities like remote-control cable TV & VCR, phone, air-con, complimentary instant coffee and private baths. Rates are 395/480 kr for singles/doubles and there's basement parking for 30 kr a day. Video rentals are available in the lobby. As it's a popular place, especially in summer, reservations are recommended. Unlike other Copenhagen hotels, breakfast is not included in the room rate, but is available in the hotel café for 40 kr.

A few blocks to the south-west is the 86-room *Cab-Inn Copenhagen* (☎ 31 21 04 00, fax 31 21 74 09), Danasvej 32, 1900 Frederiksberg C, which has the same type of rooms and the same rates as Cab-Inn Scandinavia. Both hotels have rooms accessible by wheelchair and are about a 20-minute walk from Rådhuspladsen.

The 117-room *Hotel Esplanaden* (☎ 33 91 32 00, fax 33 91 32 39), Bredgade 78, 1260 Copenhagen K, is a sister hotel to the upmarket Neptun Hotel. Located opposite Churchillparken, it's a nice choice for those who want to be near green space. The hotel is a pleasant, older place with modernised rooms that have private baths, TVs, minibars and phones. Singles/doubles cost from 655/865 kr. There's also a weekend rate (two-day minimum) that's about 100 kr cheaper.

Hotels – top end

Around Central Station The *Grand Hotel* (☎ 31 31 36 00, fax 31 31 33 50), Vesterbrogade 9, 1620 Copenhagen V, is just north of Central Station. This century-old hotel was renovated a few years ago and all 146 rooms have private baths, minibars, TVs and phones. Non-smoking rooms are available. Singles/doubles cost from 700/930 kr. There's a bar and restaurant on site.

Despite its rather nondescript facade and lobby, the *Hotel Imperial* (☎ 33 12 80 00, fax 33 93 80 31), Vester Farimagsgade 9, 1606 Copenhagen V, has one of the best reputations for service among Copenhagen's 1st-class hotels. The 163 rooms have modern décor with desks, small sitting areas, phones, cable TVs and minibars. Rates begin at 1105/1450 kr for singles/doubles. It's opposite Vesterport station.

The 471-room *Sheraton Copenhagen Hotel* (☎ 33 14 35 35, fax 33 32 12 23), Vester Søgade 6 (Postboks 337), 1601 Copenhagen V, near the Tycho Brahe Planetarium, is a well-regarded chain hotel with all the expected Sheraton facilities including a health club, concierge and secretarial services. Cheapest are the twin-bed lower-floor rooms which cost 1282/1472 kr for singles/doubles, while the executive king-size bedrooms go for 1662/1852 kr.

The *SAS Royal Hotel* (☎ 33 14 14 12, fax 33 14 14 21), Hammerichsgade 1, 1611 Copenhagen V, is a centrally located 266-room multistorey hotel. Rooms are modern with full amenities and 24-hour room service. The hotel has an SAS ticket office, a centre for business travellers, restaurants, a nightclub and a fitness centre. Many of the upper-floor rooms have good city views, some overlooking Tivoli. The standard rate is 1395/1895 kr for singles/doubles. Except from 1 June to 31 August, there's also a weekend rate of around 1000/1200 kr with advance booking. For information on senior citizen discounts, see the SAS hotels under 'Elsewhere in Copenhagen' in this section.

Rådhuspladsen & Around The *Hotel Kong Frederik* (☎ 33 12 59 02, fax 33 93 59 01), Vester Voldgade 25, 1552 Copenhagen V, is a classic hotel with turn-of-the-century character, dark woods, antique furnishings and paintings of Danish royalty. The 110 rooms are comfortable and have TVs, phones, minibars and hair dryers. Singles/doubles begin at 1350/1650 kr. The hotel is well regarded for this price category.

The *Palace Hotel* (☎ 33 14 40 50, fax 33 14 52 79), Rådhuspladsen 57, 1550 Copenhagen, is in an interesting period building. The 159 rooms are spacious and each has a TV, phone, room safe, minibar and desk. There's an old-fashioned décor with upholstered chairs, heavy curtains and brass lamps. The cheapest rooms face the rear without views, but they are also the quietest. It'd be a pleasant place to stay if the price was right and in recent times the management has taken to dropping the rates about 40% to last-minute customers when the hotel is not full. The regular rates begin at 1325/1525 kr for singles/doubles. The front rooms, which overlook Rådhuspladsen, cost 1725 kr.

Nyhavn & Around The *Hotel City* (☎ 33 13 06 66, fax 33 13 06 67), Peder Skramsgade 24, 1054 Copenhagen K, is a smaller hotel with 85 standard 1st-class rooms, each with cable TV, private bath, phone and trouser press. Most have two single beds, placed side by side. Weekday rates begin at 750/970 kr for singles/doubles year round. The hotel, which is a Best Western affiliate, also has a more tempting weekend rate of 550/650 kr on Friday, Saturday and Sunday nights from 1 October to 1 May. About a five-minute walk from the hydrofoil docks, the location is convenient for those travelling by boat to Malmö in Sweden or Bornholm.

For nautical atmosphere, it's hard to beat the waterfront *Copenhagen Admiral Hotel* (☎ 33 11 82 82, fax 33 32 55 42), Toldbodgade 24-28, 1253 Copenhagen K, located between Nyhavn and Amalienborg Palace. The hotel occupies a renovated 18th century granary and is replete with brick archways and sturdy old beams of Pomeranian pine. The 365 rooms have a nice blend of period charm and modern conveniences, including TVs, desks, couches and bathrooms with bidets. The junior suites are split level, with a queen bed in the loft and a sitting area with sofa bed below. The hotel has a sauna, solarium and restaurant. Regular rooms cost 845/1040 kr for singles/doubles. Junior suites cost 1180 kr for one or two people, 1310 kr for four people. Breakfast is an extra 90 kr.

The 82-room *71 Nyhavn Hotel* (☎ 33 11 85 85, fax 33 93 15 85), Nyhavn 71, 1051 Copenhagen K, is another hotel in a renovated 200-year-old harbour-side warehouse. Although it has also incorporated some of the building's period features, such as exposed wooden beams, it's not on a par with the Copenhagen Admiral Hotel. Rooms and views vary; some of the lower-priced rooms are quite ordinary, while the waterfront corner suites (2250 kr) are pleasant and have great views of both the harbour and Nyhavn canal. Standard rooms cost 950/1350 kr for singles/doubles. There's a weekend rate of 675/950 kr with a two-night minimum.

The *Sophie Amalie Hotel* (☎ 33 13 34 00, fax 33 32 55 42), Sankt Annæ Plads 21, 1250 Copenhagen K, is popular with business travellers. The 134 rooms are modern and have the standard amenities including desks, bathtubs and cable TV. Regular rooms cost 865/1040 kr for singles/doubles. Much more interesting are those 6th floor deluxe rooms which have a harbour view and are split level; there's a living room with a sofa bed on the lower level and a loft bedroom above. The deluxe rooms cost 1180 kr for one or two people, 110 kr more for a third person. Breakfast is an extra 90 kr. The hotel sometimes offers a 10% discount for payment by cash or travellers' cheque.

The *Neptun Hotel* (☎ 33 13 89 00, fax 33 14 12 50), Sankt Annæ Plads 14, 1250 Copenhagen V, is a well-regarded 1st-class hotel located a block north of Nyhavn. The most refined Copenhagen hotel affiliated with the Best Western chain, it has 118 rooms and 145 suites. All have TVs, phones, elec-

tronic room safes, minibars, trouser presses etc. Singles/doubles begin at 990/1235 kr.

The *Phoenix* (☎ 33 95 95 00, fax 33 33 98 33), Bredgade 37, 1260 Copenhagen K, a block north-east of Nyhavn, is one of the better-value deluxe hotels in the city. It has 212 plush rooms with heavy carpets, upholstered chairs, chandeliers and the like. There's a restaurant and pub on site. Rates for singles/doubles start from 990/1450 kr.

Visiting celebrities generally opt for the *Hotel d'Angleterre* (☎ 33 12 00 95, fax 33 12 11 18), Kongens Nytorv 34, 1050 Copenhagen K, which has chandeliers, marble floors and a history dating back to the 17th century. Rates are Copenhagen's highest, beginning at 1850/2050 kr for singles/doubles. Despite its lengthy history, the hotel has changed hands a number of times in recent years and it no longer enjoys the solidly pre-eminent reputation it once had among Copenhagen's top hotels.

Elsewhere in Copenhagen Copenhagen's four SAS hotels offer senior citizens discounts equivalent to their age: 65-year-olds get a 65% discount, 90-year-olds get a 90% discount, and so on. When two persons stay in the same room, the age of the eldest determines the discount level. This '65 Plus' rate is valid seven days a week year round, but a limited number of rooms are available at this rate, so advance booking is essential.

SAS offers all travellers a 'Weekend Freedom' rate of about 40% off the regular rate that's valid Friday to Sunday except in June, July and August. These rates must be booked in advance. There's no extra charge for children under 15 years of age.

All three of the following SAS hotels have modern rooms with TVs, phones, minibars, hair dryers, trouser presses and the like, and all offer non-smoking rooms.

The 542-room *SAS Scandinavia Hotel* (☎ 33 11 23 24, fax 31 57 01 93), Amager Blvd 70, 2300 Copenhagen S, is a high-rise hotel south of Christianshavn. The hotel has free parking, services for business travellers, 24-hour room service, a pool and fitness centre, squash courts, several restaurants, a bar and Copenhagen's only casino. Singles/doubles cost 1095/1545 kr.

The 166-room *SAS Falconer Hotel* (☎ 31 19 80 01, fax 31 87 11 91), Falkoner Allé 9, 2000 Frederiksberg, Copenhagen, is west of central Copenhagen near the S-train's Frederiksberg station. The hotel, which is a popular convention spot, has a large banquet hall, health club, restaurant and bar. Some rooms have been specially adapted for the disabled. Singles/doubles cost 1095/1375 kr.

About two km north of the airport is the 196-room *SAS Globetrotter Hotel* (☎ 31 55 14 33, fax 31 55 81 45), 171 Engvej, 2300 Copenhagen S. There are services for business travellers, a restaurant and bar, indoor pools, a fitness centre and limited free airport shuttle service on weekdays. Singles/doubles cost 1095/1395 kr.

PLACES TO EAT
Central Station
DSB operates five eateries at Central Station. You wouldn't come here from elsewhere to eat, but they're convenient if you're already at the station. The cheapest is *Spise Hjørnet*, a cafeteria open from 6.30 am to 10 pm, which offers a daily hot special for 35 kr on weekdays, 45 kr on weekends. These are filling meals, but unexciting. You can also make your own single-serving salad from a limited salad bar for 21 kr, bread included.

City Pizza & Burger, on the upper level at the west end of the station, has a pretty good pizza-and-salad buffet every day from 11.30 am to 11 pm for 58 kr, as well as lasagne and burgers for around 50 kr.

The upper-end station restaurant is *Restaurant Bistro* (☎ 33 14 12 32), which has a full Danish buffet from 11.30 am to 10 pm, including fried fish, ham sliced from the bone, meatballs, cold fish dishes such as herring and smoked salmon, salads and desserts. It's a good spread, but not gourmet quality, and thus on the pricey side at 134 kr. A limited buffet of just the cold fish dishes and bread costs 70 kr.

Café på Balkonen, open from 6.30 am to 11 pm, offers a breakfast special of a roll, Danish pastry, egg and coffee for 32 kr or a

lunch special of three smørrebrød sandwiches with a Carlsberg draught beer for the same price.

Restaurant Grillen features roast beef and steaks from 5 to 11 pm. From June to August there's a special two-course lunch for 85 kr served from 11.30 am.

Central Station also has a *McDonald's*, a small fruit stand and a supermarket open daily from 8 am to midnight. The *Kringlen* bakery, in the north-east corner of the station, has good breads and pastries and is open from 6.30 am (7 am on Sunday) to 9 pm.

Around Central Station
Centrum Smørrebrød, Vesterbrogade 6, has a window full of different smørrebrød creations sold as takeaways. Even if you're not hungry it's worth passing by just to see what can be conjured up from a slice of bread.

Restaurant Shezan (☎ 31 24 78 88), Viktoriagade 22, on the corner of Viktoriagade and Istedgade, serves authentic Pakistani food from 11 am to 11.30 pm daily. Vegetarian dishes such as dal rajmahn or chana curry cost 35 kr, while a range of chicken and lamb dishes cost 45 to 60 kr. It's a popular, albeit smoky, restaurant. If you want something quieter, the *Indus Restaurant* (☎ 31 24 23 73) on the opposite corner also has Pakistani food with similar prices and hours.

Rådhusarkaden, an indoor shopping centre on Vesterbrogade near Rådhus, has an *Irma* grocery store and the *Conditori Hans Christian Andersen*, which has good sandwiches, pastries and coffee.

Restaurant Koh-I-Noor (☎ 31 24 64 17), Vesterbrogade 33, has candlelight dining and a tasty Indian buffet that includes curried lamb, beef and chicken dishes, nan bread, soup and salad for 79 kr from 5 to 10 pm nightly. There's also an à la carte menu, including vegetarian dishes, priced around 65 to 80 kr. The kitchen stays open until midnight, later on weekends. It's a good choice for an inexpensive evening out and they don't push pricey beverages.

Merhaba Restaurant (☎ 31 22 77 21), Abel Cathrinesgade 7, about 10 minutes walk east of Central Station, is an immensely popular Turkish eatery with good food and honest prices. You can get shish kebab and salad for 50 kr and tandoori king prawns or various curries for around 80 kr, but the best value are the fixed-price meals. Each night there's a three-course meal for 49 kr that includes a starter, main dish and dessert and a 10-course meal for 79 kr. Expect to share a table; most seat about a dozen people, so it's a nice opportunity to rub elbows with the Danes. Merhaba is open nightly from 5 pm; there's belly dancing on Friday and Saturday.

Another nearby Turkish restaurant that attracts a crowd is *Alanya* (☎ 31 31 92 33), Vesterbrogade 35, which has a dinner buffet of 14 cold and 14 hot traditional Middle Eastern dishes, including calamari, chicken, lamb and salads, for 59 kr from 4 pm to midnight daily. There's a smaller but still substantial lunch buffet for 49 kr from 11 am to 4 pm.

Frugtkælderen at Vesterbrogade 27 is a good little fruit and vegetable store which sells bulk nuts and dried fruit at reasonable prices and also has feta cheese and Turkish food items.

Scala

Scala, on Vesterbrogade opposite Tivoli, is a large multi-storeyed complex chock full of restaurants, fast-food eateries and bakeries. The offerings range from the ubiquitous *McDonald's* to ethnic food stalls and steak and seafood restaurants. The food stalls, which are clustered on the ground floor, are ringed with counters and stools, so you can either eat in or order takeaway. Most of Scala's food stalls are deli-style, with the food cooked in batches and replenished as it sells, though a few places cook to order.

Not surprisingly, Scala is popular with local office workers so expect it to be fairly packed at the height of the lunch hour. If you get there a little before noon you can beat the crowd and also get the food at its freshest.

For value consider *Strecker's*, which has a tempting chilli con carne sweetened with apples and served with salad for 30 kr or half a chicken and chips for 45 kr. The *Frisk Pasta* stall also has filling food at reasonable

prices, with pasta dishes served with salad for about 40 kr and a nice focaccia for 20 kr.

If you don't mind spending a little more you can get a tasty made-to-order meal at *Matahari*, a busy little stall that has a variety of wok-cooked East Asian dishes for around 50 kr. *La Mer*, at the back of the complex, has fresh fish and chips for 35 kr until 5 pm, for 50 kr in the evening. The *City Rock Café*, opposite La Mer, specialises in burgers and beer. For open-face smørrebrød, the local favourite is *Th Sørensen*, while the nearby *Høyers Bageri* has the best pastries.

A good choice for a more relaxing meal is the *Restaurant Graabrødre*, which has a 150-gram steak for just 35 kr at lunch (until 5.30 pm) and a three-course meal at dinner for 100 kr. Restaurant Graabrødre is located on the 3rd floor of Scala, as are other sit-down restaurants serving Chinese, Japanese, Brazilian and Mexican food.

Tivoli

Tivoli boasts 29 places to eat. These range from simple self-service cafés serving typical amusement park fare to some of the city's more respected eating establishments. You'll need to pay Tivoli admission (or have a valid Copenhagen Card) to eat at any of these places – and they're only open during the Tivoli season. Depending upon the restaurant, the kitchen generally stays open until 11 or 11.30 pm; the restaurants close at midnight, the time that Tivoli closes.

A fun spot with relatively moderate prices is *Hercegovina* (☎ 33 15 63 63), which specialises in Bosnian and Hercegovinian food and often has a roaming accordion, guitar and fiddle trio performing ethnic music. In the evenings there's a nice buffet that includes lamb, fish and roast suckling pig. From 5 to 6 pm and again after 9 pm the buffet costs 99 kr, with a glass of wine included; outside those hours it costs 149 kr. Dine on the balcony and you'll be able to watch Tivoli's pantomime ballet perform below.

Another good-value moderately priced restaurant is the *Promenaden* (☎ 33 14 68 16), which enjoys a view of the open-air stage and has moderately priced beef dishes, such as spareribs (100 kr) and steaks (130 kr), with a salad included.

If money is not an issue, *Divan 2* (☎ 33 12 51 51) is widely considered Tivoli's finest restaurant for both food and service. In operation since Tivoli opened in 1843, this fine-dining restaurant serves gourmet French food and has a vintage wine collection. Its sister restaurant, *Divan 1* (☎ 33 11 42 42), has a similar history and garden setting and also enjoys a reputation for good food but with a menu that emphasises Danish and international fare. A meal at either Divan could easily set you back a good 500 kr.

Belle Terrasse (☎ 33 22 11 36), another well-regarded, expensive French restaurant, has a delightful solarium setting overlooking Tivoli's pond.

The latest addition to Tivoli's eateries is Denmark's first *Hard Rock Café* (☎ 33 12 50 28), which features burgers and other American-style fare.

Strøget & Around
Strøget has an abundance of cheap eateries including hot-dog, hamburger and ice-cream stands and numerous hole-in-the-wall kebab joints selling felafels for around 25 kr.

For a cheap treat try *Shawarma Grill House* at the west end of Strøget, a two-minute walk from Rådhuspladsen. This bustling, unpretentious eatery makes an excellent shawarma (27 kr), a pitta-bread sandwich of shaved beef and lamb that's topped with a sesame paste and yoghurt dressing. There are also felafels, kebabs and shish tawook (grilled chicken). It's open from 11 am to 11 pm daily and has a sit-down counter on the ground floor, a dining room upstairs. A more mundane option in the same price range can be found at the nearby *McDonald's*, where a Big Mac will set you back 28 kr.

Best of the area's numerous pizzerias is *Peppe's Pizza* (☎ 33 32 59 59), Rådhuspladsen 57, which offers an all-you-can-eat pizza and salad buffet from 11 am to 4 pm daily for 37 kr. This popular Norwegian chain pizzeria has a nice setting in the base-

ment of an older building with open brick and timber posts. The simpler pizzas cost 100 kr for a small or 135 kr for a large, the latter big enough for three. They serve Tuborg on tap and stay open until at least 11 pm on weekdays and until 1 am on Friday and Saturday.

For a bargain, check the little *Café de Paris* pizzeria at Vimmelskaftet 39, which has a reasonable pizza and salad buffet for only 29 kr at lunch and 39 kr at dinner. In the same arcade is *Firenze* (☎ 33 12 50 85) with Italian dishes and *Hana Kyoto* (☎ 33 32 22 96) with Japanese food; both places have moderate prices.

McGrails, in the basement on the northeast corner of Gammel Torv, is a small health-food store selling cheese, tofu, snacks, breads and sweets.

There are a few bakeries on Strøget, one of the best being *Reinh van Hauen*, which is at the western end, between McDonald's and Brasilko.

The *Magasin du Nord* department store, a block south of Østergade at the eastern end of Strøget, has a good bakery and grocery store on the 1st floor and a cafeteria on the 4th floor.

La Glace, a classic konditori at Skoubogade 3, has been serving tea and fancy cakes to afternoon socialites for more than a century. It's open from 8 am to 5 pm on weekdays, from 9 am on Saturday.

On the west side of Højbro Plads is a *Haagen-Dazs* shop that sells ice cream by the scoop or in takeaway pre-packed containers; the square also has a hot dog stall, a fruit stand and an outdoor café.

One of our favourite Copenhagen lunch spots is *RizRaz* (☎ 33 15 05 75), just south of Strøget at Kompagnistræde 20, and conveniently around the corner from Use It. At this little basement café you can feast on a superb Mediterranean-style vegetarian buffet, including felafels, pizza, hummus, tabouli and vegetable salads, for only 39 kr daily from 11.30 am to 4.30 pm. At dinner, served from 4.30 to 10 pm (until 11 pm on Friday and Saturday), the buffet costs 59 kr and includes vegetarian chilli, pasta and moussaka. You can also order from the menu: lamb kebabs, grilled fish or fried calamari cost 89 kr, and this includes the buffet as well.

Abundant in local flavour is *Café Sorgenfri* (☎ 33 11 58 80), Brolæggerstræde 8, a smoky corner pub serving good cheap Danish food. Traditional cold dishes like pickled herring or salted meat on liverpaste cost around 35 kr. Hot dishes, including the house speciality of roast pork, average 50 kr. Or jump in and sample it all with a variety plate (95 kr) that includes herring, shrimp, roast pork, meatballs with beets, cheese and other items. The kitchen is open from noon until 9 pm daily.

Chinese Restaurant Shanghai has good Chinese food at reasonable prices and a nice balcony view overlooking both Gammel Torv and Nytorv. There's a variety of lunch dishes for 45 kr that are available from 11 am to 3 pm and a few three-course meals for 98 kr that are served until 10.30 pm.

Nearby is *Huset med det Grønne Træ* (☎ 33 12 87 86), 20 Gammel Torv, at the north-west corner of the old square and beside the linden tree from which it takes its name. This charming little lunch café, which is in a period building that dates from 1796, offers quintessential Danish flavour with smørrebrød sandwiches, draught beer and a dozen brands of snaps. Sandwiches begin at 30 kr, a lunch plate costs 95 kr. It's open from 11 am to 3 pm Monday to Friday.

Brasilko (☎ 33 11 12 05), at Frederiksberggade 28, has an attractive upper-floor dining room overlooking Strøget and reasonably priced food considering its rather formal setting. At lunch, from 11.30 am to 4 pm, you can get smørrebrød sandwiches from 30 kr or a lunch plate of cheese, fish fillet, shrimp and a small steak for 65 kr. At both lunch and dinner there are various burgers and steaks on the menu for 70 to 168 kr, including a salad bar. It's open from 11 am to 11 pm daily.

Restaurant Bali (☎ 33 11 08 08), just off Kongens Nytorv at Lille Kongensgade 4, offers authentic Indonesian and Malaysian food. The restaurant specialises in 'taffel-style' meals which combine a variety of curried meat and vegetable dishes, accompanied with rice, salad, chutney and condiments. These full meals, including a mixed Indonesian and Malay curry version, cost 138 kr. It's open daily from noon to midnight.

The *Brasserie on the Square* (☎ 33 14 40 50), in the lobby of the Palace Hotel at Rådhuspladsen 57, has a Danish buffet from noon to 2.30 pm daily that includes five herring dishes, salmon paté and salads. While it's not an elaborate affair, it has a mildly upmarket setting and is a reasonable deal at 98 kr.

A sure bet for fine dining is *Restaurant Nouvelle* (☎ 33 13 50 18), 34 Gammel Strand, one of only five restaurants in Denmark to receive a Michelin star. It serves a sophisticated mix of Danish and French nouvelle cuisine with an emphasis on fresh seafood. The best value is usually the fixed-price meal, a four-course affair that's priced around 400 kr at dinner. There's also a three-course lunch for 225 kr and an extensive à la carte menu. Reservations should be made as far in advance as possible. The restaurant, which is a couple of blocks south of Strøget, is open from 11.30 am to 3 pm Monday to Friday and from 5.30 to 10 pm Monday to Saturday.

Gråbrødre Torv

Gråbrødre Torv (Greyfriars' Square), between Strøget and the Latin Quarter, has a handful of popular restaurants grouped around a cobblestone square.

For a quiet dinner out, consider *Peder Oxe* (☎ 33 11 00 77) on Gråbrødre Torv which offers fine dining with a cosy Danish country ambience. It's open from 11.30 am to 10.30 pm and specialises in hearty meat dishes, served with a salad buffet, for 90 to 150 kr. Copenhagen's oldest monastery, built in 1238, was on this site and the restaurant's wine cellar retains part of the old stone foundations.

There's also a nice atmosphere at *Jensen's Bøfhus*, one of a Danish chain of steak restaurants, which is nearby in another period house fronting Gråbrødre Torv. While the food is rather average, it's a more affordable affair. At lunch, from 11.30 am to 4 pm, you can get a steak and baked potato for 39 kr. At dinner there's a good chicken dish with a reasonable salad buffet for 79 kr. Dinner steaks average 100 kr except on weekends when there's usually a 180-gram 'steak-69' special for 69 kr.

If you prefer a non-chain restaurant, *Restaurant Graabrødre* (☎ 33 32 83 83), at the east side of Gråbrødre Torv, has decent steaks at reasonable prices. At lunch, served from 11.30 am to 5.30 pm, you can get a 200-gram steak for 43 kr. At dinner there's a special two-course meal for 89 kr and a three-course meal for 98 kr; the main dishes change monthly but there's usually both a fish and meat dish to choose between.

The trendy *Pasta Basta* (☎ 33 11 21 31), immediately south of Gråbrødre Torv at Valkendorfsgade 22, has a pleasant contemporary setting and good pasta. Its mainstay is a self-service buffet of about a dozen cold pasta and salad dishes for 69 kr. You can also order from the menu, which has various hot pasta dishes served with the likes of mussels, salmon or lamb; most are priced from 60 to 100 kr, or just 30 kr if ordered along with the cold pasta buffet. The restaurant is open from 11.30 am to 3 am on weekdays, to 5 am on weekends, and is a popular spot with night owls looking for a late meal or drink.

Latin Quarter & Around

Hellas (☎ 33 14 05 00), a Greek restaurant at Fiolstræde 21, has a pleasant atmosphere and a hard-to-beat lunch buffet of Greek salads and hot dishes for 32 kr from noon to 4 pm. From 5 to 11 pm there's a more elaborate dinner buffet or a three-course moussaka meal for 98 kr. You can also order from the menu, with main dishes averaging 75 kr. It's open daily except on Sunday.

Klaptræet, a 2nd-floor café at Kultorvet 13, is a student haunt with burgers, chilli con carne and salads for under 50 kr. There's also a daily home-made soup with bread for 28 kr. It's open daily from 10 am to midnight. Kultorvet itself becomes a popular beer

garden in summer, with some of the nearby businesses, including Klaptræet, setting up tables in the square and selling beer on tap.

An old favourite for traditional Danish food at moderate prices is *Det Lille Apotek* (☎ 33 12 56 06), tucked in the basement at Store Kannikestræde 15. Various plate meals that include pickled herring, fish fillet and open sandwiches cost 50 to 100 kr at lunch and there's a three-course dinner for 138 kr. It's open from 11 am (from noon on Sunday) to at least midnight daily, though the kitchen usually closes at 10.45 pm.

Ristorante Italiano (☎ 33 11 12 95) at Fiolstræde 2, at the back of Vor Frue Kirke, has authentic Italian food and décor. There are good-value lunch specials, including lasagne or calamari served with a glass of wine for 50 kr, and a dinner menu that ranges from 39 kr pizzas to a 139 kr three-course steak meal. In summer they have outdoor café tables, which make for a pleasant place to dine on a sunny day.

Café Sommersko (☎ 33 14 81 89), Kronprinsensgade 6, open from 9 am to midnight daily, draws a high-energy university crowd and has 50 different brands of beer. The varied menu includes Mexican chicken or an omelette with salad for about 50 kr and Thai-marinated scampi with jasmine rice for 70 kr. At breakfast you can get inexpensive French toast or yoghurt with muesli, and they also have nice desserts including tiramisu.

A good place to rub elbows with the locals is *Wessels Kro*, a small neighbourhood pub at Sværtegade 7, which serves a 500-gram steak with baked potato and salad for 58 kr from 5 to 10 pm on Wednesday, Saturday and Sunday. It can get a bit smoky, but if you like big steaks, you can't beat the price.

Mei Chiang (☎ 33 93 89 48), Gothersgade 129, a pleasant Chinese restaurant opposite the entrance to the Botanical Gardens, has 10 lunch specials for 35 to 45 kr from noon to 4 pm daily. Dinner costs about double that. It's open to 11 pm.

Peppe's Pizza (☎ 33 13 22 15), opposite Kongens Have at 101 Gothersgade, has a recommendable pizza-and-salad buffet for 37 kr that's available from noon to 4 pm daily. You can also get good pizzas to order throughout the day until 11 pm. The cost for a cheese pizza is 60 kr for a one-person deep-pan variety, 100 kr for a regular medium and 135 kr for a large.

St Gertruds Kloster (☎ 33 14 66 30), at Hauser Plads 32 just off Kultorvet, is an elegant restaurant in a former medieval monastery, sections of which date from the 14th century. The most popular of the four dining rooms is the one occupying the cellar which has arched brick walls and is lit by 1500 candles. The restaurant specialises in fresh seafood. Starters, including smoked salmon, lobster and escargot, are priced from 100 to 200 kr, while main dishes cost around 200 kr. There's also a fixed-price, three-course 'business dinner' for 360 kr. The kitchen is open from 5 to 11.30 pm nightly; reservations are requested.

The main city produce market is at Israels Plads, a few minutes walk west of Nørreport station. Stalls are set up from Monday to Friday to 5 pm and on Saturday, when it also doubles as a flea market, to 2 pm.

Nørrebrogade

Indian Corner (☎ 31 39 28 02), at Nørrebrogade 59, is a pleasant little restaurant with very good Indian food at moderate prices. Vegetarian dishes cost 45 to 50 kr, meat curries are a few kr more and tandoori or tikka chicken cost around 70 kr. Add another 20 kr for rice. It's open from 4 to 11 pm daily except on Tuesday.

Quattro Fontane (☎ 31 39 39 31) at Guldbergsgade 3, a few minutes east of Nørre All, has good Italian food at reasonable prices. There are numerous pizza and pasta dishes costing around 50 kr and a few meat dishes for 70 to 110 kr. There's also a 19 kr children's menu with spaghetti, lasagne, pizza and fish & chips. It's open for dinner only, from 4 to 11.30 pm daily.

If Quattro Fontane is full there are a couple of other options a few minutes walk to the east, on Sankt Hans Torv at its intersection with Fœlledvej. There you'll find the Indian restaurant *New Delhi* and the Pakistani restaurant *Neelam* directly opposite each other.

Both have à la carte dishes beginning around 50 kr, though Neelam sometimes offers a full daily meal for that price as well. They're open from 4 to 11 pm daily.

Mexicali (☎ 31 39 47 04), Åboulevard 12, has Mexican vegetarian dishes such as a cheese burrito or enchilada with rice for 75 to 80 kr and meat dishes from 85 to 100 kr. The restaurant has a pleasant Mexican décor and is open from 5 pm to midnight daily. It's about a 20-minute walk north-west of central Copenhagen on the way to Nørrebro.

The Nørrebrogade area has a couple of health-food stores: at Nørrebrogade 57 there's a *Naturbutik* with an array of bulk and pre-packaged foods, teas and vitamins, and at Blågårdsgade 33, *Solsikken* has the usual health-food products along with produce, wine and crystal sections.

Nyhavn

In the summer season the restaurants that run along the north side of the Nyhavn canal bring tables out onto the streets, effectively turning them into a line of pavement cafés.

Apart from the hot dog wagon that customarily sets up at the inner canal, the cheapest eats on Nyhavn are at *Pizzabageren*, on the corner of Nyhavn and Toldbodgade, which has simple salads, pittabread sandwiches, hot dogs, burgers and chips. While this hole-in-the-wall eatery isn't particularly notable, you can quiet your stomach for 30 kr or so.

For a thoroughly Danish experience, don't miss the herring buffet at *Nyhavns Fœrgekro* (☎ 33 15 15 88), an old atmospheric restaurant right on the canal at Nyhavn 5. There are 10 different kinds of herring including baked, marinated and pickled herrings, with condiments to sprinkle on top and bread and boiled potatoes to round out the meal. The all-you-can-eat buffet costs 68 kr and is available from 11.30 am to 4 pm daily. If you're not a herring lover, there's also a variety of smørrebrød for 22 to 53 kr each. Dinner, which is served from 5 to 11.30 pm, is more expensive, with a mix of Danish and French dishes.

Leonore Christine (☎ 33 13 50 40) at

Nyhavn 9 offers quality food at high prices in a cosy historic building fronting the canal. A sister operation of the city's highly reputed Restaurant Nouvelle, the menu features a mingling of French and Danish dishes, with starters and desserts priced around 100 kr and à la carte main dishes around 250 kr. It's open from noon to 3 pm and 6 to 10 pm. Reservations are often necessary.

ENTERTAINMENT

Copenhagen is a 24-hour party city. For free entertainment simply stroll along Strøget, especially between Nytorv and Højbro Plads, which in the late afternoon and evening is a bit like an impromptu three-ring circus of musicians, magicians, jugglers and other street performers.

There are scores of backstreet cafés and clubs with live music. As a general rule, entry is often free on weeknights, while there's usually a cover charge on weekends or any time someone special is playing. Danes tend to be late-nighters and many places don't really get going until midnight.

A good place to stop for a beer or coffee while getting the latest on what's happening around the city is *Kul-Kaféen* (☎ 33 32 17 77), Teglgårdsstræde 5, a 'culture information café' run by energetic youth volunteers. In addition to maintaining an entertainment calendar, they also organise their own events including concerts, poetry readings and exhibits.

Music & Dance Clubs

Copenhagen Jazz House (☎ 33 15 26 00), Niels Hemmingsensgade 10, is the city's leading jazz spot, featuring top Danish musicians and sometimes international performers. The music – mainly bebop, new jazz and fusion jazz – starts at 8.30 pm on weekdays, 9.30 pm on weekends. Admission is generally 50 to 70 kr, but occasionally as much as 150 kr. There's a disco (30 kr) from 1 to 5 am on Thursday, Friday and Saturday that helps support the jazz programme.

La Fontaine (☎ 33 11 60 98), Kompagnistræde 11, is a hang-out for swing and mainstream jazz musicians, including visit-

ing artists who sometimes end up jamming together. This is a casual late-night spot, open from 9 pm to 7 am nightly.

The smoky *Sofies Kælder* (☎ 31 54 29 45), at Sofiegade 1 in Christianshavn, usually has rock music during the week, but it's popular for its long tradition of Sunday afternoon (3 to 6 pm) jazz concerts.

The Nørrebro area has a number of entertainment and meeting spots. *Café Rust* (☎ 31 35 00 33), Guldbergsgade 8, attracts a college-age crowd and usually has good bands on Tuesday and Thursday, when there's a moderate cover charge, and a disco on Friday and Saturday when admission is free; the action begins at 9.30 pm.

Bananrepublikken (☎ 35 36 08 30), a café at Nørrebrogade 13, is a friendly spot that attracts a mixed-age crowd and has live music from 'around the equator' such as salsa, calypso and flamenco, with the biggest nights on Thursday and Saturday, when it stays open until at least 4 am; the cover charge ranges from 20 to 70 kr. Another happening place in the neighbourhood is *Barcelona* (☎ 31 35 76 11), a café at Fælledvej 21, which often has live music and no cover charge.

Mojo (☎ 33 11 64 53), Løngangstræde 21, is a hot spot for blues, with entertainment nightly from 8 pm (from 4 pm on Sunday) until at least 4 am. The cover charge varies with the group, and is sometimes free.

The Melon, Løngangstræde 39, is the place to go for reggae and roots music (on Thursday); on weekends they generally have rock. It's open from 10 pm to 5 am Thursday to Sunday. The cover charge varies with the group.

Musik Loppen (☎ 31 57 84 22) in Christiania is a popular Christianshavn spot with live music that ranges anywhere from techno-rock to Latin and Danish pop. It's open from 9 pm to 2 am on Wednesday and Thursday, when admission is generally free, and from 10 pm to 5 am on Friday and Saturday, when admission usually costs 40 to 60 kr.

Huset, Rådhusstræde 13, the home of Use It and the site of the first 1960s squatters'

COPENHAGEN

settlement, is now an alternative cultural centre with cafés, a cinema, a theatre and two nightclubs. Huset's *Musikcafén* (☎ 33 15 20 02), which usually has funk, soul or rock music and attracts an international crowd, is open from 9 pm to 2 am on weekdays, to 5 am on Friday and Saturday. Admission averages 50 kr. Also in Huset is *Barbue*, which features techno, trash, hip-hop and avant-garde jazz. Barbue is open from 10 pm to 2 am on weekdays, and until 5 am on weekends. Admission is usually 30 to 50 kr.

Ballet, Opera & Theatre

The Royal Danish Ballet and the Royal Danish Opera perform at Det Kongelige Teater (the Royal Theatre) at Kongens Nytorv. The season runs from mid-August to late May, skipping the main summer months.

An English-language brochure with the season schedule is available at the tourist office, or call ☎ 33 15 22 20 for schedule information. If booking from abroad, you can charge the tickets to a credit card and have them mailed to you. For bookings and information call ☎ 33 14 10 02 between 1 and 7 pm Monday to Saturday, or fax 33 12 36 92. Tickets range from 40 to 340 kr.

There are also a few smaller theatres in Copenhagen which have performances of popular international plays and musicals; programmes are published in the daily newspapers and in *Copenhagen This Week*.

Of special interest for children are the marionette shows that are given during the months of June, July and August at the east side of Kongens Have, the public gardens near Rosenborg Slot. The shows last about half an hour and begin at 2 and 3 pm daily, except on Monday. There's no admission charge to the show or the gardens.

Tivoli Tivoli's Concert Hall is the venue for symphony orchestra, violin, string quartet and other classical music performances by both Danish and international musicians. There's also a ballet festival each season featuring top international troupes, as well as cabaret performances.

Tickets are sold weekdays at the Tivoli Billetcenter (☎ 33 15 10 12), Vesterbrogade 3.

Tivoli also has numerous performances that are free (after paying the general Tivoli admission), including the Italian-influenced Commedia Dell'Arte pantomime which performs at 7.45 and 9.45 pm, except on Sunday and rainy days, at the open-air theatre near the Vesterbrogade entrance.

Booking Offices ARTE (☎ 38 88 22 22, fax 38 88 22 23), Hvidkildevej 64, sells tickets for theatre performances and concerts throughout Denmark from 10 am to 4 pm Monday to Friday.

The ARTE kiosk, on the corner of Fiolstræde and Nørreport, sells half-price theatre and concert tickets for same-day Copenhagen performances; it's open from noon to 7 pm Monday to Friday and from noon to 3 pm on Saturday.

Gay Scene

Copenhagen has one of the liveliest gay and lesbian scenes in Europe.

Some of the more popular meeting places are the *Cosy Bar* (☎ 33 12 74 27), Studiestræde 24, a busy late-night place that attracts mostly men and is open from 11 pm to 6 am daily, and the *Café Babooshka* (☎ 33 15 05 36), Turensensgade 6, a lesbian hangout that's open from 4 pm to 1 am Monday to Saturday and has drinks, light meals and a Friday disco. *Sebastian* (☎ 33 32 22 79), Hyskenstræde 10, is a bar and café that attracts a mixed gay and lesbian crowd and is open from noon to 1 am daily.

For dance clubs, *After Dark* (☎ 33 11 06 20) at Studiestræde 31 is known for its drag shows but it attracts both men and women; it's open from 11 pm to 5 am Wednesday to Saturday. The adjacent *Metro Place de Clichy* is predominantly frequented by gay men heavily into leather and is open from 11 pm to 6 am Thursday to Saturday.

Copenhagen has about two dozen other gay bars, clubs and cafés, nearly half of them concentrated along Studiestræde in the two blocks between Vester Voldgade and Nørregade. For a complete list pick up a copy

Copenhagen Jazz Festival

The Copenhagen Jazz Festival is the biggest entertainment event of the year, with 10 days of music beginning on the first Friday in July. The festival features a range of Danish and international jazz, blues and fusion music. It's a cornucopia of more than 400 indoor and outdoor concerts, with music wafting out of practically every public square, park, pub and café from Strøget to Tivoli.

'Great Jazz' concerts, which in recent years have featured performers like trumpeter Wynton Marsalis and saxophonist Sonny Rollins, cost around 170 kr, while the cover charge in small clubs usually ranges from 30 to 50 kr. Most of the outdoor concerts are free; get hold of a festival programme and you can plan your own jazz tour. For schedules, fees and ticket information, contact Copenhagen Jazz Festival (☎ 33 93 20 13, fax 33 93 44 13), Kjeld Langesgade 4A, 1367 Copenhagen K. ■

of *PAN magazine*, which is available at gay businesses, including the above clubs. This monthly gay newspaper also has information on gay organisations, saunas, cinemas and other businesses. There's an annual English-language version that is published each June.

Ørsteds Parken, a couple of blocks north-west of Studiestræde, is a popular gay cruising site; there are even 'nesting boxes' in the trees that are stocked with condoms. Note, however, that anti-gay youth gangs occasionally come through the park as well.

In addition to the aforementioned clubs, there's also the *Bøssehuset* (Gay House; ☎ 31 95 98 72) in Christiania, which has gay theatre and other cultural events.

The national organisation for gays and lesbians, called Landsforeningen for Bøsser og Lesbiske, or LBL (☎ 33 13 19 48), has its headquarters at Knabrostræde 3 in central Copenhagen.

Radio Rosa, at 98.9 MHz, has gay and lesbian programmes from 3 to 5 pm and from 9.30 to 11.30 pm daily.

For information on the city's two gay hotels, see the earlier Places to Stay section.

Free Concerts

Throughout the summer, numerous free concerts are held in city parks and squares. The biggest of these concerts are those sponsored by the city breweries and held on Saturday or Sunday afternoons from late May to mid-August at Femøren park on the coast of Amager. The music is rock or jazz, usually top Danish groups play, and each summer there's at least one concert with a big-name international performer such as BB King. Bring your own food, but the time-honoured custom is to buy drinks at the concerts as it helps the sponsors offset the costs. Femøren can be reached via bus Nos 12 or 13.

Cinema

There are about 20 screens showing first-release movies in the cinemas along Vesterbrogade between Central Station and Rådhuspladsen. Tickets generally range from 50 to 60 kr, though the price can be as low as 30 kr in the daytime and on Monday evenings. As elsewhere in Denmark, movies are shown in their original language with Danish subtitles.

Casino

If you want to try your hand with the high rollers, the *Casino Copenhagen* at the SAS Scandinavia Hotel in Amager has slot machines, blackjack tables, stud poker and both American and French roulette. It's open daily from 2 pm to 4 am; admission is restricted to those aged 18 and older.

THINGS TO BUY

Along Copenhagen's main shopping street, Strøget, you can find numerous speciality shops selling everything from clothing to Danish porcelain and electronics.

Danish amber can be purchased at reasonable prices from one of the many jewellery shops along Strøget; your best bet is to do a little window shopping before you buy.

The Sweater Market, at Frederiksberggade 15 on Strøget, has quality Scandinavian sweaters, mostly priced from 800 kr.

For sleek audio equipment, there's a Bang & Olufsen shop at Østergade 3, at the east end of Strøget.

China, Silver & Glass
Denmark's best-known, and most expensive, porcelain, silver and glassworks are under the umbrella of Royal Copenhagen Ltd. All three products have their main shops along Strøget and boast some interesting displays that are worth a look whether you're a shopper or not.

Royal Copenhagen Porcelain, which is famous for its Flora Danica pattern, is at Amagertorv 6, in a imposing circa 1616 Renaissance house near Højbro Plads.

The Georg Jensen shop, next door at Amagertorv 4, features quality silver work, including cutlery, candle holders, jewellery and designer art pieces.

The third operation, Holmegaard Glass & Crystal, sells fine crystal glasses and handblown vases and bowls from the 300-year-old Karel van Manders mansion at Østergade 15.

Books & Stamps
Book lovers and collectors will find good browsing in the antique bookshops along Fiolstræde in the block running between Krystalgade and Øster Voldgade.

For information on shops that sell new English-language books, see Bookshops under Information earlier in this chapter.

Stamp collectors can buy commemorative stamps from the Postens Frimærke Center, Vesterbrogade 67, from 10 am to 3.30 pm on weekdays (to 6 pm on Thursday).

Department Stores
Copenhagen's largest department store, Magasin du Nord, covers an entire city block at the south-west side of Kongens Nytorv and has everything from clothing and luggage to a bookshop and a grocery store.

Illums Bolighus, at Amagertorv 10 on Strøget, has stylish Danish design furniture, continental quilts, ceramics, silverware and glass, but is also a good place to look for simple gifts, such as a quality toy or a stainless steel cheese slicer.

Airport Shops
Copenhagen Airport has 30 tax-free shops selling a wide range of products, including men's and women's clothing, continental quilts, Royal Copenhagen porcelain, Georg Jensen silverware, jewellery, watches, toys, travel bags, skin creams, photographic and audio equipment, lingerie, chocolates and, of course, alcohol. Most of the shops are open from 6 am to 11 pm daily.

GETTING THERE & AWAY
Air
Copenhagen Airport is Scandinavia's busiest hub, serving more than 13 million passengers a year with flights to nearly 150 destinations. There are daily direct flights to Copenhagen from numerous cities in Europe, Asia and North America, as well as a handful of Danish cities. More detailed information on flying to and from Copenhagen is in the Getting There & Away chapter.

Copenhagen Airport Copenhagen's modern international airport is in Kastrup, nine km south-east of the city centre. It has a large shopping area, a children's playground and a dozen eateries and bars, most located in the transfer area. There's also a simple minihotel for transfer passengers, with showers, saunas and 15 rooms where you can nap and pay by the hour.

You'll find a full-service Den Danske Bank on the 2nd floor of the departure hall that's open weekdays from 9.30 am to 4 pm as well as foreign exchange booths in the departure, arrival and transfer halls that are open daily from 6.30 am to 10 pm. The VAT refund bureau is on the 2nd floor of the departure hall next to the bank.

There's a post office in the international terminal between the arrival and departure halls that's open from 10 am to 5 pm Monday to Friday. In the transfer hall there's a Telecom Center with long-distance phone, fax, photocopy and postal services that's open from 7.45 am to 10 pm daily.

It's a sprawling airport, so when you get off the plane grab one of the free and ubiquitous baggage trolleys to cart your luggage around.

Lockers that cost 20 kr for 24 hours can be found in the arrival hall of the international terminal and in the domestic terminal. There's also a left-luggage room in the international terminal between the departure and arrival halls where you can leave luggage for 20 kr per piece per day.

If you're waiting for a flight, note that this is a 'silent' airport and there are no boarding calls, although there are plenty of monitor screens throughout the terminal.

Airline Offices Most airline offices are north of Central Station near the intersection of Vester Farimagsgade and Vesterbrogade. The SAS ticket office, in the SAS Royal Hotel, is open weekdays to 5.30 pm.

The following are the city locations of some of the major airlines flying into Copenhagen:

Aer Lingus
    (☎ 33 12 60 55), Vesterbrogade 1C
Air France
    (☎ 33 12 76 76), Vesterbrogade 1A
Alitalia
    (☎ 33 12 88 50), Vesterbrogade 6D
British Airways
    (☎ 33 14 60 00), Rådhuspladsen 16
Delta Air Lines
    (☎ 80 01 01 70), Nyropsgade 47
Finnair
    (☎ 33 12 08 55), Nyropsgade 47
Iberia
    (☎ 33 12 22 22), Jernbanegade 4
Icelandair
    (☎ 33 12 33 88), Vester Farimagsgade 1
KLM
    (☎ 31 51 26 26), Copenhagen Airport
LOT
    (☎ 33 14 58 11), Vester Farimagsgade 21
Lufthansa
    (☎ 33 37 73 33), Vester Farimagsgade 7
SAS
    (☎ 32 32 68 08), Hammerichsgade 1

Singapore Airlines
    (☎ 33 14 34 56), Vester Farimagsgade 9
Swissair
    (☎ 33 12 80 90), Vester Farimagsgade 6

Bus

Buses to Bornholm and to Ystad and Malmö in Sweden leave from Bernstorffsgade in front of Central Station. Buses to Prague and numerous other European cities, including Paris, Frankfurt and Amsterdam, also leave from Central Station. Buses to the Swedish cities of Halmsted and Kristianstad depart from Copenhagen Airport in Kastrup. More information is in the Getting There & Away chapter.

Buses to Århus (☎ 86 78 48 88) leave from Valby station and buses to Aalborg (☎ 33 25 74 11) leave from the Herlev station; both buses require reservations.

Train

All long-distance trains arrive and depart from Central Station, a huge complex with eateries and numerous services, including money exchange, a telephone office, a post office and a supermarket. There are lockers in the lower level near the Reventlowsgade exit and 15 kr showers at the underground toilets opposite the police office.

Car & Motorbike

The main highways into Copenhagen are the E20 from Jutland and Funen, the E47 from Helsingør and Sweden. If you're coming from the north on the E47, exit onto Lyngbyvej (route 19) and continue south to get into the heart of the city.

Car Rental The following companies have booths at the airport in the international terminal. Each also has an office in central Copenhagen:

Avis (☎ 33 15 22 99), Kampmannsgade 1
Budget (☎ 33 13 39 00), Nyropsgade 6
Europcar/Interrent (☎ 33 11 62 00), Gyldenløvesgade 17
Hertz (☎ 33 12 77 00), Ved Vesterport 3
Pitzner (☎ 33 11 12 34), Trommesalen 4

Hitching

Although hitching is not very good and we don't recommend it, if you want to try your luck it's best to start outside the city centre. For rides north, take bus No 1 to Vibenhus Runddel, at the north-west corner of Fælledparken in the Østerbro area. If you're heading towards Funen, take the S-train's line A to Ellebjerg station, at the south-western outskirts of the city. Keep in mind that it's illegal to hitch on motorways throughout Denmark.

Use It has a free message board that attempts to link up drivers and riders. Interstop (☎ 33 33 08 25), Kjeld Langesgade 14, provides a similar service but charges riders a fee of 0.10 kr per km (maximum 120 kr), plus 0.20 kr per km to the driver.

Boat

The Oslo ferry departs from Copenhagen at 5 pm daily and the Bornholm ferry departs at 11.30 pm nightly. Both leave from Kvæsthusbroen, north of Nyhavn, which can be reached by bus No 28. Boats to Malmö leave from Havnegade, south of Nyhavn; take bus Nos 27 or 26E. Ferries to Swinoujscie, Poland, leave from Nordre Toldbod, east of the Kastellet. Details are in the Getting There & Away chapter.

GETTING AROUND
To/From the Airport

The airport is 15 minutes and about 120 kr from the city centre by taxi. A bit slower is the SAS airport bus which makes frequent, though sometimes packed, runs from Central Station for 35 kr. If your baggage is light, you could also take local bus No 32 (15 kr) which runs frequently between Rådhuspladsen and the airport and takes about 35 minutes.

Bus & Train

Copenhagen has an extensive public transit system consisting of a metro rail network called S-train, whose 10 lines pass through Central Station (København H), and a vast bus system called HT, whose main terminus is nearby at Rådhuspladsen.

Buses and trains use a common fare system based on the number of zones you pass through. The basic fare of 10 kr for up to two zones covers most city runs and allows transfers between buses and trains on a single ticket as long as they're made within an hour. Third and subsequent zones cost 5 kr more with a maximum fare of 35 kr for travel throughout North Zealand. DSB state railways are also included in the common fare system as far north as Helsingør, west to Roskilde and south to Køge.

On buses, you board at the front and pay the fare to the driver (or stamp your clip card in the machine next to the driver). On S-trains, tickets are purchased at the station and then punched in the yellow time clock on the platform before boarding the train.

In place of buying a single destination ticket, you can buy a clip card (*klippekort*) good for 10 rides in two zones for 70 kr (three zones for 95 kr) or get a 24-hour ticket good for unlimited travel in all zones for 65 kr. Passengers who are stopped and found to be without a stamped ticket can receive a fine of 500 kr.

Children under age seven travel free, while those aged seven to 12 travel at half price.

All rides on Copenhagen's regional buses and trains are free for those holding a valid Copenhagen Card.

Trains and buses run from about 5 am (6 am on Sunday) to around 12.30 am, though buses continue to run through the night (charging double fare) on a few main routes.

The free Copenhagen city maps distributed by the tourist office and by Use It show bus routes (with numbers) and are very useful for finding your way around the city. If you plan to use buses extensively, you might want to buy HT's hefty timetable book *Busser og tog* (30 kr), which comes with a colour-coded bus route map.

Throughout this Copenhagen chapter we list the bus numbers of some of the more frequent buses to individual destinations, but since there can be as many as a dozen buses passing any particular place, our listing is often only a partial one.

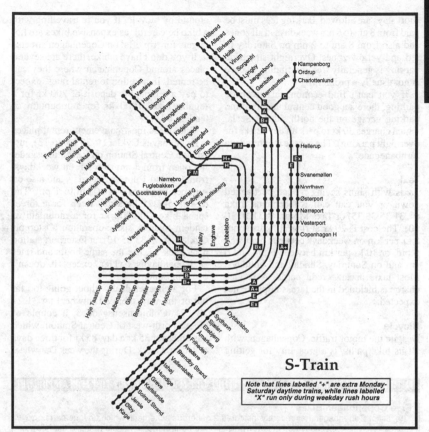

S-Train

Note that lines labelled "+" are extra Monday-
Saturday daytime trains, while lines labelled
"X" run only during weekday rush hours

For information on buses you can call ☎ 36 45 45 45, for trains ☎ 33 14 17 01.

For information on sightseeing buses, including a good-value public bus that tours the city centre, see the Organised Tours section earlier in this chapter.

Car & Motorbike

With the exception of the weekday-morning rush hour, when traffic can bottleneck coming into the city (and vice versa around 5 pm), traffic in Copenhagen is usually manageable. Getting around by car is not problematic, other than for the usual

challenge of finding an empty parking space in the most popular places.

To explore sights in the centre of the city, you're best off on foot or using public transport, but a car is quite convenient for reaching suburban sights.

Parking For streetside parking, buy a ticket from a kerbside billetautomat (an automated ticket machine) and place it inside the windscreen. Search out a blue, green or yellow zone where parking costs 4, 6 or 9 kr an hour respectively, with a 10-hour maximum; in red zones it's a steep 15 kr an hour and only short stays are allowed. Parking fees must be paid from 8 am to 6 pm weekdays in all zones and also from 8 am to 2 pm on Saturday in red and yellow zones. Overnight streetside parking is generally free and finding a space is not usually a problem.

If you can't find economical streetside parking, there's a good central underground parking garage on the north side of Scala, which charges 30 kr to park all day (25 kr for overnight parking). The garage is entered via Jernbanegade.

Taxi

Taxis with signs saying *fri* can be flagged down or you can call Københavns Taxa (☎ 31 35 35 35) or Taxa Motor (☎ 31 10 10 10). The cost is 20 kr at flagfall, plus about 8 kr per km on weekdays between 6 am and 6 pm, or 10 kr per km between 6 pm and 6 am and on Saturday, Sunday and holidays. Most taxis accept credit cards. A service charge is included in the fare, so tips are not expected.

Bicycle

Despite the motor traffic, Copenhagen, with all its bike paths, is a great city for getting around by bicycle. If you're travelling with a bike be careful, as expensive bikes are hot targets for 'rip offs' on Copenhagen streets.

If you don't have a bike, there are several places around Copenhagen where they can be rented. In addition to rental rates, expect to pay a refundable deposit of 200 kr for a regular bike, 1000 kr for a mountain or tandem bike.

One of the most convenient rental places is Københavns Cykler (☎ 33 33 86 13), just outside Central Station on Reventlowsgade. It's open from 8 am to 6 pm on weekdays, from 9 am to 1 pm on Saturday, and also on summer Sunday from 10 am to 1 pm. The cost is 50/225 kr a day/week for a three-speed bike, 200/900 kr for a mountain or tandem bike. A sister operation, Østerport Cykler (☎ 33 33 85 13), at Østerport station near track 13, has the same hours and rates as Københavns Cykler, except it doesn't open on Sunday.

For a cheaper deal without going too far out of the way, there's Danwheel (☎ 31 21 22 27), Colbjørnsensgade 3, a couple of blocks north-west of Central Station, which has bikes for 35 kr a day, 85 kr for three days or 165 kr a week. During the week Danwheel

Free Copenhagen Bikes

The city of Copenhagen has recently instituted a generous scheme in which anyone can borrow a bicycle for free. It's motivated in part by an effort to control motor vehicle traffic in the heart of the city, and its sponsors include the city council, private businesses and the local tourism office. During the first year of operation there were some 1000 bikes available.

While the bicycles are not streamlined and are certainly not practical for long-distance cycling, that's part of the plan – use of the cycles is limited to the city centre. To deter theft and minimise maintenance, the bicycles have a distinctive design that includes solid spokeless wheels with puncture-free tyres. The bikes can be found at about 100 widely scattered street stands in public places, including S-train stations. Each has a front-carrying basket that could fit a daypack or a bag of groceries.

The way it works is that if you're able to find a free bicycle, you deposit a 20 kr coin in the stand to release the bike. When you're done using the bicycle, you can return it to any stand and get your 20 kr coin back. ∎

This symbol marks Danish cycling routes

is open from 9 am to 5.30 pm, and from 9 am to 2 pm on weekends and holidays.

Except during weekday rush hours (from 6 to 9 am and from 3 to 6 pm), you can carry bikes on the S-trains for 11 kr. You can load your bicycle in any carriage that has a cycle symbol, provided that no more than two bikes are in each carriage and that you stay with the bike at all times. On the route between Hillerød and Helsingør there are no rush-hour restrictions.

For more information on cycling, see Cycling in the Activities section earlier in this chapter.

Boat

For information on getting around Copenhagen's waterfront by boat, see Canal Tours in the Organised Tours section earlier in this chapter.

Around Copenhagen

Many places in the greater Copenhagen area make for quick and easy excursions from the city. The following places offer a good variety of outings to woodlands, lakes, beaches and historic areas. For other day-trip possibilities that are farther afield, see the North Zealand chapter.

DRAGØR

If Copenhagen begins to feel crowded, consider an afternoon excursion to Dragør, a quiet maritime town on the island of Amager, a few km south of the airport. In the early 1550s King Christian II allowed Dutch farmers to settle in Amager to provide his court with flowers and produce, and Dragør still retains a bit of Dutch flavour.

Along the waterfront are fish shops, smokehouses, a sizeable fishing fleet and the **Dragør Museum**, a half-timbered house holding ship models and period furnishings. The museum is open Tuesday to Sunday, in the afternoons only, and costs 10 kr.

A fun way to spend time is to simply wander the narrow, winding cobblestone

streets leading up from the harbour, which are lined with the thatch-roofed, mustard-coloured houses that comprise the **old town**.

One interesting little ramble is to go north on the harbour-side Strandlinien, turn west on Toldergade where you'll pass the site of the old customs house at No 6, and continue up to Badstuevælen, an old square with some attractive houses dating from the 1790s (houses No 9 and 12). You could continue south from the square and then turn east on Strandgade to get back to the harbour.

There are a few restaurants near the waterfront, including an open-air café in the historic *Dragør Strandhotel* which has dishes such as pasta, pizza and calamari at moderate prices.

To get to Dragør take bus Nos 30 or 33 (15 kr) from Rådhuspladsen, a 35-minute ride.

CHARLOTTENLUND

Charlottenlund is a well-to-do coastal suburb just beyond the northern outskirts of Copenhagen. For being so close to the city, it has a decent **sandy beach**, albeit the smokestacks of Hellerup to the south are part of the backdrop.

Just inland of the beach is the moat-encircled **Charlottenlund Fort**, which now harbours a camping ground (see Camping under Copenhagen Places to Stay) and a moderately expensive seaview restaurant. There's not much to see of the old fort other than some cannons, but it's still a pleasant place, with wading ducks and lots of birdsong.

Danmarks Akvarium, an aquarium at Kavalergården 1, is 500 metres north of the beach on the inland side of the road. By Scandinavian standards it's a fairly large aquarium and the collection, which is labelled and well-presented, includes cold-water fish, tropical fish, nurse sharks, sea turtles, crocodiles and piranhas. It's open daily from 10 am to 6 pm (to 4 or 5 pm in the low season). Admission is 45 kr for adults and 25 kr for children. There's a cafeteria.

From the aquarium parking lot a path leads 200 metres west to **Charlottelund Slotshave**, an attractive three-storey manor

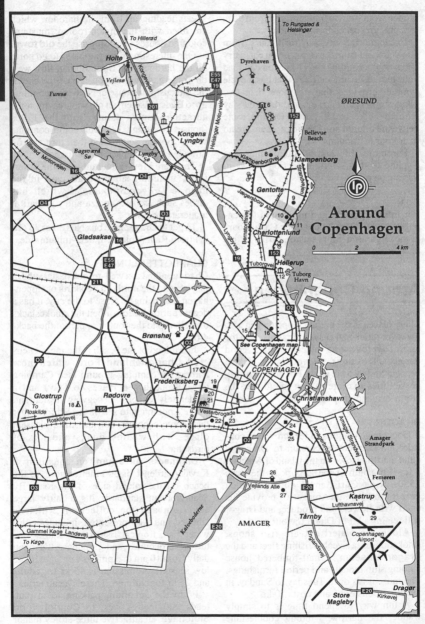

Around
Copenhagen

PLACES TO STAY		OTHER			
				10	Danmarks Akvarium
				12	Eksperimentarium
4	Lyngby Vandrerhjem	1	Holte Havn (Boat	15	Zoologisk Museum
11	Charlottelund Strand-		Rentals)	16	Parken
	park & Charlottelund	2	Frederiksdal (Boat	17	Frederiksberg Hospital
	Fort/Beach		Rentals)	20	Royal Copenhagen
13	Bellahøj Vandrerhjem	3	Frilandsmuseet		Porcelain Factory
14	Bellahøj Camping	5	Københavns Golfklub	21	Copenhagen Zoo
18	Absalon Camping	6	Eremitagen		(Zoologisk Have)
19	SAS Falconer Hotel	7	Bakken	22	Carlsberg Brewery
24	SAS Scandinavia Hotel	8	Klampenborg Galop-	23	Vesterbro Svømmehal
26	Copenhagen/Amager		bane	25	Københavns Universitet
	Vandrerhjem	9	Charlottenlund Trav-	27	Bella Center
28	SAS Globetrotter Hotel		bane	29	Airport Terminal

house that's now used for offices. Walkways lead around the park-like grounds, making for an enjoyable stroll if you're already in the area.

If you're interested in horse races, Charlottenlund's other 'sight' is **Charlottenlund Travbane**, a trotting track that's open on Wednesday evenings and weekend afternoons.

Bus No 6 from central Copenhagen goes by the beach, aquarium and trotting track.

KLAMPENBORG

Klampenborg, only 20 minutes from Central Station on the S-train's line C, is a favourite spot for Copenhageners on family outings.

A few hundred metres east of Klampenborg station is **Bellevue beach**, a sandy beach that gets packed with sunbathers in summer.

A 10-minute walk west from Klampenborg station is the 400-year-old **Bakken**, the world's oldest amusement park. A blue-collar version of Tivoli, it's a honky-tonk carnival of bumper cars, roller coasters, slot machines and beer halls. It's open from 2 pm to midnight daily from late March to late August. Entry is free. Children's rides cost 5.50 kr, adult rides from 14 to 20 kr, and there are discounted multi-use passes.

Bakken is at the southern edge of **Dyrehaven** (more formally called Jægersborg Dyrehave), an expansive 1000-hectare woodland of beech trees and meadows

crossed with an alluring network of walking and cycling trails. Dyrehaven was established as a royal hunting ground in 1669 and has evolved into the capital's most popular picnicking area. Dyrehaven also contains the **Københavns Golfklub**, an 18-hole golf course, and **Klampenborg Galopbane**, a horse-racing track immediately south of Bakken.

At the centre of Dyrehaven is the old manor house **Eremitagen**, a good vantage point for spotting herds of grazing deer, which are especially abundant in the meadows west of the house. In all, there are about 2000 deer in the park, mostly fallow deer, but also red deer and Japanese sika deer. Among the red deer are a few rare white specimens that were imported from Germany in 1737 and are now extinct there. Eremitagen can be reached by walking two km north of Bakken along the main route, Christiansholmsvej, although it can also be reached from numerous other points in the park as most of the largest trails lead out like spokes from Eremitagen.

Hackney coaches provide horse-drawn rides into the park from the Dyrehaven entrance just north of the railway station. The cost is 100 kr for 15 minutes; the coaches carry up to five passengers, but it's most romantic with two! If you want to explore by cycle, bikes can be rented at Klampenborg station.

There are a number of eating possibilities in Klampenborg. Numerous places in

Bakken sell simple carnival-style fare. For a nice sit-down restaurant there's the popular *Peter Lieps Hus*, a few minutes walk north of Bakken near the corner of Fortunvej and Christiansholmsvej, which serves smørrebrød sandwiches, game specialities and other Danish food at moderate prices.

LYNGBY

Lyngby's main sight is **Frilandsmuseet**, a sprawling open-air museum of old countryside dwellings, workshops and barns that have been gathered from sites around Denmark. The buildings are intended to give a sense of Danish rural life as it was in various regions and along different social strata. Consequently, the houses range from rather grand affairs to meagre, sod-roofed cottages. There's a light schedule of demonstrations such as folk dancing, wool spinning and weaving, mostly occurring on weekends, particularly on Sunday.

Opening hours are from 10 am to 5 pm from late March to September and from 10 am to 3 pm in October; it's closed on Monday and in winter. Admission is 30 kr for adults,

free for children under 16. The museum, at Kongevejen 100, is a 10-minute signposted walk from Sorgenfri station, which is 25 minutes from Central Station on the S-train's line B. You can also take bus Nos 184 or 194, both of which stop at the entrance.

The Lyngby area also has a number of **lakes**, including Furesø, the deepest lake in Denmark. It's possible to rent row boats for 50 kr an hour at Holte Havn (☎ 42 42 04 49), a restaurant at 22 Vejlesøvej, and row around either Furesø or the smaller Vejlesø, which are connected by a channel. Holte Havn is open from 10 am to midnight and is near the S-train Holte station, two stops north of Sorgenfri.

If you prefer canoeing, Frederiksdal (☎ 42 85 67 70) at Nybrovej 520 (by the locks) rents canoes as well as row boats for use on the river Mølleåen and the lakes Lyngbysø, Bagsværdsø and Furesø, all of which are interconnected. The rental cost is 48 kr an hour, 120 kr for three hours. Frederiksdal is open from 10 am to 9 pm. To get there, get off at the S-train's Lyngby station and take bus No 191.

North Zealand

Considering its proximity to Copenhagen, the northern part of Zealand is surprisingly rural, with small farms, wheat fields and beech woodlands. It also has fine beaches and some notable historic sights.

One of the most popular day trips from Copenhagen is a loop tour taking in Frederiksborg Castle in Hillerød and Kronborg Castle in Helsingør, with a stop at Fredensborg Palace in between. With an early start you might even have time to continue on to one of the north shore beaches or stop off at the Louisiana modern art museum in Humlebæk on the way back to the city. (The Copenhagen Card allows free admission to some of these attractions. For more information see the Copenhagen Card aside in the Copenhagen chapter.)

However, if you're not tight for time, North Zealand has a number of destinations that invite a longer stay. You could even hop on a ferry in Helsingør and skip over to Sweden for about the same price as a bottle of beer!

If you're driving between Helsingør and Copenhagen ignore the motorway and take the coastal road, Strandvej (route 152), which is far more scenic.

Information on Charlottenlund, Klampenborg and Lyngby, which are just north of Copenhagen proper, is in the Around Copenhagen section at the end of the Copenhagen chapter.

HIGHLIGHTS

- The lakeside Frederiksborg Castle with its lavish interior (Hillerød)
- Louisiana, Denmark's top modern art museum (Humlebæk)
- The summertime Roskilde Festival, northern Europe's largest rock music event
- Roskilde's cathedral, which houses the tombs of 37 Danish kings and queens
- Kronborg Castle, the setting for Shakespeare's *Hamlet* (Helsingør)
- The unhurried feel of the fishing hamlets along the north coast
- Sandy beaches at Hornbæk and Tisvildeleje

Inland Towns

The inland area of North Zealand, sometimes referred to as the heartland, has two towns of special interest to visitors, Hillerød and Fredensborg.

HILLERØD

Hillerød, 30 km north of Copenhagen, is a small town centred around a grand lakeside castle, Frederiksborg Slot. The main route through town, Slotsgade, leads directly from the central square, Torvet, to the castle gate.

Although the town, which is an administrative centre and transportation hub for North Zealand, isn't notably quaint in itself, Hillerød can be a good place to break for the night. Not only is there a commendable low-priced hotel, the light on the russet-red castle is particularly lovely in the evening. You can get picturesque views of the castle by following the waterside path that skirts the castle

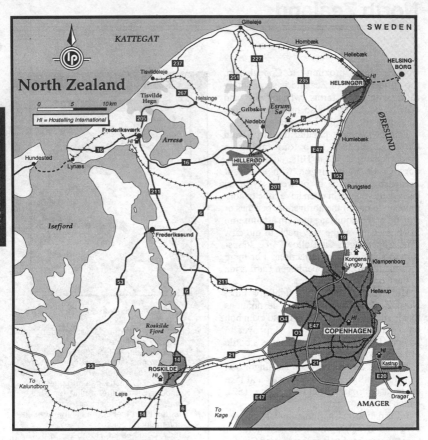

lake and provides an alternative route to
Slotsgade. If you feel like taking a longer
stroll there are some paths through Slotshaven, an expansive privet garden immediately north of the castle and lake.

The little *Frederiksborg* ferry sails across
the castle lake about every 30 minutes daily
from May to September, landing at three
small piers: one just north of Torvet, another
behind the tourist office and the third north
of the castle on the road to Slotshaven. It
costs 15 kr for adults, 5 kr for children, or is
free with the Copenhagen Card (as is the
castle).

Information

The Hillerød Turistbureau (☎ 42 26 28 52),
Slotsgade 52, 3400 Hillerød, is 75 metres
east of the castle entrance. It's open from
9 am to 4 pm on weekdays and 10 am to 1 pm
on Saturday, except from June to August
when it's open from 9 am to 6 pm on weekdays and 10 am to 5 pm on Saturday.

Frederiksborg Slot

Frederiksborg Slot (Frederiksborg Castle) is
an impressive Dutch Renaissance castle that
spreads across three islets at the east side of
lake Slotsø. The oldest part of Frederiksborg

Slot dates from the reign of Frederik II, after whom the castle is named, but most of the present structure was built in the early 1600s by Frederik II's more extravagant son, Christian IV.

As you enter the main gate, you'll pass old stable buildings dating from the 1560s and then cross over a moat to the second islet, where you'll enter an expansive central courtyard with a grandly ornate Neptune fountain. The relatively modest wings that flank either side of the fountain once served as residences for court officers and government officials. A second bridge crosses to the northernmost islet, the site of the main body of the castle, which served as home to Danish royalty for more than a century.

Frederiksborg Slot was ravaged by a fire in 1859. The royal family, unable to undertake the costly repairs, decided to give up the property. Carlsberg beer baron JC Jacobsen then stepped into the scene and spearheaded a drive to restore the castle as a national museum, a function it still serves today.

The sprawling castle has a magnificent interior with gilded ceilings, wall-sized tapestries, paintings, memorabilia and antiques. The exhibits occupy 70 rooms. The richly embellished Riddershalen (Knights Hall) and the coronation chapel, where Danish monarchs were crowned from 1671 to 1840, are alone worth the admission fee. The chapel, incidentally, was spared serious fire damage and has the original interior that was commissioned by Christian IV, including a lavish hand-carved altar and pulpit made by Mores of Hamburg in 1606 and a priceless Compenius organ. The organ is played each Thursday from 1.30 to 2 pm.

Frederiksborg Slot is open daily from 10 am to 5 pm, May to September; from 10 am to 4 pm in April and October; and from 11 am to 3 pm the rest of the year. Admission costs 30 kr for adults and 5 kr for children, or is free with a Copenhagen Card. Outside opening hours visitors are still free to stroll around the grounds and enter the castle courtyard.

If you arrive at Hillerød station by train or bus, follow the signs to Torvet and then continue north-west along Slotsgade to the castle, a 15-minute walk in all. If you arrive by car, there's free parking west of the castle off Frederiksværksgade.

Places to Stay

There's a small three-star camping ground, *Hillerød Camping* (☎ & fax 42 26 48 54), at Dyrskuepladsen, 3400 Hillerød, about a 20-minute walk directly south of the castle along Slangerupgade. It's open from May to mid-September and charges 44 kr per person. There are cooking facilities and a coin laundry, and cabins and caravans can be rented.

KFUM's Missionshotel (☎ 42 26 01 89, fax 42 26 01 68), Slotsgade 5, 3400 Hillerød, is an older, unpretentious 23-room hotel with a classic guesthouse ambience, complete with wallpapered guest rooms, Victorian lamps and a TV lounge with upholstered chairs. The rooms vary, but most have a wash basin, desk and two single beds that can be arranged as a double. It's in an ideal location, just south of Torvet and midway between the railway station and the castle. Singles/doubles cost 200/300 kr, plus 100 kr extra if you want a room with a private bath.

Places to Eat

There are a number of inexpensive places to eat on Slotsgade, a few minutes walk from the castle. At Slotsgade 38 is a *McDonald's*, 200 metres farther east is an *Irma* grocery store and just beyond that is *Gonzales Cantina* at Slotsgade 27D, which has the best pizza in town. Gonzales also has good-value 29 kr lunch specials (from 11 am to 4 pm) including spaghetti, pizza, fish or beef, while at other times generous calamari or beef dishes with salad and chips cost around 50 kr, and pitta-bread sandwiches cost 25 kr.

Getting There & Away

The S-train (A & E lines) runs every 10 minutes from Copenhagen to Hillerød (35 kr), a 40-minute ride. Trains from Hillerød run east to Helsingør (30 kr), north to Gilleleje (25 kr), and west to Tisvildeleje (25 kr).

Buses also link Hillerød with North Zealand towns. Bus No 305 goes to Gilleleje; Nos 306, 336 and 339 go to Hornbæk; and Nos 336 and 339 go to Fredensborg. Hillerød's bus terminal is immediately north of its railway station.

FREDENSBORG

Fredensborg is a quiet town with a royal palace, a lakeside location and some pleasant walking tracks.

The south-east shore of Esrum Sø, Denmark's second-largest lake, borders Fredensborg and offers swimming, boating and fishing. Along the shore you can sometimes spot osprey and cormorants, while the surrounding woods are the habitat of roe deer. It's a 10-minute walk west from the palace gate along Skipperallé to Skipperhuset, where there's a lakeside restaurant, a ferry service and rowing boats for hire. The main beach is nearby. The ferry, which operates from June to August, crosses the lake twice daily, at 12.30 and 4 pm (40 kr), and can take you to Gribskov, a forested area with trails and picnic grounds that borders the west side of Esrum Sø.

Slotsgade, the road that leads directly to the castle gate, has a number of historic buildings dating from the 1700s, including the **Hotel Store Kro** at Slotsgade 6; **Villa Bournonville**, the former home of the 19th century balletmaster Auguste Bournonville at Slotsgade 9; and the **Havremagasinet** at Slotsgade 11, which once served as horse stables. The **Kunstnegården**, an art and crafts gallery a bit farther south at Slotsgade 17, was originally an inn built in 1722.

Information

Tourist Office The lobby of the hostel, at Østrupvej 3, doubles as the tourist office, where you can find racks of brochures on Fredensborg and the North Zealand area; it's open daily from 7 am to 11 pm. This informal little office can arrange bicycle rentals and provide details on obtaining a fishing licence.

Money Den Danske Bank is located at Jernbanegade 5.

Post The post office is at Helsingørvej 2 at the intersection with Jernbanegade.

Fredensborg Slot

Fredensborg Slot (Fredensborg Palace), the royal family's residence during most of the summer, was built in 1720 by King Frederik IV. It was named Fredensborg, which means Peace Palace, to commemorate the peace which Denmark had recently achieved with its Scandinavian neighbours. The palace certainly reflects the more tranquil mood of the day and is largely in the style of a country manor house, an abrupt contrast to the moat-encircled fortresses of Kronborg and Frederiksborg castles that preceded it.

The main mansion was designed by the leading Danish architect of the day, JC Krieger, and is in Italian baroque style with marble floors and a large central cupola. It's fronted by an expansive octagonal courtyard framed by two-storey buildings.

Partly because of its spread-out design, the palace is not as impressive a sight as other Danish royal palaces in North Zealand. Fredensborg's interior can only be visited during July (guided tours cost 10 kr and take place every half-hour between 1 and 5 pm), when the royal family takes their holiday elsewhere. At other times in the summer, when the queen is in residence, you might want to time your arrival to catch the changing of the guard that takes place just before noon.

The palace is backed by 120 hectares of **wooded parkland** that's crisscrossed with trails and open to the public year round. Take a stroll through **Normandsdalen**, west of the palace, to a circular amphitheatre with 70 life-size sandstone statues of Norwegian folk characters – fishermen, farmers etc – in traditional dress. If you continue a few minutes west from there you'll reach lake Esrum Sø, which is skirted by another trail.

To get to the palace from the railway station take a left onto Stationsvej and then turn right onto Jernbanegade, which merges with Slotsgade near the palace gate; the whole walk takes about 10 minutes.

Places to Stay

The hostel, *Fredensborg Vandrerhjem*, (☎ 42 28 03 15, fax 42 28 16 56), Østrupvej 3, 3480 Fredensborg, is just 300 metres south of the castle. Most of the 88 beds are in double rooms with a desk, sink and private toilet, while the showers are in the hall. The hostel staff claim you'll never have to share a room with anyone you're not travelling with and there are no limits on the length of stay. There's a TV room, a playroom with toys and darts, a garden room and a guest kitchen. The cost is 84 kr per person. It's open year round. To get there turn west off Slotsgade at Hotel Store Kro and continue for about 50 metres.

Just outside the palace gate is *Hotel Store Kro* (☎ 42 28 00 47, fax 42 28 45 61), Slotsgade 6, 3480 Fredensborg, a classic inn the earliest parts of which were built by King Frederik IV in 1723 to accommodate palace guests. No two rooms are alike, but all have traditional décor as well as a private bathroom, TV, phone and minibar. The standard rates are 850/1150 kr for singles/doubles, but in summer there's a better-value package that includes dinner for about the same price. The hotel is a member of the Romantik Hotels chain.

The *Pension Bondehuset* (☎ 42 28 01 12), Sørupvej 14, Box 6, 3480 Fredensborg, a converted farmhouse dating from the early 1700s, is an interesting option if you're looking for a rural getaway. It's got a lakeside location on the western outskirts of Fredensborg, classic manor house furnishings and rowing boats for guests to use. Rooms have private baths and cost 410/665 kr for singles/doubles with breakfast or 600/1075 kr with full board.

Places to Eat

There's a good fruit stand and bakery, *Poggenborgs Bageri*, at Jernbanegade 20, next to the *Irma* grocery store, about halfway between the railway station and the palace. A moderately priced Chinese restaurant, *Den*

Fredelige Kinesiske Stue, is opposite the bakery at Jernbanegade 19.

For a splurge, consider a meal at the *Hotel Store Kro*, which has an engaging Old World charm and very good food. At lunch, you can get a grilled fetta cheese salad, a club sandwich or a crayfishburger for a reasonable 70 kr, or a two-course meal for 195 kr. Dinner is a three-course meal for 295 kr that changes nightly, featuring creative Danish dishes with the likes of smoked trout on asparagus salad, venison in wine sauce and a grape-marzipan dessert tart; children under 12 eat for half price.

Getting There & Away

Fredensborg is midway on the railway line between Hillerød (12 minutes, 10 kr) and Helsingør (20 minutes, 25 kr). Trains run from early morning until after midnight, departing from Hillerød at 41 minutes after the hour and from Helsingør at 33 minutes after the hour; there are extra trains during weekday rush hours.

Bus Nos 336 and 339 leave Fredensborg station for Hillerød at 40 minutes past the hour, stopping en route at Fredensborg Slot; the bus takes 20 minutes and costs 10 kr.

Øresund Coast

The Øresund Coast, the eastern shore of North Zealand, extends north from Copenhagen to the Helsingør area and is largely a run of small seaside suburbs and yachting harbours. It is the Øresund (the Sound) that connects the Baltic Sea in the south with the Kattegat in the north and separates Denmark from Sweden. On clear days you can look across the sound and see southern Sweden on the opposite shore.

Partly because of the exclusive homes along the waterfront, the local promotion authorities sometimes grandly refer to this area as the Danish Riviera. In reality its main appeal to visitors lies not in its beaches but in two museums, one dedicated to author Karen Blixen, the other to modern art.

RUNGSTED

The coastal town of Rungsted is the site of Rungstedlund, the estate which houses the Karen Blixen museum.

Rungstedlund was originally built as an inn around 1500. King Karl XII of Sweden stayed at the inn around 1700 and the Danish lyric poet Johannes Ewald, who wrote Denmark's national anthem, was a boarder from 1773 to 1776. The property was later turned into a private residence and in 1879 was purchased by Karen Blixen's father, Wilhelm Dinesen. Karen was born at Rungstedlund in 1885 and lived there off-and-on until her death in 1962.

The tourist office is in the white pavilion on Rungstedvej, not far from its intersection with Strandvej.

Karen Blixen Museet

Karen Blixen's former home, now a museum, is furnished much the way she left

---

Karen Blixen

Karen Blixen was born Karen Christenze Dinesen on 17 April 1885 in Rungsted, a well-to-do community north of Copenhagen. She studied art in Copenhagen, Rome and Paris. In 1914, when she was 28 and eager to escape from the confines of her bourgeois family, she married her second cousin Baron Bror von Blixen-Finecke, after having a failed love affair with his twin brother Hans. It was a marriage of convenience – she wanted his title and he needed her money.

The couple then moved to Kenya and started a coffee plantation which Karen was left to manage. The baron, who had several extramarital affairs, eventually infected Karen with syphilis. She came home to Denmark for medical treatment, but subsequently returned to Africa and divorced the baron in 1925.

In 1932, after her coffee plantation had failed and the great love of her life, Englishman Denys Finch-Hatton, had died in a tragic plane crash, Karen Blixen left Africa and returned to the family estate in Rungsted, where she began to write. Danes were slow to take to Blixen's writings, in part because she consistently wrote about the aristocracy in approving terms and used an old-fashioned idiomatic style that some thought arrogant. Her insistence on being called 'Baroness' also took its toll on her popularity in a Denmark bent on minimising class disparity.

Following rejection by publishers in Denmark and England, her first book, *Seven Gothic Tales*, a compilation of short stories set in the 19th century, was published in New York in 1934 (under the pseudonym Isak Dinesen) and was so well received that it was chosen as a Book-of-the-Month selection. It was only after her success in the USA that Danish publishers took a serious interest in her works.

In 1937, Blixen's landmark *Out of Africa*, the memoirs of her life in Kenya, was published in both Danish and English. This was followed by *Winter's Tales* in 1942, *The Angelic Avengers* in 1944, *Last Tales* in 1957, *Anecdotes of Destiny* in 1958 and *Shadows on the Grass* in 1960. Three of Blixen's books were published after her death: *Daguerreotypes and Other Essays*, *Carnival: Entertainments and Posthumous Tales* and *Letters from Africa 1914-1931*. Two of Blixen's works were turned into the Oscar-winning films *Out of Africa* and *Babette's Feast*.

A few years before her death, Blixen arranged for her estate to be turned over to the private Rungstedlund Foundation. For years the foundation had only enough money to maintain the grounds as a bird sanctuary, but the posthumous book sales that were spurred by the success of the films made it possible to turn her former home into a museum which opened in 1991. ∎

it and contains photographs, paintings, Masai spears and shields and other African mementoes including the gramophone that Blixen's lover, Denys Finch-Hatton, gave her. On the desk in her study, beside a photograph of Denys, is the old Corona typewriter Blixen used to write her novels.

One wing of the museum, a converted carriage house and stables, has a library of Blixen's books in many languages, a café, a bookshop and a small theatre featuring audio-visual presentations on Blixen's life. The grounds contain gardens and a wood, part of which has been set aside as a bird sanctuary. Blixen lies buried in a little clearing shaded by a sprawling beech tree, her grave marked by a simple stone slab inscribed with just her name.

From May to September the museum is open daily from 10 am to 5 pm. From October to April it's open from 1 to 4 pm on Wednesday, Thursday and Friday and from 11 am to 4 pm on Saturday and Sunday. Admission is 30 kr for adults, free for children, and free with a Copenhagen Card.

The museum is at Strandvej 111, opposite the yacht harbour and 1.25 km from the railway station. To get there, walk north from the railway station, turn right at the lights onto Rungstedvej and then at its intersection with Strandvej go south about 200 metres and you'll come to the museum; the whole walk takes about 15 minutes.

Getting There & Away

All Copenhagen-Helsingør trains stop at Rungsted. The fare is 25 kr from Helsingør, 35 kr from Copenhagen. DSB, the national railway, offers a special ticket that includes museum admission and return fare from Copenhagen for 65 kr.

HUMLEBÆK

The coastal town of Humlebæk has a couple of boat harbours, bathing beaches and some wooded areas, but the main focus for visitors is the Louisiana museum.

Louisiana

Louisiana, Denmark's most renowned modern art museum, is on a seaside knoll in a strikingly modernistic complex with sculpture-laden grounds. The sculptures on the lawns, which include works by Henry Moore, Alexander Calder and Max Ernst, create an engaging interplay between art, architecture and landscape. Louisiana is a fascinating place to visit even for those not passionate about modern art.

The museum's permanent collection, mainly paintings and graphic art from the postwar era, are creatively displayed and grouped. There are sections on constructivism, abstract expressionism, minimal art, pop art, COBRA-group artists and staged photography. Some of the more prominent Danish artists represented are Asger Jorn, Robert Jacobsen and Richard Mortensen.

The museum also has top-notch temporary exhibits, which in recent years have featured such diverse themes as an Andy Warhol retrospective, Toulouse-Lautrec & Paris, Claude Monet, and the works of the controversial American photographer Robert Mapplethorpe. The museum also presents concerts and films and has a shop and café.

Louisiana museum is one km from Humlebæk station, a 10-minute signposted walk north on Strandvej. It's open daily year round from 10 am to 5 pm, to 6 pm on weekends and to 10 pm on Wednesday. Admission costs 48 kr for adults, 15 kr for children, and is free with the Copenhagen Card. Fees can be higher for special exhibitions. DSB offers a Louisiana excursion ticket for 85 kr that includes the museum admission and the return train fare from Copenhagen.

Places to Eat

There are a number of simple eating options along Strandvej just outside Humlebæk station. To the south of the station is *Slagter Bagger*, a deli with inexpensive sandwiches as well as cheeses and meats sold by weight. Adjacent is a fruit stand and around the corner is a small grocery store that carries fresh bread and other bakery products. To the

NORTH ZEALAND

north of the station there's a pizzeria, *La Strada*.

If you're looking for a place to have a picnic lunch, immediately east of Louisiana museum there's a bench on the cliffs and steps leading down to a rocky beach.

Getting There & Away

Trains leave Copenhagen a few times each hour for Humlebæk, a ride which takes 30 minutes if you catch the fast train (which leaves Central Station weekdays at 11 minutes past the hour) and costs 35 kr. The train from Helsingør takes 13 minutes and costs 15 kr. Though its not as fast, you could also take bus No 388 which runs between Copenhagen and Helsingør.

HELSINGØR

Helsingør (Elsinore), at the narrowest point of the Øresund, the strait that separates Denmark from Sweden, has long been a busy port town. Indeed with ferries shuttling to and from Sweden 24 hours a day, this is the world's busiest shipping channel, a virtual water highway crossed with ships carrying everything from passengers and cargo to tour buses and railway cars.

Although Swedish shoppers on day trips comprise many of Helsingør's visitors (which accounts for the plethora of liquor shops near the harbour), the town has enough sightseeing possibilities to make for a half day of enjoyable touring.

Helsingør has maintained some of its historic quarters, including a block of old homes and warehouses known as Sundtoldkarreen (Sound Dues Square), at the north-east end of Strangade. Helsingør's top sight, perched across the harbour at the north side of town, is the imposing Kronborg Slot, made famous as the Elsinore Castle in Shakespeare's *Hamlet*.

Information

Tourist Office The Helsingør Turistbureau (☎ 49 21 13 33, fax 49 21 15 77), Havnepladsen 3, 3000 Helsingør, is opposite the railway station. Apropos of being at a port of entry, it offers a wide range of services,

including booking accommodation, renting bikes (40 kr a day) and selling camping passes, hostel association cards and phonecards. From 15 June to 31 August it's open from 9.30 am to 7 pm, Monday to Friday, and 10 am to 6 pm on Saturday, while the rest of the year it's open from 9.30 am to 5 pm on weekdays and from 10 am to 1 pm on Saturday.

Money Den Danske Bank, at Stengade 55, is open from 9.30 am to 4 pm Monday to Friday (to 6 pm on Thursday).

Post The post office, at the south-east side of the railway station, is open from 9 am to 5 pm, Monday to Friday, and from 9 am to 1 pm on Saturday.

Other Facilities There are lockers, where you can store your bags while you tour the town, at both Helsingør station and the ScandLines ferry terminal on Færgevej.

There's a coin laundry, Vasketeria, on Strandgade just west of the Rådmand Davids Hus café. It's open from 7 am to 9 pm daily and it costs 31 kr to wash a load of clothes.

Stengades Apotek, a pharmacy, is at Stengade 46.

Walking Tour

This pleasant little walk through the oldest parts of Helsingør makes a scenic, and virtually direct, route to Kronborg Slot. Begin the walk at the north side of the tourist office up Brostræde, a pedestrian alley, and then continue north along Sanct Anna Gade.

You'll soon come to the 15th century gothic cathedral **Sankt Olai Kirke**, which occupies the block between Stengade and Sankt Olai Gade. The cathedral has an ornate altar and baptistry and is open to the public from 10 am to 4 pm (until 2 pm in winter); admission is free.

The **Helsingør Bymuseum**, at Sanct Anna Gade 36, was built by the monks of the adjacent monastery in 1516 to serve as a sailors' hospital and had stints as a poorhouse and town library before being converted to a history museum in 1973. The hodgepodge of

NED FRIARY

NED FRIARY

NED FRIARY

NED FRIARY

NED FRIARY

A	B	C
D		
E		

North Zealand
A: North Zealand house
B: Windmill, Frilandsmuseet, Lyngby
C: Gatehouse of Ledreborg manor house

D: Frederiksborg Slot, Hillerød
E: Frederiksborg Slot, Hillerød

North Zealand
Top: Eremitagen, the manor house at Dyrehaven, Klampenborg
Bottom: Deer in the field adjacent to Eremitagen, Dyrehaven, Klampenborg

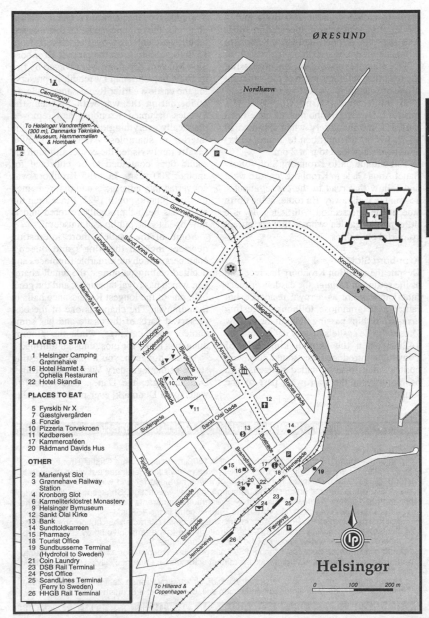

ØRESUND

Nordhavn

Campingvej

To Helsingør Vandrerhjem
(300 m), Danmarks Tekniske
Museum, Hammermøllen
& Hornbæk

Grønnehavevej

Kronborgvej

Sanct Anna Gade

Lundegade

Marienlyst Allé

Allégade

Kronborgvej

Kongensgade

Stjernegade

Bjergegade

Sanct Anna Gade

Sophie Brahes Gade

Axeltorv

Sankt Olai Gade

Sudergade

Brostræde

Fiolgade

Bramstræde

Havnegade

Stengade

Strandgade

Jernbanevej

Færgevej

To Hillerød &
Copenhagen

Helsingør

0   100   200 m

PLACES TO STAY

1 Helsingør Camping
   Grønnehave
16 Hotel Hamlet &
   Ophelia Restaurant
22 Hotel Skandia

PLACES TO EAT

5 Fyrskib Nr X
7 Gæstgivergården
8 Fonzie
10 Pizzeria Torvekroen
11 Kødbørsen
17 Kammercaféen
20 Rådmand Davids Hus

OTHER

2 Marienlyst Slot
3 Grønnehave Railway
   Station
4 Kronborg Slot
6 Karmeliterklostret Monastery
9 Helsingør Bymuseum
12 Sankt Olai Kirke
13 Bank
14 Sundtoldkarreen
15 Pharmacy
18 Tourist Office
19 Sundbusserne Terminal
   (Hydrofoil to Sweden)
21 Coin Laundry
23 DSB Rail Terminal
24 Post Office
25 ScandLines Terminal
   (Ferry to Sweden)
26 HHGB Rail Terminal

exhibits includes about 200 dolls and a model of Helsingør as it appeared in 1801. The museum is open daily from noon to 4 pm and entry costs 10 kr.

The **Karmeliterklostret**, encompassing the red brick buildings north of the museum, is one of Scandinavia's best-preserved medieval monasteries. King Christian II's mistress, Dyveke, is thought to have been buried at the monastery when she died in 1517. It's open from noon to 3 pm (10 kr) and there's a guided tour at 2 pm.

To continue on to Kronborg Slot, follow Sanct Anna Gade to Kronborgvej, turn right and follow that road to the castle, about a 15-minute walk away. En route, at the north side of the intersection with Allégade, is a little public garden whose flowers attract colourful butterflies.

Kronborg Slot

Despite the attention Kronborg has received as the setting of *Hamlet*, the castle's primary function was not as a royal residence but rather as a grandiose tollhouse, wresting taxes from ships passing through the narrow Øresund. The castle's history dates from the 1420s, when the Danish king Erik of Pomerania introduced the 'sound dues' and built a small fortress, called Krogen, on a promontory at the narrowest part of the sound.

Financed by the generous revenue of shipping tolls, the original medieval fortress was rebuilt and enlarged by Frederik II from 1574 to 1585 to form the present Kronborg Slot. Much of Kronborg was ravaged by fire in 1629, but Christian IV rebuilt it, preserving the castle's earlier Renaissance style. In 1658, during the war with Sweden, the Swedes occupied Kronborg and removed practically everything of value, leaving the interior in shambles. After that, Danish royalty rarely visited the castle, although the sound dues continued to be collected for another 200 years. In 1785 Kronborg was converted into a barracks and that remained its chief function until 1922. Since then the castle has been thoroughly restored and is now open to the public as a museum.

Some of the castle's more interesting quarters include the king's and queen's chambers, which have marble fireplaces and detailed ceiling paintings; the small chamber, which has royal tapestries; and the great hall, one of the longest Renaissance halls in Scandinavia. The chapel is one of the best preserved parts of the castle and has some choice wood carvings, while the gloomy dungeons make for most unusual touring.

In the dungeon you'll pass the resting statue of the legendary Viking chief Holger Danske (Ogier the Dane), who is said to watch over Denmark, ever-ready to come to

---

To Be or Not To Be

When Shakespeare penned his tragedy *Hamlet* in 1602, he used Elsinore Castle (Kronborg Slot) as its setting. There is no evidence that Shakespeare ever visited Helsingør, but when the stately Kronborg Slot was completed in 1585, word of it was heralded far and wide and it apparently struck Shakespeare as a fitting setting. Although the play was fiction, Shakespeare did include two actual Danish nobles in his plot – Frederik Rosenkrantz and Knud Gyldenstierne (Guildenstern), both of whom had visited the English court in the 1590s.

The fact that Hamlet, the Prince of Denmark, was a fictional character, has not deterred legions of sightseers from visiting 'Hamlet's Castle'. Indeed, due to the fame given it by Shakespeare, Kronborg is the most widely known castle in all of Scandinavia.

During the past few decades, Kronborg Slot has been used many times as the setting for staged performances of *Hamlet*, featuring such prominent actors as Sir Laurence Olivier, Richard Burton and Michael Redgrave.

However, a recent cinematic version of *Hamlet*, directed by Franco Zeffirelli and starring Mel Gibson as the prince, was filmed not on Danish soil, but rather at a Scottish castle. ■

her aid should the hour of need arise. The low-ceilinged dungeon includes areas that once served as soldiers' quarters and store-rooms for salted fish, which these days are homes for nesting bats!

Also in the castle is the **Handels-og Søfartsmuseet** (Danish Maritime Museum), a collection of ship models, paintings, nautical instruments and sea charts illustrating the history of Danish shipping and trade. Model ship enthusiasts will find it interesting. The remains of the original Krogen fortress can be seen in the masonry of the museum's showrooms Nos 21 and 22.

Both the castle and maritime museum are open from 10.30 am to 5 pm, May to September; from 11 am to 4 pm in April and October; and from 11 am to 3 pm, November to March (closed on Monday from October to April).

You can cross the moat and walk around the castle courtyard for free; tour the chapel, dungeon and royal quarters for 30 kr (10 kr for children); or get a combined ticket that includes the maritime museum for 45 kr (15 kr for children). The Copenhagen Card covers the maritime museum (which alone costs 25 kr), but no other castle sights.

Kronborg is a one-km walk from Helsingør railway station (see the above Walking Tour for a suggested route), but you can also take the Hornbæk-bound train to Grønnehave and walk a few minutes east to the castle.

Outskirts of Town

About 1.5 km north-west of the town centre is **Marienlyst Slot**, a three-storey manor house open to the public from noon to 5 pm daily. It was built in 1763 in the Louis Seize neoclassical style by French architect NH Jardin and encompasses parts of an early summer house constructed by King Frederik II. The interior exhibits include local paintings and silverwork. Admission is 20 kr for adults and free for children. The Hornbæk-bound train stops at Marienlyst station, just north of the manor house.

If you'd like to examine turn-of-the-century technological inventions, the

Danmarks Tekniske Museum at Nordre Strandvej 23, opposite the hostel, displays early gramophones, radios, automobiles and a 1906 Danish-built aeroplane that's claimed to be the first plane flown in Europe (it stayed airborne for 11 seconds!). It's open daily from 10 am to 5 pm; admission is 20 kr for adults and 10 kr for children. The museum is a short walk east from the Højstrup railway station or take bus No 340.

Hammermøllen, five km west of Helsingør centre in the village of Hellebæk, is an old smithy that was founded by King Christian IV and used to make muskets for the Kronborg arsenal. The current building, which dates from 1765, has also functioned as a water wheel-operated copper mill and textile mill. It's open daily, except on Monday, from 10 am to 5 pm. Admission costs 10 kr for adults and 5 kr for children.

Places to Stay

The two-star *Helsingør Camping Grønnehave* (☎ & fax 49 21 58 56), Campingvej 1, 3000 Helsingør, is on the beach about 1.5 km north-west of the town centre. Open all year round, it has 100 sites, a kiosk, cooking facilities and a coin laundry. The nightly cost is 42 kr per person. To get there take the Hornbæk-bound train or bus No 340 from Helsingør station, get off at Marienlyst station and walk south to Campingvej.

For a 25 kr booking fee, the tourist office will find you a room in a private home, starting at 150/280 kr for a single/double.

The hostel, *Helsingør Vandrerhjem*, (☎ 49 21 16 40, fax 49 21 13 99), Nordre Strandvej 24, 3000 Helsingør, is two km north-west of the town centre in a renovated coastal manor house. The 200-bed hostel is open year round except for the months of December and January. Most of the rooms have private baths and just two to six beds, and many are equipped for the disabled. Dorm beds cost 64 to 85 kr. There's a beach nearby, and sailboard rental and water skiing can be arranged at the hostel. From Helsingør railway station catch bus No 340 or take the Hornbæk-bound train and walk north-west from Marienlyst station.

The cheapest hotel in town is the 40-room *Hotel Skandia* (☎ 49 21 09 02, fax 49 26 54 90) at Bramstræde 1, 3000 Helsingør. This friendly, family-run place has large, clean singles/doubles for 300/500 kr with shared bath, or 400/640 kr with private bath, breakfast included. There are no phones or TV but if you request one of the north-facing topstorey rooms (No 48 is a good choice) there's a view of the castle.

The nearby 36-room *Hotel Hamlet* (☎ 49 21 05 91, fax 49 26 01 30), Bramstræde 5, 3000 Helsingør, has smaller rooms that are simple and a bit worn with private bath, phone and TV for 495/695 kr for a single/double.

Places to Eat

The Helsingør DSB railway station and the adjacent ferry terminal have food kiosks and places serving inexpensive eats.

Kammercaféen, in the old customs house behind the tourist office, has reasonably priced sandwiches, drinks and live entertainment. A block to the south at Strandgade 70 is *Rådmand Davids Hus*, a popular café in a 300-year-old half-timbered house. The special is the 54 kr 'shopping lunch', a big plate of traditional Danish foods, typically salmon paté, salad and slices of lamb, cheese and bread, which is available from 10 am to 6 pm, Monday to Saturday. Although it can be a bit smoky, this friendly place has a cobblestone garden courtyard which is a pleasant place to dine on sunny days. The café also sells takeaway Underground ice cream, one of Denmark's best brands of natural ice cream.

For something more upmarket, *Ophelia*, in the nearby Hotel Hamlet, has a traditional atmosphere and Danish-French cuisine. A daily special two-course lunch costs 98 kr and a three-course evening meal is 188 kr.

Otherwise, head for Axeltorv square, four blocks north-west of the railway station, which has a dozen places to eat as well as beer gardens selling Helsingør's own Wiibroe pilsner. *Kødbørsen*, a butcher shop at the south side of Axeltorv, makes takeaway smørrebrød sandwiches for 13 kr.

For sit-down fast food, *Fonzie*, at the north side of the square, has an extensive menu that includes burgers, barbecued chicken, salads and pizza, all for around 30 kr. Moderately priced Italian food can be found at *Pizzeria Torvekroen* on the west side of the square. *Gæstgivergården*, on the north side of the square, is candle-lit and pub-like and serves more traditional Danish fare, ranging from smørrebrød to fish, at moderate prices.

For something out of the ordinary, there's *Fyrskib Nr X*, a 19th century lightship moored outside Kronborg Slot, which has Danish cuisine and fine wines.

Getting There & Away

Helsingør is 64 km north of Copenhagen and 24 km north-east of Hillerød. There's free parking without any limit in the carpark at the side of Færgevej, a few minutes' south of Helsingør railway station, and parking with a three-hour limit in the carpark north-east of the tourist office.

Train The Helsingør railway station has two rail terminals: the main DSB terminal for national trains and the HHGB (Helsingør-Hornbœk-Gilleleje Banen) terminal for the private railway which runs along the north coast. DSB trains to and from Copenhagen run at least twice hourly from early morning to around midnight (55 minutes, 35 kr). DSB trains to and from Hillerød (30 minutes, 30 kr) run at least once hourly until a little after midnight. The HHGB train from Helsingør to Gilleleje runs an average of twice hourly (37 minutes, 30 kr), with the last train pulling out of Helsingør at 10.54 pm.

Boat For information on the frequent boats to Helsingborg, Sweden (25 minutes, 18 kr by ferry; 20 minutes, 35 kr by hydrofoil), see the Getting There & Away chapter in the front of the book. Visitors arriving by train can make a beeline to the ScandLines ferry office by walking through the back of the DSB railway station.

North Coast

The north coast of Zealand, also known as the Kattegat coast, is a pleasant mix of dunes, heathlands and coastal woodlands. Its development is limited to a handful of small fishing towns which date back to the 1500s, their backstreets bordered by half-timbered thatch-roofed houses and tidy flower gardens. Although the towns have only a few thousand residents in winter, the population swells with throngs of swimmers and sunbathers in summer.

HORNBÆK

Hornbæk has the best beach on the north coast, a vast expanse of soft white sands that run the entire length of the town. It's backed by sand dunes with beach grass and thickets of *Rosa rugosa*, a wild pink seaside rose that blooms all summer. Even though it borders the town, the beach is pleasantly undeveloped, with all commercial facilities on the inland side of the dunes.

Poet Holger Drachmann, who died in Hornbæk in 1908, is memorialised with a harbour-side monument. These days the salty fishermen, who Drachmann often wrote about, share their harbour with scores of sailing boats and yachts.

From the railway station, it's a five-minute walk directly down Havnevej to the harbour.

An Inspiring Rescue

In 1774, Hornbæk fishermen came to the rescue of British captain Thomas Brauwn, whose ship was in distress offshore. These Danes, braving treacherous seas, so inspired their country folk that a popular play, *Fiskerne*, was written about them by the lyricist poet Johannes Ewald. A song taken from the play became Denmark's national anthem. The rescue was also immortalised by the painter CW Eckersberg, who used it as a theme in a number of his paintings. ■

Climb the dunes to the left and you're on the beach.

Information

Tourist Office The Hornbæk Turistbureau is inside the library (☎ 49 70 47 47, fax 49 70 41 42), Vester Stejlebakke 2A, 3100 Hornbæk. To get there take the walkway at the side of Den Danske Bank on Hornebyvej. The tourist office is open from 2 to 7 pm on Monday, Tuesday and Thursday; from 10 am to 4 pm on Wednesday and Friday; and from 10 am to 1 pm (to 3 pm in summer) on Saturday.

Other Facilities The post office is opposite the railway station. There's a coin laundry a few minutes walk east of the Super Brugsen supermarket on Nordre Strandvej. There are public toilets and showers at the harbour. Den Danske Bank is on Hornebyvej opposite the northern end of Skolebakken.

Things to See & Do

The beach is without a doubt Hornbæk's main attraction and has good swimming conditions and plenty of space for sunbathing. If you're interested in windsurfing, contact Surfudlejning (☎ 42 20 33 75) at Drejervej 3. Those interested in chartering a boat to go fishing should contact the tourist office or the harbourmaster's office at the south side of the harbour. You can rent bicycles at Piccadilly Café.

If you're up to an enjoyable nature stroll, **Hornbæk Plantage**, a public woodland which extends along the coast 3.5 km east from Hornbæk, has numerous interconnecting trails branching out from either side of route 237. There are wild roses along the coast and pine trees and flowering scotch broom inland. One trail follows the coast from Lochersvej in Hornbæk to the eastern end of the plantage. Other trails go inland, including one that leads to Hornbæk Camping. There are several areas along Nordre Strandvej (route 237) where you can park a car and start your wanderings. A free forestry map, *Vandreture i Statsskovene,*

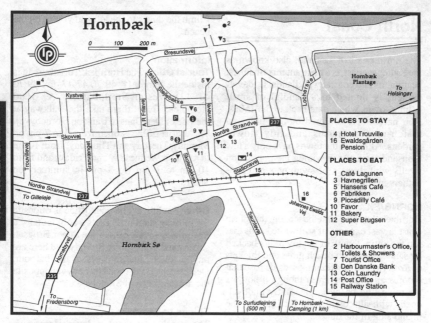

Hornbæk Plantage, shows all the trails and is available from the tourist office.

Places to Stay

There's a one-star camping ground, *Hornbæk Camping* (☎ 42 20 02 23, fax 42 20 23 91), Planetvej 4, 3100 Hornbæk, on the outskirts of town off Sauntevej, about 1.5 km south-east of the centre. It has a coin laundry, group kitchen and heated cabins for rent. The cost to pitch your tent is 40 kr per person. It's open from late March to mid-September.

Ewaldsgården Pension (☎ & fax 42 20 00 82), Johannes Ewalds Vej 5, 3100 Hornbæk, south-east of the railway station and about a 10-minute walk from the harbour, is a delightful pension in an early 18th century country house. The interior is light and airy with a cosy mix of antiques and cottage-style furnishings. All 12 rooms have a wash basin, while showers and toilets are in the hall. There's a guest kitchen for simple preparations such as sandwiches and coffee, and

four lounge areas where guests can relax. Singles/doubles cost 325/495 kr, breakfast included; a couple can sometimes share a small room for 395 kr. The friendly owners, Tom and Helle Laursen, are good sources of information on the greater Hornbæk area.

Hornbæk's biggest hotel is the 50-room *Hotel Trouville* (☎ 42 20 22 00, fax 42 20 18 27), Kystvej 20, 3100 Hornbæk, just inland of the dunes on the west side of town. Rooms have TV, phone, balcony and private bath and cost 600/720 kr for singles/doubles, breakfast included. The hotel has an indoor swimming pool, sauna, solarium, bar and an expensive restaurant. It's part of the Best Western chain.

If you're interested in renting a summer house by the week, the main local agent is Hornbækgruppen (☎ 42 20 20 20, fax 42 20 20 94), Hornebyvej 62E, 3100 Hornbæk.

Places to Eat

Down at the harbour, there's a little store, a

fish market and *Havnegrillen*, a fast-food stand selling hot dogs, burgers, fish sandwiches and Underground ice cream. Also at the harbour is *Café Lagunen*, which has simple lunch fare such as sandwiches for 30 kr and omelettes and salads for around 50 kr, as well as more expensive steak and fish dishes.

The *Piccadilly Café*, at Nordre Strandvej 336, diagonally opposite the Super Brugsen, has inexpensive burgers, sandwiches and grilled chicken with chips.

Hansens Café is in the town's oldest house, a sod-roofed half-timbered building at Havnevej 19, and has a pleasant pub like atmosphere. The hand-written menu changes daily but you can expect to find reasonably priced Danish food averaging 60 to 100 kr.

If you want good fresh fish at moderate prices, join the locals at the *Fabrikken*, a restaurant and bar at Vester Stejlebakke 2D. Food is served from 6 to 10 pm.

You can pick up groceries at the *Super Brugsen* or at the nearby *Favør* market at Nordre Strandvej 349. There's a bakery midway between the two.

Getting There & Away

Trains from Helsingør to Hornbæk (22 minutes) run an average of twice hourly every day, while bus No 340 (28 minutes) does the same route an average of once hourly. Either way it's 15 kr.

GILLELEJE

Zealand's northernmost town, Gilleleje has lots of attractive straw-roofed houses as well as the island's largest fishing harbour. Despite its size the harbour has a certain timeless character, filled with small blue-hulled fishing boats.

Much of what the town has to offer to visitors is in one way or another connected with fishing. This includes smokehouses along the harbour and a little dockside fish auction that can be viewed by early risers.

It's a five-minute walk north from the railway station down to the harbour. Although not on par with those at Hornbæk or Tisvildeleje, there are public beaches on either side of town.

Information

Tourist Office The Gilleleje Turistbureau (☎ 48 30 01 74, fax 48 30 34 74) is in the town centre at Hovedgade 6, 3250 Gilleleje, 200 metres east of the railway station. It's open from 10 am to 5 pm (to 6 pm in midsummer), Monday to Saturday, from May to August; and from 9 am to 4 pm on weekdays and 9 am to noon on Saturday the rest of the year.

Money Den Danske Bank is at Vesterbrogade 6 in the centre of town.

Post The post office is at Stationsvej 6 just north of the railway station.

Things to See & Do

The local fishing museum, **Gilleleje Museums Skibshal** at Hovedgade 49, about 400 metres east of the tourist office, has a fisherman's house from 1850 and displays about the lives of fisherfolk from the Middle Ages forward.

Midway between the tourist office and the museum, on the north side of Hovedgade, is the **Gilleleje Kirke**, originally built from shipwrecked timbers in the early 1500s to minister to seamen. The church has a 17th century hand-carved pulpit and a painted altar dating from 1834. In 1943 Danish Jews waiting to be rowed across to neutral Sweden took refuge in the church attic; a displayed Medal of Merit from the Jewish community honours the local efforts.

The **Gilleleje Museum**, in the old schoolhouse at Rostgårdsvej 2, 200 metres south of the tourist office, has some Stone and Bronze Age relics consisting mainly of pottery shards, as well as simple displays of latter-day artefacts.

There are **coastal trails** heading in each direction from the town centre. The trail to the west, which starts near the intersection of Nordre Strandvej and Vesterbrogade, leads about 1.75 km to a stone memorial for the philosopher Søren Kierkegaard who used to make visits to this coast.

The trail to the east, which begins off Hovedgade at the east side of the fishing museum, leads 2.5 km to the site where two lighthouses with coal-burning beacons were erected in 1772. In 1899 the western lighthouse was modernised with rotating lenses and the eastern one, no longer needed, was abandoned. In 1980 the eastern lighthouse, **Nakkehoved Østre Fyr**, was restored as a museum. You can get to this lighthouse on the coastal footpath or by turning north off route 237 onto Fyrvejen.

The two town museums and the lighthouse are open only from 2 to 5 pm, Tuesday to Sunday, from mid-June to mid-September; a single ticket costing 15 kr (free for children) covers all three sights.

Places to Stay

There's an inland camping ground, *Gilleleje Camping* (☎ 49 71 97 55), at Bregnerødvej 21, 3250 Gilleleje, three km south-east of the town centre.

The Gilleleje tourist office books double rooms in private homes for about 200 kr.

The 25-room *Hotel Strand* (☎ & fax 48 30 05 12), Vesterbrogade 4, 3250 Gilleleje, is in the centre of town, a short walk from the harbour. There are three rooms that are a tad small but have two twin beds, a desk and private shower (toilets are in the hall) and are a good deal at 200/350 kr for singles/doubles, including a simple breakfast. Other rooms are larger and more modern with balcony, private bath, TV and phone and cost 400/600 kr without breakfast or 450/700 kr with breakfast.

Places to Eat

Rogeriet Bornholm, a smokehouse on the harbour, sells smoked fish by the piece; a smoked mackerel makes a tasty snack and costs about 10 kr. At the nearby *Adamsen's Fisk* you can get deli items such as rollmops, shrimp salad and smoked salmon for takeaway.

Hos Karen & Marie, at Nordre Havnevej 3, is an excellent little seafood restaurant in a period building overlooking the harbour. At lunch there's a great sampler plate that includes pickled herring, dill-marinated salmon, butter-fried plaice, pork tenderloin and brie for 108 kr. There are also à la carte fish dishes from around 65 kr. At dinner, prices range from 98 kr for a vegetarian plate to 150 kr for fish. It's open from 11 am to 3 pm for lunch and 5 to 10 pm for dinner from Monday to Saturday, and from 11 am to 9 pm on Sunday.

Getting There & Away

Trains run from Hillerød to Gilleleje (31 minutes, 25 kr) about twice hourly on weekdays, once hourly on weekends, and from Helsingør to Gilleleje (37 minutes, 30 kr) an average of twice an hour every day. There's no rail link between Gilleleje and Tisvildeleje, but all the north coast towns are linked by bus. Bus No 340 connects Gilleleje with Hornbæk (20 minutes, 18 kr) and Helsingør (50 minutes, 30 kr). Bus No 363 connects Gilleleje with Tisvildeleje, but is a rather roundabout hour-long ride (24 kr). Gilleleje's bus and railway station are adjacent to each other.

TISVILDELEJE

Tisvildeleje is a pleasant little seaside village with an invitingly slow pace, a wonderful hostel and fine nature walks. It's bordered by a broad stretch of sandy beach that's backed by low dunes; the nearest beach is just a short walk from the railway station but the most glorious sweep is at the road's end, one km west of the village centre. That beach has a large carpark, a changing room and toilets.

Inland of the beach is Tisvilde Hegn, a windswept forest of twisted trees and heather-covered hills that extends southwest from Tisvildeleje for more than eight km. Much of this enchanting forest was planted in the 18th century to stabilise the sand drifts that were threatening to turn the area into desert.

Information

Both the post office and the seasonal tourist office (☎ 42 30 74 51), Banevej 8, are in the

Tisvilde railway station. The tourist office is open from 1 June to 31 August from 10 am to 5 pm, Monday to Saturday.

Walks in Tisvilde Hegn

From the beach parking area at the end of road you can walk, either along the beach or on a dirt path through the woods, about three km south to Troldeskoven, an area of old trees that have been sculpted by the wind into such haunting shapes that the area has been nicknamed the Witch Wood. On the way make a short detour east at Brantebjerg for a nice hill-top view.

Tisvilde Hegn has many other trails, including one to Asserbo Slotsruin, the ruins of a former manor house and 12th century monastery, which are near the southern boundary of the forest. The south-western part of Tisvilde Hegn merges with Asserbo Plantage, a wooded area that borders lake Arresø. Trail maps are available free from the tourist office.

Places to Stay

The cheery 272-bed hostel, *Tisvildeleje Vandrerhjem*, (☎ 42 30 98 50, fax 42 30 98 97) at Bygmarken 30, 3220 Tisvildeleje, is one km east of the town centre and within walking distance of a sandy beach that's shallow and safe for children. This hostel is the centrepiece of the new Sankt Helene complex, which conducts nature courses and thematic holidays for schoolchildren and other groups. It encompasses 12 hectares of grounds that include jogging paths, trails, tennis courts, sports fields and playgrounds. Most of the complex is accessible by wheelchair.

Hostel accommodation is in modern quarters, each with four beds, a little sitting area and a bathroom. It costs 85 kr for a dorm-style bed or 250/275 kr to have the room as a single/double. There are also cabins with up to five beds that can be rented for 300 kr and apartments accommodating four to six people that rent by the week for 1800 to 4800 kr, depending on the season. Campers can set up a tent in the field adjacent to the reception office for 20 kr, including use of the showers

and kitchen. The hostel is open year round but reservations are often essential from May to mid-September. There's a kiosk and a reasonably priced restaurant serving three meals a day. If coming by train, get off at the Godhavns station, one stop before Tisvilde station; the hostel is just north of the tracks. By car, turn north on Godhavnsvej.

The tourist office maintains a list of a few local homes with rooms for rent at prices from 100/150 kr for singles/doubles and can also help with booking summer cottages.

The 29-room *Tisvildeleje Strand Hotel* (☎ 42 30 71 19, fax 42 30 71 77), Hovedgaden 75, 3220 Tisvildeleje, is in the centre of town and within walking distance of the beach. Singles/doubles cost 325/500 kr without bath or 425/700 kr with bath, breakfast included.

A more interesting option is *Helenekilde* (☎ 42 30 70 01), Strandvejen 25, 3220 Tisvildeleje, a beachside pension about a 10-minute walk from town. There are lounges and a dining room with water views. Most of the 25 guest rooms have balconies and private baths and cost 460/660 kr for singles/doubles, breakfast included, though there are some singles without bath for 320 kr.

Places to Eat

Olifanten, in the town centre at the intersection of Hydrobakken and Hovedgaden, is a popular lunch spot with takeaway or eat-in burgers and other fast food, as well as espresso, cappuccino and wine.

There's a bakery on the north side of Hovedgaden, just east of Olifanten, and a deli, *Tisvildeleje Delikatessen*, on the opposite side of the road at 61 Hovedgaden.

The *Tisvildeleje Caféen*, at Hovedgaden 55, is open for lunch and dinner and has specials between 55 and 75 kr and steak or lamb dishes with chips and salad from around 100 kr.

The *Tisvildeleje Strand Hotel* has an expensive restaurant with starters and desserts for around 50 kr and main dishes including fish from about 130 kr.

NORTH ZEALAND

Getting There & Away

Trains run between Hillerød and Tisvildeleje (31 minutes, 25 kr) once an hour, with a few extra trains in early morning and late afternoon.

Getting Around

Bicycles can be rented in the town centre at the Hydro petrol station, Hovedgaden 53, a few minutes walk west of the railway station. It's open in summer from 7 am to 10 pm and has single-speed bikes for 35/175 kr a day/week, three speeds for 45/250 kr and tandem bikes for 100/400 kr. The hostel also rents bicycles and charges 40/150 kr for a day/week.

Fjord Towns

North Zealand has two interlinking fjords, the Isefjord and the Roskilde Fjord, that connect to the Kattegat at the town of Hundested. Hundested is a jumping-off point for visitors going on to central Jutland. The largest towns in the region, Frederiksværk and Frederikssund, border the Roskilde Fjord and are along the route for those driving between Tisvildeleje and Roskilde.

HUNDESTED

Hundested, on the mouth of the Isefjord, is a ferry port, with boats making the 90-minute crossing to Grenaa in Jutland a few times a day. The ferry costs 98 kr for adults and 380 kr for a car and driver; call Driftsselskabet (☎ 42 33 96 88) for reservations.

The main sight in Hundested is the home built by Knud Rasmussen (1879-1933), Denmark's most famous arctic explorer, which has been turned into a museum, the **Knud Rasmussens Hus**. Located near the lighthouse, at Knud Rasmussensvej 9, it has Rasmussen's original furnishings, although the thousands of archaeological artefacts that he collected on his expeditions are kept at the Nationalmuseet in Copenhagen.

The Lynæs area, a few km south of Hundested, is a **windsurfing** mecca with good

wind conditions as well as shallow-water areas suitable for beginners. Lynæs Surfcenter (☎ 47 98 01 00) at Lynæs Havnevej has windsurfing gear for hire and offers windsurfing lessons in both English and German. There's a train from Hillerød to Hundested that runs hourly and takes 45 minutes.

FREDERIKSVÆRK

Frederiksværk, at the north side of the Roskilde Fjord, is Denmark's oldest industrial town, founded in 1756 by order of King Frederik V, from whom the town takes its name. A canal was dug between the Roskilde Fjord and lake Arresø to provide water power for mills, a gunpowder factory and a cannon foundry.

Fittingly, Frederiksværk's two museums, both near the canal in the centre of town, are dedicated to the town's industrial history. The **Frederiksværk Bymuseum** on Torvet has artefacts and displays on Frederiksværk's early industries, while the open-air **Krudtværksmusset** (Gunpowder Factory Museum) at Krudtværks Alleén consists of period buildings equipped with the original machinery and a working water mill.

The town sits along the western shore of Arresø, which at 41 sq km is Denmark's largest lake; there are excursion boat tours of the lake on summer afternoons.

If you need to spend the night here, the town has a combination hostel and camping ground, *Frederiksværk Vandrerhjem & Campingplads* (☎ 42 12 07 66) at Strandgade 30, within walking distance of the railway station. Frederiksværk is on the rail line between Hundested (18 minutes) and Hillerød (28 minutes).

FREDERIKSSUND

Frederikssund, at the narrowest part of the Roskilde Fjord, is an industrial town that's best known to visitors for the **Viking play** that's performed from late June to early July by a troupe of 250 local residents. The performance takes place in an open-air theatre that's within walking distance of the S-train station. The cost is 75 kr for admission, plus 100 kr if you want to join the feast that follows the play. For information or bookings call Vikingespillene (☎ 42 31 06 85).

Also in town is the **JF Willumsens Museum** at Jenriksvej 4, which contains paintings, sculpture and drawings by Jens Ferdinand Willumsen (1863-1958), one of Denmark's leading symbolists. The museum also has some works by other artists which belonged to Willumsem's private collection.

Frederikssund is at the end of the S-train's M line, a 50-minute (35 kr) ride from Copenhagen.

Roskilde

Roskilde, Denmark's first capital, was a thriving trade centre throughout the Middle Ages. It was also the site of Zealand's first Christian church, built by Viking king Harald Bluetooth in 980 AD.

In 1026 King Canute I, in a fit of anger over a chess match, had his brother-in-law Ulf Jarl assassinated in that church. Ulf's widow and Canute's sister, Estrid, arranged to have the wooden stave church where her husband was ambushed torn down, and then donated property for the construction of a new stone church. The foundations of that early stone church are beneath the floor of the current-day Roskilde cathedral. Estrid,

and her son Svend Estridsen, are amongst the multitude of Danish royalty buried in the cathedral.

As the centre of Danish Catholicism, medieval Roskilde not only had a cathedral but nearly 20 churches and monasteries. After the Reformation swept Denmark in 1536 the monasteries and most of the churches were demolished. The town, which had been in decline since the capital moved to Copenhagen in the early 15th century, saw its population shrink radically.

Today Roskilde is a likeable, low-profile town with about 50,000 inhabitants. Only 30 km east of Copenhagen, Roskilde is on Denmark's main east-west train route.

Information

Tourist Office The Roskilde Turistbureau (☎ 42 35 27 00, fax 42 35 14 74) is at Gullandsstræde 15, Postboks 278, 4000 Roskilde. In July and August it's open from 9 am to 6 pm, Monday to Friday; 9 am to 3 pm on Saturday; and 10 am to 2 pm on Sunday. The rest of the year it's open from 9 am to 5 pm on weekdays (to 4 pm on Friday in autumn and winter) and from 10 am to 1 pm on Saturday.

Money There are a couple of banks along Algade just east of Torvet.

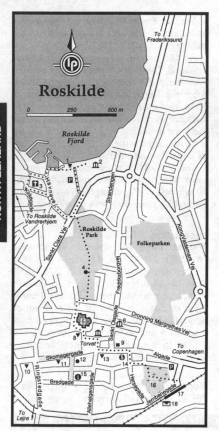

Roskilde

0   250   500 m

Roskilde
Fjord

Roskilde
Park

Folkeparken

To
Frederikssund

To Roskilde
Vandrerhjem

Torvet

Skomagergade

Bredgade

Dronning Margrethes Vej

Algade

To
Copenhagen

To
Lejre

Post The post office is at Jernbanegade 3 on the south-west side of the railway station.

Walking Tour

Roskilde's most notable sights are within walking distance of each other. The **Roskilde Domkirke** is on Torvet, a 10-minute walk north-west of the railway station; to get there, cut diagonally across the old churchyard and go left along Algade then continue through town.

From the cathedral, you can take a 15-minute walk through an extended green belt of city parks all the way down to **Viking-eskibshallen,** the Viking ship museum. The route begins on the north side of the cathedral and crosses a field where wildflowers seasonally blanket the unexcavated remains of Roskilde's original **medieval town**. The rectangular depression at this site marks the spot where the 12th century church Sankt Hans Kirke was torn down during the Reformation.

After visiting the Viking ship museum, a five-minute walk west along the harbour will bring you to the **Sankt Jørgensbjerg quarter**, where the cobbled walkway Kirkegade leads through a neighbourhood of old straw-roofed houses and into the courtyard of the hill-top **Sankt Jørgensbjerg Kirke**. This church, the nave of which dates from the 11th century, is one of the oldest in Denmark.

Roskilde Domkirke

Though most of Roskilde's medieval buildings have vanished in fires over the centuries, this imposing cathedral still dominates the city centre. Started in 1170 by Bishop Absalon, the Roskilde Domkirke has been rebuilt and added onto so many times

NORTH ZEALAND

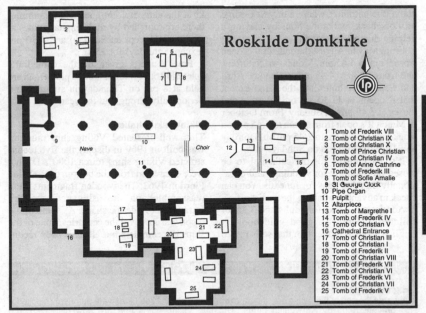

Roskilde Domkirke

1 Tomb of Frederik VIII
2 Tomb of Christian IX
3 Tomb of Christian X
4 Tomb of Prince Christian
5 Tomb of Christian IV
6 Tomb of Anne Cathrine
7 Tomb of Frederik III
8 Tomb of Sofie Amalie
9 St George Clock
10 Pipe Organ
11 Pulpit
12 Altarpiece
13 Tomb of Margrethe I
14 Tomb of Frederik IV
15 Tomb of Christian V
16 Cathedral Entrance
17 Tomb of Christian III
18 Tomb of Christian I
19 Tomb of Frederik II
20 Tomb of Christian VIII
21 Tomb of Frederik VII
22 Tomb of Christian VI
23 Tomb of Frederik VI
24 Tomb of Christian VII
25 Tomb of Frederik V

Nave
Choir

NORTH ZEALAND

that it represents a millennium of Danish architectural styles.

The cathedral has tall spires, a splendid interior and the crypts of 37 Danish kings and queens. Some of the crypts are spectacularly embellished and guarded by marble statues of knights and women in mourning, while others are simple unadorned coffins. There's something quite awesome about being able to stand next to the bones of so many of Scandinavia's most powerful historical figures.

Of particular interest is the chapel of Christian IV, off the north side of the cathedral. It contains the coffin of Christian IV flanked by his young son, Prince Christian, and his wife, Anne Cathrine, as well as the brass coffins of his successor, Frederik III, and his wife, Queen Sofie Amalie. The bronze statue of Christian IV beside the entranceway is the work of Bertel Thorvaldsen, while the huge wall-size paintings, encased in trompe l'oeil frames, were

done by Wilhelm Marstrand and include a classic scene depicting Christian IV rallying the troops aboard the ship *Trinity* during the 1644 battle of Kolbergerheide.

Some of the cathedral's finest pieces were installed by Christian IV, including the intricately detailed pulpit made of marble, alabaster and sandstone in 1610 by Copenhagen sculptor Hans Brokman.

The enormous gilt 'cupboard-style' altarpiece, made in 1560 in Antwerp, has 21 plates that depict the story of the life of Christ. The story of how it came to Roskilde is as interesting as the piece. Apparently when the altar was being sent to its intended destination of Gdansk, its shipper attempted to cheat on the sound dues in Helsingør by grossly undervaluing it, and the shrewd customs officer, asserting his right to acquire items at their valuation price, snapped up the altarpiece.

An unusually lighthearted item is the cathedral's early 16th century clock, poised above the entrance, where a tiny St George on horseback marks the hour by slaying a yelping dragon.

From May to August the cathedral is open from 9 am to 4.45 pm, Monday to Saturday, and from 12.30 to 4.45 pm on Sunday. April and September hours are the same except that it opens at 11.30 am on Saturday and closes at 3.45 pm on Sunday. From October to March it's open from 10 am to 2.45 pm on weekdays, 11.30 am to 2.45 pm on Saturday and 12.30 to 3.45 pm on Sunday.

It's not unusual for the cathedral to be closed on Saturday for weddings and occasionally on other days for funerals. You can check in advance by calling the tourist office.

Admission is 6 kr for adults and 3 kr for children. There is a good guidebook in English, French or German that sells for 20 kr at the cathedral entrance and in summer there are tours led by multilingual guides at 11.30 am (except on Sunday) and 1.30 pm (except Saturday) for 25 kr.

Free concerts given on the cathedral's splendid 16th century baroque pipe organ are held at 8 pm on Thursday in summer and periodically throughout the year.

Vikingeskibshallen

This well-presented Viking ship museum was built in 1969 to display the five reconstructed Viking ships (circa 1000 AD) that were excavated from the bottom of Roskilde Fjord in 1962. The wooden fragments were reassembled on site using new skeleton frames to provide the shape. As some of the wood was lost over the centuries, none of the ships are complete but all have been recon-

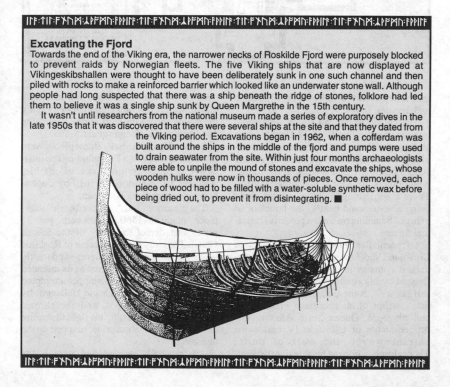

Excavating the Fjord

Towards the end of the Viking era, the narrower necks of Roskilde Fjord were purposely blocked to prevent raids by Norwegian fleets. The five Viking ships that are now displayed at Vikingeskibshallen were thought to have been deliberately sunk in one such channel and then piled with rocks to make a reinforced barrier which looked like an underwater stone wall. Although people had long suspected that there was a ship beneath the ridge of stones, folklore had led them to believe it was a single ship sunk by Queen Margrethe in the 15th century.

It wasn't until researchers from the national museum made a series of exploratory dives in the late 1950s that it was discovered that there were several ships at the site and that they dated from the Viking period. Excavations began in 1962, when a cofferdam was built around the ships in the middle of the fjord and pumps were used to drain seawater from the site. Within just four months archaeologists were able to unpile the mound of stones and excavate the ships, whose wooden hulks were now in thousands of pieces. Once removed, each piece of wood had to be filled with a water-soluble synthetic wax before being dried out, to prevent it from disintegrating. ∎

structed well enough to get a sense of their original design.

The ships include an 18-metre warship of the type used to raid England and a 16.5-metre trader that may have once carried cargo between Greenland and Denmark.

Appropriately, the Viking ship museum is on the east side of the harbour, overlooking Roskilde Fjord, which forms the backdrop for the displays. The museum has a theatre showing films on the excavation and the reassembly of the ships. There's a cafeteria on site.

The museum is open from 9 am to 5 pm daily from April to October, and 10 am to 4 pm from November to March. Admission costs 30 kr for adults and 20 kr for children. In summer the museum also sponsors inexpensive fjord tours that leave on the hour from 10 am to 3 pm. Call ☎ 42 37 20 47 for more information.

Other City Museums

The **Palæet** (Palace), an attractive 18th century building fronting Torvet, is a former bishops' residence that now houses the **Museet for Samtidskunst** (Museum of Contemporary Art), a small modern art museum with changing exhibits, and **Palæsamlingerne** (Palace Collections), which contains a collection of 18th and 19th century paintings and furnishings that once belonged to wealthy Roskilde merchants. The art museum is open from 11 am to 5 pm on weekdays, noon to 4 pm on weekends; admission is 10 kr for adults and free for children. The Palace Collections are open from 11 am to 4 pm daily from mid-May to mid-September and from 1 to 3 pm on Saturday and Sunday the rest of the year; admission is 5 kr for adults and 2 kr for children.

In addition, there's the **Roskilde Museum** at Sankt Olsgade 18, which covers Roskilde's history with displays on the Viking era and the medieval period, and a room dedicated to the Danish author Gustav Wied. It's open daily from 11 am to 5 pm June to August, and from 2 to 4 pm (to 5 pm on

Sunday) the rest of the year. Admission is 10 kr for adults and free for children.

Cycling Tours

If you want to do some serious exploring of the region by bicycle you should consider picking up a copy of *Cykelruter og udflugter i Roskilde Amt*, a good detailed cycling map of Roskilde county published by Dansk Cyklist Forbund. This map, which is printed in both English and Danish language versions, suggests tours into the countryside and gives brief descriptions of the places you'll encounter along the way. It costs 50 kr and can be purchased at the Roskilde tourist office and in bookshops.

Places to Stay

Most travellers visit Roskilde on a day trip, but should you want to stay overnight, the tourist office books rooms in private homes for 125/250 kr for singles/doubles, plus a 25 kr booking fee; an optional breakfast costs 40 kr per person. They can book rooms in town, in the suburbs and on farms.

The hostel, *Roskilde Vandrerhjem*, (☎ 42 35 21 84, fax 46 32 66 90), Hørhusene 61, 4000 Roskilde, is three km west of the city centre. Take bus No 601 or 604 from the railway station. The 114 dorm-beds cost 70 to 80 kr, while family rooms for one to four people cost 160 to 320 kr. It's open from 1 May to 1 October.

In the city centre is the *Hotel Prindsen* (☎ 42 35 80 10, fax 42 35 81 10), Algade 13, 4000 Roskilde, which claims to be Denmark's oldest continuously operating hotel. First opened in 1695, its guest list reads like a who's who of great Danes, running the gamut from King Frederik VII to Holger Drachmann and Hans Christian Andersen. As befits an old hotel, the rooms are different sizes and have varied décor but all have a private bath, phone, cable TV and minibar. Singles/doubles cost 695/795 kr, breakfast included. There's a restaurant, bar and sauna. The hotel is a member of the Best Western chain and has a slightly discounted weekend rate.

Places to Eat

On Skomagergade, the pedestrian street that runs west from Torvet, there are a few cafés and a number of fast-food joints selling pizza, burgers and hot dogs. *Mesterslagteren*, a butcher shop just off the west end of Skomagergade, has simple smørrebrød for 7 kr and more substantial sandwiches and quiche for 15 kr. The *S Supermarket*, a large grocery store with a good fruit section, has a rooftop cafeteria with an interesting city view and a varied menu that includes salads or sandwiches for around 20 kr, and steak and chips for 45 kr.

Den Gamle Bagergård, a bakery at Algade 6, has good pastries and inexpensive takeaway sandwiches. On Wednesday and Saturday mornings there's a market on Torvet selling fresh produce as well as handicrafts and flowers.

For a treat, the atmospheric *Raadhus-Kælderen*, in the cellar of the old town hall (circa 1430), has tempting lunch deals from 11 am to 5 pm, including pork tenderloin, fish fillet with shrimp and asparagus, or pasta seafood salad with home-made bread, for around 60 kr. Evening meals are more expensive and include poached salmon, scampi and various meat dishes for around 150 kr.

If you're looking for food down by the Viking ship museum the *Fiskevognen*, a trailer on the west side of the harbour, sells fishcakes (6 kr), shrimp (100 grams for 10 kr) and fried fish; there are a few picnic tables nearby.

Getting There & Away

Trains from Copenhagen to Roskilde are frequent (25 minutes, 35 kr). If you're continuing to Odense the same day you can stop over for free. There are lockers at the railway station.

If you're coming from Copenhagen by car, route 21 leads to Roskilde. Upon approaching the city, exit onto route 156, which leads into the centre. You might be able to find parking north of the railway station, but if not, there's plenty of parking down by the Vikingeskibshallen.

Getting Around

Bicycles can be rented from JAS Cykler (☎ 42 35 04 20), Gullandsstræde 3, from 9 am to 5.30 pm on weekdays and from 9 am to 2 pm on Saturday.

LEJRE

The countryside on the outskirts of Lejre, a village eight km south-west of Roskilde, has two sightseeing attractions that could be combined in an afternoon outing.

Lejre Forsøgscenter

This 'archaeological experimental centre' contains a reconstructed Iron Age village where Danish families can volunteer to spend their summer holidays as 'prehistoric families' using technology and dressed in clothing from that period. The reconstructed houses they live in and the tools they use are modelled on finds from archaeological excavations around Denmark.

The centre, which is a popular destination for school outings, also has craft demonstrations and a small 'cottage-farm' area where the lives of 19th century Danish farmers are re-enacted. In summer children can paddle dug-out canoes and partake in a few other hands-on activities such as grinding flour. Although the centre is open from 1 May to the last Sunday in September, from 10 am to 5 pm daily, the majority of the activities take place in midsummer, when the live-in families are present.

One of biggest events is the Iron Age cavalry, a drama featuring men in Iron Age dress on Icelandic horses, which takes place a few times each season.

Admission to Lejre Forsøgscenter (☎ 46 48 08 78) is 45 kr for adults and 25 kr for children.

Ledreborg

This grand manor house, set on a knoll overlooking 80 hectares of lawns and woods, was built by Count Johan Ludvig Holstein in 1739 and has been home to the Holstein-Ledreborg family ever since. The interior has hardly changed since the house was originally decorated and consequently it's considered one of the finest manor houses in Denmark.

Visitors are required to put on booties at the entrance so as not to damage the marble and parquet floors. The house is chock full of antique furniture, gilded mirrors, chandeliers, oil paintings and wall tapestries. One of the most superb rooms is the banquet room, which was designed by architect Nicolai Eigtved, the designer of Copenhagen's Amalienborg Palace. Also in the house is a chapel constructed by JC Krieger in 1745, which served as the parish church until 1899.

Ledreborg (☎ 46 48 00 38) is open to visitors from 11 am to 5 pm daily from June to August and from 11 am to 5 pm on Sunday

in May and September. Admission is 45 kr for adults and 20 kr for children.

Getting There & Away

From Roskilde, it's a short train ride to Lejre station where the seasonal bus No 233 (10 kr) continues to both Ledreborg and Lejre Forsøgscenter.

If you have your own transport, from Roskilde take Ringstedvej (route 14), turn right on route 155 and then almost immediately make a left onto Ledreborg Allé. Follow the signs to Ledreborg, six km away, where a long drive lined by century-old elm trees leads to the entrance. The Lejre Forsøgscenter is two km farther on along the same road.

Southern Zealand

Steeped in history, southern Zealand has played an important role since the Viking era. It was a stomping ground in medieval times for significant historical characters such as Bishop Absalon and the royal Valdemar family. In the 17th century the area was the stage for some of the most important battles of the lengthy wars between Denmark and Sweden. The most pivotal loss in Danish history was played out here in 1658 when Swedish King Gustave marched across southern Zealand en route to Copenhagen and forced a treaty that nearly cost Denmark its sovereignty.

Today the region contains a mix of peaceful towns, rural villages and patchwork farmland. Highlights of southern Zealand include two notably engaging towns, Køge and Sorø; one of Denmark's most impressive Viking sites, the 1000-year-old ring fortress at Trelleborg; and some interesting medieval churches.

If you're travelling across the region from Køge to Korsør with your own transport, the rural route 150 makes a fine alternative to zipping along on the E20 motorway. Not only is it a slower, greener route but it will take you right into the most interesting towns and villages.

KØGE

Køge has a rich history that dates from 1288, when it was granted its municipal charter by King Erik VI. With its large natural harbour, Køge quickly developed into a thriving fishing and trade centre.

In 1677 one of the most important naval engagements of the Danish-Swedish wars was fought in the waters off Køge. Known as the Battle of Køge Bay, it made a legend of Danish admiral Niels Juel, who resoundingly defeated the attacking Swedish navy and thwarted their attempted invasion.

Today the harbour still plays an important role in Køge's economy, having been developed into a modern commercial facility.

HIGHLIGHTS

- Sorø, a charming town with a rich cultural past
- The fascinating Viking ring fortress at Trelleborg
- The well-preserved historic quarter in the town of Køge
- The rural hamlet of Vallø, with its castle and woodland
- Sankt Bendts Kirke, Ringsted's medieval church

While parts of the city have been industrialised, Køge has done a superb job of retaining the period character of its central historic quarter. The narrow streets that radiate from Torvet, the town square, are lined with old buildings, some that survived a sweeping fire in 1633 and many others that were built in the construction boom spawned by that blaze.

Information

Tourist Office The Køge Turistbureau (☎ 53 65 58 00, fax 53 65 59 84), near Torvet, at Vestergade 1, 4600 Køge, distributes a free

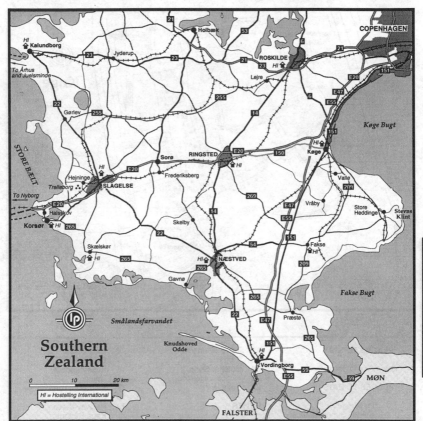

Southern
Zealand

0   10   20 km

HI = Hostelling International

70-page booklet, with English and German translations, that describes the town's sights. The office is open from 9 am to 5 pm on weekdays year round. Saturday opening hours are from 9 am to 5 pm from June to August and from 10 am to 1 pm the rest of the year.

Money There's a Unibank on Torvet, just east of Kirkestræde.

Post The post office is at Jernstøbervænget 2, on the west side of town. It's open from 10 am to 5 pm on weekdays (5.30 pm on Thursday) and from 10 am to 1 pm on Saturday.

Laundry There's a coin laundry at the Torvet end of Nyportstræde.

Walking Tour
Most of Køge's finest historic sites are within easy walking distance of each other. A pleasant little stroll of these sites can be made in about an hour, although if you take your time, stopping at the church and the two museums along the way, you could easily turn it into a half-day outing.

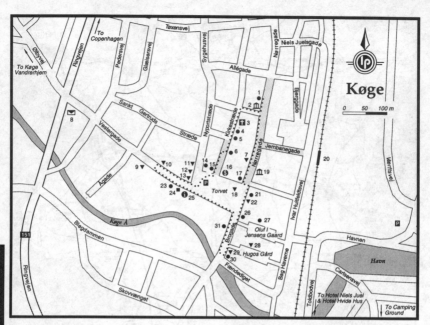

Køge

0   50   100 m

PLACES TO STAY

24 Centralhotellet

PLACES TO EAT

7   La Mirage
9   Kvickly Supermarket &
    Cafeteria
10 Richters
    Gæstgivergaard &
    No 16 Vestergade
11 Ritz Burger Boss
12 La Fontaine

13 Torve Konditoriet
18 Fruit Hut
22 Butcher Shop
28 Hugos Vinkjælder
29 Bella Napoli

OTHER

1   Goldsmith Shop
2   Køge Skitsesamling
3   Sankt Nicolai Kirke
4   Library
5   1527 House
6   Køge Børneasyl

8   Post Office
14 Coin Laundry
15 Kirkestræde 3
16 Unibank
17 Kioge Huskors Plaque
19 Køge Museum
20 Railway Station
21 Køge Rådhus
23 Vestergade 7
25 Tourist Office
26 Køge Apotek
27 Køge Galleriet
30 Brogade 23
31 Brogade 16

Begin the walk at Torvet by making a short detour west along the first block of **Vestergade**. There are two notable half-timbered houses in this area: house **No 7**, which dates from the late 1500s, and **No 16** (the Richters Gæstgivergaard restaurant), a remarkably well-preserved merchant's house dating from 1644, with old hand-blown glass in the doors and intricately carved detail on the

timbers. From here you can return back to Torvet and head north on Kirkestræde.

At **Kirkestræde 3**, just metres from Torvet, is the house built by Oluf Sandersen and his wife Margareta Jørgensdatter in 1638, as duly noted in the lettering above the gate. Other timber-frame houses include Kirkestræde 13, which dates from the 16th century, and Kirkestræde 10, a 17th century house which has served as a kindergarten, **Køoge Børneasyl**, since 1856. The oldest half-timbered house in Denmark, a modest little place constructed in 1527 with a brick front, is at **Kirkestræde 20**. It's followed by **Sankt Nicolai Kirke** (the church and the two museums in this walking tour are detailed in the sections that follow).

If you turn right onto Katekismusgade, you'll immediately come to the **Køge Skitsesamling** art museum. In the grounds near the museum are a number of sculptures, including a bronze of a young boy with a scurrying lizard by Svend Rathsack.

Immediately north of the museum, at Nørregade 31, is an attractive red timbered house built in 1612 that now holds a **goldsmith shop**. Continuing south on Nørregade, you'll pass more houses built in the early 17th century at Nos 5 and 4; the latter holds the **Køge Museum**.

Look for the plaque marked **'Kiøge Huskors'** (Kiøge and Kjøge are old spellings of Køge) on the green corner building at Torvet 2, which honours the victims of a witch hunt in the early 1600s. Two residents of an earlier house on this site were among those burned at the stake.

Along the east side of Torvet is the yellow neoclassical **Køge Rådhus**, which is said to be the oldest functioning town hall in Denmark. At the rear of this complex is a building erected in 1600 to serve as an inn for King Christian IV on journeys between his royal palaces in Copenhagen and Nykøbing. The contemporary sculpture in the courtyard was created by Jens Flemming Sørensen.

At Brogade 1, opposite the south-east corner of Torvet, is the **Køge Apotek**, a chemist shop which has occupied this site since 1660. Proceeding south, at Brogade 7 is **Oluf I Jensens Gaard**, a courtyard containing a collection of typical 19th century merchant buildings; one of these now houses the **Køge Galleriet**, a local art gallery.

At Brogade 19 there's an older courtyard, **Hugos Gård**, with some 17th century structures and a medieval brick building from the 14th century. The former wine cellar of the latter building now houses a wine bar, Hugos Vinkjælder, that could make an enjoyable place to stop for a break. In the adjacent courtyard, at Brogade 17, workers unearthed a buried treasure in 1987 – an old wooden trunk filled with more than 30 kg of 17th century silver coins, the largest such find ever made in Denmark. Some of these coins are now on display at the Køge Museum.

The circa 1638 building at **Brogade 23** is decorated with cherubs carved by the famed 17th century artist Abel Schrøder. If you cross the street and return back to Torvet along the west side of Brogade, you'll pass Køge's longest timber-framed house at **Brogade 16**, a yellow brick structure erected in 1636 by the town mayor.

Sankt Nicolai Kirke

This church on Kirkestræde, two blocks north of Torvet, is named after St Nicholas, the patron saint of mariners. At the east end of the church tower there's a little brick projection called the Lygten, which for centuries was used to hang a burning lantern to guide sailors returning to the harbour. It was from atop the church tower that Christian IV kept watch on his naval fleet as it successfully defended the town from Swedish invaders during the Battle of Køge Bay.

The church dates from 1324, but was largely rebuilt in the 15th century. Most of the ornately carved works that adorn the interior were added later, including the altar and pulpit which date from the 17th century. Sankt Nicolai Kirke is open on weekdays from 10 am to 4 pm from mid-June to late August and from 10 am to noon the rest of the year.

Køge Museum

The Køge Museum, at Nørregade 4, occupies a lovely building dating from 1610 that was once a wealthy merchant's home and store. It now holds a few dozen exhibit rooms illustrating the cultural history of the town and surrounding region. As well as the expected period furnishings and artefacts, there's an interesting hodgepodge of displays ranging from a Mesolithic-era grave to hundreds of recently discovered silver coins, part of a huge stash thought to have been hidden during the Swedish wars of the late 17th century. The museum also has a desk used by Danish philosopher NFS Grundtvig, who lived on the outskirts of Køge, and a windowpane onto which Hans Christian Andersen, during an apparently stressed-out stay at a nearby inn, scratched the words 'Oh God, Oh God in Kjøge'.

From June to August the museum is open from 10 am to 5 pm daily; the rest of the year it's open from 2 to 5 pm on weekdays and from 1 to 5 pm on weekends and holidays. Admission is 10 kr for adults and 5 kr for children.

Køge Skitsesamling

The Køge Skitsesamling (Art and Sketch Collection), at Nørregade 29, is a unique art museum that specialises in outlining the creative process from an artist's earliest concept to the finished work. The displays include the original drawings, clay models and mock-ups of a number of 20th century Danish artists. The museum also has a section dedicated to the works of Danish newspaper cartoonists as well as temporary exhibits. Admission is 15 kr for adults and free for students and children.

Cycling Tours

The Dansk Cyklist Forbund (Danish Cyclists' Union) puts out a free brochure, available in English at the tourist office, of five suggested cycling tours of the greater Køge area. These range in length from a six-km route that goes to Danish philosopher NFS Grundtvig's grave to a 40-km tour that includes Vallø Slot.

Places to Stay

The closest camping to the town centre is at *Køge Strand* (☎ 53 65 07 69, fax 53 65 59 84), Søndre Badevej, 4600 Køge, at the south side of the harbour. This two-star facility, on a beach with an industrial backdrop, charges 38 kr per person and is open from mid-April to 30 September. It's about a 20-minute walk south from the railway station,

via Toldbodvej, Carlsensvej and Strandpromenaden.

The 100-bed *Køge Vandrerhjem* (☎ 53 65 14 74, fax 53 66 08 69), Vamdrupvej 1, 4600 Køge, is in a quiet neighbourhood two km north-west of the town centre. The hostel has friendly staff and is open all year round, except for the holiday period from Christmas to New Year's. Both dorm beds and double rooms cost 69 kr per person. To get there from the Køge railway station, take bus No 210, get off at Agerskovvej and follow the signs to the hostel, 400 metres away.

The tourist office can book rooms in private homes for 130 to 150 kr per person, plus a 25 kr booking fee.

The fittingly named *Centralhotellet* (☎ 53 65 06 96, fax 53 65 59 84), adjacent to the tourist office at Vestergade 3, 4600 Køge, has 13 rooms above a small bar and in a separate wing out back. The rooms, which are straightforward but adequate, cost 230/410 kr for singles/doubles with shared bath or 510 kr for doubles with private bath, breakfast included.

Hotel Niels Juel (☎ 56 63 18 00, fax 56 63 04 92), Toldbodvej 20, 4600 Køge, near the inner harbour, a couple of blocks south of the railway station, is a modern 50-room hotel affiliated with the Best Western chain. The rooms, which have private bath, TV, phone and minibar, cost 740/940 kr for singles/doubles, breakfast included.

There's a second Best Western, the *Hotel Hvide Hus* (☎ 53 65 36 90, fax 53 66 33 14), Strandvejen 111, 4600 Køge, near the beach at the less developed south end of town. It has 127 modern rooms starting from 615/850 kr for singles/doubles, although there's a special discounted summer rate of 695 kr for a double.

Places to Eat

Torve Konditoriet, a good bakery at the west side of Torvet, has a café on the second floor with reasonable prices and a view of the square. The adjacent *La Fontaine*, Torvet 28, is a simple café with coffee, cappuccino, beer and good 15 kr sandwiches; it's open until at least midnight every day.

The *Ritz Burger Boss*, at Torvet 22, adjacent to Ritz Discotek (a disco open on Friday and Saturday from 10 pm to 5 am), sells burgers and hot dogs until 10 pm on weekdays and 4 am on weekends.

On the east side of Torvet you'll find a good fruit hut and a butcher shop with a deli and tempting smørrebrød sandwiches. There's a produce, cheese and flower market at Torvet open on Wednesday and Saturday mornings, and a Kvickly supermarket on Vestergade

Bella Napoli, at Brogade 21, is a popular and somewhat upmarket Italian restaurant with pizza and pasta dishes for 40 to 70 kr. It's open from 11 am to 10.30 pm. Cheaper pizza (30 kr) can be found at *La Mirage*, a largely takeaway pizzeria on Nørregade, which has a couple of tables and late hours.

Richters Gæstgivergaard, Vestergade 16, is a fine-dining restaurant in a half-timbered building dating from 1644. It has Danish and German main dishes from 95 to 168 kr and starters for about half that. In summer it also has a casual open-air courtyard where there's often live music.

A nice place for a drink is *Hugos Vinkjælder*, in the courtyard at Brogade 19. This cosy little wine bar, in the cellar of a medieval brick building that dates from the 14th century, sells half a bottle of wine for a reasonable 50 kr and also has beer. It's open from 10 am to 11 pm on weekdays, and to 1 am on Friday and Saturday.

Getting There & Away

Train Køge is at the end of the E line, the southernmost point of greater Copenhagen's S-train network. Trains from Copenhagen run three times an hour, take 38 minutes and cost 35 kr. Køge is also on the train line between Roskilde (25 minutes, 30 kr) and Næstved (34 minutes, 35 kr).

Car Køge is 42 km south-west of Copenhagen and 25 km south-east of Roskilde. If you're coming by car take the E47/55 from Copenhagen or route 6 from Roskilde and then pick up route 151 south into the centre of Køge. There's parking on Torvet with a one-hour limit during business hours and less-restricted parking off Havnen, north of the harbour.

VALLØ

Vallø is a charming little hamlet with cobblestone streets, a dozen mustard-yellow houses and an attractive moat-encircled Renaissance castle, Vallø Slot. Situated in the countryside about seven km south of Køge, Vallø makes an enjoyable little excursion for those looking to get off the beaten path. If Old World character and mildly eccentric surroundings appeal, it could also be a fun place to spend the evening.

Vallø Slot

The red-brick Vallø Slot (Vallø Castle) dates from 1586 and retains most of its original style, even though much of it was rebuilt following a fire in 1893.

The castle has a rather unique history. On her birthday in 1737, Queen Sophie Magdalene, who owned the estate, established a foundation that turned Vallø Slot into a home for 'spinsters of noble birth'. Until a few decades ago, unmarried daughters of Danish royalty who hadn't the means to live in their own castles or manor houses were allowed to take up residence at Vallø, supported by the foundation and government social programmes.

In the 1970s, bowing to changing sentiments that had previously spared this anachronistic niche of the Zealand countryside, the foundation amended its charter to gradually make the estate more accessible to the general public. For now, the castle remains home solely to half a dozen blue-blooded women who had taken up residence prior to 1976.

Vallø Slot is surrounded by 2800 hectares of woods and ponds and 1300 hectares of fields and arable land that reach clear down to the coast. Although the main castle buildings are not yet open to the public, visitors are free to walk in the gardens and the adjacent woods.

Hestestalden, the stables at Vallø Slot, has an exhibition on the history of the castle

SOUTHERN ZEALAND

that's open in summer only, from 11 am to 4 pm daily. A Køge Museum ticket allows free admission.

Places to Stay & Eat

Vallø Slotskro (☎ 56 26 70 20), Slotsgade 1, 4600 Køge, is a 200-year-old inn that sits just outside the castle gate. There are 11 pleasantly decorated rooms. Most cost 520/675 kr (breakfast included) for singles/doubles and have TV, phone and shower, but there are also two small rooms without baths that are a bit cheaper, as well as a suite with a jacuzzi that's more expensive.

The inn's restaurant serves traditional Danish cuisine with a French accent. From noon to 4 pm, there's a full lunch plate with herring, meat, salmon paté, cheese and fresh fruit for 110 kr and a few lighter offerings for around 70 kr. A fixed-price three-course dinner costs 195 kr; otherwise main dishes of fish, veal or chateaubriand average 150 kr.

Getting There & Away

Take the train to Vallø station, two stops south of Køge, and from there it's a pleasant stroll east down a tree-lined country road 1.25 km to the castle.

By car take route 209 south from Køge, turn right onto Billesborgvej and then left (south) onto Valløvej, which leads to Slotsgade. By bike, there's a cycle route from Køge that leads into Valløvej.

RINGSTED

Situated at a crossroads in central Zealand, Ringsted was an important market town during the Middle Ages and also served as the site of the *landsting*, a regional governing assembly. The town grew up around the Sankt Bendts Kirke, which was built during the reign of King Valdemar I (1157-82). This historic church still marks the town centre and is Ringsted's most interesting sight.

Immediately east of the church is Torvet, the central square, which has a statue of Valdemar I sculpted by Johannes Bjerg in the 1930s, as well as three sitting stones that were used centuries ago by the landsting members.

Information

The friendly Ringsted Turistbureau (☎ 53 61

The Dagmar Cross

Queen Dagmar, the first wife of King Valdemar II, was born a princess in Bohemia. Although she lived in Denmark for only a few years before her premature death in 1212, she was much beloved by the Danes and is revered in several ballads as a kind, good-hearted woman.

In 1683, as Queen Dagmar's tomb was being removed from Sankt Bendts Kirke in Ringsted, a small gold cross with finely detailed enamel work was found at the site. Now known as the Dagmar Cross, it is thought to date from 1000 AD. One side shows Christ with arms outstretched on the cross and the other side depicts him with the Virgin Mary, John the Baptist, St John and St Basil.

This perfectly preserved cross of Byzantine design is now in the Nationalmuseet in Copenhagen. It has been widely replicated as a pendant by Ringsted jewellery shops and is popularly worn as a necklace by brides who marry in Sankt Bendts Kirke. ■

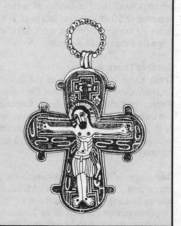

34 00, fax 53 61 64 50) is at Sankt Bendts-gade 10, 4100 Ringsted, opposite Sankt Bendts Kirke. From May to August it's open from 9 am to 5.30 pm on weekdays and from 9 am to 2 pm on Saturday; in winter it's open from 9 am to 2 pm, Monday to Friday.

Sankt Bendts Kirke

This imposing church was erected in 1170 by Valdemar I, partly to serve as a burial sanctuary for his murdered father, Knud Lavard, who had recently been canonised by the Pope as a saint, and partly as a calculated move to shore up the rule of the Valdemar dynasty and intertwine the influences of the Crown and the Catholic church.

Although Sankt Bendts Kirke was substantially restored in the early 1900s, it retains much of its original medieval style and still incorporates travertine blocks from an 11th century abbey church that had earlier occupied the same site.

The nave has magnificent frescoes, including a series on King Erik IV (known as Erik Ploughpenny, for the despised tax he levied on ploughs), which were painted in about 1300 in a failed campaign to get the assassinated king canonised. These frescoes show Queen Agnes, seated on a throne; on her left is a scene of Ploughpenny's murderers stabbing the king with a spear, while the right-hand scene depicts the king's corpse being retrieved from the sea by fishermen.

Sankt Bendts Kirke was a burial place for the royal family for 150 years. In the aisle floor beneath the nave (in order from the font) are flat stones marking the tombs of Valdemar III and his queen, Eleonora; Valdemar II, flanked by his queens Dagmar and Bengærd; Knud VI; Valdemar I, flanked by his queen, Sofia, and his son Christoffer; and Knud Lavard. Also buried in the church is Erik VI (Menved) and Queen Ingeborg, whose remains are in an ornate tomb in the chancel, and King Birger of Sweden and his queen Margarete, who occupy the former tomb of Erik Ploughpenny. Some of the tombs, including the empty one that once held Queen Dagmar, have been disturbed over the centuries to make room for later burials. A few of the grave relics removed from these tombs can be found in the museum chapel, along with a copy of the Dagmar Cross (see the Dagmar Cross boxed aside).

The church also has some interesting carved works, including pews from 1591 (note the dragons on the seats near the altar), an elaborate altarpiece from 1699 and a pulpit from 1609. The oldest item in the church is the 12th century baptismal font which, despite its historical significance, once served a stint as a flower bowl in a local garden.

The church is open daily from 10 am to noon and 1 to 5 pm from May to mid-September; it's open from 1 to 3 pm the rest of the year.

Ringsted Museum

This small museum of local cultural history, which includes a restored 1814 Dutch windmill, is on the east side of town at Køgevej 37, within walking distance of Torvet and the railway station. Opening hours are from 11 am to 4 pm, Tuesday to Sunday. Admission is 15 kr.

Places to Stay

The 78-bed hostel, *Ringsted Vandrerhjem* (☎ 53 61 15 26, fax 53 61 34 26), Sankt Bendtsgade 18, 4100 Ringsted, is in the town centre just a block north of Sankt Bendts Kirke. Dorm beds cost 80 kr. From June to August, you can book a private room for one to four people for 320 kr. Outside those months, private rooms cost 180/260 kr for singles/doubles, plus 50 kr for each additional person. Each room has a private bathroom. The hostel is closed from 20 December to 10 January.

The tourist office books rooms in private homes for an average of 150 kr per person, including breakfast; there's no booking fee.

Places to Eat

There are a number of places to eat near Sankt Bendts Kirke. *Raadhuskroen* at Sankt Bendtsgade 8, opposite the church, is a pub-style restaurant with average Danish fare.

ᛁᚦᛖ·ᛏᛁᚱ·ᚠᛉᚾᛗ·ᛉᛈᚠᛗᚾ·ᚠᛈᛈᛁᚦᛖ·ᛏᛁᚱ·ᚠᛉᚾᛗ·ᛉᛈᚠᛗᚾ·ᚠᛈᛈᛁᚦᛖ·ᛏᛁᚱ·ᚠᛉᚾᛗ·ᛉᛈᚠᛗᚾ·ᚠᛈᛈᛁᚦᛖ·ᛏᛁᚱ·ᚠᛉᚾᛗ·ᛉᛈᚠᛗᚾ·ᚠᛈᛈᛁᚦᛖ

Bishops & Bricks

Shortly after the end of the Viking era, two things happened that had a significant and lasting impact on church architecture in Denmark. First, King Sweyn II (1047-74) found himself deep in a power struggle with the Archbishop of Bremen, the leader of the Danish church. To weaken the influence of the archbishop, the king divided Denmark into eight separate dioceses, which set the stage for a flurry of new church and cathedral building.

In the 12th century the art of brick-making was introduced to Denmark from northern Italy and Germany. Before that, most churches were constructed with wood or calcareous tufa and rough stone. The use of bricks allowed for construction on a much larger scale and within a few decades grand churches were being built all around Denmark. Some of the buildings from this era still stand today, including the stalwart churches of Sorø and Ringsted and the cathedrals in Roskilde and Århus. ■

ᛁᚦᛖ·ᛏᛁᚱ·ᚠᛉᚾᛗ·ᛉᛈᚠᛗᚾ·ᚠᛈᛈᛁᚦᛖ·ᛏᛁᚱ·ᚠᛉᚾᛗ·ᛉᛈᚠᛗᚾ·ᚠᛈᛈᛁᚦᛖ·ᛏᛁᚱ·ᚠᛉᚾᛗ·ᛉᛈᚠᛗᚾ·ᚠᛈᛈᛁᚦᛖ·ᛏᛁᚱ·ᚠᛉᚾᛗ·ᛉᛈᚠᛗᚾ·ᚠᛈᛈᛁᚦᛖ

Their speciality is spareribs; two ribs with a selection from their simple salad bar and a baked potato cost 75 kr.

Just a couple of minutes walk south is *Burger Plads*, at Sankt Hansgade 11, which has burgers and pitta-bread sandwiches, and *Italy & Italy*, at Torvet 1, which has authentic, moderately priced pizza, pasta, calamari and meat dishes.

Getting There & Away

Ringsted is on route 150 and just off the E20 motorway, 27 km west of Køge and 16 km east of Sorø. Roskilde is 30 km to the north via route 14.

There are numerous trains throughout the day to Ringsted from Roskilde (18 minutes, 24 kr) and Næstved (20 minutes, 24 kr). Ringsted's town centre is a 10-minute walk north of the railway station.

Getting Around

Bicycles can be rented from Nørregade's Cykelforretning (☎ 53 61 33 52), at Nørregade 34, north of the church.

SORØ

Bordered by lakes and woodlands, Sorø is a delightful little town steeped in history. Bishop Absalon established a Cistercian monastery here in 1161, six years before he founded Copenhagen. The bishop and four Danish monarchs lie buried in Sorø Kirke,

the church that Absalon erected on the monastery grounds.

After the Reformation, when Catholicism was banned and church properties were turned over to the Crown, King Frederik II set aside the monastery grounds to be used as a school. His successor, King Christian IV, developed it into the Sorø Academy of Knights, an élite school dedicated to the education of the sons of the nobility.

The great Danish playwright Ludvig Holberg (1684-1754), a summer resident in Sorø and a patron of the academy, helped revive the school during faltering times by bequeathing his substantial estate. Other significant men of letters had connections with the academy, including the poet and novelist BS Ingemann (1789-1862), who taught literature here for three decades from 1822.

During Denmark's 'golden age' of national romanticism (1800-50), Sorø became a haunt for some of the country's most prominent cultural figures, including Bertel Thorvaldsen, NFS Grundtvig and Adam Oehlenschläger.

Sorø is a pleasant destination with an interesting air of culture and history. The streets of the town centre are thick with old timber-framed houses, and the academy grounds and surrounding lakeside park are open to the public.

Information

Tourist Office The Sorø Turistbureau (☎ 57

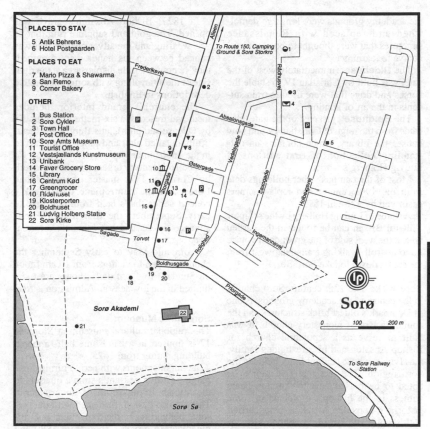

PLACES TO STAY
5 Antik Behrens
6 Hotel Postgaarden

PLACES TO EAT
7 Mario Pizza & Shawarma
8 San Remo
9 Corner Bakery

OTHER
1 Bus Station
2 Sorø Cykler
3 Town Hall
4 Post Office
10 Sorø Amts Museum
11 Tourist Office
12 Vestsjællands Kunstmuseum
13 Unibank
14 Favør Grocery Store
15 Library
16 Centrum Kød
17 Greengrocer
10 Tidehuset
19 Klosterporten
20 Boldhuset
21 Ludvig Holberg Statue
22 Sorø Kirke

Sorø

SOUTHERN ZEALAND

82 10 12, fax 57 82 10 13), in the town centre at Storgade 15, 4180 Sorø, has brochures on Sorø and the region, and can help with everything from exchanging money after hours to suggesting cycling tours. It's open from 9 am to 5 pm, Monday to Saturday (to noon on Saturday in the low season).

Money There are several banks in town, including a Unibank at Storgade 22, opposite the tourist office.

Post The post office is at Rådhusvej 6, a few minutes south of the bus station.

Sorø Akademi
Although it's no longer reserved for the sons of the nobility, the Sorø Akademi remains a prominent Danish school. The extensive grounds are owned by a private foundation, while the school itself is funded by the state.

The south end of Sorø's main street, Storgade, leads directly to the academy via **Klosterporten**, the medieval gate that once served to cloister monks from the outside world.

Although both the gate and the Sorø church date from the Middle Ages, other monastery buildings which once occupied the academy grounds were long ago demolished and replaced with Renaissance structures that were thought to be more conducive to learning.

The **Ridehuset**, immediately west of the gate, was built by Christian IV to stable the horses and dogs that were used to train students in the art of hunting.

The **Boldhuset**, just east of the gate, also dates from the reign of Christian IV and now houses the library, which contains an outstanding collection of first editions of Ludvig Holberg's works.

Most of the campus' other buildings date from the 19th century and replace others destroyed by a fire in 1813.

A statue of Ludvig Holberg by the sculptor Vilhelm Bissen can be found in the garden area at the west side of the grounds. If you're up to a stroll, walking trails lead west from the statue down to lake Sorø Sø.

Sorø Kirke The 12th century Sorø church, in the centre of the academy grounds, is one of Denmark's oldest brick structures and the country's largest monastery church. It was built to serve as a sepulchral church for Bishop Absalon and his prestigious family, the Hvides, whose landholdings included the Sorø region. The fact that five monarchs opted to be buried next to Absalon bears witness to the bishop's prominence; some historians consider Absalon, who carried both sceptre and sword, to be the most significant Danish statesman of medieval times.

The church stands largely as Absalon erected it, in the Romanesque style typical of Cistercian monasteries. Its huge central nave is flanked by two aisles. At the end of the left aisle is the marble sarcophagus of Ludvig Holberg.

Bishop Absalon lies at rest directly behind the main altar; keeping him company are the sarcophagi of kings Valdemar IV, Christopher II and Oluf III. Queen Margrethe I, the architect of the 1397 Union of Kalmar that brought Norway and Sweden under Danish rule, was originally buried here as well, but her remains were later transferred to the Roskilde cathedral.

In 1827, Bishop Absalon's grave was opened. The gold and sapphire ring that he was wearing and the silver chalice that was cupped between his hands were removed; they're now in a little display area at the right side of the altar, along with some interpretive descriptions in English.

The church's grand interior includes medieval frescoes, a six-metre-high crucifix by Odense sculptor Claus Berg and a beautifully detailed altar and pulpit, both carved in the 1650s in baroque style.

The 16th century organ, which was rebuilt by Christian IV's master organist Johan Lorenz, is the centrepiece of a weekly concert series that's held from late June to early September; the tourist office sells advance tickets and has schedule information.

From mid-May to early September the church is open to visitors from 10 am (noon on Sunday) to 4 pm daily; hours are more limited in the low season. Admission is free.

Sorø Amts Museum
This regional cultural museum at Storgade 17 is housed in a handsome half-timbered building dating from 1625.

It contains rooms with period furnishings, ranging from a peasant's simple quarters to the stylish living room of an aristocrat. There's also a room furnished with the personal belongings of the romanticist poet BS Ingemann, a grocer's shop from 1880 and displays of period costumes, old bottles and archaeological finds. It's open from 1 to 4 pm, Tuesday to Sunday (from 10 am in summer); admission is 10 kr for adults and free for children.

Vestsjællands Kunstmuseum
Another worthwhile spot is the Vestsjællands Kunstmuseum (Art Museum of West Zealand), which is in a period building at Storgade 9. Its varied collection of regional art runs the gamut from medieval church pieces and stodgy portraits by CW Eckersberg to wildly expressionist modern art. It's open from 10 am to 4 pm daily from mid-

May to mid-August and from 1 to 4 pm the rest of the year. Admission is free.

Other Things to See & Do
Inside the courtyard at Storgade 7 is an attractive timber-framed Renaissance building constructed by Christian IV which now houses the town's **bibliotek** (library).

From Torvet, consider taking a walk down **Søgade**, an inviting street with leaning half-timbered mustard-yellow houses, with red tiled roofs. You can follow this street down to the lake and its garden-like setting, where there are trails in both directions.

Places to Stay
Sorø Camping (☎ 53 63 02 02, fax 57 82 11 02), Udbyhøjvej 10, 4180 Sorø, borders lake Pedersborg Sø at the north-west side of town, about 150 metres north of Slagelsevej. This three-star camping ground is wheelchair accessible and has a coin laundry, kitchen, playground and miniature golf. Pitching a tent costs 42 kr per person and there are a few cabins that can be rented at reasonable rates. Open all year round, the camping ground is a 20-minute walk from town along a lakeside trail; bus No 234 (10 kr) stops nearby.

Antik Behrens (☎ 53 63 53 52), Absalonsgade 19, 4180 Sorø, a 10-minute walk from the town centre, is a private home with three comfortable double rooms for 300 kr and a single room for 175 kr, breakfast included. The owner is a former antiques dealer and the breakfast room is so laden with period paintings and furniture that it resembles a museum.

Hotel Postgaarden (☎ 53 63 22 22, fax 53 63 22 91), Storgade 25, 4180 Sorø, is an inn-style hotel with a 300-year history. The 23 rooms are pleasantly simple with private bath, desk and phone; TVs are available on request. Most of the town's sights are within a few minutes walk. Rates are 450/650 kr for singles/doubles, breakfast included.

The *Sorø Storkro* (☎ 53 63 56 00, fax 53 63 56 06), Abildvej 100, 4180 Sorø, is a modern 94-room hotel in a rural setting about two km north-west of town on the way to Slagelse. The rooms are comfortable with

cable TV, minibar and private bath. There's a sauna, indoor pool, restaurant and bar. Standard rates are 650/850 kr for singles/doubles; however 'inn cheques', available at the tourist office, can reduce the rate a bit.

Places to Eat
There are a few places to get inexpensive eats along Storgade near the Hotel Postgaarden. Opposite the hotel is *Mario Pizza & Shawarma*, a hole-in-the-wall place selling cheap pizza and pitta-bread sandwiches. Just south of it is *San Remo*, a more standard pizzeria with pasta and lasagne for 29 kr at lunch and pizza from 31 kr any time of the day. Across the street is the *Corner Bakery*, which has good breads and pastries. There's another cluster of fast-food places a few minutes farther south on Storgade near Torvet, as well as a greengrocer and the *Centrum Kød*, a butcher shop with a deli and takeaway smørrebrød.

For a romantic treat, the *Hotel Postgaarden* has a candlelit restaurant with an engaging traditional atmosphere. At dinner the speciality is a medieval style of cooking in which flat stones are heated to 120°C and brought to your table for cooking slices of 'stonebeef'; prices vary depending upon the amount of meat you order, but you can eat well for less than 150 kr; salad and potatoes are included. At lunch, served from 11.30 am to 5 pm, you can get standard combination plates of traditional Danish foods, including smoked salmon, herring and meatballs, priced from 50 to 125 kr.

Getting There & Away
Sorø is 15 km east of Slagelse and 16 km west of Ringsted via route 150 or the E20. The Sorø railway station is in Frederiksberg, two km south of Sorø's centre; bus Nos 806 and 807 (10 kr) run between Sorø and the railway station at least hourly. The trains run about once hourly to Sorø from Slagelse (10 minutes, 18 kr) and Ringsted (8 minutes, 18 kr). There's also a bus service (No 234) between Sorø and Slagelse. The bus station is on Rådhusvej between Absalonsgade and Fægangen.

Getting Around
Sorø Cykler (☎ 53 63 42 01), at Storgade 38, rents bicycles.

SLAGELSE
Slagelse is best known to visitors as the starting point for trips to nearby Trelleborg. Although Slagelse doesn't have any particular allure, there are a couple of local sights you could take in if time permits and it's an agreeable place to stay if you need to break for the night.

The town centre is dominated by Sankt Mikkels Kirke (St Michael's), a gothic-style church built of brick in the early 1300s. To the east of the church is Nytorv, the main commercial square.

Information on Trelleborg is in the section that follows Slagelse.

Information
Tourist Office Slagelse Turistbureau (☎ 53 52 22 06, fax 53 52 86 87), Løvegade 7, 4200 Slagelse, is a 10-minute walk south of the railway station and a few hundred metres west of Nytorv. It's open from 9 am to 5 pm, Monday to Saturday, from mid-June to August; and from 10 am to 5 pm on weekdays and 10 am to 1 pm on Saturday the rest of the year.

Money There are several banks around town, including Den Danske Bank at Nytorv 1.

Post The post office is immediately east of the railway station.

Slagelse Museum
This local museum at Bredgade 11, a short walk south-west of Nytorv, displays the craft and industrial history of Slagelse, with the old tools and workshops of a grocer, barber, butcher, blacksmith etc, and rooms of period furniture. It's open in summer from noon to 4 pm daily, and all year round on Saturday from 3 to 5 pm. Admission is 10 kr.

Ruins of Antvorskov
The brick ruins of Antvorskov, a medieval monastery founded by King Valdemar I in 1164, are about two km south of the town centre. Antvorskov's most significant role in history is its connection with Hans Tausen, the renegade monk who took his monastic training here. Hans was vexed by the excessive privilege he found at Antvorskov, which was one of the wealthiest monasteries in Denmark and open only to the sons of nobility. After a study tour abroad, during which he heard Martin Luther preaching in Wittenburg, Germany, Hans returned to Antvorskov, where on Maundy Thursday in 1525 he delivered a fiery speech that helped spark the Danish Reformation.

Following the Reformation, Antvorskov was confiscated by the Crown and became a favourite hunting manor for King Frederik II, who died here in 1588. Eventually it was sold off and the buildings, including the old monastery church, were demolished.

About half of the former monastery grounds are now buried under the E20 motorway, but some of the brick remains of the original foundations can still be seen. A couple of interpretive plaques at the site detail the ruins. While historically significant, the ruins aren't overwhelmingly interesting in themselves and are out of the way if you don't have your own transport. You can get there by taking Slotsalléen from the town centre to its end; then turn right and go about 200 metres to the carpark opposite Munkebakken.

Places to Stay
The adjacent *Slagelse Campingplads* and *Slagelse Vandrerhjem* (☎ 53 52 25 28, fax 53 52 25 40) are under the same management at Bjergbygade 78, 4200 Slagelse, two km south of the railway station. The two-star camping ground is open from 1 April to 30 September and charges 41 kr per person. Hostel dorm beds cost 70 kr, while family rooms for one to six people range from 160 to 420 kr. The hostel is closed from mid-December to mid-January. There are also cabins for 390 kr that can sleep up to six, and a coin laundry. You can take local bus No 303 (10 kr), or take a taxi (about 35 kr), from the railway station.

The tourist office can arrange rooms in private homes for about 100 kr per person, with a 10 kr booking fee.

The *Hotel Slagelse* (☎ 53 52 01 72), Sondre Stationsvej 19, 4200 Slagelse, an older 40-room hotel near the railway and bus stations, has straightforward singles/doubles without bath for 230/460 kr or 330/580 kr with bath, breakfast included.

Hotel Frederik den II (☎ 53 53 03 22, fax 53 53 46 22), Idagårdsvej 3, 4200 Slagelse, is a modern hotel near the intersection of route 22 and the E20, at the south side of town. The rooms are comfortable, with private bath, TV, phone, coffee maker etc. There's a pleasant little sauna and a good breakfast is included. The standard rate is a pricey 745/995 kr for singles/doubles, but Best Western promotions can cut that rate substantially. The hotel is adjacent to a large shopping complex called Bilka.

Places to Eat
For something healthy and quick there's *Café Grønne*, opposite Sankt Mikkels Kirke at the south-eastern side of Nytorv square, which has focaccia sandwiches (25 kr) and quality gelato (13 kr for a double scoop).

There are a number of other restaurants bordering the church and Nytorv, including *Nat Toget*, Gammel Torv 8, a pleasant pub-style place with pizza, pasta and beef dishes; *Siang Jiang*, on the square, with moderately priced Chinese food; and the more upmarket *Nytorv 2*, which has Danish meat and fish dishes for around 75 to 125 kr. There's a *Netto* grocery store just south of Nytorv.

Getting There & Away
Slagelse is at the intersections of routes 150 and 22 and along the E20 motorway. It's 37 km south-east of Kalundborg and 19 km north-east of Korsør.

Slagelse is on the main east-west rail line between Copenhagen and Jutland and thus has frequent rail services. From Slagelse, it's 33 minutes (41 kr) to Roskilde and 12 minutes (18 kr) to Korsør.

Getting Around
Bicycle rentals can be arranged at the tourist office or from the nearby HJ Cykler (☎ 53 52 28 57), Løvegade 46.

TRELLEBORG
Trelleborg, in the countryside seven km west of Slagelse, is the best preserved of the four Viking ring fortresses in Denmark.

At the entrance to Trelleborg is a reconstructed Viking house, built in Viking stave style, using rough oak timbers erected above mud floors. The inside has earthen benches of the type used by warriors for sleeping and a central hearth with a simple opening in the roof for venting smoke.

There's a museum with exhibits of pottery and other items excavated from the fortress grounds and a 20-minute video on Trelleborg's history that runs in turn in Danish, English and German. There are usually a few costumed interpreters, chopping wood for a fire or giving archery demonstrations to Danish schoolchildren, but the highlight is just strolling the grounds.

You can walk up onto the grassy circular rampart and readily grasp the geometric design of the fortress. From atop the rampart, Trelleborg appears strikingly symmetrical and precise; cement blocks have been placed to show the outlines of the elliptical house foundations. Grazing sheep wandering in from the surrounding farmland imbue the scene with a timeless aura. A few interpretive plaques in English describe burial mounds and other features along the way.

Trelleborg (☎ 53 54 95 06), on Trelleborg Allé, is open from 10 am to 5 pm daily. It's a fairly compact site and you could easily take it all in during an hour-long visit. Admission is 30 kr for adults and 15 kr for children. There's a café and gift shop.

Getting There & Away
To get to Trelleborg from Slagelse with your own transport, take Strandvejen to its end at the village of Hejninge (where there's an attractive church with early 15th century

frescoes) and then follow the signs to Trelleborg, one km farther.

Bus No 312 from Slagelse to Trelleborg takes 12 minutes and costs 10 kr. On summer weekdays the bus to Trelleborg leaves Slagelse bus station at 8.06 am and 12.06, 3.46 and 5.06 pm; in the opposite direction, buses leave Trelleborg for Slagelse at 7.38 and 9.31 am and 2.31 and 6.31 pm. During the school year the bus is about twice as frequent. On Saturday there's only one bus from Slagelse to Trelleborg, at 1.06 pm (and no later return bus), and there are no buses on Sunday.

A good alternative to relying on the bus is to cycle your way across the rural countryside between Slagelse and Trelleborg. The Slagelse tourist office rents bicycles and has an English-language brochure describing points of interest along the way.

KORSØR

Situated at the narrowest point of the Store Bælt (Great Belt), the channel that separates Zealand and Funen, Korsør takes much of its character from its strategic location. The town boomed in the 1850s with the construction of the Zealand railroad, of which Korsør is the western terminus. The railroad and the linking ferry and shipping services continue to be an economic mainstay for the town.

Although Korsør is not a prime tourist destination, a lot of travellers pass through as it has the main rail (via ferry) and boat connections to Funen.

Korsør is divided in half by an inland bay (Korsør Nor) and connected with a single bridge (Halsskovbroen) over which routes 150 and 265 cross. Both the train ferries and the car ferries leave from the northern half of the city, while in the commercial centre, the

Trelleborg's Precise Design

Trelleborg's military origins are visible in its precise mathematical layout and use of the Roman foot (29.33 cm) as a unit of measure.

The Trelleborg compound consists of two wards that encompass about seven hectares in all. The inner ward is embraced by a circular earthen rampart that is six metres high and 17 metres thick at its base. Four gates, one at each point of the compass, cut across the rampart. The gateways are crossed by two streets, one east-west, the other north-south, which has the effect of dividing the inner ward into four symmetrical quadrants. In Viking times, each quadrant contained four long elliptical buildings that surrounded a courtyard. Each of the 16 buildings was exactly 100 Roman feet long and contained a central hall and two smaller rooms.

Following the arc along the exterior of the inner rampart was an 18-metre-wide ditch; two bridges spanned the ditch, crossing over to the outer ward. This outer ward contained a cemetery with about 150 graves and 15 houses, each of which was 90 feet long and lined up radially with its gable pointing towards the inner rampart. A second earthen ward separated the outer ward from the surrounding countryside. ∎

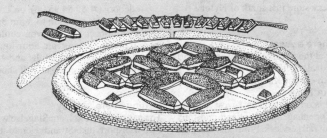

Southern Zealand
- Top: Viking Age ramparts and former longhouse sites, Trelleborg
- Left: Field of rapeseed (mustard) flowers in bloom
- Right: Bicycle in central square, Præsto

NED.FRIARY

NED FRIARY

NED FRIARY

NED FRIARY

Møn & Lolland
Top Left: People walking along the beach at the foot of Møns Klint chalk cliffs, Møn
Top Right: Elmelunde Kirke, Elmelunde, Møn
Bottom Left: Frescoes, Elmelunde Kirke, Møn
Bottom Right: Pub, Sakskøbing, Lolland

restaurants and sights of interest are in the southern half. It's about one km from the railway station, on the northern side of the bridge, to Torvet, the town square, on the southern side. If you want to leave your bags and explore town, there are 10 kr lockers at the railway station.

Information
The Korsør Turistbureau (☎ 53 57 08 03, fax 53 57 00 21) at Nygade 7, 4220 Korsør, is open from 10 am to 5 pm, Monday to Friday, and from 10 am to 1 pm on Saturday; it opens one hour earlier in summer.

Things to See
The **Fæstningen** (Fortress) tower, which is on the south side of the harbour and clearly visible from the railway station, is Korsør's main sight and one of Denmark's few remaining medieval towers. The tower is about 24 metres high and nine metres wide and is built of monkstone, a type of oversized brick. This tower, and a powderhouse built by King Christian IV in 1610, are the remains of a castle that once stood on the site. The half-timbered building adjacent to the tower was built in the early 18th century as a naval commander's home and now contains the local history archives.

Also within the fortress grounds is the **Korsør By-og Overfartsmuseum** (Korsør Town & Ferry Service Museum), which has ship models and other displays portraying the history of the ferries and icebreakers that have crossed the Store Bælt over the past two centuries. It's open from 10 am to 4 pm, Tuesday to Sunday; admission is 8 kr for adults and 2 kr for children.

Kongegården, in the town centre at Algade 25, is a small art museum that has one floor dedicated to the works of Harald Isenstein, a Jewish sculptor who fled Nazi Germany in the 1930s. There are also temporary exhibits of regional work. It's open daily from 10 am to 4 pm (to 8 pm on Wednesday). Admission is free. The museum is in a neighbourhood of interesting 18th century buildings.

Places to Stay
Halsskovhavn Camping (☎ & fax 53 57 09 23), Revvej 185, 4220 Korsør, is just south of the DSB car ferry harbour and the E20 terminus. This two-star facility charges 40 kr per person and has a kitchen, a coin laundry and a view of the water. It's open from 1 April to 1 October.

The hostel, *Korsør Vandrerhjem* (☎ 53 57 10 22, fax 58 35 68 70), Tovesvej 30F, 4220 Korsør, is on the quiet eastern outskirts of town, about one km north-east of the railway station. Built in the mid-1980s, this modern hostel has 20 four-bed rooms, each with a private shower and toilet. It's open year round except from mid-December to mid-January. Dorm-style beds cost 85 kr, while private rooms cost 200 kr for one person and up to 300 kr for four people. There are cooking facilities and it's accessible by wheelchair.

The tourist office books rooms in private homes for 120 to 170 kr per night.

The *Jens Baggesen Hotel* (☎ 58 35 10 00, fax 58 35 10 01), south of the fortress at Batterivej 3, 4220 Korsør, is a 42-room hotel in a converted period warehouse. Rooms have private bath, phone and TV with multilingual programmes. The regular rate is 560/830 kr for singles/doubles, but there's a special summer rate of 600 kr for doubles, breakfast included.

Places to Eat
The kiosk at the railway station sells sandwiches, pastries, hot dogs and light beer.

The main restaurant area is on the south side of the harbour, a little over a km from the station. In the town centre, near the intersection of Nygade and the pedestrian walkway Algade, you'll find two bakeries, two supermarkets and a couple of pizzerias. Best bet amongst them is *Galaxsi Pizza*, at Algade 33, which is open daily until 11 pm and has various pizzas for 35 kr, moussaka for 63 kr and a good selection of lunch specials for 39 kr.

Getting There & Away
Korsør is at Zealand's western end of the

E20, which picks up again on the opposite side of the Store Bælt at Nyborg on Funen. Until the Store Bælt bridge is completed, all crossings between Zealand and Funen are by boat.

As Korsør is on the main rail line between Zealand and Funen, there are frequent train services to Copenhagen (65 minutes, 106 kr) and Odense (95 minutes, 98 kr).

Rail Ferries If you're travelling by train the Store Bælt crossing is included in your fare on a through ticket. Once you reach Korsør's harbour-side railway station, the IC trains roll right onto the ferries, whereas on most IR trains you walk onto the docked boat and then off the ferry and onto a waiting train upon reaching the other side of the channel. For more information on rail services see the train section of the Getting Around chapter.

Car Ferries In addition to the rail ferries, DSB operates a car ferry across the Store Bælt every 30 minutes (24 hours a day) on weekdays, with slightly fewer late-night sailings on weekends. The DSB car ferries leave from Halsskov Færgehavn, where the E20 terminates, at 15 and 45 minutes after the hour, and arrive an hour later in Nyborg's Knudshoved harbour, where the E20 picks up again. The cost is 280 kr for a car with up to five passengers, or 130 kr for a motorcycle and two passengers. In the opposite direction, boats leave Knudshoved on the hour and half-hour. Reservation numbers are ☎ 53 57 15 17 in Halsskov and 65 31 40 54 in Knudshoved.

The ferry operated by Vognmandsruten (☎ 53 57 02 04) is cheaper. It leaves Korsør from the harbour just north of the railway station on the hour an average of 20 times a day, arriving 70 minutes later in Nyborg. The cost is 63 kr for adults (bicycles are free), 25 kr for children, 110 kr for a motorcycle with up to two people, and 235 kr for a car and all its passengers. In the opposite direction, boats leave Nyborg on the half-hour.

For information on the ferries from Korsør to Kiel in Germany, see the Getting There & Away chapter in the front of the book.

Getting Around
Bus Bus No 502 connects the town centre with the railway station (10 kr).

Bicycle Bicycles can be rented for 45 kr a day from Svend Eriks Cykler & Symaskiner (☎ 53 57 04 29), in the centre of town at Algade 35.

KALUNDBORG

If you're heading directly to Jutland from Zealand, Kalundborg is the main jumping-off point. The railway line ends at the central harbour, so if you're going to Århus you can walk off the train and right onto your ferry or catamaran. The ferry to Juelsminde leaves from Sydhavn, at the south side of the harbour; to get there from the railway station, walk east on Østre Havnevej and then follow the road south along the waterfront.

If you have time to spare before catching a ferry, consider a stroll over to Vor Frue Kirke, an intriguing medieval church and Kalundborg's only major site of interest.

Things to See
The **Vor Frue Kirke** was erected in the late 12th century and with its five towers stands as one of the most unique medieval churches in Denmark. It was built as a castle church by Esbern Snare, Bishop Absalon's brother, using a Byzantine-like design based upon the Greek cross. The cross shape takes the form of a square central tower connected by cross appendages to four equidistant octagonal towers. The church was originally part of an extensive fortress, but in 1658 the townspeople tore down the fortress walls to minimise the risk of an attack by the Swedes. The church is on Adelgade, just west of Torvet and a short walk north-west from the harbour. The site of Snare's castle is in **Ruinparken**, a few minutes farther west, but there's little left to decipher amongst the ruins.

If you make a loop around the church via Præstegade and Adelgade, you'll pass through the oldest part of town, where there are cobbled streets and 16th century homes; the one at Adelgade 23 houses the **Kalund-**

borg-og Omegns Museum, the local history museum.

Places to Stay & Eat
The new 118-bed hostel, *Kalundborg Vandrerhjem* (☎ 59 56 13 66, fax 59 56 46 26), Stadion Allé 5, 4400 Kalundborg, is just north-west of Ruinparken, within walking distance of the railway station and the ferries to Århus. Dorm beds cost 80 kr and there are also family rooms. It's open year round.

There are restaurants in the town centre and snack bars on the ferries.

Getting There & Away
Kalundborg is at the terminus of routes 22 and 23, some 51 km north of Korsør and 69 km west of Roskilde.

Train Trains between Copenhagen and Kalundborg operate at least once an hour throughout the day. The journey takes 1¾ hours and costs 77 kr. A free en route stop in Roskilde is allowed – just tell the conductor when you board.

Boat The fastest way to zip over to Århus is by Cat-Link's (☎ 89 41 20 20) sleek catamaran ferry that takes just 80 minutes. The fare is 150 kr for adults, 75 kr for children, 360 kr for a car with up to four passengers, 200 kr for a motorcycle with driver, and 20 kr for a bicycle. On weekdays it leaves Kalundborg at 8.30 am, noon and 4, 7.30 and 10.30 pm and leaves Århus at 6.45 and 10.15 am and 2, 5.45 and 9 pm. On Sunday there's no early morning crossing and on Saturday there's no late evening crossing.

The DSB (☎ 33 15 15 15) car ferry operates between Kalundborg and Århus three to six times a day, takes three hours and 10 minutes, and costs 245 kr for a car and driver (300 kr with three passengers, 330 kr with five).

KattegatBroen (☎ 75 69 48 00) operates a car ferry from Kalundborg to Juelsminde three to five times a day. It takes three hours and costs 70 kr for adults, 35 kr for children, 40 kr for a motorcycle, 200 kr for a car

driver and 275 kr for a car with up to five passengers.

NÆSTVED
Located at the mouth of the Suså river, the town of Næstved has been an important trading centre since medieval times. Industry grew following the introduction of the railroad in the 19th century and with the later dredging of a new commercial harbour.

With nearly 45,000 residents, Næstved is the largest town in southern Zealand. The town centre has a few interesting historic buildings, including two medieval gothic churches, all within easy walking distance of each other.

Orientation
The bus and railway station are together on Farimagsvej, opposite its intersection with Jernbanegade. To get to Axeltorv, the central square, take Jernbanegade west to Sankt Mortens Kirke and then continue west on Torvestræde; it's a walk of about five minutes in all. All the town's sights are within a few minutes walk of Axeltorv.

Information
Tourist Office The Næstved Turistbureau (☎ 53 72 11 22) is a few blocks south of Axeltorv at Det Gule Pakhus, Havnegade 1, 4700 Næstved. From mid-June to August it's open from 9 am to 5 pm, Monday to Friday, and from 9 am to 2 pm on Saturday; in the low season it closes at 4 pm on weekdays and at noon on Saturday.

Money There are a few banks in the town centre including a Jyske Bank opposite Sankt Mortens Kirke at Østergade 2.

Post The post office is at the south side of the railway station on Farimagsvej.

Sankt Peders Kirke
This large gothic church dominates the square Sankt Peders Kirkeplads. Just south of Axeltorv, it features notable 14th century frescoes, including one depicting King Valdemar IV and Queen Helvig kneeling

before God. The Latin inscription to the left of the king reads, 'In 1375, the day before the feast of St Crispin, King Valdemar died, do not forget it'. The church is open from 10 am to noon Tuesday to Friday year round; from May to August it's also open in the afternoons from 2 to 4 pm. Admission is free.

Sankt Mortens Kirke
Also built of brick, this smaller church, midway between the railway station and Axeltorv, has a strikingly similar design to Sankt Peders Kirke. The interior has period frescoes and a six-metre-high altar created by the master Næstved carver Abel Schrøder in 1667. The pulpit, which dates from the early 17th century, is thought to have been carved by Schrøder's father. The church is open from 9 to 11 am, Monday to Friday, year round and also from 2 to 5 pm from mid-June to mid-September. Admission is free.

Næstved Museum
The Næstved Museum has two sections. Fittingly, the local history section is in Næstved's oldest building, the 14th century Helligåndshuset (House of the Holy Ghost) at Ringstedgade 4, north of Axeltorv. It contains 13th and 14th century church carvings and exhibits of farm, trade and peasant life from Næstved's past. The museum's second section, Boderne, at Sankt Peders Kirkeplads, displays Næstved silverwork, Holmegaard glass and locally made pottery. Both are open from 10 am to 4 pm, Tuesday to Sunday; a combination ticket is 20 kr for adults and free for children.

Other Central Sights
Constructed in 1493, **Kompagnihuset** on Kompagnistræde, a minute's walk southeast of Sankt Peders Kirke, is said to be the only medieval guild hall remaining in Denmark. This timber-framed building was recently restored and can be appreciated from the outside, but the interior is not open to the public.

Apostelhuset, a half-timbered medieval building on Riddergade, just south of Sankt

Mortens Kirke, takes its name from the 13 wooden exterior braces that separate the windows, each carved with the figure of Christ or one of the 12 apostles. Dating from about 1510, they are some of the oldest and best preserved timber-frame carvings in Denmark.

Also with roots in the medieval period is the old town hall, **Rådhuskirken**, which is on the south side of Axeltorv.

The town's most novel curiosity is Denmark's smallest equestrian statue, a tiny bronze atop a tall brick pedestal that depicts Næstved's founder, Peder Bodilsen. It's located in Hjultorv square, just north of Axeltorv.

Holmegaards Glasværker
If you have your own transport you might want to drive out to Fensmark, about eight km north-east of Næstved, to visit the Holmegaards Glasværker (Holmegaard Glassworks). Founded in 1825, Holmegaard is Denmark's principal producer of quality glass. On weekdays, visitors can see glass blown by hand and view the automated factory where bottles are produced. There's also a shop and a little museum. It's open from 9.30 am to noon and 12.45 to 1.30 pm, Monday to Thursday, and from 9.30 am to noon on Friday. Admission is free.

Canoeing
The Suså river, which has calm waters that make for good canoeing, runs through the west side of town. You can rent canoes for around 40 kr an hour from Suså Kanoudlejning (☎ 53 64 61 44) at Slusehuset, located at the southern end of Rådmanshave, a green zone north of the town centre.

Places to Stay
Næstved Vandrerhjem & Camping (☎ 53 72 20 91, fax 53 72 56 45), Frejasvej 8, 4700 Næstved, is a combined hostel and one-star camping ground. The 81-bed hostel, which is open to individuals from mid-March to mid-November, has dorm beds for 60 kr and family rooms for one to four people from 200 to 240 kr. Camping in the hostel grounds,

allowed from 15 May to 15 September, costs 30 kr per person. Cooking facilities and bicycle rentals are available. It's a 15-minute walk from the railway station and town centre; to get there, go south from the station and then continue east on Præstøvej.

The tourist office maintains a list of private rooms in the greater Næstved area, beginning at 120/240 kr for singles/doubles.

Hotel Vinhuset (☎ 53 72 08 07, fax 53 72 03 35), Sankt Peders Kirkeplads 4, 4700 Næstved, is an 18th century hotel that has recently been renovated but retains its period character. It's got a prime location on the square directly opposite Sankt Peders Kirke. The rooms have private bath, phone, TV and minibar, and begin at 450/690 kr for singles/doubles.

Places to Eat

The *DSB restaurant* at the railway station has moderately priced food. *Sesam Burger* at Jernbanegade 13, a few minutes walk west of the railway station, has pizza and burgers. There's a *Kvickly* grocery store about 100 metres farther west on Jernbanegade and *Bager Cafeen*, a konditori with pastries and sandwiches, at the intersection of Jernbanegade and Kattebjerg.

The central square, Axeltorv, has hot dog and ice-cream stands and there's a *Grøntland* greengrocer with fresh fruit. For something more upmarket you can try one of the two restaurants at the *Hotel Vinhuset*.

Getting There & Away

Næstved is 25 km south of Ringsted and 28 km north of Vordingborg, at the crossroads of routes 14, 22, 54 and 265. It's on two train routes from Roskilde, one via Køge (37 minutes, 35 kr) and the other via Ringsted (20 minutes, 24 kr).

PRÆSTØ

This seaside village, at the south side of the Præstø Fjord, largely retains the look of a sleepy 19th century provincial town. It has a small centre with older homes and handsome buildings that can make for a pleasant hour or so of wandering. However the main activity is at the yacht harbour, which spreads along the north side of the town centre. While foreign tourists are few, Præstø attracts plenty of Danish visitors, particularly sailors with their own boats.

Information

Tourist Office The Præstø Turistbureau (☎ 55 99 11 90), at Jernbanevej 22, 4720 Præstø, is open on weekdays from 9 am to 4 pm year round, and in summer from 9 am to 2 pm on Saturday as well.

Money There's a Unibank at Adelgade 72 and Den Danske Bank is at Adelgade 92.

Post The post office is north of the tourist office on Jernbanevej.

Things to See & Do

Just south of the Hotel Frederiksminde is **Præstø Kirke**, a church with a north nave dating from the 13th century. Before the Reformation it was an abbey church for monks of the order of St Anthony. Each of its two naves has an altar; most notable is the detailed altarpiece in the south nave, which was created by Abel Schrøder in 1657. The religious philosopher NFS Grundtvig was the parish rector here from 1821 to 1822.

The **Brandværnsmuseum** (Fire Brigade Museum) on Havnevej boasts Denmark's oldest (1761) horse-drawn fire engine, a collection of other restored fire engines and blaze-related paraphernalia.

The waters around Præstø are mostly shallow – a challenge for yachters but quite

---

Off With His Head

The old Rådhus building in Præstø's cobbled town square once served not only as the town hall, but also as a combined jail and courthouse.

It was here that a notorious criminal, Balle-Lars, was held in 1860 before his head was chopped off in what turned out to be Denmark's last execution by decapitation. ■

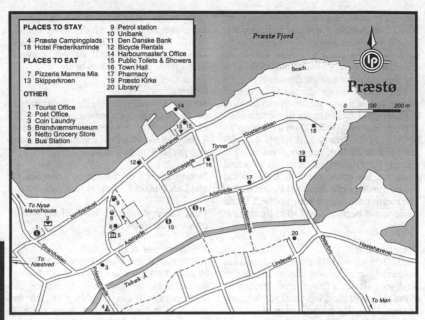

PLACES TO STAY
4 Præstø Campingplads
18 Hotel Frederiksminde

PLACES TO EAT
7 Pizzeria Mamma Mia
13 Skipperkroen

OTHER
1 Tourist Office
2 Post Office
3 Coin Laundry
5 Brandværnsmuseum
6 Netto Grocery Store
8 Bus Station
9 Petrol station
10 Unibank
11 Den Danske Bank
12 Bicycle Rentals
14 Harbourmaster's Office
15 Public Toilets & Showers
16 Town Hall
17 Pharmacy
19 Præsto Kirke
20 Library

suitable for waders. There's a good public **strand** (beach) for children below the Hotel Frederiksminde at the north-east side of the peninsula.

A km north-west of town is the private **Nysø manor house**, built in the 1670s. Although it has a rather severe exterior, giving it the appearance more of a town hall than a grand manor, it has an interesting history. Baroness Christine Stampe, who owned Nysø in the mid-1800s, opened it as a retreat to many Danish writers and artists, including sculptor Bertel Thorvaldsen who set up a studio here. Nysø now contains the **Thorvaldsen-samlingen**, a collection of Thorvaldsen's works.

Places to Stay
Præstø Campingplads (☎ 55 99 11 48) at Spangen 2, 4720 Præstø, is a simple one-star facility 300 metres from the centre of town. It costs 35 kr per person to pitch a tent and

cabin rentals can also be arranged. It's open from mid-April to mid-September.

The *Hotel Frederiksminde* (☎ 55 99 10 42, fax 55 99 17 65), Klosternakken 8, 4720 Præstø, built in 1868, is a pleasant Victorian hotel on a seaside knoll. Singles/doubles cost 400/500 kr with private bath or 275/300 kr with shared bath, breakfast included. The 21 rooms are all different, some quite spacious, some with ocean views, others with balcony; all have TV and phone.

Places to Eat
The friendly *Pizzeria Mamma Mia* at Adelgade 45, in a quaint courtyard off Jernbanevej, has good pizzas from 39 kr. Lasagne and other pastas start around 60 kr (39 kr from noon to 5.30 pm) and there are also more-expensive fish and meat dishes. It's open from 4 to 10 pm on Sunday and from noon to 11 pm on other days.

Down at the harbour in the attractive old customs house is *Skipperkroen*, which has good, if expensive, fish dishes. A light lunch will cost 120 kr, a full lunch 168 kr and dinner a bit more. You can also order à la carte. It's open daily from noon to 8 pm.

The *Hotel Frederiksminde* usually offers a special two-course meal for 100 kr in its seaside dining room; it's popular with tour groups.

Getting There & Away

Route 265 passes Præstø on its way to Næstved (25 km) and Møn (26 km). Bus No 808 connects Præstø with Næstved and Møn. There are no train services to Præsto.

VORDINGBORG

Strategically located on the strait between Zealand and Falster, Vordingborg played an important role in Denmark's medieval history. It was the royal residence of King Valdemar I, whose ascension to the throne in 1157 marked the end of a contentious period of rebellion and served to reunite the Danish kingdom, and it continued to be a favoured residence of other kings in the Valdemar reign. With its large natural harbour, Vordingborg also served as the staging ground for Bishop Absalon's late 12th century military campaigns against the Wends of eastern Germany.

The Jutland Code, which codified traditional law and was thus one of the most important doctrines of the Middle Ages, was sanctioned by King Valdemar II in Vordingborg in 1241. Today, virtually every schoolchild in Denmark can recite the code's preamble 'Mæth logh skal land byggiæs' (With law shall a land be built).

During the 15th century, Vordingborg slipped from importance, in part because the Kalmar Union had so greatly expanded Danish rule elsewhere in Scandinavia that the royal family now took little interest in Vordingborg.

Vordingborg is today a modest, modern town (population 10,000) whose best known sight is its 14th century Goose Tower. It's also the jumping-off point for trips to Møn if you're travelling by public transport.

Information

Tourist Office The Vordingborg Turistbureau (☎ 55 34 11 11, fax 55 34 03 08) at Algade 96, 4760 Vordingborg, just east of the Gåsetårnet (Goose Tower), is open from 9 am to 4 pm, Monday to Friday, and from 9 am to noon on Saturday. In midsummer it stays open to 5 pm on weekdays and 2 pm on Saturday.

Money There are several banks on Algade, including a Jyske Bank at Algade 57 and a Den Danske Bank at Algade 61.

Post The post office is north of the railway station at Ärsleffsgade 1.

Things to See & Do

The 14th century **Gåsetårnet** (Goose Tower), once part of a huge royal castle and fortress, is Scandinavia's best preserved medieval tower and the only intact structure remaining from the Valdemar era. The name stems from 1368, when Valdemar IV placed a golden goose on top of the tower to express his scorn for the German Hanseatic League's declaration of war. The rest of the fortress, including seven other towers, has been demolished over the centuries but the 36-metre-high Gåsetårnet was spared because of its function as a navigational landmark. The tower can be climbed for a good view of the surrounding area.

On the old fortress grounds, there's also a botanical garden and the **Sydsjællands Museum**, southern Zealand's regional history museum which has a Stone Age collection as well as Middle Age and Renaissance displays that include trade and craft exhibits, church decorations and textiles.

Both the museum and tower are open from 10 am to 5 pm daily from June to August and from 10 am to 4 pm, Tuesday to Sunday, the rest of the year. The admission fee, 20 kr for adults and 8 kr for children, covers both sights. To get there from the railway station, walk north to the nearby post office and then turn south-east on Algade. Algade terminates at Slotstorvet, which fronts the old fortress grounds.

SOUTHERN ZEALAND

A few minutes walk to the west at Kirketorvet is the church **Vor Frue Kirke**, which has a nave dating from the mid-1400s, frescoes and a baroque altarpiece carved by Abel Schrøder in 1642. It's open from 10 am to noon.

Walking Track If you're up to a walk, **Knudshoved Odde**, the narrow 15-km-long peninsula west of Vordingborg, offers some hiking opportunities in an area known for its 'Bronze Age landscape'. The peninsula also has a small herd of American buffalo brought in by the Rosenfeldt family, who own the property. There's a carpark (10 kr) about halfway down the peninsula, where the trail begins.

Places to Stay & Eat
The hostel, *Vordingborg Vandrerhjem* (☎ 53 77 50 84, fax 55 34 09 55), Præstedgårdsvej 8, 4760 Vordingborg, in the countryside about two km north of town, has dorm beds for 65 kr. The hostel rents bicycles and is accessible by wheelchair. It's open year round except from mid-December to early January.

The tourist office books rooms in private homes for 130 kr per person.

The 65-room *Hotel Kong Valdemar* (☎ 53 77 00 95, fax 53 77 07 95), Algade 101, 4760 Vordingborg, is at Slotstorvet. Singles/doubles with private bath, phone, TV and minibar cost 545/680 kr, but there are also a few singles with shared bath for 395 kr. The hotel has a restaurant, lounge and sauna.

There are numerous cafés and restaurants on Algade, the town's main commercial street. These include two inexpensive pizzerias, *Xanthos Pizzeria & Café* at Algade 16 and *Pizzeria Roma* at Algade 80, and also a fine Chinese restaurant, *China House*, at Algade 69.

Getting There & Away
Vordingborg is 28 km from Næstved via route 22 and 13 km from Møn via route 59. By train, Vordingborg is 80 minutes (77 kr) from Copenhagen and 20 minutes (24 kr) from Næstved. If you're en route to Møn, you'll need to switch from the train to the bus at Vordingborg station; see the Møn chapter for more details.

Møn, Falster & Lolland

The three main islands south of Zealand – Møn, Falster and Lolland – are all connected with Zealand by bridges. Møn is known for its unique chalk cliffs and Falster has fine white-sand beaches. Lolland, the largest of the three islands, has a handful of scattered sights that are only practical to explore if you have your own transport. All three islands are predominantly rural and, except for Møn's rolling hills, the terrain is largely flat and monotonous.

Møn

Although its main allure is the spectacular white cliffs of Møns Klint on the east coast, Møn is a thoroughly appealing island. The scenery is rustic and the pace slow; the entire island has only 11,000 residents. There are good beaches, prehistoric passage graves and medieval churches with outstanding frescoes.

Møn's interior is largely given over to fields of rapeseed, grains and sugar beets, although agriculture has been in decline since the island's only sugar refinery closed in the early 1990s. Møn's rich clay soil has given rise to numerous pottery shops, and *keramik* signs are commonplace along its country roads.

Travellers using public transport should note that the island lacks a train system and the bus service is sketchy. Still, for those with time to explore, Møn offers a generous dose of what Danes call 'lovely nature'.

GETTING THERE & AWAY
Route 59 connects southern Zealand with Møn.

As there's no rail service to Møn, travellers using the train need to take the Copenhagen-Nykøbing F line to Vordingborg in southern Zealand and from there

switch to a bus. Trains from Copenhagen to Vordingborg (85 minutes, 77 kr) leave an average of once an hour from early morning to around midnight.

Bus No 62 to Stege (45 minutes, 36 kr) coordinates with the trains, leaving Vordingborg about once an hour. The service for both is more frequent during weekday rush hours and less regular on weekends.

GETTING AROUND
Møn's main road is route 287, which cuts across the centre of the island from east to west. There are lots of narrow rural roads

MØN

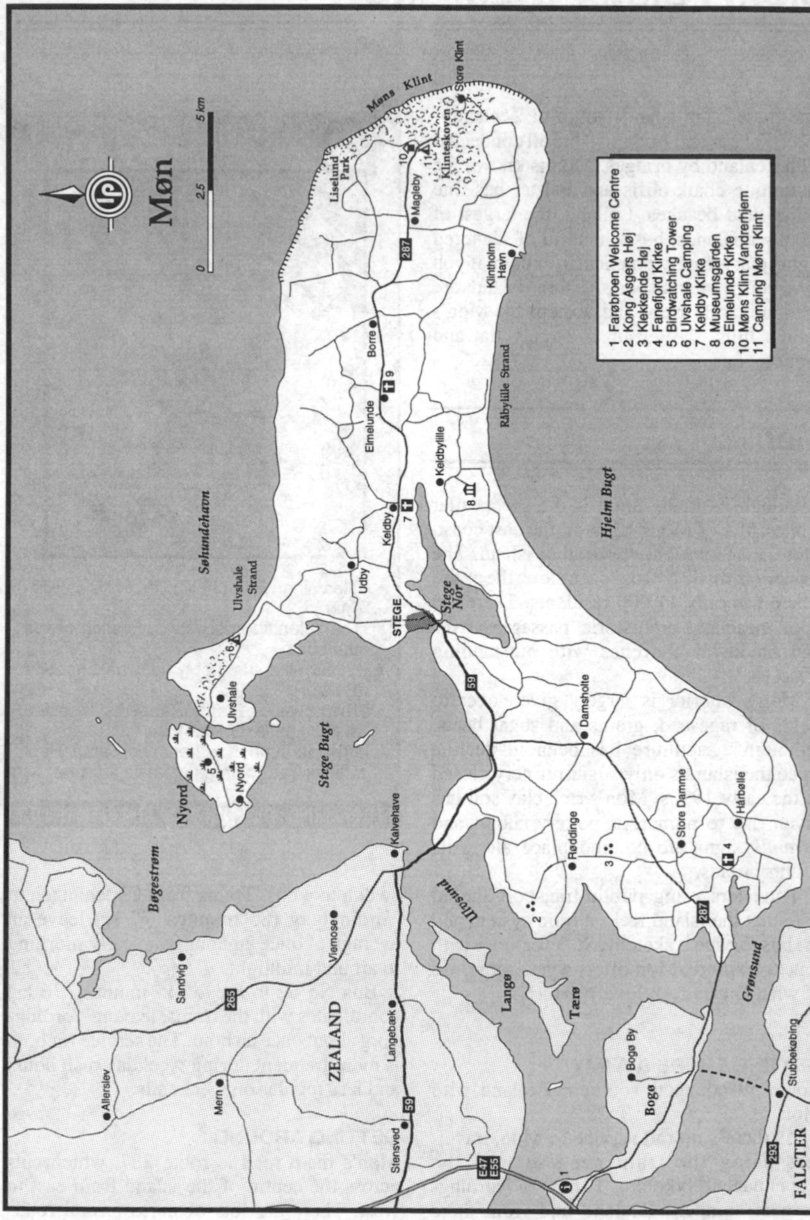

Møn

0   2.5   5 km

Møns Klint
Store Klint
Liselund Park
Klinteskoven
Magleby
Klintholm Havn
287
Borre
Elmelunde
Keldbylille
Keldby
Ulvshale Strand
Udby
STEGE
Stege Nor
Ulvshale
Nyord
Nyord
Stege Bugt
Kalvehave
Damsholte
Råddinge
Store Damme
Hårbølle
287
Ulvsund
Lange
Tærø
Grønsund
Bøgø By
Bøgø
Stubbekøbing
Sandvig
V
Viemose
Langebæk
Mern
Stensved
59
Allerslev
265
E47
E55
293
ZEALAND
FALSTER
Bøgestrøm
Sehundehavn
Råbylille Strand
Hjelm Bugt
MØN

1 Farørbroen Welcome Centre
2 Kong Asgers Høj
3 Klekkende Høj
4 Fanefjord Kirke
5 Birdwatching Tower
6 Ulvshale Camping
7 Keldby Kirke
8 Museumsgården
9 Elmelunde Kirke
10 Møns Klint Vandrerhjem
11 Camping Møns Klint

branching off route 287 that can be slow-going but fun to explore.

Bus

Møn's bus station is in Stege, the departure point for all bus routes. Fares depend on the number of zones travelled, with the highest fare between Stege and any other point on Møn being 24 kr. Frequency varies with the day of the week and the season.

The most frequent service is bus No 52, which goes from Stege to Klintholm Havn via Elmelunde and Magleby about hourly on weekdays and every couple of hours on weekends. Magleby is the most easterly town with year-round bus service, but from late June to mid-August the seasonal bus No 54 goes from Stege to Møns Klint at least six times a day on weekdays and four times daily on weekends. Bus No 53 runs from Stege to Ulvshale and No 64 runs from Stege to Bogø.

Cycle Routes

There's a signposted bike path between Stege and Møns Klint, and another from Stege to Bogø. The tourist office distributes a pamphlet called *Cykelture på Møn* that maps out six suggested cycling tours of the island, which collectively take in all of the island's major sights.

Bicycles can be rented in Stege at Kurt's Cykler (☎ 55 81 10 60), Lendemarke Hovedgade 12, and at Rent-a-Sport (☎ 55 81 84 94) at the old sugar refinery, Stege Sukkerfabrik. Prices begin at 35/200 kr a day/week.

STEGE

Stege is the main town and commercial centre of Møn. Most visitors to Møn will at least pass through Stege, as it has the bus terminal, tourist office and other central facilities. It also has the island's best selection of reasonably priced places to eat, most of which can be found along Storegade, the main shopping street.

During the Middle Ages, Stege was one of Denmark's wealthiest provincial towns, thanks to its position as a central market for the lucrative herring fisheries. The entire town was once surrounded by fortress walls; remnants of the ramparts can still be found, including a section near the camping ground.

In the mid-19th century, a large sugar mill was erected on the west side of town, but with the demise of the sugar beet industry the mill has been converted into a fledgling business zone.

Information

Tourist Office Møns Turistbureau (☎ 55 81 44 11, fax 55 81 48 46), Storegade 2, 4780 Stege, adjacent to the bus station, has information on the entire island. It books beach cottages and rooms in island farmhouses and also sells a few inexpensive publications on topics such as Møn's passage graves. From mid-June to 31 August it's open Monday to Saturday from 9 am to 6 pm, and on Sunday from 10 am to noon; the rest of the year it's open Monday to Friday from 9 am to 5 pm and on Saturday from 9 am to noon.

Money There are a couple of banks in Stege centre, including a Unibank at Storegade 23. All banks are open Monday to Friday from 9.30 am to 4 pm (to 6 pm on Thursday).

Post The post office, opposite the tourist office, is open Monday to Friday from 10 am to 5 pm and on Saturday from 10 am to noon.

Stege Kirke

The oldest part of the Stege church was built in Romanesque style in the early 13th century by Møn's ruler, Jakob Sunesen, a member of the powerful Hvide family that controlled much of southern Zealand. In the late 15th century this 60-metre-long church was expanded to its present dimensions, with a main nave flanked by two smaller naves, each with high vaulted ceilings and pointed arch windows.

Noteworthy are the primitive-style ceiling frescoes, some with whimsical jester-like characters, including one of a hunter with a pack of dogs that are chasing a fox and hare. The frescoes, which were covered with whitewash centuries earlier, were exposed and restored in 1892. (For more information

MØN

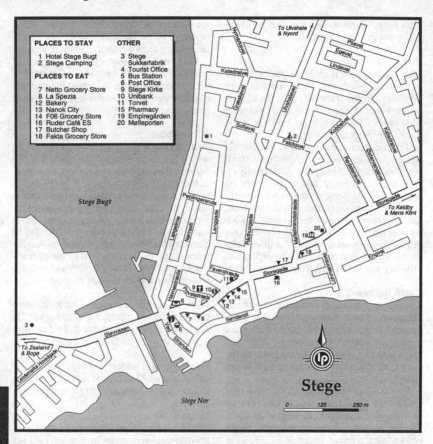

PLACES TO STAY	OTHER
1 Hotel Stege Bugt	3 Stege
2 Stege Camping	Sukkerfabrik
	4 Tourist Office
PLACES TO EAT	5 Bus Station
	6 Post Office
7 Netto Grocery Store	9 Stege Kirke
8 La Spezia	10 Unibank
12 Bakery	11 Torvet
13 Nanok City	15 Pharmacy
14 F06 Grocery Store	19 Empiregården
16 Ruder Café ES	20 Mølleporten
17 Butcher Shop	
18 Fakta Grocery Store	

see the following Church Frescoes boxed aside.) The church also has a splendidly carved pulpit dating from 1630, with reliefs of biblical scenes. Each relief is separated by a narrow vertical panel depicting virtues such as hope and truth, and below each of these is a grotesque little caricature mask to serve as a reminder of the horrors that await the unvirtuous.

The church, on Provstestræde, is open free to the public until 5 pm daily.

Empiregården

Møn's museum has two sections, one in Stege and the other near Keldbylille village. The Stege section, called the Empiregården, is at Storegade 75 and covers local cultural history. There are fossilised sea urchins, archaeological finds from the Stone Age to the Middle Ages, old coins, pottery and displays of 19th century house interiors. It's open Tuesday to Sunday from 10 am to 4 pm. Admission is 15 kr for adults, free for children.

Mølleporten

Of the three medieval gates that once allowed entry into the town, Mølleporten

(Mill Gate) on Storegade still stands and is considered one of the best preserved town gates in all of Denmark. The gate's construction bears a resemblance to the Stege church tower, both made of red brick and distinctively lined with horizontal strips of white chalk from Møns Klint.

Places to Stay

Stege Camping (☎ 55 81 53 25), Falcksvej, 4780 Stege, a small municipality-owned, one-star camping ground, is 500 metres north of the town centre. It's open from 1 May to 31 August and costs 36 kr per person.

Hotel Stege Bugt (☎ 55 81 54 54, fax 55 81 58 90), Langelinie 48, 4780 Stege, a small, modern, three-storey motel-style place, is 600 metres north of the tourist office. The 27 rooms have private bath, TV, phone and minibar, and many have balconies with views over the water. Singles/doubles cost 400/600 kr, breakfast included.

Places to Eat

There's a good bakery at Storegade 36 and three grocery stores elsewhere along Storegade.

Nanok City, a simple burger and steak place at Storegade 30, has a changing daily meal for 37 kr. It's open Monday to Friday from 11 am to 9 pm.

Ruder Café ES, at Storegade 68, is an appealing café with light eats such as salads, sandwiches, burgers and stuffed potatoes for around 30 kr. It's an afternoon place in the low season but open from 10 am to 10 pm daily in the summer.

Stig's Slagterforretning, a butcher shop at Storegade 59, has takeaway smørrebrød sandwiches and deli-style salads and is open until at least 5 pm on weekdays and to 1 pm on Saturday.

La Spezia, at Storegade 10, is a pleasant restaurant with good Italian food at reasonable prices. You can get the island's best pizza or half a chicken with chips for 40 kr, lasagne and pastas for around 50 kr. It's open daily from 11 am to 10 pm, but try to avoid peak hours as it gets crowded.

ULVSHALE & NYORD

The ocean side of the Ulvshale peninsula, six km north of Stege, has one of Møn's best beaches and a primeval forest that's one of the few virgin woods left in Denmark. The main road, Ulvshalevej, runs right along the beach, called Ulvshale Strand. If you're travelling by car, there's a carpark shortly before the camping ground, but you can also park along the road. The forest, which has a network of walking trails, begins north-west of the camping ground and extends to the end of the peninsula, where there's a bridge to the island of Nyord.

Nyord has been connected to the Møn mainland for only a decade, a situation that served to safeguard the island from development. Now, its little one-lane bridge boasts Møn's only traffic light! Its sole village, also named Nyord, is a characteristic 19th century hamlet of old thatched houses. There's a yacht harbour, a small octagonal church (circa 1846) and a little red-brick hut called Møllestangen where villagers once kept watch over the sound to make sure no boats came through without first stopping at Nyord to hire a pilot.

Much of the island, particularly the eastern side, is given over to marshland and offers excellent bird-watching opportunities. There's a bird-watching tower on the north side of the road about a km after the bridge. The bridge itself is also a good bird-watching site, as is the marsh on the Ulvshale side.

Some of the birds spotted in the area are arctic terns, kestrels, rough-legged hawks, ruffs, snow buntings, avocets, swans, black-tailed godwits, curlews and various ducks.

Places to Stay & Eat

Ulvshale Camping (☎ 55 81 53 25), at Ulvshalevej 236, 4780 Stege, is a two-star municipality-owned camping ground right at the beach and on the main road in Ulvshale. The cost is 36 kr per person. It's open from April to September.

Fætter Fiks café and bistro, opposite Ulvshale Strand at Ulvshalevej 151, is a popular place that serves reasonably priced food. Fish & chips, or schnitzel with roasted

⏐⎯⏐

Church Frescoes

Møn's churches are enlivened with some of the best preserved frescoes in Denmark. A vivid form of peasant art, the paintings are so splendid that the churches can be likened to medieval art galleries. The frescoes, which served as a means of describing the Bible to illiterate peasants, run the gamut from light-hearted Genesis scenes to grotesque demons and the fires of hell.

Frescoes are created by painting with watercolours on newly plastered, still-wet walls or ceilings, which allows the colours to penetrate deep into the plaster before it dries. The frescoes in the Stege church were painted solely in black and ochre-red while those in the other Møn churches employ a fuller range of colour.

Møn's frescoes were whitewashed over in the 17th century by Lutheran ministers who thought they too closely represented Catholic themes of the pre-Reformation days. In many cases a protective layer of dust separated the frescoes from the whitewash. Ironically, the whitewashing served to preserve this medieval art from soiling and fading, rather than obliterating it. The whitewash wasn't removed from most of the churches until the 20th century, at which time the frescoes were restored by artists under the auspices of Denmark's national museum.

As you visit Møn's churches you may notice a similar style in many of the frescoes. This is because most of those that date to the 15th century were painted by the same artist, whose exact identity is a mystery but who has come to be known over the centuries as the *Elmelundemesteren* (Elmelunde master). This artist used distinctive warm earth tones: russet, mustard, sienna, brick red, chestnut brown, soft grey and pale aqua. ∎

⏐⎯⏐

potatoes, will set you back a mere 50 kr and there are cheaper burgers and salads.

In Nyord, the little general store sells ice cream, beer and groceries and there's a fast-food kiosk at the harbour.

KELDBY

The Keldby area, about five km east of Stege, is marked mainly by its roadside church, but there's also a small farm museum three km south of route 287.

Keldby Kirke

Keldby's brick church, the nave of which dates from the early 13th century, has a splendid collection of fresco paintings splashed across its walls, arches and ceiling. The frescoes cover a period of two centuries with the oldest (1275) decorating the chancel walls and depicting scenes from the book of Genesis. Scores of other expressionistic scenes, from the vivid sacrifice of Cain and Abel to a large mural of doomsday, make this one of the most intriguing collection of church frescoes to be found in Denmark. The church pulpit was carved in 1586. You'll find an interesting tombstone at the north side of

the chancel that dates from 1347 and shows three nobles in period dress.

The church is open from 7 am to 5 pm from April to September, and from 8 am to 4 pm in the winter.

Museumsgården

This low-key museum, in a four-winged farmhouse at Skullebjergvej 15, south of Keldbylille, depicts life on a small Møn farm in the 19th century. Essentially it's an old farmstead that remained in the same family for generations and was turned over to the Møns Museum after its bachelor owner, Hans Hansen, died in 1964. The drive to it is suitably through fields of sugar beets and wheat. The museum is open from May to October, from 10 am to 4 pm Tuesday to Sunday. Admission is 15 kr for adults, free for children.

ELMELUNDE

Elmelunde is a small, rural hamlet with an appealing pension and an ancient church, both on the main road between Stege and Møns Klint. The bus stops right in front.

Elmelunde Kirke

Elmelunde Kirke is one of Denmark's oldest stone churches, with the section around the choir dating from around 1080. The nave was lengthened during the Romanesque period and the lower section of the tower was added around 1300. It has wonderful frescoes, ranging from Adam and Eve's expulsion from Eden at the rear of the church to heavenly scenes above the altar. The altar itself is intricately carved and painted and dates from 1646, while the pulpit, the weight of which is carried by a figure of the apostle Peter, dates from 1649. The three-pointed vaults over the nave were added in 1460 and painted by the Elmelunde master. The church is open from 8 am to 5 pm.

Places to Stay & Eat

The *Pension Elmehøj* (☎ 55 81 35 35, fax 55 81 32 67), Kirkebakken 39, 4780 Stege, right next door to the Elmelunde Kirke, could make for a convenient base as it's equidistant to Stege, Møns Klint and Klintholm Havn. The owners, Møn-born Brit and her Australian husband, Jonathan Olifent, have taken a former home for the elderly and turned it into a friendly, good-value pension. There are 25 rooms, all with shared toilets and showers. Singles/doubles cost 220/370 kr, breakfast included. There's a shared kitchen, a TV lounge and a few bicycles that can be rented for 25 kr a day. The pension is accessible by wheelchair, complete with a lift.

With advance notice, you can have a two-course dinner for 80 kr at the pension, and a simple inexpensive lunch is usually available as well.

Otherwise the nearest restaurant is *Kaj Kok*, on the main road at Klintevej 151, 1.75 km west of the pension. Kaj Kok has good although pricey steak and schnitzel, as well as light eats such as chicken with chips for 50 kr.

MØNS KLINT & KLINTESKOVEN

The chalk cliffs at Møns Klint were created 5000 years ago when the calcareous deposits from eons of seashells were uplifted from the ocean floor. The gleaming white cliffs rise sharply 128 metres above an azure sea, presenting one of the most striking landscapes in Denmark. The cliffs are a repository for fossilised Cretaceous-period shells, many of them from creatures long extinct.

Møns Klint is a popular destination for Danish tourists. The main visitor area, Store Klint, contains a cafeteria, a hotel, a carpark and a couple of souvenir shops. There are also picnic grounds in the woods above the cliffs, but none of this detracts from the natural beauty of the cliffs themselves.

You can walk down the cliffs to the beach and directly back up again in about 30 minutes, or walk along the shoreline in either

---

Møns Klint's Unusual Flora

The unusual soil at Møns Klint has given rise to a unique ecosystem. The beech trees along this coast keep their fresh spring-green hue throughout the summer, thanks to the soil's high calcareous content which inhibits the uptake of iron and magnesium, elements essential to darkening leaf colour.

The calcareous soil also provides ideal conditions for orchids. The Klinteskoven wood that back the cliffs is habitat to 20 species of orchids, the greatest variety to be found anywhere in Denmark. The flowering season is from May to August. The grassy hills in the Mandemarke area at the south side of the wood are particularly abundant with wild orchids.

Two of the more beautiful flowers are the pyramidal orchid (*Anacamptis pyramidalis*), which has a mounded, multiblossomed pink head, and the dark red helleborine (*Epipactis atrorubens*), which has an oval leaf and a tall stem with numerous crimson flowers. Look but don't touch, as many of the orchids are rare and all are protected. ■

direction and then loop back up through a thick forest of wind-gnarled beech trees for a hardier walk of about 1½ hours. Either way, start on the path directly below the cafeteria – it's a quick route to the most scenic stretch of the cliffs.

You needn't limit your hiking to the coast. Klinteskoven (Klinte Forest), the wood that extends three km inland from the cliffs, is crisscrossed by an extensive network of footpaths and horse trails. Although most people start the trails from the cliffs, if you're staying at the camping ground, there's a trail from there as well. One interesting track leads a km west of Store Klint to Timmesø Bjerg, where castle ruins on the hill top date back to around 1100 AD. Other trails lead to lakes, marshes, ancient barrows and old-growth forests where deer run free.

Rent A Horse (☎ 55 81 22 26) at Langebjergvej 1, near the hostel, offers two-hour guided horseback tours of the Møns Klint area for 150 kr.

Places to Stay & Eat

Camping Møns Klint (☎ 55 81 20 25, fax 55 81 27 97), Klintevej 544, 4791 Borre, which borders the Klinteskoven woods, is opposite the hostel. This three-star camping ground has a 25-metre swimming pool, a guest kitchen, free hot showers, a coin laundry and bicycle rentals. There's a simple grill with hot dogs, fish & chips and the like, and a shop selling fresh bread, beer and other basics. It costs 44 kr per person and is open from 1 April to 31 October.

The hostel, *Møns Klint Vandrerhjem* (☎ 55 81 20 30, fax 55 81 28 18), Langebjergvej 1, 4791 Borre, is in a former hotel three km north-west of Møns Klint. The hostel has a pleasant location, right on a lake, with lots of shade trees and scurrying hares. The 32 rooms have 120 beds in all. Dorm beds cost 70 kr, double rooms 190 kr. Breakfast is available; there's a guest kitchen; and a small shop sells snacks, soft drinks and beer. It's open from mid-April to 1 November. In the summer you can take the Møns Klint bus, but the rest of the year the nearest

bus is No 52, which stops in Magleby, 2.75 km west of the hostel.

The 18-room *Hotel Store Klint* (☎ & fax 55 81 90 08), Stengårdsvej 6, 4791 Borre, is the only place to stay right at Møns Klint. This classic little three-storey hostel is perched above the cliffs and a stone's throw from the cafeteria where you check in. Singles cost 325 kr, doubles from 450 to 525 kr, depending on the room and view. The bathrooms are shared. Breakfast is included.

The cafeteria at Møns Klint, which is open from 10.30 am to 6 pm, has simple food such as soup and bread for 35 kr and chicken or fish with chips for 55 kr. There's a little kiosk below the cafeteria where you can get ice cream.

If you'd like to stay in a small manor-house hotel, *Liselund Slot* (☎ 55 81 20 81, fax 55 81 21 91), Langebjergvej 6, 4791 Borre, occupies a classic 19th century home in the midst of an expansive estate that's been turned into a park of lawns, duck ponds and gardens. There are 14 rooms with private bathrooms that cost 550/750 kr for singles/doubles, breakfast included. There's also a fine dining restaurant with à la carte prices from 100 kr. Liselund is near the coast, two km north of the hostel.

KLINTHOLM HAVN

Klintholm Havn is a pleasant little harbour-side village with a long sandy beach. Half tourist, half local, there's one harbour filled with working fishing boats and an adjacent harbour given over to yachts, many belonging to German tourists.

This one-road village has a bank that's open for two hours in the morning, a grocery store, a handful of eateries, a souvenir shop, a large harbour-side resort and a little seaside kro or inn.

Beyond that, it's mostly the beach, which extends in both directions from the two harbours. The section that runs east is particularly appealing and pristine, with light grey sand backed by low dunes; it can be a fun place for strolling and also has the best surf. The safest swimming is found along the west side. There are public toilets and showers at the marina.

Places to Stay
Klintholm Søbad (☎ 55 81 91 23), Thyravej 19, 4791 Borre, is a small kro with half a dozen huts that can accommodate a small family and cost 525 kr. There are also a couple of rooms in the kro with shared bath that cost 300/400 kr for singles/doubles.

Danland/Feriehotel Østersøen (☎ 55 81 90 55, fax 55 81 90 56), 4791 Borre, is a large condominium resort spread across the artificial peninsula that separates the two harbours. It's modern, albeit project-like, and has a pool, sauna, restaurant, coin laundry and other conveniences. The 79 units have two bedrooms, a bathroom, kitchen and TV. The complex rate system varies with the season, with the highest prices in summer when the cheapest rooms (those without sea views) cost somewhere around 700 kr.

Places to Eat
There are half a dozen restaurants along the waterfront road, ranging from a beachside hot-dog-and-burger joint to the high-priced *Ålekroen*, which serves some of Møn's best fish dishes.

For a typically Danish experience, try the *Klintholm Søbad*, which has an ocean-view dining room and standard meat and potato dishes at moderately expensive prices; there are also some lighter eats such as fish or chicken and chips for 50 kr.

If you want to rub shoulders with the fishers and other locals, head for *Hyttefadet*, a lively watering hole that also serves light meals and occasionally has music.

For the best value of all, take the coastal road 200 metres east of the fishing harbour to *Klintholm Røgeri*, where you can buy smoked and fried fish by the piece, get an inexpensive beer and sit down to feast at picnic tables.

WESTERN MØN
The western end of Møn is largely farmland cut by narrow backcountry roads. It has a few worthwhile historic sights but you'll need your own transport to visit them, as there's no public bus system.

Passage Graves
Møn's two best-known Stone Age passage graves, Kong Asgers Høj and Klekkende Høj, are not far from each other at the west side of the island. Both are about two km from the village of Røddinge and marked by signs.

Kong Asgers Høj is in a farmer's field north-west of Røddinge on Kong Asgers Vej; you can clearly see the mound from the road. This is Denmark's largest passage grave, with a burial chamber that's 10 metres long and more than two metres wide. Bring a torch (flashlight) and watch your head!

Klekkende Høj, south-east of Røddinge, is the only double passage-grave mound on Møn. It has two side-by-side entrances, each leading to a seven-metre-long chamber.

Fanefjord Kirke
The Fanefjord Kirke, overlooking the Fanefjord, was built around 1250 in early Gothic style. The current church still incorporates parts of the original structure, but there have been a number of additions over the centuries. The church has superb frescoes; the oldest, which date from 1350 and can be seen at the rood arch, depict a scene of St Christopher carrying Christ across a fjord. Most of the other frescoes date from around 1450 and were created by the Elmelunde master, whose mark (which resembles a stick man with rabbit ears) can be seen on a rib in the north-eastern vault. (See the Church Frescoes boxed aside earlier in the chapter for more information.) The

Stone Age burial mounds

MØN

church is open daily from 8 am to 6 pm (from 9.30 am on Sunday).

BOGØ

The island of Bogø, west of Møn, is connected to Møn by a causeway and to Zealand and Falster via the impressive Farø bridges.

The Bogø chocolate factory, well known throughout Denmark, is here, as is a Dutch windmill built in 1852 and a Gothic church. A car ferry, dating back to the days when Bogø had no causeways or bridges, still shuttles between the south side of the island to Stubbekøbing in Falster.

Near the on-ramp to the Farø bridges is the **Farøbroen Welcome Centre** with a cafeteria, a road-theme museum (Vejmuseum, admission 10 kr), money exchange and toilets. There's also a tourist office where you can load up on brochures from 9 am to 5 pm daily (to 8 pm in summer). The cafeteria has a good-value lunch buffet, served daily to 3.30 pm, with boiled shrimp, crisp salad and various hot and cold dishes for 68 kr.

Falster

The island of Falster is almost entirely given over to agriculture and its roads literally slice across farmers' fields. While the interior can get repetitious, Falster's south-east coast is a summer haven, lined with lovely white-sand beaches that are a magnet for German and Danish holiday-makers.

If you're poking around Falster, the island's rural hamlets and small towns offer a few sights, including a **tractor museum** in Eskilstrup, a **motorcycle and radio museum** in Stubbekøbing, a restored **windmill** in Gedesby and **frescoes** by the Elmelunde master at the church in Nørre Alslev.

The E55 motorway runs the length of the island; for those travelling by bicycle, there are bike lanes along the motorway in both directions.

NYKØBING F

With a population of 25,000, Nykøbing F is

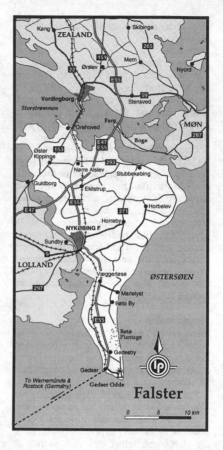

Falster

Falster's only large town. The 'F', incidentally, stands for Falster, and is used to differentiate the town from Denmark's two other Nykøbings, one in Zealand, the other in Jutland.

Nykøbing F tore its grand medieval castle down in the 18th century (you can see a model of it in the Museet Falsters Minder) and with few exceptions the town has a predominantly modern facade. Still, if you need to stay over there's a hostel, a relatively cheap hotel and some low-key sights of local interest.

Torvet, the town centre, is a 10-minute walk west of the railway station.

Information

The Nykøbing Turistbureau (☎ 54 85 13 03, fax 54 85 10 05), just south of Torvet at Østergågade 7, 4800 Nykøbing F, is open Monday to Saturday year round; hours vary with the season.

The post office is at the north side of the railway station.

Things to See & Do

There's an old **watertower**, called Nykøbing F Vandtårn, off Østergågade, just south of the tourist office, that you can climb for a bird's-eye view of the town. In the summer it's open Monday to Friday from 11 am to 3 pm, on Saturday to noon; in the winter it's open Monday, Wednesday and Friday until 2 pm. Admission is 10 kr.

The **Museet Falsters Minder**, the local history museum, is in one of Nykøbing F's oldest houses, a half-timbered building that dates from around 1700. The house itself is referred to as Czarens Hus because the Russian tsar Peter the Great stayed here en route to Copenhagen in 1716. It's on the corner of Langgade and Færgestræde, at the west side of Torvet. From May to mid-September it's open Tuesday to Saturday from 10 am to 4 pm and on Sunday from 2 to 4 pm; the rest of the year it's open Tuesday to Sunday from 2 to 4 pm.

The town also has a fire engine museum, **Brandmuseum**, at Vendersgade 6, that's open Monday to Wednesday from 11 am to 3 pm and also on Saturday morning. Admission is 10 kr.

The **Nykøbing F Folkepark Zoo**, a children's zoo at Østre Allé 97, one km east of the railway station, has flamingos, goats, deer, llamas and other animals. It's open daily from 9 am to 8 pm in the summer, from 9 am to 4 pm in the winter; admission is free.

On the outskirts of town the **Middel-aldercentret** (Medieval Centre), at Ved Hamborgskoven 2, Sundby, has displays demonstrating medieval technology. There's a large wooden catapult, a smithy, a pottery and a few medieval-style reconstructions. It's open only from mid-May to 30 September, Tuesday to Saturday from 10 am to 4 pm and on Sunday from 11 am to 5 pm. Admission is 35 kr for adults and 15 kr for children. The medieval centre is across the bridge in Lolland; bus No 2 from the Nykøbing F railway station stops about 500 metres away.

Places to Stay

Falster's only hostel is the 94-bed *Nykøbing Falster Vandrerhjem* (☎ 54 85 66 99, fax 54 82 32 42), Østre Allé 110, 4800 Nykøbing F, one km east of the railway station and opposite the zoo. It has dorm beds for 80 kr, singles/doubles for 175/220 kr, and is open from mid-January to mid-December. Bus No 42 (6 kr) stops out front.

Just south of the hostel is the three-star *Nykøbing F Camping* (☎ 54 85 45 45, fax 54 82 32 42), Østre Allé 112, 4800 Nykøbing F, which charges 35 kr per person and is open from May to mid-September.

The tourist office books rooms in private homes for 110 kr per person.

Teaterhotellet (☎ 54 85 32 77, fax 54 85 22 40) is a small central hotel at Torvet 3, 4800 Nykøbing F, with 38 straightforward rooms that cost 275/415 kr for singles/doubles with shared bath, 315/440 kr with private bath, breakfast included.

Places to Eat

The Nykøbing F railway station has a kiosk with fresh fruit; a snack bar with drinks, ice cream and sandwiches; and a full *DSB Restaurant* that's open from 11 am to 9.30 pm and has a daily meal with coffee for 38 kr.

There are half a dozen simple places to eat on Torvet with the special of the day priced between 38 and 55 kr. There's a pizzeria, a *Kvickly* grocery store and a bakery on the pedestrian street Jernbanegade, about midway between the railway station and Torvet.

Getting There & Away

Nykøbing F is 128 km south-west of Copenhagen and 24 km north of Gedser. The north-south E55 motorway goes directly

FALSTER

through Nykøbing F, while route 9 connects Nykøbing F to Lolland via the Frederik IX bridge.

Trains leave Copenhagen hourly for Nykøbing F, take two hours and cost 95 kr.

The bus stop is at the south side of the railway station.

Getting Around
Bicycles can be hired at the railway station for 30 kr a day.

MARIELYST
The most glorious stretch of beach in Falster is at Marielyst which, with 6000 summer cottages, ranks as one of Denmark's prime holiday areas. It has all of the expected beach resort offerings, including numerous places to eat and drink and a variety of places to stay from camping grounds to a chain hotel. Although Marielyst draws lots of visitors in the summer, the beach extends for many km with easy access to its entire length so there's no need to feel crowded.

Information
Tourist Office The Marielyst Turistbureau (☎ 54 13 62 98, fax 54 13 62 99), Marielyst Strandvej 54, 4873 Væggerløse, in the town centre, is open in the summer Monday to Saturday from 9 am to 5 pm and the rest of the year on weekdays from 9 am to 4 pm and on Saturday from 10 am to 2 pm.

Money The Unibank at Marielyst Strandvej 54 is open in the summer Monday to Friday from 10 am to 3 pm and in the low season Tuesday to Friday from 10 am to 12.30 pm.

Laundry There's a coin laundry on Marielyst Strandvej between Natravnevej and Hjejlevej.

Cycling
A bike path runs along top of the dunes the

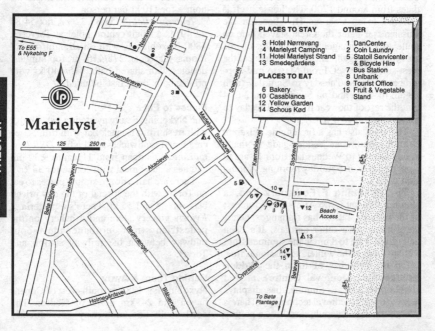

PLACES TO STAY
3 Hotel Nørrevang
4 Marielyst Camping
11 Hotel Marielyst Strand
13 Smedegårdens

PLACES TO EAT
6 Bakery
10 Casablanca
12 Yellow Garden
14 Schous Kød

OTHER
1 DanCenter
2 Coin Laundry
5 Statoil Servicenter
  & Bicycle Hire
7 Bus Station
8 Unibank
9 Tourist Office
15 Fruit & Vegetable
  Stand

length of the beach, which makes it easy to get around and explore the coast. This bike path isn't limited to Marielyst but continues 12 km south, through a coastal forest (Bøtø Plantage) and clear down to Gedesby Strand, near the southern tip of the island.

Bicycles can be rented from Statoil Servicenter (☎ 54 13 60 80) at Marielyst Strandvej 40 for 30/150 kr a day/week.

Places to Stay

Marielyst's most central camping ground is *Smedegårdens* (☎ 54 13 66 17, fax 54 13 66 16), Bøtøvej 5, 4873 Væggerløse. It's a simple place, but there are cooking facilities and showers and it's but a two-minute stroll to the beach or the town centre. It's open from 1 May to 15 September and costs 44 kr per person.

The other camping ground in town is *Marielyst Camping* (☎ 54 13 53 08), Marielyst Strandvej 36, 4873 Væggerløse, about 800 metres from the beach, in a field with hedges that offer some privacy. It's open from Easter (March/April) to 1 October and costs 36 to 44 kr, depending on the month.

The tourist office maintains a list of rooms in private homes that cost on average 150/300 kr for singles/doubles. They can also help with booking small apartments for around 1800 kr a week and summer houses from 3000 to 15,000 kr a week. There are no booking fees. You can also book cottages from DanCenter (☎ 54 13 65 00), Marielyst Strandvej 15.

The *Hotel Marielyst Strand* (☎ 54 13 68 88), Marielyst Strandvej 61, 4873 Væggerløse, a short stroll from the beach, has straightforward rooms for 350/450 kr for singles/doubles, 100 kr more for a room with a private bath.

The *Hotel Nørrevang* (☎ 54 13 62 62, fax 54 13 62 72), Marielyst Strandvej 32, 4873 Væggerløse, part of the Best Western chain, is Marielyst's most upmarket hotel and has some nice touches including a thatched reception building. There are 26 standard rooms with private bath, TV and phone and 57 apartments, with kitchen and balcony, which can accommodate two to six people.

Rates begin at 595/795 kr for singles/doubles, but there are various package plans and discounts.

Places to Eat

Marielyst is filled with cafés, hot-dog stands and ice-cream shops, including a fast-food stand on the corner of Bøtøvej and Marielyst Strandvej.

A good alternative to junk food is offered by *Schous Kød*, 200 metres down Bøtøvej, which sells inexpensive cod cakes, fish & chips (25 kr), half a baked chicken with chips (35 kr) and other deli foods for takeaway. There's a little fruit and vegetable stand next door.

There's a good bakery 50 metres west of the tourist office that's open daily from 7 am to 5 pm.

The *Yellow Garden* steak house, at Bøtøvej 1, has steaks from 69 to 99 kr, chicken or fish with chips for around 40 kr and a Danish lunch buffet from 11 am to 3 pm for 59 kr.

Casablanca, a popular café on Marielyst Strandvej, often has jazz on weekends, and usually has a daily special such as spareribs, potatoes and salad for around 60 kr.

The *Hotel Nørrevang* has an expensive fine-dining restaurant with international fare.

Getting There & Away

From the Nykøbing F railway station, it's a 25-minute (18 kr) bus ride to Marielyst. Buses are fairly frequent, particularly on weekdays; you can catch bus Nos 40, 41 or 45. If you prefer to pedal your way to Marielyst, DSB rents bicycles at the Nykøbing F railway station.

GEDSER

Gedser, at the tip of Falster, is Denmark's southernmost point, but is otherwise unremarkable and most visitors simply zip right through town on their way to a waiting ferry.

The only sights are a little toy museum with dolls and old wooden toys, and a private railway museum open only on Wednesday

FALSTER

and Saturday, both on Stationsvej within walking distance of the ferry.

If you want to grab a meal, there are a couple of simple cafés in town on Langgade, north of the post office. The tourist office is just west of the post office and adjacent to the toy museum.

There is a nice stretch of beach, Gedesby Strand, a few km east of Gedser, but it's largely a residential and summer cottage community with none of the transient-visitor services found in Marielyst.

Getting There & Away

Gedser is 152 km south of Copenhagen. Both the railway station and the E55 motorway terminate right at the ferry dock.

Trains leave Gedser for Nykøbing F (20 minutes, 24 kr) about half a dozen times a day, usually in coordination with the ferry service.

In the summer, bus No 45 runs between Gedser and Marielyst (12 kr) and continues on to Nykøbing F.

There are daily car ferries from Gedser to Warnemünde and Rostock in Germany; information is in the Getting There & Away chapter.

Lolland

Lolland has some of Denmark's best farming land, much of it planted in sugar beets. Being a farm belt it's not an immensely interesting area for touring but it does have a few scattered sights, including a safari park and a notable auto museum.

Maribo, in a little lake district in central Lolland, is the most appealing of Lolland's towns. Sakskøbing, nine km east of Maribo, has a watertower painted with a cheery smiling face, and Nakskov, at the western end of Lolland, has a few half-timbered waterfront warehouses and a couple of other minor sights.

Rødbyhavn, a little harbour-side town in the south, grew up in the 1960s after a direct ferry service was initiated to Puttgarden,

Germany. That ferry service now provides the linkage for the inter-Europe E47 highway between Germany and Denmark.

GETTING THERE & AWAY
Bus & Train

There are two rail lines in Lolland. The main east-west route cuts across the centre of Lolland and is operated by the private company Lollandsbanen. These trains run between Nykøbing F and Nakskov, a trip of just 47 minutes, stopping en route in Sakskøbing and Maribo. Service is about hourly during the week but much less frequent on weekends. Lollandsbanen also operates a limited bus service on the island; the most useful route, No 560, runs from Nykøbing F to Nakskov via Nysted and Rødby.

The other rail line, from Rødby to Nykøbing F, is run by DSB. Trains, which take just 23 minutes, leave Rødby several times a day in conjunction with the Puttgarden ferry service; in most cases the train continues from Nykøbing F on to Copenhagen.

Boat

Route 9 cuts across central Lolland 61 km from Nykøbing F in the east to Tårs in the west. There are no services at Tårs; it's simply a car-ferry terminal.

SFDS operates the car ferry between Tårs and Spodsbjerg (in Langeland) every 30 minutes during peak hours and once an hour in the early morning and late evening. The last ferry in either direction leaves at 11.30 pm, except on Saturday when it leaves at 9.30 pm. The cost is 250 kr for a car with up to five passengers. For reservations call ☎ 53 93 13 23 in Tårs and ☎ 62 50 10 22 in Spodsbjerg.

For information on the ferry to Puttgarden, Germany, see the Getting There & Away chapter in the front of the book.

AALHOLM SLOT & AUTOMOBIL MUSEUM

Aalholm Slot, one of northern Europe's oldest inhabited castles, belonged to Danish royalty until 1725 when it was put up for

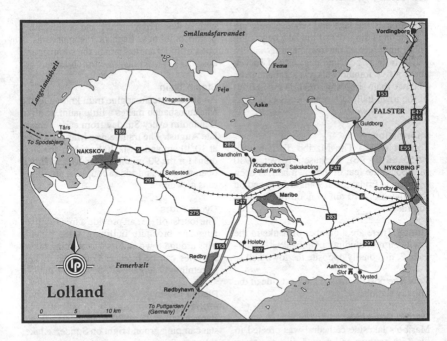

auction and sold to the Raben family. The estate's history goes back to the 12th century, while the oldest sections of the current castle date from the 14th century. King Christopher II was imprisoned in his own dungeon here in 1332 by his half-brother, Count Johan the Mild.

Its current owner, the baron JO Raben-Levetzau, has opened the 40-room castle to the public. Visitors are shown some of the lavishly furnished rooms as well as the dungeon and torture chamber.

Near the castle is the baron's Aalholm Automobil Museum, which has four cavernous halls holding about 200 antique cars, one of Europe's largest collections. Rare models include a 1900 Decauville, a 1902 Renault, a 1903 Ford Model A, a 1904 Cadillac, a 1911 Rolls Royce and a 1926 Bugatti. An 1850 steam train gives rides around the grounds.

The castle and museum are at the west side of the small town of Nysted, which is con-

nected to Nykøbing F via route 297 and to Saksøbing via route 283. Both are open daily from 11 am to 5 pm in June, July and August, and on weekend afternoons in spring and autumn. Admission to each costs 50/20 kr for adults/children; there's a combination ticket for 90/35 kr.

MARIBO

If you decide to break for a night in Lolland, the town of Maribo, the geographical and commercial centre of the island, is an agreeable place. It has a choice setting, nestled around the northern arm of a large inland lake, Søndersø. A historic cathedral sits on the eastern shore, while Bangshave, a wood thick with beech trees, sits on the western shore.

The town centre, Torvet, is marked by Maribo's neoclassical 19th century Rådhus (town hall), which is fronted by a water fountain and backed by a few 18th century timber-frame houses. Beyond that the main

LOLLAND

attraction is the lake and woods; there are trails along both sides of the lake beginning only minutes from the town centre.

The railway/bus station is north of Torvet, about a five-minute walk via Jernbanegade. The two main shopping streets begin in front of the town hall; Østergade leads east, Vestergade leads west.

Information
Tourist Office The Maribo Turistbureau (☎ 53 88 04 96), Rådhuset, Torvet, 4930 Maribo, at the rear of the town hall, is open Monday to Friday from 9 am to 5 pm and on Saturday from 10 am to noon (to 3 pm in summer).

Money There are a number of banks in the town centre including a Unibank at Vestergade 2, diagonally opposite the town hall.

Post The post office is at the west side of the railway station.

Maribo Domkirke
Maribo's lakeside cathedral was erected in the 15th century and named, like the town itself, after the Virgin Mary. The cathedral was once part of a larger complex that included the convent where the daughter of King Christian IV, Leonora Christine, spent the last years of her life after her release from imprisonment in Copenhagen Castle in 1685. She is buried in the cathedral; for a peek into her crypt join one of the cathedral tours that are given at 2 pm daily. Maribo Domkirke is 200 metres south-west of Torvet.

Museums
Maribo has a couple of small museums. The **Storstrøms Kunstmuseum**, beside the railway station on Jernbanepladsen, has a collection of regional art from the 18th to the 20th century. The adjacent **Lolland-Falster Stiftsmuseum** exhibits church art and some social displays, including one on migrant farm labourers. The **Frilandsmuseum** on Meinckesvej 5, in the Bangshave area a km south-west of town, is an open-air museum

with a wooden windmill and a few other period buildings. Each of the museums is open from 10 am to 5 pm in the summer and costs 10 kr for adults, free for children.

Steam Train
An antique steam engine train known as the Museumsbanen makes a little jaunt north to Bandholm every Sunday from early June to late August. The train leaves Maribo station at 10.30 am and costs 30 kr (15 kr for children) for the 90-minute return trip. In July it operates daily and adds a couple of afternoon runs as well.

Cycle Tours
The tourist office can provide a free English-language brochure outlining three bicycle trips around town and its surrounding lakes. Bicycles can be hired at Østergade Cykelforretning, Østergade 40, for 35 kr a day.

Places to Stay
Maribo Sø Camping (☎ 53 88 00 71), Bangshavevej 25, 4930 Maribo, is a three-star camping ground right on Søndersø lake, about a 20-minute walk from the town centre. It has kitchen and laundry facilities, a TV lounge and is accessible by wheelchair. The cost is 44 kr per person; there are also a few cabins for 150 kr plus the per-person charge. It's open from mid-March to the end of September.

The *Maribo Vandrerhjem* (☎ 53 88 33 14, fax 53 88 32 65), Søndre Boulevard 82B, 4930 Maribo, about two km south-east of Torvet, is a new 97-bed hostel near lake Søndersø that's open all year round. Dorm beds cost 70 kr, while a family room for four costs 280 kr. There's a lakeside trail to the town centre.

Ebsens Hotel (☎ 53 88 10 44), Vestergade 32, 4930 Maribo, is a small hotel just a few minutes walk from the railway station and Torvet. While the rooms are straightforward, the hotel is pleasant enough and relatively cheap at 230/390 kr for singles/doubles with shared bath, 390/550 kr with private bath.

Hotel Hvide Hus (☎ 53 88 10 11, fax 53 88 05 22), Vestergade 27, 4930 Maribo, is a modern 69-room lakeside hotel 500 metres west of Torvet. A member of the Best Western chain, the rooms have private bath, minibar, TV and lakeview balcony and cost from 595/695 kr for singles/doubles.

Places to Eat

There's a bakery on Vestergade just east of the Ebsens Hotel.

Omer's Pizza Bar, at Vestergade 13A, has pizza, pasta, burgers, salads and shawarma sandwiches.

Restaurant China House, above the Fakta grocery store at Vestergade 4, has fixed-price lunches for 45 to 55 kr from 12.30 to 4.30 pm.

The *Restaurant Bangs Have* on Bangshavevej, in an old manor house east of Maribo Sø Camping, has a pleasant lakeside setting with a view of the cathedral across the water. It's open from noon to 9 pm and has a daily two-course special for 85 kr as well as an à la carte menu.

KNUTHENBORG SAFARI PARK

The Knuthenborg Safari Park, seven km north of Maribo via route 289, is a large drive-through safari park with free-roaming zebra, giraffes, rhinoceroses, antelopes, llamas, ostriches and other exotic creatures. The park, which occupies the lawns of what was once Denmark's largest privately held estate, is enclosed by a seven-km-long wall. In addition to the free-roaming animals there are 500 varieties of trees and flowering bushes, an aviary, an enclosed tiger section and some simple amusement rides for young children. There's a hot dog stand and a cafeteria-style restaurant. It's open from 9 am to 6 pm daily from late April to late September. Admission costs 70 kr for adults and 35 kr for children.

Bornholm

Bornholm (population 45,000) is a delightful slow-paced island that makes for a nice getaway. Lying 200 km east of Copenhagen, it's connected to the capital by a daily ferry service – however, Bornholm is closer to Germany and Sweden than it is to the rest of Denmark and thus sees more foreign tourists than Danish visitors.

It's a pleasantly varied island. The centre of Bornholm is a mixture of wheat fields and forests, the coast is dotted with small fishing villages and there's a scattering of half-timbered houses throughout. The northern part of Bornholm has sea cliffs and a rocky shoreline, while the south coast has long stretches of powdery white sand. Not only is Bornholm geographically separated from the rest of Denmark, but its granite-based geology is also unique and it has many varieties of plants that grow nowhere else in Denmark.

Notable attractions include Bornholm's fortified 12th century round churches; its picturesque little harbour towns, particularly Gudhjem and Svaneke; the ruins of the medieval fortress Hammershus; and the island's extensive network of bicycle trails.

Bornholm is also renowned for its smokehouses. Be sure to try Bornholm's smoked

HIGHLIGHTS

- Unique 12th century round churches
- Cycling along the island's numerous cycling trails
- Coastal ruins of the 13th century fortress Hammershus Slot
- Dueodde's fine white sand dunes and beach
- Unspoiled harbourside villages of Gudhjem and Svaneke
- Christiansø, an offshore island with a well-preserved 17th century character

herring, *bornholmers*, and the nearby island of Christiansø's spiced herring, considered the best in Denmark.

Bornholm's Round Churches

Unique among Bornholm's sights are its four 12th century *rundkirke* (round churches), constructed with two-metre-thick whitewashed walls and black conical roofs. The churches were built at a time when pirating Wends from eastern Germany were ravaging coastal areas throughout the Baltic Sea. Thus, the churches were designed not only as places of worship but also as refuges against enemy attacks – the upper storeys served as a shooting galleries. Each church was built about two km inland, and all four are sited high enough on knolls to offer a lookout to the sea. Fittingly, these bold churches have a stern, ponderous appearance, more typical of a fortress than as a place of worship.

Another unique architectural feature of the churches is their detached belfries, made of stone and tarred timber. All four churches are still used for Sunday services and are also open to visitors from Monday to Saturday. ■

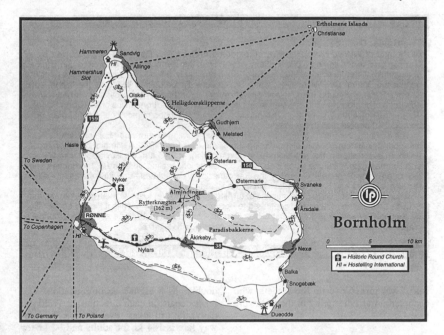

HISTORY

Bornholm's rich history, which goes back at least 5000 years, has been traced through Bronze Age burial mounds, rock engravings and monoliths. During the Iron Age, Bornholm served as a trade centre for the Baltic region. Excavated items, including numerous Roman coins, indicate that trade between Bornholm and the rest of Europe was widespread.

During the Middle Ages, Bornholm was administered by the Bishop of Lund (Lund was then Danish territory, but is now part of southern Sweden), who ruled Bornholm from Hammershus, an expansive fortress on the island's north coast.

During the wars between Sweden and Denmark in the mid-17th century, Bornholm fell into Swedish hands, along with Danish territories at the southern end of the Swedish mainland. In 1658, when it looked likely that the island might be become a permanent part of Sweden, the Swedish commandant on

Bornholm, Colonel Printzenskjöld, was murdered in an uprising. The rebels, led by Bornholm native Jens Kofoed, went on to expel the Swedish garrison from Bornholm and in 1660 returned the island to Danish rule. As a consequence, during this period when Denmark's borders were substantially eroded by Swedish conquest, a defiant Bornholm managed to prevail as Denmark's easternmost province.

Peace in the 18th century brought prosperity to the island and to merchants who built timber-framed mansions along waterfront villages like Svaneke and Rønne. Many of those harbour-side homes still stand today.

During WW II Bornholm, like the rest of Denmark, was occupied by the Nazis. However when Germany surrendered to the Allies on 4 May 1945, the German commander on Bornholm refused to step down. As a result the Soviets bombed Rønne and Nexø in the days that followed, causing heavy damage to those towns. On 9 May the

The Soviet Occupation
At the end of WW II, when Germany surrendered to the Allies, Bornholm was occupied by a German garrison of some 20,000 soldiers. At that time, the German naval commander in charge of Bornholm, Captain von Kamptz, fearful of Soviet reprisals, insisted on surrendering his troops only to the British. On 7 May 1945, when Soviet surveillance planes flew over the island, von Kamptz fired off a round from his anti-aircraft guns. Later that day the Soviets returned with a squadron of bombers, which released their loads onto the harbourfront towns of Nexø and Rønne. There was no warning given to the islanders, who were still in the midst of celebrating the war's end, and 10 people died in the attack.

The Soviets gave the Germans until 10 am the next morning to surrender, but von Kamptz held his ground, insisting once again on turning the island over to the British. He did, however, order a civilian evacuation of the two towns. The next morning, at 9.45 am, the Soviets attacked Nexø and Rønne again, this time using incendiary bombs which levelled one-third of the houses and damaged many of the rest. On 9 May, the Germans finally capitulated and within a matter of days the Nazi soldiers had been repatriated from the island.

After the Germans were gone, instead of turning Bornholm over to the Danish government, the Soviets built up their forces and continued to occupy the island. For a while it looked as if Stalin was going to wrap Bornholm within his Iron Curtain – but in March 1946 he abruptly announced plans to withdraw and within a month all the Soviet troops had left. ■

island was turned over to the Soviets, who occupied it until the spring of the following year.

GETTING THERE & AWAY
Bornholm can be reached by air, by boat or by a bus/boat combination.

Air
Mærsk Air (☎ 32 32 68 28) has several flights a day between Copenhagen and Rønne. If you fly on certain midday flights from Monday to Friday the cost is 595 kr return, which is otherwise the standard one-way fare. For more information on air travel see the Getting Around chapter in the front of the book.

The airport, Bornholms Lufthavn, is five km south-east of Rønne, on the road to Dueodde. Bus No 7 stops on the main road in front of the airport.

Boat & Bus
To/From Copenhagen Bornholmstrafikken (☎ 33 13 18 66 in Copenhagen, 56 95 18 66 in Rønne) has an overnight ferry between Copenhagen and Rønne. This can be a very economical way to get to Bornholm, since it

doubles as a night's accommodation. The boats depart (in each direction) at 11.30 pm daily; the trip takes seven hours. The one-way fare is 184 kr for adults and 92 kr for children. Add 60 kr for a dorm bunk, 144 kr per person for a double cabin inside (177 kr for a cabin outside), or spread out your sleeping bag in the TV lounge free of charge. It costs 51 kr to take a bicycle, 187 kr for a motorcycle and 379 kr for a car. The boat has lockers, a cafeteria and a sit-down restaurant. There are also lockers at the ferry terminals.

Bornholmstrafikken also has departures daily, except on Wednesday, at 8.30 am from Copenhagen and 3.30 pm from Rønne between late June and mid-August, as well as a few daytime departures on weekends in the shoulder season. The cost is the same as the overnight boat.

Flyvebådene (☎ 33 12 80 88) offers high-speed hydrofoil connections between Copenhagen and Rønne for 159 kr for adults and 90 kr for children. The trip takes 4½ hours. The boats leave Copenhagen daily at 9 am and 5 pm and depart from Rønne at 8 am and 4 pm.

Another option is Bornholmerbussen's (☎ 44 68 44 00) bus No 866, which goes from Copenhagen's Central Station to Ystad in Sweden, where it connects with a ferry to Rønne. The service runs twice daily, takes 5½ hours and costs 160 kr for adults and 80 kr for children.

To/From Sweden Bornholmstrafikken (☎ 56 95 18 66 in Rønne, 41 11 80 65 in Ystad) runs ferries daily between Rønne and Ystad. Boats depart from Ystad at 11.15 am and 7.15 pm and depart from Rønne at 8 am and 4 pm. In summer there are one or two extra sailings daily. The journey takes 2½ hours. The cost is 107 kr for adults, 54 kr for children and 190 kr for a car. On Tuesday, Wednesday and Thursday a car with up to five people costs 500 kr.

Especially during the winter there can be some very cheap discounts between Sweden and Rønne, and throughout the year the cost of a same-day return fare is equivalent to the one-way fare; this is all geared to encourage Swedish shoppers.

There's also a summertime boat service between Simrishamn (Sweden) and Allinge (Bornholm), though the schedule varies a bit from year to year. For details, contact Bornholms Terminalen (☎ 414 143 45) in Simrishamn or the Bornholms Velkomst-center (☎ 56 95 95 00).

To/From Germany There are ferries to Bornholm from Sassnitz and Neu Mukran (Rügen).

DFO HansaFerries (☎ 56 48 00 01 in Bornholm, 38 39 26 41 80 in Sassnitz) departs from Sassnitz daily from June to mid-September at 10 am and from Rønne at 5 pm, with an extra sailing on Saturday. The rest of the year sailings are only on Tuesday and Saturday. The trip takes four hours. The one-way fare is 80/40 kr for adults/children from June to mid-September, and 40/20 kr for adults/children the rest of the year. The cost for a car (including up to five passengers) is 538 kr, except on summer weekends, when it's 807 kr.

The Neu Mukran-Rønne route, run by Bornholmstrafikken (☎ 56 95 18 66 in Rønne, 38 39 23 52 26 in Neu Mukran),

operates six times a week in summer and a little less frequently the rest of the year. The schedule varies with the day of the week; the trip takes 3½ hours. The one-way fare (or same-day return fare) is 100/50 kr for adults/children from June to August and 50/25 kr the rest of the year. Depending on the day of the week and the season, it costs from 399 to 690 kr to take a car with up to five passengers included.

To/From Poland Polferries (☎ 936 3006 in Swinoujscie, ☎ 56 95 10 69 in Rønne) runs a ferry between Poland and Bornholm on Saturday from late June to late August. The trip takes six hours, with the boat leaving Swinoujscie at 10 am and departing from Rønne at 5.30 pm. The one-way/return fare is 155/250 kr for adults, 80/125 kr for children, 155/250 kr for a car, or 530/840 kr for a car and five passengers.

GETTING AROUND
Bus

Bornholms Amts Trafikselskab (called BAT for short) operates a good, inexpensive bus service around the island. Fares, which are based on a zone system, cost 7.50 kr per zone, with the maximum fare set at 10 zones. You can save money by buying a bus pass called RaBATkort from the bus driver for 60 kr, which is good for 10 zones of travel and can be used for multiple rides and by more than one person. There's also a one-day pass for 90 kr that allows unlimited travel. Buses operate all year, but schedules are less frequent in winter.

In summer, bus No 7 leaves from the Rønne ferry terminal every two hours from 8 am to 6 pm and travels anticlockwise around the island, stopping at Dueodde beach and all major coastal villages before terminating at Hammershus Slot. Other buses make direct runs from Rønne to Nexø, Svaneke, Gudhjem and Sandvig.

Standard fares include 21.50 kr from Rønne to Åkirkeby (bus No 5 or 6); 30 kr from Rønne to Sandvig (bus No 1) or Gudhjem (bus No 3); and 37.50 kr from

Rønne to Svaneke (bus No 4), Nexø (bus No 6) or Dueodde (bus No 7).

In midsummer, BAT runs special sightseeing buses – the Den Grønne Bus goes to places of environmental interest; the Bondegårdsbussen visits farms; and the Kunsthåndværkerbussen stops at craft studios. For details contact the main bus office (☎ 56 95 21 21).

Car & Motorbike
Car rentals are expensive on Bornholm. Even with advance reservations, expect to pay a good 600 kr a day for short-term rental, although the rates can drop a bit if you keep the car for a longer period.

Avis has an office in Rønne at Rønne Autoudlejning ApS (☎ 56 95 22 08), Snellemark 19, and will allow visitors to drop off the car after hours. Avis, Hertz (☎ 30 54 32 13) and Interrent (☎ 56 95 43 00) have booths at the airport.

Cycle Routes
Cycling is a great way to get around, as Bornholm is crisscrossed by 200 km of bike trails. Some of the trails are built over former rail routes, some slice through forests and others parallel highways. Together they connect Bornholm's largest towns, cross a wide variety of landscapes and lead to most of the island's sightseeing attractions.

There are bike routes running from Rønne to Allinge, from Rønne to Helligdomsklipperne, from Rønne to Åkirkeby and Nexø, from Rønne to Dueodde and Nexø, from Rønne through the Almindingen forest to Årsdale, from Allinge to Åkirkeby, from Helligdomsklipperne to Gudhjem, from Gudhjem to Åkirkeby and Dueodde, and from Nexø to Svaneke. An extension of the latter trail, from Svaneke to Gudhjem, is expected to be completed by 1997.

If you don't feel like pedalling the entire way, you can carry your bike on public buses for an additional 19 kr.

Bicycle Rental
Bicycles can be rented at various places around the island for about 50/200 kr a day/week for a three-speed bike and 65/350 kr a day/week for a mountain bike. Two of the larger Rønne rental shops are Cykel-Centret (☎ 56 95 06 04) at Søndergade 7 and Bornholms Cykeludlejning (☎ 56 95 13 59) at Nordre Kystvej 5. Elsewhere on the island, most hostels and camping grounds rent bicycles, and tourist offices and hotels can also arrange rental for you.

RØNNE
Rønne is Bornholm's administrative centre and largest town. It has 15,000 residents, one-third of the island's total population.

Spread around a large natural harbour, Rønne has been the island's commercial centre since the Middle Ages. Over the years the town has expanded and taken on a more suburban look, but the old harbour-side district still retains many of its older houses and can be a pleasant place to stroll.

Despite the fact that Rønne is commonly regarded more as a watering hole and shopping locale for Swedes on day trips than as a sightseeing destination, it has a couple of local museums and nearby attractions and can be a pleasant-enough place to begin or end a longer tour of the island.

Information
Tourist Office The tourist office, Bornholms Velkomstcenter (☎ 56 95 95 00, fax 56 95 95 68), Nordre Kystvej 3, 3700 Rønne, a few minutes walk from the harbour, has information on all of Bornholm. Opening hours vary with the season and boat schedules, but are usually from 7 am to 10.15 pm (sometimes as late as 12.30 am) from June to August, and from 9 am (from 1 pm on weekends) to 6 pm in spring and autumn.

Other There's a Unibank at Store Torv. The post office is on the south side of Lille Torv. The hospital, Bornholms Centralsygehus (☎ 56 95 11 65), is on Sygehusvej at the south end of town.

Walking Tour
A good place to begin a walking tour of Rønne's older quarters is at **Store Torv**,

BORNHOLM

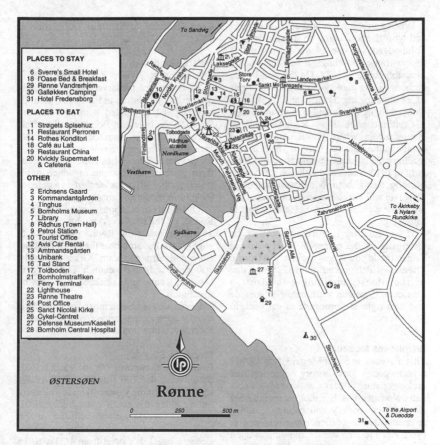

PLACES TO STAY

6 Sverre's Small Hotel
18 I'Oase Bed & Breakfast
29 Rønne Vandrerhjem
30 Galløkken Camping
31 Hotel Fredensborg

PLACES TO EAT

1 Strøgets Spisehuz
11 Restaurant Perronen
14 Rothes Konditori
18 Café au Lait
19 Restaurant China
20 Kvickly Supermarket
& Cafeteria

OTHER

2 Erichsens Gaard
3 Kommandantgården
4 Tinghus
5 Bornholms Museum
7 Library
8 Rådhus (Town Hall)
9 Petrol Station
10 Tourist Office
12 Avis Car Rental
13 Amtmandsgården
15 Unibank
16 Taxi Stand
17 Toldboden
21 Bornholmstraffiken
Ferry Terminal
22 Lighthouse
23 Rønne Theatre
24 Post Office
25 Sanct Nicolai Kirke
26 Cykel-Centret
27 Defense Museum/Kasellet
28 Bornholm Central Hospital

ØSTERSØEN

Rønne

0   250   500 m

which once served as the military parade ground. Now the central commercial square, it's the site of a **public market** on Wednesday and Saturday mornings all year round. On the east side of the square, at Store Torv 1, is **Tinghus**, a neoclassical building dating from 1834 that formerly held Rønne's city hall, courthouse and jail.

Continue up Store Torvegade and turn left on Laksegade, an older street with a number of attractive period houses built in the early 19th century. You can tour one of them, **Erichsens Gaard** at Laksegade 7, a merchant's house dating from 1806 that has been

turned into a museum (15 kr), complete with period furnishings; it's open daily from 10 am (from noon on Sunday) to 5 pm.

At the end of Laksegade turn left onto Storegade and at No 42, you'll find the **Kommandantgården**, a restored stone structure that was built to house Bornholm's military commander. A block farther south, at Storegade 36, is **Amtmandsgården**, a half-timbered structure that dates from the late 1700s and is now the Bornholm prefect's residence. Jens Kofoed, who liberated Bornholm from the Swedes in 1658, was born in a house that once stood on this site.

BORNHOLM

When you reach Rådhusstræde, turn right and you'll soon come to **Toldboden**, at Toldbodgade 1, one of the town's oldest timber-framed buildings; it was constructed as a storehouse in 1684. On the wall by the harbour-facing gable you can spot figurines of two menacing Dalmatians flanking a cloaked figure that is said to represent Satan.

Continue back down Rådhusstræde to Havnebakken where you'll pass a quaint octagonal **lighthouse** built in 1880, before reaching the attractive **Sankt Nicolai Kirke**, built in 1915. South of the church is **Bombehusene**, a neighbourhood that encompasses Kapelvej and Kirkestræde; this is one of the areas that was levelled by Soviet bombers in May 1945.

If you continue east from the church on Østergade, at the corner of Østergade and Teaterstræde you'll pass the restored **Rønne Theatre**, which was built in 1823 and is one of the oldest functioning theatres in Denmark. Continue north onto Nellikegade and turn right at Tornegade to get back to Store Torv.

Bornholms Museum

This museum, at Sankt Mortensgade 29, has a hodgepodge local-history collection that includes nature displays, antique toys, excavated Roman coins, Bornholmer grandfather clocks, local pottery and paintings, and a re-created doctor's office from an earlier era. From April to October the museum is open from 10 am to 5 pm, except on Sunday when it's open from 1 to 5 pm. In winter it's open on Tuesday, Thursday and Sunday afternoons only. Admission is 20 kr.

Forsvarsmuseet

Forsvarsmuseet (the Defence Museum) is located in the 17th century citadel called Kastellet, at the south side of Rønne near the hostel. It has the usual old armaments and military uniforms as well as displays on the bombing of Rønne and Nexø by the Soviets at the end of WW II and their subsequent occupation of the island. From May to September the museum is open from 10 am to 4 pm, Tuesday to Saturday. Admission is 15 kr.

Nylars Rundkirke

The attractive Nylars Rundkirke, built in 1150, is the best preserved and most easily reached round church in the Rønne area. Its central pillar is painted with 13th century frescoes, the oldest in Bornholm. The frescoes depict scenes from the Creation myth, including Adam and Eve's expulsion from the Garden of Eden. The cylindrical nave has three storeys, the top one of which has a watchman's gallery that served as a defence lookout in medieval times.

The church is about seven km from Rønne, on the road to Åkirkeby. It's only a 15-minute ride from Rønne on bus No 6; alight at the bus stop near the Dagli Brugsen store and turn north on Kirkevej for the 300-metre walk to the church. The bike path between Rønne and Åkirkeby also goes by the church.

From May to September the church is usually open from 9 am to 6 pm, Monday to Saturday; admission is free.

Places to Stay

Galløkken Camping (☎ 56 95 23 20), Strandvejen 4, 3700 Rønne, is 750 metres south of the Rønne Vandrerhjem in a pleasant setting along the south coast bike trail. It costs 40 kr per person for a tent site, or 250 kr for a four-person cabin (bring your own sleeping bags). It's open from 1 May to 15 September. Bicycle rentals are available for 50/195 kr a day/week.

The tourist office books private rooms for 140 to 175 kr a person, depending on the category of the room.

The 160-bed *Rønne Vandrerhjem* (☎ 56 95 13 40, fax 56 95 01 32) at Arsenalvej 12, 3700 Rønne, a little over a km south of the centre, is a 20-minute walk or a 30 kr taxi ride from the harbour. The hostel is open from late March to 1 November. The rate for a dorm bed is 75 to 84 kr, while family rooms range from 110 kr (one person) to 450 kr (six people).

l'Oase Bed & Breakfast (☎ 56 95 12 15),

NED FRIARY

NED FRIARY

Bornholm
Top: Fishing boat in Svaneke Harbour
Bottom: Rapeseed (mustard) field in mist

Bornholm
Top: Østerlars Rundkirke
Bottom: Fish market, Nexø
Right: View of great tower, Christiansø Fortress

run by Edith Lærkesen, consists of two rooms with bath above the Café au Lait, at Snellemark 22, 3700 Rønne. One room has a small balcony, a view and a TV and costs 425/550 kr for singles/doubles from late June to late August and 375/450 kr the rest of the year. The other, which is smaller and has a skylight, goes for 250/375 kr in the high season and 200/275 kr in the low season. There's a shared refrigerator and coffee maker and guests are provided with bread, coffee and tea to make their own breakfasts.

Also at the low-end of the price range is the 11-room *Sverre's Small Hotel* (☎ 56 95 03 03, fax 56 95 03 92), centrally located at Sankt Mortensgade 42B, 3700 Rønne. singles/doubles with shared bath are 220/330 kr in the low season and 270/430 kr from mid-June to late August. Rooms with private bathroom are 110 kr more. There's a small restaurant and bar (with jazz and dancing on weekends) on the ground level; breakfast is included in the rates.

Hotel Fredensborg (☎ 53 95 44 44, fax 53 95 03 14), Strandvejen 116, 3700 Rønne, the area's most upmarket hotel, is on a quiet knoll in a wooded coastal section at the south end of Rønne. A modern hotel affiliated with the Best Western chain, all 72 rooms have the standard resort amenities, including TV, trouser press and minibar. It has a sauna, pool, a tennis court, billiards and cycle rentals. Rates begin at 640/840 kr for singles/doubles.

Places to Eat

The ferry terminal has an upstairs cafeteria with reasonably priced snacks and pastries. If you're taking the overnight ferry to Copenhagen, the restaurant on the boat offers a good-value evening buffet with a few hot dishes, salad items, cheeses and the requisite smoked herring for 49 kr.

Rothes Konditori, opposite the central bus stop at Snellemark 41, has pastry, coffee and sandwiches.

There are a number of hamburger, hot dog and fast-food eateries along Store Torv and there's an inexpensive cafeteria in the nearby *Kvickly* supermarket.

Café au Lait, Snellemark 22, is a wine bar and café with a garden courtyard. It's a good place to take a relaxing break with a slice of apple pie and coffee or a glass of chardonnay. It's closed on Wednesday, but is otherwise open from 2 to 11 pm most days.

Restaurant Perronen, opposite the tourist office, has lasagne with salad (from a salad bar) for 48 kr, and steaks with salad for about double that. It's open for breakfast from 6.30 to 10 am, for lunch from noon to 3 pm and for dinner from 6 to 9 pm.

Strøgets Spisehuz, Store Torvegade 39, has a cosy atmosphere and good food at reasonable prices. There's a 'lunch des hauses' of Danish dishes and a daily special both for around 50 kr, as well as steaks for around 100 kr. The kitchen is open from 11 am to 10 pm, Tuesday to Saturday, and from noon to 10 pm on Sunday.

Restaurant China, Tornegade 6, has a standard array of Chinese dishes at moderately high prices. The kitchen is open from noon to 9 pm.

For a splurge, the *Hotel Fredensborg*, Strandvejen 116, has a well-regarded restaurant serving expensive Scandinavian fare.

ÅKIRKEBY

Åkirkeby is an inland town with a mix of old half-timbered houses and newer less distinctive homes.

The town takes its name from its main sight, the 12th century Romanesque stone church **Aa Kirke**, which is built on a granite knoll overlooking the surrounding farmland. The largest church on Bornholm, its crossroads location made it a convenient island-wide place of assembly. Although it has been altered and renovated in recent centuries, the church interior still holds a number of historic treasures, including a 13th century baptismal font of carved Gothic sandstone that depicts scenes of Christ and features Runic script. The ornate pulpit and altar date from around 1600 and are notable for their fine detail. For a 360° view of the township, climb the 22-metre-high bell tower, but watch your head on the low ceilings en route! Admission to the church is 4 kr. It's open Monday to Saturday, from 10 am to 4 pm in spring and autumn and from 9.30 am to 5 pm in summer.

A carpark and the tourist office are at the east side of the church on Jernbanegade. There's a konditori-style bakery north of the carpark and a better bakery directly behind the tourist office. The post office and the town centre are 150 metres east of the tourist office.

About two km south of Åkirkeby centre, at Grammegaardsvej 1, is the **Bornholms Automobilmuseum**, a small museum with 1920s vintage cars and motorcycles. It's open Monday to Saturday from 1 to 4 pm from May to October. Admission is 25 kr.

INTERIOR WOODLANDS

Bornholm has the distinction of being the most wooded county in Denmark, with one-fifth of the island covered with woodlands. Beech, fir, spruce, hemlock and oak are predominant. There are three main forested areas, each laid out with walking trails (pick up free maps at the tourist office). A single bicycle trail connects them all.

Almindingen, the largest forest (2412 hectares), is in the centre of the island and can be reached by heading north from Åkirkeby. Almindingen is the site of Bornholm's highest point, the 162-metre hill **Rytterknægten**, which has a lookout tower called Kongemindet that can be climbed for a view of the surrounding area.

Paradisbakkerne (Paradise Hills) is two km north-west of Nexø and has wild deer and a trail that passes an ancient, monolithic gravestone. **Rø Plantage**, about five km south-west of Gudhjem, has a terrain of heathered hills and woodlands.

DUEODDE

Dueodde, the southernmost point of Bornholm, is a vast stretch of white-sand beach backed by woodlands and dunes. Its soft sand is so fine grained that it was once used in hourglasses and old-fashioned ink blotters.

There's no real village at Dueodde – the bus stops at the end of the road where there's

a hotel, a restaurant, a couple of kiosks and a footpath to the beach.

Dueodde is a true beach-bum hang-out. The only 'sight' is a **lighthouse**, a short walk west along the beach; it's open in summer, when you can climb the 197 stairs for 4 kr.

The beach is a good place for children – the water is generally calm and is shallow for a good 100 metres out, after which it becomes deep enough for adults to swim.

Places to Stay

Møllers Dueodde Camping (☎ 56 48 81 49, fax 56 48 81 69), Duegårdsvej 2, 3730 Nexø, is open from 15 May to 20 September. This three-star camping ground is in a wooded area five minute's walk north-east of the bus stop. Camping costs 42 kr per person, plus 20 kr per site. Cabins equipped with cooking facilities cost from 1330 to 2380 kr per week, depending upon the season, with the latter rate from mid-June to mid-August. Bicycle rentals are available and there's a small store.

The beachside *Dueodde Vandrerhjem & Camp Ground* (☎ 56 48 81 19, fax 56 48 81 12), at Skrokkegårdsvejen 17, 3730 Nexø, borders the beach and is a 10-minute walk east of the bus stop. The hostel has simple rooms with private bath that cost 350 kr for one to four people from late June to early August. Smaller rooms with shared bath cost 280 kr. For the rest of the season, rates depend upon the number of people in the room and are 160/240 kr for singles/doubles with private bath or 140/190 kr with shared bath. There are level grassy tent sites shaded by pine trees and camping costs 40 kr per person plus 16 kr per tent. Caravans can be hired. There's a coin laundry, guest kitchen and playground. It's open from 1 April to 1 October.

The *Dueodde Badehotel* (☎ 56 48 86 49, fax 56 48 89 59), Sirenevej 2, 3730 Nexø, right at the bus stop, is a modern apartment-style hotel that rents units by the week for 2890 to 5635 kr, depending on the season. The one-bedroom units have TV, phone and sofa bed in the living room and can sleep up to five people. There's a coin laundry, tennis court and sauna.

Places to Eat

There are a couple of kiosks selling ice cream, hot dogs and snacks at the end of the road opposite the bus stop.

Also at the end of the road is the *Granpavillonen*, which has a lunch-time burger, salad and chips plate for 52 kr and Danish plates for about double that. At dinner, main dishes range from chicken for 62 kr to grilled salmon for 142 kr.

The *Dueodde Badehotel* has a small café with salads and sandwiches for around 25 kr.

The *Dueodde Vandrerhjem* has a cafeteria serving simple, inexpensive meals and a minimart with ice cream and a few basic supplies.

SNOGEBÆK

A quaint seaside village of older homes, Snogebæk makes a nice little detour if you're travelling by car or bike between Dueodde and Nexø. Down by the water, on Hovedgade, you'll find a shop that has quality hand-blown glass for reasonable prices; immediately next to it is a fish market and smokehouse where you can get smoked herring, mackerel and salmon. The end of the road beyond the glassworks is a good site for spotting migratory ducks and other waterbirds. If you want to explore more, there's a coastal trail leading north along the beach.

NEXØ

Nexø (also spelt Neksø) is Bornholm's second-largest town. It has a large modern harbour where both Danish and foreign fishing vessels unload their catch. The harbour, and much of the town, was reconstructed after being destroyed by Soviet bombings in WW II. Despite taking a back seat to more touristed towns like Gudhjem and Svaneke, Nexø has its fair share of picturesque buildings.

One of them, built in 1796 from Nexø sandstone (once a major export of the town), holds the **Nexø Museum**. Located opposite the waterfront at Havnen 2, the museum has exhibits on the town's history with an emphasis on fishing and shipping, its main industries. Particularly notable are the recon-structed old fishermen's houses. It's open (10 kr) Monday to Friday from 2 to 5 pm and on Saturday from 10 am to 1 pm.

The home where author Martin Andersen Nexø lived in his childhood is now a **museum** on the corner of Andersen Nexøvej and Ferskeøstræde, at the south side of town. Those interested in Nexø's life will find photos of the author, some of his letters and other memorabilia. It's open (15 kr) Monday to Saturday from May to October from 10 am to 4 pm.

While Nexø's waterfront is industrial, two km south of town there's a popular seaside area called **Balka** which has a gently curving white-sand beach.

Information

Tourist Office The Nexø-Dueodde Turist-bureau (☎ 56 49 32 00, fax 56 49 43 10), Åsen 4, 3730 Nexø, is in the centre of town two blocks inland of the harbour and has information on both Nexø and Dueodde.

Money There are a couple of banks on Torvet, the central square, just south of the tourist office.

Places to Stay

Most people don't stay in Nexø, but rather at the beaches to the south. However, there is one place to stay in town, the *Nexø Sømandshjem* (☎ 56 49 24 40), or Seaman's Home, at Købmagergade 27, 3730 Nexø. This new church-affiliated, alcohol-free hotel is simple but tidy and comfortable. Single rooms cost 210/330 kr with shared/private bath, while double rooms cost 360/475 kr, breakfast included. Non-guests can use the shower here for 12 kr, and there's a coin laundry.

Hotel Balka Strand (☎ 56 49 21 50, fax 56 49 36 99), Boulevarden 9A, 3730 Nexø, 200 metres from Balka's sandy beach, has double rooms as well as cheery apartments, all with modern décor. Rates are per person and vary with the season, from 385 to 530 kr. There's a sauna, pool, tennis court, bar and restaurant.

Also in Balka is the *Hotel Balka Søbad*

(☎ 56 49 22 25, fax 56 49 22 33), Vester Strandvej 25, 3730 Nexø, a friendly beachside hotel with 106 rooms in modern two-storey buildings. The rooms are large with various configurations, but all have at least two twin beds, a sofa bed and a balcony; some have a separate second bedroom. Rates vary with the season, beginning at 375 to 545 kr per person. There's a sauna, pool, tennis court, bar and restaurant.

Places to Eat
In the centre of Nexø, near the bus stop at Købmagerade 12, there's a large *Kvickly* supermarket which has a bakery, deli, cafeteria and a good produce section. It's the place to stop if you want to pack a lunch for the beach.

The *Nexø Sømandshjem* at Købmagergade 27 has a cafeteria open to the public. The set menus change daily, but feature typical Danish fare; lunch costs 35 kr and dinner is 45 kr. It's open daily from 8 am to 9 pm.

The *Hotel Balka Strand* offers a two-course dinner for 98 kr or three courses for 128 kr; there's usually a choice of meat or fish and a salad buffet. On Wednesday there's a cabaret dinner show for 168 kr.

The *Hotel Balka Søbad* has a restaurant with a three-course dinner and salad buffet for 125 kr.

SVANEKE
Svaneke is an appealing town of red-tiled 19th century buildings which has won international recognition for maintaining its historic character; in 1975 it was awarded the prestigious Council of Europe's gold medal for town preservation. The **harbourfront** is lined with mustard-yellow, half-timbered, former merchants' houses, some of which have been turned into restaurants and hotels.

Another good area for period buildings is near the **Svaneke church**, a few minutes walk south of Torv, the town square. The church, which has a rune stone, dates to 1350, although it was largely rebuilt in the 1880s.

If you're interested in crafts, there are half a dozen pottery shops spread around town, and at Glastorvet in the town centre there's a handicrafts collective and a workshop where you can watch glass being blown.

The easternmost town in Denmark, Svaneke gets reliable breezes and consequently has a number of **windmills**. On the north side of town you'll find an old post mill (a type which turns in its entirety to face the wind) and a Dutch mill, as well as an unusual three-sided water tower designed by architect Jørn Utzon in 1951. On the main road three km south of Svaneke, in the hamlet of Årsdale, there's a working windmill where corn is ground and sold.

Information
Tourist Office The Svaneke Turistbureau (☎ 56 49 63 50, fax 56 49 70 10), at Rådhus, Storegade 24, 3740 Svaneke, is open in summer from 9.30 am to 4.30 pm, Monday to Friday, and from 9 am to 2 pm on Saturday; in the off season it's open on weekdays only.

Other There's a Unibank at Nansensgade 5 and the post office is at Postgade 2. You can rent bicycles for 45/175 kr a day/week at Boss Cykler, Søndergade 14.

Places to Stay
Svaneke has two three-star camping grounds that are open from mid-May to mid-September. Each is about one km from the town centre and each has a coin laundry, TV lounge, playground, kiosk, and caravans for hire.

Hullehavn Camping (☎ & fax 56 49 63 63), Sydskovvej 9, 3740 Svaneke, 400 metres south of the hostel, has the more natural settin. To stay here it costs 41 kr per person plus 5 kr per tent.

Møllebakkens Familie Camping (☎ 56 49 64 62), Møllebakken 8, 3740 Svaneke, is by the roadside along the coast on the north side of town and charges 44 kr plus 10 kr per tent.

The 176-bed *Svaneke Vandrerhjem* (☎ 56 49 62 42, fax 56 49 73 83), Reberbanevej 9, 3740 Svaneke, a km south of the centre, is a pleasant chalet-like facility that was com-

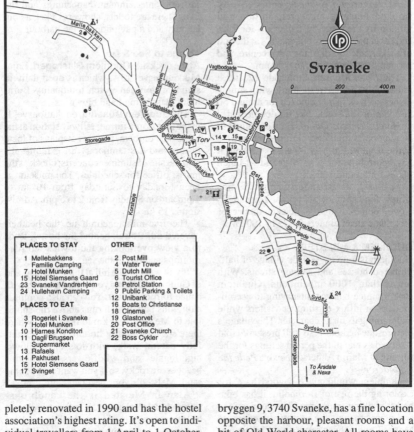

PLACES TO STAY

1. Møllebakkens
   Familie Camping
7. Hotel Munken
15. Hotel Siemsens Gaard
23. Svaneke Vandrerhjem
24. Hullehavn Camping

PLACES TO EAT

3. Rogeriet i Svaneke
7. Hotel Munken
10. Hjarnes Konditori
11. Dagli Brugsen
    Supermarket
13. Rafaels
14. Pakhuset
15. Hotel Siemsens Gaard
17. Svinget

OTHER

2. Post Mill
4. Water Tower
5. Dutch Mill
6. Tourist Office
8. Petrol Station
9. Public Parking & Toilets
12. Unibank
16. Boats to Christiansø
18. Cinema
19. Glastorvet
20. Post Office
21. Svaneke Church
22. Boss Cykler

pletely renovated in 1990 and has the hostel association's highest rating. It's open to individual travellers from 1 April to 1 October. Dorm beds cost 85 kr, while doubles cost 250 kr. There's a coin laundry and the hostel is right on the bus route.

The tourist office books rooms in private homes for 250 kr a person.

The *Hotel Munken* (☎ 56 49 61 12, fax 56 49 61 24), Storegade 12, 3740 Svaneke, is a small restaurant and hotel with unpretentious rooms. Rates are 350/500 kr for singles/doubles, breakfast included.

The 50-room *Hotel Siemsens Gaard* (☎ 56 49 61 49, fax 56 49 61 03), Havne-bryggen 9, 3740 Svaneke, has a fine location opposite the harbour, pleasant rooms and a bit of Old World character. All rooms have private bath, TV, phone and refrigerator. Rates are 420/560 kr for singles/doubles, breakfast included.

Places to Eat

The best place to buy groceries is at the *Dagli Brugsen* supermarket on Nensensgade near Torv. On Torv you'll find *Hjarnes Konditori*, which has bakery items, coffee and tea, and *Rafaels*, which has moderately priced pizza and Italian food. *Svinget*, just south of Torv

BORNHOLM

on Postgade, has hot dogs and other fast food.

At *Rogeriet i Svaneke* you can buy smoked herring, mackerel, shrimp and salmon by the piece, or fish cakes for 7 kr, and eat at picnic tables outside. It's at the end of Fiskergade, north of the town centre, and is open daily from 9 am to 6.30 pm.

The *Hotel Munken*, Storegade 12, has a reasonably priced restaurant with simple dishes such as fish or chicken for around 60 kr and more elaborate fare for double that.

Hotel Siemsens Gaard, Havnebryggen 9, is a popular outdoor dining spot with a harbour view. From 11.30 am to 4.30 pm it has smørrebrød for 32 to 70 kr and set-lunch plates for around 100 kr.

Pakhuset, at Brænderigænget 3, has simple food at moderate prices. You can get a two-course calamari or chicken dinner for 59 kr, and steak dinners for 75 to 100 kr.

GUDHJEM & MELSTED

Gudhjem is a pretty seaside village of half-timbered houses and sloping streets. With fewer than 1000 inhabitants, Gudhjem strikes a nice balance, managing to accommodate an influx of summer visitors while maintaining its rustic character. The village's picturesque harbour is so well preserved that it served as one of the period settings for the filming of Martin Andersen Nexø's *Pelle the Conqueror*.

Gudhjem would make a good base for exploring the rest of Bornholm; it has bike paths, walking trails, good bus connections and places to stay, the nearby attractions of Melsted and a boat service to Christiansø. Gudhjem is also an enjoyable place to just wander about and soak up the atmosphere.

Information

Tourist Office The Gudhjem Turistbureau (☎ 56 48 52 10, fax 56 48 52 74) is at Åbogade 9, 3760 Gudhjem, a block inland of the harbour.

Money & Post There's a Unibank at Brøddegade 6 and the post office is at Brøddegade 19.

Other The Christiansø boat ticket office at the harbour has a notice board with rooms for rent, entertainment happenings and the like. There are toilets, showers (5 kr), a coin laundry and a pay phone at the harbour.

Things to See & Do

At the dockside **Gudhjem Glasrøgeri**, Enjar Mikkelsensvej 13A, which is open daily in summer, you can watch top-quality Bornholm glass being hand blown.

The **Gudhjem Museum**, on Stationsvej 1, in the handsome former railway station at the south side of town, features displays of local history and has temporary art exhibits. It's also the site of summer concerts; check at the tourist office for schedules. The museum is open Monday to Saturday from 10 am to 4 pm and on Sunday from 2 to 5 pm. Admission is 15 kr.

The five-minute climb up the heather-covered hill **Bokul**, behind the hostel, leads to a view overlooking the town's red tiled rooftops and out to the sea.

If you walk up the hill at the south-east end of Gudhjem harbour you'll find a bench with a nice **harbour view**. You can also continue along this path which runs above the shoreline to Melsted, two km to the south, where there's a little **sandy beach**. It's a delightfully natural walk, with lots of swallows, nightingales and wildflowers. Gudhjem's beaches are rocky, so if you want to see some sand, Melsted's your best bet.

Also in Melsted is the **Landbrugsmuseet**, Melstedvej 25, an agricultural history museum in old farm buildings where costumed interpreters tend animals and demonstrate traditional farming techniques. It's open from 10 am to 5 pm (closed on Monday) from mid-May to late October. Admission is 20 kr.

In summer, the boat *Thor* (☎ 58 48 51 65) makes regular sailings (10.30 am, 1.30 and 2.30 pm) along the rocky coastline from Gudhjem to Helligdomsklipperne for 50 kr return.

Places to Stay

The nearest camping ground is *Sletten*

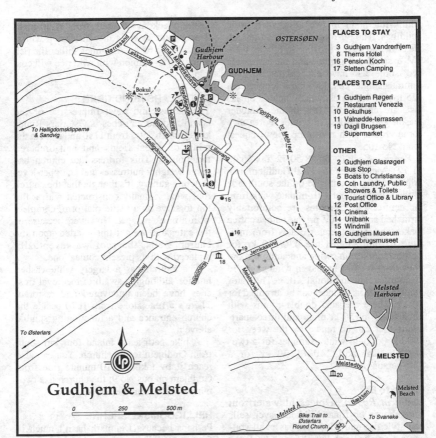

Gudhjem & Melsted

PLACES TO STAY
3 Gudhjem Vandrerhjem
8 Therns Hotel
16 Pension Koch
17 Sletten Camping

PLACES TO EAT
1 Gudhjem Røgeri
7 Restaurant Venezia
10 Bokulhus
11 Valnødde-terrassen
19 Dagli Brugsen Supermarket

OTHER
2 Gudhjem Glasrøgeri
4 Bus Stop
5 Boats to Christiansø
6 Coin Laundry, Public Showers & Toilets
9 Tourist Office & Library
12 Post Office
13 Cinema
14 Unibank
15 Windmill
18 Gudhjem Museum
20 Landbrugsmuseet

0   250   500 m

Camping (☎ 56 48 50 71, fax 56 48 42 56), Melsted Langgade 45, 3760 Gudhjem, near the coast a 15-minute walk south of Gudhjem harbour. It costs 42 kr per person to camp and there are cabins and caravans that can be rented for 300 kr. This two-star camping ground, which is open from mid-May to mid-September, has a kiosk and is within walking distance of a grocery store.

The centrally located *Gudhjem Vandrerhjem* (☎ 56 48 50 35, fax 56 48 56 35), Ejnar Mikkelsensvej 14, 3760 Gudhjem, is in an attractive tile-roofed building opposite the harbour-side bus stop. It has dorm beds

for 80 kr and also books about 20 private rooms, most in nearby homes, for 250 kr a double. Breakfast is available for an additional 38 kr and dinner for 40 kr. The hostel, which is also known as Sct Jørgens Gaard, is open to groups and individuals all year round. Reception is at a small grocery store on Løkkegade, about 75 metres north-west of the hostel. The hostel rents 18-speed mountain bikes for 60 kr a day, with discounts for longer rentals.

Therns Hotel (☎ 56 48 50 99, fax 56 48 50 69), Brøddegade 31, 3760 Gudhjem, a short walk from the waterfront, is a friendly family-run hotel in two adjacent historic buildings. The 30 rooms vary but they are pleasant and clean. Most have private bath, TV, a small refrigerator and an extra sofa bed; some also have kitchenettes. In midsummer, singles cost 400 kr and doubles cost 525 to 650 kr. Rates, which include breakfast, are about 10% less in the shoulder season and 20% less in winter. For a nice corner room with a rooftop view request room No 105.

Pension Koch (☎ 56 48 50 72, fax 56 48 51 72), Melstedvej 15, 3760 Gudhjem, is a bright, cheery guesthouse on the south side of the village, about a 10-minute walk from the centre. All 12 rooms are comfortably furnished and have TV, private bath, a coffee maker and a refrigerator. Rates from mid-June to mid-August are 430/540 kr for singles/doubles; in spring and autumn room rates drop by 100 kr and in winter they're discounted an additional 10%. The rates include breakfast; dinner can be arranged for 80 kr. There are also double rooms with kitchenette for 50 kr more and three apartments that can be rented by the week for 1900/2600 kr in winter/summer for a two-person unit and 2400/3200 kr for a four-person unit.

Places to Eat
Gudhjem Røgeri, a pleasant waterfront smokehouse on Ejnar Mikkelsensvej, sells deli-style fish and salads and has an all-you-can-eat smoked fish buffet for 68 kr. From June to August it's open from 10 am to midnight and has live folk music nightly; in spring and autumn it closes at 5 pm.

Valnødde-terrassen, at Brøddegade 20, has only average food but prices are cheap and there's a bit of a view. You can get fish and chips for 35 kr or a steak dinner for 60 kr.

The popular *Restaurant Venezia* at Brøddegade 33 has good Italian food, including pizzas and pastas, at moderate prices.

If you're looking for an upmarket Danish restaurant in a traditional setting, *Bokulhus*, at Bokulvej 4, is well regarded for its fish

dishes. Weekdays at lunch, from 11.30 am to 5 pm, you can get a nice fish soup with a baguette for 65 kr. At dinner, either the fish of the day or salmon with wild rice will cost 135 kr.

ØSTERLARS RUNDKIRKE
The largest and most impressive of the island's round churches is Østerlars Rundkirke, which dates from 1150 and is set in the midst of wheat fields and half-timbered farmhouses. This fortress-like church has seven weighty buttresses and an upper-level shooting gallery. It's thought that the church roof was originally constructed with a flat top to serve as a battle platform, complete with a brick parapet. However, because of the extensive weight this exerted upon the church walls, the roof was eventually replaced with its present conical one.

The church has a largely whitewashed interior, although a swath of medieval frescoes have been uncovered and restored. There's a rune stone from 1070 beside the church entrance and a functioning sundial above it.

A bike path leads inland four km south from Gudhjem to the church. You can also reach it by taking a 10-minute ride from Gudhjem on bus No 9; the church is a two-minute walk from the bus stop.

HELLIGDOMSKLIPPERNE
Perhaps because Denmark hasn't much in the way of hills or lofty rocks, those that it does have are almost revered. Such is the case with Helligdomsklipperne (Sanctuary Cliffs), where moderately high **coastal cliffs** of sharp granite rock formations attract sightseers. Located about five km north of Gudhjem, on the east side of the main coastal road, the Helligdomsklipperne area also has **nature trails** and an art museum.

Bornholms Kunstmuseum, a century-old museum in a stylish new building, exhibits paintings by artists from the Bornhorn School, including Olaf Rude, Oluf Høst and Edvard Weie, who painted in the first half of the 20th century. There are also works by other Danish artists, including paintings of Bornholm by Skagen artist Michael Ancher. The museum is open daily from 10 am to 5 pm from April to October and from 1 to 5 pm on Tuesday, Thursday and Saturday the rest of the year. Admission is 25 kr for adults and free for children under 16. There's a café on site. Buses stop in front of the museum (bus No 2 from Rønne or Sandvig and bus No 7 or 9 between Gudhjem and Sandvig).

For information about the sightseeing boat to Helligdomsklipperne, see the Gudhjem section.

SANDVIG

Sandvig is a quiet little seaside hamlet with attractive older homes, many fronted by rose bushes and tidy flower gardens. About four blocks deep and one km wide, it's an easy place to stroll about on foot. There's a nice sandy beach right in town, where you'll also find tennis courts and an indoor pool.

Three km south-west of Sandvig is Bornholm's best known sight, Hammershus Slot. There are enjoyable walking trails in the Hammeren area between Sandvig and Hammershus Slot. For details, see the Hammeren and Hammershus Slot sections that follow.

Allinge, the larger and more developed half of the Allinge-Sandvig municipality, is two km south-west of Sandvig. Although not as quaint as Sandvig, Allinge has the lion's share of commercial facilities, including banks, grocery stores and the area tourist office.

Seven km south-east of Sandvig, in the small village of **Olsker**, is the slenderest of the island's four round churches. If you take the inland bus to Rønne, you can stop off en route to visit the church or catch a passing glimpse of it as you ride by.

Places to Stay & Eat

Sandvig Familie Camping (☎ 56 48 04 47), Sandlinien 5, 3770 Allinge, on the north side of Sandvig, is backed by heathered hills and has an ideal location just minutes from the beach, restaurants and nature trails. This three-star camping ground charges 41 kr per person, has a coin laundry and is within walking distance of the bus stop. It's open from mid-May to mid-September.

The *Sandvig Vandrerhjem* (☎ 56 48 03 62), Hammershusvej 94, 3770 Allinge, open from 1 June to 1 October, has a pleasant rural location. Located between Hammershus and Sandvig, it's a 10-minute walk to the ruins, and a bit longer to Sandvig; the public bus stops 100 metres from the hostel. Dorm beds cost 80 kr, while family rooms cost start at 320 kr. Breakfast is available for 38 kr, but other meals are not served.

There are numerous moderately priced pensions in Sandvig. *Pension Langebjerg* (☎ 56 48 02 98, fax 56 48 22 98), Langebjergvej 7, Sandvig, 3770 Allinge, has 24 cosy rooms. Those with shared bath start from 210/390 kr for singles/doubles. The pension has a bus stop outside and is about 300 metres from the beach.

For a full listing of pensions, contact the Nordbornholms Turistbureau (☎ 56 48 00 01, fax 56 48 02 26), Kirkegade 4, 3770 Allinge, which covers the Sandvig area.

There's a reasonably priced cafeteria by the beach and a number of restaurants near the camping ground. *Ella's Konditori* at Strandgade 42, about 100 metres south of the camping ground, has a pleasant setting. There are several lunch dishes for 50 kr, while at dinner, tuna salad, fish fillet or a half-chicken with chips cost 60 to 80 kr.

HAMMERSHUS SLOT

The impressive 13th century castle ruins of Hammershus Slot, dramatically perched on top of a sea cliff, are the largest in Scandinavia. It is thought that construction was begun around 1250 by the Archbishop of Lund, who wanted a fortress to protect his diocese against the Crown, which at that time was engaged in a power struggle with the church. In the centuries that followed, the castle was enlarged, with the upper levels of the square tower having been constructed during the mid-1500s.

Eventually, improvements in naval artillery left the fortress walls vulnerable to attack and in 1645 the castle temporarily fell to Swedish troops after a brief bombardment. Hammershus not only served as a military garrison but also as a prison; from 1660 to 1661 King Christian IV's daughter, Leonora Christina, was imprisoned here on treason charges along with her husband, Corfitz Ulfeldt.

In 1743 the Danish military abandoned Hammershus and many of the stones were carried away to be used as building materials elsewhere. Still, there's much to see – you shouldn't miss a stroll through these extensive fortress ruins.

Looking north from the coastal sections of the ruins you can see Hammer Havn, a little harbour that was originally built to carry quarried rock to Germany but now shelters yachts, and Hammeren, the rocky jut of land in the background that's set aside as a nature reserve.

Getting There & Away

There's an hourly bus to Hammershus Slot from Sandvig, but the most enjoyable way to get there is via footpaths through the hills of Hammeren – a wonderful hour's hike. The well-trodden trail begins by Sandvig Familie Camping and the route is signposted.

HAMMEREN

Hammeren, the hammerhead-shaped crag of granite at the northern tip of Bornholm, is crisscrossed by walking trails that lead through hillsides thick with purple heather. Some of the trails cross inland, others are along the coast.

In addition to just wandering about, you can take trails between Sandvig and Hammershus Slot. The shortest route to Hammershus goes along the inland side of Hammeren and passes Hammer Sø, Bornholm's largest lake, and Opalsøen, a deep lake at the bottom of an old quarry. A longer and more windswept route goes along the rocky outer rim of Hammeren, passes a lighthouse at Bornholm's northernmost point and continues south along the coast to a harbour, Hammer Havn.

From Hammershus Slot there are trails heading south through another heathered landscape, in a nature area called Slotslyngen, and east through public woodlands to Moseløkke granite quarry. Moseløkke is also the site of a small museum where traditional rock-cutting techniques are demonstrated. It's open weekdays in summer from 10 am to noon and 1 to 4 pm; admission is 10 kr for adults and free for children.

The whole area is a delight for people who enjoy nature walks. For a detailed map of the trails and terrain, pick up the free *Hammeren og Hammershus, Slotslyng* forestry brochure at one of the island's libraries or tourist offices.

CHRISTIANSØ

Tiny Christiansø is a charmingly preserved 17th century fortress island an hour's sail north-east of Bornholm. The largest of a cluster of small granite islands known collectively as Ertholmene, Christiansø has an intriguing history.

A seasonal fishing hamlet since the Middle Ages, Christiansø fell briefly into Swedish hands in 1658, after which Christian V decided to turn the island into an invincible naval fortress. Bastions and barracks were built; a church, school and hospital followed. Christiansø became the Danish Navy's forward position in the Baltic, serving to monitor Swedish trade routes and in less congenial times as a base for attacks on Sweden.

In 1808 the British Navy, keen on capturing Christiansø for its strategic significance, bombarded the island but withdrew after it were unable to make a landing. The island also played an infamous role in Danish history when a prison was built in 1825 to house political prisoners, the most famous of whom was Dr Dampe, an insurgent who rallied against the despotism of King Frederik VI.

By the 1850s Christiansø was no longer needed as a base against Sweden and the navy withdrew. Soldiers who wanted to stay on as fishermen were allowed to live as free tenants in the old cottages. Their offspring, and a few latter-day fisherfolk and artists, currently comprise Christiansø's 140 residents. The entire island is an unspoiled reserve – there are no cats or dogs, no cars and no modern buildings. Instead there's a simple continuity of old stone-block fortifications and attractive yellow-washed houses.

Christiansø is connected to its smaller sister island, **Frederiksø**, by a footbridge.

Græsholm, the island north-west of Christiansø, is a wildlife refuge and an important breeding ground for razorbills, guillemots and other seabirds.

All of the Ertholmene Islands, including Christiansø and Frederiksø, serve as spring breeding grounds for as many as 2000 eider ducks. Because the ducks nest near coastal paths, visitors should take care not to scare the mothers away from their nests, as predator gulls will quickly attack the unattended eggs. Also, conservation laws strictly forbid the removal of any plants in this unique ecosystem.

Things to See & Do
A leisurely walk around both Christiansø and Frederiksø exploring the sights takes a couple of hours, making this destination ideal for a day trip.

The two main 'sights' are at the two stone circular defence towers. The **Lille Tårn** (Little Tower), on Frederiksø, dates from 1685, and is the site of the **local history museum**. The ground floor holds fishing supplies, hand tools and iron works, while upstairs there are cannons, period furnishings, models and a display of local flora and fauna. It's open afternoons daily from mid-May to the end of September. Admission is 7 kr.

Christiansø's **Store Tårn** (Great Tower), which was built in 1684, is an impressive structure that measures a full 25 metres in diameter. The tower's century-old **lighthouse** offers a splendid 360° view of the island; for 4 kr you can climb to the top.

The main activity on Christiansø is the walk along the fortified stone walls and cannon-lined batteries that surround the perimeter of the island. There are skerries (rocky islets) with nesting seabirds and a secluded **swimming cove** on Christiansø's east side.

One of the watercolourists who lives and works on the island is Henning Køie, who has a shop on the east side of Christiansø, a few minutes walk south of the Store Tårn.

Places to Stay & Eat
Christiansø Gæstgiveriet (☎ 56 46 20 15, fax 56 46 20 86), 3740 Christiansø, built in 1730 as the naval commander's residence, is the island's only inn. It has half a dozen singles/doubles with shared bath for 280/380 kr, including breakfast, and is open from 1 May to mid-September.

The inn also coordinates camping in a small field at the Duchess Battery in summer (25 kr), but because of the limited space, camping can be difficult to book.

There's a moderately priced restaurant at the inn and a small grocery store and snack shop nearby.

Getting There & Away
Boats sail to Christiansø from Allinge and Gudhjem in season, while the mail boat from Svaneke makes the trip all year round.

From Gudhjem, the boat leaves at 10.20 am daily from early May to late September, departing from Christiansø for the return trip at 2.20 pm. There are additional sailings from Gudhjem at 9.40 am and 12.15 pm daily from mid-June to mid-August.

From Allinge, the boat leaves at 1 pm, Monday to Friday, from early May to late September, departing from Christiansø at 4.20 pm.

From Svaneke, the boat leaves at 10 am on weekdays, departing from Christiansø at 2.30 pm from mid-April to October and at 1.30 pm the rest of the year.

All boats charge 120 kr return on a day trip and 190 kr for an open return. Children aged 4 to 11 years pay 60/95 kr for day trip/open return.

BORNHOLM

Funen

Funen (Danish: Fyn) is the name of Denmark's second largest island as well as the name of the county (Fyn Amt) that includes Funen island and about 90 neighbouring islands. While most of these neighbouring islands are small and privately owned, the largest three – Ærø, Langeland and Tåsinge – have appealing seaside towns and make fine destinations in themselves. All of Funen county has a bucolic character, with picturesque rural scenery and thatched farmhouses throughout.

The main railway line from Copenhagen runs straight through Odense, Funen's main city, and westward to Jutland, but it would be a shame to zip through without stopping to explore more of Funen. Outside of Odense, places of special merit are the Egeskov castle, the historic maritime town of Faaborg and the unspoiled island of Ærø.

Store Bælt (Great Belt), the channel that separates Zealand and Funen, can currently only be crossed by boat. Both car and train ferries make frequent crossings between Korsør in Zealand and Nyborg in Funen. If you're travelling by train, note that the IC trains roll right onto the ferries, whereas on most IR trains you walk onto the boat and then off onto a waiting train upon reaching the other side of the channel. (For more information about Denmark's train system see the Getting Around chapter.)

Cycle Routes

Funen is an attractive place for cycling, with pleasant scenery and some gentle hills. In all, Funen county is crisscrossed with 1175 km of marked bike paths, some leading into the countryside and others parallelling the main routes between major towns.

Cykelnetværk Fyn, in cooperation with the Funen county government, puts out an excellent Funen cycling guide that comprises a 50-page booklet and detailed 1:100,000 maps. The booklet describes 20 cycling routes around Funen, Langeland and

HIGHLIGHTS

- Ærøskøbing's leaning half-timbered houses (Ærø)
- Faaborg, an enjoyable small town of cobblestone streets
- Egeskov castle, a splendid Renaissance castle with a moat encircling it
- The city of Odense and its interesting cathedral and museums
- Cycling through Funen's undulating countryside of farms and villages
- Hopping on a boat to one of the small islands off Funen's southern coast

Ærø, including distances, difficulty and sightseeing spots along the way. It can be bought at local bookshops or tourist offices for 75 kr. Look carefully when you pick it up, as there are three versions: English, Danish or German.

Odense

Odense, which translates as 'Odin's shrine',

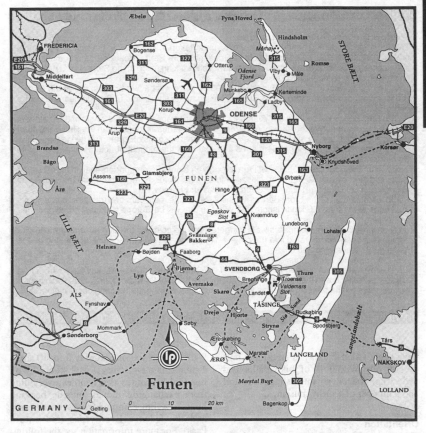

Funen

was named for the powerful Nordic god of war, poetry and wisdom. The city's history dates back to pre-Viking times, with the first known reference to Odense appearing in a letter written in 988 by the German emperor Otto III.

Although by the mid-1700s Odense was the largest provincial town in Denmark, with 5000 inhabitants, it was the only major Danish town without a harbour and thus failed to benefit directly from the maritime trade that prospered in coastal towns such as Faaborg. In 1800, in the largest construction project of that era, a canal was dug to connect

Odense to the Odense Fjord, five km to the north. With the new sea link, Odense grew as an industrial city whose products ranged from refined sugar to textiles.

Odense is now Denmark's third largest city (population 173,000), the capital of Funen county and a transportation hub for the region.

The city makes much ado about being the birthplace of Hans Christian Andersen though in actuality, after a fairly unhappy childhood, Andersen got out of Odense as fast as he could.

Whatever Andersen's experiences may

IᚱᚠᛁᛏIᚱᛁᚠᛜᚾᛗᛁᚨᛈᚠᛗᚾᛁᚠᚦᛈIᚱᛁᛏIᚱᛁᚠᛜᚾᛗᛁᚨᛈᚠᛗᚾᛁᚠᚦᛈIᚱᛁᛏIᚱᛁᚠᛜᚾᛗᛁᚨᛈᚠᛗᚾᛁᚠᚦᛈIᚱᛁᛏIᚱᛁᚠᛜᚾᛗᛁᚨᛈᚠᛗᚾᛁᚠᚦᛈIᚱ

World's Largest Suspension Bridge

The most ambitious engineering scheme ever undertaken in Denmark is the bridge and tunnel project that is currently being constructed across the Store Bælt (Great Belt), the body of water that separates Zealand and Funen. The construction is taking place at the Store Bælt's narrowest point, which has a width of 18 km.

When the project is completed in the late 1990s, there will be two bridges, called the Østbro (East Bridge) and the Vestbro (West Bridge), linking at the little island of Sprogø near the centre of the Store Bælt.

The East Bridge will be the world's largest suspension bridge, with a total length of 6790 metres. It has a free span above the fairway of 1624 metres, 214 metres longer than the Humber Bridge in England, which previously boasted the world's longest suspension span. The two towers of the East Bridge reach a height of 254 metres and stand as the highest structures ever erected in Scandinavia.

Beneath the East Bridge, trains will run through an eight-km-long undersea twin tunnel which is being drilled by a state-of-the-art closed-shield tunnel borer of the same genre that was used to construct the Channel Tunnel between England and France.

On the other half of the Store Bælt span, the West Bridge, both cars and trains will cross above the water. Measuring 6.6 km in length, the West Bridge will be Europe's longest combined road and railway bridge.

This being Denmark, aesthetics were budgeted into the cost and the Danes' renowned flair for design has been incorporated into the project. Despite its record-setting dimensions, the bridge has a gentle geometric appeal.

If you care to learn more about the nitty gritty of construction, exhibition centres (30 kr admission) have been opened on each side of the Store Bælt, one at Halsskov ferry harbour (at Korsør) in Zealand and the other at Knudshoven ferry harbour (at Nyborg) in Funen. Each centre has displays on the project as well as vantage points for viewing the ongoing construction. ■

IᚱᚠᛁᛏIᚱᛁᚠᛜᚾᛗᛁᚨᛈᚠᛗᚾᛁᚠᚦᛈIᚱᛁᛏIᚱᛁᚠᛜᚾᛗᛁᚨᛈᚠᛗᚾᛁᚠᚦᛈIᚱᛁᛏIᚱᛁᚠᛜᚾᛗᛁᚨᛈᚠᛗᚾᛁᚠᚦᛈIᚱᛁᛏIᚱᛁᚠᛜᚾᛗᛁᚨᛈᚠᛗᚾᛁᚠᚦᛈIᚱ

have been, Odense today is an affable university city with lots of bike paths and pedestrian streets, an interesting cathedral and a number of worthy museums.

Orientation

The tourist office, at Rådhus, is a 10-minute walk south from the railway station. The cathedral is on Klosterbakken, two minutes from the tourist office, and most other sights are also in the city centre within walking distance of each other. The central bus transit point is in front of the cathedral.

Information

Tourist Office The Odense Turistbureau (☎ 66 12 75 20, fax 66 12 75 86), Rådhuset, 5000 Odense C, is open from 9 am to 7 pm Monday to Saturday, and from 11 am to 7 pm on Sunday from 15 June to 31 August. In the low season it's open Monday to Friday from 9 am to 5 pm and on Saturday from 10 am to 1 pm. This busy office is well stocked with regional brochures and handles everything from exchanging money outside banking hours to selling camping passes, hostel cards and the Odense Eventyrpas (Adventure Pass). For more information see the following Odense Eventyrpas boxed aside.

Money There's a Unibank at the north end of Kongensgade and a number of banks on Vestergade, including Den Danske Bank opposite Rådhus.

Post The main post office is north-east of the railway station at Dannebrogsgade 2. There's also a branch in the centre at Gråbrødrestræde 1, open Monday to Friday to at least 5 pm and on Saturday to 1 pm, but it generally has longer queues.

PLACES TO STAY

6 Odense Plaza Hotel
7 Hotel Domir
8 Ydes Hotel
12 Det Lille Hotel
16 City Hotel
18 SAS HC Andersen Hotel
30 Grand Hotel Odense

PLACES TO EAT

11 Bager'From
13 Pizza Express
21 Birdy's Café
   & Boogies

24 Naturkost
26 Den Gamle Kro
29 Målet
32 Big Store Supermarket
34 Raadhusbageriet
36 Burger King
37 Délifrance
39 McDonald's
41 Jensen's Bøfhus
42 Mona Rosa
47 Mekong Restaurant
48 Arkaden

OTHER

1 Jernbanemuseet

2 Main Post Office
3 Regional Bus Terminal
4 Railway Station
5 Avis Car Rental
9 Europcar Car Rental
10 Unibank
14 Odense Slot
15 Carl Nielsen Museet
   & Odense Koncerthus
17 Casino Odense
19 Police
20 HC Andersens Hus
22 Montergården
23 Fyns Kunstmuseum
25 Vor Frue Kirke
27 Cykel Biksen

28 Antique Shops
31 Gråbrødre Kloster
33 Post Office
35 Brandts Klædefabrik
38 Kilroy Travels
40 Cotton Club
43 Den Danske Bank
44 Tourist Office & Rådhus
45 Central Bus
   Transit Point
46 Sankt Knuds Kirke
49 James Dean Dansebar
50 HC Andersens
   Barndomshjem
51 Library
52 Boat Dock

Kottesgade

Kochsgade

Thomas B Thriges Gade

Østre Stationsvej

Kongens Have

Vestre Stationsvej

Jernbanegade

Hans Tausensgade

Kongensgade

Koststevej

Dronningensgade

Vindegade

Slotsgade

Sskt Gertrude Stræde

Stålstræde

Gravene

Nørregade

Hans Jensen Stræde

Bangs Boder

Claus Bergs Gade

Hans Mule's Gade

Sortebrødre

Østergade

Overgade

Nedergade

Nørrestade

Frue Kirkestræde

Vestergade

Klaregade

Vindegade

Pantheonsgade

Brandts Passage

Vintapperstræde

Mageløs

Klosterbakken

Filosofgangen

Sendre Boulevard

Odense Å

Munke Mose

To Den Fynske
Landsby (museum),
Odense Camping,
Faaborg & Odense Zoo

HC Andersen
Haven

Kronprinsensgade

Hunderupvej

Tvergade

Albanigade

To Café
Frederik

To
Nyborg

Odense

0   100   200 m

To Odense Vandrerhjem

Allegade

To Svendborg

FUNEN

ᛁᚠᛖ᛫ᛏᛁᚠ᛫ᚠᛣᚾᛈᛣ᛫ᚨᛈᚠᛈᚾ᛫ᚠᛈᛈᛁᚠᛖ᛫ᛏᛁᚠ᛫ᚠᛣᚾᛈᛣ᛫ᚨᛈᚠᛈᚾ᛫ᚠᛈᛈᛁᚠᛖ᛫ᛏᛁᚠ᛫ᚠᛣᚾᛈᛣ᛫ᚨᛈᚠᛈᚾ᛫ᚠᛈᛈᛁᚠᛖ᛫ᛏᛁᚠ᛫ᚠᛣᚾᛈᛣ᛫ᚨᛈᚠᛈᚾ᛫ᚠᛈᛈᛁᚠᛖ

Odense Eventyrpas

Odense has an Eventyrpas (Adventure Pass) which allows free entry into most of the city sights, including those at Brandts Klædefabrik, Fyns Kunstmuseum, Den Fynske Landsby, the two Hans Christian Andersen museums, the Carl Nielsen museum and Møntergården. It gives a 50% reduction on Jernbanemuseet and a 25% reduction on the zoo and the Odense Åfart riverboat. The pass also provides unlimited free use of buses and trains within city limits.

The pass is a bargain at 50 kr for one day or 90 kr for two days (half price for children). The pass can be purchased at the tourist office, the railway station or at any city museum. ■

ᛁᚠᛖ᛫ᛏᛁᚠ᛫ᚠᛣᚾᛈᛣ᛫ᚨᛈᚠᛈᚾ᛫ᚠᛈᛈᛁᚠᛖ᛫ᛏᛁᚠ᛫ᚠᛣᚾᛈᛣ᛫ᚨᛈᚠᛈᚾ᛫ᚠᛈᛈᛁᚠᛖ᛫ᛏᛁᚠ᛫ᚠᛣᚾᛈᛣ᛫ᚨᛈᚠᛈᚾ᛫ᚠᛈᛈᛁᚠᛖ᛫ᛏᛁᚠ᛫ᚠᛣᚾᛈᛣ᛫ᚨᛈᚠᛈᚾ᛫ᚠᛈᛈᛁᚠᛖ

Travel Agency Kilroy Travels (☎ 66 17 77 80), Pantheonsgade 7, specialises in youth and discount travel.

Library The library, adjacent to the cathedral, has a few English-language foreign newspapers, including London's *Daily Telegraph* and *Observer*. It's open Monday to Friday from 11 am to 6 pm and on Saturday from 10 am to 4 pm.

Pharmacy There's a 24-hour chemist, Ørnen Apoteket, at Vestergade 80.

Walking Tour

The following route takes in many of the city's historic sights and museums. Although the walk itself takes only about an hour, if you stop at all the sights along the way you could easily pass the better part of a day. (The major sights listed in this walk are given more detail later in this section.)

Start at **Rådhus**, the town hall, which is predominantly of 1950s vintage. From May to September tours take place Monday to Thursday at 2 pm and cost 10 kr.

From Rådhus head east on Overgade and then turn right onto **Nedergade**, a cobblestone street with leaning half-timbered houses and antique shops.

At the end of Nedergade, a left turn onto Frue Kirkestræde will bring you to **Vor Frue Kirke**, Odense's oldest church, which dates back to the 13th century. It has a rather plain, whitewashed interior, though there's an ornate baroque pulpit and a baptismal font that date from the mid-17th century. It's open

daily, except Sunday, from 10 am to 3 pm in summer and from 10 am to noon the rest of the year.

From the church turn left on Overgade, where you'll soon reach **Møntergården**, the city museum, and then turn right onto Claus Bergs Gade, where you'll pass the city's only casino. Immediately north is the **Odense Koncerthus** (Concert Hall) and a museum dedicated to composer Carl Nielsen.

Just past the casino, turn left onto Ramsherred (which quickly changes to Hans Jensens Stræde) to reach **HC Andersens Hus**, the main museum dedicated to Hans Christian Andersen. The museum is in a pleasant neighbourhood of narrow cobbled streets and old tile-roofed houses. If you desire some green space there's a little park with a duck pond south of the museum.

Continue down Hans Jensens Straede, cross Thomas B Thriges Gade and follow Gravene to Slotsgade to reach the **Fyns Kunstmuseum**, Odense's notable fine arts museum. Turn left, then proceed down Jernbanegade to Vestergade. Along the way you'll pass the site of **Gråbrødre Kloster**, a former medieval Franciscan monastery that has been converted into a home for the aged.

When you reach Vestergade, turn east back to Rådhus and then go south to **Sankt Knuds Kirke**, Odense's historic cathedral. Opposite the cathedral, turn onto Sankt Knuds Kirkestræde and then go south on Munkemøllestræde, where you'll pass **HC Andersens Barndomshjem**, the writer's childhood home.

Loop back around on Klosterbakken and

at the south side of the library take the path into the **HC Andersen Haven**, a riverside park which has a statue of him. You can walk north through the park to get back to your starting point at Rådhus.

Sankt Knuds Kirke

Odense's 12th century gothic cathedral is one of the city's most interesting sights. It boasts an ornate gilded altar dating from 1520 that's considered the finest work of the master woodcrafter Claus Berg. An intricately detailed triptych, the altar stands five metres high and has nearly 300 carved figures, most depicting the life and death of Christ, although the bottom row also works in King Hans on the left and Queen Christine on the right. It was Queen Christine, a friend of Berg's, who commissioned the work. Berg also created the large limestone sepulchral monument bearing the king and queen's portraits in bas-relief.

Still, the cathedral's most intriguing attraction lies in the basement beneath the altar where you'll find a glass case containing the 900-year-old skeleton of King Canute (Knud) II and another displaying the skeleton of his younger brother Benedikt. An inconspicuous set of stairs leads from the right side of the altar down to these basement treasures.

A few metres west of the coffins, steps lead down to the remains of St Alban's church, which stood on this site before the cathedral was built. It was at the altar of St Alban's that Canute II and his brother Benedikt were killed during a tax revolt.

From mid-May to mid-September the cathedral is open Monday to Saturday from 10 am to 5 pm, and from June to August it's also open on Sunday from 11.30 am to 3.30 pm. The rest of the year it's open Monday to Saturday from 10 am to 4 pm (to 2 pm on Saturday between October and March). There's no admission charge.

HC Andersens Hus

This museum, on a cobbled pedestrian street at Hans Jensens Stræde 39, depicts Hans Christian Andersen's life story through a barrage of memorabilia – though the presentation doesn't always match up to the author's rich imagination. There's a room with slide presentations on Andersen's life, a reconstruction of his Nyhavn (in Copenhagen) study, displays of his fanciful silhouette-style paper cuttings and a voluminous selection of his books, which have been translated into 79 languages from Azerbaijani to Zulu.

The museum is open daily from 9 am to 6 pm from June to August and 10 am to 4 pm from September to May. Admission costs 20 kr for adults and 10 kr for children.

HC Andersens Barndomshjem

In the city centre, at Munkemøllestræde 3, the HC Andersens Barndomshjem has a couple of rooms of exhibits in the small childhood home where Andersen lived from

---

King Canute – the Unsaintly Saint

King Canute (Knud) II reigned over Denmark from 1080 to his untimely death six years later. A ruthless tyrant, Canute II had led Viking raids abroad and instituted numerous taxes at home, often using brutal methods to collect them.

In 1086 Canute II, trying to evade a crowd of angry farmers who had pursued him from Jutland, fled into St Alban's church in Odense in an attempt to take sanctuary. There, while kneeling before the altar, he was killed by the attacking mob.

Although less than saintly, in 1101 Canute II was canonised Canute the Holy by the pope in a move to secure both the crown and church in Denmark. Despite being Denmark's first saint, Canute the Holy has never been widely popular and his name is still invoked as a term of abuse among farmers in Jutland. ∎

1807 to 1819. It's open daily from 10 am to 5 pm from June to August and 11 am to 3 pm from September to May. Admission costs 5 kr for adults and 2 kr for children.

Fyns Kunstmuseum

The Fyns Kunstmuseum (Funen Art Museum), in a stately Graeco-Roman building at Jernbanegade 13, contains a quality collection of Danish art, from paintings of the old masters to abstract contemporary works. Among the museum's 2500 works of art are paintings by Jens Juel, PS Krøyer, Vilhelm Hammershøi, Asger Jorn and Richard Mortensen. A local highlight is the collection by the Fynboerne (Funen Group), which includes Fritz Syberg, Peter Hansen and Johannes Larsen.

It's open year round from 10 am to 4 pm daily. Admission costs 15 kr for adults and 5 kr for children.

Carl Nielsen Museet

This museum, in the Odense Koncerthus (Odense Concert Hall) at Claus Bergs Gade 11, details the career of Odense native son Carl Nielsen (1865-1931), Denmark's best-known composer. Nielsen's music career began at the age of 14 when he became a trumpet player in the local military band. Four years later he moved to Copenhagen to undertake formal music studies and shortly after, in 1888, his first orchestra work, *Suite for Strings*, was performed at Tivoli concert hall. It was critically acclaimed and since that time has become a regular piece in the Danish concert repertory. Nielsen's music includes six symphonies, several operas and numerous hymn tunes and popular songs, some with patriotic themes.

The chronologically based exhibition details not only the life of Nielsen, but also that of his wife, sculptor Anne Marie Brodersen. Displays include Brodersen's works and studio and Nielsen's study and piano. There's an auditorium where you can listen to Nielsen's music.

It's open year round from 10 am to 4 pm daily. Admission costs 15 kr for adults and 5 kr for children.

Møntergården

This city museum, at Overgade 48, has displays of Odense's history dating back to the Viking Age and a number of 16th and 17th century half-timbered houses that you can walk through. There are numerous rooms with period furnishings, medieval exhibits, church carvings, local archaeological finds and a good coin collection spanning nearly a millennium. It's open daily from 10 am to 4 pm. Admission is 15 kr for adults and 5 kr for children.

Jernbanemuseet

Train buffs shouldn't miss the 19th century locomotives at the Jernbanemuseet (Railway Museum), just behind the railway station. It has a re-created station of the late 1800s and about two dozen engines and saloon cars, including a royal carriage that once belonged to King Christian IX. There's also a model train section.

Opening hours are from 10 am to 4 pm daily in summer and 10 am to 1 pm in winter. Admission costs 20 kr for adults and 10 kr for children.

Brandts Klædefabrik

This former textile mill on Brandts Passage has been converted into a cultural centre with three museums, an art academy, a cinema, a music library and a couple of restaurants.

The **Danmarks Grafiske Museum/ Dansk Pressemuseum** (Danish Museum of Printing/Danish Press Museum) portrays the development of printing in Denmark over the last three centuries. One facet of the museum covers old-fashioned lithography, engraving, bookbinding and paper making, while the other concentrates on newspaper production. Former workers, now retired, re-enact the techniques they used in their working days (such as end-paper marbling and setting cold type), demonstrating processes that have now been made obsolete by modern presses and computerised equipment.

The **Museet for Fotokunst** (Museum of Photographic Art) is Denmark's only museum dedicated solely to photography. It has one floor with a permanent collection and a second floor with changing exhibitions by both national and international photographers.

The **Kunsthallen**, a modern art gallery, has four large halls with changing exhibitions largely dedicated to new trends in the visual arts. There's also a videotheque with a library of art videos that can be viewed for free.

The three museums are open Tuesday to Sunday from 10 am to 5 pm, and also on Monday in July and August. Admission is 25 kr to the art gallery, 20 kr each to the other museums, or you can get a joint ticket to all three for 40 kr (10 kr for children).

Odense Slot

Kongens Have, the park directly opposite the railway station, is the site of Odense Slot (Odense Castle), a two-storey building with red-tiled roofs and a cobbled courtyard. Modest as castles go, it was erected in 1720 by King Frederik IV to serve as a royal residence during his visits to Odense. The king died here in 1730, a victim of tuberculosis. Odense Slot was later converted to a governor's residence and now serves as administrative offices for the local municipal and county governments. It's not open for touring, but the grounds can be strolled.

Den Fynske Landsby

This is a delightful open-air museum whose furnished period buildings are laid out like a small country village of the mid-1800s, complete with barnyard animals, a duck pond, apple trees and flower gardens. There are about two dozen thatched houses and farm buildings in all, including a windmill, watermill and smithy, which have been gathered from rural areas in Funen.

The museum is in a green zone four km south of the city centre; bus Nos 21 and 22 stop in front.

In summer you can also take the boat operated by Odense Åfart (see Boat in the Odense Getting Around section) and get off at Erik Bøghs Sti, from where it's a refreshing 15-minute woodland walk south-east along the river to Den Fynske Landsby.

The museum is open daily between 1 April and mid-October from 10 am to 5 pm, until 7 pm in summer. Admission is 20 kr for adults and 10 kr for children. Activities ranging from beer brewing to crop harvesting are scheduled on weekends and in midsummer.

Odense Zoo

This zoo, bordering the river Odense Å at Sondre Boulevard 83, is two km south of the city centre. It's currently rather small, with penguins, tigers, giraffes, kangaroos, reindeer and other penned-up creatures, but there are plans to expand the grounds (and the cages) and turn it into Denmark's second largest zoo.

It's open from 9 am to 7 pm in July, from 9 am to 6 pm in May, June and August, and from 9 am to either 4 or 5 pm the rest of the year. Admission is 40 kr for adults and 20 kr for children. You can get there via buses 31 or 32. The Odense Åfart (see Boat in the Odense Getting Around section) also stops at the zoo, or you could walk the entire way along the wooded riverside path that begins at Munke Mose.

Places to Stay

Camping *Odense Camping* (☎ 66 11 47 02, fax 65 91 73 43), Odensevej 102, 5260 Odense S, is a two-star camping ground in a wooded area not far from Den Fynske Landsby, 3.5 km south of the city centre. It has cooking and laundry facilities and cabins for hire. The cost for pitching a tent is 40 kr per person. You can get there via bus No 41 or 91.

Hostels & Hotels – bottom end The hostel, *Odense Vandrerhjem* (☎ 66 13 04 25, fax 65 91 28 63), Kragsbjergvej 121, 5230 Odense M, is in an exclusive suburb two km south-east of the centre. The hostel buildings, formerly a manor house, surround a cobbled courtyard and have pleasant half-timbered exteriors, while the interiors are renovated and the rooms modern. A dorm bed costs 74 kr. The 168 beds are mostly in four-bed rooms but there are also a few doubles that can be booked for 200 kr. It's open from mid-February to the end of November. Bus Nos 61 or 62 can drop you 150 metres from the hostel; take the driveway lined with linden trees.

The tourist office books rooms in private homes at 175/250 kr for singles/doubles, plus a 25 kr booking fee.

The 14-room *Det Lille Hotel* (☎ & fax 66 12 28 21), Dronningensgade 5, 5000 Odense C, a 10-minute walk west of the railway station, is a pension-like place that has straightforward rooms with shared bath for 220/350 kr, breakfast included.

Hostels & Hotels – middle The 38-room *Hotel Domir* (☎ 66 12 14 27, fax 66 12 17 82), Hans Tausensgade 19, 5000 Odense C, has a convenient location just minutes from the railway station. The rooms are cheery with TV, phone, desk and private bath (some have waterbeds!) for 360/480 kr. There are also a couple of very small rooms for 310/410 kr. Breakfast is included.

Also good value is the nearby *Ydes Hotel* (☎ 66 12 11 31, fax 66 12 17 82), Hans Tausensgade 11, 5000 Odense C. It has two dozen compact but very clean and modern rooms with TV, desk and private bath for 290/430 kr for singles/doubles and a few rooms with shared bath for 260/390 kr. A simple continental breakfast is included.

The *City Hotel* (☎ 66 12 12 58, fax 66 12 93 64), Hans Mules Gade 5, 5000 Odense C, is about a 15-minute walk from the railway station and city centre. This is a contemporary hotel with 43 modern rooms, each with private bath, phone, TV and hair drier. Singles/doubles cost 595/695 kr, breakfast included.

Hostels & Hotels – top end The *Odense Plaza Hotel* (☎ 66 11 77 45, fax 66 14 41 45), Østre Stationsvej 24, 5000 Odense, is a small hotel in a period brick building 150 metres south-east of the railway station. The rooms have leather chairs and the standard Best Western-chain amenities including mini-

bars, trouser presses and TV. The staff are friendly and there's a pleasant sunroom where a better-than-average breakfast is served. The standard rates are 720/895 kr for singles/doubles. There's also a special 680 kr rate valid on weekends (Friday to Sunday) and in summer that covers up to two adults and two children, breakfast included.

The city's other historic hotel, the centrally located *Grand Hotel Odense* (☎ 66 11 71 71, fax 66 14 11 71), Jernbanegade 18, 5100 Odense C, has rather standard rooms with minibars, TV, phone, desk and private bath with bathtubs for 895/995 kr for singles/doubles. From mid-June to mid-August there's a weekend rate (Friday and Saturday) of 550/730 kr for singles/doubles. Parking is an additional 40 kr.

The *SAS HC Andersen Hotel* (☎ 66 14 78 00, fax 66 14 78 90), Claus Bergs Gade 7, 5000 Odense C, is a modern four-storey brick hotel a few minutes walk from Andersen's birthplace. The rooms have modern amenities, including TV, phone and minibars. There's a sauna, solarium and billiards as well as a casino on site. Singles/doubles cost 690/890 kr. It's part of the Radisson chain and there are occasionally cheaper promotional rates.

Places to Eat
Inexpensive Bakeries and cheap fast food are easy to find all around the city. *Raadhusbageriet*, opposite the tourist office, has good pastries and big 20 kr sandwiches made with wholegrain bread. The *Bager From* at Kongensgade 59 also has good takeaway sandwiches. You can get French bakery products at *Délifrance* on Kongensgade, opposite *McDonald's* and *Burger King*.

Café Biografen at Brandts Klædefabrik is a popular student haunt with inexpensive pastries, coffees, light meals and beer. It's open from 11 am to at least midnight daily, though the kitchen closes at 9 pm. At the back side of the complex is the quieter *Brandt's Café & Restaurant*, which has sandwiches and salads at reasonable prices, chilli con carne, lasagne and pastas for around 50 kr, as well as coffees, wine and beer. It's open from 11 am to 11 pm most days, with slightly different hours on weekends.

Another popular student spot is *Birdy's Café*, Nørregade 21, which has Mexican food and is open Monday to Saturday from 6 pm to at least 2 am. Nachos or tostadas cost 44 kr, while an enchilada with rice and salad costs 55 kr.

Pizza Express, Vindegade 73, has 26 varieties of thin-crusted takeaway pizza for 37 kr as well as 25 kr pitta bread sandwiches. It's open from 3 to 11 pm daily, except on Friday and Saturday when it stays open until 5 am.

The *Big Store Supermarket* on Slotsgade has a bakery with good croissants (4.50 kr) and a large inexpensive cafeteria with tempting smørrebrød sandwiches and various full meals for around 35 kr. The railway station has a small supermarket open until midnight daily. There's a well-stocked health-food shop, *Naturkost* at Gravene 8, that's open Monday to Friday from 9 am to 5.30 pm and on Saturday until 1 pm.

Middle There are numerous moderately priced restaurants and cafés along both Vestergade and Kongensgade, many of which chalk up daily specials. One good spot to start is the *Arkaden* complex, on the corner of Vestergade and Kongensgade, which has Greek, Italian, Spanish, Brazilian and a few other ethnic restaurants offering lunch specials for around 50 kr and full dinners for about 100 kr.

Jensen's Bøfhus, Kongensgade 10, is one of the more popular places in town, with grilled chicken and steaks from around 80 kr at dinner. There's also a good salad buffet that can be had as a meal in itself for 29 kr. At lunch, from 11.30 am to 4 pm, there's a steak and potatoes special for 34 kr. It's open to 11 pm daily.

Målet, a sports pub and restaurant at Jernbanegade 17, specialises in Danish and German food, featuring 10 different kinds of schnitzel, all priced at 65 kr. It's open until 10 pm for food, to 11 pm for drinks.

Mona Rosa, Vintapperstræde 4, is a pleasant restaurant with a mixed Mexican and Italian menu. At lunch, from 11.30 am to 3.30 pm, a 150-gram steak, pizzas, various pasta dishes or a burrito with rice cost 39 kr. At dinner an enchilada or vegetarian burrito cost 85 kr, while beef dishes average 120 kr; a salad bar is included at dinner and is available at lunch for an additional 35 kr.

Mekong Restaurant, at Albanitorv 3, has a mix of western and Vietnamese fare including chicken and chips for 48 kr, curry dishes for 68 kr and a daily meal that includes salad and dessert for 98 kr. It's open nightly from 4 to 10.30 pm (on Friday and Saturday from noon).

Top End *Restaurant Rosenhaven*, in the Odense Plaza Hotel at Østre Stationsvej 24, is a popular little place serving Danish-French cuisine, with a two-course dinner for 168 kr and a three-course meal for 198 kr.

Den Gamle Kro, at Overgade 23, is in a period building dating from 1683 and has traditional Danish fare. There are a few dining rooms; the most atmospheric is the one in the brick-vaulted cellar. Expect lunch to cost about 125 kr, and dinner to be around 200 kr.

Entertainment

The outdoor amphitheatre at *Brandts Klædefabrik* is a venue for free summertime rock, jazz and blues concerts, particularly on Saturday. *Café Biografen*, at Brandts Klædefabrik, screens first-run movies for just 25 kr.

The *Cotton Club*, Pantheonsgade 5, is the place to hear jazz on weekends. University students hang out at *Boogies*, a dance spot at Nørregade 21, open from 10 pm to 5 am daily.

The *James Dean Dansebar* at Mageløs 12 is a bar that has night-time dancing to mostly recorded rock music and is open Monday to Saturday from noon to 5 am and on Sunday from 5 pm to 5 am. The *Crazy Daisy*, a disco at Klingenberg 14, is another popular dance spot.

The outdoor cafés on Vintapperstræde are good for a quiet evening drink.

On a splashier scale there's the *Casino Odense*, at the SAS hotel at Claus Bergs

Gade 7, where for a 40 kr entry fee you can try your luck at blackjack, roulette and slot machines. It's open from 7 pm to 4 am daily.

Symphony orchestra and other classical music performances are given at the *Odense Koncerthus*, Claus Bergs Gade 9; the programme commonly includes works by Carl Nielsen. The tourist office can provide the current schedule.

Gay & Lesbian Venues The gay and lesbian organisation Lambda (☎ 66 17 76 92) has a weekend disco in the basement of Vindegade 100. At other times *Café Frederik*, Brogade 3, is a popular meeting place for the gay community, open from 4 pm to 1 am daily.

Things to Buy

You can find a variety of clothing and speciality shops in the city centre along Kongensgade and Vestergade. For antiques, Kramboden at Nedergade 24 has an interesting hodgepodge of items including porcelain, toys, glass and pewter. Borsen Antikvardboghandel, next door at Nedergade 26, sells old books.

Getting There & Away

Odense is 34 km west of Nyborg, 44 km north-west of Svendborg, 37 km north-east of Faaborg and 50 km east of the Jutland bridge.

Air Mærsk Air has direct flights to Copenhagen and Billund.

Bus Regional buses leave from the bus station, Dannebrogsgade 6, at the rear of the railway station. There are buses from Odense to all major towns on Funen (see individual destinations for bus information).

Train Odense is on the main railway line between Copenhagen (2½ hours, 130 kr) and Århus (1¾ hours, 118 kr), and the service is frequent throughout the day. The only other Funen train route makes an hourly run between Odense and Svendborg (one hour, 41 kr).

Car & Motorbike Odense is at the north side of the E20; you can exit the E20 into the city via route 9, 43 or 168. Odense is connected to Nyborg via route 160 and the E20, to Kerteminde via route 165, to Jutland via the E20, to Faaborg via route 43 and to Svendborg via route 9.

Car Rental The following companies have booths at the airport and in Odense:

Avis (☎ 66 14 39 99), Østre Stationsvej 31
Europcar (☎ 66 14 15 44), Kongensgade 69
Hertz (☎ 66 14 90 96), Hjallesevej 21

Getting Around

To/From the Airport The airport in on route 327, 12 km north-west of Odense. Airport buses leave from the SAS HC Andersen Hotel 50 minutes prior to scheduled departures and cost 50 kr.

Bus In Odense you board city buses at the back and pay the driver (10 kr) when you get off.

It will generally work out better to pick up a 24-hour bus pass, which costs just 25 kr and can be purchased at the tourist office or the railway station. For information on a local transport/sightseeing pass see the Odense Eventyrpas boxed aside earlier.

Car & Motorbike Outside rush hour, driving in Odense is not difficult, though many of the central sights are on pedestrian streets and it's best to park your car and explore on foot.

Near the city centre, parking is largely metered, with a fee of 5 kr an hour from 9 am to 5 pm on weekdays and to noon on Saturday. Outside those hours it's free. There are carparks near the west side of Rådhus, in the area around Brandts Klædefabrik and at the north side of the Carl Nielsen museum.

Taxi Taxis are readily available at the railway station or can be ordered by phoning Odense Taxa (☎ 66 15 44 15) or Odense Taxi (☎ 66 12 27 12).

Bicycle You can rent bikes at Cykel Biksen

FUNEN

(☎ 66 12 40 98), Nedergade 14, between 8 am and 6.30 pm on weekdays, or at the less-central Per's Cykler Odense (☎ 66 14 84 85) at Vesterbro 95, about a km west of the centre via Vestergade.

Boat From 1 May to 15 August the Odense Åfart (☎ 65 95 79 96) runs a little covered boat down the Odense Å (Odense River) to Erik Bøghs Sti, a landing in the woods at Fruens Bøge. The boat departs from Munke Mose, on the south-west side of the city centre, at 10 and 11 am and 1, 2, 3 and 5 pm. You can take it as a 70-minute return excursion in itself, or break your journey at the zoo or the woods. The cost is 24 kr one way, 36 kr return, one-third less for children.

Around Funen Island

The island of Funen, nicknamed 'Denmark's garden island', is largely rural and green, with rolling woodlands, pastures, wheat fields and lots of old farmhouses. The terrain is gentler in the north, where it eventually levels out to marshland, and hillier in the south. During May, the landscape is ablaze with solid patches of yellow rapeseed flowers.

NYBORG

Nyborg is the Funen terminal for car and train ferries crossing the Store Bælt. While most people pass right through the town without pause, seeing no more than its industrial harbourfront, for those with time to spare Nyborg can make an enjoyable stop on a cross-island journey.

The most appealing part of town is around Torvet, where there's an attractive brick Rådhus, the remains of a medieval castle and some classic half-timbered houses. All are within a few hundred metres of each other and but a 10-minute walk west of the railway station. There's parking at Torvet.

There are white-sand beaches running along the Store Bælt at the east side of town about 1.5 km from the centre.

Tourist Office

The Nyborg Turistbureau (☎ 65 31 02 80, fax 65 31 03 80), Torvet 9, 5800 Nyborg, at the central square, is open from 9 am to 5 pm Monday to Saturday between 15 June and 31 August, and from 9 am to 4.30 pm Monday to Friday and 9 am to noon on Saturday the rest of the year.

Nyborg Slot

Nyborg Slot (Nyborg Castle) was one of a half-dozen strategically located fortresses erected in the late 12th century to secure Denmark's coast. In 1282 King Erik V, under pressure from nobles who wanted to limit royal power and safeguard individual rights, signed an important charter here which established an annual parliament known as the Danehof. The castle was used as a royal residence for centuries and was the birthplace of King Christian II.

The fortress once had an enclosing defence wall and four corner towers but only part of the original structure remains. Two of the towers fell victim to earlier modifications and in 1870 most of the ramparts were torn down to make room for the town's expansion.

Still, what remains is fun to explore. The Danehof Room, where the Danehof met, has walls painted with an intriguing three-dimensional cube design which appears strikingly contemporary despite the fact it was done in the 1500. Here and in other rooms you'll find old royal paintings, suits of armour, antique guns and swords. You can climb a spiral staircase to the loft and walk along the running boards past the machicolations through which boiling tar was once poured down onto attacking Swedes.

The castle is open from 10 am to 5 pm daily from June to August and from 10 am to 3 pm Tuesday to Sunday the rest of the year. Admission is 20 kr for adults and 10 kr for children.

Mads Lerches Gård

This engaging half-timbered merchant's house, built in 1601 at Slotsgade 11, just south of the fortress grounds, holds local cultural history exhibits. Some of its 30 rooms have period furnishings, others the usual odds-and-ends collection of old toys, model ships, antique tools etc. It's open the same hours as the castle and costs 10 kr for adults, 5 kr for children.

Vor Frue Kirke

Vor Frue Kirke, Nyborg's central church, dates back to 1388 although it's been altered numerous times over the years, most extensively in 1870. Its beautifully detailed baroque pulpit was carved in 1653 by Anders Mortensen of Odense. From left to right the pulpit sections depict the birth of John the Baptist, Christ's baptism, the Transfiguration, the Resurrection and the Ascension. There's also a wooden baptismal font dating from 1585. The church, which is on Gammel Torv, is open (via the southern door on Korsbrødregade) from 9 am to 6 pm in summer and from 9 am to 4 pm the rest of the year.

Places to Stay

Nyborg Camping (☎ 65 31 02 56), Hjejlevej 99, 5800 Nyborg, is a popular three-star camping ground on a white-sand beach about two km east of the town centre. Run by the municipality, it's accessible by wheelchair and has guest kitchens, a common room with TV, a minimarket and a view of the new Store Bælt bridge. The cost is 43 kr per person. There are also a few four-person cabins that rent for 275 kr.

The *Nyborg Vandrerhjem* (☎ 65 31 27 04, fax 65 30 26 04), Havnegade 28, 5800 Nyborg, is at the east side of the main harbour, a km from Torvet and 300 metres from the railway station and the train-ferry port. It's a rather utilitarian facility with 88 beds in four-bed rooms, each with a toilet and shower. The hostel is accessible by wheelchair, has laundry facilities and costs 85 kr per person. It's open from mid-January to mid-December.

The tourist office maintains a list of a half-dozen homes with private rooms in the Nyborg area; most charge 100 kr per person. The cheapest in-town hotel is the

Missionshotellet (☎ 65 30 11 88, fax 65 30 11 33), Østervoldgade 44, 5800 Nyborg. It has 26 straightforward rooms, a bit worn but fine. Those with sinks but without baths cost 260/420 kr for singles/doubles, while those with private bath cost 360/550 kr. Ask for room No 14 or 15 as they have large harbourview balconies.

Hotel Hesselet (☎ 65 31 30 29, fax 65 31 29 58), Christianslundsvej 119, 5800 Nyborg, one of Funen's most exclusive hotels, has a pleasant location between the woods and ocean, two km north-east of town. The 46 rooms have modern amenities and in most cases ocean views. There's an indoor swimming pool, billiards, a library and a hearthside lounge. A member of the Relais & Chateaux chain, prices begin at 880/1280 kr for singles/doubles, though there's a slightly cheaper weekend rate.

There's also a large and rather standard Best Western hotel, the *Hotel Nyborg Strand* (☎ 65 31 31 31, fax 65 31 37 01), Østerøvej 2, 5800 Nyborg, to the north of the Hotel Hesselet. Its 247 rooms cost 640/840 kr although there are weekend rates and other promotions that can bring the cost of a double down to 650 kr.

Places to Eat

Café Anton, at Mellemgade 25, a block north of the pedestrian street Kongegade, is an inviting spot to relax over a beer or cappuccino.

Pomona Pizza, Kongegade 22, has pitta bread sandwiches and pizzas from 29 kr as well as burgers, salads, grilled chicken and chips. There's a fruit shop just east of the pizzeria. *Gertz Conditori* at Kongegade 16 has pastries and sandwiches for both eat-in and takeaway.

You can get inexpensive smørrebrød and simple hot dishes for takeaway at *Jyttes Smørrebrød* at Korsgade 4, on the street that runs south from Torvet, and smoked fish by the piece at *Fiskehallen*, Korsgade 11.

For some place more upmarket in the town centre, try the atmospheric *Restaurant Østervemb* at Mellemgade 18, which specialises in fresh fish and home-style Danish food.

For the area's ultimate splurge, there's the *Hotel Hesselet*, a couple of km north-east of town, which has a candle-lit oceanfront dining room and a French flair. The five-course dinner of the day costs 495 kr, or you can select three courses from the menu for 325 kr.

Getting There & Away
Nyborg is 34 km east of Odense, a 20-minute (30 kr) train ride away. Trains run an average of twice an hour.

Nyborg marks the eastern end of the E20 on Funen; the E20 picks up again across the Store Bælt at Korsør on Zealand. Until the Store Bælt bridge is completed, all crossings between Zealand and Funen are by boat. If you're travelling by train the crossing on the DSB train ferry is included in your fare on a through ticket.

DSB and the private company Vognmandsruten both operate car ferries across the Store Bælt; in all, there are nearly 70 runs a day. For information on fares, see Getting There & Away in the Korsør section of the Southern Zealand chapter.

KERTEMINDE
Kerteminde is a seaside town with a pleasant slow pace and a couple of sights of local interest. While it still has a few fishing boats, the town's waterfront has largely been given over to leisure craft, with yachters comprising a fair number of Kerteminde's visitors.

Although Kerteminde is fronted by a harbour and a long marina, there are sandy beaches on both sides of town. Nordstranden, the north beach, extends from the north end of the marina, while Sydstranden, the south beach, begins at the south side of the harbour. A statue of Amanda the fishergirl, a town symbol of sorts, stands at the south side of the Langebro bridge, which crosses the Kerteminde Fjord connecting the north and south sides of Kerteminde.

Information
Tourist Office The helpful Kerteminde Turistbureau (☎ 65 32 11 21, fax 65 32 18 17), Strandgade 1B, 5300 Kerteminde, has a wide range of brochures and rents bicycles for 45/270 kr a day/week. From 15 June to 31 August it's open from 9 am to 5 pm Monday to Saturday; the rest of the year it's open from 9 am to 4 pm Monday to Friday and from 9 am to noon on Saturday.

Money There are a few banks in the town centre, including a Bikuben at Langegade 6 and an Amtssparekassen at Langegade 33.

Post The post office is in the centre on Strandvejen, immediately south of the bus station.

Museums
The local history museum **Farvergården**, at Langegade 8 in the town centre, is in an interesting half-timbered farm building built in 1630. Many of the rooms remain as they would have been in centuries past, with period furnishings, pottery, paintings, and there is also a cellar full of dusty butter churns, washboards and candles. It's open from 10 am to 4 pm. Admission is 15 kr for adults, free for children.

The **Johannes Larsen Museet**, Møllebakken 14, at the north side of town, is in the artist's former home, and retains its original furniture and décor. Larsen (1867-1961), one of the Fynboerne painters, is known for his paintings of wildlife and provincial Danish scenes. Also here is the **Svanemøllen windmill** which dates from 1853, and a modern 15-room exhibition centre with paintings by several dozen artists. It's open from 10 am to 5 pm daily from June to August; from 11 am to 4 pm on Wednesday, Saturday and Sunday from November to February; and from 10 am to 4 pm Tuesday to Sunday the rest of the year. Admission costs 30 kr for adults, free for children. This museum has parking spaces for the disabled only; other travellers with cars should park at the carpark at the corner of Hindsholmvej and Marinavejen.

Romsø

For a quiet outing, consider a visit to the island of Romsø, a 30-minute boat ride from Kerteminde. The only residents are the boatman's family, a few hundred deer and numerous rabbits and birds. You can walk around the 109-hectare island on a three-km coastal trail, take the trails inland or just soak up the solitude. Bring a picnic lunch.

The Romsø-Båden boat service takes passengers to the island on Wednesday and Saturday, departing from Kerteminde at 9 am and from Romsø at 3.30 pm. Reservations are required (☎ 65 32 13 77). The return trip costs 75 kr for adults and 40 kr for children.

The same boat service also offers a 'fjord tour' (50 kr) of Kerteminde, Ladby and Munkebo from 10 am to noon on Tuesday.

Places to Stay

Kerteminde Camping (☎ 65 32 19 71, fax 65 32 23 27), opposite the beach at Hindsholmvej 80, 5300 Kerteminde, is a three-star camping ground about 1.5 km north of the town centre. The cost is 43 kr per person. There's a kiosk, laundry facilities and huts that rent for 250 kr for two people.

The hostel, *Kerteminde Vandrerhjem* (☎ 65 32 39 29, fax 65 32 39 24), Skovvej 46, 5300 Kerteminde, is at the edge of a pleasant wooded area that's just a five-minute walk from a sandy beach and 15 minutes from the centre of town. The 30 rooms each have four beds, a shower and toilet. The facilities include a guest kitchen, a laundry room and a living room with fireplace and TV. The cost is 85 kr per person. It's open from mid-January to 30 November.

The tourist office can book rooms for 200 to 250 kr a double but most are a few km from the centre, including a place in Ladby.

The *Tornøes Hotel* (☎ 65 32 16 05, fax 65 32 48 40), right on the harbour at Strandgade 2, 5300 Kerteminde, has 25 basic rooms, each with a TV, phone and desk. Singles/doubles cost 360/460 kr with shared bath, 460/660 kr with private bath.

Places to Eat

Madhjørnet, in the centre on the corner of Vestergade and Langegade, has hearty food at honest prices. Everything is takeaway. There's a daily special, such as spareribs or fish, that always comes with potatoes and often salad, for 30 to 35 kr, as well as cheaper salads and sandwiches.

Pizza Hot, next door at Langegade 9, has pizza mainly for takeaway, although there's a small stand-up counter where you could eat in. There's a bakery nearby on Langegade a few doors to the north. The *Super Brugsen* on Hindsholmvej, opposite Rådhus, is a large grocery store with a deli.

There are two eateries at the marina, both with good water views. At the south side is the cafeteria-style *Restaurant Sejlklub*, which has a daily meal for 68 kr and cheaper hot dogs and sandwiches. Somewhat fancier is the *Marinaen Restaurant*, at the marina's north side, which offers omelettes for 40 kr and a Danish plate of pickled herring, fish fillet, beef slices and the like for 85 kr.

The *Tornøes Hotel* has a rather elegant restaurant with a nice harbour view and main courses that begin around 100 kr. The restaurant specialises in fish and meat dishes, but also has smørrebrød.

At the top end is *Rudolf Mathis*, Dosseringen 13, a waterside restaurant at the south side of Kerteminde harbour. It specialises in fresh seafood and is widely regarded as one of Funen's best restaurants.

Getting There & Away

Kerteminde is on route 165, 19 km north-west of Nyborg and 21 km north-east of Odense.

There's hourly bus service connecting Kerteminde with Odense (bus Nos 885 and 890) and Nyborg (bus Nos 891 and 892); both routes take about 35 minutes and cost 24 kr.

LADBYSKIBET

The remains of a 22-metre-long Viking ship has been preserved in Ladby, at the site where it was excavated in 1935. The ship was buried in the 10th century, as the tomb of a Viking chieftain, and covered with an earthen mound. Although it was not uncommon for high-ranking Vikings to be buried in their wooden ships, along with supplies considered to be of use in the afterlife, the Ladby ship is the only Viking Age ship burial site thus far uncovered in Denmark.

Unlike the spectacularly preserved Viking ships dug from clay burial sites in Norway and now on display in Oslo, all the wooden planks from the Ladby ship, which was buried in turf, have decayed. What is preserved is the impression of the hull moulded into the earth, along with iron nails, an anchor and the partial remains of the dogs and horses that were buried with their master. The little Ladbyskibet museum was erected around the excavation and from the exterior resembles a burial mound.

It's open year round except Monday from 10 am to 6 pm from May to September and from 10 am to 3 pm from October to April. Admission is 20 kr for adults, free for children.

Getting There & Away

In the little village of Ladby, four km southwest of Kerteminde via Odensevej, turn north onto Vikingevej (look for the Vikingeskibet sign), a one-lane road that ends after 1.2 km at a parking area. From there it's a five-minute walk along a dirt path to the mound, which is in a farmer's field.

Local bus No 482 makes the six-minute trip from Kerteminde to the village of Ladby (10 kr) several times a day on weekdays.

HINDSHOLM

The Hindsholm peninsula, which stretches north from Kerteminde, is a rural area of small villages with 16th century churches and old farmhouses. Two of the more attractive villages, Viby and Måle, are at the southern end of the peninsula, only a 15-minute drive from Kerteminde.

Farther north, in Mårhøj, is Funen's largest single-chamber **burial mound**, which dates from 200 BC and has a 10-metre-long chamber that visitors can walk into.

At the northernmost tip is **Fyns Hoved**, an island-like extension of the Hindsholm peninsula that's connected by a narrow causeway. You can walk to the edge of its 25-metre cliffs (high by Danish standards) where there's a view of the north Funen coast and, on a clear day, Jutland and Zealand as well.

There's a bus service from Kerteminde that connects the villages of Hindsholm, ending about a km shy of Fyns Hoved. However, the best way to visit laid-back Hindsholm is by bicycle. There's a regional loop cycle route from Kerteminde to Fyns Hoved that could make a good day-long bike tour. You can get more information on cycling from the Kerteminde tourist office.

EGESKOV SLOT

Egeskov Slot is a Renaissance castle complete with moat and drawbridge. Egeskov, literally 'oak forest', was built in 1554 in the middle of a small lake on top of a foundation of thousands of upright oak trunks.

While it's most impressive from the outside, you can also tour the castle interior. It has antique furnishings, grand period paintings and an abundance of hunting trophies that include elephant tusks and the skins and heads of tigers, cheetahs and other rare and endangered creatures. Apparently the former owner, Count Gregers Ahlefeldt-Laurvig-Bille, was one of the more active African big game hunters of his day.

The expansive 15-hectare park surrounding the castle was designed in the mid-1700s and includes century-old privet hedges, free-roaming peacocks, topiary and manicured English gardens.

However, not all is formal – you can laugh your way through the bamboo grass labyrinth, dreamed up by the contemporary Danish poet-artist Piet Hein. A sign at the entrance of this three-metre-high maze admonishes visitors 'Don't be afraid. We inspect the maze thoroughly each autumn' – in actuality most people make it through in about 15 minutes.

Also on the castle grounds there is an antique car museum that displays about 300 period cars; a motorbike museum; a children's playground; and an old-time smithy, where the forge is sometimes fired up for demonstrations.

From May to September the castle is open from 10 am to 5 pm daily. From June to August the grounds and museums (but not the castle interior) are open from 9 am to 6 pm. Admission to the grounds, the labyrinth and the museums costs 50 kr, while admission to the castle interior is an additional 45 kr. Children pay half price.

Getting There & Away
Egeskov Slot is two km west of Kvændrup on route 8. From Odense take the Svendborg-bound train to Kvændrup station (41 kr) and continue on foot or by taxi. Alternatively you could take bus No 801 from Odense to Kvændrup Bibliotek (32 kr) and there catch bus No 920, which stops in front of the castle (it's a 700-metre walk to the entrance) on its way between Faaborg and Nyborg.

FAABORG
In the 17th century, Faaborg was a bustling harbour town with one of Denmark's largest fleets. Home to only 6000 people today, Faaborg retains many vestiges of that earlier era and its picturesque cobbled streets and leaning half-timbered houses make for delightful walking. It has two notable museums, one dedicated to town history and the other to regional art. Faaborg also has a central hostel and a couple of small reasonably priced hotels, making it an appealing place to break journey.

Information
Tourist Office The Faaborg Turistbureau (☎ 62 61 07 07, fax 62 61 33 37), Havnegade 2, 5600 Faaborg, has general brochures and sells cycling maps and telephone cards. From 15 June to 31 August it's open from 9 am to 5 pm Monday to Friday and from 10 am to 6 pm on Saturday; the rest of the year

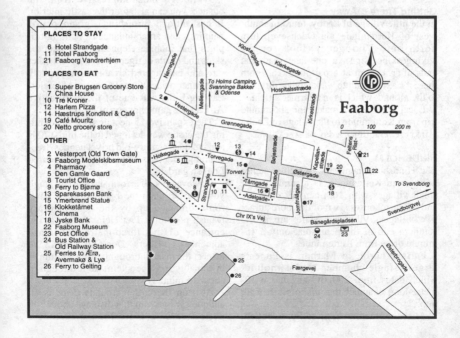

PLACES TO STAY
6 Hotel Strandgade
11 Hotel Faaborg
21 Faaborg Vandrerhjem

PLACES TO EAT
1 Super Brugsen Grocery Store
7 China House
10 Tre Kroner
12 Harlem Pizza
14 Hæstrups Konditori & Café
19 Café Mouritz
20 Netto grocery store

OTHER
2 Vesterport (Old Town Gate)
3 Faaborg Modelskibsmuseum
4 Pharmacy
8 Den Gamle Gaard
8 Tourist Office
9 Ferry to Bjørnø
13 Sparekassen Bank
15 Ymerbrønd Statue
16 Klokketårnet
17 Cinema
18 Jyske Bank
22 Faaborg Museum
23 Post Office
24 Bus Station & Old Railway Station
25 Ferries to Ærø, Avernakø & Lyø
26 Ferry to Gelting

Faaborg

it's open from 10 am to 5 pm Monday to Saturday.

Money There are a few banks in the centre, including a Sparekassen at the north side of Torvet and a Jyske Bank at Østergade 36.

Post The post office is at Banegårdspladsen 4, just east of the bus station. It's open Monday to Friday from 10 am to 5 pm and on Saturday from 10 am to noon.

Walking Tour

You can explore Faaborg's older quarters by taking a short walking tour around the town centre. Beginning at Torvet, walk west along Torvegade to Holkegade, a narrow winding street of half-timbered houses that still looks much as it did in the mid-1700s. Two of Holkegade's period buildings have been turned into museums. At Holkegade 1 is **Den Gamle Gaard** museum (see the following description), while at Holkegade 2 there's the **Faaborg Modelskibsmuseum** (25 kr), a museum dedicated to model ships and Faaborg's seafaring past.

At the end of Holkegade, turn left on Havnegade, where you'll pass the harbour which brimmed with merchant ships during Faaborg's heyday. Turn north on Strandgade and then east at Torvet onto Adelgade, a street lined with restored 19th century homes. On the block between Adelgade and Tårngade is the **Klokketårnet**, a belfry that was once part of a medieval church and now serves as the town's clock tower; in summer there's usually a pensioner on site who'll let you climb the tower for 2 kr.

Proceed west on Tårngade, a cobbled lane lined with attractive period houses and hollyhock-trimmed doorways. On the east side of Torvet you'll find the **Ymerbrønd statue**; based on a Nordic creation myth, the controversial statue, which shows a man, child and cow entwined, created a minor uproar when it was unveiled in 1913.

Den Gamle Gaard

This well-presented museum, just west of Torvet at Holkegade 1, is in a circa 1725

timber-framed merchant's house that retains its original character with few alterations. The 22 rooms are arranged to show how a wealthy merchant lived around 1800, with part of the house holding the family quarters and other sections housing workshops and storerooms. The museum is full of intriguing antiques, from furniture, porcelain and toys to maritime items and a hearse carriage. One room contains personal items that belonged to Riborg Voigt, a merchant's daughter with whom Hans Christian Andersen had a brief relationship and a lifelong infatuation. The momentoes include one of Andersen's business cards and a curling lock of his hair. The museum is open daily from mid-May to mid-September from 10.30 am to 4.30 pm and admission costs 20 kr.

Faaborg Museum

This museum, in an attractive neoclassical building at Grønnegade 75, contains Denmark's best collection of Funen art, with works by Peter Hansen, Johannes Larsen, Poul Christensen and Fritz Syberg. Also on display is sculptor Kai Nielsen's original sandstone Ymerbrønd, the bronze copy of which stands on Torvet. The museum is open daily, from 10 am to 5 pm in summer, from 10 am to 4 pm in spring and autumn and from 11 am to 3 pm during winter. Admission is 20 kr.

Other Things to See & Do

Svanninge Bakker, the countryside north of Faaborg, has some pretty rolling hills, amusingly dubbed the Funen Alps by local tourism authorities. There are cycling and walking trails, a golf course and a restaurant.

Vesterport (West Gate), a brick town gate that was erected in the 15th century to allow entry into the city, still spans the road on Vestergade, 500 metres north-west of Torvet. It's one of only a handful of such gates remaining in Denmark. The gate owes its existence primarily to Faaborg's economic decline in the 19th century, a time when many town gates elsewhere in Denmark were torn down to make room for wider roads and municipal expansion.

On Sunday in summer, the antique train **Veterantoget** makes a leisurely run from the old Faaborg railway station north to Korinth. The trip lasts from 1.30 to 3.30 pm and costs 30 kr. In July there's also a journey to Odense on Wednesday that leaves at 10.50 am and costs 75 kr. Children pay half price on both trips.

Places to Stay

There are half a dozen camping grounds within a 10 km radius of Faaborg. The closest, *Holms Camping* (☎ 62 61 03 99, fax 62 61 33 63), Odensevej 54, 5600 Faaborg, is on route 43, one km north of the town centre. A two-star facility, it's open from 1 May to 30 September and costs 38 kr per person.

The 79-bed hostel, *Faaborg Vandrerhjem* (☎ 62 61 12 03, fax 62 61 35 08) at Grønnegade 71-72, 5600 Faaborg, occupies two handsome historic buildings, one a former public bathhouse and the other half-timbered. Dorm beds cost 74 kr. The hostel is open from 1 April to 1 October and has a convenient location near the Faaborg Museum.

The tourist office can provide a brochure listing private rooms in the greater Faaborg area. Prices vary from 125 to 250 kr for singles and from 200 to 280 kr for doubles.

Hotel Strandgade (☎ 62 61 20 12), Strandgade 2, 5600 Faaborg, an 11-room hostelry near Torvet, has pleasant-enough rooms with bath (but no breakfast) for 225/350 kr for singles/doubles. Call ahead as the reception is open limited hours, particularly on weekends.

Hotel Faaborg (☎ 62 61 02 45, fax 62 61 08 45), Torvet 15, 5600 Faaborg, in a period brick building overlooking the central square, has 10 nicely renovated rooms, each with private bath, TV and a small kitchenette with refrigerator and hot plates. There's a small bar and a restaurant on the ground floor. Singles/doubles cost 375/525 kr; breakfast is an optional 50 kr more.

For a large hotel with standard tourist amenities there's the *Interscan Hotel Faaborg Fjord* (☎ 62 61 10 10, fax 62 61 10 17), Svendborgvej 175, 5600 Faaborg, on the eastern outskirts of town. It has 131 modern rooms as well as a restaurant, pool, sauna, solarium and billiards room. Standard rates are 695/795 kr for singles/doubles, but there are often cheaper weekend and summer promotions.

Places to Eat

There are numerous places to eat in Faaborg, most of them within a few minutes walk of Torvet, the central square.

Early-risers can head for *Hæstrups Konditori & Café*, on Torvegade at the east side of Torvet, which opens daily at 6.30 am and has good bakery items, juice and milk for takeaway, and a café at the side where you can eat in.

Harlem Pizza at Torvegade 10 has good pizza with a wide range of toppings priced between 29 and 45 kr, as well as reasonably priced pitta bread sandwiches, lasagne and spaghetti. It stays open until at least 3 am from Thursday to Saturday and until 10 pm on other days.

The popular *China House*, just south of Torvet at Strandgade 4, has lunch specials for 40 to 50 kr that are served until 4 pm and à la carte Chinese dishes at moderate prices at dinner.

Café Mouritz, Østergade 27, has good cakes and coffees, and simple hot dishes like lasagne or a half a chicken with salad and chips for around 45 kr. The café also serves beer, wine and mixed drinks and on warm summer days it extends onto the pedestrian street with pavement tables.

Tre Kroner at Strandgade 1 has a charming old-fashioned character and traditional Danish food at moderate prices. For expensive food with a French influence there's the restaurant at the nearby *Hotel Faaborg*, which specialises in seafood.

Getting There & Away

Faaborg is 27 km west of Svendborg and 37 km south of Odense.

Bus Faaborg has no train service. Buses from Odense (Nos 960, 961 or 962) cost 42 kr, take 1¼ hours and run at least hourly from sunrise to around 11 pm. Buses from Svendborg (No 930) are also frequent throughout the day, running at least hourly, and take 40 minutes. Faaborg's bus station is on Banegårdspladsen, at the old railway station on the south side of town.

Car & Motorbike Getting to Faaborg by car is straightforward; from the north, simply follow route 43, which is called Odensevej as it enters the town. From Svendborg, route 44 leads directly west into Faaborg, entering the town as Svendborgvej. Route 8 ends 10 km west of Faaborg at Bøjden, from where a car ferry (☎ 33 15 15 15) runs seven times a day from 7 am to at least 7 pm (30 kr per person or 205 kr for a car and five passengers) to Fynshav on Als, Jutland.

Boat Ferries run to and from Faaborg daily to the island of Ærø and to Gelting, Germany. Information on boats to Gelting is in the Getting There & Away chapter. Information on boats to Ærø is in the Ærø Getting There & Away section later in this chapter.

There are also ferries from Faaborg to the nearby offshore islands of Bjørnø, Lyø and Avernakø; information is in the section that follows.

Getting Around
Bicycles can be rented at Bjarnes Cykler (☎ 62 61 24 61), Svendborgvej 69, and at the Faaborg Vandrerhjem.

BJØRNØ, LYØ & AVERNAKØ
If you're looking for a quiet getaway while you're in the Faaborg area, consider a day trip to one of the three small offshore islands, Bjørnø, Lyø and Avernakø. All three islands are rural, unspoiled and connected by a daily ferry service to Faaborg. If you're interested in staying overnight, contact the Faaborg tourist office which can arrange B&B-style stays with a local family.

The nearest and smallest island, Bjørnø, three km south of Faaborg, is just three km long and a km wide. It has one small village with about 40 inhabitants, most of whom make a living from farming. You can walk

around the island, but otherwise it's a bit of a sleeper.

Lyø, about 10 km south-west of Faaborg, is the most heavily populated of the islands – with all of 150 residents. Roughly four km long and two km wide, it has a small village perched in the middle of the island, with half-timbered houses, a school and a church with an unusual circular churchyard. It also has a few scattered sights, including a bell stone at the west side of the island, and enough narrow roads to make for an interesting cycling day trip.

Avernakø, six km south of Faaborg, is shaped a bit like a pair of spectacles, with two oval-shaped sides, both about four km long, which are connected by a thin rim of land. There's a small village, Avernak, on the north-west side of the island and scattered farmsteads throughout. In all, about 120 people live on Avernakø.

Getting There & Away
The MS *Lillebjørn* (☎ 30 66 80 50), a little 20-passenger boat, makes six crossings between Faaborg and Bjørnø on weekdays, a few less on weekends. It takes about 20 minutes; the return trip costs 22 kr for adults, 11 kr for children. Bicycles cost an additional 12 kr return.

The MF *Faaborg II* (☎ 62 61 23 07) carries 150 passengers and 12 cars and operates between Faaborg, Avernakø and Lyø at least six times daily. From Faaborg it takes between 30 minutes and an hour to get to your destination, depending on which island the boat pulls into first. It costs 45 kr return (30 kr for children), plus 15 kr for a bicycle or 45 kr for a motorbike.

Because the roads are narrow, visitors are not encouraged to bring cars over to Avernakø or Lyø, and there's no car ferry to Bjørnø.

SVENDBORG
During the 19th century Svendborg was a busy harbour town whose nearly two dozen shipyards produced almost half of all wooden-hulled ships built in Denmark. AP Møller, one of the world's largest shipping

FUNEN

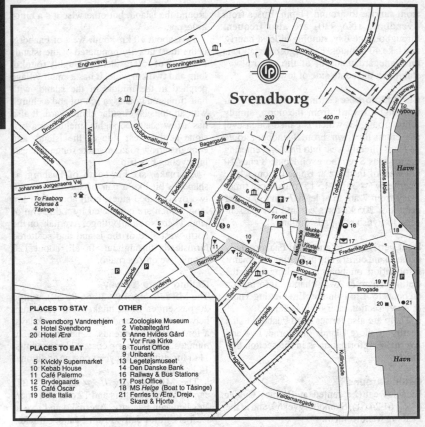

Svendborg

0   200   400 m

PLACES TO STAY
3 Svendborg Vandrerhjem
4 Hotel Svendborg
20 Hotel Ærø

PLACES TO EAT
5 Kvickly Supermarket
10 Kebab House
11 Café Palermo
12 Brydegaards
15 Café Oscar
19 Bella Italia

OTHER
1 Zoologiske Museum
2 Viebæltegård
6 Anne Hvides Gård
7 Vor Frue Kirke
8 Tourist Office
9 Unibank
13 Legetøjsmuseet
14 Den Danske Bank
16 Railway & Bus Stations
17 Post Office
18 MS Helge (Boat to Tåsinge)
21 Ferries to Ærø, Drejø,
    Skarø & Hjortø

companies, got its start in Svendborg during that period. With its excellent port facilities, Svendborg also became the site of foundries, tanneries, tobacco processing plants and mills.

Today Svendborg, south Funen's largest municipality (population 40,000), remains an industrial city with commercial port facilities and two of Denmark's largest food processing companies. It also has a couple of shipyards that still build wooden ships and provide repair services to the scores of yachts that ply the south Funen waters.

Svendborg has a few nicely restored buildings in the city centre and along the waterfront, but overall the less-developed islands around Svendborg – such as Tåsinge and Ærø – hold far more allure.

Information
Tourist Office The Svenborg Turistbureau (☎ 62 21 09 80, fax 62 22 05 53), Centrumpladsen, 5700 Svendborg, in the city centre, has information on all of south Funen. From 15 June to 31 August it's open Monday to Friday from 9 am to 7 pm, and on Saturday from 9 am to 5 pm; the rest of the year it's open Monday to Friday from 9

Funen
Top: Window, Den Fynske Landsby open-air museum, Odense
Bottom: Ymerbrønd statue by Kai Nielsen, Faaborg
Left : Nyborg Museum, Nyborg

NED FRIARY

NED FRIARY

Funen
Top: Gatehouse at Valdemars Slot, Tåsinge
Bottom: Tranekær Slot, Langeland

am to 5 pm and on Saturday from 10 am to 1 pm.

Money There are several banks in the city centre including a Unibank on Gåsestræde, south of the tourist office, and Den Danske Bank a few minutes walk from the railway station on the corner of Brogade and Møllergade.

Post The post office is at the south side of the railway station.

Things to See
Near Torvet you'll find two attractive period structures. The handsome brick church, **Vor Frue Kirke**, was originally erected in the 13th century in Romanesque style although subsequent alterations have given it a gothic appearance. The church has a late 16th century pulpit and altar and is open from 8 am to 4 pm in summer; from 8 am to noon in winter. Just west of the church is the city's oldest secular building, **Anne Hvides Gård**, a large and lovely timber-framed house that dates from 1560. It's now a local history museum displaying antiques, including locally made pottery, silverware and glass. It's open (15 kr) from 10 am to 5 pm in summer, with slightly shorter low season hours.

The other city sights are mainly of local interest. There's **Viebæltegård** (20 kr), Grubbemøllevej 13, a former poorhouse that exhibits its old workshops and some archaeological finds; **Legetøjsmuseet** (30 kr), a toy museum at Sankt Nicolaigade 18; and the **Zoologiske Museum** (10 kr) at Dronningemaen 30, which displays the usual stuffed birds and mammals, as well as the skeleton of a baleen whale that beached on Tåsinge. All three museums are open from 10 am to 5 pm in summer, with slightly shorter hours in winter.

Places to Stay
The nearest camping grounds are on Tåsinge, on the south side of the Svendborg sound; for details see the Tåsinge section.

The hostel, *Svendborg Vandrerhjem* (☎ 62

21 66 99, fax 62 20 29 39), Vestergade 45, 5700 Svendborg, is in a pleasantly renovated 19th century iron foundry in the city centre. The building, in which L Lange & Co produced kitchen stoves from 1850 to 1984, now also contains a small stove museum. The hostel has 34 double rooms, 28 three-bed rooms and 21 four-bed rooms, each with a shower and toilet. Dorm beds cost 85 kr. Open year round except during the Christmas and New Year holidays, it has laundry facilities, conference rooms and bicycle rentals.

Hotel Ærø (☎ 62 21 07 60), Brogade 1, 5700 Svendborg, opposite the Ærø ferry dock, has 13 clean, straightforward rooms for 200/400 kr. Common toilets and showers are off the hall.

Popular with business people, the *Hotel Svendborg* (☎ 62 21 17 00, fax 62 21 90 12), Centrumpladsen 1, 5700 Svendborg, is a newly renovated midsize hotel in the city centre. Rooms have TV, phone and private bath and cost 550/650 kr for singles/doubles.

Places to Eat
There's a *DSB restaurant* at the railway station and a number of inexpensive restaurants within a five-minute walk south-east along Brogade (which becomes Gerritsgade after the first block).

Café Oscar, on the corner of Brogade and Korsgade, has a pizza and beer special for 40 kr. A block and a half farther west, on the north side of Gerritsgade, is *Kebab House*, which has inexpensive burgers, kebabs and pitta bread sandwiches. About 100 metres farther west, at Gerritsgade 25, is *Brydegaards*, a konditori-style bakery with café tables and simple eats. On the next block west is *Café Palermo*, which has pizza, lasagne, spaghetti and a few Greek dishes such as souvlaki for around 40 kr; there's a lunch special from 11 am to 4 pm for 29 kr.

The *Hotel Ærø*, at the ferry dock, has a pleasant dining room with a hearty daily special, such as Danish beef and potatoes, for 68 kr. Otherwise most dishes are in the 90 to 140 kr price range at dinner, a bit cheaper at lunch.

Bella Italia, a pleasant Italian restaurant at Brogade 2, north of the Hotel Ærø, has pizza and spaghetti for 44 to 70 kr and more expensive meat and seafood dishes.

There's a *Kvickly* supermarket with a bakery and a cafeteria-style restaurant at Vestergade 20.

Getting There & Away
For most travellers, Svendborg is the transit point between Odense and the south Funen islands. Svendborg is 44 km south-east of Odense via route 9, 33 km south-west of Nyborg via route 163 and 27 km east of Faaborg via route 44.

Bus & Train Trains leave Odense for Svendborg at 15 minutes past the hour; the trip takes one hour and costs 41 kr. There's frequent bus service from Svendborg to Faaborg and other Funen towns. Buses leave from in front of the railway station, which is two blocks north-west of the ferry dock.

Boat Ferries to Ærøskøbing depart five times a day; the last boat leaves Svendborg at 10.30 pm in summer, 9 pm in winter. For more information see the Ærø section.

For information on the M/S *Helge*, which sails between Svendborg and Tåsinge, see the Tåsinge section.

DREJØ, SKARØ & HJORTØ
Many of Svendborg's visitors are yachters who sail the protected waters along the south Funen coast. Three popular local sailing spots are the small offshore islands of Drejø, Skarø and Hjortø, all 10 to 15 km south-west of Svendborg.

Camping is allowed on all three islands; Drejø has a restaurant and grocery store, while Skarø has a small food shop and a snack bar with beer, ice cream and simple grilled items.

Drejø, with about 100 inhabitants, is the largest island, long and narrow, extending about five km in length and comprising a total of 412 hectares. Its small central town, Drejø By, was devastated during a Midsummer Eve bonfire in 1942 when an ember

landed on the vicarage's thatched roof – within minutes, 17 closely clustered half-timbered farmhouses had burned to the ground. Despite the fire, Drejø still has some attractive period houses and a community church that dates from 1535. The island is largely given over to moors and meadows (home to the endangered fire-bellied toad) and has a large protected harbour with good mooring facilities.

Skarø, population 25, is shaped something like a rabbit's head, consists of 189 hectares and reaches just nine metres at its highest point. Part of the island's salt meadows are set aside as a bird sanctuary, habitat to about 50 species of breeding birds each summer. Skarø has mooring space for about 50 boats.

Hjortø, population 15, is the smallest of the three islands, just two km at its widest point. It's free of cars and motorbikes, attracts lots of seabirds and shorebirds, and has some protected beaches. The island can be walked around in just a couple of hours. About 25 boats can moor in Hjortø's harbour.

Getting There & Away
If you don't have your own boat, it's possible to visit these islands on a day trip via small ferries that leave from Svendborg's harbour. The Hjortø ferry (☎ 62 54 12 08) generally has two sailings daily, while the ferry to Drejø and Skarø (☎ 62 21 02 62) runs three to four times a day. Sailing times take 50 to 90 minutes, depending on the island and the route. The return trip costs 40 kr for adults, 20 kr for children, 10 kr for a bicycle. For more details, call the ferry direct or pick up the current timetable at the tourist office.

TÅSINGE
Tåsinge, the fourth largest island in Funen county, is connected by bridge to both Svendborg and Langeland. Most of the island is typically rural, a mix of woods and open fields.

The island's main road, route 9, cuts straight across Tåsinge, but it's well worth making a loop detour through the north-east quarter of the island where you'll find

Tåsinge's main sights: the old sea captains' village of Troense and the 17th century castle Valdemars Slot.

Troense is a well-to-do seaside village with lots of quaint thatched houses and a small yachting harbour. The main activity for visitors is just strolling around and admiring the period homes; two particularly interesting streets are Grønnegade and Badstuen. There's also a small maritime museum, the Søfartsmuseum (20 kr) at Strandgade 1, housed in the old village schoolhouse (circa 1790), which still has its rooftop belfry. The museum exhibits paintings, photos, model ships, figureheads and items from China brought back by local merchant ships in the 19th century.

From Troense the tree-lined Slotsalléen leads south-east to **Valdemars Slot**, (Valdemar's Castle) which was originally constructed by King Christian IV in 1639 for his son Valdemar. In 1677 the castle was transferred to the naval commander Niels Juel as part of the payment for his victory in the decisive Battle of Køge Bay; Juel's heirs still own the property today.

The main building, a brick manor house, is open to the public as a museum. About 20 of its rooms can be toured to see period furniture, walls hung with tapestries and royal portraits, and a few of Juel's personal belongings. It's open from 10 am to 5 pm daily from May to September and on weekends in the low season. Admission is 45 kr for adults and 20 kr for children.

The road from Troense passes right through the castle's two decorative gatehouses, which are open 24 hours a day. There's no admission charge to the castle grounds, which have a pond and a tea pavilion, or to the sandy beach just outside the castle's southern gate.

About a km south-west of the castle, look for a grand oak tree in a field on the north side of the road. Called **Ambrosius Egen** (Ambrosius' Oak), the tree, which is marked by a plaque, is named for Ambrosius Stub, a romantic poet who worked at Valdemars Slot around 1700 and who composed many of his verses while relaxing beneath the shade of

this tree. The oak tree is thought to be at least 500 years old and has a girth of nearly seven metres.

The small village of **Bregninge**, on route 9, has a windmill with a restaurant inside and the Bregninge Kirke, a church that dates from medieval times. One of the church's three votive ships was built in 1727 as a replica of the battleship sailed by Admiral Niels Juel in the Battle of Køge Bay, but the main attraction is the panoramic view from the church tower, which at 72 metres is the highest point on the island. The tower is open from 8 am to 4 am Monday to Saturday and costs 5 kr. There's a local history museum, Tåsinge Skipperkjem og Folkemindesamling, nearby which costs 15 kr.

Landet, three km south of Bregninge, also has a medieval church, most notable for the churchyard graves of the famous lovers Elvira Madigan and Sixten Sparre, who died in a suicide pact in 1889.

Places to Stay

There are four camping grounds on Tåsinge. Closest to Svendborg is the seaside *Vindebyøre Camping* (☎ 62 22 54 25, fax 62 22 54 26), Vindebyørvej, Tåsinge, 5700 Svendborg, a three-star facility with a coin laundry, TV lounge and guest kitchen. It costs 45 kr per person and is open from mid-April to mid-September. The local ferry boat *Helge* docks out front.

Cheapest is *Tåsinge Camping* (☎ 62 54 13 27), Sundbrovej 130, Tåsinge, 5700 Svendborg, on route 9 at the south-east side of Tåsinge. It's a small friendly place open from May to September, with basic facilities and a snack bar. It costs 33 kr in a tent and there are a couple of huts for 175 kr plus the per-person fee.

The *Det Lille Hotel* (☎ 62 22 53 41), Badstuen 15, 5700 Svendborg, is an old half-timbered guesthouse in the village of Troense, with a coffee lounge, quiet garden and bicycles for rent. It has eight rooms with shared baths from 280/420 kr for singles/doubles, breakfast included. There's a slight reduction for stays of two days or more.

FUNEN

Also in the village of Troense is the *Hotel Troense* (☎ 62 22 54 12, fax 62 22 78 12), Strandgade 5, Tåsinge, 5700 Svendborg, perched above the harbour 100 metres west of the maritime museum. Its 30 rooms have TV, phone and private bath and cost 420/620 kr, breakfast included. The hotel is part of the Dansk Kroferie association and accepts 'Inn Cheques'. (See the Hotel Schemes information in the Accommodation section of the Facts for the Visitor chapter.)

Places to Eat
The *Hotel Troense*, on the main road in the village of Troense, has a three-course lunch for 120 kr; otherwise fish and meat main dishes range from 115 to 170 kr. There's also a second dining area with a cheaper *småretter* (small courses) menu. Nearby, between the hotel and the museum, is an ice-cream shop with hot dogs, burgers and chips, and there's a bakery and minimarket opposite the museum.

At Valdemars Slot, the *Restaurant Valdemars Slot* in the main manor house has a changing menu with lunch dishes such as salmon piccata or saffron fish soup priced from about 100 to 120 kr, while main dishes at dinner are about double that. Also on the grounds is a cheaper snack-type restaurant and a picturesque seaside tea pavilion where you can get beverages and cakes.

Getting There & Away
Route 9 connects Tåsinge to Svendborg on Funen and to Rudkøbing on Langeland; there are bike paths the entire way.

The Svendborg city bus operates between the city and Tåsinge, but the most enjoyable public transport option is the vintage ferry boat M/S *Helge* (☎ 62 50 25 00), which runs five times a day from June to August. The boat leaves Svendborg harbour at 9 and 11 am and 1.30, 3.30 and 5.30 pm. Ten minutes later it docks at Vindebyøre on the northern tip of Tåsinge and then crosses back across the sound to Christiansminde, a beach area at the east side of Svendborg. The boat continues on to Troense and then to Valdemars Slot. Return departures from Valdemars Slot

are at 9.55 and 11.55 am and 2.25, 4.25 and 6.25 pm. The *Helge* also operates the three midday sailings during the last three weeks in May. Fares range from 10 to 30 kr one way (children half price), depending on the distance. Bicycles cost an extra 10 kr.

Langeland

Langeland is a long, narrow island with good beaches, cycling and bird-watching. It has an unhurried provincial character with small farming villages and a countryside dotted by windmills, both modern and vintage. There are ceramic shops and galleries selling local handicrafts all around the island.

Langeland's only large town, Rudkøbing, has a handful of historic sights, but the island's most frequented visitor attraction is the medieval castle at Tranekær.

GETTING THERE & AWAY
Route 9, via the Langeland bridge, connects Langeland to Tåsinge and Svendborg. Buses make the 25-minute, 20-km run from Svendborg to Rudkøbing at least hourly, more frequently on weekdays.

Boat There are frequent daily ferries from Rudkøbing to Marstal in Ærø (see Getting There & Away in the Ærø section); from Spodsbjerg to Tårs in Lolland (see the Lolland Getting There & Away section); and from Bagenkop to Kiel in Germany (see the Getting There & Away chapter).

GETTING AROUND
Route 305 runs from Lohals to Bagenkop, nearly the full north-south length of the island.

Bus
Note when boarding buses that the following routes are all marked No 910, so you'll need to confirm with the driver in which direction the bus is headed. Buses travel from Rudkøbing north to Lohals and south to

Langeland

RUDKØBING

Rudkøbing is Langeland's commercial centre and main town, with a population of 5000. It's also the departure point for ferries to Ærø, which leave from the ferry harbour at the west side of the town centre. North of the ferry harbour is a fishing harbour, followed by a 260-berth yacht harbour that attracts German boaters in summer and Danes year round.

Information
Tourist Office You can pick up information on the entire island from the Langelands Turistbureau (☎ 62 51 35 05, fax 62 51 43 35), Torvet 5, 5900 Rudkøbing. From mid-June through to 31 August it's open Monday to Saturday from 9 am to 5 pm, the rest of the year Monday to Friday from 9.30 am to 4.30 pm and on Saturday from 9.30 am to 12.30 pm.

Money There's a Unibank on Østergade 39 that's open Monday to Friday from 9.30 am to 4 pm (Thursday to 6 pm).

Post The post office, at Brogade 13, is open Monday to Friday from 10 am to 5 pm and on Saturday from 9.30 am to noon.

Things to See & Do
Rudkøbing can appear rather nondescript from the ferry harbour, but it's well worth a closer look. Just east of Havnegade, the main harbour road, are a series of one-lane carriage roads that date from medieval times and are lined with period houses. Three of the most interesting streets – Ramsherred, Smedegade and Vinkælddergade – can be combined in a pleasant 15-minute stroll between Havnegade and Brogade.

The town also has a few sights along its main street, which begins inland of the harbour as Brogade and changes to Østergade after Torvet. On Brogade, just east of Ramsherred, is a **statue of HC Ørsted**, the Danish physicist who was instrumental in the development of the electromagnetic theory. Across the street at Brogade 15 is the old Rudkøbing Apotek, the site where Ørsted

Bagenkop roughly once an hour (about half as often on weekends), connecting all of Langeland's major villages en route. There's also a bus service between Rudkøbing and Spodsbjerg, but it only runs three to five times a day.

Bicycle
There are separate asphalt bike paths from the Rudkøbing area running north to Lohals, east to Spodsbjerg and south to Bagenkop. In Rudkøbing you can rent bicycles at the cycle shop at Ørstedsgade 5 or at the yacht harbour.

FUNEN

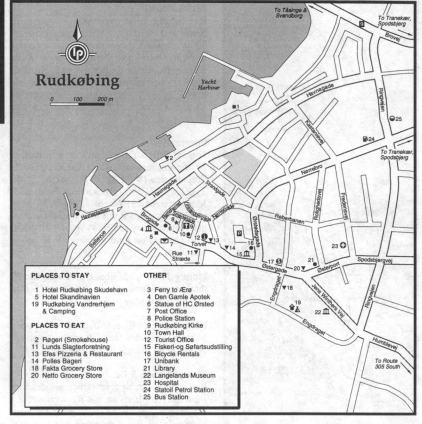

Rudkøbing

0   100   200 m

PLACES TO STAY

1 Hotel Rudkøbing Skudehavn
5 Hotel Skandinavien
19 Rudkøbing Vandrerhjem
   & Camping

PLACES TO EAT

2 Røgeri (Smokehouse)
11 Lunds Slagterforetning
13 Efes Pizzeria & Restaurant
14 Polles Bageri
18 Fakta Grocery Store
20 Netto Grocery Store

OTHER

3 Ferry to Ærø
4 Den Gamle Apotek
6 Statue of HC Ørsted
7 Post Office
8 Police Station
9 Rudkøbing Kirke
10 Town Hall
12 Tourist Office
15 Fiskeri-og Søfartsudstilling
16 Bicycle Rentals
17 Unibank
21 Library
22 Langelands Museum
23 Hospital
24 Statoil Petrol Station
25 Bus Station

was born. It now houses the small museum **Den Gamle Apotek**, which contains two replicas of the interiors of pharmacy shops, one from the 18th century and another from the 19th century. In summer it's open Monday to Friday from noon to 5 pm. Admission is 10 kr for adults, free for children.

A block farther on Torvet is the 19th century town hall backed by the town church, **Rudkøbing Kirke**. The church dates from the early 12th century, although most of the current building is from the post-Reformation era. At Østergade 25 there's the

Fiskeri-og Søfartsudstilling, a nautical museum with fishing gear, dinghies and model ships. In summer it's open Monday to Friday from 10 am to 5 pm and on Saturday from 10 am to 2 pm, closing an hour earlier the rest of the year; admission is free.

The **Langelands Museum**, about 500 metres farther east at Jens Winthers Vej 12, is the island's history museum. It primarily displays archaeological finds from Langeland and Ærø but also has a collection of 18th century glass, silver and furniture.

It's open year round from 10 am to 4 pm Monday to Thursday, and from 10 am to 2 pm on Friday; it's also open on summer weekends. Admission costs 15 kr for adults, free for children.

Places to Stay

Langeland's only hostel, *Rudkøbing Van-drerhjem & Camping* (☎ & fax 62 51 18 30), Engdraget 11, 5900 Rudkøbing, has a convenient location just a km east of the harbour and a 10-minute walk from Torvet. Dorm beds cost 66 to 84 kr, depending upon whether the bathroom is off the room or in the hall, while singles/doubles cost 168/212 kr. You can pitch a tent in the field at the side of the hostel for 30 kr per person. The hostel is open from 1 March to 30 November.

The tourist office maintains a list, with brief descriptions, of about 25 private homes with rooms for rent. Some are in villages, others on farms; about a third are in the Rudkøbing area, the rest spread around the island. Prices are generally 100 to 150 kr per person.

Hotel Skandinavien (☎ 62 51 14 95), Brogade 13, 5900 Rudkøbing, a five-minute walk from the Rudkøbing ferry dock, is the best bottom-end hotel deal. It has nine simple rooms above a restaurant that cost 235/310 kr for singles/doubles with shared bath or 295/390 kr with private bath.

The *Hotel Rudkøbing Skudehavn* (☎ 62 51 46 00, fax 62 51 49 40), Havnegade 21, 5900 Rudkøbing, is a comfortable condominium-style hotel fronting the yacht harbour. There are 33 two-storey buildings, each with a couple of units that can be rented as a two-room apartment with a kitchen or as separate hotel rooms. Either way, all have private bath and many also have harbourfront balconies with fine sunset views. Rooms with twin beds, TV, phone and balcony cost 520/675 kr for singles/doubles, while simpler rooms with a queen sofa bed cost 405/575 kr. Both rooms together as an apartment cost 850 kr in summer (with a two-day minimum) and 500 to 625 kr the rest of the year (with no minimum stay). Breakfast is included in the hotel room rates. There's a large indoor pool, a sauna, tennis and billiards.

Places to Eat

There's a *Fakta* grocery store on Engdreget, just a few minutes walk from the hostel. Along the harbourfront you'll find a couple of grill restaurants with snacks and beer and a *røgeri* selling smoked fish.

There are a number of more substantial options near Torvet. *Hotel Scandinavien* at Brogade 15 has an old-fashioned restaurant with a daily meal for 55 kr. *Lunds Slagter-foretning*, a butcher shop on Torvet opposite the tourist office, has a deli with inexpensive sandwiches and salads for takeaway.

Efes Pizzeria & Restaurant, just east of the tourist office at Østergade 5, has pitta bread sandwiches for 30 kr and lasagne or pizza for 45 kr. *Polles Bageri*, a bakery at Østergade 11, opens at 6.30 am with fresh pastries and coffee.

The *Hotel Rudkøbing Skudehavn*, at the yacht harbour, has a restaurant with a nice harbour view. At lunch sandwiches, salads and Danish dishes are 40 to 85 kr. At dinner most fish and meat main courses cost 110 to 155 kr but there's often a special, such as mixed grill and salad, for around 75 kr.

NORTHERN LANGELAND

Northern Langeland has a run of small villages separated by farmland. There's an occasional sign for organic produce and a few roadside windmills but the main sights are at Tranekær, a quiet village surrounding a lovely medieval castle.

You could continue travelling north from Tranekær to Lohals, a fair-sized village at the northern tip of Langeland. It and the neighbouring seaside area of Hov have a couple of camping grounds and hotels, but Lohals lacks the charm of Tranekær and the beaches are better in the south.

Tranekær

Tranekær has a quaint character with numerous timber-framed houses but its dominant sight is the salmon-coloured **Tranekær Slot** which, reflected in its swan pond, has the appearance of something torn from the pages of a fairy tale.

The castle dates to around 1200 AD and

was once the centrepiece of a royal estate that included more than half of Langeland. Although it's been altered several times, most recently in 1862, Tranekær Slot has been in the same family since 1659. Its current owner, Count Preben Ahlefeldt-Laurvig, still maintains it as a residence so the castle interior cannot be toured, but much of the grounds have been converted into a sculpture park called **Tickon** that's open to the public.

The park, the main path of which circles the castle pond, contains the environmental works of 14 international artists who have used straw, stones and sticks to give their works a distinctively Nordic appearance. In addition, 70 different types of exotic trees, ranging from Norway spruce to California sequoia, are marked by numbers and identified in the corresponding park brochure. It costs 15 kr (free for children) to walk around the castle grounds and view the sculptures; after hours, drop your coins into the box.

In the old water mill opposite the castle is **Tranekær Slotsmuseum**, which has exhibits on the history of the castle and Tranekær village. It's open from mid-May to 30 September, from 10 am to 5 pm Monday to Friday and from 1 to 5 pm on Sunday. Admission is 15 kr for adults, free for children.

One km north of the castle is **Tranekær Slotsmølle**, an attractive Dutch windmill dating from 1846. It's been restored as a museum and, wind permitting, still grinds flour. It has the same opening hours and fees as Tranekær Slotsmuseum.

Places to Stay The half-timbered village kro, the *Tranekær Gæstgivergaard* (☎ 62 59 12 04), Slotsgade 74, 5953 Tranekær, 200 metres south of the castle, dates from 1802 and retains its period ambience. There are 16 straightforward guest rooms that cost 450/550 kr for singles/doubles with private bath, 300/400 kr with shared bath, breakfast included.

Sundgården (☎ 62 59 15 55, fax 62 59 13 02), Slotsgade 10, 5953 Tranekær, a km south of the castle, is an appealing B&B that

specialises in healthy vegetarian holidays for those looking to de-stress and unwind. The rooms are pleasantly simple, with shared toilet and shower, and can be rented on a nightly basis for 225/450 kr for singles/doubles, breakfast included. However, most people come for the week and take full board for 2675 kr. Meals are prepared with organic fruits and vegetables.

Places to Eat The *Café Herskabsstalden*, a large café in the grounds fronting the castle, has simple food such as grilled chicken or fish with chips, omelettes, burgers and hot dogs, all for 50 kr or less. It's open in summer from 10 am to 9 pm and in spring and autumn from 11 am to 8 pm.

For some place fancier, the restaurant at the *Tranekær Gæstgivergaard*, Slotsgade 74, has a solidly traditional setting and offers a Danish lunch plate for 98 kr.

SOUTHERN LANGELAND

Southern Langeland has the island's best beaches, several passage graves and a couple of bird sanctuaries.

Heading south from Rudkøbing, you'll pass a number of small villages. Three km south-east of Lindelse is **Skovsgaard**, a publicly owned estate that contains an old manor house and an organic farm, complete with a windmill and thatched farm buildings. The stable is now a carriage museum with 25 horse-drawn vehicles, ranging from a wedding carriage to farm wagons. The scenic grounds can be strolled for free, while the museum can be entered daily except on Saturday for 18 kr.

A few km away, just south of Kædeby, is **Kong Humbles Grav**, the largest long dolmen on Langeland. Dating from approximately 3000 BC, the barrow is edged with 77 stones, extends 55 metres in length and has a single burial chamber. Its size has given rise to local folklore that a king was buried here, although historians give little credence to the tale. The dolmen is on private property in a field of grain and rapeseed, but visitors are free to walk to the site along a path that begins near the whitewashed Humble church. To get to the dolmen walk north-east from the carpark, which is just past the church, and bear left at the first intersection; follow that trail past the farmhouses, a walk of about 20 minutes each way.

If the vegetation isn't too high you can also see the site from route 305 about 150 metres south of Kædeby; the mounded dolmen is about 800 metres east of the road.

The village of **Humble**, the little commercial centre of southern Langeland, has a bank, a coin laundry, a pizzeria and a 24-hour cash-operated OK Benzin station with the cheapest petrol on the island. Humble is also the turn-off for Ristinge.

Ristinge, a little seaside village with thatched houses, is bordered by a long stretch of sandy beach that's backed by dunes with beach grass and wild roses. Despite being the island's favourite bathing area, Ristinge is pleasantly low-key, its main visitor facility being the camping ground.

At the south end of the island is **Bagenkop**, an attractive fishing village that has a ferry service to Kiel, Germany. Just beyond Bagenkop at the southernmost tip of the island is **Dovns Klint**, an area of 16-metre-high cliffs and pebbly beaches that's popular with bird-watchers during the autumn southern migration. About 500 metres north of the cliffs is **Gulstav Mose**, a marshy bird sanctuary that provides habitat to hawks, herons, ducks, reed buntings and small songbirds. East of the sanctuary is the adjacent woodlands **Gulstav Skov**. All three sites are connected by footpaths. Another area of interest to bird-watchers is **Tryggelev Nor**, a coastal nature reserve with a sighting tower that's midway between Bagenkop and Ristinge.

Places to Stay & Eat The *Ristinge Camping & Feriecenter* (☎ & fax 62 57 13 29), Ristingevej 104, 5932 Humble, a three-star camping ground, is within walking distance of the beach in Ristinge. There are 250 sites at 42 kr per person, four-person cottages for 1700 kr a week, bicycle rentals, a grocery store, cafeteria and hot dog stand. It's open from mid-April to 1 September.

The nearest hotel to Ristinge is the little *Humble Hotel* (☎ 62 57 11 34, fax 62 57 11 24), Ristingevej 2, 5932 Humble, in Humble centre, which has four rooms with private bath for 430/595 kr, breakfast included.

The larger villages, such as Humble and Bagenkop, have bakeries, grocery stores and at least a couple of places where you can stop and get a meal.

Ærø

Well off the beaten track, Ærø is an idyllic island with small villages, rolling hills and patchwork farms. It's a great place to tour by bicycle – the country roads are enhanced by thatched houses and old windmills, and the island has ancient passage graves and dolmens to explore.

Ærø is a popular destination for yachters and each of the three main towns – Ærøskøbing, Marstal and Søby – has a modern marina. Sailing is so popular that, with a total of 800 berths, there are four times as many yacht moorings as there are hotel rooms. Each of the three towns also has a commercial harbour with a ferry service.

GETTING THERE & AWAY
Det Ærøske Færgetrafikselskab operates year-round car ferries to Søby from Faaborg, to Ærøskøbing from Svendborg, and to Marstal from Rudkøbing. All run an average of five times a day, take about an hour and charge 53 kr for adults, 25 kr for children, 15 kr for a bike, 30 kr for a motorbike and 120 kr for a car. If you have a car it's a good idea to make reservations, particularly on weekends and in midsummer – even if you can only call a few hours before the sailing, do so, as the stand-by line at the dock will give priority to those on the waiting list. The phone numbers are: ☎ 62 61 14 88 in Faaborg; ☎ 62 52 10 18 in Svendborg; ☎ 62 53 17 22 in Rudkøbing and ☎ 62 52 40 00 in Ærø.

There is also a ferry (☎ 62 58 17 17)

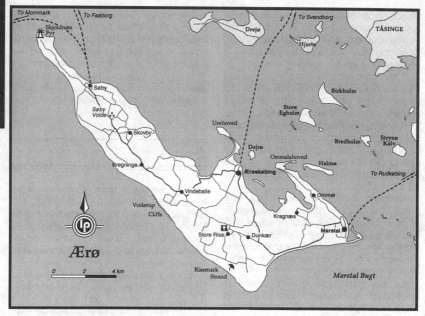

Ærø

0   2   4 km

Marstal Bugt

between Søby and Mommark (in Als on Jutland) which runs daily from April to September and on weekends the rest of the year. The frequency, from two to six times a day, depends upon the season and the day of the week. It takes one hour and has the same fares as the other car ferries.

For information on the passenger ferry between Marstal and Kiel, Germany, see the Getting There & Away chapter.

GETTING AROUND
Bus
Fyns Amt (☎ 66 15 61 62) operates a bus from Marstal to Søby via Ærøskøbing. It runs hourly on weekdays, leaving Marstal at 30 minutes past the hour from 5.30 am to 7.30 pm. It takes about an hour to get from one end of the island to the other. Saturday and Sunday buses are about half as frequent and depart five minutes earlier, with the first bus leaving Marstal at 9.25 am. The best deal is to get a pass for unlimited one-day travel,

which costs 46 kr for adults and 23 kr for children.

Car
Cars can be rented at Q8 Service (☎ 62 53 18 55), Havnen, Marstal, and at Ærø Auto-Center (☎ 62 53 13 02), Skolevej 12, Marstal.

Cycle Routes
There are three signposted cycle routes on Ærø. Cycle route 91 begins at Marstal and continues along the south side of the island up to Søby, while cycle route 90 runs along the north side of the island from Søby to Ærøskøbing and continues as route 92 from Ærøskøbing to Marstal. If you were to make the entire route as a circular tour of the island it would be a distance of about 65 km, a hardy outing considering the island's hilly terrain.

Ærø's tourist offices can provide a free detailed cycling map of the island, which has a brief description of sights along the routes. The county-wide cycle guide and map sold by Cykelnetværk Fyn also covers cycling on Ærø.

Bicycle Rental You can rent bicycles in Ærøskøbing at Pilebækkens Cykelservice (☎ 62 52 11 10), Pilebækken 7, and Den Gamle Isenkram (☎ 62 52 26 27), Søndergade 4; in Marstal at Nørremark Cykelforretning (☎ 62 53 14 77), Møllevejen 77; and in Søby at Søby Cykelforretning (☎ 62 58 18 42), Langebro 4. The camping ground in Ærøskøbing and the island's two hostels also rent bikes. The going rate is 40 kr a day, with a slight discount for longer rentals.

ÆRØSKØBING

A prosperous merchants town in the late 1600s, Ærøskøbing has been preserved in its entirety. Its narrow cobblestone streets are tightly lined with 17th and 18th century houses, many of them are gently listing half-timbered affairs with handblown glass windows, decorative doorways and streetside hollyhocks.

In addition to its engaging historic character, Ærøskøbing has a central location and good accommodation options, which makes it an ideal base for a stay on Ærø.

Information

Tourist Office The Ærøskøbing Turistbureau (☎ 62 52 13 00, fax 62 52 14 36) is in the centre at Torvet, 5970 Ærøskøbing. From 15 June to 31 August it's open Monday to Saturday from 9 am to 5 pm; the rest of the year it's open Monday to Friday from 9 am to 4 pm and on Saturday from 9 am to noon.

Money There's an Amtssparekassen bank at Torvet.

Post The main post office, on the north side of town at Statene 6, is open Monday to Friday from 11 am to 4.30 am and on Saturday from 11 am to 1 pm.

Things to See & Do

In keeping with the town's character, sights are low-key. The main attraction is **Flaskeskibssamlingen**, in the former poorhouse at Smedegade 22. The museum is dedicated to the lifetime work of Peter Jacobsen, a local sailor nicknamed Bottle Peter for the 1700 ships-in-a-bottle he created before dying in 1960 at the age of 86. In addition to the model ships, many of which are in handblown bottles, the museum also contains other local folk art. It's open daily from 10 am to 4 pm. Admission costs 10 kr.

There are two other local museums. The **Ærø Museum**, Brogade 3, has antique furnishings and other historical items including a collection of mid-19th century paintings. It's open daily, except Monday, from 10 am to 3 pm from mid-May to mid-September and from 1 to 3 pm from mid-April to mid-May. Admission is 10 kr.

Hammerichs Hus, a half-timbered house at Gyden 22, has a collection of antiques, china and period furnishings from Funen and Jutland collected by sculptor Gunnar Hammerich. It's open from 11 am to 3 pm from Wednesday to Monday between 1 June and 31 August. Admission is 10 kr. Children pay half price at all three museums.

Otherwise, the main activity is wandering the quaint streets with their tidy houses – it's all a bit like winding the clock back a century or two. The **oldest house** in town, circa 1645, is at Søndergade 36. Other fine streets for strolling are Vestergade and Smedegade; there's a particularly picturesque little house known as the **Dukkehuset** (Doll's House) at Smedegade 37.

Places to Stay

The three-star *Ærøskøbing Campingplads* (☎ 62 52 18 54, fax 62 52 14 36), Sygehusvej 40, 5970 Ærøskøbing, open from 1 May to 30 September, is near a shallow beach just a km from the town centre. The fee is 40 kr per person. Four-person cabins with hot plates and refrigerator cost from 770 to 1155 kr a week, depending on the size. Outside of midsummer, it's possible to book the cabins for weekend stays for 500 kr. There's a kitchen, laundry room, TV lounge and facilities for disabled campers.

The tourist office maintains a list of islanders who rent out rooms in private homes throughout Ærø for 150/200 kr singles/doubles; about half a dozen of the homes are in Ærøskøbing. The office can also book houses, cottages and flats by the week.

The 84-bed hostel, *Ærøskøbing Vandrerhjem* (☎ 62 52 10 44, fax 62 52 16 44), Smedevejen 15, 5970 Ærøskøbing, is 750 metres from the town centre on the road to Marstal. It's open from 1 April to 30 September. Dorm beds cost 65 to 72 kr, while private rooms for one to six people cost between 130 and 432 kr.

Det Lille Hotel (☎ 62 52 23 00), Smedegade 33, 5970 Ærøskøbing, is a cosy family-run hotel on one of the town's most historic streets and it's good value. There are six pleasant rooms with sink and desk for 260/395 kr for singles/doubles, breakfast included. Bathrooms are in the hall.

The timber-framed, 43-room *Hotel Ærøhus* (☎ 62 52 10 03, fax 62 52 21 23), Vestergade 38, 5970 Ærøskøbing, has an old-fashioned character right down to the creaky hallways and fine china at the breakfast table. Singles/doubles cost 240/405 kr for rooms with shared bath, 430/640 kr for those with private bath. Breakfast is included. The hotel is part of the Dansk Kroferie association and accepts 'Inn Cheques'. (See the Hotel Schemes information in the Accommodation section in the Facts for the Visitor chapter.)

Places to Eat

On Vestergade, just west of the ferry dock, you'll find a small grocery store and a number of places to eat. The *Ærø Burger Bar* at Vestergade 41 serves simple fare including ice cream, burgers, hot dogs, and chicken or fish with chips. For fancier ice cream, there's *Vaffelbageriet* at Vestergade 21, which specialises in fresh-baked waffle cones. There's a bakery in the town centre at Vestergade 62, just a block north of Torvet.

In summer, you can sit outside on the main square at *Torve-Caféen*, Torvet 7, and have pastries, light meals and a glass of beer or wine – there's music from 8.30 pm.

Det Lille Hotel, in a former sea captain's house at Smedegade 33, has a small restaurant with reasonably priced dinners, such as chicken with salad and chips, from around 50 kr.

The *Hotel Ærøhus*, Vestergade 38, has a pleasant dining room with a moderately expensive menu of Danish food. For the best value choose from the daily two-course specials for 95 kr or from the light-eats menu which has some filling dishes such as fish fillet and potatoes for around 60 kr.

MARSTAL

Marstal, at the eastern end of the island, is Ærø's most modern-looking town though it too has a nautical character with a maritime museum, shipyard and yacht harbour.

While Marstal is a quiet place today, until the 19th century it was one of the region's busiest harbours, with more than 300 merchant ships pulling into port annually. The sea was such an integral part of people's lives that even the gravestones at the seaman's church on Kirkestræde are engraved with maritime epitaphs, the most frequently quoted being 'Here lies Christen Hansen at anchor with his wife; he will not weigh until summoned by God.'

There's a reasonably good beach, half sandy and half rocky, on the south side of town, about a 15-minute walk from the centre.

Information

Tourist Office The Marstal Turistbureau (☎ 62 53 19 60, fax 62 53 30 35), Havnegade 5, 5960 Marstal, is a five-minute walk south of the harbour. From mid-June to August it's open Monday to Friday from 10 am to 5 pm and on Saturday from 10 am to 3 pm; in July it's also open on Sunday from 10 am to noon. Low-season hours are Monday to Friday from 9 am to 4 pm.

Money There's an Amtssparekassen bank on

Kongensgade 28, the road that runs west from the harbour.

Post The post office, at Havnegade 1, is open Monday to Friday from 11 am to 5 pm and on Saturday from 11 am to 1 pm.

Laundry Ærø Mønt-og Færdigvask is a self-service coin laundry at Kirkestræde 39.

Marstal Søfartsmuseum
The Marstal Søfartsmuseum, on the corner of Havnegade and Prinsensgade, has a collection of maritime paraphernalia including paintings and models of some of the schooners and brigs that filled the town harbour during its heyday. It's open daily from 9 am to at least 5 pm in summer and on weekdays from 10 am to 4 pm the rest of the year. Admission is 25 kr.

Places to Stay
The three-star *Marstal Camping* (☎ 62 53 36 00), Egehovedvej 1, 5960 Marstal, is behind the yacht harbour, a km south of the ferry harbour. The camping ground occupies a quiet grassy area just minutes from the water. It's open from 1 April to 1 October. The camping cost is 41 kr per person, and there are also cabins for rent from 770 to 1155 kr a week.

The 82-bed hostel, *Marstal Vandrerhjem* (☎ 62 53 10 64, fax 62 53 10 57), Færgestræde 29, 5960 Marstal, is in a renovated municipal office on the corner of Havnegade and Færgestræde. It's a good central location, 500 metres south of the ferry harbour and within walking distance to restaurants and the beach. Dorm beds cost 74 kr, while private rooms for one to four people cost from 148 to 296 kr. It's open from 1 May to 1 September.

The *Hotel Marstal* (☎ 62 53 13 52), Dronningestræde 1A, 5960 Marstal, just a few minutes walk south-west of the harbour, has six simple rooms above a restaurant, all with shared bath for 250/350 kr for singles/doubles, breakfast included.

An alternative place to stay is *Biokol* (☎ 62 53 18 12), 5960 Marstal, a small organic farm commune in Kragnæs, a few km west of Marstal, which allows travellers to stay in exchange for working on the farm.

Places to Eat
At the ferry harbour there's a small food shop and a grill restaurant with inexpensive burgers, pizza and other simple eats.

For something a little more substantial, the restaurant at the *Hotel Marstal*, Dronningestræde 1A, has a varied menu, ranging from half a chicken with salad and chips for 48 kr to steak dishes for around 100 kr. There's also a daily special that includes soup and a main dish for 75 kr.

There's a bakery west of the tourist office at Prinsensgade 11 and a *Super Brugsen* grocery store with a deli and good produce and wine sections on the corner of Kirkestræde and Skovgyden about 300 metres west of the ferry harbour.

For cheap beers, head for *Minde* at Kongensgade 13, about 100 metres west of the ferry harbour.

STORE RISE
The village of Store Rise, at the island's centre, has an attractive church that dates from medieval times, although much of the current structure is from the 17th century. The churchyard is surrounded by a medieval circular wall and contains graves that are separated from each other by hedges. The church interior includes an ornately carved altar from the late gothic period.

In the field behind the church is **Tingstedet**, a 54-metre-long Neolithic passage grave that is thought to be at least 5000 years old. The cup-like markings in the largest stone near the church indicate the grave may have belonged to a fertility cult. The footpath from the church is marked and it takes only a few minutes to get there.

A couple km south of the village is **Risemark Strand**, the best of Ærø's few sandy beaches.

SØBY
Søby has a shipyard, which is the island's biggest employer, a sizeable fishing fleet and

a popular yacht harbour. It's a pleasant enough place with some thatched houses but the town doesn't pack the same charm as Ærøskøbing and most of its visitors are yachters.

Five km beyond Søby, at Ærø's northern tip, is **Skjoldnæs Fyr**, a 19th century granite-block lighthouse with a narrow stairway that you can climb for 4 kr to admire the seaview at the top. A few minutes walk beyond the lighthouse is a pebble beach.

Søby Volde, the mounded-over earthen ramparts that once were part of an 12th century fortress, are along the main cross-island road, about three km south of Søby. The hilltop site offers a good vista of western Ærø with its fields, windmills and distant ocean view.

Information

Tourist Office In summer, a branch tourist office (☎ 62 58 13 88) is open at Søby harbour weekdays from 10 am to 4 pm.

Post The post office, at Havnevejen 19, is open Monday to Friday from noon to 4.30 pm and on Saturday from 11 am to 1 pm.

Places to Stay & Eat

Søby Camping (☎ 62 58 14 70), Vitsø 10, 5985 Søby, a small two-star facility about a km west of town, is open from 1 May to 15 September. The fee is 36 kr per person. There are caravans for hire at 800 kr weekly.

The town has two small hostelries, each with half a dozen guest rooms with shared bath. *Larsen's Pensionat & Café* (☎ 62 58 27 00), Havnevejen 12, 5985 Søby, charges 185/310 kr for singles/doubles, while *Søby Kro* (☎ 62 58 10 06), Østerbro 2, 5985 Søby, charges 150/280 kr.

Finn's Bageri, Nørrebro 2, has fresh bread and pastries from 6.30 am. *Cafeteria Øen*, at the yacht harbour, has sandwiches, light meals, coffee, beer and wine. You can get Danish-style meals at the *Søby Kro*.

Southern Jutland

The Jutland (Danish: Jylland) peninsula, the only part of Denmark connected to the European mainland, was originally settled by the Jutes, a Germanic tribe whose forays included invading England in the 5th century.

Jutland's southern boundary has long been a fluid one. It was last redrawn in 1920, when Germany returned part of the Schleswig region to Denmark following a postwar plebiscite on self-determination.

Southern Jutland has a few well-preserved historic towns, the most notable of which is Ribe. However, many southerly towns tend to be modern and nondescript, in part due to the destruction unleashed during the border wars with Germany.

As is the case throughout Jutland, the bulk of the land is given over to fields and pastures, with only sporadic patches of woodland. The east coast of southern Jutland is cut by deep fjords while the west coast is bordered by marshland and moors.

ESBJERG

Esbjerg, the youngest city in Denmark, owes its rise to the territorial losses that beleaguered Denmark in the 19th century. Following the loss of the Schleswig and Holstein regions to Germany in 1864, farmers in Jutland suddenly needed a new export harbour for shipping grain to England. To serve that purpose the coastal town of Esbjerg was founded in 1868, on a site that had previously been farmland.

Esbjerg's port opened in 1874 and within only a few decades the town's population had grown to nearly 20,000. It's now Denmark's fifth largest city, the centre of Denmark's North Sea oil activities and the country's largest fishing harbour. Witness to the latter is sometimes found in the fishy odour that wafts up from the harbour on warm, breezy days.

Although Esbjerg has its fair share of turn-of-the-century buildings, it lacks the intrigue

HIGHLIGHTS

- Ribe, Denmark's oldest and best preserved town
- Quaint Møgeltønder village and its lavish church
- The island of Rømø, a haven for windsurfers
- Denmark's largest folk music festival held in Tønder each August
- Sønderborg with its seaside castle and 1864 battlefield sites
- The unspoiled island of Fanø

found in the medieval quarters of other Danish cities and isn't on the itinerary of most travellers unless they're heading by ferry to or from the UK.

Orientation

Torvet, the city square where Skolegade and Torvegade intersect, is bordered by cafés, a bank, the post office and the tourist office. The railway and bus stations are about 300 metres east of Torvet, while the ferry terminal is one km south. Trains that meet the ferries continue down to the harbour.

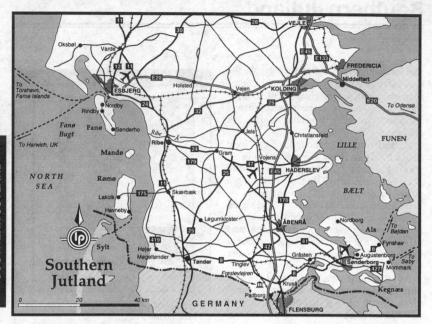

Information

Tourist Office The Esbjerg Turistkontor (☎ 75 12 55 99, fax 75 12 27 67), Skolegade 33, 6700 Esbjerg, is open from 9 am to 5 pm Monday to Saturday, except in the low season when it closes at 1 pm on Saturday.

Money There are many banks in the centre, including a Den Danske Bank on Torvet, south of the post office. A Unibank and a Jyske Bank can be found around the corner on Kongensgade.

Post The post office, at Torvet, is open Monday to Friday from 9 am to 5 pm (9 am to 5.30 pm on Thursdays) and on Saturdays from 9 am to noon.

Newspapers & Magazines There's a good newsstand in the Midt-I shopping centre, at the intersection of Kongensgade and Torvet, which carries the *International Herald-Tribune*, the *Observer*, the *European*, *USA Today* and other foreign newspapers.

Library The library, at Nørregade 19, has a reading room with foreign newspapers and magazines and is open Monday to Friday from 10 am to 7 pm and from 10 am to 2 pm on Saturday.

Laundry There's a coin laundry on the corner of Danmarksgade and Englandsgade.

Pharmacy Krone Apoteket, at Kongensgade 36, is open 24 hours a day.

Things to See & Do

There are a few local museums to explore, or you could pick up a walking-tour map at the tourist office and stroll along a route that traces Esbjerg's architectural development, unassuming as it is. Opposite the tourist office, in the centre of Torvet, stands a **statue**

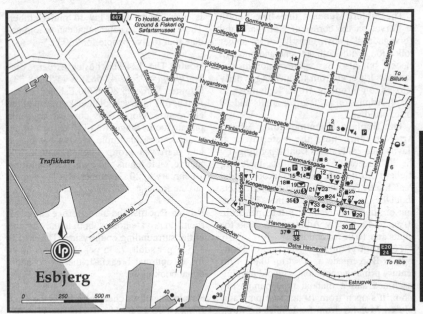

Esbjerg

0   250   500 m

Trafikhavn

SOUTHERN JUTLAND

PLACES TO STAY			
8	Park Hotel		
14	Hotel Britannia		
16	Hotel Bell-inn		
18	Hotel Ansgar		
25	Cab-Inn		

PLACES TO EAT	
4	Café Biografen
10	Netto Grocery Store
11	Bakery
17	Restaurant Munkestuen
22	Café Chr Ix
23	Flannigan's
26	Italiano Express

27	Jensen's Bøfhus
28	Café Bageriet
29	English Pub
31	Droob Supermarket
33	McDonald's
34	Peking Grill
36	Føtex Supermarket

OTHER	
1	Police Station
2	Esbjerg Museum
3	Library
5	Bus Station
6	Railway Station
7	Coin Laundry
9	Avis Car Rental

12	Tourist Office
13	Hertz Car Rental
15	Public Toilets
19	Post Office
20	Den Danske Bank
21	Torvet
24	Midt-I Shopping Centre
30	Bogtrykmuseet
32	Krone Apoteket
35	Unibank
37	Esbjerg Vandtårn
38	Esbjerg Kunstmuseum
39	Ferries To England & The Faroe Islands
40	Ferry To Fanø
41	Lightship

of King Christian IX, who reigned in 1899 when Esbjerg obtained its municipal charter.

The **Esbjerg Vandtårn** (Esbjerg Water-tower), two blocks south of Torvet at Havnegade 22, was erected in 1897 by town architect CH Clausen who incorporated medieval features in an attempt to give Esbjerg a more historic look. For a view of the city and harbour, you can climb the tower (10 kr) from 10 am to 4 pm daily in summer and on Saturday and Sunday in the low season.

The **Esbjerg Museum**, three blocks north of Torvet on the corner of Nørregade and Torvegade, is known mostly for its amber collection, with both ancient and modern pieces, but also has some minor history exhibits. It's open from 10 am to 4 pm daily (closed on Monday from September to May). Admission is 20 kr for adults and 10 kr for children.

The **Esbjerg Kunstmuseum** (Esbjerg Art Museum), near the watertower at Havnegade 20, features Danish paintings by the 20th century COBRA artists, including Richard Mortensen, Robert Jacobsen and Per Kirkeby (See the Arts section in the Facts about the Country chapter for more information on this art movement.). It's open from 10 am to 4 pm daily. Admission is 20 kr for adults and 10 kr for children.

The **Bogtrykmuseet** (Museum of Printing), at Borgergade 6, is set up like a 19th century printing operation, with old printing machines and a manual type composing room. It's open from 10 am to 4 pm daily (closed Monday from September to May). Admission is 15 kr for adults and 8 kr for children.

The **Fiskeri-og Søfartsmuseet** (Museum of Fishing & Shipping) at Tarphagevej, four km north-west of the city centre, has an aquarium with 50 species of fish, an outdoor seal pool (feeding times at 11 am and 2.30 pm) and various fisheries exhibits. It's open daily from 10 am to 8 pm in summer, from 10 am to 6 pm in spring and autumn and from 10 am to 4 pm in winter. Admission costs 40 kr for adults and 20 kr for children. Take bus No 3, 6 or 11.

There's also an old wooden **lightship** down at the harbour that can be visited for 10 kr between 10 am and 4 pm daily from May to September.

Places to Stay

Camping The one-star *Ådalens Camping* (☎ 75 15 88 22, fax 75 13 93 74), Gudenåvej 20, 6710 Esbjerg, five km north of the city via route 447 or bus No 2, is the nearest camping ground. It charges 35 kr per person, has cooking facilities and a coin laundry, and

is open from mid-May to mid-October. There are also 16 cabins that can accommodate four to five people for 200 kr.

Hostel The 124-bed hostel *Esbjerg Vandrerhjem* (☎ 75 12 42 58, fax 75 13 68 33), Gammel Vardevej 80, 6700 Esbjerg, is in a former folk high school three km north of the city centre. Dorm beds cost 80 kr, while private rooms range from 150 kr for a single to 300 kr for a quadruple. Meals are available and there's a group kitchen, sauna, TV lounge, table tennis and gym. It's open from 1 February to 20 December. Bus No 4 stops out the front.

Private Rooms The tourist office can book rooms in private homes, both in the city and in the surrounding countryside. The cost is 125 kr per adult, 75 kr per child, plus 30 kr for an optional breakfast; there's no additional booking fee.

Hotels The city's cheapest hotel is the *Park Hotel* (☎ 75 12 08 68), Torvegade 31, 6700 Esbjerg, two blocks north of Torvet, which has seven small and simple rooms with shared bath at 250/440 kr for singles/doubles. Rates are higher if you want breakfast.

Just a few hundred yards east is the 30-room *Hotel Bell-Inn* (☎ 75 12 01 22, fax 75 13 16 40), Skolegade 45, 6700 Esbjerg, which has some pleasant rooms with shared bath for 325/490 kr, including a light breakfast. Check the rooms first, as they're not all the same.

A *Cab-Inn* hotel (☎ 75 18 16 00, fax 75 18 16 24), a member of the Copenhagen chain, has recently opened at Skolegade 14, 6700 Esbjerg. Rooms have the usual Cab-Inn amenities, including a bathroom, phone and TV, and cost 395/480 kr for singles/doubles – a good price for Esbjerg if you're looking for a modern room with private bath. Breakfast is available for an extra 40 kr.

A popular mid-range choice is the *Hotel Ansgar* (☎ 75 12 82 44, fax 75 13 95 40), Skolegade 36, 6700 Esbjerg, which has a good central location and comfortable singles/doubles from 475/680 kr with private bath. There are also a couple of singles with shared bath for 350 kr. A good breakfast is included. The hotel is a member of the Dansk Kroferie association.

The *Hotel Britannia* (☎ 75 13 01 11, fax 75 45 20 85), Torvet, 6700 Esbjerg, is a modern Best Western affiliated hotel in the centre of the city. All 79 rooms have private bath, minibar, phone, and TV with video; the hotel has a pub, two restaurants and conference facilities. Standard rates, which include breakfast, are 700/840 kr for singles/doubles, but there's a weekend and summer rate of 630/650 kr.

Places to Eat

Kongensgade Restaurants, cafeterias and grocery stores can be found east of Torvet on Kongensgade, the main pedestrian shopping street. The friendly *Café Bageriet*, a bakery a couple of blocks south of the railway station at Kongensgade 7, is a good place to get cheap coffee and pastries if you're stumbling off an early-morning train.

The dark-wood *English Pub* at Kongensgade 10 is, as billed, an English-style pub complete with darts, a pool table and live TV broadcasts of British football. In addition to more than 50 types of beer (including English, Irish and Scottish brews on tap), the pub also offers English snacks such as steak & kidney pies (18 kr).

Jensen's Bøfhus, a chain steakhouse restaurant at Kongensgade 8, has a good-value steak lunch for 34 kr served weekdays from 11 am to 4 pm. At other times grilled chicken and steak dishes begin at about double that price. Around the corner on Englandsgade 23 is *Italiano Express* with both eat-in and takeaway pizza (delivery available within five km of the city centre).

The *Droob* supermarket on the corner of Kongensgade and Englandsgade has a cafeteria with cheap eats, including two hot dogs with chips for 22 kr and a daily meal for 30 kr. The *Midt-I* shopping centre on Kongensgade and Torvet has a konditori-style bakery and a cafeteria. There's a *McDonald's* on Kongensgade 40, opposite

the south side of Torvet. *Peking Grill*, next to McDonald's, has takeaway Chinese meals for around 35 kr.

Torvet There are two pleasant and rather large restaurants on the east side of Torvet; despite their size both manage to maintain a café-like atmosphere and on warm summer days both set out tables on Torvet. *Café Chr IX* has cappuccino, croissants, sandwiches, pizza and pasta, while the adjacent *Flannigan's* has a more Danish menu. At either place you can get sandwiches for around 30 kr and hot dishes for about double that.

Elsewhere in Esbjerg *Biblioteks Caféen*, the cafeteria in the public library at Nørregade 19, has inexpensive food, including good salads and a 15 kr soup and bread combo.

Opposite the library at Finsensgade 1 is the *Café Biografen*, which has sandwiches, light dishes, cakes, coffee and beer.

Restaurant Munkestuen, a cosy upmarket restaurant in a century-old building at Smedegade 21, has reasonably priced salads, light dishes and traditional Danish lunches as well as more expensive fish and meat courses.

Føtex, a modern supermarket near the harbour, at the intersection of Havnegade and Kronprinsensgade, has a simple family restaurant with a Wiener schnitzel, salad and chips plate for 35 kr and a children's burger and chips plate for 20 kr.

There's another bakery and a *Netto* grocery store in the centre on Skolegade, just east of the tourist office, and a *DSB Restaurant* at the railway station.

Entertainment

Café Biografen (☎ 75 45 09 22) at Finsensgade 1 is a popular student haunt with live music – commonly jazz, blues or rock – and a cover charge ranging from free to around 30 kr, depending on the band.

The *English Pub* (☎ 75 45 40 60) at Kongensgade 10 has live music – often Irish or Scottish folk musicians – a few times weekly. *Café Chr IX* on Torvet sometimes has music in the evening as well.

Getting There & Away
Esbjerg is 77 km north-west of Tønder, 59 km south-west of Billund and 92 km west of the Funen-Jutland bridge.

Air Maersk Air operates seven flights daily between Esbjerg and Copenhagen. The normal one-way fare is 705 kr. For information on stand-by and discounted return tickets, see the Getting Around chapter.

There are flights from Esbjerg to the UK cities of Aberdeen, Edinburgh and Manchester via Business Air, which can be booked through Mærsk Air.

Train High-speed IC trains depart from Esbjerg for Copenhagen (4½ hours, 189 kr) every two hours on weekdays, from 5.15 am to 7.28 pm; the trains are less frequent on weekends. There's also an overnight sleeper train that departs from Esbjerg for Copenhagen each day at 25 minutes after midnight. In addition, there are hourly regional trains between Esbjerg and Fredericia (70 minutes, 65 kr), where you can change to an IC train running between Århus and Copenhagen.

There's also a train service that runs north to Struer (2¼ hours, 106 kr) and south to Ribe (35 minutes, 30 kr) and Tønder (1½ hours, 59 kr).

Car & Motorbike If you're driving into Esbjerg, the E20, the main expressway from the east, leads directly into the heart of the city and down to the ferry harbour. If you're coming from the south, route 24 merges with the E20 on the outskirts of the city. From the north, route 12 makes a beeline into the city ending at the harbour.

There's a Hertz car rental office (☎ 75 12 60 88) at the Hotel Brittania and an Avis office (☎ 75 13 44 77) at Skolegade 15. Both also have booths at the airport, but there's a hefty surcharge on airport rentals.

Boat For details of ferry services to the UK and the Faroe Islands see the Getting There

& Away chapter. For information on boats to Fanø, see the following Fanø Getting There & Away section.

Getting Around
To/From the Airport The airport is nine km east of the city centre. A public bus runs about once an hour between the two.

Bus Most city buses can be boarded at the stop on the north side of the railway station. The cost is 10 kr per ride, or you can buy a 68 kr card good for 10 rides.

Car & Motorbike There's free central parking with a two-hour limit west of the Hotel Brittania (enter from Danmarksgade) and free parking with no time limit at the carpark on Nørregade east of the library.

Bicycle Bikes can be hired from Skrænten Cycle Hire (☎ 75 45 75 05), at Skrænten and Kirkegade, at the north side of town.

FANØ
Fanø, just 15 minutes by ferry from Esbjerg, is a long flat island with a landscape dominated by heathland, dunes and broad sandy beaches. The two main villages, at opposite ends of the island, are Nordby and Sønderho, both of which have narrow streets and attractive period houses.

The best beaches are on the exposed north-western side of the island in the area around Fanø Bad and Rindby Strand. At the north side of Fanø Bad is Soren Jemsens Sand, a three-km-long sand spit that can be explored on foot, while the packed-sand beach extending to the south is open to both pedestrians and cars. Windsurfers take to the beach south of Rindby Strand.

Fanø has attempted to hold onto its traditions more strongly than other parts of Denmark. As recently as the 1960s, some of Fanø's elderly women still wore the traditional island costume, which consisted of multiple skirts and a scarf that could be folded down as a face mask to protect against blowing sand. During island festivals, such as the Fannikerdage which takes place in

A Cunning Deal

Until 1741 the island of Fanø was crown property, but when King Christian VI, who was undertaking construction projects across Denmark, found the royal coffers running dry he decided to sell it. He put the island up for auction, much to the chagrin of the Fanø natives, who were convinced that wealthy Ribe merchants would purchase it and impose hefty taxes.

According to one oft-told story, on the eve of the auction, Fanø's attractive young women lured the would-be bidders to a night of drink and merriment and, while they were distracted, wound the men's watches back an hour. When the auction took place the next morning at 8 am, only a contingent of Fanø islanders and a single lord from Tønder appeared. The Tønder lord was forcibly squeezed behind a door by a crowd of Fanø men, and the Fanø islanders put in the sole bid.

This bit of local lore aside, history does record that the Fanø islanders were able to piece together enough money to buy their island from the crown. Along with the land, the deed also bestowed the right to own and build ships and in the next 150 years nearly a thousand sailing vessels were constructed on Fanø. ■

Nordby in early July, you can see these costumes being worn and enjoy local folk music and dancing.

Information

Tourist Office The Fanø Turistbureau (☎ 75 16 26 00, fax 75 16 29 03), Havnepladsen, Nordby, 6720 Fanø, is at the ferry harbour in Nordby. From early June to early September it's open Monday to Friday from 8.30 am to 6 pm, on Saturday from 9 am to 5 pm on Sunday from 9 am to 7 pm. In the low season it's open Monday to Friday from 8.30 am to 5.30 pm and on Saturday from 9 am to 1 pm.

Money In Nordby there's a Den Danske Bank at Hovedgaden 74 and a Fanø Spare-og Lannekasse bank at Hovedgaden 51.

Post The post office, Hovedgaden 15, Nordby, is open Monday to Friday from 10 am to 5 pm and on Saturday from 10 am to noon.

Things to See & Do

Fanø has a surprising number of local sights.

In Nordby, 200 metres west of the tourist office at Hovedgaden 28, there's the **Fanø Skibsfarts-og Dragtsamling**, a museum of ship models, maritime displays and local costumes. The **Fanø Museum**, 300 metres to the east on the corner of Skolevej and Hovedgaden, is another local history museum, this one concentrating on period furnishings.

In Sønderho's centre, within a few minutes walk of each other, there's a small art museum, the **Fanø Kunstmuseum**, which features paintings of Fanø; **Hannes Hus**, a 17th century sea captain's home, complete with period décor; and the 18th century church **Sønderho Kirke**, known for its 14 votive ships. Half a km north of Sønderho centre, on the road to Nordby, is a picturesque century-old **windmill**.

Most of the sights on Fanø are seasonal; the hours fluctuate a bit, but all are open afternoons in summer. Admission to the church is free; the other sights cost 10 kr, except for the art museum which is 15 kr.

The centre of the island, midway between Nordby and Sønderho, has a 1162-hectare wooded area called **Fanø Kiltplantage** that is crisscrossed with walking trails and provides habitat for deer, rabbits and birds.

Places to Stay

There are nine camping grounds on Fanø, most of which have cabins for rent in addition to tent and caravan sites. About a km north of Nordby is *Tempo Camping* (☎ 75 16 22 51), Strandvejen 34, Nordby, 6720 Fanø, which is open from mid-May to mid-September. If you prefer to be closer to the beach, *Feldberg Strand Camping* (☎ 75 16

24 90, fax 75 16 33 33), Rindby Strand, 6720 Fanø, is within walking distance of Rindby Strand and is open from mid-April to mid-September. *Camping Klitten* (☎ & fax 75 16 40 65), Sønderho Strandvej 3, Sønderho, 6720 Fanø, at the northern outskirts of Sønderho, is open all year round. All three have group kitchens, coin laundries and fees of 37 kr per person.

The cheapest of the island's handful of hotels is the 12-room *Kellers Hotel* (☎ 75 16 30 88), Strandvejen 48, 6720 Fanø, north of Nordby on the beach road. Singles/doubles start at 200/300 kr with shared bath, 275/375 kr with private bath, breakfast included. It's open from late March to late October.

For an intimate upmarket place to stay there's the *Sønderho Kro* (☎ 75 16 40 09), Kropladsen 11, Sønderho, 6720 Fanø, a small inn that dates from 1722. It's a member of the Relais & Chateaux chain and has eight rooms with private bath from 540 to 1090 kr.

The *Danland Feriehotel Vesterhavet* (☎ 75 16 32 77, fax 75 16 61 04), Fanø Bad, 6720 Fanø, a three-storey resort complex right on the beach, has 146 flats that cost 625 to 835 kr a day in midsummer, less in the low season.

For information on booking summer holiday homes, contact the tourist office.

Places to Eat
There are bakeries and simple cafés in Nordby, Fanø Bad and Sønderho. The *Tempo Center* near Tempo Camping, at Strandvejen 27 in Nordby, has a supermarket, coin laundry and amusement arcade – a potentially convenient combo!

The *Danland Feriehotel Vesterhavet*, on the beach at Fanø Bad, has a café with fish & chips, lasagne and similar fare for around 40 kr and a *Den Grimme Ælling* restaurant that features an all-you-can-eat buffet for 70 kr at lunch, 100 kr at dinner.

The *Sønderho Kro*, at Kropladsen 11 in Sønderho, has an expensive restaurant with traditional Danish décor and food.

Getting There & Away
DSB (☎ 75 13 45 00 on Fanø, 75 12 00 00

in Esbjerg) shuttles a car ferry between Nordby and Esbjerg from early morning to after midnight, departing two to three times an hour in the middle of the day. The return fare is 22 kr for adults, 11 kr for children, 70 kr for a motorbike with driver and 240 kr for a car with up to five passengers.

Getting Around
Bus There's a local bus service from the ferry dock that runs about every 40 minutes in summer, connecting Nordby with Fanø Bad (10 kr), Rindby Strand (10 kr) and Sønderho (15 kr).

Bicycle Bicycles can be hired in Nordby from Havnekiosken (☎ 75 16 21 20), the kiosk next to the tourist office, and from Fanø Cykelhandel (☎ 75 16 25 13) at Hovedgaden 96. Fanø Cykelhandel also has branches at Rindby and Fanø Bad.

RIBE
Ribe, the oldest town in Denmark, is full of historic sites. Recent excavations, which unearthed a number of silver coins, indicate that a market town existed on the north side of the Ribe Å (Ribe River) as far back as 700 AD. In 850, Saint Ansgar built the first church in Ribe and the town began to grow. During the Viking era, Ribe, linked to the sea by its river, flourished as a centre of trade between the Frankish Empire and the Scandinavian states to the north.

In the 12th century the Valdemar dynasty fortified the town, building a castle and establishing Ribe as one of the king's Jutland residences.

In the late medieval period, as power shifted to eastern Denmark, Ribe's importance declined. A sweeping fire in 1580 devastated much of the town and in the century that followed the incessant wars with Sweden strangled trade and further impoverished Ribe. Meanwhile the Ribe Å silted up and the town's population dropped off. With the founding of the port city of Esbjerg in 1868, Ribe was completely bypassed.

Ironically, in terms of preservation, Ribe's economic misfortunes have served to spare

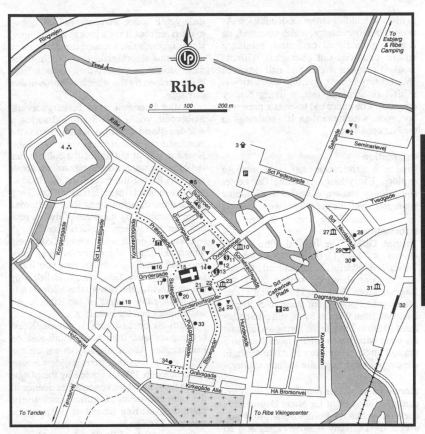

PLACES TO STAY		9	Pinocchio Pizzeria	15	Ribe Domkirke
		12	Vægterkælderen	17	Old Grammar School
3	Ribe Vandrerhjem	19	Firenze Pizzeria	20	Hans Tausens Hus
12	Hotel Dagmar &	25	Rådhus Conditoriet	22	Den Gamle Rådhus
	Vægterkælderen			23	Ribe Legetøjsmuseum
16	Backhaus	**OTHER**		24	Memorial Tablet
18	Hotel Sønderjylland			26	Sct Catharinæ Kirke
21	Den Gamle Arrest	2	Coin Laundry	27	Ribe Kunstmuseum
		4	Riberhus Slotsbanke	28	Library
PLACES TO EAT		5	Flood Column	29	Post Office
		7	House Built In 1580	30	Cinema
1	Kvickly Supermarket	10	Quedens Gaard	31	Ribes Vikinger
6	Sælhunden	11	Den Danske Bank	32	Railway Station
8	Weis Stue (Restaurant	13	Tourist Office	33	Tårnborg Manor House
	& Guest Rooms)	14	Torvet	34	Puggaard

its historic buildings from modernisation. As a result the town centre, which surrounds an imposing medieval cathedral, retains a unique centuries-old character. With its crooked cobbled streets and half-timbered 16th century houses, ambling about Ribe is a bit like stepping into a living history museum. The entire old town is a preservation zone, with more than 100 buildings in the National Trust.

Orientation

Ribe is a tightly clustered place, easy to explore. Everything, including the hostel and railway station, is within a 10-minute walk of Torvet, the central square.

Information

Tourist Office The helpful Ribe Turistbureau (☎ 75 42 15 00, fax 75 42 40 78), Torvet 3, 6760 Ribe, is conveniently located on the central square beside the Hotel Dagmar. From 15 June to 31 August it's open Monday to Friday from 9 am to 5.30 pm, Saturday from 9 am to 5 pm, and on Sunday from 10 am to 2 pm. In the spring and autumn it's open Monday to Friday from 9 am to 5 pm and on Saturday from 10 am to 1 pm. In winter, weekday hours are slightly shorter.

Money There's a Den Danske Bank on Overdammen, just east of the Hotel Dagmar. It's open on weekdays from 9.30 am to 4 pm, except on Thursday when it closes at 5.30 pm.

Post The Ribe post office, at Sct Nicolajgade 12, is open Monday to Friday from 10 am to 5 pm and on Saturday from 10 am to noon.

Laundry There's a coin laundry at the Kvickly supermarket at Seminarievej 1.

Walking Tour

You can make an enjoyable loop route of central Ribe's historic sights in a walk that takes a couple of leisurely hours.

The walk begins at Torvet and follows Overdammen east to Fiskergade. On Fisker-

gade you'll notice many **alleys** leading east to the riverfront. Take a look at the 'bumper' stones on the house corners; the alleys are so narrow that the original residents installed these stones to protect their houses from being scraped by the wheels of horse-drawn carriages.

At the intersection of Fiskergade and Skibbroen, you'll find Stormflodssøjlen, a wooden **flood column** which marks the numerous floods that have swept over Ribe. Note the ring at the top of the column that indicates the water's depth (six metres above normal!) during the record-setting flood of 1634 which claimed hundreds of lives. While these days low-lying Ribe is afforded more protection by a system of dykes, residents are still subject to evacuation.

Continue north-west along Skibbroen, which skirts the old medieval quay, now lined with small motorboats. Here you'll also find the *Johanne Dan*, an old sailing ship designed with a flat bottom that allowed it to sail the shallow waters of the Ribe Å; it's sometimes open for boarding.

From Skibbroen turn south on Korsbrødregade and then head south-east on Præstegade. About halfway down on the right, you'll pass this street's oldest house, constructed in 1580, as noted by the plaque above the door; it was once the residence of the cathedral curate. Continue back to the **cathedral**, skirting around its western side and onto Skolegade.

On the corner of Skolegade and Grydergade is an **old grammar school** that first opened in the early 16th century. On the opposite side of Skolegade is the two-storey **Hans Tausens Hus**, which dates from the early 17th century and is Denmark's oldest bishops' residence.

From Skolegade continue south on Puggårdsgade, a cobbled street lined with older homes. The timber-framed brick house on the corner of Sønderportsgade and Puggårdsgade has an interesting 2nd storey which overhangs the road. A couple of buildings down on the left is **Tårnborg**, a 16th century manor house that now serves as a local government office. On the same side of the street, but a little farther south, is a half-timbered house dating to 1550.

When you reach Gravsgade go right for about 50 metres and along the north side of the street you'll come to the brick **Puggaard**, a canon's residence that was constructed around 1400. From there turn around and go east on Gravsgade and then turn north on Bispegade.

On the corner of Bispegade and Sønderportsgade, you'll find a **memorial tablet** to Maren Spliid, who was burned at the stake on 9 November 1641, a victim of witch-hunt persecutions.

From that corner continue north past **den gamle rådhus** (the old town hall) and back to your starting point at Torvet, where you can finish off your walk with a frosty beer or an ice cream.

Ribe Domkirke

The town's dominant landmark, Ribe Cathedral, stands as a fine testament to Ribe's prominent past. The diocese of Ribe was founded in 948, but its original cathedral was a modest wooden building. In 1150, Ribe's Bishop Elias, with the financial backing of the royal family, began work on a more stately stone structure.

The new cathedral was constructed primarily of tufa, a soft porous rock, quarried near Cologne and shipped north along the Rhine River. It took a century for the work to reach completion. Although later additions added a number of gothic features, the core of the cathedral remains decidedly Romanesque, a fine example of medieval Rhineland influences.

One notable feature is the original 'Cat's Head' door at the south portal of the transept, which has detailed relief work, including a triangular pediment portraying King Valdemar II and Queen Dagmar positioned at the foot of Jesus and Mary. At noon and 3 pm the church bell plays the notes to a folk song about Queen Dagmar's death during childbirth.

The cathedral's interior décor is a hodgepodge of later influences. Among the highlights are an organ whose facade was designed by the renowned 17th century sculptor Jens Olufsen and an ornate altar created in 1597 by Odense sculptor Jens Asmussen. You can find frescoes dating from the 16th century along the north side of the cathedral, while in the apse are modern-day frescoes, stained-glass windows and seven mosaics created in the 1980s by artist Carl-Henning Pedersen.

For a towering view of the countryside, climb 27 metres up the cathedral tower, which dates from 1333. A survey of surrounding marshland makes it easy to understand why the tower once doubled as a lookout station for floods. It's open June to August from 10 am to 6 pm, in May and September from 10 am to 5 pm and during the rest of the year from 11 am to 3 pm (on Sunday and holidays it opens at noon). The admission of 5 kr for adults, 1 kr for children, covers both the cathedral and the tower.

Sct Catharinæ Kirke

Sct Catharinæ Kirke (St Catherine's Church), about a five-minute walk east of Torvet, was founded by Spanish Blackfriars in 1228. The original church, built on reclaimed marshland, eventually collapsed and the present structure dates from the 15th century. Of the 13 churches that were built in Ribe during the pre-Reformation period,

---

Sepulchral Monuments

In the Renaissance period, arranging for burial inside Ribe Cathedral became trendy among those wealthy enough to afford the floor space. Most of these graves are marked by simple carved stones in the aisles, but there are also more ostentatious memorials and chapels containing the remains of bishops and other distinguished citizens of the day. The highest ranked bones within the confines of the cathedral are those of King Christopher I, who was buried in 1259 directly beneath the great dome in the middle of the sanctuary. ■

St Catherine's and the cathedral are the only survivors.

In 1536 the Reformation forced the friars to abandon St Catherine's and in the years that followed the compound served various functions, including those of an asylum for the mentally ill and a wartime field hospital. The abbey is currently used as housing for the elderly.

In the 1920s the church was restored at a tremendous cost due to its still-faulty foundations and in 1932 it was reconsecrated. It has a delicately carved pulpit dating to 1591 and an ornate altarpiece from 1650. The church is open from 10 am to noon year round and from 1 to 4 pm in winter and 1 to 5 pm in summer. Admission is free to the church and 2 kr to the adjacent garden courtyard.

Den Gamle Rådhus
This building, opposite the south-eastern corner of the cathedral, dates from 1496, making it the oldest town hall in Denmark. In addition to being the site of council meetings it also houses a small collection of historical artefacts, including medieval weapons and the executioner's axe. Before entering the town hall, take a look at the highest point of its gable – in recent years it's been the nesting site for a pair of storks. It's open from 1 to 3 pm daily in summer and on weekdays only in May and September. Admission is 5 kr.

Quedens Gaard
The Quedens Gaard, on the corner of Overdammen and Sortebrødgade, is a history museum in a half-timbered former merchant's house, whose oldest wing was built in 1583. Part of the house retains merchant's furnishings from the early 17th century; other rooms exhibit furniture and crafts from earlier periods and trade and industry displays of more recent times. It's open in summer from 10 am to 5 pm daily; the rest of the year it's open daily, except Monday, from 11 am to 3 pm (11 am to 1 pm in midwinter). Admission is 10 kr for adults and 3 kr for children.

Ribes Vikinger
Ribes Vikinger (The Vikings of Ribe), opposite the railway station, is a new 2500-sq-metre museum with displays of Ribe's Viking and medieval history. One exhibition hall reproduces a marketplace in 800 AD, complete with a cargo-laden Viking ship, while another hall portrays a late-medieval scene of the town centre. There are also excavated artefacts, a multimedia project depicting a Viking ship tour of the old trade routes, a museum shop and a café. It's open from 10 am to 5 pm in summer and from 10 am to 4 pm the rest of the year (closed on Monday in winter). Admission is 30 kr for adults and 15 kr for children.

Ribe Vikingecenter
The new Ribe Vikingecenter, three km south of the town centre at Lustrupvej 4, is affiliated with the Ribes Vikinger Museum. Open in summer only, the Vikingecenter has attempted to recreate a slice of life in Viking era Ribe during the various reconstructions, including a 34-metre Fyrkat-style longhouse. The staff, who dress in period clothing, cook over open fires and demonstrate Viking-era crafts like pottery and amber working.

It's open from 11 am to 4 pm daily, except Friday, from mid-June to mid-August. Admission is 30 kr for adults and 15 kr for children. There are plans to offer Viking performances on midsummer evenings; contact the museum (☎ 75 41 16 11) or the tourist office for more details.

Ribe Kunstmuseum
Ribe Kunstmuseum, in a 19th century villa at Sct Nicolajgade 10, is one of the oldest art museums in Denmark and consequently has acquired a good collection, particularly of the 19th century Danish Golden Age painters. There are works by Abildgaard, Juel, Eckersberg, Købke and Lundbye. Among the museum's more notable paintings is Michael Ancher's *Christening in Skagen Church*. The museum is open from 11 am to 5 pm daily from mid-June to mid-September and from 1 to 4 pm daily, except Monday, the

rest of the year. Admission is 20 kr for adults and free for children under 16.

Other Things to See & Do

A costumed **night watchman** makes his rounds from Torvet at 8 and 10 pm from June to August and you can follow him as he sings his way through the old streets. The 'tour' starts in front of the Weis Stue restaurant and proceeds south from Torvet. It's an unabashedly touristy scene that's both fun and free. In May and during the first half of September the watchman makes the rounds once each night at 10 pm.

Ribe Legetøjsmuseum, just south-east of the cathedral, has a collection of 19th and 20th century antique toys, including porcelain dolls. It's open from 10 am to 5 pm daily in summer, and on afternoons only from Sunday to Thursday in winter. Admission is 25 kr for adults and 15 kr for children.

Riberhus Slotsbanke, a km north-east of town, is the moated site of a former 12th century royal castle; it served as a fort until the 17th century and then was dismantled for its stones. At the south-western corner of the grounds is a statue of Queen Dagmar.

Places to Stay

Camping *Ribe Camping* (☎ 75 41 07 77, fax 75 41 00 01), Farupvej 2, 6760 Ribe, is in a field about two km north of Ribe centre. A three-star facility, it's open year round and charges 45 kr per person. There are also 13 cabins that can be hired for up to four people at 250 kr in the low season and 350 kr from June to September. The camping ground has a laundry room, TV lounge, kiosk and reasonably priced cafeteria.

Hostel The modern 152-bed *Ribe Vandrerhjem* (☎ 75 42 06 20, fax 75 42 42 88), Sct Pedersgade 16, 6760 Ribe, has very helpful management and a good in-town location. The hostel overlooks a quiet marsh and is within walking distance to the main sights. Dorm beds in a four or six-bed room cost 85 kr if there's a private bath and 77 kr if the bath is shared by two rooms. A double room costs 250/215 kr with private/shared

bath, a triple 300/250 kr and a quadruple 340/308 kr. Many of the rooms are accessible by wheelchair. Common facilities include a kitchen, sitting areas and TV lounge. Breakfast is available for 38 kr, while dinner can be taken as one course (45 kr) or two courses (60 kr). Advance reservations are recommended. The hostel is open to individual travellers from 1 February to 30 November.

Private Rooms The tourist office has a brochure that lists about two dozen private accommodation options, mostly rooms, in the greater Ribe area. Some are in the town centre while others are on the outskirts and would require a car; at least one is on a farm. Rates vary, but 150/225 kr for singles/doubles is about average in the centre and 100/175 kr is average for places five to eight km from town. You can make a booking yourself or, for a small fee, the tourist office will handle it for you.

If you arrive when the tourist office is closed you might call the Kristensens (☎ 75 42 28 63) at Tornskadevænget 10, who have a couple of comfortable guest rooms in their suburban home, two km north of town; the rate is 125/185 kr for singles/doubles.

Hotels & Inns *Hotel Sønderjylland* (☎ 75 42 04 66) at Sønderportsgade 22, 6760 Ribe, 300 metres west of Torvet, has five rooms above a small family-run pub. Though they vary a bit, the rooms are generally tidy and old-fashioned with lace curtains in the skylights and clean bathrooms down the hall. The rate is 200/400 kr for singles/doubles, breakfast included.

There are also two in-town restaurants that rent similar 2nd-storey rooms: *Weis Stue* (☎ 75 42 07 00) at Torvet and *Backhaus* (☎ 75 42 11 01) at Grydergade 12. Both charge 200/400 kr for singles/doubles including breakfast.

One of the more unusual places to stay is *Den Gamle Arrest* (☎ 75 42 37 00, fax 75 42 37 22), Torvet 11, 6760 Ribe, in the old jail house opposite the cathedral. Originally built as a curate's residence, it was converted to a jail in 1893 and continued to serve that function until 1989. In 1992 it was renovated into an 11-room hotel. There's a certain austere quaintness in entering your room through the old steel doors but, as might be expected, converted jail cells make rather cramped quarters. Rooms with individual washbasins, but with a shared bath in the hall, cost 360/440 kr for singles/doubles, while those with private bath are priced from 640 kr.

The red-brick *Hotel Dagmar* (☎ 75 42 00 33, fax 75 42 36 52), at Torvet 1, 6760 Ribe, in the centre of Ribe opposite the cathedral, dates from 1581, giving it claim to being the oldest hotel in Denmark. This hotel, which has been carefully restored to retain its period character, has 50 rooms each with a double bed, private bath, TV, phone and minibar. Rates, which include breakfast, begin at 625/825 kr for singles/doubles.

Places to Eat

Pinocchio Pizzeria, Overdammen 9, has good pizza and pasta dishes that are served with a fresh salad buffet for 59 kr. You can also get just the salad buffet, which includes fetta cheese, olives, tomatoes and rolls, for 29 kr. It's open from 11 am to 10 pm. Another good Italian restaurant is *Firenze Pizzeria*, Skolegade 6, which stays open until 11 pm and has pizza and pasta from 50 kr.

For a delightful old-fashioned dining experience try the *Weis Stue* at Torvet, a leaning half-timbered tavern with wooden plank tables that dates from 1704. At lunch, served from 11.30 am to 5 pm, a traditional Danish meal that includes fish, shrimp and caviar costs 65 kr. You can also get a Danish beef or fried herring plate throughout the day for 75 kr and various dinner specials from around 100 to 150 kr.

Sælhunden, opposite the harbour at Skibbroen 13, also has a cosy atmosphere and good Danish food. This popular restaurant serves a nice seafood stew or a Danish beef dish for around 65 kr and seafood and steak dishes for around 100 kr. The fried plaice with shrimp and mussels (112 kr) is a local favourite. The kitchen is open from

noon to 8.45 pm; on clear summer days you can dine outdoors.

The historic Hotel Dagmar has an elegant and expensive main dining room as well as a more affordable basement restaurant, *Vægterkælderen*, which shares the same kitchen but has less fastidious service and a simpler menu. In the basement you can order light dishes for around 75 kr (children's plates for 32 kr), a two-course set menu of traditional Danish fare for 125 kr or the daily fish special for a few kr more. Vægterkælderen is also a popular spot for a relaxing drink. The kitchen is open from noon to 10 pm, while the bar is open until 2 am.

In season there's an *Underground Ice Cream* stand in the square fronting the Hotel Dagmar. In summer there are also simple café tables set up on the square where you can sit and enjoy a cold beer.

The *Rådhus Conditoriet*, a couple of minutes walk south-east from Torvet at Hundegade 2, has both takeaway and eat-in bakery items, as well as coffee and simple eats. The *Kvickly* supermarket, at the north side of town and about a five-minute walk from the hostel, has an inexpensive cafeteria.

Getting There & Away

Train Trains to Ribe run hourly on weekdays and slightly less frequently on weekends to Esbjerg (40 minutes, 30 kr) and Tønder (50 minutes, 41 kr).

Car Ribe is 30 km south of Esbjerg via route 24 and 47 km north of Tønder via route 11.

Getting Around

Car & Motorbike There's parking with a two-hour limit near the cathedral and parking with no limits at the end of Sct Pedersgade, near the hostel.

Bicycle Bicycles can be hired at the Ribe Vandrerhjem, Sct Pedersgade 16, for 40 kr a day.

RØMØ

Rømø, the largest Danish island in the North Sea, extends 17 km from north to south and about six km across. Lying off the coast midway between Ribe and Tønder, it's connected to the Jutland mainland by a 10-km causeway that passes over scenic marshland with grazing sheep and wading waterbirds.

For more than a hundred years Rømø, just five km north of Sylt, has been a popular summer resort for German tourists, though in the low season Rømø is a windswept sleeper.

The western side of the island, exposed to the North Sea, is lined with expansive sandy beaches that attract scores of windsurfers. The busiest beach area is at Lakolk, on the central west coast. Lakolk 'village' is essentially a large strip-mall shopping centre and a camping ground on the inland side of the dunes. Although Lakolk is separated from the beach by just 100 metres, the beach itself is more than a km wide, so it's a pretty hefty walk over the sand flats to the water's edge, particularly at low tide. Some people drive out, but be careful not to park your car in an incoming tide zone.

Despite a few unsightly caravan parking areas, most of Rømø is a rural scene with thatched houses, open spaces and the scent of the sea heavy in the air. The main settlements are on the east coast in the seven-km stretch from the causeway bridge south to the harbour-side village of Havneby.

Rømø is rich in bird life and its west coast also provides habitat for about 1500 seals, which haul out onto sandbanks to sunbathe during the day. The north-western corner of the island is a restricted military zone.

Information

Tourist Office The Rømø Turistbureau (☎ 74 75 51 30, fax 74 75 50 31), Havnebyvej 30, Tvismark, 6792 Rømø, is on the east side of the island, a km south of the causeway. It's open in summer from 9 am to 5 pm on weekdays and from 9 am to 4 pm on weekends, with shorter low-season hours.

Money There's a Den Danske Bank just west of Havneby harbour on Vestergade and two other banks on the main road about 500 metres from the harbour.

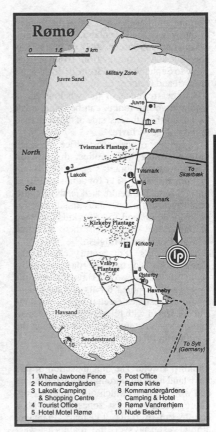

Rømø

1 Whale Jawbone Fence
2 Kommandørgården
3 Lakolk Camping & Shopping Centre
4 Tourist Office
5 Hotel Motel Rømø
6 Post Office
7 Rømø Kirke
8 Kommandørgårdens Camping & Hotel
9 Rømø Vandrerhjem
10 Nude Beach

Post The post office, two km south of the causeway in Kongsmark, is open Monday to Friday from 9 to 11 am and 1 to 4 pm and on Saturday from 9 am to noon.

Things to See & Do

The **Kommandørgården**, a handsome sea captain's house dating from 1748, maintains much of its original décor, including 4000 Dutch wall tiles, and has displays on local history which, in Rømø, was heavily tied to the sea. In the 18th century a disproportionately high number of Rømø men served as sea captains (*kommandører*) on

German and Dutch whale ships that hunted in the waters off Greenland. The museum, 1.5 km north of the causeway on Juvrevej, is open Tuesday to Sunday from 10 am to 6 pm (May to September) and from 10 am to 3 pm in April and October.

Another remnant of the whaling era, a **whale jawbone fence**, can be found a km farther north on the east side of the main road in the village of Juvre.

At the rear of the tourist office is a small **nature centre** with modest displays on island flora and flora. It's open from 10 am to 4 pm and costs 15 kr for adults and 10 kr for children. The centre also leads **wetland ecology tours** almost daily in summer for 40 kr for adults and 15 kr for kids; most are in Danish and German but there are some midsummer tours in English.

The island's 18th century church, the **Rømø Kirke**, is on the main road in Kirkeby, about midway between Havneby and the causeway. It's noted for its unique Greenlandic gravestones erected by sea captains and decorated with reliefs of their boats and families; these stones can be seen lining the north wall of the church yard.

Walking Tracks The inland section of this flat island has trails through heathered moors and wooded areas which offer quiet hiking. There are three forest zones, each with a couple km of trails: Tvismark Plantage, along Vesterhavsvej, the main east-west road; Kirkeby Plantage, on the west side of Kirkeby; and Vråby Plantage, a less diverse area dominated by pines that's about a km farther south.

Water Activities Water activities are centred along the west coast, with the main **windsurfing** zone at the south side of Lakolk. Almost all windsurfers arrive with their own equipment, so rentals are hard to find – for the latest, ask at the tourist office or the Lakolk camping ground.

There's a **nude beach** in the Sønderstrand area, at the south-western tip of the island; to reach it, take Søndersvej to its western end,

from where it's a two-km hike across the sand flats to the ocean.

Places to Stay
Lakolk Camping (☎ 74 75 52 28), Lakolk, 6792 Rømø, on the west coast beach at Lakolk, charges 41 kr and is open from mid-April to mid-September. It also has some four-person huts that cost 200 kr per day in the low season, 380 kr in summer. *Kommandørgårdens Camping* (☎ 74 75 51 22) in Østerby, behind and managed by the hotel of the same name, charges 35 kr per person and is open year round. Both are three-star camping grounds with full facilities and have food shops and restaurants nearby.

The 91-bed *Rømø Vandrerhjem* (☎ 74 75 51 88), Lyngvenen, 6792 Rømø, on the south-eastern side of the island near Havneby, is in a delightful traditional building with a thatched roof. The hostel is open from 15 March to 1 November and has dorm beds for 65 to 75 kr and doubles from 150 kr.

The 40-room *Hotel Motel Rømø* (☎ 74 75 51 14), Gamle Færegevej 1, 6792 Rømø, just south of the tourist office, is a simple motel-style place with good-value singles/doubles with bath from 245/295 kr, breakfast included.

The *Hotel Kommandørgårdens* (☎ 74 75 51 22, fax 74 75 59 22), Havnebyvej 201, 6792 Rømø, in Østerby, is the biggest hotel on the island. It has 80 rooms with private bath from 415/595 kr for singles/doubles, breakfast included, and 87 apartments from 1500 to 4800 kr a week, depending on the size and season. There's a large pool, restaurants, tennis courts and a minimarket.

The vast majority of Rømø's accommodation is found in some 1300 summer houses that are scattered around the island. Prices vary, with rates for a simple six-person, cabin-like place starting from 1400 to 3000 kr per week, depending on the season. A ritzier chalet would cost roughly twice that. The tourist office can provide a catalogue with photos and prices of the houses and can handle the bookings. Other agencies specialising in summer rentals are DanCenter (☎ 74 75 61 81), Vestergade 3, 6792

Rømø, and Dansk Familieferie (☎ 74 75 55 00), Søvej 2, 6792 Rømø.

Places to Eat
There are a couple of fast-food places near the harbour in Havneby, but a better choice is the nearby *Rømø Røgeri*, which sells smoked herring and cooked shrimp by the kilo and has a small café with reasonably priced fish dishes. *Frisk Super* on Vestergade in Havneby is a good place to pick up groceries and fresh bakery items such as chocolate-chip scones. Next door is *Europa*, which has pizzas, Italian food and Greek dishes at moderate prices. There are also grocery stores and a bakery in Østerby, within walking distance of the hostel.

Café Therese at the Kommandørgårdens hotel and camping ground in Østerby, has a varied menu that includes burgers for 30 kr, chicken with chips for 40 kr and pizzas and pastas for around 50 kr. The café has live pop or folk music nightly in summer, with no cover charge. There's also a more expensive sit-down restaurant at the hotel.

There's a supermarket, a bakery and numerous eateries at the shopping centre fronting the camping ground at Lakolk; these include hot-dog stands, pizzerias, steak-houses and cafeterias.

Getting There & Away
Rømø is 14 km west of the town of Skærbæk, on route 175. It's a 30-minute drive via route 11 to either Ribe or Tønder.

Bus No 29 runs from Skærbæk to Havneby (35 minutes, 10 kr) about hourly on weekdays, less frequently on weekends. From Skærbæk there's train service to Ribe, Tønder and Esbjerg about once an hour.

The Rømø-Sylt Linie (☎ 74 75 53 03) operates car ferries between Havneby and Germany's island of Sylt (one hour, 32 kr) at least six times a day.

Getting Around
Bus From late May to early September bus No 29/591 makes a 20-minute trip from Havneby up the east coast road and over to Lakolk. There are 10 runs on weekdays, four on weekends. It costs 10 kr to go anywhere on the island.

Bicycle The best choice, if you don't have your own transport, is to rent a bicycle, as Rømø is notably flat and small enough to explore. You can rent bikes at the grocery store opposite the camping ground in Lakolk for 30/120 kr a day/week, in Havneby from Garni at Nørre Frankel 15 for 30/150 kr, and in Østerby at the Kommandørgården camping ground for 40/200 kr.

TØNDER
Tønder, just four km north of the German border, is an historic town that retains a few curving cobblestone streets lined with half-timbered houses.

Tønder's town charter was issued in 1243. Although it's surrounded by marsh today, it was once a busy market town with access to the sea. Because it's low-lying, Tønder has always been subject to serious flooding and in medieval times it was nearly swept away altogether. In the 16th century a network of dykes was erected to protect the town from flooding but the dykes also contributed to the alteration of the tidal flats and the seas eventually receded, leaving the town landlocked.

By the 18th century Tønder was again prospering, as it had become the centre of a high-quality lace industry which, at its peak, employed some 12,000 workers in the greater Tønder area. Many of the town's finest houses were erected by wealthy lace merchants.

These days Tønder's high point is during the last weekend of August when the Tønder Festival (☎ 74 72 46 10), one of Denmark's largest folk festivals, brings a multitude of international and Danish musicians to town for more than 40 concerts.

Information
Tourist Office The Tønder Turistbureau (☎ 74 72 12 20, fax 74 72 09 00) is in the centre of town at Torvet 1, 6270 Tønder. In summer it's open from 9.30 am to 5.30 pm on weekdays and from 9.30 am to 3 pm on Saturday; the rest of the year it's open from

9 am to 4 pm on weekdays and from 9 am to noon on Saturday.

Money There are a couple of banks near Torvet, the central square.

Post The post office at Vestergade 83, a few minutes walk north of the railway station, is open Monday to Friday from 10 am to 5 pm and on Saturday from 9.30 am to noon.

Things to See & Do

Some of the town's most picturesque streets for period houses are off Søndergade, just a couple of minutes walk south of Torvet. The best preserved is the cobbled Uldgade.

The **Tønder Museum** has regional historic objects including a collection of delicate Tønder lace, period furniture and Dutch wall tiles. The adjacent **Sønderjyllands Kunstmuseum** (South Jutland Art Museum) features Danish surrealist and modern art, mostly of lesser-known artists. Both are at Kongevej 55, a 10-minute walk east of the railway station, and are open from 10 am to 5 pm from May to October and from 1 to 5 pm in winter, but closed on Monday all year round. Admission is 10 kr for adults and 5 kr for children.

The **Kristkirken**, the large church at the north-east side of Torvet, dates from the late 16th century. The 47.5-metre tower, from an earlier church that once stood on this site, doubled as a navigational marker in the days when Tønder was connected to the sea. The church interior has some impressive carvings and paintings, including a font from 1350, a pulpit from 1586 and a series of memorial tablets from around 1600. It's open Monday to Saturday from 10 am to 4 pm.

Den Gamle Apotek, on Torvet at Østergade 1, is noted mainly for its elaborate 1671 baroque doorway that's flanked by two lions. Also worth a look is the old-fashioned interior, which was a pharmacy until 1989 and is now largely a gift shop.

You can rent **paddle boats** (25 kr for half an hour) on the river near the Hostrups Hotel.

Places to Stay

Tønder Campingplads (☎ & fax 74 72 18 49), immediately east of the hostel at Holmevej 2, 6270 Tønder, is a three-star facility with a coin laundry, cooking facilities and a kiosk. The camping charge is 44 kr per person. There are also 23 cabins. It's open from 1 April to 1 October and is part of a sports centre (Tønder Fritidscenter) that includes tennis courts, a swimming pool and squash courts.

The *Tønder Vandrerhjem* (☎ 74 72 35 00, fax 74 72 27 97), Sønderport 4, 6270 Tønder, is on the east side of the town centre, about a 15-minute walk from the railway station and just five minutes from Torvet. The hostel is a rather nondescript facility but the rooms are comfortable, all with four beds and a private bath. The cost is 80 kr for a dorm bed and 150/200 kr for singles/doubles. It's open to individuals from 1 February to 20 November. There's a guest kitchen and bicycle rentals.

The tourist office can provide a list of rooms in private homes in the Tønder area, costing an average of 140/200 kr for singles/doubles. Some are in the centre, others in the outskirts, including one in Møgeltønder. You can either call on your own or have the tourist office make a reservation for a 10 kr fee.

The older *Hostrups Hotel* (☎ 74 72 21 29, fax 74 72 07 26), Søndergade 30, 6270 Tønder, a few minutes walk south-east of Torvet, has 23 comfortable rooms, most with private bath, desk and TV. Singles cost from 280 to 485 kr, doubles from 305 to 600 kr.

The *Hotel Tønderhus* (☎ 74 72 22 22, fax 74 72 05 92), Jomfrustien 1, 6270 Tønder, opposite the Tønder Museum, is a modern brick building with 50 standard motel-style rooms with private bath, TV and phone. Singles/doubles start at 475/575 kr, breakfast included.

Places to Eat

Choices are limited and many people simply drive south to Germany where food is cheaper. Otherwise your best bet for restaurants is around Torvet.

Torve Bistroen, a café on Torvet, has fish

NED FRIARY

NED FRIARY

Southern Zealand
Top: Cobblestone street in Ribe
Bottom: Waterfront at sunset, Sønderborg

NED FRIARY

NED FRIARY

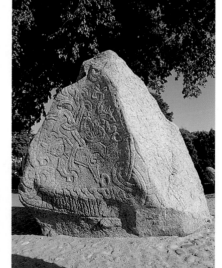
NED FRIARY

Central Jutland
Top: Reconstructed historic buildings, Den Gamle By open-air museum, Århus
Left: Statue of Sitting Bull, built of 1.2 million lego blocks, Legoland
Right: Viking-era rune stone, Jelling

& chips, vegetarian omelettes and pasta for around 40 kr, as well as smørrebrød, burgers and salads. In the same building is *Torvets Restaurant*, a more expensive sit-down restaurant with a varied menu of meat and fish dishes that average around 100 kr including salad. There's a market selling produce and cheese at Torvet on Tuesday and Friday mornings.

A short walk east of Torvet is *Pizzeria Italiano*, at Østergade 40, which has good pizza and pasta dishes from around 60 kr and fish dishes for about 100 kr. Just west of the pizzeria is a *bakery*. For cheap eats there's *Spisehuset Asian* at Østergade 37, which has Chinese dishes for 39 kr and some inexpensive grilled items.

Another cheap place to eat is the *Kvickly* supermarket on Plantagevej, but it's out of the way, a km north-west of the post office. It has a daily meal, such as fish & chips, for 28 kr and other inexpensive cafeteria food. The supermarket also has a kiosk with good takeaway sandwiches for 15 to 20 kr.

Hagge's Musik Pub, at Vestergade 80 opposite the post office, has 'pub grub' and Danish and Irish draught beer; it's also a popular venue for live music, especially folk, blues and jazz.

Getting There & Away

Tønder is on route 11, four km north of Germany and 77 km south of Esbjerg.

The railway station is on the west side of town, a km from Torvet via Vestergade. Trains run every hour on weekdays and slightly less frequently on weekends from Ribe (50 minutes, 41 kr) and Esbjerg (1½ hours, 59 kr).

MØGELTØNDER

If you're in the Tønder area, don't leave without first visiting the fetching village of Møgeltønder.

The centre of the village is the cobbled main street Slotsgade, which is lined with period brick houses sporting thatched roofs and colourful wooden doors. At the western end of Slotsgade is **Schackenborg**, a small castle that was presented by the crown to Field Marshal Hans Schack in 1661 following his victory over the Swedes in the battle of Nyborg. Members of the Schack family have occupied the castle ever since. While the castle building is not open to the public, the moat-surrounded grounds on the opposite side of the street have been turned into a small public park that visitors are free to roam.

At the eastern end of Slotsgade is the **Møgeltønder Kirke**, which has one of the most lavish church interiors in Denmark. The Romanesque nave dates from 1180 and the baptismal font from 1200, but the church has had numerous additions – the gothic choir vaults are from the 13th century, the tower dates from 1500 and the chapel at the north side was added in 1763. The interior is rich in frescoes, gallery paintings and ceiling drawings. Here too is one the oldest church pipe organs in Denmark, dating from 1679. The elaborately detailed gilt altar dates from the 16th century; it's flanked by a 17th century pulpit and a 'countess bower', a balcony with private seating for the Schack family, who owned the church from 1661 until 1970. The church is open daily from 8 am to 5 pm (until 4 pm from October to March).

Places to Stay & Eat

The *Schackenborg Slotskro* (☎ 74 73 83 83, fax 74 73 83 11), Slotsgaden 42, 6270 Tønder, in the village centre, has 11 suitably simple rooms from 300/475 kr for singles/doubles. The inn has both a coffee shop and an upmarket Danish restaurant, while there's a small place at the western end of Slotsgade selling bakery items, ice cream and snack foods.

Getting There & Away

Møgeltønder is four km west of Tønder via route 419.

Bus No 66 connects Tønder with Møgeltønder about once an hour on weekdays, less frequently on weekends; it takes 10 minutes and costs 10 kr.

SOUTHERN JUTLAND

SOUTHERN JUTLAND

HØJER

If you're heading onward to Rømø from Møgeltønder you'll pass through Højer, a rural market town that once served as a port for shipping south Jutland cattle. Only a few metres above sea level, Højer is bordered by marshland and is protected by an extensive network of sluice gates and dykes, some of which date from the 16th century.

While it's not a must-see town, Højer does have some distinctive red-brick houses with thatched roofs and claims the only thatched town hall in Denmark. The main site, in the centre of town next to the tourist office, is a nicely restored Dutch windmill from 1857 that houses a little local history museum. It's open from 10 am to 4 pm daily from April to October; admission costs 10 kr for adults and 5 kr for children.

If you're interested in bird-watching, the coastal marshland west of Højer is a rich habitat for wading birds, sea birds and shore birds.

Getting There & Away

Højer is on route 419, seven km west of Møgeltønder. Bus No 66 connects Højer with Møgeltønder (10 kr) and Tønder (20 kr).

KOLDING

Kolding is Jutland's fifth largest city, with a population of 59,000. Despite an industrial edge, Kolding has a pleasant centre with a castle and some attractive historic buildings.

Akseltorv, the central square, is the site of **Borchs Yard**, a decorative Renaissance building dating from 1595. Pedestrian streets radiate in all directions from Akseltorv. Helligkorsgade, a few minutes walk south of Akseltorv at the end of Østergade, is a pleasant street for a stroll. There you'll find a cluster of picturesque buildings, including Kolding's **oldest house**, a timber-framed affair built in 1589 at Helligkorsgade 18. Just west of Akseltorv, on the other side of the rådhus, is **Sankt Nicolai Kirke**, a medieval church that was largely rebuilt in the 19th century. It's not grandly interesting but it does have a late 16th century altar and pulpit and entry is free.

Information

Tourist Office The Kolding Turistbureau (☎ 75 53 21 00, fax 75 53 48 38), Akseltorv 8, 6000 Kolding, is open Monday to Saturday from 9.30 am to 5.30 pm, except in the low season when it closes at 1 pm on Saturday.

Money & Post There's a Den Danske Bank on the south side of Akseltorv and a post office at the railway station.

Koldinghus

The town's main landmark is Koldinghus, a castle fortress immediately north of Akseltorv. The first fortress on this site was built in 1268 by King Erik V to guard the border between Denmark and the Duchy of Schleswig. The oldest preserved parts of the current castle, the north and west wings, date from around 1440. The castle's distinctive tower was added around 1600 by Christian IV, who had spent much of his childhood at Koldinghus.

In 1808, Spanish troops stationed at Koldinghus during the Napoleonic Wars tried to fight off the chilly Danish weather by building a roaring fire in one of the castle's hearths; the fire got out of hand, engulfing a defective chimney, and the castle went up in flames. Koldinghus was left in ruins until 1890, when the north wing was restored to house a museum. The work continued piecemeal over nearly a century and in 1935 the Christian IV tower was rebuilt. The exterior now has an 18th century baroque appearance while the castle interior has the original gothic and Renaissance influences innovatively fused with modern Scandinavian architecture.

The castle, which has church sculpture, paintings, period furnishings and historic exhibits, including one on the Schleswig wars, can be toured from 10 am to 5 pm daily from April to September and during the rest of the year from noon to 3 pm on weekdays and 10 am to 3 pm on weekends. Admission is 30 kr for adults, free for children under 16.

Kunstmuseet Trapholt

The Kunstmuseet Trapholt, Æblehaven 23, is on the eastern outskirts of the city on the north side of the Kolding Fjord. Opened in 1988, this is one of Denmark's largest museums dedicated to 20th century art. The fine arts collection includes works by Richard Mortensen, Anna Archer, Franciska Clausen and Egill Jacobsen. The applied arts section shows the influence of Danish design on ceramics, textiles and furniture. It's open from 10 am to 5 pm daily from May to September, and in winter from noon to 4 pm on weekdays and 10 am to 4 pm on weekends. Admission is 22 kr for adults, free for children under 16. Bus No 4 runs between the railway station and the museum about every 20 minutes.

Places to Stay

The *Vonsild Camping & Feriecenter* (☎ 75 53 47 25, fax 75 52 45 29), Vonsildvej 29, 6000 Kolding, is a three-star facility on the southern outskirts of Kolding. It's open year round and charges 45 kr per person.

The *Kolding Vandrerhjem* (☎ 75 50 91 40, fax 75 50 91 51), Ørnsborgvej, 6000 Kolding, is a km north-west of the city centre. It's a simple place, with 18 family rooms and one dorm. Dorm beds cost 70 kr, while family rooms cost from 140 kr for singles up to 420 kr for six people. The hostel is open from 1 February to 1 December.

The *Hotel Kolding* (☎ 75 52 50 00, fax 75 54 23 30) is an old-fashioned hotel right on the central square at Akseltorv 5, 6000 Kolding. The 40 rooms have private baths and are reasonably priced from 255/370 kr for singles/doubles, plus 40 kr for an optional continental breakfast.

Another older hotel with some character is the *Saxildhus* (☎ 75 52 12 00, fax 75 53 53 10), Banegårdspladsen, 6000 Kolding, opposite the railway station. Its 95 rooms each have a private bath, phone, TV and minibar and start at 345/445 kr for singles/doubles.

Places to Eat

There's a market on Akseltorv on Tuesday and Friday from 7 am to 1.30 pm where you can buy produce and cheese.

The pizzeria *Den Italienske*, at the Hotel Kolding at Akseltorv 5, has pleasant sit-down dining with a good pizza buffet for 39 kr; after 4 pm it costs 59 kr but includes a salad bar. You can also order pizza and pasta dishes à la carte or have the salad bar alone for 25 kr.

Café Paraplyen on Adelgade, just west of Akseltorv, has cheap eats including sandwiches for 12 kr and lasagne with salad for double that. West of the café is a *Fakta* grocery store and to the east there's a fast-food place selling burgers and chicken.

For a more relaxing setting, *Den Blå Café* at Slotsgade 4, a block south of Akseltorv, has pavement tables and beer, coffee and snacks.

Den Grimme Ælling, in the Saxildhus hotel building at Banegårdspladsen, opposite the railway station, has an all-you-can-eat buffet of herring, salads, cheeses and a few hot dishes for 70 kr at lunch and a more elaborate buffet for 100 kr at dinner. You can add on unlimited beer or wine to the meal for another 30/100 kr at lunch/dinner.

Getting There & Away

Train There are regular train services from Kolding south to Padborg on the German border (70 minutes, 65 kr) and north all the way to Frederikshavn (four hours, 189 kr). There's a second line to Esbjerg (55 minutes, 53 kr).

Car Kolding is 92 km east of Esbjerg and 82 km north of the German border. The E20 and the E45 connect Kolding with other major towns in Jutland. If you're travelling leisurely by road north to south, route 170 is a pleasant alternative to the E45.

HADERSLEV

Haderslev, with a population of about 30,000, is an appealing town at the head of the Haderslev Fjord. Established as a market town in the 13th century, it has a nicely

SOUTHERN JUTLAND

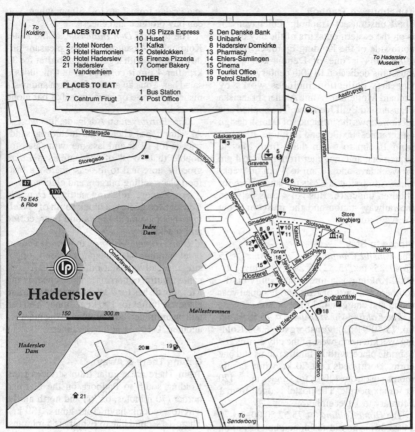

PLACES TO STAY

2 Hotel Norden
3 Hotel Harmonien
20 Hotel Haderslev
21 Haderslev
   Vandrerhjem

PLACES TO EAT

7 Centrum Frugt

9 US Pizza Express
10 Huset
11 Kafka
12 Osteklokken
16 Firenze Pizzeria
17 Corner Bakery

OTHER

1 Bus Station
4 Post Office

5 Den Danske Bank
6 Unibank
8 Haderslev Domkirke
13 Pharmacy
14 Ehlers-Samlingen
15 Cinema
18 Tourist Office
19 Petrol Station

Haderslev

restored centre. In addition to the fjord the town also borders a lake, the Haderslev Dam, which offers some good canoeing opportunities.

The Haderslev tourist office goes a long way in welcoming visitors. Every day in summer, the office schedules an outing at 10 am. On some days it's a free guided walking tour of the town. On other days there's a canoe trip on the lake, a fishing expedition or a visit to a local dairy farm; the cost of each of these is 40 kr for adults, 20 kr for children. For outings outside the town, you'll need your own transport.

Information

Tourist Office The Haderslev Turistbureau (☎ 74 52 55 50), Sønderbro 3, 6100 Haderslev, is open from 9 am to 5 pm on weekdays and from 9.30 am to 2.30 pm on Saturday from mid-June to 31 August, closing in the low season at 4 pm on weekdays and 12.30 pm on Saturday. The office keeps a letter box stocked with tourist brochures when it's closed.

Money There are five banks along Nørregade, including a Unibank at No 30 and a Den Danske Bank at No 23.

Post The post office in the town centre at Gravene 8 is open Monday to Friday from 9.30 am to 5 pm and on Saturday from 9.30 am to noon.

Walking Tour

The town's oldest quarters, in the streets surrounding Torvet, can readily be explored in a short walking tour. Begin at the tourist office, which is in a handsome building dating from 1776; here you can pick up the free English-language brochure *A Stroll Through the Old Part of the City* which describes every nook and cranny along the way.

You'll find some of the nicest period buildings along Højgade and on Torvet, a cobbled square bordered by half-timbered buildings and filled with sculptures by Erik Heide.

A short stroll north-east of Torvet will bring you to the **Ehlers-samlingen** (Ehlers Collection) at Slotsgade 20, a museum specialising in Danish pottery from the Middle Ages until 1900, when the regional distinctions in Danish pottery style began to erode. The museum is in an attractive timber-framed building dating from 1577 that still has some of its original decorative painted wall panels. It's open (10 kr) from 10 am to 5 pm on weekdays and from 2 to 5 pm on weekends; it's closed on Monday year round and on Wednesday and Friday in the low season.

If you return from Slotsgade via Store Klingbjerg and Lille Klingbjerg you'll pass by some other older houses.

Haderslev Domkirke

Haderslev's cathedral, on a knoll above Torvet, is the most imposing building in town. Parts of the cathedral, including the transept and nave, date from the mid-1200s, while other additions were made in the centuries that followed. It's said that in 1525 the cathedral became the site of the first Lutheran teachings in Denmark.

The church has an impressive interior. Particularly notable is the altar which has a crucifix from about 1300 and alabaster figures of the 12 apostles from around 1400. There's also a grand Sieseby organ and a baptismal font dating from 1485. The most intriguing decorations are the memorial tablets lining the walls, which are richly embellished with skulls, crossbones and other ghostly detail. The cathedral is open from 10 am to 5 pm (from 11.30 am on Sunday) between May and September, and from 10 am to 3 pm in winter; admission is free.

In summer, concerts are given on the church organ at 4.30 pm on Friday (free) and at 8 pm on Tuesday (60 kr).

Haderslev Museum

This museum at Dalgade 7, a km north-east of Torvet, has exhibits on southern Jutland's archaeological history as well as a small open-air museum with a windmill and a few other period buildings. From June to August it's open Monday to Friday from 10 am to 5 pm and weekends from noon to 5 pm; the rest of the year it's open Tuesday to Sunday from 1 to 4 pm. Admission is 10 kr for adults, free for children.

Places to Stay

The 102-bed *Haderslev Vandrerhjem* (☎ 74 52 13 47, fax 74 52 13 64), Erlevvej 34, 6100 Haderslev, is a 10-minute walk west of the tourist office, on the southern shore of the Haderslev Dam. Dorm beds cost 68 kr, while private rooms cost from 120 kr for singles to 408 kr for six people. The hostel, which is open from February to November, has a playground and canoes for rent.

Cheapest of the town's three hotels is *Hotel Haderslev* (☎ 74 52 60 10, fax 74 52 65 42), Damparken, 6100 Haderslev, which is right on the shore of the Haderslev Dam, between the hostel and tourist office. The 70 rooms each have a private bath, TV, video, minibar and phone. Many of the rooms have pleasant water views, as does the hotel restaurant. Singles/doubles cost 425/550 kr, breakfast included.

The 28-room *Hotel Harmonien* (☎ 74 52 37 20, fax 74 52 44 51), Gåskærgade 8, 6100

Haderslev, has singles/doubles with TV, phone and private bath from 455/655 kr.

More upmarket is the *Hotel Norden* (☎ 74 52 40 30, fax 74 52 40 25), Storegade 55, 6100 Haderslev, about 500 metres north-west of Torvet. It has an indoor swimming pool and rooms with modern amenities including minibars and videos. Singles/doubles start at 625/835 kr. There's a bar, restaurant and conference facilities.

Places to Eat
There are numerous places to grab a bite near Torvet, all convenient for sightseeing.

On Nørregade, in the first block north of Torvet you'll find *US Pizza Express* with sandwiches and kebabs for 20 kr and pizza by the slice. Directly opposite at Nørregade 6 is *Kafka*, a trendy alternative café with good coffee and a variety of dishes for 40 kr or less, including pasta, omelettes, chilli con carne and vegetarian specials. On the far corner of the block is *Centrum Frugt*, a large fruit and vegetable stand.

On Apotekergade opposite the cathedral is *Osteklokken*, a good health food shop with grocery items, fresh produce, cheeses and a full line of vitamins and teas. For bread and pastries try the *Corner Bakery*, a block south of Torvet on Lavgade.

Firenze Pizzeria, at the south side of Torvet, is an Italian restaurant with pizza and pasta for 60 kr, and meat and fish dishes for 100 to 145 kr. It's open from noon to 2.30 pm Monday to Saturday and from 5 to 11 pm nightly.

Huset at Nørregade 10, just north of Kafka, is a music café serving up beer and wine with live rock and blues.

Getting There & Away
Haderslev is 31 km south of Kolding via route 170 or E45 and 51 km east of Ribe via routes 24 and 47. There's a large carpark beside the tourist office with free parking and no time limit.

Bus DSB bus Nos 33, 35 and 37 run frequently between Haderslev and Vojens (21 minutes, 12 kr), which has the nearest

railway station. Bus 34 runs hourly between Haderslev and Kolding, taking 45 minutes.

Getting Around
You can hire bicycles at Bosack (☎ 74 52 07 54), Sønderbro 7, near the tourist office.

KRUSÅ & PADBORG
Kruså, a Danish outpost on the border with Germany, is lined with service stations, money exchange facilities and sex shops.

A more sombre landmark is found just east of Kruså at Padborg, the site of **Frøslev-lejren** (Frøslev Camp), an internment camp opened near the end of WW II to detain members of the growing Danish Resistance. Built to prevent the deportation of Danes across the border, Frøslev Camp held 12,000 prisoners during its nine months of operation.

The camp buildings now house a collection of displays and museums. The tower complex holds the Frøslevlejrens Museum, which depicts the Danish Resistance movement and daily prison life at Frøslev, while other buildings house exhibits by the Danish Red Cross (in the former infirmary), Amnesty International, the United Nations and branches of the Danish defence forces. On a lighter note there's also an exhibit on local wildlife.

The Frøslevlejrens and Red Cross museums are open in midsummer from 10 am to 5 pm daily and in the low season from 9 am to 4 pm Tuesday to Friday and 10 am to 5 pm on weekends; closed in December and January. Combined admission to these two museums is 20 kr for adults and 5 kr for children. The camp's other exhibits are open from 9 am to 5 pm daily between April and October; admission to the UN museum is 10 kr, while the others are free.

Frøslevlejrens is at the north-western outskirts of Padborg at Lejrvejen 83, a km west of the E45 (take exit 76) and just five km north of the German border.

SØNDERBORG
Sønderborg is an agreeable seaside town with a population of nearly 30,000. It traces

its origins to medieval times when King Valdemar the Great erected a castle fortress along the waterfront. The town grew up around the castle and with its good natural harbour prospered as a fishing and trade centre.

Sønderborg played a notable role in Denmark's history as the site of the last Danish resistance in the German invasion of 1864. The Danish loss at the pivotal Battle of Dybbøl, fought on the western outskirts of town, marked the beginning of a German occupation in the region that continued until the end of WW I. One legacy of that 1864 battle is Sønderborg's predominantly modern appearance; the heavy artillery bombardment that took place during that fighting left much of the town in rubble.

Today Sønderborg has a distinctively peaceful appearance and caters in equal measure to German and Danish tourists.

Orientation

Sønderborg spreads along both sides of the Als Sund (Als Sound), which is spanned by two bridges. The town centre and the castle are to the east, on the island of Als, while the Dybbøl section and the railway terminal are on the west side, which is part of mainland Jutland. There's a small sandy beach right in town along the south side of the castle.

Information

Tourist Office The Sønderborg Turistbureau (☎ 74 42 35 55, fax 74 42 57 47), Rådhustorvet 7, 6400 Sønderborg, is on the main town square. It's open Monday to Friday from 9 am to 4 pm on Saturday from 9 am to noon.

Money & Post There's a post office, a Den Danske Bank and a Unibank along the pedestrian street Perlegade, immediately north of Rådhustorvet.

Things to See & Do

The town's dominant sight is the waterfront **Sønderborg Slot**, a castle whose history dates from the 12th century, when it was constructed as a circular fortress to defend

against marauding Wends. The deposed king Christian II was held captive here from 1532 to 1549 – not in the dungeon, but in comfortable royal chambers. The castle has been rebuilt over the years, with its current baroque design dating from 1718. Of special interest is the chapel, built in 1568 by the dowager queen Dorothea, widow of Christian III, as it is Denmark's first Lutheran chapel and one of Europe's oldest preserved royal chapels.

The castle now holds the **Museet på Sønderborg Slot**, which has exhibits on the wars of 1848 and 1864, the maritime history of Sønderborg, medieval church art and the German occupation of Denmark. It's open from 10 am to 5 pm daily from May to September, with shorter low-season hours. Admission is 15 kr for adults, free for children.

Dybbøl, on the east side of the Als Sund, was the site of the most important battle in the Danish-German war of 1864. Today the **Historiecenter Dybbøl Banke**, a history centre at Dybbøl Banke 16, has a multimedia display commemorating the bloody battle that marked the fall of southern Jutland to the Germans. The reconstructed windmill **Dybbøl Mølle**, on the opposite side of the street, was damaged in the battle of 1864 and is now a national historic site. Admission is 15 kr to the mill and 40 kr to the history centre. Both are open spring to autumn from 10 am to 5 pm.

Places to Stay

Sønderborg Camping (☎ & fax 74 42 41 89), Ringgade 7, 6400 Sønderborg, is in a wooded area near the yacht harbour, a km south-east of the town centre. It's open from mid-April to mid-September and charges 40 kr per person.

The modern *Sønderborg Vandrerhjem* (☎ 74 42 31 12, fax 74 42 56 31), Kærvej 70, 6400 Sønderborg, a km north of the centre, is almost motel-like with comfortable guest rooms, a lounge with a fireplace, a coin laundry, sauna and sports fields. Most of the 42 rooms have just four beds, and all have private baths and double-entry doors to ensure quiet. Dorm beds cost 80 kr, while singles/doubles cost 195/250 kr. The hostel is accessible by wheelchair and is open from February to November.

Sønderborg's cheapest hotel is the 13-room *Hotel Arnkilhus* (☎ 74 42 23 36), about 500 metres north of the centre at Arnkilgade 13, 6400 Sønderborg. Simple singles/doubles cost 195/325 kr with a bath in the hall, 260/410 kr with a private bath. Breakfast is included and there's a TV lounge.

In a prime location opposite the castle is *Scandic Hotel Sønderborg* (☎ 74 42 19 00, fax 74 42 19 50), Rosengade 2, 6400 Sønderborg, a 1st-class hotel with a restaurant, lounge, sauna and indoor swimming pool. The 95 rooms each have a private bath, phone, TV, minibar etc and cost 745/845 kr for singles/doubles, breakfast included. This chain has various schemes and holiday plans that can bring the rate down to 595 kr.

Places to Eat

An atmospheric place to dine that won't burn a hole in your wallet is *Jensens Bøfhus*, a chain steakhouse in a half-timbered building at Løkken 24, at the north side of the centre. The best deal is the chain's standard 29 kr steak lunch, while dinner prices begin at about double that.

A block to the east on the pedestrian street Perlegade you'll find, from north to south: *Mika*, a large grocery store with good produce and a cheap cafeteria; *Restaurant Sønderjylland*, a sit-down restaurant with fish and meat dishes from around 60 kr; an ice-cream shop; and *Centrum Frugt*, a large fruit shop.

If you continue walking south you'll find a couple of kebab-style fast-food places near the rådhus.

Bella Italia, at Lille Rådhusgade 31, is an upmarket Italian restaurant with pleasant candlelight dining. Pizzas start at 50 kr and pastas at 60 kr, while fish dishes are about double that and steaks top out at 175 kr.

Tortilla Flats, north of the castle at Brogade 2, is a popular place with decent Mexican food, good-sized servings and reasonable prices. A chicken enchilada with beans and a small green salad costs 78 kr, while various combination plates average at about 100 kr.

Getting There & Away

Sønderborg is 30 km north-east of the border crossing at Kruså, via route 8.

Air The airport is six km north of town. The commuter airline Cimber Air has a few direct flights daily to Copenhagen. The normal one-way fare is 680 kr. For information on stand-by and discounted return tickets, see the Getting Around chapter.

Train Sønderborg is connected by numerous trains a day to Kolding (1¾ hours, 83 kr) and the rest of Jutland. It's also possible to go from Sønderborg to Padborg (41 kr), changing trains in Tinglev; with a good connection it takes about an hour.

Getting Around

Bicycles can be rented at Cykelsmeden (☎ 74 42 36 60), Torvet 7, Ulkebøl.

AROUND ALS

The 33-km-long island of Als is separated from the Jutland mainland by the narrow Als Sund. Its only large town, Sønderborg (see the previous section), sits at the south-western corner of Als; the rest of the island is a quiet provincial region of small farming villages. There are more than a dozen camping grounds spread along the coast, with the best beaches in the south. Tourist sights are limited but many of the villages have small churches of varying antiquity that can be visited and there's a dolmen and a Viking burial site on the east coast at Blommeskobbel.

Augustenborg, eight km north-east of Sønderborg along route 8, is one of Als' more easily accessible and interesting villages. It has a compact centre whose main street begins at the gate of the **Augustenborg Slot**, an 18th century baroque palace that now serves as a psychiatric hospital; the grounds are open to all, as is the courtly palace chapel. The Augustenborg Turistbureau (☎ 74 47 17 20) is at Storegade 28, just 300 metres west of the palace in a picturesque circa-1769 house. Nearby you'll find a bakery and a couple of cafés where you could grab something to eat.

For those with their own transport the area around **Kegnæs**, the island at the southern tip of Als, can make an enjoyable little outing with its gently pastoral countryside and sandy beaches. Fifteen km south-east of Sønderborg via route 427, Kegnæs is connected to the rest of Als by a short causeway. At the north-eastern side of the causeway there's a long sandy beach with the island's most popular seaside camping ground, *Drejby Camping* (☎ 74 40 43 05), which has 500 spaces, cabins, a grill-style eatery and a minimarket. On Kegnæs, a km west of the causeway, is a hilltop **lighthouse** that can be climbed (4 kr) for a coastal view. If you want to try your luck at angling, the fishing is said to be good at the western end of Kegnæs, but otherwise the only place on the island that you're likely to encounter any company is at the beach.

Getting There & Away

On weekdays bus No 13 leaves from the Sønderborg bus station on the hour for Augustenborg (12 minutes), while bus No 11 runs about every two hours from Sønderborg, via Augustenborg, to Fynshav (30 minutes), where there's a ferry service to Funen (see the Faaborg Getting There & Away section). There's also a ferry from Mommark to Søby on Ærø (see the Ærø Getting There & Away section for details).

As bus services are sketchy to the more rural parts of Als, a pleasant alternative for those without their own transport is to rent a bike in Sønderborg. The tourist office can provide a map with suggested cycling tours.

Central Jutland

Central Jutland covers a broad swath of Denmark extending from Fredericia in the south to the Limfjord in the north. The west side is an expansive plain of windswept moors, bordered by a coastline of beach flats and sand dunes. Although this western region was predominantly wild heathland until the 19th century, much of it has now been turned into pasture and sugar beet fields. The more protected east side of central Jutland has rich fertile land, small farms, a coastline indented with shallow fjords, and the largest cities and towns.

East Central Jutland

This section of Jutland has two significant – but quite dissimilar – destinations. Children who have grown up playing with Lego will undoubtedly want to make a beeline for Legoland, Jutland's most visited attraction, while adults travelling without kids are likely to find the main point of interest in Jelling, one of Denmark's most important historic sites.

FREDERICIA

Fredericia is an industrial city of 29,000 people that's notable mainly for its old fortified ramparts. The town dates from 1650 when King Frederik III began construction of the fortress to guard the narrow sound between Jutland and Funen. Over the centuries the Fredericia fortress played a role in the frequent wars between Denmark and its neighbours. In the winter of 1657 Swedish troops, en route to Copenhagen, overran the fortress and killed the entire garrison before marching across the frozen waters of the Lille Bælt. The most celebrated battle fought here took place two centuries later when, in 1849, an unsuccessful German assault on Fredericia halted the northward advance of Schleswig-Holstein troops.

HIGHLIGHTS

- Århus, Denmark's second-largest city, for its museums and cafés, and sights dating back to Viking times
- Den Gamle By, the largest open-air museum in Denmark (Århus)
- Hiking and canoeing in the Lake District
- Remains of the 'bog people' at Silkeborg and Århus museums
- The amusement park Legoland, for families with children
- Historic rune stones at the Jelling church
- Trails through the heather-covered hills of Rebild Bakker
- Summertime Viking play at Hobro's Viking fortress

ᚠᚤᚾᛗᛦᛣᛈᛈᛗᚾᛦᚠᛈᛈᛁᛁᚠᛏᛁᛁᚠᚠᚤᚾᛗᛦᛣᛈᛈᛗᚾᛦᚠᛈᛈᛁᛁᚠᛏᛁᛁᚠ

Orientation

The railway and bus stations are together on the west side of the centre. To get to the tourist office walk north from the station, turn right on Vesterbrogade and follow it to the ramparts, and then take the old town gate at Danmarks Port through the rampart wall to Danmarksgade. The walk takes about 10 minutes.

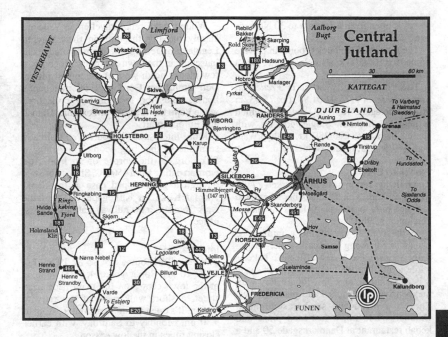

Information

Tourist Office The Fredericia Turistbureau (☎ 75 92 13 77, fax 75 93 03 77), Danmarksgade 2A, Box 248, 7000 Fredericia, is open in summer from 8.30 am to 6 pm on weekdays and from 9 am to 5 pm on Saturday. The rest of the year it's open from 8.30 am to 5 pm on weekdays and from 10 am to 1 pm on Saturday.

Money & Post The post office is on the north side of the railway station. There's a Jyske Bank at Danmarksstræde 22, a few minutes walk south-east of the tourist office.

Things to See & Do

The old earthen **ramparts** of the Fredericia fortress remain largely intact, forming a mounded park-like green belt around the oldest section of the city. The ramparts extend about two km and are topped with scattered war memorials, cannons and a foot-

path. You can get the best overview of it all from the top of the rampart wall at the western end of Denmarksgade, where there's a water tower that can be climbed in summer. An English-language brochure detailing the history of different parts of the wall is available at the nearby tourist office.

The other main sight is the **Fredericia Museum** (15 kr), which displays local military and civilian history in an attractive collection of historic buildings at Jernbanegade 10, just a few minutes walk south of the railway station. It's open daily from 11 am to 5 pm in summer, from noon to 4 pm Tuesday to Sunday the rest of the year.

Places to Stay

The 112-bed *Fredericia Vandrerhjem* (☎ 75 92 12 87, fax 75 93 29 05) is about 1.5 km south-west of the railway station at Skovløbervænget 9, 7000 Fredericia. Dorm beds cost 75 kr and private rooms cost from 150 kr for one person up to 450 kr for six. The hostel is open from 2 January to 30 November.

The tourist office books rooms in private homes for 100/200 kr a single/double, plus a 25 kr booking fee.

The cheapest city hotel is *Fredericia Sømandshjem* (☎ 75 92 01 99, fax 75 93 25 90), Gothersgade 40, 7000 Fredericia, which is near the harbour. Singles/doubles with shared bath cost 280/380 kr, with private bath 440/540 kr, breakfast included.

Places to Eat

The railway station has a minimarket, a *DSB Restaurant* and a cheap snack bar where you can get pitta bread sandwiches or half a chicken for 29 kr.

In the centre, you'll find a number of places to eat along Danmarksgade. Diagonally opposite the tourist office is a bakery, while a block to the west at Danmarksgade 8 is *Harlekin*, a large fast-food eatery with inexpensive sandwiches and plate lunches. There's a pizza and steak restaurant at Danmarksgade 36, a fast-food pizza and kebab restaurant at Danmarksgade 50 and a standard pizza and sandwich shop at Danmarksgade 55. A few blocks south from Danmarksgade at Gothersgade 39 is the English-style pub *You'll Never Walk Alone* which serves British draught beers, sandwiches and snacks.

Getting There & Away

Fredericia is at the north side of the E20, 80 km from Nyborg and 92 km from Esbjerg.

Train Fredericia has frequent train services, being on both the north-south line between Padborg and Frederikshavn and the busy Copenhagen-Århus route. Train fares are 53 kr to Odense, 77 kr to Padborg or Århus and 166 kr to Copenhagen.

VEJLE

Vejle, at the head of the Vejle Fjord, has a population of 50,000. In the 19th century, after the railway was extended here, Vejle became a centre for iron foundries, cotton mills and food processing plants.

While most foreign travellers in Vejle are simply passing through on their way to Legoland or Jelling, there are two adjacent museums in the town centre on Flegborg, a few blocks north-west of the tourist office. **Den Smidtske Gård**, a 1799 merchant's house, holds the local history collection, while **Vejle Kunstmuseum** exhibits Danish and European art.

More interesting, if you haven't already seen one of the 'bog people' in Århus or Silkeborg, is the corpse of an **Iron Age woman** dating from 450 BC. She can be seen through a glass-topped case at the Sankt Nicolai Kirke on Kirkegade, a 10-minute walk from either the railway station or tourist office.

Information

The Vejle Turistbureau (☎ 75 82 19 55, fax 75 82 10 11), Søndergade 14, 7100 Vejle, is in the town centre on the main pedestrian street, a short walk west of the railway station. It's open in summer from 9.30 am to 5.30 pm Monday to Saturday, with earlier closing times in the low season.

Places to Stay & Eat

If you need to break for the night, Vejle has a hostel (☎ 75 82 51 88) south-east of the city at Gammel Landevej 80 and a camping ground (☎ 75 82 33 35) north-east of the city; the tourist office books rooms in private homes for 105 kr per person; and there are a few moderately priced hotels in the centre.

You'll find the usual bakeries, cafés and restaurants in the central streets around the tourist office and the nearby Rådhustorvet.

Getting There & Away

Vejle is off the E45, 73 km south-west of Århus and 30 km north of Kolding.

Vejle has frequent train service, as it's on the main Jutland line and is also the terminus for the north-westward line to Jelling, Herning and Holstebro. From Vejle it takes 45 minutes (59 kr) to Århus, 36 minutes (35 kr) to Kolding and one hour (53 kr) to Herning.

JELLING

Jelling is a small town with a rich history. Although its sleepy rural character gives few hints to its past, Jelling once served as the royal seat of King Gorm the Old, the first in a millennium-long chain of Danish monarchs that continues unbroken to this day. The site of Gorm's ancient castle remains a mystery, but other vestiges of his reign can still be found at the Jelling Church. The church is in the centre of town right on route 442 and just a two-minute walk due north of the railway station along Stationsvej.

Information

The Jelling Turistbureau (☎ 75 87 13 01) is west of the church at Gormsgade 4, 7300 Jelling. It's open daily from 10 am to 4 pm mid-May to the end of August and from 10 am to 6 pm in July.

Jelling Kirke

The Jelling Church, erected around 1100 AD, is one of Denmark's most significant historic sites. Inside this small whitewashed church you'll find some vivid (although unauthentically restored) 12th century **frescoes** that are among the oldest in Denmark. The main attraction, however, sits just outside the church door where there are two well-preserved **rune stones**.

The smaller stone was erected in the early 900s by King Gorm the Old, in honour of his wife. The larger one, raised by Gorm's son, Harald Bluetooth, is adorned with the oldest representation of Christ found in Scandinavia and reads:

Harald king bade this be ordained for Gorm his father and Thyra his mother, the Harald who won for himself all Denmark and Norway and made the Danes Christians.

Harald Bluetooth did, in fact, rout the Swedes from Denmark and begin the peaceful conversion of Denmark to Christianity, away from the pagan religion celebrated by his father. The larger stone, commonly dubbed 'Denmark's baptismal certificate',

not only represents the advent of Christianity but also bids a royal farewell to the ancient gods of prehistoric Denmark. One side of the stone, which shows a snake coiled around a mythological creature, is thought to symbolise this change of faith.

Two huge **burial mounds** flank the church. The barrow at the north side had long been speculated to contain the bones of King Gorm and Queen Thyra. However, when it was excavated in 1820, no human remains were found. In 1861, King Frederik VII oversaw the excavation of the southern mound, but again only a few objects were found, with no mortal remains among them.

In the 1970s, a team of archaeologists excavated beneath the Jelling Church itself and this time hit pay dirt. They found the remains of three earlier wooden churches, the oldest of which is thought to have been erected by Harald Bluetooth. A burial chamber was also unearthed at this time and human bones and gold jewellery discovered. The jewellery was consistent with pieces that had been found earlier in the northern burial mound. Archaeologists now believe that the skeletal remains found beneath the church are those of King Gorm, who had originally been buried in the northern mound but was later reinterred by his son. Presumably, Harald Bluetooth, out of respect, moved his parents' remains from pagan soil to a Christian place of honour within the church. The bones of Queen Thyra have yet to be found.

Items found during the excavation, as well as replicas of the rune stones (brightly painted, as the originals are thought to have been), are displayed at the national museum in Copenhagen.

Viking Play

For 10 days in late June, a local theatre group performs a Viking-theme play near the shores of lake Fårup Sø, at the southern outskirts of Jelling. A 15-metre-long replica of a Viking ship is sailed on the lake as part of the drama. Tickets cost 75 kr for adults and 20 kr for children and can be reserved by calling ☎ 75 87 27 20.

CENTRAL JUTLAND

Places to Stay & Eat

The three-star *Friluftsbadets Camping* (☎ 75 87 16 53, fax 75 87 20 82), Mølvangvej, 7300 Jelling, is right in town, a km west of the church. It's open from early April to mid-September and charges 46 kr per person.

The *Jelling Kro* (☎ 75 87 10 06, fax 75 87 11 76), Gormsgade 16, 7300 Jelling, 100 metres north of the tourist office, has a daily two-course meal for 95 kr and six rooms with shared bath for 275/375 kr a single/double, breakfast included.

The *Super Brugsen* supermarket, just west of the church on Mølvangvej, has a delicatessen with takeaway items. The *Jelling Bageri* at Vejlevej 22, about a five-minute walk east of the church, has croissants, burgers and sandwiches.

Getting There & Away

Jelling is 10 km north-west of Vejle via route 442.

Train Jelling is on the railway line between Vejle and Struer, with trains at least hourly on weekdays, slightly less frequently on weekends. From Vejle to Jelling, the train takes 15 minutes and costs 18 kr. There's also an hourly bus service between Vejle and Jelling (bus No 211), but it takes a few minutes longer.

LEGOLAND

Legoland, a km north of the small inland town of Billund, is Denmark's most visited tourist attraction outside of Copenhagen. A 10-hectare theme park built from plastic Lego blocks, Legoland has hosted some 25 million visitors, more than half of them from abroad, since it opened in 1968.

Legoland has its own bank, post office, tourist office, hotel and restaurants, and even its own airport.

The park's main attraction is a Lilliputian world of 42 million plastic blocks arranged into miniature cities as well as scenes with Lego pirates and safari animals. Most replicas are on a scale of 1:20 and include such scenes as the medieval town of Ribe, the Amalienborg palace in Copenhagen and a handful of easily recognisable international sights like Amsterdam, Bergen and the Parthenon.

At times the park employs as many as 30 'builders' who spend their days snapping together the creations. The tallest piece, modelled after the Statue of Liberty in New York, reaches a height of nearly 10 metres and contains 1.4 million Lego blocks. The most elaborate piece is the three-million-block Port of Copenhagen exhibit, which features electronically controlled ships, trains and cranes.

Legoland also has amusement rides geared mostly for children, including Ferris wheels, merry-go-rounds, miniature trains and boats – all included in the admission price. The only ride that charges an extra fee (25 kr) is the traffic school, a mini driving course with little electric cars.

There's also an antique puppet and doll collection complete with an elaborate six-sq-metre dollhouse castle and some theme-park sections such as Legoredo, a small Wild West town with a few costumed gunslingers and American Indians in feather headdresses.

Legoland (☎ 75 33 13 33) is open daily from mid-April to the end of September. Opening hours are from 10 am to 8 pm (until 9 pm from July to mid-August). Admission costs 90 kr for children ages 3 to 13 and 100 kr for adults. If you visit in July, a prime time for European holiday-makers, try to come on the weekends as the busiest days, and longest queues, are from Monday to Thursday.

Note that the activities and rides generally shut down about two hours before Legoland closes, and that there's no admission charge after the rides stop. In this evening period when the gates are open gratis to the public you can still view the Lego block sights – so for those just curious to see what the park is all about it's an ideal time to swing by for a free stroll.

Information

The Billund Turistbureau (☎ 75 33 19 26, fax 75 35 31 79), Postbox 46, 7190 Billund, is inside Legoland but has an entrance that faces the road and is open year round. Mid-summer opening hours are from 9 am to 9 pm daily, and during the rest of the Legoland season is open from 10 am to 6 pm. Winter hours are shorter.

Places to Stay

Billund FDM Camping (☎ 75 33 15 21, fax 75 35 37 36), Ellehammer Allé 2, 7190 Billund, adjacent to the hostel, is one of Denmark's largest camping grounds, with 550 sites. It's also one of the few Danish camping grounds with a four-star rating and has a full range of amenities from a coin laundry to lounges and playground facilities. The camping charge is 44 kr per person and it's open all year round.

The 268-bed *Billund Vandrerhjem* (☎ 75 33 27 77, fax 75 33 28 77), Ellehammer Allé, 7190 Billund, is a new hostel that's only 400 metres east of the Legoland gate. Dorm beds cost 85 kr, while family rooms cost from 225 kr for one person to 375 kr for five people. It's open year round except from 15 December to 15 January.

Opposite Legoland park, but connected by an overhead walkway, is the 127-room *Hotel Legoland* (☎ 75 33 12 44, fax 75 35 38 10), Aastvej 10, 7190 Billund. The rooms have a private bath, TV, phone and minibar and cost 610/875 kr for singles/doubles, including breakfast and a discount on the park entrance fee.

A cheaper option is the *Hotel Svanen* (☎ 75 33 28 33, fax 75 35 35 15), Nordmarksvej 8, 7190 Billund, a motel-style place 500 metres south-east of Legoland, in the same neighbourhood as the hostel and camping ground. It has 24 modern rooms with phone, TV and private bath for 475/575 kr, breakfast included.

Places to Eat

Legoland park has about a dozen food stands and restaurants. Among them are the *Waffle Bakery*, which has homemade waffles and jam; *Oasen*, which has hot dogs, burgers and ice cream; the *Drive Inn*, with sandwiches and pizza; the *Grill House*, specialising in grilled steaks and kebabs; the *Saloon*, which features draught beer and spareribs; the *Ristorante*, with pizza and pasta dishes; and the *Cafeteria* which, not surprisingly, has cafeteria fare.

The hostel has its own café serving three meals a day and there are restaurants at both hotels.

Getting There & Away

Billund is on route 28, 59 km north-east of Esbjerg and 28 km west of Vejle. There's no train service. If you're travelling by train, the most common route is to get off at Vejle and to catch a bus from there.

Air Mærsk Air (☎ 75 33 22 44) has numerous daily flights to Billund from Copenhagen. It also provides a daily international service to Billund from London, Amsterdam, Brussels, Stockholm and Frankfurt, and a twice-weekly summertime service flying from the Faroe Islands.

In addition, New Air (☎ 75 35 33 77) flies to Billund from Manchester, Birmingham, Stavanger and Bergen; KLM (☎ 75 33 81 11) flies from Amsterdam; Sabena (☎ 75 33 22 04) flies from Brussels; and Braathens Safe (☎ 75 35 33 78) flies from Oslo.

Bus Seasonal bus tours, which include same-day return fares and entrance to Legoland, are available from a number of Danish cities. From Vejle (☎ 75 82 97 66) the cost is 155/110 kr for adults/children, from Århus (☎ 86 12 16 00) it's 162/147 kr and from either Esbjerg or Fanø (☎ 75 16 26 00) it's 160/115 kr.

There's also a frequent public bus service from Vejle to Legoland (30 minutes) and a once-hourly bus from Esbjerg to Legoland (1½ hours).

In addition you could hop on one of the airport buses, timed to meet scheduled flights between Billund airport and Århus (1½ hours) and Odense (1½ hours); the Odense bus makes a stop in Fredericia.

Getting Around

To/From the Airport Billund's airport, which sits right outside Legoland's gate, not

Lego

Lego got its start more than 60 years ago when a local carpenter, Ole Kirk Christiansen, tried his hand at making wooden toys to earn income during a Depression-era construction slump. In 1934, after a couple of years of making pull-toys and piggy banks, Ole selected the business name Lego, a contraction of the Danish words *leg godt*, meaning 'play well', and expanded his line to four dozen toy designs.

In the late 1940s, Lego became the first company in Denmark to acquire a plastics injection-moulding machine and began making plastic interlocking blocks called 'binding bricks', the forerunner of today's Lego blocks. In 1960, when Lego's wooden-toy warehouse went up in flames, the company decided to concentrate solely on plastic toys. By that time Lego blocks had become the most popular children's toys in Europe.

Lego continued to expand. In 1969 it created the Duplo series for younger children, with bricks twice as long and twice as wide as basic Lego blocks. Later, Lego introduced little vehicles, wooden families and complex theme sets of trains, pirate ships and the like. While there are now advanced kits that incorporate motors and fancy gadgets, the basic appeal of Lego continues to be the simple interlocking blocks that can be snapped together in endless creative combinations.

Lego is still a family-run business, today headed by Ole Kirk's grandson, but it's grown into one of Denmark's best-known companies and Europe's largest toy manufacturer. Lego now has 42 branches on six continents. It's estimated that in the past half-century some 300 million children worldwide have at one time or another played with Lego toys. ∎

only services Legoland but because of its central Jutland location has grown into Denmark's second busiest airport.

Århus

Århus, Denmark's second largest city, has just over a quarter of a million residents. The cultural centre of Jutland, it's a lively university city with one of Denmark's best music and entertainment scenes – everything from symphony performances and theatre to a thriving night-owl café life.

Århus boasts a well-preserved historic quarter and plenty to see and do, ranging from good museums and intriguing old churches in the city centre to woodland trails and beaches along the city outskirts. Some of the highlights are Den Gamle By, a quality open-air museum; Vor Frue Kirke, which has Denmark's oldest chapel; Århus Cathedral, Denmark's largest church; and the Moesgård Museum, which has notable Bronze and Iron Age collections and an enjoyable trail through a landscape rich in prehistoric sights.

History

On the centre of Jutland's east coast, Århus has been an important trade centre and seaport since Viking times. Originally named Aros, meaning at 'the river mouth', archaeological excavations indicate Århus was founded around 900 AD, when a semicircular rampart was constructed at the waterfront. The rampart, only a few city blocks in diameter, enveloped the area where the current cathedral, theatre and casino now stand. (Remnants of the original city can be seen in the excavated basement of the Unibank west of the cathedral.)

In medieval times Århus' central location often left it thick in conflict with neighbouring states; King Sweyn II of Denmark and King Magnus of Norway engaged in a major battle off Århus in 1043, and just a few years later, in 1050, Århus was ravaged by the Norwegian warrior-king Harald Hardrada. In the decades that followed its prosperity was kept in check by raids from other rival

Vikings and attacks by fearsome Wend pirates.

Over the next centuries, stability was slowly achieved and Århus grew as a centre of trade, art and religion. Its large, protected harbour became increasingly important. In the 18th century Århus flourished as a transport hub for central Jutland, and indeed, virtually all regional roads and railway lines still lead to the city.

An ongoing dispute between Århus and the national government led the city to found its own university in 1928. However, by the time the new campus was ready to open its doors in 1933, the national government had come around to recognise and support the university. Today students at Århus University, along with those at Århus' engineering college, dental school, business college, music academy and school of architecture, account for nearly 40,000 of the city's 265,000 residents. Århus University's best-known student of recent times was Denmark's Crown Prince Frederik who studied law and political science there before entering a postgraduate programme at Harvard University.

Orientation

Århus is fairly compact and easy to get around. The railway station (Århus Hovedbanegård) is on the south side of the city centre. The pedestrian shopping streets of Søndergade and Sankt Clements Torv lead to the cathedral in the heart of the old city. The small streets around the cathedral are filled with cafés, pubs and restaurants.

Information

Tourist Office Tourist Århus (☎ 86 12 16 00,

Viking dragonhead motif of eastern Jutland

fax 86 12 95 90), Rådhuset, 8000 Århus C, is south of the city hall on Park Allé. From mid-June to early September it's open from 9 am to 7 pm Monday to Friday, from 9.30 am to 5 pm Saturday and from 9.30 am to 1 pm Sunday. The rest of the year it's open Monday to Friday from 9.30 am to 4.30 pm (to 5 pm from May to mid-June) and from 10 am to 1 pm on Saturday.

Money There's a Sydbank at the front of the railway station and many more banks along Søndergade. There's also a Unibank near the cathedral at Sankt Clements Torv 6 and a Midtbank near the harbour on the corner of Åboulevarden and Mindebrogade.

Post The main post office is beside the railway station. It's open Monday to Friday from 9 am to 6 pm and from 10 am to noon on Saturday.

Travel Agency Kilroy Travels (☎ 86 20 11 44), Fredensgade 40, specialises in youth and discount travel.

Bookshops The GAD bookshop on Søndergade, south of McDonald's, has a good English-language travel section as well as novels and general-interest books about Denmark. At Frederiks Allé 53, near the health-food shop Sundhedskost, there's a shop specialising in second-hand English books. Foreign newspapers are sold at the stand opposite the railway station.

Library You can read foreign newspapers at the main public library, a large modern facility off Vester Allé. This is also a good place to pick up various free trail brochures published by Skov og Naturstyrelsen, the forestry department. The library is open from 10 am to 7 pm Monday to Thursday, 10 am to 6 pm on Friday and 10 am to 2 pm on Saturday.

Laundry The Quick Vask, a coin laundry at Guldsmedgade 27, is open from 7.30 am to 9.30 pm.

CENTRAL JUTLAND

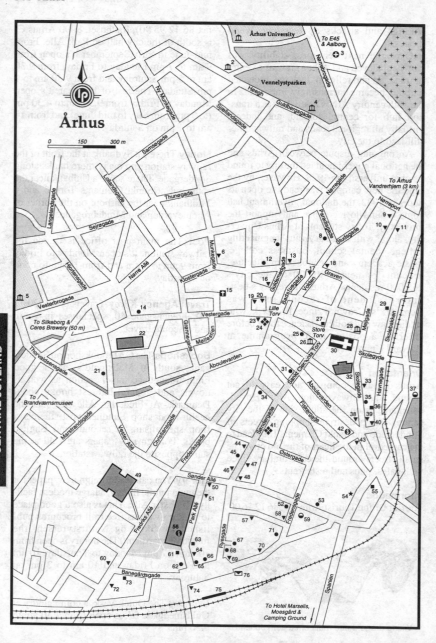

Århus University

To E45
& Aalborg

Vennelystparken

Narrebrogade

Høegh

Guldbergsgade

Ny Munkegade

Sjællandsgade

Samsøegade

Lollandsgade

Thunøgade

Langelandsgade

Sejrøgade

Nørre Allé

Hortensgade

Klostergade

Munkegade

Vesterbrogade

To Silkeborg &
Ceres Brewery (50 m)

Grønnegade

Møllestien

Vestergade

Åboulevarden

Thorvaldsensgade

To
Brandværnsmuseet

Marstrandsgade

Vester Allé

Christiansgade

Fredensgade

Vester Allé

Sønder Allé

Park Allé

Frederiks Allé

Banegårdsgade

Paradisgade

Studsgade

Nørregade

Nørreport

To Århus
Vandrerhjem (3 km)

Graven

Volden

Badstuegade

Guldsmedgade

Lille
Torv

Store
Torv

Sankt Clemens Torv

Åboulevarden

Fiskergade

Mejlgade

Skolebakken

Skolegyde

Skolegade

Havnegade

Rosensgade

Sønder Allé

Østergade

Spanien

Frederiksgade

Ryesgade

To Hotel Marselis,
Moesgård &
Camping Ground

0   150   300 m

Århus

PLACES TO STAY

27 Hotel Royal & Casino
29 Hotel Windsor
36 Århus City Sleep-In
55 Hotel Atlantic
61 Ansgar Missions Hotel
63 Hotel Ritz
73 Eriksens Hotel

PLACES TO EAT

6   Naturkost
9   Kulturgyngen &
    Musikcaféen
10 Gallorant Kif-Kif
11 Hornitos
13 Hougaard Konditori
16 Pizza Hut
17 Ajam
18 Café Drundenfuss
19 Café Smagløs
20 Munkestuen
23 Jacob's Bar BQ
29 Fiskekælderen
33 Rosita's Cantina
38 Færgekroen
39 El Greco
40 Asian House
43 Italia
44 McDonald's

46 Super Brugsen Super-
    market
47 Greengrocers
48 China Wok House
50 Special Smørrebrød
51 Bakery
57 Jensen's Bøfhus
58 China Town
60 Føtex Supermarket
64 Guldhornet
69 Loft Konditori
70 Café Hollywood
72 Sundhedskost
74 Fruit Stand

OTHER

1   Naturhistorisk Museum
2   Steno Museet
3   Århus Kommunehospital
4   Århus Kunstmuseum
5   Den Gamle By
7   Coin Laundry
8   Café Paradis & Cinema
12 Blitz
14 V58
15 Vor Frue Kirke
21 Huset Musikteater
22 Library
24 Magasin du Nord
25 Løve Apotek

26 Unibank & Vikinge-
    Museet
28 Besættelses-Museet &
    Kvindemuseet
30 Århus Domkirke
31 Glazzhuset
32 Århus Teater
34 Telefon Torv
35 Fatter Eskil
37 Kalundborg Boats
41 Salling Department
    Store
42 Midtbank
45 GAD Bookstore
49 Musikhuset Århus
52 Kilroy Travels
53 Europcar Car Rental
54 Police Station
56 Tourist Office & Århus
    Rådhus
59 Bus Station
62 SAS Ticket Office
65 Newspaper Stand
66 Jernbane Apotek
67 Biografen
68 Dan Foto
71 Asmussen Cykler
75 Railway Station
76 Post & Telegraph Office

CENTRAL JUTLAND

Pharmacy A conveniently located pharmacy is the Jernbane Apotek, opposite the railway station, open Monday to Friday from 9.30 am to 7.30 pm and on Saturday from 9.30 am to 1 pm. The Løve Apotek, Store Torv 5, opposite the Hotel Royal, is open 24 hours.

Emergency Dial 112 for police or ambulance and ☎ 86 20 10 22 for emergency medical services. Århus Kommunehospital on Nørrebrogade has a 24-hour emergency ward.

The Krisecenter for Voldsramtekvinder (☎ 86 15 35 22) helps women in crisis and can provide overnight safe haven.

Film & Photography Dan Foto on Ryesgade, just north of the railway station, will develop a roll of 24 prints for 49 kr with a three-day wait, 69 kr in 24 hours or 99 kr in an hour. It also carries print film, slide film and camera accessories.

Central Museums

Den Gamle By Den Gamle By (The Old Town) is a fine open-air museum with 75 restored buildings brought here from around Denmark and reconstructed as a provincial town, complete with a functioning bakery, silversmith, bookbinder etc. Most of the buildings are half-timbered 17th and 18th century houses but there's also a watermill, a windmill and a few buildings from the turn of the century.

Den Gamle By is on Viborgvej, a 20-minute walk from the city centre, and open daily all year round. Hours are from 9 am to 6 pm from June to August, from 9 am to 5 pm in May and September, from 10 am to 4 pm in the shoulder season and from 11 am to 3 pm in winter. Admission is 40 kr for adults and 12 kr for children. After hours, however,

ᚠᛉᚾᛈᛁ᛫ᚪᛈᚠᛈᚾᛁ᛫ᚠᛈᛈᛁᛁᚠ᛫ᛏᛁᚠ᛫ᚠᛉᚾᛈᛁ᛫ᚪᛈᚠᛈᚾᛁ᛫ᚠᛈᛈᛁᛁᚠ᛫ᛏᛁᚠ᛫ᚠ

Århus Pass

Århus has a city pass that allows unlimited transport on municipal buses and admission to most city sights, including Den Gamle By, Århus Kunstmuseum, the Mosegård museum, the two university museums, the fire brigade museum, the women's museum and Tivoli Friheden.

The cost for a two-day pass is 110 kr for adults and 55 kr for children aged 15 and under. A seven-day pass costs 155/75 kr for adults/children. The pass can be purchased from hotels and the tourist office. ∎

ᚠᛉᚾᛈᛁ᛫ᚪᛈᚠᛈᚾᛁ᛫ᚠᛈᛈᛁᛁᚠ᛫ᛏᛁᚠ᛫ᚠᛉᚾᛈᛁ᛫ᚪᛈᚠᛈᚾᛁ᛫ᚠᛈᛈᛁᛁᚠ᛫ᛏᛁᚠ᛫ᚠ

you can walk through the old cobbled streets for free – this is a delightful time to visit as the crowds are gone and the light is ideal for photography, but you won't be able to enter individual buildings. Bus Nos 3, 14 and 25 pass the museum.

Vikinge-Museet Pop into the basement of Unibank, Sankt Clements Torv 6, for a look at artefacts from the Viking village that was excavated at this site in 1964 during the bank's construction. The excavated artefacts date from 900 to 1400 AD, indicating that this neighbourhood was one of the first areas settled in Århus. The display includes photos of the excavation, a skeleton, a reconstructed house, thousand-year-old carpenter's tools and pottery. It's open during banking hours: 9.30 am to 4 pm Monday to Friday, 9.30 am to 6 pm Thursday. Admission is free.

Besættelses-Museet The old city hall at Domkirkeplads 5, which served as the Gestapo headquarters during WW II, now contains the Besættelses-Museet (Occupation Museum). Located in the basement of the building, it details the Danish Resistance movement through photo displays, tableaus, guns and a few instruments of torture. This volunteer-run museum is generally open from 10 am to 4 pm daily in summer and on Saturday and Sunday the rest of the year.

Admission is 15 kr for adults and 5 kr for children.

Kvindemuseet Also at Domkirkeplads 5 is Kvindemuseet (Women's Museum), which features changing exhibits on the culture and history of women. This is also a good place for women travellers to meet Danish women involved in the feminist movement. It's open from 10 am to 5 pm daily between June and September, and from 10 am to 4 pm Tuesday to Sunday the rest of the year. Admission is 15 kr for adults, 10 kr for teenagers and free for children 12 and under.

Århus Kunstmuseum This museum, at Vennelystparken south of the university, has a comprehensive collection of 19th and 20th century Danish art. There's also a foreign collection, predominantly of German and American art, and periodic special exhibits. It's open from 10 am to 5 pm Tuesday to Sunday. Admission costs 20 kr for adults (except during special exhibits when it's 30 kr), and is free for children. Take bus No 1, 2, 3 or 6 to Nørreport.

University Museums There are two museums at Universitetsparken, the grounds of the Århus University. The **Naturhistorisk Museum** has a large collection of domestic and foreign stuffed birds and animals, many set in dioramas. There are also displays on Danish ecology, evolution and minerals. Opening hours are from 10 am to 5 pm in July and August, and from 10 to 4 pm the rest of the year; closed on Monday from November to March. Admission is 25 for adults, free for children.

The **Steno Museet** is a science history museum, with exhibits on medicinal herbs, anatomy and medicine. The museum also has a planetarium with shows at 11 am and 1 and 3 pm. Admission to the museum is 30 kr for adults, free for children. The planetarium shows cost 30 kr for adults and 20 kr for children. It's open from 10 am to 4 pm Tuesday to Sunday, and 10 am until 5 pm in July and August.

Numerous buses go to the university, including Nos 2, 3 and 11.

Churches

Århus Domkirke Århus Cathedral is Denmark's longest, with a lofty nave that spans nearly 100 metres. Its construction began around 1200 AD and took 100 years to complete. In the 15th century the cathedral was transformed from its original Romanesque style to its current gothic one. At that time, the roof was raised over the nave, the landmark clock-tower was erected, high gothic windows were installed and the chancel was extended.

Like other Danish churches, Århus Cathedral was once richly decorated with frescoes which served to convey biblical parables to illiterate peasants. After the Reformation in 1536 church authorities, who felt the frescoes represented Catholicism, had them all whitewashed. Many of these frescoes, which range from tormented scenes of hell to fairy-tale-like paintings, have now been uncovered and restored. North of the altar there's a delightfully detailed one of St George, the patron saint of knights, slaying a dragon as a grateful princess looks on; the Arabic numbers in the corner date it from 1497.

The ornate gilt altarpiece, a five-panel pentaptych, was made in Lubeck by the renowned woodcarver Bernt Notke. In its centre panel, to the left of the Madonna and child, is a gaunt-faced St Clement, for whom the cathedral was dedicated. Clement, rather ironically, became the patron saint of sailors by having the inauspicious fate of drowning at sea with an anchor around his neck. The anchor, which has come to symbolise St Clement, can be found in many of the cathedral decorations.

Other items worth special attention are the bronze baptismal font from 1481; the finely carved Renaissance pulpit from 1588; the magnificent baroque pipe organ from 1730;

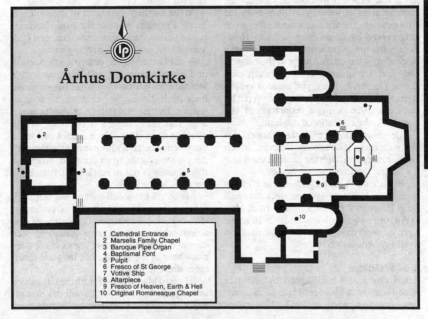

Århus Domkirke

1 Cathedral Entrance
2 Marselis Family Chapel
3 Baroque Pipe Organ
4 Baptismal Font
5 Pulpit
6 Fresco of St George
7 Votive Ship
8 Altarpiece
9 Fresco of Heaven, Earth & Hell
10 Original Romanesque Chapel

the large 18th century votive ship; and the baroque sepulchre in the Marselis family chapel.

The cathedral is open from 9.30 am to 4 pm from May to September and from 10 am to 3 pm from October to April. It's closed on Sunday. As with all churches, there's no touring allowed during funerals, wedding and other services. Admission is free.

Vor Frue Kirke This church is like a Russian *matryoshka* doll, opening to reveal multiple layers beneath the surface. It was here that the original Århus Cathedral was erected shortly after 1060 when King Sweyn II, bent on weakening the power of the archbishop who led the Danish church, divided Denmark into eight separate dioceses, one of which was Århus. The cathedral was constructed of rough stone and travertine and stood until about 1240, when it was replaced by the current Vor Frue Kirke.

Built of red brick, this church has a largely whitewashed interior although the chancel has a few exposed frescoes that depict the coats of arms of wealthy families from the 14th century. There's also a detailed triptych altar carved by Claus Berg in 1530. However, the main treasure, in the church basement, is the vaulted crypt of the original cathedral, the oldest surviving church interior in Denmark. The crypt, entered via the stairs beneath the chancel, was uncovered by chance in 1956 during a restoration of Vor Frue Kirke by the national museum.

The church has yet another chapel, this one with early 16th century frescoes, which can be entered through the garden courtyard; it's behind the first door on the left.

Set back on Vestergade, Vor Frue Kirke is open from 10 am to 4 pm on weekdays and from 10 am to 2 pm on Saturday from May to August; in winter it's open from 10 am to 2 pm on weekdays and 10 am until noon on Saturday. Admission is free.

Århus Rådhus

Århus city hall was designed by architect Arne Jacobsen, a pioneer of Danish modernism, and completed in 1942. This rather controversial building, which has always elicited strong opinions, has a ponderous, functional design and is topped by a rectangular clock-tower whose outer skeleton resembles forgotten scaffolding. The outer facade is of dark Norwegian marble, while the inside has light open spaces. On weekdays at noon and 4 pm (mid-June to mid-September) you can take the lift (5 kr) up the tower for a view, or at 11 am take a guided tour (10 kr), which includes the tower.

Southern Outskirts

Marselisborg About two km south of the city centre is the start of a large wooded area that stretches down along the coast for nearly 10 km. The woods changes names several times, but generally the northern end is known as Marselisborg, the midsection as Moesgård and the southern part as Fløjstrup, names taken from the estates that once owned each section of the woods. The entire green belt has numerous wooded trails suitable for hiking, cycling and horse riding.

At the northern perimeter of the woods is Tivoli Friheden amusement park; Stadionhallen, Århus' main sports stadium; and Jysk Væddeløbsbane, a horse racing track.

A km farther south, near the intersection of Carl Nielsens Vej and Kongevejen, is **Marselisborg Slot**, a big white manor house built in 1902 that is occasionally used in summer by the royal family. When the queen is in residence, there's a changing of the guard at noon. The palace cannot be toured but you can catch a glimpse of it, along with the palace guards, from the road; when the royal family is not in residence the grounds are open to the public.

About 1.5 km south-east of Marselisborg Slot, on the main road south, is **Dyrehaven** (Deer Park), an enclosed section of the woods where you can see fallow deer, sika deer and wild pigs. There are wild roe deer elsewhere in the woods, but they are much more difficult to spot.

To get to Marselisborg from the city centre take Spanien (route 451) south to Strandvejen, the coastal road. Bus No 19 runs from the Århus railway station south along the coastal road.

Tivoli Friheden If you're travelling with children who are getting tired of old churches and museums, consider a skip to this amusement park, two km south of the city centre. It's on Skovbrynet, at the northern edge of the Marselisborg woods, which is reached via Strandvejen; you can get there on bus No 4. The park contains carnival-style rides, clown shows, flower gardens, fast-food eateries, cafés and a small casino section of slot machines for wayward adults. It's open from 1 to 10 pm daily from late April to late August and 1 to 11 pm in midsummer. Admission costs 22 kr for adults and 10 kr for children.

Moesgård The Moesgård area, eight km south of the city centre, makes for an absorb-

ing half-day outing. The main focal point is the **Forhistorisk Museum Moesgård** (Moesgård Prehistoric Museum), which has quality displays from the Stone Age to the Viking Age, including flint axes and tools, pottery and a roomful of **rune stones**. The most unique exhibit, displayed in a glass case, is the 2000-year-old **Grauballe Man**, found preserved in a nearby bog in 1952. The dehydrated, leathery body is amazingly intact, right down to its red hair and fingernails. The museum is open from 10 am to 5 pm daily from 1 May to late September, from 10 am to 4 pm Tuesday to Sunday the rest of the year. Admission is 30 kr for adults, free for children.

An enjoyable **walking trail** dubbed the 'prehistoric trackway' leads from behind the museum through fields of wildflowers, grazing sheep and beech woods down to **Moesgård Strand**, Århus' best sandy beach.

Graubelle Man

The Grauballenmanden (Graubelle Man), now displayed at the Moesgård Museum, was discovered in April 1952 in a peat bog near the village of Graubelle, 35 km west of Århus. He died around 80 BC, a slash across his throat indicating he may have been the victim of a murder or execution. It's possible that he was the object of some sort of ritualistic sacrifice, perhaps killed as an offering to one of the pagan gods thought responsible for warding off plagues and assuring abundant harvests.

The Graubelle Man was about 30 years old when he died. Tannic acids and iron deposits in the bog preserved his body and literally tanned his hide, giving his skin a brown, leather-like appearance.

Two millennium after the Graubelle Man's last supper, scientists were able to discover a great deal about his eating habits by examining his stomach, which contained remnants of a porridge of barley and rye, as well as 66 different types of seeds. ∎

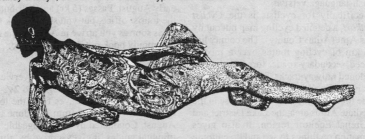

CENTRAL JUTLAND

The trail, marked by red-dotted stones, passes reconstructed historic sights including a dolmen, burial cists and an Iron Age house. Before you start off, pick up the detailed English-language trail brochure (10 kr) at the museum. You can walk one way and catch a bus from the beach back to the city centre, or do the trail both ways as a five-km loop.

Bus No 6 from Århus railway station terminates at the museum, and bus No 19 terminates at Moesgård Strand; both buses run twice an hour.

Det Danske Brandværnsmuseum
The Danish Fire Brigade Museum, one of Europe's largest museums of its kind, has more than 100 antique fire-fighting vehicles, both horse-drawn and engine-driven. It's open from 10 am to 5 pm Tuesday to Saturday. Admission is 40 kr for adults and 15 kr for children. It's at Tomsagervej 23, five km west of the city centre and just off Viby Ringvej. The museum can be reached by bus No 12 or 18.

Activities
Hiking & Cycling The Århus Kommune distributes the detailed brochure *Nature Around Århus-South* that maps out suggested tours for hiking and cycling in the green space south of the city. This brochure, which has short but interesting titbits on local flora, fauna and history, can be picked up at the tourist office for 10 kr. Be sure to ask for the English-language version.

Specifically for cyclists is the *Cyclist Turistkort*, a detailed cycling map put out by Århus Amt (Århus County). The county has 1200 km of cycling routes over a mix of surfaced secondary roads, forest paths and abandoned railway tracks. The cycling map, available in English, suggests various countywide touring routes, including those in the immediate Århus area, the Lake District and the Grenaa/Ebeltoft region. It also gives information on things to see and do en route and has a few useful tips, such as the location of cycle repair shops. The map costs 80 kr

and can be purchased at tourist offices and bookshops.

Swimming There are sandy beaches on the outskirts of Århus. The most popular one to the north is Bellevue, about four km from the city centre via bus No 6 or 16, while the favourite to the south is Moesgård beach, eight km from the centre via bus No 19.

Other Sports The tourist office has a Tourist Århus/Sport programme (☎ 86 12 16 00) that can arrange a variety of sporting activities, including horse riding, sailing, tennis, golf and windsurfing.

Meet the Danes The tourist office can arrange for foreign travellers to meet with a Danish family at home for tea and conversation. Because they try to match people with similar interests, it's best to request the 'Meet the Danes' programme a day or two in advance. There are no fees.

A special programme designed specifically for foreign students who want to meet Danish students is administered by the International Student Centre, Niels Juels Gade 84. Call ☎ 89 42 17 99 for information and activity schedules.

Organised Tours
Ceres Brewery Tours of the Ceres Brewery, on Vesterbrogade opposite Den Gamle By, are given at 2 pm on Wednesday, except in December; additional tours are given at 9 am on Tuesday and Thursday from late June to early August. Passes (5 kr) are distributed at the tourist office, but you should pick them up as soon as you arrive in Århus as the tours commonly book out days in advance.

Sightseeing Tour For a good overview of the city consider taking the guided 2½-hour public bus tour that leaves from the tourist office at 10 am daily from mid-June to 31 August. Conducted by knowledgeable multilingual guides, it gives a drive-by glimpse of the main city sights and a more detailed tour of the cathedral. At 45 kr it's a good deal as it includes entry into Den Gamle By and also leaves you with a 24-hour bus pass.

Places to Stay

Camping The nearest camping ground is *Blommehaven Camping* (☎ 86 27 02 07, fax 86 27 45 22), Ørneredevej 35, Århus, which has a nice beach-side setting in the Marselisborg woods, five km south of the city centre. Rated three-star, it has cooking facilities, a coin laundry, a minimart with fresh bread, and cabins and caravans for rent from 200 kr a day. The camping charge is 44 kr per person. It's open from early April to mid-September. From Århus railway station you can take bus No 19 (which stops out front) or No 6 (which stops 400 metres away).

Hostel & Private Rooms The 145-bed *Århus Vandrerhjem* (☎ 86 16 72 98, fax 86 10 55 60), Marienlundsvej 10, 8240 Risskov, is in a renovated 1850s dance hall in the midst of the Risskov woods, four km north of the city centre. Dorm beds cost 70 to 85 kr, while family rooms are available from 225 kr for one person to 464 kr for six people. Take bus No 1, 6, 9 or 16; from the bus stop it's a 300-metre walk east along Marien-lundsvej. The hostel is open from 20 January to 20 December. There are hiking trails through the woods and down to the ocean.

The new *Århus City Sleep-In* (☎ 86 19 20 55, fax 86 19 18 11), Havnegade 20, 8000 Århus C, is a great alternative place to stay. Run by the same people who operate Kulturgyngen, the city youth and culture centre, it has a good location near the harbour and is within easy walking distance of the cathedral and other central sights. The building was originally a seaman's hotel, so the sleeping quarters are hotel rooms rather than large dorms and the facilities are good. You can share a room dorm-style for 75 kr or get a private room with your own bath for 240 kr a single or double. The latter comes made up, while in the dorms you can rent a pillow and sheets for 30 kr if you don't have your own. There's a big guest kitchen, a TV room, a pool table and laundry facilities. Breakfast

is available for 25 kr. Reception is open 24 hours and advance reservations are accepted.

The tourist office books rooms in private homes for 120 kr a person, plus a 25 kr booking fee.

Hotels *Eriksens Hotel* (☎ 86 13 62 96, fax 86 13 76 76), Banegårdsgade 6, 8000 Århus C, is a pleasant family-run hotel a few minutes west of the railway station. The 18 rooms are straightforward and vary a bit but most have a desk, a washbasin, two single beds and a couch that can be used as a third bed; baths are off the hall. Singles/doubles cost 315/400 kr, breakfast is an optional 30 kr more per person. Rooms facing the rear are quieter.

The 36-room *Hotel Windsor* (☎ 86 12 23 00), near the harbour at Skolebakken 17, 8000 Århus C, has tidy rooms at reasonable prices. Singles/doubles with phone and washbasin but baths off the hall cost 325/465 kr, while rooms with private baths cost 395/540 kr.

For something more upmarket in the centre, the best value is the 170-room *Ansgar Missions Hotel* (☎ 86 12 41 22, fax 86 20 29 04), at Banegårdsplads 14, 8100 Århus C. Rates are 315 kr for a single room with a shared bath, from 440/540 kr for singles/ doubles with private bath. For 100 kr more there are quiet courtyard-fronting rooms in the rear that have a pleasantly old-fashioned décor, cable TV and deep bathtubs. Breakfast is included in the rates; there's guest parking for an additional 20 kr a day.

Opposite the Ansgar and just north of the railway station is the *Hotel Ritz* (☎ 86 13 44 44, fax 86 13 45 87), Banegårdsplads 12, 8100 Århus C. A member of the Best Western chain, this older 70-room hotel has an appearance that's a throwback to the 1950s. Singles/doubles cost 610/710 kr, though cheaper weekend rates are sometimes available.

The *Hotel Atlantic* (☎ 86 13 11 11, fax 86 13 23 43), Europaplads 12, 8000 Århus C, between the bus station and the harbour, has 102 modern rooms with private bath, TV, phone and minibar. The standard rates are pricey at 895/995 kr for singles/doubles, but the hotel occasionally hangs a sign outside advertising four-bed rooms for as little as 595 kr. Breakfast is included in the rates and there's free guest parking and a rooftop restaurant.

The historic *Hotel Royal* (☎ 86 12 00 11, fax 86 76 04 04), Store Torv 4, Box 43, 8100 Århus C, on the same square as the cathedral, is the city's most expensive hotel. Its casino and deluxe rooms cater to high rollers; singles/doubles frilled up with amenities including a private fax, cost 1400/1650 kr. There are also 'standard' rooms with minibar, TV, video and the like for 1045/1225 kr.

The *Hotel Marselis* (☎ 86 14 44 11, fax 86 11 70 46), Strandvejen 25, 8000 Århus C, is in a well-to-do suburb three km south of the city centre. A member of the Best Western chain, this 100-room hotel fronts the beach on one side and the forest on the other. The rooms, which have modern amenities, including ocean-view balcony, TV and minibar, cost 920/1120 kr for singles/doubles from Sunday to Thursday. On Friday and Saturday there's a weekend rate of 650 kr that covers two adults and two children. All rates include breakfast. The hotel has a pool, sauna, billiards room, bar and restaurant.

Places to Eat

Railway Station Area There are a number of eating options within easy walking distance of the railway station.

The station itself has a small supermarket open to midnight; a *DSB Restaurant* with the usual menu, including a daily meal for 35 kr; and a *DSB Minibar* with hot dogs, burgers and beer. There's a fruit stand out the front while across the street is *Loft Konditori*, a good bakery with a small dining room that opens for breakfast at 7 am every day except Sunday.

A two-minute walk from the station is *Guldhornet*, a pavement solarium restaurant at the Hotel Ritz with a Danish lunch special that includes smoked herring, salted salmon, roast beef and a salad buffet for 70 kr. Dinner is nearly twice as expensive.

Café Hollywood, a few minutes walk east of the railway station at Banegårdsgade 47, has a changing daily meal on weekdays – it can be anything from spaghetti to a Middle Eastern plate or Spanish paella – for just 40 kr. There are also half a dozen salads for the same price and sandwiches for around 30 kr. If you need to pass time while waiting for a train, the café has a pool table and bar. It's open from 11 am to at least midnight (to 10 pm for food).

The nearby *China Town*, opposite the bus station at Fredensgade 46, has a pleasant atmosphere. There are 10 daily lunch specials for under 50 kr served until 4 pm each day. At dinner, there's a four-course meal for around 100 kr and an à la carte menu with standard Chinese dishes averaging 75 kr. It's open from noon to 11 pm daily.

Jensen's Bøfhus, Rosenkrantzgade 23, has a nice all-you-can-eat salad bar for just 29 kr and a 150-gram steak lunch that's served daily from 11.30 am to 4 pm for 34 kr. Dinner dishes, which include salad, range from chicken breast (79 kr) to sirloin (129 kr).

There's a health-food shop, *Sundhedskost*, at Frederiks Allé 49, that's open on weekdays only. The *Fotex* supermarket, diagonally opposite Sundhedskost, has a bakery and deli that can make for a cheap takeaway meal.

Central Area If you're up for Danish open sandwiches, *Special Smørrebrød* at Sønder Allé 2 has a wide variety of smørrebrød at moderate prices. The *China Wok House*, a casual Chinese restaurant at Sønder Allé 9, usually has a few inexpensive specials as well as pitta bread sandwiches.

In the first block of the pedestrian street Søndergade there's a *Super Brugsen* supermarket, a greengrocer (at the entrance of Hafnia Arkaden) and a *McDonald's* that's open to midnight. The *Salling* department store, a bit farther north on Søndergade, has a supermarket in its basement, a bakery and an upstairs 'bistro' with sandwiches and a salad bar.

Huset, a café and restaurant at the Huset cultural centre at Vester Allé 15, on the west side of the city centre, has quiet outdoor dining and cheap prices. On weekdays from noon to 8 pm you can get sandwiches for 20 kr and good salads for 35 kr. From 5 to 8 pm there's also a more substantial menu that includes a daily meal for 45 kr and grilled fish for 65 kr.

Italia, at Åboulevarden 9, is an Italian restaurant with a wood-fired pizza oven. It has pizza and pasta dishes from about 50 kr, meat and fish dishes for around 100 kr and various Italian desserts such as tiramisu and gelato. It's open daily from noon to 11 pm, except on Sunday when it opens at 5 pm.

Rosita's Cantina, Skolegade 21, is a long-established Mexican restaurant with a full menu, including beef enchilada and chicken tostada plates with rice and beans for 89 kr. It's open from 5 pm nightly. Upstairs in the same building is *Liberty*, a moderately priced 'American' sparerib and steak restaurant. Nearby there's a Greek restaurant, *El Greco* at Skolegade 27, and a Cantonese restaurant, *Asian House* at Mindebrogade 2; both have three-course dinners for under 100 kr.

Northside Cafés & Restaurants The narrow streets of the old quarter north of the cathedral are thick with cafés serving Danish, Middle Eastern, Mexican and other ethnic foods at moderate prices. *Café Drudenfuss*, on the corner of Graven and Studsgade, is one of the more popular meeting places; it has inexpensive sandwiches and empanadas (Chilean meat pies) and reasonably priced beer and wine. *Ajam*, on the opposite corner at Klostergade 1, has good Lebanese meals for around 90 kr.

For a different type of scene, step into *Hougaard Konditori*, on the corner of Klostergade and Guldsmedgade, an old-fashioned place where high society gossips over afternoon tea and fine chocolate-covered pastries.

The popular *Munkestuen* at Klostertorv 5 is a smokey hole-in-the-wall café serving excellent Danish food at cheap prices, including a daily dinner for 60 kr. Meals are served from noon to 8 pm, though the bar stays open to around midnight. If Munkestuen is full, the next-door *Café Smagløs* serves good-value meals such as lasagne or chilli con carne with salad and bread for 40 kr. On the opposite side of the same square is Denmark's first *Pizza Hut*, which serves the chain's standard pizzas, pastas and salads from 11.30 am to 11 pm daily.

Jacob's Bar BQ, in an historic merchant's house at Vestergade 3, is a popular and often boisterous place known for its grilled steaks, which begin at around 100 kr. There are also fish, lamb and kebab dishes priced from around 75 kr. It's open daily from 11 am to after midnight.

Naturkost, at Gammel Munkegade 4, is a small health-food shop with a good selection of natural foods, including juices, vitamins, produce and snack items.

The countercultural *Kulturgyngen* at Mejlgade 53, serves hearty portions of good food, offering a different vegetarian dinner and a different fish or meat dinner each night for 40 to 50 kr. There's also a lunch special for 25 kr, as well as cakes, coffees and other drinks. Meals are served from 10 am to 5 pm and 6 to 9 pm Monday to Saturday, but it's open for drinks and conversation to at least midnight and commonly to 2 am.

Nearby, the cosy *Gallorant Kif-Kif* at Mejlgade 41 is open nightly from 5 pm and has Middle Eastern dishes such as vegetarian couscous or shish kebab with salad and hummus for 70 kr. It also offers takeaway pitta bread sandwiches for 25 kr.

Hornitos, inconspicuously tucked in a corner at the end of the courtyard at Mejlgade 46B, makes authentic Chilean empanadas for takeaway only. These delicious pies, which come in chicken, lamb, beef and vegetarian spinach versions, cost 25 kr alone or 30 kr with a salad. There are also a couple of plate meals for a few kr more. It's open from 11 am to 9 pm Monday to Saturday.

The café at the *Kvindemuseet* (Women's Museum), Domkirkeplads 5, is a casual place for women to meet over coffee, cakes and sandwiches. There's also a changing daily meal for 30 kr. It's generally open the same hours as the museum, from 10 am to 5 pm (closed Monday in winter), although on summer evenings it sometime stays open to midnight.

Fiskekælderen, Skolebakken 17, at the Hotel Windsor, is a fine-dining restaurant specialising in fresh fish and shellfish. It's open for dinner only, from 5 to 10 pm daily. Main dishes start (à la carte) at 72 kr (for fried plaice with potatoes) and go up to 165 kr. There's also a daily special of two courses for 168 kr, three courses for 198 kr.

Entertainment

Being a university city, there's always a lot happening in Århus. For detailed listings of current events, music and other entertainment, pick up *Ugen Ud*, *Tjek Århus* or the tourist office's *What's On in Århus*, all of which are free.

Music Clubs Much of Århus' vibrant music scene is centred around backstreet cafés, such as *Fatter Eskil* (☎ 86 12 79 45), Skolegade 25, which plays good blues music from 10 pm most nights with a cover charge of about 25 kr.

Musikcaféen (☎ 86 76 03 44) and *Gyngen* (☎ 86 19 22 55) at Mejlgade 53 are part of Kulturgyngen, a youth and culture centre that occupies a renovated factory at the north side of the city centre. Both places offer an interesting alternative scene with a wide range of music that includes jazz, reggae, rock, Afro and salsa. Entry is sometimes free, often 20 to 30 kr, and occasionally as high as 70 kr if someone special is performing.

There's usually something going on at *Husets Musikteater*, (☎ 86 12 27 95), which is part of Huset, a good-energy cultural centre at Vester Allé 15. It has rock, jazz, folk and ethnic music concerts; the cover charge is generally 30 to 70 kr.

Another happening venue is *Blitz* (☎ 86 12 94 11) at Klostergade 34. It houses Rokken, which has live rock and dance music, and two discos. On Thursday entry is free if you arrive by 12.30 am, while on Friday and Saturday there's usually a 40 to 50 kr cover charge.

V58, a jazz dance club at Vestergade 58, has both live music and DJs, playing mainly modern jazz, acid jazz, salsa, rap and soul. It's open on weekends and the cover is usually 20 to 40 kr.

Crazy Daisy (☎ 86 18 08 55), Frederiksgade 29, dubs itself an 'Old English rock n' roll pub' and has dancing nightly from midnight to 5 am.

Glazzhuset (☎ 86 12 13 12) at Åboulevarden 1 generally attracts an older crowd with folk, country and blues, and an occasional cabaret. *Café Paradis* (☎ 86 13 71 11), Paradisgade 7, boasts the city's longest hours (from 9 pm to at least 5 am) and has one of the cheapest cover charges: free during the week, 20 kr on weekends; it's closed on Monday.

Musikhuset Århus Århus' modern concert centre, Musikhuset Århus, is in the city centre off Fredriks Allé. It contains two concert halls, the larger of which seats 1500, and is the arena for numerous events including dance, opera, musicals and concerts. Events range from performances by the city symphony orchestra to international pop and jazz stars. The foyer, which houses the ticket office and a café, commonly has some sort of free musical performance, so if you're strolling by it's worth checking out. A monthly programme schedule is available from the ticket office (☎ 89 31 82 10), which is open from 11 am to 9 pm daily.

Theatre The Århus Theater on Bispetorv, at the south side of the cathedral, is a splendid century-old building richly embellished with gargoyles and other decorative elements, including a scene from a Holberg play painted across the front gable. Jutland's largest theatre, it has five stages, a permanent theatre troupe of 35 actors and an affiliated drama school. In addition to performing its own repertoire, from early September to mid-June, there are also performances by students of the drama school and by visiting actors. For schedule information call ☎ 86 12 26 22.

Gay & Lesbian Venues The main gay and

lesbian hangout is the *Pan Club*, (☎ 86 13 43 80), a café and disco at Jægergårdsgade 42, a short walk south-west of the railway station. The café is open Monday to Friday from 4 pm to at least 2 am and on Saturday from 8 pm to 6 am. The disco is open Wednesday and Thursday from 11 pm to 3 am on, and Friday and Saturday from 11 pm to 5 am.

There are gatherings for lesbians sometimes held at *Sappho*, a women's centre at Mejlgade 71.

The *A-Men's Club*, for gay men into leather, has periodic discos and other events; call ☎ 86 19 10 89 for information.

Færgekroen, at Skolegade 32, is a gay-friendly café that has food, drinks and music.

LBL (☎ 86 13 19 48), Landsforeningen for Bøsser og Lesbiske, the national organisation for gays and lesbians, has its Århus branch at Jægergårdsgade 42 and is open from 5 to 7 pm.

Cinema There are several cinemas in Århus, all showing films in their original languages with Danish subtitles. Tickets typically cost from 30 to 50 kr, with reduced rates on Wednesday. The four-screen Biografen (☎ 86 13 70 90), centrally located at Sankt Knuds Torv 1, generally features first-run Hollywood movies. Øst for Paradis (☎ 86 19 31 22), a four-screen cinema at Paradisgade 7, mainly shows European films.

Casino If you have extra cash to gamble with, there's the Royal Scandinavia Casino, at the Hotel Royal. It has two sections, one with slot machines and other electronic games, and a more formal 'classic hall' with American roulette, French roulette and blackjack. Entrance to the latter requires formal dress; ask about borrowing a jacket at the door. It's open from 2 pm to 4 am daily, restricted to those 18 and older, and there's an admission fee of 40 kr.

Things to Buy
Department Stores & Speciality Shops
The city's largest department stores are the huge Magasin du Nord, which takes up an

Århus Festival
The nine-day Århus Festival, or Århus Festuge, bills itself as Denmark's largest annual multicultural festival. It's held the first week of September, encompassing weekends at both ends, and includes scores of events at indoor and outdoor venues around Århus. Activities include contemporary and classical music performances, theatre, ballet, modern dance, opera, films and sports. The biggest non-music event is the Marselis Run, a six-km (or 12-km) run through the Marselisborg woods, which attracts close to 20,000 runners of all ages. The tourist office can provide a schedule, or call Musikhuset Århus (☎ 86 31 82 70), which coordinates the festival. ■

entire block between Vestergade and Åboulevarden, and Salling at Søndergade 27, which has 30 departments. Both stores carry just about anything you can imagine, from gourmet foods to designer clothing, Danish silverware and tax-free gift items.

Søndergade, a busy pedestrian shopping street, has numerous speciality shops, many selling fashionable clothing. Other shops and boutiques specialising in both Danish design and imported clothing are thick along Badstuegade and Volden, streets which run north from Lille Torv.

If you're looking for luggage, Kjærulff Lædervarer, at Guldsmedgade 21, north of Lille Torv, has a good variety of bags and suitcases at reasonable prices.

Crafts Telefon Torv, a small pedestrian square off the northern end of Søndergade, has a few open-air stalls where university students sell carved pipes, jewellery and other simple handicrafts.

More traditional items, including pottery, handblown glass and wooden toys, can be found in shops along Møllestien, a cobbled street east of the library. These include Glasmenageriet, a glassworks gallery at Møllestien 48; Gavlhuset, a shop that sells its own Danish and raku-style earthenware at Møllestien 53; and a mixed crafts shop at Møllestien 57. All are open on weekday afternoons and generally from 10 am to 1 pm on Saturday.

Antiques There are several antiques shops north of the cathedral; you'll find two of them close by at Graven 16 and 24 and another at Mejlgade 24, 50 metres north of its intersection with Graven. These shops carry everything from old furniture, silver and china to rare books.

Getting There & Away

Air The Århus airport, which is in Tirstrup, 44 km north-east of Århus, is primarily a domestic airport. SAS operates about a dozen flights to and from Copenhagen on weekdays, half as many on weekends. The one-way fare is 595 kr every day, while the return fare is 595 kr in midweek and 840 kr from Friday to Sunday. SAS also operates an afternoon flight from Århus to London (for more details see the Getting There & Away chapter earlier).

Billund airport, just an hour away from Århus by bus, is the main link between Jutland and the rest of Europe, with direct flights to Amsterdam, Frankfurt, Brussels, Stockholm and a number of cities in Norway and the UK. For information see the Legoland section earlier in this chapter.

The SAS ticket office, on Park Allé near the Århus railway station, is open weekdays from 9 am to 4.30 pm.

Bus All long-distance buses stop at the Århus bus station, which is a five-minute walk east of the railway station. The bus station has lockers, a small grocery store, a DSB Café and a food kiosk.

Express buses (☎ 86 78 48 88) run a few times daily between Århus and Copenhagen's Valby station via a channel crossing at Ebeltoft. The trip takes 4½ hours and costs 140 kr.

Train Trains to Århus, via Odense, leave Copenhagen hourly from early morning to 8 pm (4½ hours, 201 kr) and there's a night

train at 11.30 pm. There's also an hourly train service to Frederikshavn (3½ hours, 142 kr) as well as trains east to Grenaa and west to the Lake District (see those sections for more details).

Car & Motorbike The main highways to Århus are the E45 from the north and south and route 15 from the west. The E45 curves around the western edge of the city as a ring road. There are a number of turn-offs from the ring road into the city, including Åhavevej from the south and Randersvej from the north.

Boat DSB car ferries (☎ 86 18 17 88) sail three to six times a day between Århus and Kalundborg. They take 3¼ hours and cost 75 kr per passenger, 245 kr for a car and driver or 300 kr for a car with three people. For a motorbike and driver the cost is 190 kr.

The fastest way to cross to Kalundborg is by Cat-Link's (☎ 89 41 20 20) sleek catamaran ferry that takes just 80 minutes and operates four to five times a day. The fare is 150 kr for adults, 75 kr for children, 360 kr for a car with up to four passengers and 200 kr for a motorcycle with driver.

Getting Around

To/From the Airport The airport bus to Århus railway station costs 50 kr, a taxi about 375 kr.

Bus Århus has an extensive public bus system with frequent services throughout the city. Most city buses stop in front of the railway station or around the corner from it on Park Allé. Tickets are bought from a machine in the back of the bus for 12.50 kr and are good for unlimited rides within the time period stamped on the ticket (about two hours) and you can change buses as often as you like. You can also buy a 24-hour pass good for bus travel in Århus municipality alone for 45 kr, or one valid throughout Århus County, which includes Grenaa and the Lake District, for 75 kr. There are also 70 kr klippekort tickets that are valid for nine rides. The klippekort and passes can be bought at newsstands and the tourist office.

Car & Motorbike A car is quite convenient for getting to sights such as Moesgård on the city outskirts, though the city centre is best explored on foot.

Århus has numerous billetautomats (parking meters) along its streets. Parking generally costs 1 kr per seven minutes, with a three-hour maximum, between 8 am and 6 pm Monday to Thursday, from 8 am to 8 pm Friday and from 8 am to 2 pm on Saturday. Outside those hours you can park free of charge.

There are carparks at Magasin du Nord and Salling department stores, which charge roughly the same price as the billetautomats.

Cars can be rented from:

Avis (☎ 86 16 10 99), Jens Baggesensvej 88A
Europcar (☎ 86 12 35 00), Sønder Allé 35
Hertz (☎ 86 19 18 12), Silkeborgvej 4

Taxi Taxis are readily available at the railway station. You can also get a taxi by phoning ☎ 89 48 48 48 or 86 16 47 00.

Bicycle You can rent bicycles for 50 kr for the first day and 35 kr for additional days at Asmussen Cykler (☎ 86 19 57 00), Fredensgade 54, near the bus station. It also sells quality bikes and accessories and is open from 10 am to 5.30 pm on weekdays and 9 am to noon Saturday.

The Århus City Sleep-In (☎ 86 19 20 55), Havnegade 20, is planning to offer bicycle rentals for around the same price.

The Lake District

The Lake District (Danish: Søhøjlandet), the closest thing Denmark has to hill country, is a popular 'active holiday' spot for Danes, with good canoeing, cycling and hiking. The scenery is pretty, but placid and pastoral rather than stunning. The district contains the Gudenå, Denmark's longest river; Mossø,

Jutland's largest lake; and Yding Skovhøj, Denmark's highest point – none of which are terribly long, large or high!

SILKEBORG

Silkeborg, population 35,000, is the Lake District's largest and youngest town. It was founded in 1846 when Michael Drewsen – whose statue graces the town square – built a paper mill on the east side of the river. The mill and other industries still form the backbone of the economy. Because of its modern facade, the town may seem a bit bland but it has a pretty setting, bordered by both a river (the Remstrup Å) and a lake (the Silkeborg Langsø). If you're strolling the town at night, walk down by the rådhus, where a colour-lit fountain spurts up from the lake.

Information
Tourist Office The Silkeborg Turistbureau (☎ 86 82 19 11, fax 86 81 09 83), Godthåbsvej 4, 8600 Silkeborg, is a few minutes walk north-east of Torvet, the town square. From mid-June to 31 August it's open Monday to Saturday from 9 am to 5 pm, while the rest of the year it closes Monday to Friday at 4 pm and on Saturday at noon.

Money There are a number of banks on Vestergade, a block west of Torvet, including a Unibank at Vestergade 13 and a Jyske Bank at Vestergade 16.

Other Facilities The post office is just east of the railway station. There's a pharmacy at Vestergade 9 and a coin laundry at Hostrupsgade 21.

Silkeborg Museum
This quality regional museum of cultural history is housed in the 18th century Hovedgården manor house, the oldest building in town. Its Bronze and Iron Age collections include pottery, flint daggers and jewellery, most found in nearby peat bogs. There are also trade workshops from the turn of the century, including those of a cooper, dentist and shoemaker, and a good glass collection.

CENTRAL JUTLAND

PLACES TO STAY

14 Hotel Dania
29 Hotel Louisiana
31 Silkeborg Vandrerhjem

PLACES TO EAT

5   Netto Grocery Store
10 Bakery
13 Føtex Supermarket
18 Hjørten
21 Café Den Goe Fe
22 Italiano Pizzeria

23 Piaf
24 Heksekosten Health
    Foods
25 Bakery

OTHER

1   Night-lit Fountains
2   Petrol Station
3   Rådhus
4   Tourist Office
6   Slusekiosken Canoe
    Rentals
7   Hjejlen Boat Dock

8   Hospital
9   Silkeborg Museum
11 Torvecentret
12 Local Bus Stand
15 Pharmacy
16 Unibank
17 Jyske Bank
19 Cinema
20 Coin Laundry
26 Daghøjskolen Cycle
    Rentals
27 Railway & Bus Stations
28 Post Office
30 Police

Central Jutland
Top: Reconstructed Viking-style longhouse, Vikingegården Fyrkat, Hobro
Middle: Autumn hayfields outside Ry, Lake District
Bottom: Århus Theatre, Århus

NED FRIARY

NED FRIARY

NED FRIARY

Northern Jutland

Left: The Buried Church (Tilsandede Kirke), Skagen
Top: Viking grave in the shape of a ship, Lindholm Høje, Aalborg
Bottom: Fresco in Buldolfi Domkirke, Aalborg

However the museum's main attraction is **Tollund Man**, an Iron Age man in his late 30s who came to an untimely end in 200 BC. His blackened, leather-like body, complete with a rope still around his neck, was discovered in a nearby bog in 1950. He was apparently hanged as a sacrifice to the gods. When discovered, Tollund Man was wearing only a sheepskin cap and a simple leather belt. The face is so amazingly well preserved that you can count the wrinkles in his forehead.

The museum, on Hovedgårdsvej east of the town centre, is open from 10 am to 5 pm daily from May to mid-October, and from noon to 4 pm on Wednesday, Saturday and Sunday in winter. Admission costs 20 kr for adults and 5 kr for children.

Silkeborg Kunstmuseum

The Silkeborg Kunstmuseum (Silkeborg Museum of Art) on Gudenåvej, one km south of the town centre, features the works of native son Asger Jorn and other modern artists. Built upon Jorn's private collection, it contains about 200 paintings and sculptures and scores of prints and drawings. The emphasis is on 20th century art including early expressionism, spontaneous abstract art of the 30s and 40s, and the COBRA movement that followed. Among the artists whose works are on display are Jean Dubuffet, Carl-Henning Pedersen, Richard Mortensen and Per Kirkeby. The museum is open from 10 am to 5 pm between April and October, from noon to 4 pm in winter, but closed on Monday all year round. Admission is 30 kr for adults, free for children.

Aqua

Aqua, an aquarium complex at Vejsøvej 55, at the south side of town, displays fish, otters, cormorants and other fauna found in a freshwater environment. It's open from 10 am to 6 pm daily in summer, from 10 am to 4 pm Tuesday to Sunday in winter. Admission costs 40 kr for adults and 20 kr for children.

Hiking & Canoeing

To get to **Nordskoven**, a beech forest with hiking and cycling trails, simply walk over the old railway bridge down by the hostel.

You can rent **canoes** for 210 kr a day at a few places around town, including the camping grounds and at Slusekiosken (☎ 86 80 08 93) at the harbour. In addition to just touring for the day, it's possible to paddle through the Lake District and spend nights at lakeside camping areas. The canoe rental shops can help you plan an itinerary.

Places to Stay

Indelukkets Camping (☎ 86 82 22 01, fax 86 80 50 27), Vejlsøvej, 8600 Silkeborg, one km south of the art museum, is near the river and surrounded by woods. It has a coin laundry, a group kitchen, and cabins and caravans for hire. There are similar facilities at the lakeside *Silkeborg Sø-Camping* (☎ 86 82 28 24, fax 86 80 44 57), Århusvej 51, 8600 Silkeborg, which is 1.5 km east of the town centre. Both camping grounds are open from early April to mid-September, are rated three-star and charge 45 kr per person in the high season, 38 kr in the low.

The 100-bed *Silkeborg Vandrerhjem* (☎ 86 82 36 42, fax 86 81 27 77) Åhavevej 55, 8600 Silkeborg, has a scenic riverbank location and is a 10-minute walk east of the railway station. It's open from 1 March to 1 December, with dorm beds for 85 kr and private rooms for 180/240 kr a single/double. The hostel offers an unusually good breakfast for 38 kr and there's a coin laundry.

The tourist office has a list of about a dozen private homes with rooms from 100 to 160 kr for singles, 180 to 280 kr for doubles. For a 20 kr fee the office will book a room for you, or you can take the list and call on your own.

The 85-room *Hotel Dania* (☎ 86 82 01 11, fax 86 80 20 04), Torvet 5, 8600 Silkeborg, is an old-fashioned hotel with front rooms that overlook the town square and quieter rear rooms that overlook the lake. The rooms are large, the décor is simple but not austere, and all have private bath and three-channel TV. Singles/doubles cost 565/690 kr, breakfast included.

Also in town is the *Hotel Louisiana* (☎ 86 82 18 99, fax 86 80 32 69), Christian 8 Vej, 8600 Silkeborg. It has 27 comfortable, modern rooms with private bath, satellite TV, phone and minibar. Singles/doubles cost 690/795 kr, though there are sometimes discounted rates of 525/650 kr. Breakfast is included. There's a sauna, fitness facilities and a restaurant.

Places to Eat

There are several drinking spots and restaurants on Nygade. *Heksekosten* at Nygade 28 sells health food, natural teas and vitamins.

A good place for lunch is *Café Den Goe Fe*, Nygade 18, a casual alternative café with both meat and vegetarian dishes. The prices are reasonable and the menu includes salads, chilli con carne and pitta bread sandwiches.

Italiano Pizzeria at Nygade 34 is open for dinner with candlelight dining. Pizza costs from 45 kr, pasta from 55 kr. Nearby at Nygade 31 is *Piaf*, a trendy café and restaurant with a French flair. It has a daily special for 64 kr and a three-course meal for 178 kr.

The *Føtex* supermarket at Torvet has an inexpensive bakery and a cafeteria with good-value specials – you can get a solid meal for under 30 kr.

There's a fast-food eatery at the bus station, with burgers, hot dogs, chicken and chips. The *Asian Restaurant* in the adjacent Torvecentret has a rooftop view, standard Chinese dishes for around 80 kr and lunch specials for half that.

Hjørten at Tværgade 4 is a decent steak restaurant with a pleasant setting of dark woods and exposed-beam ceilings. From 11.30 am to 5 pm there are lunch deals such as a meat pie with salad for 35 kr and a 150-gram steak for 49 kr. At dinner, steak prices are 80 to 140 kr and include a good salad bar. There's also an inexpensive children's menu.

The restaurant at the *Hotel Dania* on Torvet has numerous lunch specials, including salads, for 40 to 50 kr from noon to 5 pm. At dinner it features beef dishes for around 100 kr.

Getting There & Away

Silkeborg is 37 km south of Viborg via route 52, and 43 km west of Århus via route 15.

Bus Long distance buses leave from the west side of the railway station. The express bus No 913E makes a 48-minute run between Silkeborg and Århus (42 kr) a couple of times daily; the frequent regional bus Nos 112 and 113 also go to Århus, but they take 1¼ hours.

Train Hourly trains connect Silkeborg with Skanderborg (30 minutes, 30 kr) and Århus (45 minutes, 47 kr) via Ry.

Getting Around

There's metered parking along the streets in the town centre and numerous carparks, including on both the north and west sides of rådhus and at the Torvecentret.

Bus There are numerous bus routes around Silkeborg. All local buses leave from the bus stand on Fredensgade. Tickets cost 8 kr per ride if you're going direct, 10 kr if you need a transfer.

Taxi For a taxi call Silkeborg Taxi (☎ 86 80 60 60).

Bicycle Bicycles can be hired at Daghøjskolen (☎ 86 81 13 99), Toldbodgade 29, and at Cykel-Klubben (☎ 86 82 26 33), Frederiksberggade 1. The hostel and the camping grounds can also arrange bicycle rentals.

RY

A smaller town in a more rural setting than Silkeborg, Ry is a good place from which to base your exploration of the Lake District. Although there aren't really any notable sights in the town centre, there are lots of options for activities and excursions into the surrounding countryside.

Information

Tourist Office The Ry Turistbureau (☎ 86 89 34 22, fax 86 89 35 52) is in the railway station at Klostervej 3, 8680 Ry. It's open in summer from 9 am to 5 pm on weekdays and from 8 am to 4 pm on Saturday. In the low season, opening hours are from 9 am to 4 pm on weekdays and from 9 am to noon on Saturday.

Other Facilities The post office is north of the railway station and there's a Den Danske Bank nearby at Klostervej 2.

Activities

If you want to explore the surrounding lakes and rivers, Ry Kanofart (☎ 86 89 11 67), Kyhnsvej 20, rents canoes for 50/220 kr an hour/day.

The tourist office arranges tours on summer weekdays to Himmelbjerget (Tuesday), Gammel Ry (Wednesday) and there's a canoe tour to Om Kloster (Thursday) – costs vary with the tour.

There's also a fledgling windsurfing operation, Søhøjlandets Surfskole (☎ 86 89 28 05), that offers three-hour beginner courses for 295 kr and rents gear for 80 kr an hour.

Hiking The Ry tourist office has an English-language brochure (15 kr) that maps out and briefly describes 10 hikes in the Ry area. One of the nicest hikes from Ry is the two-hour, seven-km walk to Himmelbjerget. The starting point for the hike is the dirt road that begins off Rodelundvej about 400 metres south of the Ry bridge. The path, which is signposted, leads to the Himmelbjerget boat dock before climbing the hill to the tower.

Cycling Tour A good half-day outing is to cycle from Ry to **Boes**, a tiny hamlet with picturesque thatched houses and bounteous flower gardens. From there continue through the countryside to **Om Kloster**, the ruins of a medieval monastery. There's just enough brick and rocks left to show what the monastery was once like. In the underground tombs, where the high altar once stood, you can peer through glass-topped enclosures at the 750-year-old skeleton of Bishop Elafsen of Århus and the bones of many of his

abbots. There's also a small museum with more skulls and monastery artefacts.

Om Kloster is open from 9 am to 6 pm between May and August, with earlier closing times in spring and autumn. It's closed in winter and on Monday all year round. Admission costs 25 kr for adults and 10 kr for children. The whole trip from Ry and back is about 18 km.

Places to Stay

The lakeside *Sønder Ege Camping* (☎ 86 89 13 75), Søkildevej 65, 8680 Ry, is a km north of town. Rated three-star, it charges 45 kr per person and has full facilities, including a coin laundry, and caravan and cabin rentals. It's open from 1 April to 1 October.

On the same bathing lake, fronting a popular beach, is *Ry Vandrerhjem* (☎ 86 89 14 07, fax 86 89 28 70), Randersvej 88, 8680 Ry. To get there from the railway station cross the tracks, turn left and go 2.5 km; or take the infrequent bus No 104. Dorm beds cost 75 kr, private rooms 105/140 kr for singles/doubles. The hostel is open all year round and has canoe rentals.

The tourist office books private rooms in about a dozen homes around Ry for 125 kr per person; there's no booking fee. They can also help you book cottages in the Ry area, most of which sleep four people, from around 2200 kr a week.

In town is the *Ry Park Hotel* (☎ 86 89 19 11, fax 86 89 12 57), Kyhnsvej 2, 8680 Ry. It has 78 rooms with modern amenities, including TV, phone and minibar. The hotel has an indoor swimming pool, sauna and restaurant. Rates range from 395 to 595 kr for singles, and from 595 to 795 kr for doubles.

Places to Eat

The best place to eat in the town centre is *Alberto*, Randersvej 1, a popular café serving fresh vegetarian food, good salads and tasty chicken or lamb dishes for around 50 kr, beef dishes for 60 kr. They also have cappuccino, wine and other drinks.

Gyda Slagter, a butcher shop opposite the railway station, has inexpensive sandwiches, fried fish by the piece and a few other takeaway items. There's a bakery next door to the butcher shop and a health-food shop at Klostervej 6. *Pizzeria Italia*, on the eastern side of the train tracks at Skanderborgvej 3, has pizza from 45 kr.

The restaurant at the *Ry Park Hotel*, Kyhnsvej 2, has traditional Danish food, with starters from 35 kr and main dishes from around 100 kr.

Sønder Ege, near the camping ground at Søkildevej 69, has a nice view and Danish dishes for around 100 kr.

Getting There & Away

Ry is on route 445, 24 km south-east of Silkeborg and 35 km from Århus.

Hourly trains connect Ry with Silkeborg (20 minutes, 24 kr) and Århus (30 minutes, 35 kr). There's also a bus from Århus but it takes twice as long and costs 38 kr.

Getting Around

Ry Cykel (☎ 86 89 14 91), Skanderborgvej 19, rents bikes for 45 kr a day.

HIMMELBJERGET

The Lake District's most visited spot is the whimsically named Himmelbjerget (Sky Mountain) which, at just 147 metres, is one of Denmark's highest hills. The hilltop is crowned with a 25-metre tower erected in 1875 and offers a fine 360° view of the lakes and surrounding countryside, which is part woodland, part farmland. On a clear day it's quite a lovely scene. Admission to the tower costs 5 kr.

There are marked hiking trails in the area, including one that leads a km down to the lake, where there's a dock for the lake boats and a cafeteria that has live jazz music in summer.

The parking area for Himmelbjerget has a hotel and restaurant as well as a couple of souvenir kiosks. It's a five-minute walk from the carpark to the hilltop tower.

Places to Stay & Eat

The *Hotel Himmelbjerget* (☎ 86 89 80 45), Ny Himmelbjergvej 20, 8680 Ry, is a pleasantly rustic lodge with 18 rooms that have shared bath and cost 260/380 kr for singles/doubles, breakfast included.

Tårn Caféen, the restaurant at the hotel, has a nice view of the woods and reasonable prices. Half a chicken with chips and salad will set you back 50 kr. There's also a kiosk with fast food.

Getting There & Away

Himmelbjerget is a 10-minute ride west of Ry via route 445. Bus No 104 goes from Ry railway station to Himmelbjerget a few times a day, but check the schedule first with the tourist office as not every bus makes the stop. Himmelbjerget can also be reached by a pleasant seven-km hike from Ry or by a scenic boat ride.

Boat The *Hjejlen* (☎ 86 82 07 66), a paddle steamer that sails from Silkeborg to Himmelbjerget during summer, leaves Silkeborg at 10 am and 1.45 pm. It takes 1¼ hours and costs 57 kr return or 38 kr one way; children's tickets are half price. The same company also operates an ordinary boat on this route three to six times a day, depending on the month.

A Paddle Steamer Cruise

The *Hjejlen*, one of the world's oldest operating paddle steamers, has been faithfully plying the waters of the Lake District since it was first launched in 1861. King Frederik the VII was among the passengers on that inaugural cruise.

Built by the Burmeister & Wain shipyard in Copenhagen, the boat is such an antique that when it was time for an engine overhaul a few years back, an engineer had to be called out of retirement to do the work.

These days the boat makes a couple of daily runs shuttling tourists from Silkeborg to Himmelbjerget during the summer season. The 15-km route takes in a wealth of river and lake scenery along the way and is one of the most popular outings in the Lake District. ■

There are also boats (☎ 86 89 16 70) from Ry to Himmelbjerget daily in summer, leaving Ry at 10 am, noon and 2 pm and leaving Himmelbjerget an hour later. The cost is 33 kr one way, 48 kr return, 18/27 kr for children.

Djursland & Mols

Djursland and Mols are the names, respectively, of the northern and southern halves of the large peninsula north-east of Århus. It's a pleasant area of gently rolling hills and farmland interspersed with patches of woodland. There are small villages and a scattering of old manor houses throughout. The main destinations are the towns of Ebeltoft and Grenaa with their fine white-sand beaches which attract summer tourists.

There are a handful of other sites around the peninsula that could also be toured. The southern town of Rønde has the ruins of **Kalø Slot**, a coastal brick fortress erected in the early 1300s. The Swedish king Gustav Vasa was a prisoner here in 1519. While those who like to soak up history should enjoy this site, all that's left is the outline of the fortress foundation and the partial remains of one of the towers.

For a different sort of experience, there's **Djurs Sommerland**, an amusement park with water shoots and slides and other recreational activities geared towards children. It's about 20 km east of Grenaa on Randersvej 17 in Nimtofte.

There's some particularly pretty countryside along the eastern side of the peninsula. If you're travelling by bicycle or car between Ebeltoft and Grenaa, consider taking the unfrequented rural route that leads through Dråby and continues as the easternmost through road north.

EBELTOFT
Ebeltoft is an enjoyable tourist town whose centre of cobbled pedestrian streets is lined with souvenir shops, cafés and ice-cream stands.

In medieval times, Ebeltoft was a successful market town, trading with Zealand, Germany and Sweden. The town's prosperity came to an abrupt end in 1659 when the Swedish navy sacked Ebeltoft and torched its merchant fleet. It wasn't until the 1960s, when the Swedes reinvaded – this time as tourists – that the economy shook off three centuries of stagnation. The central town quarters are more historic than modern, the streets around the old town hall are thick with old timber-framed brick buildings topped with red-tiled roofs.

The town sits on a calm, protected bay that's fringed with white-sand beaches; you'll find a nice stretch right along Strandvejen, the coastal road that leads north into town. Another bathing area begins at the south side of Ebeltoft, just below the harbour.

Orientation
The tourist office, the *Fregatten Jylland* and the harbour are along Strandvej. Torvet, with the town hall, library and museum, are a five-minute walk to the north. Jernbanegade links the two areas.

Information
Tourist Office The Ebeltoft/Mols Turistbureau (☎ 86 34 14 00, fax 86 34 05 28), Strandvejen 2, 8400 Ebeltoft, is open in summer from 10 am to 6 pm Monday to Saturday and 11 am to 3 pm Sunday. The rest of the year opening hours are Monday to Friday from 9 am to 4 pm and on Saturday from 10 am to 1 pm.

Money There are four banks on Jernbanegade, including a Unibank at Jernbanegade 7, about 100 metres east of the tourist office.

Post The post office, on the waterfront north of the tourist office, is open Monday to Friday from 9.30 am to 5 pm and on Saturday from 9 am to noon.

Things to See
Ebeltoft's old rådhus, which claims to be Denmark's smallest town hall, is a quaint

half-timbered building erected in 1789. Located on Torvet, it now houses the **Ebeltoft Museum**, a worthwhile little museum that exudes a sense of the town's history. It's open from 10 am to 5 pm daily in summer and from 11 am to 3 pm Tuesday to Sunday in spring and autumn. Admission costs 15 kr for adults and 5 kr for children.

At the harbour is **Fregatten Jylland**, a 19th century wooden frigate that has recently undergone a costly restoration. You can visit it, along with a retired lightship, from 9 am to 7 pm daily in summer and from 10 am to 5 pm in the low season. Admission is 40 kr for adults and 20 kr for children.

The **Ebeltoft Kirke** dates from at least 1301, when the town received its charter from King Erik VI. The church has a 13th century sandstone font and a few simple early-16th century frescoes, including a drawing of the *Maria*, a Danish warship that was used to attack Sweden in 1517. The church is about a 10-minute walk south from Torvet via Overgade; the door is generally unlocked during the day and entry is free.

Missers Dukkemuseum, a little doll museum, is just west of the church at Grønningen 15 that's open from 2 to 4 pm daily; admission is 20 kr for adults and 10 kr for children.

Another attraction is the **Glasmuseum**, Strandvejen 8, which displays both decorative and functional works in glass. It's open from 10 am to 5 pm (until 7 pm in summer) and costs 30 kr for adults and 5 kr for children.

Places to Stay

There are several camping grounds in the Ebeltoft area. *Vibæk Camping* (☎ 86 34 12 14), Strandvej 23, 8400 Ebeltoft, is on a white-sand beach a km north of town. It's a two-star facility with the usual amenities, including a laundry room and kitchen. Open all year round, the camping charge is 42 kr per person. There are also a handful of caravans and cabins for hire from 1200 kr a week, plus the daily camping charge.

The 72-bed *Ebeltoft Vandrerhjem* (☎ 86 34 20 53, fax 86 34 20 77), Søndergade 43, 8400 Ebeltoft, is a small hostel in a residential neighbourhood south of the centre, a 10-minute walk from the harbour and Torvet. It has dorm beds for 70 kr as well as more expensive family rooms. The hostel's open from 1 March to 1 November.

Hotel Ebeltoft (☎ 86 34 10 90), Adelgade 44, 8400 Ebeltoft, a small hotel in the centre, has 10 straightforward rooms with shared baths. Singles/doubles cost 250/400 kr, breakfast included.

Ebeltoft also has two expensive hotels each with modern facilities, including a pool, sauna and restaurant. The 72-room *Hotel Ebeltoft Strand* (☎ 86 34 33 00, fax 86 34 46 36), Nedre Strandvej 3, 8400 Ebeltoft, is on a rocky shoreline 500 metres north of the town centre. The rooms, which each have private bath, TV, phone, minibar and a terrace or balcony, cost 670/985 kr for singles/doubles, breakfast included.

The 100-room *Hotel Hvide Hus* (☎ 86 34 14 66, fax 86 34 49 69), Strandgårdshøj 1, 8400 Ebeltoft, a few minutes walk from the waterfront north of the centre, has similarly appointed rooms for 610/810 kr for singles/doubles, breakfast included.

Places to Eat

There's a cafeteria at the street side of the tourist office, with moderately priced fish & chips and similar fare.

In the centre you'll find a few places to eat along Adelgade between Jernbanegade and Torvet, including *Gryden*, at Adelgade 32, which has smørrebrød and pizza; the *Café Sommerdrømme*, in the Vigen courtyard at Adelgade 5, which has four daily lunch options, such as a Mexican beef plate or fish fillet, from 45 to 65 kr; and *Torvet Burger*, on the opposite side of the street, with cheap fast food.

For somewhere with more atmosphere, there's *Mellem Fyder*, Juulsbakke 3, in a half-timbered house just south of Torvet and the old town hall. It has good-value lunches from 11.30 am to 4 pm, including chicken or beef with salad and chips for 49 kr. At dinner, à la carte dishes begin at 65 kr.

Getting There & Away

Ebeltoft is on route 21, 54 km east of Århus and 38 km south-west of Grenaa.

Bus Bus No 123 runs between Århus and Ebeltoft hourly on weekdays, less frequently on weekends; it takes 1½ hours and costs 42 kr. The bus stops in front of the Ebeltoft tourist office. There's also a regular bus service (No 351) between Ebeltoft and Grenaa.

Boat Mols-Linien (☎ 89 52 52 52 in Ebeltoft, ☎ 59 32 32 32 in Zealand) operates a car ferry between Ebeltoft and Sjællands Odde, in north-western Zealand. The boats run seven to 11 times a day and take 1¾ hours. The cost is 86 kr for adults, 43 kr for children, 175 kr for a motorcycle with two people and 330 kr for a car with up to four passengers.

Getting Around

Bicycles can be hired from L&P Cykler (☎ 86 34 47 77) at 5 Nørregade and from Tur Cyklen (☎ 86 34 01 44) at Ebeltoft Maritime Ferieby at Øervej.

GRENAA

Grenaa, at the eastern tip of Jutland, is a relatively young town, having largely taken its present form in the late 19th century when its commercial harbour was dug and a rail link was established with the rest of Jutland. It now serves as a port for ferries to Zealand and Sweden.

Grenaa is divided into two sections. The centre of town, three km inland from the harbour, has Torvet, the main square, with the town hall, town church and the usual mix of shops, restaurants and bakeries. The railway station is two blocks east of Torvet. A second commercial area is built up along the inland side of the harbour and has similar services, including banks and eateries. The harbour is a sizeable complex with a popular yachting marina, the ferry docks and a fishing port.

A wide inviting beach, backed by gentle sand dunes, runs south from the harbour for nearly seven km. The inshore waters are shallow and popular with families who flock here on warm summer days.

Information

Tourist Offices The Djurslands Turistforening (☎ 86 32 12 00, fax 86 32 70 28), Torvet 1, 8500 Grenaa, is open in summer from 9 am to 5 pm on weekdays and from 9 am to 1 pm on Saturday. The rest of the year it's open from 9 am to 4 pm on weekdays and from 10 am to 1 pm on Saturday.

There's also a branch tourist office (☎ 86 30 93 88) opposite the harbour that's open daily from 10 am to 5 pm (10 am to 2 pm on Sunday) from June to August.

Money There's a Den Danske Bank at Strandgade 1, opposite the fishing harbour, and a couple of banks on Torvet in the town centre.

Post The post office is at Stationplads 2, west of the railway station; it's open from 10 am to 5 pm on weekdays and from 9 am to noon on Saturday.

Things to See & Do

While the main attraction is the beach, there are also a couple of other sights that can be taken in.

The **Kattegatcentret** at the harbour, north of the marina, is a modern aquarium with several tanks of cold-water and tropical fish, including sharks. It's open daily in summer from at least 10 am to 6 pm and in winter from 10 am to 4 pm. Admission costs 50 kr for adults and 35 kr for children.

The regional history museum, **Djurslands Museum & Dansk Fiskerimuseum** at Søndergade 1, is in a large timber-framed merchant's house on the south side of Torvet. It has antique toys, ceramics, coins, local archaeological finds and displays on the Danish fishing industry, including a collection of model ships. It's open in summer from Monday to Friday from 10 am to 4 pm and on weekends from 1 to 4 pm; winter opening hours are from 1 to 4 pm Tuesday to Friday and on Sunday. Admission is 20 kr for adults, free for children.

Places to Stay

Polderrev Camping (☎ 86 32 17 18, fax 86 30 95 55), Fuglsangvej 58, 8500 Grenaa, is opposite the beach about two km south of the harbour. Open all year round, it has a three-star rating and a grocery store, restaurant, large group kitchen, laundry room and cabins for rent. The per-person camping charge is 45 kr.

The 108-bed hostel *Grenaa Sportel og Vandrerhjem* (☎ 86 32 66 22, fax 86 32 12 48), Ydesvej 4, 8500 Grenaa, is at a sports centre about 1.5 km south-east of the town centre. Dorm beds cost 85 kr, family rooms cost from 250 kr for singles to 340 kr for four people. The hostel is accessible by wheelchair and serves three meals a day. It's closed from Christmas to New Year's Day.

The tourist office can provide a list of private rooms in the Grenaa area, with rates beginning around 100 kr per person. It can also provide information on beach-side holiday cottages that rent by the week in summer.

The *Hotel Grenaa Strand* (☎ 86 32 68 14), opposite the harbour at Havneplads 1, 8500 Grenaa, is a small 16-room hotel. Singles/doubles cost 275/425 kr with shared bath and from 375/550 kr with private bath, breakfast included. Many of the rooms have TVs and phones and there's a reasonably priced restaurant.

Places to Eat

In the town centre, you'll find a number of places to eat on Lillegade, the street that runs north-west from Torvet. These include *Din Café*, a simple café with salads and sandwiches at Lillegade 10; *Ephesus*, an authentic Turkish restaurant at Lillegade 11; *Den Gyldne Krus*, a pub-style grill restaurant with a summertime pavement café at Lillegade 18; *Alberto's*, with moderately priced pizza and pasta at Lillegade 22; and *Ibs Bageri*, a bakery at Lillegade 31.

Udsigten, a cafeteria at the ferry harbour, has a water view and cheap eats such as fish & chips for 35 kr and a daily meal for 45 kr. A short walk from the harbour at Strandgade 7 is *Glimmer Grill*, a popular fast-food grill

with inexpensive hot dogs and burgers, or half a chicken and chips for 34 kr. There's a *Super Brugsen* grocery store and a bakery 100 metres to the west, on the corner of Strandgade and Strandstræde.

Getting There & Away

Grenaa is 63 km north-east of Århus via route 15, and 57 km east of Randers along route 16.

Train & Bus Train and bus services from Århus to Grenaa each make the run about every two hours. The train takes 1¼ hours and costs 53 kr; the bus (No 122) takes about 1½ hours and costs 50 kr.

Boat Driftsselskabet Grenaa-Hundested (☎ 86 30 96 88 in Grenaa, ☎ 42 33 96 88 in Hundested) operates a car ferry three to four times a day between Grenaa and Hundested in North Zealand. The trip takes 1½ hours. The cost is 98 kr for adults, 49 kr for children, 200 kr for a motorcycle with two people and 380 kr for a car and driver.

For information on boats between Grenaa and the Swedish cities of Varberg and Halmstad, see the Getting There & Away chapter.

Getting Around

You can catch local buses and get bus schedules at the DSB railway/bus station at Stationsplads 4.

Bicycles can be hired from Viggo Jensen (☎ 86 32 06 83), Strandgade 14.

GAMMEL ESTRUP

Gammel Estrup, at Randersvej 2 in the village of Auning, 33 km west of Grenaa, is an impressive estate whose history dates back to the early 1300s.

The moat-encircled manor house, along with its period furnishings, tapestries and paintings, has been turned into a museum, the **Jyllands Herregårdsmuseum**. The estate farm buildings, adjacent to the manor house, have been set aside as a separate farming museum, **Dansk Landbrugsmuseum**, which depicts the more earthy lives of those who worked the land. The farm museum has various demonstrations in season and the forge is often fired up with a blacksmith in attendance during the afternoons.

Both museums are open from 10 am to 5 pm, although from October to March the manor house has shorter hours. Admission to the manor house is 20 kr for adults and 5 kr for children. Admission to the farming museum is 20 kr for adults, free for children. Bus No 119 from Århus stops out front.

The Interior

This area has some small industrial towns and cities, as well as wooded areas and farmland. The most interesting places are the 1000-year-old Viking ring fortress in Hobro and the Rebild Bakker national park, which is part of Rold Skov, Denmark's largest public woodland area.

RANDERS

Randers is the fourth largest city in Jutland, although it has a population of just 60,000. Situated at the spot where the river Gudenå and the Randers Fjord merge, Randers' central location has made it an important trading town since its founding in 1302. In the 19th century after the railway linked Randers with the rest of Jutland, heavy industry was developed and lofty smokestacks are still a dominant feature of the skyline. Because so many highways and trains pass through Randers there's a good chance you'll pass through as well.

Orientation

The railway station is west of the city centre, about a 15-minute walk from the tourist office (go east on Jernbanegade and Tørvebryggen) or 10 minutes from Rådhustorvet via Vestergade.

Information

Tourist Office Randers Turistbureau (☎ 86 42 44 77, fax 86 40 60 04), Tørvebryggen 12, 8900 Randers, is open in summer from 9 am to 6 pm Monday to Friday and from 9 am to 3 pm on Saturday. Most of the rest of the year it's open from 9 am to 5 pm Monday to Friday and from 9 am to noon on Saturday.

Money The Jyske Bank on Rådhustorvet has an ATM that accepts major credit cards and operates until midnight.

Post The post office, north of Rådhustorvet at Nørregade 1, is open Monday to Friday from 9.30 am to 5.30 pm and on Saturday from 9 am to noon.

Things to See & Do

Although much of the city has a nondescript appearance there are some period brick and half-timbered houses. Among the oldest buildings, all dating to the late 15th century, are **Paaskesønnernes Gård**, a three-storey brick building on Rådhustorvet; **Helligåndshuset**, once part of a medieval monastery, at Eric Menveds Plads 1; and the church **Sankt Mortens Kirke** on Kirketorvet. All three are in the city centre, within a few minutes walk of each other.

The local history and art museums are at **Kulturhuset** on the east side of the city centre at Stemannsgade 2, a 10-minute walk from either Rådhustorvet or the tourist office. The history museum has a prehistory section and collections of church art, period interiors, weapons and glass. The art museum has Danish paintings from the late 19th century to the present. Each museum is open Tuesday to Sunday from 11 am to 5 pm and has an admission fee of 20 kr for adults, free for children.

Places to Stay

The *Randers Vandrerhjem* (☎ 86 42 50 44, fax 86 41 98 54), Gethersvej 1, 8900 Randers, is just west of the city centre, a 10-minute walk north of the railway station. It has 138 beds in 32 rooms. Dorm beds cost 70 kr, while private rooms cost 178/276 kr for singles/doubles. The hostel has a coin laundry and rooms accessible by wheelchair. It's open from 15 February to 1 December.

The tourist office can give you a booklet listing private homes with rooms for rent in the Randers area; prices vary, but average at around 130/225 kr for singles/doubles.

The old-fashioned *Hotel Randers* (☎ 86 42 34 22, fax 86 40 15 86), in the city centre at Torvegade 11, 8900 Randers, has 79 rooms with private bath, TV, phone and minibar from 395/695 kr for singles/doubles. There's a restaurant and lounge.

Slightly cheaper doubles can be found at the *Hotel Kronjylland* (☎ 86 41 43 33, fax 86 41 43 95), a five-minute walk east of the railway station at Vestergade 53, 8900 Randers. It has 33 renovated rooms with private bath, TV and phone that cost 425/595 kr.

Places to Eat
There's a pizzeria and a bakery opposite the railway station.

Storegade and Brødregade, which run north from the tourist office to the city centre, have a number of cafés and pubs to choose from. *Downtown Pizza*, just beyond the tourist office, has pizza for 25 kr a slice, while *Grilletten* at Storegade 6 has inexpensive burgers and kebabs. *Charles Dickens*, a pub at Storegade 9, has reasonably priced steaks, and the *Restaurant Munken* at Brødregade 23 has standard Danish food at moderate prices.

For some ethnic variety, just north of the Sankt Mortens Kirke there's *Hellas*, a Greek restaurant at Vester Kirkestræde 3; *China House* at Eric Menveds Plads; and *Pamukkale*, a Turkish dinner restaurant at Store Voldgade 7.

Getting There & Away
Randers is 76 km south of Aalborg and 36 km north of Århus via the E45 and 57 km west of Grenaa and 41 km east of Viborg via route 16.

All trains between Århus and Aalborg stop in Randers. The fare is 41 kr to Århus and 59 kr to Aalborg.

HOBRO
Hobro is best known as the site of Fyrkat, an intact 10th century Viking ring fortress.

The town, which sits at the head of the Mariager Fjord, is otherwise a rather utilitarian place with a mix of small industry and commercial facilities that serve the farms and villages in the surrounding district. Other than Fyrkat, Hobro's main claim to fame is being the site of Denmark's third largest cattle market, held at the fjord-side market hall every Wednesday morning.

Over the centuries, fires have robbed the town of its finer buildings. The oldest remaining structure is a merchant's house erected in 1821. Located at Vestergade 23, it now holds the **Hobro Museum** (15 kr), which has local history exhibits, including excavated items from Fyrkat; it's open from 11 am to 5 pm daily from April to October.

Information
Tourist Office The Hobro Turistbureau (☎ 98 52 56 66, fax 98 52 34 66), Store Torv, 9500 Hobro, is in the town centre, one km south-east of the railway station; walk east on Jernbanegade to Adelgade. It's open in summer from 9 am to 5 pm on weekdays and from 9 am to 2 pm on Saturday, closing in the low season at 4 pm on weekdays and 12.30 pm on Saturday.

Money & Post There's a Jyske Bank at Adelgade 10 and a few other banks near the tourist office. The post office is at Adelgade 8.

Fyrkat
Although it's somewhat smaller than the better-known Trelleborg fortress in southern Zealand, the 1000-year-old Fyrkat fortress outside Hobro so closely resembles Trelleborg that both are presumed to have been built by the Viking king Harald Bluetooth around 980 AD.

Fyrkat was part of an farmer's overgrown field until the 1950s when archaeologists from the national museum excavated the site. Items found during the excavation indicate that Fyrkat not only quartered about 800 Viking soldiers, but that women and children were also part of the camp life. Many of the finds were singed, suggesting that the wooden longhouses that sat within the rampart walls had been destroyed by fire, probably within a few years of the fortress' completion, and that the site was then abandoned.

Today you can walk out onto the grass-covered circular ramparts for an impressive view of the fort's symmetrical design. The four cuts in the earthen walls, all formerly gates, face the four points of the compass. Within the rampart walls the fortress is divided into four equal quadrants, each of which once had four symmetrical buildings surrounding a central courtyard. Stone blocks placed within the fortress show the foundation shape of these elongated buildings, which once housed the inhabitants of Fyrkat. Sheep grazing in the fields add a certain timeless backdrop to it all.

No structures now stand within the ramparts, but just outside is a replica Viking house that was built of oak timbers using a stave-style construction technique.

At the entrance to Fyrkat there are also some period farm buildings, including a functioning 200-year-old water mill and a half-timbered house with a pleasant old-fashioned restaurant.

Fyrkat (☎ 98 51 09 27) is three km southwest of Hobro centre, via Fyrkatvej, and about a 40 kr taxi ride from the railway station. If the weather is good, stop at the Viking farmstead (detailed in the following section) and then walk the last km to the fortress site.

Admission, which includes entrance to the water mill and the Viking house, costs 25 kr for adults and 10 kr for children. Opening hours are from 10 am to 5 pm daily from mid-April to late October. In the summer months costumed interpreters give a daily demonstration of a Viking activity such as spinning, military training or bronze casting.

Vikingegården Fyrkat To augment the Fyrkat fortress site, a Viking-style farmstead is currently under construction along Fyrkatvej, one km north of the fortress. It is believed that farms such as this sat outside

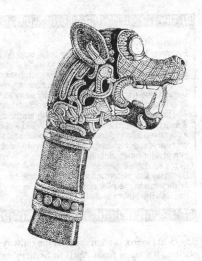

Vikings often decorated the sterns of their ships with dragonheads, which were believed to protect against the evil spirits of the sea

the fortress walls and served to provide food to the soldiers encamped within.

The goal is to construct at least eight Viking farm buildings – but since period-authentic materials and hand tools are used in the construction, the work is expected to take another five years to complete. So far a smithy, a storehouse and a 33-metre longhouse have been erected. The frame of the longhouse is made of oak that was hewn by hand using an adze, the roof is constructed of reeds fastened by willow shoots, the ridge consists of local peat and the walls are a mix of cow dung, blue clay and straw. The rich colour of the exterior walls is from a natural paint of yellow ochre and curds.

When the work is complete, demonstrations will take place at the farm, but in the meantime visitors are free to stop by, look inside the buildings and watch the construction taking place.

Places to Stay

The three-star *Hobro Camping Gattenborg* (☎ 98 52 32 88, fax 98 52 56 61), Skivevej

CENTRAL JUTLAND

ᛁᚾᚠ·ᛏᛁᚾ·ᚠᚤᚾᛗᛚ·ᛚᛈᚠᛗᚾ·ᚠᛈᛈᛁᚾᚠ·ᛏᛁᚾ·ᚠᚤᚾᛗᛚ·ᛚᛈᚠᛗᚾ·ᚠᛈᛈᛁᚾᚠ·ᛏᛁᚾ·ᚠᚤᚾᛗᛚ·ᛚᛈᚠᛗᚾ·ᚠᛈᛈᛁᚾᚠ·ᛏᛁᚾ·ᚠᚤᚾᛗᛚ·ᛚᛈᚠᛗᚾ·ᚠᛈᛈᛁᚾᚠ

Viking Play

Fyrkatspillet, a local amateur theatre troupe, presents a Viking play at Fyrkat annually during a two-week period from late May to early June. A new play is performed each season, with the staging and production handled by members of the Aalborg Theatre.

The plays are performed at the reconstructed Viking house. Although the performances are in Danish, the general theme is usually easy to follow and someone will gladly provide you with a little rundown on the plot before the action begins.

Themes commonly involve Viking kings; the most recent focused on the marriage between Sweyn Forkbeard and the strong-spirited Polish princess Swietoslawa, which was undertaken in a contrived effort to unite Denmark and Poland against the German kaiser. Whatever the storyline, you can expect beautiful damsels, sword-wielding Viking warriors, conflicts and resolutions, and lots of light-hearted laughter.

It's all quite a pleasant scene with the inviting spirit of a neighbourhood party. On Friday and Saturday the performance is accompanied by a dinner featuring lamb roasted over an open spit. Admission to the play costs 60 kr, to the play with dinner costs 130 kr. Tickets can be reserved through the Hobro tourist office. ∎

ᛁᚾᚠ·ᛏᛁᚾ·ᚠᚤᚾᛗᛚ·ᛚᛈᚠᛗᚾ·ᚠᛈᛈᛁᚾᚠ·ᛏᛁᚾ·ᚠᚤᚾᛗᛚ·ᛚᛈᚠᛗᚾ·ᚠᛈᛈᛁᚾᚠ·ᛏᛁᚾ·ᚠᚤᚾᛗᛚ·ᛚᛈᚠᛗᚾ·ᚠᛈᛈᛁᚾᚠ·ᛏᛁᚾ·ᚠᚤᚾᛗᛚ·ᛚᛈᚠᛗᚾ·ᚠᛈᛈᛁᚾᚠ

35, 9500 Hobro, is a km south of the railway station. It's open from April to September and has a food kiosk, swimming pool, TV lounge and a few cabins for rent. The camping cost is 45 kr per person.

The 116-bed *Hobro Vandrerhjem* (☎ 98 52 18 47, fax 98 51 18 47), Amerikavej 24, 9500 Hobro, is a modern hostel at a sports centre, 1.5 km east of the town centre. Dorm beds cost 75 kr, while private rooms are available from 180 kr for singles. It's open from 1 February to 1 December.

The tourist office can book a few rooms in private homes for 100/200 kr a single/double, plus a 25 kr booking fee.

The *Hotel Alpina* (☎ 98 52 28 00), Hostrupvej 83, 9500 Hobro, about a km north of the town centre, has 19 rooms with private baths that cost from 300/525 kr for singles/doubles, breakfast included.

Places to Eat

Although restaurants tend to be spread out, there are a few eateries on Adelgade, the pedestrian street that runs through the town centre. *Bæch's Conditori*, a bakery with café tables at Adelgade 38, has pastries, sandwiches and salads. *Restaurant Storm P* at Adelgade 48 has Danish beer and moderately priced food, while the *Kvickly Cafeteria* at Adelgade 14 has simple meals at inexpensive prices. You'll also find a hot dog wagon nearby on Torvet.

The most atmospheric place to eat, however, is the restaurant at Fyrkat. Here you can get cakes and coffees at reasonable prices as well as a couple of Danish country meals for around 80 kr. The restaurant is open the same hours as the fortress (see the earlier Fyrkat section).

Getting There & Away

Route 180 runs straight through Hobro, connecting it to Randers, 27 km to the south-east, and to Aalborg, 49 km to the north. The speedier E45 runs along the outskirts of Hobro, connecting it to the same cities.

Hobro is on the Frederikshavn-Århus line and has frequent train services. If you catch one of the hourly IC trains from Hobro it takes 19 minutes (24 kr) to get to Randers and 32 minutes (41 kr) to Aalborg.

REBILD BAKKER

Rebild Bakker, with its rolling heathered hills, is Denmark's only national park. In 1912 a group of Danish-Americans purchased 200 hectares of property at this site and presented it to the Danish government with three provisions. First, that it would remain in a natural state; second, that it would be open to all visitors; and third, that it would be accessible to Danish Americans for the celebration of US holidays.

To augment the park area the Danish forest service acquired adjacent woodland tracts that are now set aside as nature reserves. Collectively the area, referred to as Rold Skov, is the largest forest in Denmark. Still, don't expect vast wilderness, as it doesn't take much to lay claim to being Denmark's largest forest – the entire area accounts for only 77 sq km and at its greatest width can be walked across in a matter of hours.

Rebild Bakker is a pleasant area to stroll, its hills covered with heather, juniper, crow-berry, blueberry, cranberry, mountain tobacco and club moss, while its scrubby woods contain European aspen, beech and oak trees.

Things to See & Do

The **Lincoln Log Cabin**, just west of the carpark at the start of the trails, contains bits of Americana as seen through Danish eyes and displays on Danish emigration to the USA. The building, which is supposedly modelled on the log cabin that US president Abraham Lincoln grew up in, is itself a replica, the original having been destroyed by arsonists in 1993. Admission is 10 kr.

At the carpark is the **Spillemandsmuseet**

(Fiddlers' Museum), a simple regional museum with a varied collection of exhibits that includes fiddles, guns and traps, textiles and a 19th century kitchen. Admission is 10 kr for adults and 3 kr for children.

There are numerous walking **trails** criss-crossing the park. One pleasant four-km route begins in a sheep meadow west of the carpark. It goes past Tophuset, a small century-old thatched house that was built by the first caretakers; the Lincoln log cabin; a large glacial boulder called the Cibrere-stenen, which was sculpted in the form of a Cimbrian bull's head by Anders Bundgaard; the hollow where the 4 July festivals are held; and the 102-metre Sønderland, the park's highest hill. It's a particularly lovely area in summer and autumn when the heather adds a purple tinge to the hillsides.

Places to Stay

Safari Camping (☎ 98 39 11 10, fax 98 39 17 94), Rebildvej 17A, 9620 Skørping, is just a few minutes walk from the entrance to Rebild Bakker. This three-star facility is open year round, charges 44 kr per person and has 150 sites as well as some cabins.

The thatched *Rebild Vandrerhjem* (☎ 98 39 13 40, fax 98 39 27 40), Rebildvej 23, 9520 Skørping, has a handy location, right next to the park entrance. It has a friendly

CENTRAL JUTLAND

Danish-American Festivities

Every 4 July thousands of Danes and Americans gather at Rebild Bakker to celebrate US Independence Day. The festivities, known as the Rebild Festival, have occurred annually since 1912, except during the two world wars, and are the largest US Independence Day celebrations held outside the USA. Many of the American participants are descendants of Danish immigrants, some 300,000 of whom went to the USA in the Danish emigration boom of the late 19th and early 20th centuries.

The festivities include singing, square dancing and country music as well as speeches by prominent Danes and Americans. Among the keynote speakers in recent times have been members of the Danish royal family; US presidents Bush, Reagan and Nixon; and actors Richard Chamberlain and Danny Kaye.

While the main celebration occurs at Rebild, in the days preceding the event there are also receptions and various activities in Aalborg, where most of the participants are accommodated. More information about the Rebild Festival can be obtained from the Aalborg tourist office. ∎

management, laundry facilities and rooms accessible by wheelchair. Dorm beds cost from 55 to 75 kr and singles/doubles are 165/210 kr. The hostel has 100 beds and is open to individuals from 1 March to 1 November.

The *Rebild Bakker Hotel & Konferencecenter* (☎ 98 39 12 22, fax 98 39 24 55), Rebildvej 36, 9520 Skørping, opposite the hostel, is large and modern. The 151 rooms each have a private bath, TV, phone, minibar, desk and balcony. Rates are 705/925 kr for singles/doubles, breakfast included, but there's a good-value summer price of 425/595 kr. The hotel has an indoor swimming pool, sauna, fitness room, tennis courts, restaurant and bar.

Rold Stor Kro (☎ 98 37 51 00, fax 98 37 52 50), Vælderskoven 13, 9520 Skørping, is at the edge of the woods, two km south-west of the park entrance. Affiliated with Best Western, the rooms have private bath, TV, phone and minibar but are rather straightforward for the price, which is 545/795 kr for singles/doubles, breakfast included. There's an indoor pool and sauna.

Places to Eat

At the Rebild Bakker carpark you'll find a kiosk with ice cream, hot dogs and inexpensive chicken and chips, and a cafeteria with somewhat more substantial food including fish or roast beef with potatoes for 48 kr. Here too is *Rebild Hus*, a sit-down restaurant with main dishes costing around 100 kr and a three-course meal for 140 kr.

The *Rebild Vandrerhjem* has breakfast for 38 kr and with advance notice can also provide dinner for 40 kr.

Skørping, the nearest town to Rebild Bakker, has two bakeries near the railway station and a *Super Brugsen* grocery store 200 metres east of the station.

If you're looking for upmarket dining, the *Rold Stor Kro*, two km south-west of the park entrance, has a dining room with a pleasant view of wooded hills. The salmon with exotic greens makes a good starter and the duck a recommendable main course. A three-course dinner costs 238 kr on weekends, 154 kr from Monday to Thursday.

Getting There & Away

Route 180 runs through the Rold Skov forest, connecting Rebild Bakker with Hobro, 23 km to the south.

From Aalborg, Århus-bound trains stop in Skørping (16 minutes, 24 kr), from where it's three km west to Rebild Bakker. Bus No 104 runs between Aalborg and Rebild Bakker (45 minutes, 40 kr) via Skørping 12 times daily on weekdays, four times daily on weekends.

VIBORG

Viborg's history can be traced back to the 8th century. In 1060, it became one of Denmark's eight bishoprics and a century later, in 1150, the town was granted its municipal charter. Viborg grew into a major religious centre and prior to the Reformation had 25 churches and abbeys, although ecclesiastic remnants of that period are few.

The old part of town consists of the streets around the cathedral. Sankt Mogens Gade, which runs north between the cathedral and the tourist office, has some handsome old homes, including the Hauchs House at Sankt Mogens Gade 7 and the Willesens House at Sankt Mogens Gade 9, both dating from around 1520.

Viborg has a pleasant setting, bordering two lakes and surrounded by woods and moors. If you have your own transport, the Hald-Viborg preserve, six km south-west of Viborg, has trails through the woods, a manor house with a natural history exhibit and the ruins of a castle.

Information

Tourist Office The Viborg Turistbureau (☎ 86 61 16 66, fax 86 60 02 38), Nytorv 9, 8800 Viborg, is in the centre of town. In summer it's open Monday to Saturday from 9 am to 5 pm, while in the low season it's open Monday to Friday from 9 am to 4 pm and on Saturday from 9.30 am to 12.30 pm.

Churches

The twin-towered cathedral, **Viborg Domkirke**, a two-minute walk down the hill from the tourist office, is one of Denmark's largest granite churches. Archaeological excavations in 1974 indicate that the first church on this site was a wooden structure dating back to Viking times. A series of stone churches followed, and although there are traces of the first stone crypt from 1130, the current cathedral was virtually rebuilt in its entirety in 1876. The interior is splashed with grand frescoes painted over a five-year period (1901-1906) by artist Joakim Skovgaard. The frescoes on the nave depict scenes from the Old Testament, those on the transept depict the life of Christ and the choir frescoes feature scenes from the Resurrection and Ascension. The cathedral is open Monday to Saturday from 10 am to 4 pm in summer and from 11 am to 3 pm in winter; on Sunday it opens from noon year round. Also notable is **Søndre Sogns Kirke**, two blocks south of the cathedral. This church was built in 1230 as part of a Dominican monastery and although it's been much altered over the centuries, the original nave remains largely intact. The most interesting interior feature is an ornately carved Dutch altarpiece from 1520.

Museums

The **Skovgaard Museet**, at the south side of the cathedral at Domkirkestræde 4, has works by Joakim Skovgaard, the painter of the cathedral frescoes, but here the scenes are more varied and include nudes, portraits and landscapes. Works by friends and family members, including his father, PC Skovgaard, and his brother, Niels Skovgaard, are also on display. It's open year round from 1.30 to 5 pm, and also from 10 am to 12.30 pm from May to September.

There's a local history museum, the **Viborg Stiftsmuseum** at Hjultorvet 9, a few minutes walk south-west of the tourist office. It's open in summer from 11 am to 5 pm daily, with shorter low-season hours.

Places to Stay

Bus No 707 (seven minutes, 8 kr) can take you from the railway station to the hostel or camping ground, which are adjacent to each other on the east side of lake Søndersø.

The three-star *Viborg Sø Camping* (☎ 86

67 13 11, fax 86 67 35 29), Vinkelvej, 8800 Viborg, has full facilities including a group kitchen and coin laundry, is open from late March to late September and costs 40 kr per person.

The *Viborg Vandrerhjem* (☎ 86 67 17 81, fax 86 67 17 88), Vinkelvej 36, 8800 Viborg, is a modern 122-bed hostel with dorm beds for 75 kr and private rooms from 150 kr for singles up to 450 kr for six people. It's open to individuals from 1 March to 30 November.

The tourist office books rooms in private homes from 100/200 kr for singles/doubles.

For a moderately priced central hotel there's the *Palads Hotel* (☎ 86 62 37 00, fax 86 62 40 46), Sankt Mathias Gade 5, 8800 Viborg, a short walk north of the railway station. A member of the Best Western chain, it has 82 rooms with private baths and the usual amenities. The hotel offers a weekend and summertime family rate of 650 kr for up to two adults and two children in the same room, breakfast included. At other times the rates are a hefty 840/995 kr for singles/doubles.

Places to Eat

There are places to grab a quick meal on Vestergade, the short pedestrian street north of the tourist office. These include a bakery at Vestergade 12, the moderately priced Mexican restaurant *Tortilla Flats* at Vestergade 4 and two inexpensive cafés near the intersection of Vestergade and Gravene.

If you continue south on Gravene you'll pass a *Føtex* supermarket and at the next block reach Sankt Mathias Gade where there are more cafés and restaurants to choose from, including *Ristorante-Pizzeria Italia* at Sankt Mathias Gade 4 and the *Palads Hotel Restauranten* with Danish food at Sankt Mathias Gade 5.

Getting There & Away

Viborg is 66 km north-west of Århus via route 26 and 41 km west of Randers via route 16. Trains from Århus (70 minutes, 65 kr) run hourly on weekdays, less frequently on weekends. The railway station is about a km south-west of the tourist office.

CENTRAL JUTLAND

Cycling on the Old Military Road

Denmark's best-known cycling route extends the length of Jutland, from Padborg on the German border to Skagen at the northernmost tip of Denmark, much of the way along an historic route called the Hærvejen (Old Military Road). Established as Denmark's first national cycling route in 1989, this 440-km trail roughly traces a path that has been used for a thousand years by nomad hunters, kings' armies, cattle herders and pilgrims. The ancient roadway follows the ridge of Jutland, providing broad views and minimising the need to cross rivers and fjords.

While today parts of the Hærvejen have been swallowed up by modern motorways, there are still many stretches that maintain their ancient character as field tracks. En route, cyclists will pass through landscapes of heath and woodlands and find traces of earlier wayfarers, including barrows, old churches and rune stones.

Going at a relaxing pace, the entire route generally takes about a week – although many people opt for a smaller slice. The Dansk Cyklist Forbund puts out a series of inexpensive maps (1:100,000 scale) that cover the route and detail the sights along the way. For more information see Cycling in the Activities section of the Facts for the Visitor chapter. ■

HJERL HEDE

Six km east of the small village of Vinderup is Hjerl Hede (☎ 97 44 80 60), a large open-air museum that traces the development of a Danish village from 1500 to 1900. Scenically set against a lake and moors, it has a collection of about 40 period buildings, many of them timber-framed with thatched roofs, which were gathered from around Jutland. You can wander around and visit a forge, a dairy, a grocery shop and a village school.

From mid-June to mid-August about 100 traditionally costumed men, women and children arrive around 1 pm to 'inhabit' the village and perform old-time functions such as dipping candles and tilling the fields. There's also a small settlement where 'Stone Age people' in costume make flint instruments and pottery and practice spear fishing from dugout canoes. Additionally, Hjerl Hede has a forestry and bog cultivation museum with an old steam engine and the remains of a narrow-gauge peat railway.

It's open from 1 April to 31 October from 9 am to 5 pm, except from mid-June to mid-August when it closes at 6 pm. Because of the activities, the midsummer period is by far the most interesting time to go. Admission costs 50 kr for adults and 15 kr for children. The nearest railway station is at Vinderup.

HOLSTEBRO & HERNING

Roughly 50 km west of Viborg on route 16 is Holstebro and an equal distance southwest of Viborg on route 12 is Herning. Both Holstebro and Herning are industrial towns with populations of about 30,000 and both are on the railway line from Silkeborg.

Holstebro is an old established market town that reached its heyday in the early 1700s spurred on by a large cattle market and its convenient location on the river Storå. It has a couple of small museums, but fire has claimed most of its historic buildings.

More interesting is Herning, a town that developed in the late 19th century when the railway came chugging through. Textile mills followed, but have since been largely replaced by wood processing industries and computer technology. The community has a keen interest in the arts, there are sculptures around town and the general ambience is enlivened by the presence of a music school. The Herning Museum (10 kr) at Museumsgade 32, 300 metres south-west of the railway station, has period furnishings and tools, a prehistoric collection and an interesting section of shadow-box village scenes. The Herning Kunstmuseum (30 kr), two km east of town, has a decent collection of modern Danish art, with works by Asger Jorn, Richard Mortensen and Carl-Henning Pedersen.

The Herning tourist office (☎ 97 12 44 22) is on Bredgade 2, the main shopping street, two blocks north-west of the railway station. The Holstebro tourist office (☎ 97 42 57 00), Brotorvet 8, is on the south side of the river and about a 20-minute walk south of the railway station.

Herning has an HI hostel and both Herning and Holstebro have camping grounds and a few hotels.

Central West Coast

The central west coast, north of Esbjerg, is lined with sandy beaches, making it a popular summer holiday destination. One area particularly thick with summer cottages is Holmsland Klit, the thin neck of sand and dunes that stretches nearly 35 km from north to south, separating the North Sea from the Ringkøbing Fjord. This sandy neck, only about a km wide, has its appeal but don't expect the drive to be overwhelmingly scenic as the dunes block the ocean view almost the entire way.

The Ringkøbing Fjord attracts scores of windsurfers with conditions that are suitable for all levels, including beginners, while the North Sea side of Holmsland Klit has more challenging action for advanced windsurfers.

HENNE STRAND

Henne Strand is a small seaside resort that's especially popular with German visitors. The road into the village, Strandvejen, dead-ends at the beach and is lined with a touristy collection of souvenir shops, boutiques, restaurants, discos and pizzerias, all in a row one after the other. The grassy dunes that separate the village from the beach are dotted with summer holiday homes, including some attractive thatched cottages.

The beach itself is long and lovely. On warm summer days when the wind is calm swimmers take to the waters, although caution should be used as strong North Sea undertows can occur anywhere along the

west coast. The northern end of the beach is a popular spot for nude sunbathing.

Information

Henne Strand Turistbureau (☎ 75 25 56 00, fax 75 25 51 20), Strandvejen 436, 6854 Henne Strand, is right in the centre of the village. Next door you'll find minigolf and cycle rentals and there's a coin laundry nearby.

Places to Stay & Eat

Henne Strand Camping (☎ 75 25 50 79), Henne Strandvej 418, 6854 Henne Strand, is a three-star facility open from early April to late October. Located 300 metres east of the village centre, it's about a 10-minute walk to the beach. The camping charge is 47 kr; there's a coin laundry, cooking facilities and cabins. The site also has a 'tropicland' with a swimming pool and waterslide.

The little 44-bed *Henne Strand Van-drerhjem* (☎ 75 25 50 75), Strandvejen 458, 6854 Henne Strand, is right in the village 100 metres west of the tourist office and just minutes from the beach. It's open to individuals from late June to late August. Dorm beds cost 65 kr. There are two rooms with two beds that can be rented as doubles for 170 kr, while the other 10 rooms have four beds.

The tourist office books summer houses priced from 1500 to 6000 kr a week. Opposite the tourist office there's an agency that books rooms for 200/300 kr for singles/doubles.

Along Strandvejen you'll find a grocery store, a fish shop, hot dog stands, a couple of bakeries and numerous eateries where you can get a meal for 35 to 70 kr. The latter includes *Strand Café en Bodega* which has fish or chicken with chips for 39 kr.

Getting There & Away

Henne Strand is at the end of route 465. Almost all visitors arrive by car, but it is possible to get there by public transport. The easiest route is to take a train to Henne Strandby and from there catch a taxi, which will cost about 100 kr. Alternately you could take the train to the more northerly Nørre

Nebel and catch one of the infrequent buses (14 kr) that run from there to Henne Strand.

HVIDE SANDE

The town of Hvide Sande came into existence in 1931 with the opening of a sluice channel and lock between the Ringkøbing Fjord and the North Sea. The sluice regulates both the water level and salinity of the Ringkøbing Fjord and protects the fields on the inland side of the fjord from being flooded. The lock, which is 16.5 metres wide, allows ships to enter the fjord, which is otherwise sealed off from the sea.

The channel cuts across the centre of town and you can get a view of it all from the bridge. Hvide Sande has a busy deep-sea fishing harbour, with lots of trawlers, fish processing factories and an early morning fish auction. There's also a little fishing museum adjacent to the tourist office. Most visitors, however, aren't here for the fish, but for the wind.

Information

The Holmsland Klit Turistforening (☎ 97 31 18 66) is at the Fiskeriets Hus Museum, Nørregade 2, 6960 Hvide Sande, on the north side of the channel. It's open Monday to Friday from 10 am to 5 pm all year round and also in summer from 9 am to 5 pm on Saturday and 11 am to 4 pm on Sunday.

Windsurfing

Ringkøbing Fjord has ideal wind and water conditions and Hvide Sande attracts scores of windsurfers. There are two related windsurfing shops: Westwind Nord (☎ & fax 97 31 25 99), on the northern side of Hvide Sande, and Westwind Syd (☎ 97 31 28 99), a couple of km to the south. Both are open from April to the end of October and offer a three-hour introductory course for 350 kr as well as more comprehensive classes. They also rent gear, including wet suits for 90 kr a day and boards with rigs from 250 kr a day; weekly rates are equivalent to about three times the daily rate. The shops also rent mountain bikes for 80 kr a day.

Places to Stay

The two-star Beltana Camping (☎ 97 31 12 18, fax 97 31 33 11), Karen Brandsvej 70, 6960 Hvide Sande, is at the south side of town opposite a popular windsurfing beach. It has a nightly charge of 43 kr per person plus 10 kr per site, a TV lounge, cooking and laundry facilities and cabins for hire. It's open from mid-April to late October. There are other camping grounds to both the north and south of Hvide Sande.

The tourist office can provide a list of about a dozen places with private rooms for rent as well as information on summer cottages.

The hotel Hvide Sande Sømandshjem (☎ 97 31 10 33), Bredgade 5, 6960 Hvide Sande, has a central location, on the south side of the harbour. There are 15 straightforward singles/doubles with private bath for 250/395 kr, breakfast included.

The other in-town choice is the Hotel Holmsland Klit (☎ 97 31 16 00, fax 97 31 31 55), Nørregade 2, 6960 Hvide Sande, a 17-room motel-style place on the north side of the channel. Singles/doubles with private bath, TV, refrigerator and a coffee maker cost 425/550 kr, breakfast included.

Places to Eat

There's a bakery on the south side of town on the corner of Metheasvej and Stormgade, and one on the north side of town at Nørregade 50.

The røgeri on Metheasvej near the waterfront street Auktionsvej, on the south side of town, has crab claws and smoked fish by the piece as well as takeaway shrimp salad.

Bella Italia, Parallelvej 3, on the north side of town, has pizza from 40 kr and good tortellini and other pastas for around 60 kr.

La Barca, on the opposite side of the bridge at Søndergade 3, also has similarly priced pizza and pasta, but it's best known for its steaks, priced at around 120 kr.

If you're looking for an upmarket place to eat, Restaurant Slusen at Bredgade 3, near the harbour, has an excellent reputation for its fresh seafood. There's a daily three-course fish meal for 238 kr, as well as an à la carte menu.

Getting There & Away
Hvide Sande is on route 181. Bus No 58 runs to Hvide Sande from Ringkøbing railway station (20 minutes) and Nørre Nebel railway station (35 minutes) about once an hour on weekdays, half as frequently on weekends.

RINGKØBING
Ringkøbing, on the north side of the Ringkøbing Fjord, is an old market town that was granted its municipal charter in 1443. The town's origins were as a North Sea port, but from the 1600s shifting sands caused the mouth of the fjord to slowly migrate south and threatened to cut off Ringkøbing's access to the sea. It wasn't until the lock at Hvide Sande was built in 1931 that the town was once again assured a reliable North Sea passage.

Ringkøbing now has 8500 residents, a shipyard, some industry and the county administrative offices.

Information
The Ringkøbing Turistbureau (☎ 97 32 00 31, fax 97 32 49 00), Torvet, 6950 Ringkøbing, is in the town centre next to the church. It's open from 9.30 am to 5 pm Monday to Friday and from 9.30 am to 12.30 pm Saturday, with slightly longer summer hours.

There are two banks at Torvet and a coin laundry 300 metres to the west, on the corner of Torvegade and Godthaabs Vej. The post office is at the west side of the railway station.

Things to See
There are a few **period buildings** in the centre of town around Torvet, the oldest of which is the Hotel Ringkøbing, whose timber-framed wing dates from about 1600. The church north-west of the hotel dates in part to medieval times and has a sundial from 1728 on its western buttress.

The **Ringkøbing Museum**, Kongevejen 1, a few blocks east of Torvet, has displays on the Greenland expeditions (1906-1908) of Mylius Erichsen and such intriguing local items as a chastity belt from 1600. It's open on weekdays from 11 am to 5 pm and on Sunday afternoon; admission is 15 kr.

Places to Stay
The three-star *Ringkøbing Camping* (☎ 97 32 08 38, fax 97 32 52 08), Vellingvej 56, 6950 Ringkøbing, on the east side of town, is open year round and charges 44 kr per person.

The *Ringkøbing Vandrerhjem* (☎ 97 32 24 55, fax 97 32 49 59), Kirkevej 28, 6950 Ringkøbing, is a modern hostel at a sports centre 1.5 km north of the railway station via Holstebrovej. Open year round, there are 136 beds in 25 rooms, most with private baths. Dorm beds cost 84 kr and there are also family rooms.

The tourist office books private rooms from 100 kr per person.

The old *Hotel Ringkøbing* (☎ 97 32 00 11), Torvet 18, 6950 Ringkøbing, has 16 rooms that cost 375/550 kr for singles/doubles.

The Best Western *Hotel Fjordgården* (☎ 97 32 14 00, fax 97 32 47 60), Vesterkær 28, 6950 Ringkøbing, at the west side of town, has 92 modern rooms with private bath, cable TV and minibar and there's a sauna and indoor swimming pool. Singles/doubles cost 740/940 kr; from June to August there's a summer rate of 650 kr.

Places to Eat
There's a kiosk and *DSB Minibar* at the railway station, a smokehouse and grill at the harbour and a cafeteria at the camping ground. A central supermarket is *Super Brugsen* at Torvegade 9, on the street leading west from Torvet. There's a bakery at Øster-gade 17, east of Torvet, and another at Vester Strandgade 10, south of Torvet.

Algade, which heads east from Torvet to the museum, is lined with small shops, including *Ristorante Pizzeria Italia* at Al-gade 11, which has pizza, pasta and Italian meat dishes at moderate prices. There's a kebab stand opposite the museum.

There's a fine-dining restaurant specialising in fish at the *Hotel Ringkøbing* on Torvet and another expensive, but more contemporary, restaurant at the *Hotel Fjordgården*.

Getting There & Away
Ringkøbing is on route 15, 46 km west of Herning and nine km east of the North Sea.

Ringkøbing is on the DSB railway line between Esbjerg (1¼ hours, 59 kr) and Struer (one hour, 53 kr). Buses to Hvide Sande leave from the east side of the railway station.

There's also a little seasonal ferry, the MF *Sorte Louis*, that sails across the Ringkøbing Fjord between Ringkøbing and Hvide Sande; call ☎ 97 32 06 66 or check at the tourist office for the current schedule.

Northern Jutland

Northern Jutland, which is separated from the rest of Jutland by the Limfjord, has a coastal landscape dominated by heathlands, dunes and sandy beaches.

The region has only one large city, Aalborg, and a handful of mid-sized towns. Although road maps are peppered with the names of numerous smaller villages, these are often little more than a string of roadside houses, broken by farmland, fields of grazing sheep and the occasional petrol station.

Among the most interesting places in northern Jutland are the Lindholm Høje Viking burial ground on the northern outskirts of Aalborg, the vast shifting sand dunes of Råbjerg Mile and the arty resort town of Skagen, whose sandy tip marks Denmark's northernmost boundary.

AALBORG

Strategically situated at the narrowest point of the Limfjord, the long body of water that slices Jutland in two, Aalborg has been a bustling port since Viking times.

Today Aalborg is Jutland's second-largest city with a population of 155,000. An industrial and trade centre, Aalborg's economy is reliant upon shipbuilding, cement and steel. It is also well known to bar hoppers as the leading producer of Danish snaps, aquavit.

Although it's skipped over by most foreign travellers Aalborg has a few worthwhile sites, the paramount attraction being Lindholm Høje, Denmark's largest Viking burial ground.

Orientation

Linked by bridge and tunnel, Aalborg spreads along both sides of the Limfjord. The heart of the city and most services are on the south side, including the tourist office and the cathedral, which are a 10-minute walk from the railway and bus stations, north down Boulevarden.

HIGHLIGHTS

- Viking burial ground at Lindholm Høje (Aalborg)
- Vast stretches of deserted beaches
- The extensive sand dunes of Råbjerg Mile
- Seaside Skagen with its distinctive houses, museums and artists' community
- The 'buried church' in the dunes south of Skagen
- Windsurfing at Klitmøller

Information

Tourist Office The Aalborg Turistbureau (☎ 98 12 60 22, fax 98 16 69 22) is at Østerågade 8, Postboks 1862, 9100 Aalborg. From June to August it's open Monday to Friday from 9 am to 6 pm, and on Saturday from 9 am to 5 pm. In the low season it's open on weekdays from 9 am to 4 pm and on Saturday from 10 am to 1 pm.

Money There are a number of banks in the city centre including a Unibank opposite the Buldolfi Domkirke and a Jyske Bank at the intersection of Nytorv and Østerågade.

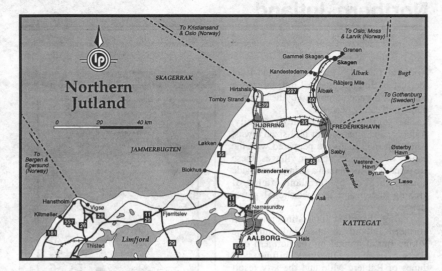

When the banks are closed, you can change money at the tourist office.

Post & Telecommunications The post office immediately west of the Buldolfi Domkirke is open from 9 am to 5.30 pm on weekdays and from 9 am to noon on Saturday. You can also make phone calls, both domestic and international, from there.

Gay Information The Aalborg branch of Landsforeningen for Bøsser og Lesbiske (LBL), the national organisation for gays and lesbians, can be reached on ☎ 98 14 10 65.

Bookshop Ginnerups Boghandel, Boulevarden 12, has books and maps on Denmark.

Laundry There's a coin laundry on the corner of Vesterbro and Borgergade.

Pharmacy Buldolfi Apotek (☎ 98 12 06 77), on the corner of Vesterbro and Algade, is open 24 hours.

Other Facilities Danes Worldwide Archives (☎ 98 12 57 93) at Arkivstræde 1, behind Vor Frue Kirke, has an archives of Danish emi-gration history and is set up to help foreigners of Danish descent trace their roots. It's open Monday to Thursday from 9 am to 4 pm and on Friday from 9 am to 2 pm.

Buldolfi Domkirke

This whitewashed cathedral, which dates from the 12th century, marks the centre of the old town. As you enter the cathedral interior from Algade, look up at the foyer ceiling to see colourful frescoes. The cathedral has some beautifully carved items, including a gilded Baroque altar and a richly detailed pulpit. Interestingly, both were created by Danish sculptor Lauridtz Jensen; apparently the altar, carved in 1689, was too flashy for the parish, so in 1692 Jensen used an older Renaissance style for the pulpit. It's open Monday to Friday from 9 am to 4 pm and on Saturday to 2 pm. Admission is free.

Aalborg Historiske Museum

The next block west from the Buldolfi Domkirke is the Aalborg Historiske Museum, a local history museum with excavated artefacts, the requisite Renaissance furnishings and fine collections of glassware and ancient Danish coins. It also has some interesting

PLACES TO STAY

2 Limfjordshotellet & Casino
31 Helnan Phønix Hotel
32 Hotel Chagall
38 Prinsens Hotel
39 Park Hotel
45 Hotel Hvide Hus

PLACES TO EAT

3 Fellini
4 Regesen
5 Jules Vernes
6 Fyrtøjet
8 Rendezvous Café
10 Romeo & Julie
12 Burger King
15 McDonald's
20 Føtex Grocery Store
24 Café Underground
25 Fast and Easy
26 Skibsted's Fish Market
34 Brugsen Supermarket
36 Bakery
37 Restaurant Akropolis

OTHER

1 Coin Laundry
7 La Bar
9 Carpark
11 Jørgen Olufsens House
13 Aalborghus Slot
14 Jyske Bank
16 Jens Bangs Stenhus
17 Old Town Hall
18 Tourist Office
19 Salling Department Store
21 Vor Frue Kirke
22 Danes Worldwide Archives
23 Pan Blue Gate
27 Buldolfi Domkirke
28 Post Office
29 Helligåndsklostret
30 Aalborg Historiske Museum
33 Unibank
35 Bookshop
40 Europcar Car Rental
41 Bus Station
42 Avis Car Rental
43 Railway Station
44 Aalborg Kongres og Kultur Center

Limfjord

Aalborg

0   100   200 m

To Lindholm Høje

Gammel Strandvej

To Aalborg Vandrerhjem, Camping Grounds & Aalborg Marinemuseum

Strandvejen

Toldbodgade

Borgergade

Vesterbro

Ved Stranden

Domhtr Ans Gade

Bispensgade

Østerågade

Nytorv

Nytorv

Slotsgade

To Aalborg Sømandshjem

Alpade

Vingårdsgade

Jernbanegade

Sankelmarksgade

Danmarksgade

Prinsensgade

Vesterbro

Boulevarden

Hjelmer Stald

Peder Barkes Gade

Rantzausgade

Danmarksgade

Niels Ebbesens Gade

Jyllandsgade

To Tivoliland (500 m)

Kildeparken

To Aalborg Tower, Aalborg Zoo, Mølleparken & Nordjyllands Kunstmuseum

NORTHERN JUTLAND

oddities, including a mid-18th century hearse embellished with skulls and cross-bones. It's open Tuesday to Sunday from 10 am to 5 pm. Admission is 10 kr for adults and 5 kr for children.

Other Central Sights

The alley between the Aalborg Historiske Museum and the cathedral leads to the rambling **Helligåndsklostret**, or Monastery of the Holy Ghost, which dates from 1431. The interior can only be visited on a guided tour arranged through the tourist office.

East of the Buldolfi Domkirke are three noteworthy historic buildings on Østerågade: the baroque-style **old town hall** (circa 1762); the five-storey **Jens Bangs Stenhus** (circa 1624) and the **Jørgen Olufsens House** (circa 1616) at Østerågade 25. The latter two are lovely Renaissance buildings, one built by a wealthy merchant, Jens Bang, and the other by a wealthy mayor, Jørgen Olufsen.

In addition, the half-timbered neighbourhoods around **Vor Frue Kirke** on Peder Barkes Gade are worth strolling through, particularly the cobbled street Hjelmerstald. **Aalborghus Slot**, near the waterfront, is more an administrative office than a castle, but there's a small dungeon you can enter for free.

Ask at the tourist office for the English-language *Good Old Aalborg* booklet, which maps out two suggested walking tours and provides details on buildings and sights along the way.

Nordjyllands Kunstmuseum

This regional museum of modern and contemporary art, at Kong Christian Allé 50, is in a marble building designed by Finnish architect Alvar Aalto. It has a fine collection of Danish art from the late 19th century to the present day, including works by JF Willumsen, Asger Jorn, Richard Mortensen and Edvard Weie. Opening hours are Tuesday to Sunday from 10 am to 5 pm year round, and in July and August it's also open on Monday. Admission is 20 kr for adults and free for children.

To get there, take the tunnel beneath the railway station which emerges into Kildeparken, a green space with statues and water fountains. Go directly through the park, cross Vesterbro and continue through a wooded area to the museum, a 10-minute walk in all.

Aalborgtårnet

The hill behind the art museum is topped with the Aalborgtårnet, an ungainly tower offering a panoramic view of the city's steeples and smokestacks. The tower is open from April to October, from 10 am to 5 pm (to 7 pm in summer), weather permitting. The ride up costs 15 kr for adults and 10 kr for children.

The tower sits on the edge of an expansive wooded area, **Mølleparken**, which has walking trails, views and the Aalborg zoo.

Aalborg Zoo

This zoo in Mølleparken, at the south-west side of the city, has some pleasant aspects including a wooded setting and a children's zoo with goats and other tame creatures which children are encouraged to touch and pat. In all, the Aalborg Zoo has 1000 animals, including elephants, zebras, tigers, giraffes, crocodiles, baboons and performing sea lions. There are golden-lion tamarins, almost extinct in the wild, which have been successfully bred here. The zoo is open daily in summer from 9 am to 6 pm, with shorter hours the rest of the year. Admission is 50 kr for adults and 20 kr for children. There's a cafeteria with moderately priced food. Bus No 1 takes you there from the city centre.

Tivoliland

This amusement park, at Karolinelundsvej on the east side of the city centre, has a roller coaster, carousel, bumper cars and about 70 other rides and attractions as well as the usual carnival food. It's open from April to September. Opening hours vary, but are from 10 am to 10 pm at the height of the season. Admission is 40 kr for adults and 20 kr for children, not including rides.

Aalborg Marinemuseum

This waterfront museum at Vestre Fjordvej 81, three km west of the city centre, features a dry-docked 54-metre submarine, a torpedo boat, model ships and various other maritime exhibits. It's open in summer from 10 am to 6 pm and in winter from 10 am to 4 pm. Admission is 35 kr for adults and 20 kr for children. Bus Nos 2 and 8 stop nearby.

Lindholm Høje

On a hill-top pasture overlooking the city, Lindholm Høje is the site of 682 graves from the Iron Age and Viking Age. Many of the Viking graves are marked by stones placed in an oval ship shape, with two larger end stones as stem and stern. Interpretive plaques on the grounds provide historical insights. It's an intriguing place to walk, and there's something almost spiritual about the site.

The **Lindholm Høje Museet** located at the site's carpark has local archaeological items and displays that attempt to a create a sense of life during Viking times. The museum is open daily from June to August from 10 am to 7 pm, and Tuesday to Sunday from 10 am to 4 pm in winter. Admission costs 20 kr for adults and 10 kr for children. The museum complex has a pleasant café with salads, sandwiches and fish & chips at reasonable prices.

The field with the gravestones is open from dawn to dusk; admission is free. Lindholm Høje is 15 minutes from Aalborg on bus No 6; cross the fence 50 metres beyond the bus stop and you're in the burial field. If you have your own transport, head north from the city centre over the Limfjord bridge to Nørresundby, following Lindholmsvej north to Hvorupvej. After Hvorupvej intersects with Vikingevej, take the first left, which will bring you up the driveway to the museum.

Organised Tours

A two-hour city bus tour with a guide who speaks both Danish and English is available at 1.30 pm in summer. It cruises past the city's main sights and stops at Lindholm Høje and the Viking museum. The tickets can be bought in advance from the tourist office and cost 30 kr for adults and 20 kr for children.

The tourist office also organises a tour of the 15th century Helligåndsklostret (Monastery of the Holy Ghost) on weekdays at 2 pm. The tours cost 25 kr for adults and 10 kr for children; only the Tuesday and Thursday guides speak English.

Places to Stay

Hostel & Camping The hostel, *Aalborg Vandrerhjem* (☎ 98 11 60 44, fax 98 12 47 11), Skydebanevej 50, 9000 Aalborg, at the marina four km west of the centre, has 35 rooms, each with four beds and a private bath. Dorm beds cost 85 kr. During the low season you can get a single/double for 165/ 230 kr. There's a TV lounge, table tennis and billiards. It's open year round except from mid-December to mid-January. Bus No 8, which operates about twice an hour, from 6 am to almost midnight, stops out front.

The hostel also operates the adjacent *Fjordparken*, a three-star camping ground with full facilities and a camping charge of 44 kr per person. It's open from 1 April to 1 October. There are also heated fjord-side cabins that sleep five for 250 kr.

Strandparkens Camping (☎ 98 12 76 29, fax 98 12 76 73), Skydebanevej 20, 9000 Aalborg, is on the east side of the marina, 300 metres from Fjordparken. It has the same rating and comparable amenities, including laundry and cooking facilities, but cheaper rates at 36 kr a night. Cabins are also available. The camping ground is open from mid-April to mid-September.

Private Rooms The tourist office can book rooms in private homes for 120 kr a person, plus a booking fee of 25 kr.

Hotels All of the following hotels include breakfast in their rates.

The *Aalborg Sømandshjem* (☎ 98 12 19 00, fax 98 11 76 97), about a km east of the centre at Østerbro 27, 9000 Aalborg, is part of a small hotel chain originally geared for seamen but now open to all. It has 54

ᛁᚱᚠ·ᛏᛁᚱ·ᚠᛉᚾᛈᛂ·ᚼᛈᚠᛈᚾ·ᚠᚦᚦᛁᚱᚠ·ᛏᛁᚱ·ᚠᛉᚾᛈᛂ·ᚼᛈᚠᛈᚾ·ᚠᚦᚦᛁᚱᚠ·ᛏᛁᚱ·ᚠᛉᚾᛈᛂ·ᚼᛈᚠᛈᚾ·ᚠᚦᚦᛁᚱᚠ·ᛏᛁᚱ·ᚠᛉᚾᛈᛂ·ᚼᛈᚠᛈᚾ·ᚠᚦᚦᛁᚱᚠ

Water of Life

Aquavit (or akvavit), which means 'water of life', is the most popular spirit produced in Denmark. There are nearly 30 types of Danish aquavit on the market, most made from fermented potato mash. During the distilling process this dry spirit is flavoured with herbs, berries or spices – the most common being caraway seeds.

Aquavit is served in special long-stemmed glasses and is not sipped, but swallowed straight in one gulp. The bottle is commonly kept in a deep chill and the liquor served so ice-cold that it frosts the glass when it is poured. In Denmark, aquavit is often followed by a chaser of beer and is usually not drunk as an aperitif but as a complement to traditional Danish meals such as smørrebrød or herring.

Most aquavit is 40% alcohol and all varieties zing with a strong fiery sensation on the way down the throat. The city of Aalborg has been producing aquavit since the 17th century and its namesake Aalborg brand is the world's most famous. ■

ᛁᚱᚠ·ᛏᛁᚱ·ᚠᛉᚾᛈᛂ·ᚼᛈᚠᛈᚾ·ᚠᚦᚦᛁᚱᚠ·ᛏᛁᚱ·ᚠᛉᚾᛈᛂ·ᚼᛈᚠᛈᚾ·ᚠᚦᚦᛁᚱᚠ·ᛏᛁᚱ·ᚠᛉᚾᛈᛂ·ᚼᛈᚠᛈᚾ·ᚠᚦᚦᛁᚱᚠ·ᛏᛁᚱ·ᚠᛉᚾᛈᛂ·ᚼᛈᚠᛈᚾ·ᚠᚦᚦᛁᚱᚠ

straightforward rooms, comfortable enough but with no particular character, for 360/475 kr for singles/doubles with private bath. There are also a few single rooms with shared bath for 275 kr. It has a TV lounge and a billiards room.

The centrally located *Prinsens Hotel* (☎ 98 13 37 33, fax 98 16 52 82), Prinsensgade 14, 9000 Aalborg, has 42 rooms with modern amenities, including TV, phone and minibar. The rooms are pleasant but many are on the small side. Weekday rates are 395/520 kr for singles/doubles with shared bath and 595/745 kr with private bath; there's a slight discount on weekends. The hotel has a sauna (25 kr extra) and a bar.

The traditional *Park Hotel* (☎ 98 12 31 33, fax 98 13 31 66), Boulevarden 41, 9000 Aalborg, has a good location opposite the railway station. Rooms are very comfortable, with deep bath tub, TV, hair drier and soft continental quilts. Ask for a courtyard room as they are free of traffic noise. Singles/doubles start at 580/700 kr.

The following hotels are all 1st class and in the city centre. In addition to the regular rates listed here, any of these hotels may offer discounted rates on weekends, in summer or when business is slow.

The old-fashioned *Helnan Phønix Hotel* (☎ 98 12 00 11 or toll-free 80 81 51 01, fax 98 16 31 66), Vesterbro 77, 9000 Aalborg, has 180 rooms with private bath, TV, phone and minibar for 815/1025 kr a single/double. There's a bar, restaurant, sauna, billiard table and fitness room.

The *Hotel Chagall* (☎ 98 12 69 33, fax 98 13 13 44), Vesterbro 36, 9000 Aalborg, has 69 rooms with private bath, TV, phone and minibar for 690/920 kr a single/double. There's a sauna, jacuzzi and also an exercise room.

The *Limfjordshotellet* (☎ 98 16 43 33, fax 98 16 17 47), Ved Stranden 14, 9100 Aalborg, is best known as the site of the local casino. The 180 rooms, some of which are set aside for nonsmokers, are modern and have private bath, minibar and TV. Singles/doubles cost 830/1050 kr.

The *Hotel Hvide Hus* (☎ 98 13 84 00, fax 98 13 51 22), Vesterbro 2, 9000 Aalborg, is a modern 200-room Best Western hotel with all the usual amenities. There's a fitness room, sauna, outdoor pool and 15th-floor restaurant. The regular rate is 700/1095 kr for singles/doubles, but there's a family rate of 650 kr from 15 June to 15 August that allows two adults and two children in the same room.

Places to Eat

Jomfru Ane Gade The best place to head at mealtime is Jomfru Ane Gade, a boisterous pedestrian street lined with restaurants and cafés with outdoor tables. In the afternoon you'll find lots of lunch deals for 30 to 50 kr, while at dinner there are three-course meals for 70 to 100 kr.

A good approach is to simply stroll the street and see what catches your fancy. Some of the choices, from north to south, include the following.

Fellini, at Jomfru Ane Gade 23, is a popular spot with pizzas from 45 kr, pastas from 60 kr and fish dishes for around 100 kr. There's a varied children's menu for just 11 kr and cheap pizza and lasagne lunch specials.

Jules Vernes, Jomfru Ane Gade 14, which spices up its menu with international dishes, has a nice lunch buffet of salad, fish, chicken and a few cold dishes for just 39 kr. For a more traditional Danish buffet, visit *Regesen*, at Jomfru Gade 16, which puts on a good lunch-time spread for 49 kr; at dinner, served from 4 pm, dishes start at 100 kr and include selections from the salad bar.

If the weather is threatening rain, consider *Fyrtøjet* at Jomfru Ane Gade 17, which has a glass-roofed courtyard and three-course lunch specials until 4 pm for 49 kr.

The *Rendezvous Café*, Jomfru Ane Gade 5, has light lunches, including 20 kr sandwiches and inexpensive pasta and salads. For cheap drinks *La Bar*, just a few metres to the north, is the hot spot.

Elsewhere The railway station has a small grocery store and a *DSB restaurant* and there's a cafeteria at the bus station.

Algade, a pedestrian shopping street a block south of the tourist office, has a few good inexpensive options. *Skibsted's Fish Market*, Algade 23, has takeaway salmonburgers and fresh fish & chips for under 20 kr. Request 'no remoulade' if you don't want it drenched in mayonnaise.

Café Underground, Algade 21, has natural ice cream, crêpes and sandwiches; it's open until 6 pm on weekdays and 2 pm on Saturday. The nearby *Fast and Easy* has cheap beer and good pizza by the slice for 12 kr; on a sunny day its courtyard is a fun place to sit and watch the shoppers parading by.

There are a few fast-food restaurants in the city centre on Østerågade, including *Burger King* and *McDonald's*. The *Salling* department store, 100 metres to the east on Nytorv, has a cafeteria with moderately priced Danish fare and a basement supermarket with a deli that has smoked fish, salads and cheeses available for takeaway. The *Føtex* grocery store, a few minutes walk farther east at Slotsgade 8, has a bakery, a fast-food kiosk with decent 15 kr sandwiches and a cafeteria with meals for around 40 kr.

Romeo & Julie, a pleasant pizzeria at Ved Stranden 5, has a steak lunch for 39 kr, a buffet of pizza, lasagne and fresh salad for 59 kr and a three-course meal with baked salmon for 99 kr. All are served from 11.30 am to 4 pm daily.

Restaurant Akropolis, Sankelmarksgade 1A, serves authentic Greek food with starters from around 30 kr and main courses such as souvlaki, moussaka and yiros for around 100 kr. It's open from noon to midnight (from 5 pm on Sunday).

A superb way to cap off the night is with a glass of wine at the smoulderingly romantic *Duus Vinkjælder*, a candlelit 300-year-old wine cellar in the Jens Bangs Stenhus on Østerågade. Open until at least midnight from Monday to Saturday, it has surprisingly reasonable drink prices and a few cheap light eats, such as burgers, chips and hot dogs.

Entertainment

Jomfru Ane Gade is a popular spot for night life. You'll find drinks, music and dancing along this street at *Rock Nielsen* and *Jomfru Ane's Danse Bar*, both open Thursday to Saturday from 9 pm to 5 am, and at *Sidegaden* and *Musikhuset Hr Nielsen*, both open daily from 11 am to 5 am.

Aalborg Kongres og Kultur Center (☎ 98 13 46 33) on Vesterbro, north of Kildeparken, is the venue for classical music, opera and ballet performances and the home of the Aalborg Symphony Orchestra.

Pan Blue Gate (☎ 98 12 22 45), a gay bar and dance club, is at Danmarksgade 27A. It's open Tuesday to Thursday from 8 pm to 1 am, on Friday from 4 pm to 4 am, and on Saturday from 10 pm to 5 am.

The Limfjordshotellet, at Ved Stranden

14, has a casino with French and American roulette, blackjack and slot machines. Entry is restricted to those aged 18 and older from 8 pm to 4 am daily. Admission is 40 kr and the dress code is 'neat, semi-formal'.

Getting There & Away

Aalborg is 112 km north of Århus and 65 km south-west of Frederikshavn.

Air SAS (☎ 98 11 61 00) operates 10 daily nonstop flights between Aalborg and Copenhagen. The one-way fare is 595 kr, while the return fare costs 595 kr in midweek and 840 kr on Friday, Saturday and Sunday. Most international flights are via Copenhagen, but Muk Air (☎ 98 19 03 88) operates a direct flight on weekdays to Oslo in Norway, for 1460 kr one way or 1860 kr with an Apex return fare.

The airport is six km north-west of the city centre; cross the Limfjord bridge and follow the signs for *lufthavn*.

An airport bus (22 kr) runs to coincide with flight times between the airport and the bus station on Jyllandsgade. A taxi between the airport and the city centre costs about 90 kr.

Bus Express buses (☎ 98 16 09 99) run daily to Copenhagen (six hours, 175 kr), Århus (2¼ hours, 98 kr) and Esbjerg (3½ hours, 156 kr).

Train Trains run about hourly to Frederikshavn (one hour, 53 kr) and a little more frequently to Århus (1½ hours, 95 kr).

Car & Motorbike The E45 bypasses the city centre, tunnelling under the Limfjord, whereas route 180 (which links up with the E45 both north and south of the city) leads into the centre.

To get to Lindholm Høje or points north from the centre of Aalborg, take route 180 (Vesterbro) which crosses the Limfjord by bridge.

Car Rental Hertz, Avis and Europcar have booths at the airport. The following companies also have offices in central Aalborg:

Avis (☎ 98 13 30 99), at the railway station
Europcar (☎ 98 13 23 55), Jyllandsgade 4

Getting Around

Bus Nearly all city buses leave from Østerågade and Nytorv, near Burger King. The bus fare is 11 kr. You can also buy a 24-hour tourist bus pass for 70 kr. The detailed city maps found in the tourist office's free *Aalborg Guide* show bus routes in blue; there's a bus information line (☎ 98 11 11 11) if you need further assistance.

Car & Motorbike Other than for a few one-way streets that may have you driving in circles a bit, Aalborg is easy to get around by car. The city has free street parking along many of its side streets, as well as metered parking in the centre. If you're unable to find a parking space, there are several large commercial carparks, including one at Ved Stranden 11 that's open 24 hours a day.

Taxi Taxis line up at the railway station and are usually plentiful at the airport around flight times. You can also call for one (☎ 98 10 10 10 or 98 12 48 00).

Bicycle Bicycles can be rented for 40 kr a day from Feriesport Aalborg (☎ 98 13 30 88), Harald Jensensvej 3, about halfway between the hostel and the railway station.

FREDERIKSHAVN

Frederikshavn, with a population of 26,000, is the largest town north of Aalborg and Jutland's busiest international ferry port.

Frederikshavn is a young town, quite modern in appearance and with few historic attractions. It has an industrial waterfront of boat terminals and shipyards, while the town centre is chock-a-block with supermarkets selling liquor, canned hams and frozen meats to Swedes and Norwegians on shopping excursions.

Although overtaxed Scandinavians may be drawn here for bargains, Frederikshavn is not terribly appealing to most other foreign travellers who generally pass right through without pause. If you have time to spare, there are a couple of local sights you could visit, the most interesting being the Bangsbomuseet.

Orientation

An overhead walkway leads from the ferry terminals to the tourist office, which sits at the edge of the central commercial district. The railway station and adjacent bus terminal are a 10-minute walk north of the ferry terminals.

Information

Tourist Office The Frederikshavn Turistbureau (☎ 98 42 32 66, fax 98 42 12 99) is opposite the harbour at Brotorvet 1, 9900 Frederikshavn. From June to August it's open Monday to Saturday from 8.30 am to 8.30 pm, and on Sunday from 11 am to 8.30 pm; in the low season it's open on weekdays from 9 am to 4 pm and on Saturday from 11 am to 2 pm.

Money There are several banks in the town centre spread out along Danmarksgade.

Post The post office, beside the railway station, is open on weekdays from 9.30 am to 5 pm and on Saturday from 9.30 am to noon.

Things to See

If you're waiting for a train, you might want to climb the nearby whitewashed **Krudt-tårnet** gun tower, a remnant of the 17th century citadel that once protected the port. Until 1974 this squat round tower stood 270 metres to the east but an expansion of the shipyards necessitated its move farther inland. Within the tower's two-metre-thick walls are a few displays of antique swords, helmets and guns, while a steep stairway leads to a top galley mounted with cannons. From April to October, it's open daily from 10 am to 5 pm; admission is 10 kr.

Frederikshavn Kirke, the church opposite the railway station, dates from 1892 and

has an altarpiece painted by Skagen artist Michael Ancher.

On Parallelvej, 500 metres west of the railway station, there's a **cultural complex** with a modest art museum, swimming pools, the public library and a café.

Bangsbomuseet

The Bangsbomuseet (Bangsbo Museum), three km south of Frederikshavn centre, is an old country estate with an eclectic mix of collections. The manor house holds local history exhibits, Victorian furniture, antique dolls and a peculiar collection of ornaments woven from human hair.

The farm buildings have old ship figureheads, military paraphernalia and exhibits on the Danish resistance to the German occupation during WW II. The museum's most intriguing exhibit is the Ellingå ship, the reconstructed remains of a 12th century Viking-style merchant ship that was dug up from a stream bed five km north of Frederikshavn.

If you're up to a walk, a gate just outside the museum leads into Dyrehaven, a wooded area that's home to red, fallow and sika deer. The museum is open daily, except on Monday in winter, from 10 am to 5 pm. Admission is 20 kr. To get there, take bus No 1 or 2 which stops near the entrance to the estate, from where it's an enjoyable 500-metre walk through the woods to the museum.

Places to Stay

Nordstrand Camping (☎ 98 42 93 50, fax 98 43 47 85), Apholmenvej, 9900 Frederikshavn, is near the coast, four km north of the town centre. It's rated four stars and has a full range of amenities. It costs 30 kr for a camping space plus 44 kr per person in the high season, or 33 kr in the low season. Cabins can also be rented. It's open from April to September. In summer there's a bus from the harbour and railway station to the camping ground.

The *Frederikshavn Vandrerhjem* (☎ 98 42 14 75, fax 98 42 65 22), Buhlsvej 6, 9900 Frederikshavn, about 1.5 km north-west of the railway station, has 130 beds and is open from 1 February to 20 December. Dorm beds, mostly in rooms with eight to 12 people, cost 53 kr. The hostel also has four-bed family rooms with private bath, which are available as doubles in the low season for 156 kr. From the ferry harbour, it's a 30-minute walk or a 45 kr taxi ride.

The tourist office books about 50 private rooms, most within a 15-minute walk of the town centre. Singles cost from 115 to 165 kr and doubles from 220 to 250 kr. There's a 25 kr booking fee.

The central *Frederikshavn Sømandshjem* (☎ 98 42 09 77, fax 98 43 18 99), Tordenskjoldsgade 15B, 9900 Frederikshavn, has 40 cheery renovated rooms with TV, washbasin and shared bath for 275/425 kr a single/double. Rooms with private bath cost 450/650 kr. Breakfast is included in the rates. It's just a few minutes walk from either the railway station or the ferry terminals.

Another relatively cheap central hotel is the 32-room *Hotel Mariehønen* (☎ 98 42 01 22, fax 98 43 40 99), Skolegade 2, 9900 Frederikshavn, just off Danmarksgade, the main pedestrian street. It has adequate rooms with washbasin and shared bath for 275/420 kr a single/double and more expensive rooms with private bath.

The town's largest hotel is the 215-room *Stena Hotel* (☎ 98 43 32 33, fax 98 43 33 11), Tordenskjoldsgade 14, 9900 Frederikshavn, which is a short walk north of the Stena Line ferry. This 1st-class hotel has a large indoor swimming pool with water slides and rooms with modern amenities such as minibar and TV. It caters largely to package tours affiliated with its ferry service to Sweden and has singles/doubles from 695/800 kr.

Places to Eat
The railway station has a kiosk selling fruit and snacks and there are simple eateries at both the railway station and ferry terminals.

There are large grocery stores near the waterfront geared to travellers who want to stock up on cheap Danish food and liquor before they leave. One of these, *Havne Super*, adjacent to the ferry harbour at

Sydhavnsvej 8, is open daily from 8 am to 9 pm and has a bistro-style restaurant serving lunch and dinner at moderate prices.

The *Damsgaard Supermarket* on Havnegade 10, behind the tourist office, also has a cafeteria. There are a number of places to eat on Havnegade and Lodsgade, one street to the north, as well as on the nearby streets of Danmarksgade and Søndergade. *Café Fanny*, at Havnegade 11, has pastries, ice cream and simple eats. Nearby on Havnegade is *Romeo & Julie*, a fast-food place with pizza and 25 kr burgers.

At Lodsgade 5 is *Europa*, a steak house and pizzeria with pizza and pasta dishes starting from around 50 kr, fish for 90 kr and a daily steak special for 80 kr. *Bacchus* at Lodsgade 8A specialises in meat and fish dishes for around 90 kr. Cheaper is the nearby *Los Gringos*, which has chilli con carne, tacos and similar Mexican fare for around 50 kr.

In the same neighbourhood, just to the west, you'll find three pizza and pasta restaurants: *Mamma Rosa* at Danmarksgade 59, *Firenze Pizzeria* at Danmarksgade 84 and *Toni Pizzeria* at Søndergade 3B.

Getting There & Away
Frederikshavn is 65 km north-east of Aalborg via the E45 and 41 km south of Skagen via route 40.

Bus & Train Frederikshavn is the northern terminus of the DSB rail line. Trains depart about hourly south to Aalborg (53 kr) and on to Copenhagen (231 kr).

Nordjyllands Trafikselskab (NT) has both a train (40 minutes) and bus service (one hour) north to Skagen (33 kr). NT sells a clip-ticket (*klippekort*) for 74 kr that's good for 110 kr worth of travel; several people can clip the same card.

NT also has a 24-hour ticket good for unlimited travel along its bus routes, which take in most of northern Jutland, including Skagen, Råbjerg Mile, Hirtshals, Hjørring and Løkken (note that some of the beach routes operate in summer only). The ticket costs 70 kr for adults and 35 kr for children.

Car As Frederikshavn is a major port of entry, there are several car rental offices. These include:

Avis (☎ 98 43 19 77), Paradiskajen 1
Europcar (☎ 98 42 31 33), Havnepladsen 5A
Hertz (☎ 98 42 86 77), Danmarksgade 15

Boat For detailed information on ferries from Frederikshavn to Gothenburg in Sweden and to Moss, Oslo and Larvik in Norway see the Getting There & Away chapter in the front of the book. For information on the ferry to Læsø, see the following Læsø section.

LÆSØ

Læsø, 28 km south-east of Frederikshavn, is a quiet island with 2400 inhabitants. Although it's only 25 km at its greatest width, this 114-sq-km island is the largest in the Kattegat. It has a landscape of small farms, heathlands, coastal meadows, dunes and sandy beaches.

Læsø is free of large resort hotels and attracts visitors looking for a low-key summer holiday. The island has a few small towns, two churches dating from medieval times, a straw-roofed maritime museum and a seaweed-roofed farm museum.

According to legend Queen Margrethe I, saved from a shipwreck off Læsø in the 14th century, rewarded her rescuers with a lovely dress and gave them the right to adapt it as an island costume. Although regional customs had largely disappeared elsewhere in Denmark by the 19th century, Læsø women wore their traditional island dress up until the post-war period and continue to wear the costumes today on special occasions.

Another island tradition continues in the making of Læsø salt, which was once an island export; it's now sold in small bags as a tourist souvenir.

The Læsø Turistbureau (☎ 98 49 92 42, fax 98 49 92 83), Fægeterminalen, 9940 Læsø, is at the ferry terminal in Vesterø Havn.

Places to Stay & Eat
There are two three-star camping grounds on Læsø. Østerby Camping (☎ & fax 98 49 80 74), Campingpladsvej 8, 9960 Østerby Havn, is on the north-east side of the island right in the village of Østerby Havn. Læsø Camping (☎ 98 49 94 95, fax 98 49 94 55), Agersigen 18, 9950 Vesterø Havn, is on the north-west side of the island, 1.5 km from the ferry terminal. Both charge 44 kr per person, are open from May to October and have cabins for rent and food kiosks.

The 90-bed Læsø Vandrerhjem (☎ 98 49 91 95, fax 98 49 91 60), Lærkevej 6, 9950 Vesterø Havn, is 500 metres from the ferry harbour. The hostel is open from February to November and charges 65 to 85 kr for dorm beds, 168 kr for a single room and 340 kr for a room for four.

The tourist office books private rooms and flats at varying rates in the villages of Vesterø Havn and Byrum.

There are bakeries, food markets and small restaurants in the main villages. You can get pizza at the hostel.

Getting There & Away
Andelsfærge-Selskabet Læsø (☎ 98 49 90 22 in Læsø, 98 42 29 49 in Frederikshavn) sails two to four times a day between Læsø and Frederikshavn all year round. The crossing takes 1½ hours. The return fare is 120 kr for adults, 80 kr for children and 350 kr for a car. There's also a special 175 kr same-day-return ticket for a car. These car fares don't include drivers or passengers.

Getting Around
Bus A public bus runs hourly on weekdays and every couple of hours on weekends between the villages of Vesterø Havn, Byrum and Østerby Havn.

Bicycle Bicycles can be rented for 40 kr a day from Jarvis Cykelservice (☎ 98 49 94 44) at Vesterø Havnegade 29 in Vesterø Havn, and from the camping grounds.

SKAGEN
Skagen was a fishing port for centuries, but

its luminous heath-and-dune landscape was discovered in the mid-1800s by artists and in more recent times by summering urbanites.

The town's older neighbourhoods are filled with distinctive yellow-washed houses, each roofed with red tiles edged with white lines. Skagen is half arty and half touristy, with a mix of galleries, souvenir shops and ice-cream parlours. The peninsula is lined with fine beaches, including a sandy stretch on the east end of Østre Strandvej, a 15-minute walk from the town centre.

Sankt Laurentii Vej, Skagen's main street, runs almost the entire length of this long thin town, never more than five minutes from the waterfront.

Information

Tourist Office The Skagen Turistbureau (☎ 98 44 13 77, fax 98 45 02 94) is in the railway/bus station at Sankt Laurentii Vej 22, 9990 Skagen. From June to August it's open Monday to Saturday from 9 am to 5.30 pm and on Sunday from 11 am to 2 pm; in the low season it's open on weekdays from 9 am to 4 pm and on Saturday from 10 am to 1 pm.

Money There are a number of banks in the town centre, including an Egnsbank Nord opposite the railway station and Den Danske Bank on the corner of Sankt Laurentii Vej and Havnevej.

Post The post office, at Christian X Vej 8, is open weekdays from 9.30 am to 5 pm and on Saturday from 9.30 am to noon.

Museums

Skagens Museum This fine museum, at Brøndumsvej 4, displays the paintings of PS Krøyer, Michael & Anna Ancher and other artists who flocked to Skagen between 1830 and 1930 to 'paint the light'. Take a close look at *Johannisfeuer*, Krøyer's turn-of-the-century work that shows a bonfire on Skagen beach; among the notable Skagen residents depicted on the left side of the painting are Anna Ancher, in a blue cape, and Holger Drachmann, in a brown cloak with a white beard and cane. The museum, just a few

minutes walk east from the tourist office, is open daily in summer from 10 am to 6 pm, to 5 pm in May and September, with shorter low-season hours. Admission is 30 kr for adults and free for children.

Michael & Anna Anchers Hus The house that Michael and Anna Ancher purchased in 1884 was turned into a museum following the death of their daughter Helga in the 1960s. Preserved much as it would have looked during the artists' lifetimes, it is of note mainly to those with a particular interest in the Anchers. It's at Markvej 2, 300 metres north-east of the tourist office, and open in summer from 10 am to 6 pm daily, with shorter low-season hours. Admission is 25 kr for adults and 5 kr for children.

Drachmanns Hus The house where poet/artist Holger Drachmann lived from 1902 until his death six years later is now a museum dedicated to his life. At Hans Baghs Vej 21, near Sankt Laurentii Vej, on the west side of the town centre, it's open from 10 am to 5 pm daily in summer, with shorter low-season hours. Admission is 15 kr for adults and 2 kr for children.

Skagen Fortidsminder Evocatively presented, this worthwhile open-air museum depicts Skagen's maritime history. It has interesting displays on Skagen's lifeboat rescue service, including dramatic black & white photos of ships in distress.

There are also the preserved homes of fisherfolk with their original furnishings, and a picturesque original Dutch windmill. Ask at the entrance for English notes on the sights, which are otherwise explained in Danish only.

The museum is a 15-minute walk from the railway station, west down Sankt Laurentii Vej, then south on Vesterled. From May to September it's open daily from 10 am to 5 pm; in March, April, October and November it's open weekdays from 10 am to 4 pm. Admission costs 25 kr for adults and 5 kr for children.

Grenen

Denmark's northernmost point is the long curving sweep of sand at Grenen, three km north-east of Skagen's centre. From the carpark, at the end of route 40, the path to the beach crosses rose-covered dunes and at its highest point passes the grave of poet Holger Drachmann (1846-1908).

It's a 30-minute walk out along the vast beach to its narrow tip where the waters of the Kattegat and Skagerrak clash and you can put one foot in each sea. Swimming is not allowed near the point, however, as strong currents have been responsible for sweeping unsuspecting bathers out to sea.

If you're short on time, you might want to walk one way and take the Sandormen in the other direction. This tractor-drawn 'bus' drives out to the point from the Grenen carpark every half-hour in summer, spending 15 minutes at the site before returning. The cost is 6 kr one way and 10 kr return.

At the carpark is the **Grenen Kunstmuseum**, an art gallery which exhibits contemporary Danish paintings with an emphasis on the seascapes of Axel Lind, who founded the museum 20 years ago. It's open daily in summer from 10 am to 6 pm and from 10 am to 4 pm in May and September.

Admission is 20 kr for adults and 10 kr for children. The 35-metre-high bronze sculpture east of the museum is *God on the Rainbow*, created by Swedish sculptor Carl Milles.

The Buried Church

The Tilsandede Kirke (Buried Church) is a whitewashed medieval church tower that still rises up above the sand dunes that buried the surrounding village and farms in the late 1700s. The church itself, once the country's largest, was closed in 1795 because of drifting sand that obscured the doorways and in 1810 it was finally torn down. The tower was left standing for its use as a navigational landmark.

The picturesque church tower and the surrounding area comprise part of Skagen Klitplantage, a nature reserve. It's five km south of Skagen, well signposted from route 40. The church is 400 metres east of the main parking area, where you'll find an ice-cream kiosk and picnic tables should you want to stop for lunch. The nicest way to get here is by bike; take Gammel Landevej from Skagen. The tower interior is open daily from 1 June to 1 September from 11 am to 5 pm. Admission is 7 kr for adults and 3 kr for children.

A Mariner's Nightmare

The waters off northern Jutland have always been extremely treacherous for mariners and have claimed many hundreds of ships over the centuries. Not only are water tempestuous and the currents strong, but the land, which is flat and devoid of landmarks, offers few bearings by which ships can be guided.

Historically, when ships did wash up on shore, local residents would go straight to work pillaging the contents and dismantling the ships for their timber. Some unscrupulous souls are even said to have hung lanterns in such a manner as to mock waterways, and in so doing would lure captains into venturing too close to the shoreline and shallow shoals.

The situation got so out of hand that in 1521 a decree was passed to control salvaging. Gallows were erected along the coast to remind would-be pillagers of the new penalty for the looting of shipwrecks.

At the same time, simple wooden seesaw-style 'lighthouses' called *vippefyret* were erected along the coastline. Each had a basket that could be pulled down and filled with coal, and a counterweight that raised the basket high where it burned throughout the night. These forerunners of present-day lighthouses helped guide ships safely around the point. Although none of the original coal lights still exist, Skagen has a reconstructed one above the beach on the north-east end of Østre Strandvej. ∎

Places to Stay

Camping There are two three-star camping grounds about 1.5 km north-east of Skagen's centre, both with a per-person charge of 46 kr in the high season or 39 kr in the low season. *Grenen Camping* (☎ 98 44 25 46), Fyrvej 16, 9990 Skagen, has a fine seaside location, some semi-private tent sites and pleasant four-bunk cabins with heater, refrigerator and comfortable foam mattresses. It's open from late April to early September. *Poul Eegs Camping* (☎ 98 44 14 70), Batterivej 31, 9990 Skagen, is inland from the beach, but like Grenen Camping has full facilities, including guest kitchens and reasonably priced cabin rentals. It's open from mid-May to early September.

Hostel & Rooms The spiffy new 100-bed hostel, *Skagen Ny Vandrerhjem* (☎ 98 44 22 00, fax 98 44 22 55), Rolighedsvej 2, 9990 Skagen, is one km west of the town centre, on the south side of the road to Frederikshavn. Dorm beds cost 60 to 85 kr, while private rooms range from 210 kr for singles to 340 kr for four people. The hostel serves three meals a day and is open from 10 February to 30 November. The facilities are accessible by wheelchair.

The tourist office books private rooms which range from 200 to 275 kr, plus a 25 kr booking fee.

Hotels & Pensions The following hotels and pensions all have bright, cosy rooms and are competitively priced; the rates given include breakfast.

The newly refurbished 35-room *Skagen Sømandshjem* (☎ 98 44 21 10, fax 98 44 30 28), near the harbour at Østre Strandvej 2, 9990 Skagen, charges 250/480 kr for singles/doubles with shared bath and 395/585 kr with private bath.

Clausens Hotel (☎ 98 45 01 66, fax 98 44 46 33), Sankt Laurentii Vej 35, 9990 Skagen, opposite the railway station, has singles/doubles with shared bath for 395/450 kr, with private bath for 550/595 kr.

The 12-room *Marienlund Badepension* (☎ 98 44 13 20) at Fabriciusvej 8, 9990 Skagen, on the older west side of town near the open-air museum, has singles/doubles for 230/430 kr, all with shared bath.

Finns Pension (☎ & fax 98 45 01 55), Østre Strandvej 63, 9990 Skagen, is a new five-room gay pension in the town centre. Rooms have shared bath and start at 275/500 kr for a single/double.

Places to Eat

There are bakeries on Sankt Laurentii Vej, the best being *Krages Bageri* at No 104. The *Super Brugsen* grocery store, at Sankt Laurentii Vej 28, a two-minute walk west of the tourist office, has a restaurant but it's not as cheap as the typical grocery-store eatery.

In general, Skagen tends to be a pricey place to eat. Havnevej, the main road connecting the harbour and the centre, has a few of the more reasonably priced spots. *Italia*, at Havnevej 5, has takeaway pizza and pasta for 49 kr and sit-down service with the same items in the 50 to 70 kr range. *Alfredo*, at Havnevej 13, has similarly priced pizza as well as grilled fish starting from around 80 kr and meat dishes for 100 kr. *Kebab House*, next to Italia, offers pitta-bread kebab sandwiches for 30 kr and a half-chicken with salad and chips for 52 kr. The *Sømandshjem* hotel, on the corner of Havnevej and Østre Strandvej, has a simple and inexpensive cafeteria.

Clausens Hotel, opposite the railway station, serves lunch from 11 am to 5 pm with a café menu that includes a half-lobster with salad and bread for 78 kr, a smørrebrød plate for 68 kr and a 300-gram steak with chips for 89 kr, all including a glass of wine or beer. At dinner, there's a three-course meal available for 195 kr.

There are two good fish restaurants right on the harbour. The popular *Pakhuset*, Rødspættevej 6, serves simple breakfast items until 11.30 am, including scrambled eggs with bacon and fried tomatoes for 28 kr. From 11.30 am to 11 pm there are reasonably priced sandwiches, various Danish fish dishes and a nice 68 kr saffron fish soup. More expensive is the *Skagen Fiske Restau-*

rant at Fiskehuskaj 13, which specialises in fresh seafood with a French accent.

Getting There & Away

Skagen is 41 km north of Frederikshavn via route 40, and 49 km north-east of Hirtshals via routes 597 and 40.

Bus & Train Either a bus or a train leaves the Skagen station for Frederikshavn (33 kr) about once an hour.

NT's seasonal Skagerakkeren bus (No 99) runs seven times daily from Skagen to Hirtshals (1½ hours, 27.50 kr) from mid-June to mid-August. That same bus also continues on to Hjørring and Løkken. In July the bus company puts together a couple of inexpensive tours to regional destinations; call ☎ 98 44 21 33 for information.

Getting Around

Bus In summer, there are buses that run between Skagen station and Grenen almost every hour (11 kr).

Taxi Taxis, available at the railway station or by calling ☎ 98 43 34 34, charge about 35 kr from Skagen's centre to Grenen. There's a phone at the kiosk in Grenen that you can use to call for a return taxi.

Bicycle Cycling is a good way to get around. Both camping grounds rent bicycles, as does Skagen Cykel (☎ 98 44 12 14), a stand at the west side of the railway station.

GAMMEL SKAGEN

Gammel Skagen (Old Skagen), four km west of Skagen, is an upmarket summer cottage community on the Skagerrak coast, known for its lovely evening sunsets. It was a fishing hamlet in centuries past, before sandstorms ravished this windswept area, forcing many of its inhabitants to move to Skagen, on the more protected east coast.

Gammel Skagen is also known as Højen. Højensvej, the main road, leads west from the hostel a half-km to the main beach and sunset spot.

Places to Stay & Eat

The hostel, *Skagen Vandrerhjem* (☎ 98 44 13 56, fax 98 45 08 17), Højensvej 32, 9990 Gammel Skagen, is a pleasant place with a variety of rooms, including some bright sunny ones. Dorm beds cost 80 kr and double rooms cost 220 kr. Breakfast is available for an extra 35 kr. The hostel is no longer affiliated with Hostelling International, so there's no need for an HI membership card. There's a kiosk on the beach where you can buy ice cream and snack items.

Getting There & Away

Bus No 79 between Frederikshavn and Skagen stops in Gammel Skagen every hour or two; there's a bus stop in front of the hostel. From Skagen centre the fare is 11 kr.

RÅBJERG MILE

Denmark's largest expanse of shifting dunes, these undulating 40-metre hills are almost large enough to disappear in and good fun to explore. The dunes, which are carried eastward about 10 metres a year by prevailing west winds, are a legacy of the 17th century deforestation and overgrazing that left northern Jutland susceptible to the ravages of sand storms. While other dunes in northern Jutland have been stabilised by the planting of beach grasses, the dunes at Råbjerg Mile have purposely been left in a migratory state.

Råbjerg Mile is 16 km south of Skagen, off route 40 on the road to Kandestederne. From mid-June to mid-August, Nordjyllands Trafikselskab runs its Skagerakkeren bus No 99 six times a day from Skagen station to Råbjerg Mile (25 minutes, 16.50 kr) and on to Hirtshals. The dunes themselves are a 750-metre walk from the Råbjerg Mile bus stop.

HIRTSHALS

Hirtshals, with a population of 7000, takes its character from its commercial fishing harbour and ferry terminal. The main street is lined with supermarkets catering to Norwegian shoppers who pile off the ferries to load up with relatively cheap Danish meats and groceries.

Although it's not a town that invites lingering, at least the hostel and camping ground are on the more scenic western side, where there are coastal cliffs and a lighthouse. If you want beaches and dunes, head south to Tornby Strand instead.

Information
The Hirtshals Turistbureau (☎ 98 94 22 20, fax 98 94 58 20) is one km south of the ferry harbour at Nørregade 40, 9850 Hirtshals. You'll find banks and a pharmacy on Jørgens Fiblers Gade, a block south of the railway station.

Nordsømuseet
The main sight in town is the Nordsømuseet (North Sea Museum), which has an aquarium exhibiting North Sea fish, an outdoor seal pool with feedings at 11 am and 3 pm, and displays on fishing. The museum is one km east of the town centre on Willemoesvej, opposite the Skaga Hotel. It's open daily from June to August from 9 am to 6 pm, and from 9 am to 4 pm on weekdays and 10 am to 5 pm on weekends the rest of the year. Admission is 45 kr for adults and 25 kr for children.

Places to Stay & Eat
The three-star *Hirtshals Camping* (☎ 98 94 25 35, fax 98 94 33 43), Kystvejen 6, 9850 Hirtshals, is in an open field on the coast about 150 metres south of the hostel. It's open from late April to mid-September and charges 45 kr per person in the high season or 38 kr in the low season.

The 72-bed *Hirtshals Vandrerhjem* (☎ 98 94 12 48, fax 98 94 56 55), Kystvejen 53, 9850 Hirtshals, is one km from the railway station on the south-west side of town. Open from March to November, it has dorm beds for 80 kr and private rooms costing from 125 kr for one person to 480 kr for six.

The cheapest hotel in town is the *Sømandshjemmet* (☎ 98 94 19 44) at Havnegade 24, 9850 Hirtshals, opposite the ferry dock. It has straightforward rooms with shared bath for 210/395 kr or with private bath for 290/480 kr.

The *Skaga Hotel* (☎ 98 94 55 00, fax 98 94 55 55) at Willemoesvej 1, 9850 Hirtshals, is a new hotel on the east side of town. The 108 rooms, which have modern amenities including private bath and TV, cost from 495/650 kr for a single/double. There's a pool, fitness room and restaurant.

There are cafés and a bakery at the north end of Hjørringgade. One of the cheaper eateries there is the *Restaurant Lilleheden*, Hjørringgade 2, which has simple dishes and a 48 kr daily special. The *Sømandshjemmet* hotel has an inexpensive cafeteria that's popular with local fishers.

Getting There & Away
Hirtshals is 49 km south-west of Skagen via routes 40 and 597, and 41 km north-west of Frederikshavn via the E39 and route 35.

Train Hirtshals' main railway station is 500 metres south of the ferry terminal, but trains connecting with ferry services continue down to the harbour. The private railway, which is operated by Hjørring Privatbaner, connects Hirtshals with Hjørring (16.50 kr), 20 minutes to the south. Trains run at least hourly, with the last departure from Hjørring to Hirtshals at 10.43 pm. From Hjørring you can take a DSB train to Aalborg (35 kr) or Frederikshavn (30 kr).

From mid-June to mid-August there's a bus from Hirtshals station to Hjørring (16.50 kr) and to Skagen (27.50 kr) six times a day.

Boat The Color Line runs year-round ferries to the Norwegian ports of Oslo and Kristiansand. See the Getting There & Away chapter in the front of the book for detailed information.

TORNBY STRAND
Tornby Strand, five km south of Hirtshals, is a lovely undeveloped stretch of beach and dunes. It generally has good swimming conditions in summer, which is the only time you can expect to find much company.

The beach sand is packed hard enough to

drive on and indeed many visitors park their cars right on the sand at the spot where they sunbathe. It's possible to drive south on the beach for about four km, at which point a river slices the beach en route to the sea.

There are plenty of possibilities for hiking on the beach, along the high mounded dunes and in the coastal woodlands that back the south side of the beach. Other than a bit of seabird watching there's nothing more to see or do here – which is what makes Tornby Strand an attractive little getaway.

Places to Stay & Eat

The family run *Munch Badepension* (☎ & fax 98 97 71 15), Tornby Strand, 9850 Hirtshals, is right on the beach at the end of Tornby Strandvej. It has a handful of rustic rooms with dune views and shared bath for 175/275 kr a single/double. The management also books cottages in the dunes. These can sleep six people for 1400 kr a week in the low season and 2600 kr in midsummer. The pension has a food store as well as a simple restaurant with an ocean view and a menu that includes salad and smørrebrød for 25 kr, spaghetti for 38 kr and a daily special for 68 kr.

Getting There & Away

Tornby Strand is five km south of Hirtshals via route 55 and Tornby Strandvej. The bus from Hirtshals to Hjørring, which operates from mid-June to mid-August, stops en route at Tornby Strand six times a day; the cost from Hirtshals is 11 kr.

HJØRRING

Hjørring, an old market town with a population of 24,000, is the capital of Vendyssel county and a regional centre with the district hospital and central rail connections.

It's a tidy town with lots of statues and bronze artwork. The oldest part of Hjørring is around Torvet, the central square, where there are three churches dating back to medieval times and a few half-timbered houses. Torvet is a 10-minute walk north from the railway station along Kongensgade and Nørregade.

While Hjørring is not generally a destination in itself, it can be an enjoyable place to spend a few hours (or break for the night) if you decide to stopover between trains or are leisurely touring around the region.

Information

Tourist Office The Hjørring Turistbureau (☎ 98 92 02 32, fax 98 92 04 52) is on Markedsgade 9, 9800 Hjørring, 750 metres east of the railway station. It's open on weekdays from 9 am to 4 pm and on Saturday from 9 am to noon, except in summer when it closes at 5 pm on weekdays and at 2 pm on Saturday.

Money & Post There are a number of banks in the centre on Østergade, just east of its intersection with Jernbanegade. The post office is at the west side of the railway station.

Churches

Hjørring is unique in that it managed to retain three medieval churches despite the consolidations that occurred throughout Denmark following the Reformation. All three churches are within 200 metres of each other, on the north side of Torvet.

The oldest, **Sankt Olai Kirke**, which dates from the 11th century, has a Romanesque chancel and a 16th century altarpiece. **Sankt Catharinæ Kirke**, the current parish church, retains traces of its medieval beginnings in the transept and has a 13th century gothic crucifix, though the church has been altered through the centuries and was largely rebuilt in the 1920s. The Romanesque **Sankt Hans Kirke** has a nave built of medieval red brick, a fresco from 1350 and an altarpiece and pulpit from the early 1600s.

Museums

The **Vendsyssel Historiske Museum** occupies an old deanery and a couple of 19th century school buildings on Museumsgade on the south side of Torvet. It covers local history from prehistoric times and has an ecclesiastical art collection, period furnishings and displays on farming. In July and

August it's open daily from 10 am to 5 pm, from 11 am to 4 pm in May and June, and from 1 to 4 pm the rest of the year. Admission is 20 kr for adults and 5 kr for children.

There's also an art museum, the **Hjørring Kunstmuseum**, a five-minute walk northeast of the railway station at Brinck Seidelinsgade 10, that's devoted to regional art and crafts. Summer opening hours are from 10 am to 5 pm and low-season hours from 11 am to 4 pm; admission is 10 kr for adults and free for children.

Places to Stay

Both the camping ground and hostel are about 2.5 km north-east of the railway station and can reached by local bus. *Hjørring Campingplads* (☎ 98 92 22 82, fax 98 91 06 99), Idræts Allé 45, 9800 Hjørring, has a three-star rating, an outdoor swimming pool and two and four-bunk cabins for rent. It's open from mid-May to mid-September and charges 42 kr per person.

The *Hjørring Vandrerhjem* (☎ 98 92 67 00, fax 98 90 15 50), Thomas Morildsvej 11, 9800 Hjørring, is a modern hostel open from 1 March to mid-October. It has 116 beds in 28 rooms, each room with a private bath. Dorm beds cost 85 kr, while family rooms range from 170 kr for an individual to 470 kr for six people.

The tourist office books rooms in private homes for about 100 kr per person; there's no booking fee.

The *Hotel Phønix* (☎ 98 92 54 55, fax 98 90 10 37), Jernbanegade 6, 9800 Hjørring, is a comfortable 70-room hotel a few minutes walk north of the railway station. It has an older section with traditional rooms and a newer section with contemporary décor. The rooms, which have private bath and TV, cost 440/590 kr for a single/double, breakfast included.

Places to Eat

The railway station has a café and kiosk. There's a small cafeteria at the bus station and a number of restaurants nearby on Jernbanegade, including *Manhattan Pizza*, which sells pizza by the slice, and *Peking Grill*, which has Chinese dishes with rice for 35 to 40 kr. You'll find another cluster of eateries around Torvet, including a pizzeria and a couple of grills selling hot dogs and burgers.

For more-upmarket dining, the *Hotel Phønix* at Jernbanegade 6 has Danish dishes, with a daily special for 79 kr and a two-course dinner for 139 kr.

Getting There & Away

Hjørring is 35 km west of Frederikshavn via route 35, and 17 km south of Hirtshals via route 55 or the E39.

Bus & Train Hjørring is on the DSB Århus-Frederikshavn rail line and is the terminus for a private rail line to Hirtshals. The train fare is 16.50 kr to Hirtshals, 30 kr to Frederikshavn and 118 kr to Århus.

The town is also served by Nordjyllands Trafikselskab, which operates bus services to Skagen, Løkken, Frederikshavn and Hirtshals. The bus station is 200 metres north-east of the railway station, near the intersection of Jernbanegade and Asylgade.

LØKKEN

Fronted by a broad sandy beach, Løkken is a small town of 1300 residents that is packed each summer by an invasion of beach-goers. Not surprisingly, its character is that of a popular resort area, more commercial than quaint, with a bustling centre of shops, ice-cream stands and cafés. While the beach is the major attraction, there's also a summertime museum, the Løkken Museum at Nørregade 12, which has exhibits on the town's history as a trade and fishing port.

Information

The Løkken Turistbureau (☎ 98 99 10 09, fax 98 99 11 59), Møstingsvej 3, 9480 Løkken, is at the south side of Torvet, the central square. There's a Jyske Bank on the north side of Torvet.

Places to Stay

There are five camping grounds at the south side of town either on or near Søndergade;

all are open in summer only. Right in the centre, a five-minute walk south of Torvet, is *Midtbyens Camping* (☎ 98 99 11 52), Jyllandsgade 2, 9480 Løkken, a small two-star place that charges 45 kr per person in the high season.

One km south of the centre is the three-star *Løkken Camping* (☎ 98 99 17 67, fax 98 99 26 80), Søndergade 69, 9480 Løkken, which has camping sites for 50 kr and 32 cabins, each with four beds and an equipped kitchen, for 1500 kr a week plus the daily per-person charges. The nearby three-star *Josefines Camping* (☎ 98 99 13 26) at Søndergade 57, 9480 Løkken, has slightly cheaper rates and an earlier opening date (mid-May).

Løkken's cheapest central hotel is the *Hotel Litorina* (☎ 98 99 10 44, fax 98 99 27 19), Søndergade 15, 9480 Løkken. It has 26 straightforward rooms that cost 235/315 kr with shared bath and 265/395 kr with private bath. Prices jump about 25% for the month of July and drop a similar amount in the low season.

Most other hotels and apartment complexes in Løkken are geared for holiday-makers planning longer stays and offer their best prices by the week. The tourist office can provide a booklet with a brief description of each place and a detailed price list.

Places to Eat
There are numerous places to eat around Torvet. *Café au Lait*, on the north side of Torvet, has good inexpensive sandwiches and some tempting coffee and cake combinations. For something more fancy, the restaurant in the *Løkken Badehotel* overlooks Torvet and has a good-value daily meal of fish, salad and potatoes for 79 kr and a steak lunch that's served until 6 pm for 49 kr. You can find a bakery on Søndergade, a block south of Torvet. The *Jansen Supermarket*, which has long opening hours, is just a minute's walk south-east of Torvet.

Getting There & Away
Løkken is on route 55, 18 km south-west of Hjørring. Buses run a couple of times a day between Løkken and Hjørring (25 minutes,

22 kr) and once a day between Løkken and Aalborg (one hour, 44 kr).

HANSTHOLM
Hanstholm is a new town built around a large commercial harbour, which was completed in 1967 and is now one of Denmark's largest fishing ports. It was originally thought that the population would quickly reach 20,000, but to date Hanstholm has only about 3000 residents.

There's no real reason to come to Hanstholm unless you're taking a boat to or from Norway. Those who do find themselves here might want to visit the lighthouse, which claimed to beam the world's most powerful beacon when erected in 1843 and now holds local history exhibits. Early risers scratching for something to do might want to watch the harbourside fish auction, which is held at 7 am on weekdays. There are also some remnants of the German occupation during WW II in Hanstholm and in the village of Vigsø to the east, which has a coastline of concrete bunkers that are slowly being washed into the sea.

Information
The Hanstholm Turistbureau (☎ 97 96 12 19, fax 97 96 21 54), Bytorvet 2, 7730 Hanstholm, is open on weekdays from 9 am to 4 pm and on Saturday from 9 am to noon, except in summer when it stays open to 4.30 pm on weekdays and to 2 pm on Saturday.

The tourist office is in Hanstholm Centret, about a km inland from the harbour. The centre also has banks, the post office, a library, a pharmacy, shops and eateries.

Places to Stay & Eat
The nearest camping ground is *Hanstholm Camping* (☎ 97 96 51 98, fax 97 96 54 70), Hamborgvej 95, 7730 Hanstholm, about five km east of the harbour, midway to Vigsø. It's open from April to September, charges 38 kr per person and has the usual three-star facilities.

At the harbour is the *Hanstholm Sømandshjem & Hotel* (☎ 97 96 11 45, fax 97 96 27 80), located at Kai Lindbergsgade 71, 7730

Hanstholm, which has 19 rooms with private bath and TV. This seaman's hotel is a utilitarian place, a bit dull but adequate. Singles range from 200 to 290 kr and doubles from 325 to 500 kr, with the higher prices applicable in summer.

The hotel has a cheap cafeteria with a 39 kr daily special (51 kr on weekends); it's a popular hang-out for local fishers but, like the town itself, doesn't draw many tourists. There's a supermarket just to the west of the hotel and a grill with ice cream and hot dogs down by the harbour.

The modern 79-room *Hotel Hanstholm* (☎ 97 96 10 44, fax 97 96 25 84), Christian Hansens Vej 2, 7730 Hanstholm, inland from the harbour and close to the Hanstholm Centret, has singles/doubles with private bath, TV, phone and minibar for 355/585 kr, breakfast included. The hotel has a restaurant and a swimming pool.

The Hanstholm Centret has a bakery, cafeteria, fast-food grill and a *Super Brugsen* supermarket.

Getting There & Away
Hanstholm is at the terminus of routes 181, 26 and 29. Thisted, 21 km to the south via route 26, has the nearest train service. Bus No 40 makes the 45-minute run to Thisted railway station from Hanstholm harbour about once an hour on weekdays and five times a day on weekends.

Information on the Fjord Line car ferries to the Norwegian cities of Bergen and Egersund is in the Getting There & Away chapter in the front of the book.

KLITMØLLER
Klitmøller is a small fishing village that attracts lots of windsurfers, both German and Danish, as it has some of North Jutland's best wind conditions. The main windsurfing spot is right in town; simply follow the main road, Ørhagevej, to the waterfront. When the winds are down there's good swimming at the beaches along the north and south sides of the village.

The landscape around Klitmøller, dunes backed by stark heathlands, continues for more than 10 km to the north and south. The section between Hanstholm and Klitmøller looks particularly barren as you zip along the road, but there are bogs and ponds inland and the entire area is an important bird reserve known as the Hanstholm Vildtreservat; human access is restricted.

Amber
Amber is fossilised tree resin that is translucent and brittle. It's usually golden yellow but can appear in other hues, most notably reddish brown. Some pieces of amber contain fossilised ferns or insects that were trapped inside the resin aeons ago when it was still sticky.

In Denmark amber is most commonly found on the west coast of Jutland. The best time to hunt for amber is in the wake of a storm or strong gale, when the amber gets stirred up from the seabed, bobs to the surface and is washed ashore. Look for it up on the beach mixed with other lightweight items like driftwood and seaweed.

Amber is not easily found by novices, however, and most first-time collectors end up with a pocketful of small yellow stones instead. There are two key identification points: amber is significantly lighter than rock and it floats in salt water; it also collects a small negative charge when rubbed and will warm to the touch after being held.

Professional amber collectors have their own tools of the trade, primarily a meshed net on a long frame with which they can snatch the amber as it's tossed around in breaking waves.

Amber is often polished and made into jewellery, particularly pendants, beaded necklaces, earrings and rings. If you're unable to find your own pieces they can be readily purchased at jewellery shops all around Denmark. ■

Windsurfing

Those interested in windsurfing can contact Windsurfing Klitmøller (☎ 97 97 56 56), near the beach at Ørhagevej 152, which hires out equipment and gives windsurfing lessons. In addition to the challenging North Sea waters, there's also the lake Vandet Sø, to the east of Klitmøller, which is a popular spot with windsurfing conditions suitable for all levels.

Places to Stay & Eat

Most visitors to Klitmøller stay in one of the three camping grounds that are right in town; the first two listed are just a few minutes walk from Ørhagevej. The two-star *Hausgård Motel & Camping* (☎ 97 97 50 85, fax 97 97 50 20), Vangvej 16, 7700 Thisted, has camping for 30 kr per person and rooms from 200 kr. *Nordsø Camping* (☎ & fax 97 97 50 71), Vangsåvej 25, 7700 Thisted, has a higher rating, more elaborate facilities and a rate of 44 kr; it also has the longest camping season, from April to late October. The third and largest is the three-star *Nystrup Camping* (☎ 97 97 52 49, fax 97 71 05 71), Trøjborgvej 22, Klitmøller, 7700 Thisted, which charges 45 kr per person. All three places have cabins for rent, minimarkets and grill-style eateries.

There's a burger bar, an ice-cream shop, a bakery, a food market and a few cafés and restaurants along Ørhagevej within a km of the waterfront.

Getting There & Away

Klitmøller is 10 km south-west of Hanstholm via route 181, and 15 km north-west of Thisted via route 557. From Klitmøller, bus No 22 goes to Thisted, which has the nearest rail connections, and bus No 24 goes to Hanstholm.

Glossary

Note that the Danish letters æ, ø and å fall at the end of the alphabet.

adgang forbudt – no trespassing
amt – county
apotek – pharmacy, chemist

bageri – bakery
billetautomat – automated parking-ticket dispenser
bro – bridge
bugt – bay
by – town
børnemenu – children's menu

campingplads – camping ground

damer – lady; often seen on restroom doors (or as 'D')
Danmark – Denmark
Dansk – Danish
domkirke – cathedral
DSB – abbreviation for Danske Statsbaner (Danish State Railroad), Denmark's national railway

EU – European Union

Fyn – Funen, both a county and an island
færegehavn – ferry harbour

gade – street
god tur – literally 'good trip' (ie Have a pleasant journey)
gård – yard, farm

have – garden
havn – harbour
herrer – gentleman; often seen on restroom doors (or as 'H')
HI – Hostelling International, the main international hostel organisation (formerly IYHF)

IC – intercity train
IR – inter-regional train

jernbane – train

Jylland – Jutland

keramik – ceramic, pottery
kirke – church
kirkegård – churchyard, cemetery
klint – cliff
kloster – monastery
konditori – a bakery with café tables
kro – inn
København – Copenhagen
køreplan – timetable

lur – Bronze Age horn

museet – museum
møntvask – coin laundry

nord – north

plantage – plantation, tree farm, woods
privat vej – private road

røgeri – fish smokehouse
rådhus – town hall

samling – collection, usually of art
Sjælland – the island of Zealand
skov – forest, woods
slagter – butcher
slot – castle
smørrebrød – open sandwich
strand – beach, shoreline
sund – sound
syd – south
sø – lake

torv, torvet – square, marketplace
tårn – tower

vandrerhjem – youth and family hostel
vej – street, road
vest – west

ø – island
øst – east

å – river

Index

Note that the Danish letters æ, ø and å fall at the end of the alphabet.

LONELY PLANET JOURNEYS

JOURNEYS is a unique collection of travellers' tales – published by the company that understands travel better than anyone else. It is a series for anyone who has ever experienced – or dreamed of – the magical moment when they encountered a strange culture or saw a place for the first time. They are tales to read while you're planning a trip, while you're on the road or while you're in an armchair, in front of a fire.

JOURNEYS books will catch the spirit of a place, illuminate a culture, recount a crazy adventure, or introduce a fascinating way of life. They will always entertain, and always enrich the experience of travel.

ISLANDS IN THE CLOUDS
Travels in the Highlands of New Guinea
Isabella Tree

This is the fascinating account of a journey to the remote and beautiful Highlands of Papua New Guinea and Irian Jaya. The author travels with a PNG Highlander who introduces her to his intriguing and complex world. *Islands in the Clouds* is a thoughtful, moving book, full of insights into a region that is rarely noticed by the rest of the world.

'One of the most accomplished travel writers to appear on the horizon for many years . . . the dialogue is brilliant' – Eric Newby

LOST JAPAN
Alex Kerr

Lost Japan draws on the author's personal experiences of Japan over a period of 30 years. Alex Kerr takes his readers on a backstage tour: friendships with Kabuki actors, buying and selling art, studying calligraphy, exploring rarely visited temples and shrines . . . The Japanese edition of this book was awarded the 1994 Shincho Gakugei Literature Prize for the best work of non-fiction.

'This deeply personal witness to Japan's wilful loss of its traditional culture is at the same time an immensely valuable evaluation of just what that culture was' – Donald Richie of the Japan Times

THE GATES OF DAMASCUS
Lieve Joris
Translated by Sam Garrett

This best-selling book is a beautifully drawn portrait of day-to-day life in modern Syria. Through her intimate contact with local people, Lieve Joris draws us into the fascinating world that lies behind the gates of Damascus.

'A brilliant book . . . Not since Naguib Mahfouz has the everyday life of the modern Arab world been so intimately described' – William Dalrymple

SEAN & DAVID'S LONG DRIVE
Sean Condon

Sean and David are young townies who have rarely strayed beyond city limits. One day, for no good reason, they set out to discover their homeland, and what follows is a wildly entertaining adventure that covers half of Australia. Sean Condon has written a hilarious, offbeat road book that mixes sharp insights with deadpan humour and outright lies.

'Funny, pithy, kitsch and surreal . . . This book will do for Australia what Chernobyl did for Kiev, but hey you'll laugh as the stereotypes go boom' – Andrew Tuck, Time Out

LONELY PLANET TRAVEL ATLASES

Lonely Planet has long been famous for the number and quality of its guidebook maps. Now we've gone one step further and in conjunction with Steinhart Katzir Publishers produced a handy companion series: Lonely Planet travel atlases – maps of a country produced in book form.

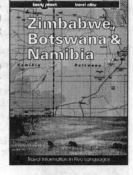

Unlike other maps, which look good but lead travellers astray, our travel atlases have been researched on the road by Lonely Planet's experienced team of writers. All details are carefully checked to ensure the atlas corresponds with the equivalent Lonely Planet guidebook.

The handy atlas format means no holes, wrinkles, torn sections or constant folding and unfolding. These atlases can survive long periods on the road, unlike cumbersome fold-out maps. The comprehensive index ensures easy reference.

- full-colour throughout
- maps researched and checked by Lonely Planet authors
- place names correspond with Lonely Planet guidebooks
  – no confusing spelling differences
- legend and travelling information in English, French, German, Japanese and Spanish
- size: 230 x 160 mm

Available now:
Thailand; India & Bangladesh; Vietnam; Zimbabwe, Botswana & Namibia

Coming soon:
Chile; Egypt; Israel; Laos; Turkey

LONELY PLANET TV SERIES & VIDEOS

Lonely Planet travel guides have been brought to life on television screens around the world. Like our guides, the programmes are based on the joy of independent travel, and look honestly at some of the most exciting, picturesque and frustrating places in the world. Each show is presented by one of three travellers from Australia, England or the USA and combines an innovative mixture of video, Super-8 film, atmospheric soundscapes and original music.

Videos of each episode – containing additional footage not shown on television – are available from good book and video shops, but the availability of individual videos varies with regional screening schedules.

Video destinations include: Alaska; Australia (Southeast); Brazil; Ecuador & the Galápagos Islands; Indonesia; Israel & the Sinai Desert; Japan; La Ruta Maya (Yucatán, Guatemala & Belize); Morocco; North India (Varanasi to the Himalaya); Pacific Islands; Vietnam; Zimbabwe, Botswana & Namibia.

Coming soon: The Arctic (Norway & Finland); Baja California; Chile & Easter Island; China (Southeast); Costa Rica; East Africa (Tanzania & Zanzibar); Great Barrier Reef (Australia); Jamaica; Papua New Guinea; the Rockies (USA); Syria & Jordan; Turkey.

The Lonely Planet TV series is produced by:
Pilot Productions
Duke of Sussex Studios
44 Uxbridge St
London W8 7TG UK

Lonely Planet videos are distributed by:
IVN Communications Inc
2246 Camino Ramon
California 94583, USA

107 Power Road, Chiswick
London W4 5PL UK

Music from the TV series is available on CD & cassette.
For ordering information contact your nearest Lonely Planet office.

PLANET TALK

Lonely Planet's FREE quarterly newsletter

We love hearing from you and think you'd like to hear from us.

When...is the right time to see reindeer in Finland?
Where...can you hear the best palm-wine music in Ghana?
How...do you get from Asunción to Areguá by steam train?
What...is the best way to see India?

For the answer to these and many other questions read PLANET TALK.

Every issue is packed with up-to-date travel news and advice including:

* a letter from Lonely Planet co-founders Tony and Maureen Wheeler
* go behind the scenes on the road with a Lonely Planet author
* feature article on an important and topical travel issue
* a selection of recent letters from travellers
* details on forthcoming Lonely Planet promotions
* complete list of Lonely Planet products

To join our mailing list contact any Lonely Planet office.

Also available: Lonely Planet T-shirts. 100% heavyweight cotton..

LONELY PLANET ONLINE

Get the latest travel information before you leave or while you're on the road

Whether you've just begun planning your next trip, or you're chasing down specific info on currency regulations or visa requirements, check out the Lonely Planet World Wide Web site for up-to-the-minute travel information.

As well as travel profiles of your favourite destinations (including interactive maps and full-colour photos), you'll find current reports from our army of researchers and other travellers, updates on health and visas, travel advisories, and the ecological and political issues you need to be aware of as you travel.

There's an online travellers' forum (the Thorn Tree) where you can share your experiences of life on the road, meet travel companions and ask other travellers for their recommendations and advice. We also have plenty of links to other Web sites useful to independent travellers.

With tens of thousands of visitors a month, the Lonely Planet Web site is one of the most popular on the Internet and has won a number of awards including GNN's Best of the Net travel award.

http://www.lonelyplanet.com

LONELY PLANET PRODUCTS

Lonely Planet is known worldwide for publishing practical, reliable and no-nonsense travel information in our guides and on our web site. The Lonely Planet list covers just about every accessible part of the world. Currently there are eight series: *travel guides*, *shoestring guides*, *walking guides*, *city guides*, *phrasebooks*, *audio packs*, *travel atlases* and *Journeys* – a unique collection of travellers' tales.

EUROPE

Austria • Baltic States & Kaliningrad • Baltic States phrasebook • Britain • Central Europe on a shoestring • Central Europe phrasebook • Czech & Slovak Republics • Denmark • Dublin city guide • Eastern Europe on a shoestring • Eastern Europe phrasebook • Finland • France • Greece • Greek phrasebook • Hungary • Iceland, Greenland & the Faroe Islands • Ireland • Italy • Mediterranean Europe on a shoestring • Mediterranean Europe phrasebook • Poland • Prague city guide • Russia, Ukraine & Belarus • Russian phrasebook • Scandinavian & Baltic Europe on a shoestring • Scandinavian Europe phrasebook • Slovenia • St Petersburg city guide • Switzerland • Trekking in Greece • Trekking in Spain • Ukranian phrasebook • Vienna city guide • Walking in Switzerland • Western Europe on a shoestring • Western Europe phrasebook

NORTH AMERICA

Alaska • Backpacking in Alaska • Baja California • California & Nevada • Canada • Hawaii • Honolulu city guide • Los Angeles city guide • Mexico • Pacific Northwest USA • Rocky Mountain States • San Francisco city guide • Southwest USA • USA phrasebook

CENTRAL AMERICA & THE CARIBBEAN

Central America on a shoestring • Costa Rica • Eastern Caribbean • Guatemala, Belize & Yucatán: La Ruta Maya • Jamaica

SOUTH AMERICA

Argentina, Uruguay & Paraguay • Bolivia • Brazil • Brazilian phrasebook • Buenos Aires city guide • Chile & Easter Island • Colombia • Ecuador & the Galápagos Islands • Latin American Spanish phrasebook • Peru • Quechua phrasebook • Rio de Janeiro city guide • South America on a shoestring • Trekking in the Patagonian Andes • Venezuela

AFRICA

Arabic (Moroccan) phrasebook • Africa on a shoestring • Cape Town city guide • Central Africa • East Africa • Egypt & the Sudan • Ethiopian (Amharic) phrasebook • Kenya • Morocco • North Africa • South Africa, Lesotho & Swaziland • Swahili phrasebook • Trekking in East Africa • West Africa • Zimbabwe, Botswana & Namibia • Zimbabwe, Botswana & Namibia travel atlas

ALSO AVAILABLE:

Travel with Children • Traveller's Tales

MAIL ORDER

Lonely Planet products are distributed worldwide. They are also available by mail order from Lonely Planet, so if you have difficulty finding a title please write to us. North American and South American residents should write to Embarcadero West, 155 Filbert St, Suite 251, Oakland CA 94607, USA; European and African residents should write to 10 Barley Mow Passage, Chiswick, London W4 4PH; and residents of other countries to PO Box 617, Hawthorn, Victoria 3122, Australia.

NORTH-EAST ASIA

Beijing city guide • Cantonese phrasebook • China • Hong Kong, Macau & Canton • Hong Kong city guide • Japan • Japanese phrasebook • Japanese audio pack • Korea • Korean phrasebook • Mandarin phrasebook • Mongolia • Mongolian phrasebook • North-East Asia on a shoestring • Seoul city guide • Taiwan • Tibet • Tibet phrasebook • Tokyo city guide

INDIAN SUBCONTINENT

Bengali phrasebook • Bangladesh • Delhi city guide • Hindi/Urdu phrasebook • India • India & Bangladesh travel atlas • Karakoram Highway • Kashmir, Ladakh & Zanskar • Nepal • Nepali phrasebook • Pakistan • Sri Lanka • Sri Lanka phrasebook • Trekking in the Indian Himalaya • Trekking in the Nepal Himalaya

SOUTH-EAST ASIA

Bali & Lombok • Bangkok city guide • Burmese phrasebook • Cambodia • Ho Chi Minh city guide • Indonesia • Indonesian phrasebook • Indonesian audio pack • Jakarta city guide • Java • Laos • Lao phrasebook • Malaysia, Singapore & Brunei • Myanmar (Burma) • Philippines • Pilipino phrasebook • Singapore city guide • South-East Asia on a shoestring • Thailand • Thailand travel atlas • Thai phrasebook • Thai audio pack • Thai Hill Tribes phrasebook • Vietnam • Vietnamese phrasebook • Vietnam travel atlas

AUSTRALIA & THE PACIFIC

Australia • Australian phrasebook • Bushwalking in Australia • Bushwalking in Papua New Guinea • Fiji • Fijian phrasebook • Islands of Australia's Great Barrier Reef • Melbourne city guide • Micronesia • New Caledonia • New South Wales & the ACT • New Zealand • Outback Australia • Papua New Guinea • Papua New Guinea phrasebook • Queensland • Rarotonga & the Cook Islands • Samoa • Solomon Islands • South Australia • Sydney city guide • Tahiti & French Polynesia • Tonga • Tramping in New Zealand • Vanuatu • Victoria • Western Australia

Travel Literature: Islands in the Clouds • Sean & David's Long Drive

MIDDLE EAST & CENTRAL ASIA

Arab Gulf States • Arabic (Egyptian) phrasebook • Central Asia • Iran • Israel • Jordan & Syria • Middle East • Turkey • Turkish phrasebook • Trekking in Turkey • Yemen

Travel Literature: The Gates of Damascus

ISLANDS OF THE INDIAN OCEAN

Madagascar & Comoros • Maldives & Islands of the East Indian Ocean • Mauritius, Réunion & Seychelles

THE LONELY PLANET STORY

Lonely Planet published its first book in 1973 in response to the numerous 'How did you do it?' questions Maureen and Tony Wheeler were asked after driving, bussing, hitching, sailing and railing their way from England to Australia.

Written at a kitchen table and hand collated, trimmed and stapled, *Across Asia on the Cheap* became an instant local bestseller, inspiring thoughts of another book.

Eighteen months in South-East Asia resulted in their second guide, *South-East Asia on a shoestring*, which they put together in a backstreet Chinese hotel in Singapore in 1975. The 'yellow bible', as it quickly became known to backpackers around the world, soon became *the* guide to the region. It has sold well over half a million copies and is now in its 8th edition, still retaining its familiar yellow cover.

Today there are over 180 titles, including travel guides, walking guides, language kits & phrasebooks, travel atlases and travel literature. The company is one of the largest travel publishers in the world. Although Lonely Planet initially specialised in guides to Asia, we now cover most regions of the world, including the Pacific, North America, South America, Africa, the Middle East and Europe.

The emphasis continues to be on travel for independent travellers. Tony and Maureen still travel for several months of each year and play an active part in the writing, updating and quality control of Lonely Planet's guides.

They have been joined by over 70 authors and 170 staff at our offices in Melbourne (Australia), Oakland (USA), London (UK) and Paris (France). Travellers themselves also make a valuable contribution to the guides through the feedback we receive in thousands of letters each year.

The people at Lonely Planet strongly believe that travellers can make a positive contribution to the countries they visit, both through their appreciation of the countries' culture, wildlife and natural features, and through the money they spend. In addition, the company makes a direct contribution to the countries and regions it covers. Since 1986 a percentage of the income from each book has been donated to ventures such as famine relief in Africa; aid projects in India; agricultural projects in Central America; Greenpeace's efforts to halt French nuclear testing in the Pacific; and Amnesty International.

'I hope we send the people out with the right attitude about travel. You realise when you travel that there are so many different perspectives about the world, so we hope these books will make people more interested in what they see. These are guidebooks, but you can't really guide people. All you can do is point them in the right direction.'
– Tony Wheeler

LONELY PLANET PUBLICATIONS

Australia
PO Box 617, Hawthorn 3122, Victoria
tel: (03) 9819 1877 fax: (03) 9819 6459
e-mail: talk2us@lonelyplanet.com.au

USA
Embarcadero West, 155 Filbert St, Suite 251,
Oakland, CA 94607
tel: (510) 893 8555 TOLL FREE: 800 275-8555
fax: (510) 893 8563
e-mail: info@lonelyplanet.com

UK
10 Barley Mow Passage, Chiswick,
London W4 4PH
tel: (0181) 742 3161 fax: (0181) 742 2772
e-mail: 100413.3551@compuserve.com

France:
71 bis rue du Cardinal Lemoine, 75005 Paris
tel: 1 44 32 06 20 fax: 1 46 34 72 55
e-mail: 100560.415@compuserve.com

World Wide Web: http://www.lonelyplanet.com